28th EDITION
WRECKS
&RELICS

KEN ELLIS

Crécy
Crécy Publishing Limited

CONTENTS

Front Cover: Tony Agar's superb NF.II HJ711 *Spirit of Val* takes a bow at East Kirkby, Lincolnshire, May 2021. *Richard Hall*
Rear Cover:
Main: Boeing 747-436 G-BNLY. Arriving at Dunsfold 5th Dec 2020. *Phil Whalley*
Middle left: Spitfire Vb BM597 (G-MKVB). Duxford, Dec 2020. *Col Pope*
Middle centre: Phantom FGR.2 XV408. Tangmere, Dec 2021. *Hugh Trevor*
Middle right: Spitfire XVI RW388. Stoke-on-Trent, Sep 2021. **Dave Murray**
Lower left: Dakota 3 ZA947. Coningsby, Jul 2021. *Richard Hall*
Title Page: Newark Air Museum's Vulcan B.2 XM594, a frequent static 'runner' to the delight of visitors. *Col Pope*

Copyright 2022 © Ken Ellis

This twenty-eighth edition published by
Crécy Publishing
1a Ringway Trading Estate, Shadowmoss Road
Manchester M22 5LH
www.crecy.co.uk

ISBN 9781800351387

Printed in Bulgaria by Multiprint

PREFACE

With the world in the throes of what is bound to be perpetual pandemonium, it may seem trivial to return to a review of Britain's aviation heritage 'sector'. But 'Lockdown' proved that our pursuits can be sanity savers and the pages that follow carry some heartening examples of people at their best. There was also plenty of time for reading: despite being slightly delayed due to the pandemic, *W&R27* was a *sell out!* This edition is still suffering from 'Covid collateral', so here's hoping that next one will be back to the 'new normal'...

As well as some incredible achievements, the 'movement' is witnessing unprecedented changes, and I've taken the opportunity to expand my rambling space to dwell on these.

Size does matter

British Airways paid off its final Boeing 747s in 2020, ending a half century of operating 'Jumbos'. Along with its predecessors, BA has a superb track-record of making sure that its retired airliners find a place where the public can experience them. Unlike the Concorde hand-out, not one 'mainline' museum appears to have been in the queue for a 747; the onus falling to enlightened operators at Cotswold, Dunsfold and St Athan to cherish these gifts. In terms of 'pulling power', a 747 ain't no Concorde, but I'd argue the lumbering giant is far, far more significant than the elite-toting hot-rod. The Boeing 747 is a social, commercial, technological, earth-shrinking phenomena and, with over 1,500 built (Concorde limped to just 20 examples) *millions* of people have sampled it. Given the big Boeing's long and varied use by British hauliers, not forgetting those powered by Rolls-Royce RB211s, it is a *national*, as well as global icon.

A Series 400 747 has a wingspan of 211ft 0in and an empty weight in the region of 351,100lb; these stats and many more explain why Britain's national museums have shied away from taking one on. The Science Museum's moribund transport aircraft collection at Wroughton, Wilts, is marooned by a sea of solar cells and the runway at Duxford won't 'take' a 747 in terms of length or 'footprint'. These precluded airborne delivery, even if there was the will and space could be found. If the Boeing can't come to the museum then why can't a sub-site of the museum *go to* the Boeing? There will come a time when one of the larger Airbus types needs considering and it looks as though once again, the nation will be relying on the 'private sector' to take the initiative. Hopefully this batch of 747s face long lives, but companies wax and wane and in that case who will step into the breach? This burgeoning responsibility needs some thought, or dare I say it, a strategy. Or should we just continue to ignore the 'Jumbo' in the room?

Trickle-down has to seep somewhere

It didn't work for Thatcher and it's going to cause many a problem for the UK's aviation museums. The economic 'trickle-down' theory centres on the belief that by making the better-off even richer, their largesse will percolate down through society thereby boosting the contents of everyone's pocket. Aye, right. Tackled in depth under Hendon on page 144, the RAF Museum is embarking on a 'trickle-down' procedure of its own, hoping that other collections will absorb what has been determined as 'over-stocking'. The preface to the 27th edition briefly mentioned this problem in a wider context, asking: "Is your Dassault Mystère really necessary?"

There may well be financial incentives to help the thinning down of the RAF Museum's fleet, but this will generate 'over-stocking' in collections further down the 'food chain'. Is it presumed that participating museums/organisations will have to jettison other airframes in order to make space – where will they go? Will the venue involved also face the same restrictions on disposal that the RAF Museum operated under? Something has to give.

The RAF Museum is not going to be the only 'national' slimming down: the Imperial War Museum, Science Museum and the Fleet Air Arm Museum – and let's not forget the National Museum of Flight Scotland – must all be watching this process very closely before embarking on similar exercises.

We've looked at the problems of preserving really big airframes. The RAF Museum, it seems, has adopted a covert but understandable policy of no longer keeping such leviathans – no Tristar, no Sentry. Further to this there are some relatively heavyweights on the 'to clear' list: Valetta, Varsity, Argosy.

The 'business end' of Argosy C.1 XP411 at Cosford, Shropshire. *Ken Ellis*

Offered for 'outward loan' (you look after it, we'll keep the title) is the 56,000lb, 115ft 0in of Argosy C.1 XP411. In every way this is a 'big ask'. It's warmly nestled in Hangar 1 at Cosford and as its new home would almost certainly need the eviction of existing exhibits for it to be accommodated in similar style it has become accustomed to. Or, is XP411 now considered to be only worthy of exposure to the wonderful British climate? There are two whole Argosies in 'captivity' at Coventry and East Midlands, both 'front-and-back loader' civilian versions and kept outdoors. The 'business end' of XP411 is its innovative clam shell rear door system. Is it time to bite the bullet and reduce XP411 to a walk-in fuselage that might well find a niche within the RAF Museum?

While we're talking sacrilege, how's this for a hypothesis? I have nothing against Jetstream T.1 XX496 currently at Cosford, but bear with me. There are four T.1s in museums in the UK (whole at Doncaster, East Midlands and Newark; a fuselage at Carlisle); that's not a bad population figure. Is is better to just take poor old XX496 *out of the picture* – to a technical institute, glamping emporium, paintball park or break it up, and let the others fly the flag? It would certainly be 'green' and cut down the 'air miles' and diminish the national 'over-stock'. Just a thought…

In other words, 'trickle-down' only works if the recipients along the chain get a say in what's coming their way and what will be required to achieve it, to the benefit of all.

You don't know what you've got until it's gone

The Tristars and 747s at Bruntingthorpe were a *commercial* venture that came to an end in the breaker's yard. That some elements of the inspiring collection of historic aircraft types that had developed at the Leicestershire airfield since the mid-1980s also faced the axe was sad, but an inevitability. A perfectly understandable *commercial* decision was taken by the owners of Bruntingthorpe, who are in business as a primary concern and are coincidentally aviation enthusiasts. This love of aviation heritage has resulted in the scaling back of the collection, thereby saving the endeavours of much of the Bruntingthorpe community. An ice-cold corporate mind would have evicted the lot, or let the bulldozers roll.

I discuss the transformation of the Bruntingthorpe skyline on page 120 and the debt the 'movement' owes to the Walton family. The vast majority of Britain's 'grass roots' aviation heritage activity relies on *someone* granting the use of a workshop, a plot of land or even an entire airfield. Most of this will be conducted on a peppercorn rent basis, or a you-scratch-mine… arrangement, or even free of charge. If you've got copies of my books *Lost Aviation Collections of Great Britain* or *Local Aviation Collections of Great Britain* (and if not, why not? – see the rear pages) you'll know that the history of aircraft preservation is littered with collections collapsing because they've lost a venue they thought was 'for keeps'. Finding a kind benefactor is a tremendous boost, but it is no excuse for the application of some pragmatism. Nothing lasts for ever, a wise preservation group will always have an eye on 'Plan B'. Those that find their 'landlord' coming up with a built-in rescue package are indeed very fortunate.

Ken Ellis
Bringing my own bottle
People's Republic of Rutland
February 2022

Dedication

This edition is dedicated in fond memory of **Roy Bonser** and **Ernie Cromie**. Perhaps best known for his exceptional book *Aviation in Leicestershire and Rutland*, Roy had an innate knowledge of the aircraft preservation community and a great knack for finding that missing component. He was a driving force in the incredible Hinckley, Leics, Boston IIIA project and it serves as a memorial to his endeavours. Forever modest, Ernie was a historian of great repute, a man of vision and quiet inspiration. His 'mark' can be found in every aspect of the Ulster Aviation Society (see Long Kesh, Northern Ireland) and all that it stands for. Blue skies, both.

29th Edition deadlines

Images by **1st December 2023**. If you are new to contributing images to *W&R*, please get in touch beforehand for details of resolution required and how best to send. **Comments and notes by 10th January 2024**. Thanks for your support!

email: **ken@sillenek.com**
or, if all else fails: **sillenek@gmail.com**
'Snail mail' via Crécy Publishing – address on page 2

Opposite page

Top: Guppy 201 F-BTGV during scrapping at Bruntingthorpe, Leics, in December 2020. The flightdeck was salvaged and is at St Athan, Wales. In the foreground is the centre section and the flightdeck of a Transaero 747. *Nigel Bailey-Underwood*
Bottom: Boeing 747-436 G-CIVB on its own hard-standing at Cotswold, Glos, December 2021. *Mark Roberts*

ACKNOWLEDGEMENTS

Overseeing the draft, adding to it and refining it were: **Dave Allport, David Bennett, John Coghill, Andy Marden**, compiler of *Military Aviation Review's* excellent *Out of Service* feature, **Alistair Ness**, monitored Scotland and via his column in the Central Scotland Aviation Group's superb *Scottish Air News*; **Nigel Price, David E Thompson**, for the north of England and other travels; **Ian Thompson**, tackled all of Ireland; **Andy Wood** looked after Lincolnshire and Yorkshire, directly and via his column in the ever-brilliant *Humberside Air Review*. That said, awl mistooks our mein and mein aloan.

The map was created by the late **Pete West**.

Cover and layouts by **Rob Taylor**. Deep respect to **Charlotte Stear** and all the team at **Crécy Publishing**.

Many thanks also go to: **Neil** and **Heather Airey**, and the team at Lakes Lightnings; **Alan Allen** Vampire and Wasp collector; **Brian Asplin; Steve Austin**, Stoneykirk Aviation Museum; **Maurice Baalham; Ray Ball; Nigel Bailey-Underwood; Philip Bedford**, South East Aviation Enthusiasts Group; **Steve Bell**, Norfolk and Suffolk Aviation Museum; **Rowland Benbrook; John Berkeley; Lyndon Blackburne**, The Provost Boys; **Kevin Bowen**, Heathrow Trident Collection; **Alec Brew**, Tettenhall Transport Heritage Centre; **Dave Brocklehurst**, Kent Battle of Britain Museum; **Ben Brown**, Sywell Aviation Museum; **Peter Budden; David J Burke**, preservation pioneer; **Ian Burningham; Ray Burrows**, Ulster Aviation Society; **Mike Cain; John Camp**, Boxted Airfield Historical Group; **Richard Capper; Russell Carter; David Charles**, North East Land Sea and Air Museums; **Richard Clarkson**, Vulcan Restoration Trust; **Ricky Clarkson; Theo Classen; Pete Coe; Philip Cole**, Medway Aircraft Preservation Society; **John Coleman**, Southend and more; **David Collins**, DH Hornet and The Stirling Aircraft Project; **Peter Colwill; Glyn Coney; Marcus** and **Carolyn Cordran**, Buccaneer 'XN979'; **Nigel Coward** and his collection; **Paul Crellin; Alan Curry; Terry Dann**, Stow Maries and other notes; **Mike Davey**, Phantom and cockpit guru; **Clive Davies**, Gloster Aviation Club and Canberra WT333; **David Davis; John Davis; Thomas Davis; Rev Timothy Day; Lewis Deal**, Medway Aircraft Preservation Society; **Gary Dean**, P-51 perfectionist; **Brian Downs; Ian Doyle; Alan Drewett**, Jet Age Museum; **Colin Durrant**, Suffolk Aviation Heritage Museum; **Tony Dyer**, Air Defence Collection; **Geoff Eastham; Mike Eastman**, Aircraft Restoration Group; **Don Ellis; Alan Eley; Simon Fage; Roger Farmer**, Fenland and West Norfolk Aviation Museum; **Ian Farquharson; Bill Fern**, South Yorkshire Aircraft Museum; **Mike Fitch**, Yorkshire Helicopter Preservation Group; **Murray Flint**, refinishing maestro; **Nick Foden**, light aircraft collector; **Ken Fostekew**, Museum of Berkshire Aviation; **Ron Fulton**, BDAC; **Mal Function**, health and safety specialist; **Graham Gaff**, East London Aviation Society and UK military master; **Paul Giblin; Dominic Goings; Bruce Gordon**, Great British Aircraft Spares; **Gilmar Green; Ian Greenhalgh; Nick Griffiths; Paul Griffiths**, Jet Age Museum; **Richard Hall**, Lightning owner and imagery; **Ian Hancock**, Norfolk and Suffolk Aviation Museum; **Ian Haskell; Andrew Hawkins**, Firefly restorer; **Graham Haynes**, Bentwaters Cold War Museum; **Mark Hazell; Robin Heaps**, Medway Aircraft Preservation Society; **Howard Heeley**, Newark Air Museum; **Richard Hentschke**, Jet Age Museum; **Phil** and **Lynn Hewitt; Norman Hobbs**, Britten-Norman Aircraft Preservation Society; **Steve Hobden; Andy Hone; Trevor Hope**: Jonathan Horswell; **Jonathan Howard**, The Aeroplane Collection and Vampire restorer; **Lee Howard** all things Yeovilton; **Ian Humphreys; Mike Hutchinson; Mike Ingham**; JLY 751V; **David S Johnstone; Tim Jones**, Slingsby Cadet cockpiteer; **John Kenyon; Dougie Kerr**, Solway Aviation Museum; **Howard King**, Martlesham Heath Control Tower Museum; **Colin Kurek**, Wight Aviation Museum; **Max** and **Ritch La Rue-Blood; Martin Law; David Legg,** Catalina Society; **Darren Lewington; Keith Lynch; Chris Mabbott; Richard Mackeen; Owen Mansfield; Roger Marley**, Hawker Demon project; **Paul Marsh; Rod Martins; Brian Matthews; Tony** and **Brenda McCarthy; Ross McNeill**, Hurricane and more; **Alan Measles; Paul Middleton; Frank Millar**, Canberra restorer; **Alf Milliken; Steve Milnthorpe**, Boston craftsman; **Robert Mitchell; Naylan Moore**, Doncaster People's Front/South Yorkshire Aircraft Museum; **John Morris**, The Aeroplane Collection; **Dave Murray; Leo Murray**, Irish notes and his own collection; **John Nixon**, Millom Heritage and Art Centre; **Geoff Nutkins**, Shoreham Aircraft Museum; **Mike Overs**, The Buccaneer Aviation Group; **Martin Painter**, Nimrod XV148; **Alan Partington**, Catford Independent Air Force; **David Peace**, Tamworth Aviation Group; **Dr I Pertbottom; John Phillips**, rotorcraft 'sleuthing' and Skeeterisms; **Mike Phipp**, Bournemouth Aviation Museum and more; **Peppa Pig; Darren J Pitcher; Nigel** and **Anne Ponsford**, Ponsford Collection; **Geoffrey Pool**, Bruntingthorpe, Hunter owner; **Col Pope**, warbirds and imagery; **Robert Pountney; Mark Presswood; Simon Pulford**, Air Pulford; **Ivor Ramsden**, Manx Aviation and Military Museum; **Alexander Rankin; Elfan ap Rees**, The Helicopter Museum; **Stuart Richardson; Paco Rivas; Norman Roberson; Mark Roberts**, Aerobilia; **Neil Rodgers; Bob Rongé; Colin Savill**, Newark's *CockpitFest* head honcho; **Rob Sawyer; Andy Shemans**, Sywell Aviation Museum; **Jim Simpson; Tom Singfield; Bill Skinner**, Thorpe Camp; **Doug Smith**, RAF Manston History Museum; **Graham Sparkes**, Hooton Park Trust; **Darren Speechley; Peter Spooner**, notes from far and wide; **Ajay Srivastava**, Royal Air Force Museum; **James Stables**, South Yorkshire Aircraft Museum and cockpiteer; **Brian Stafford**, North Coates Heritage Collection; **Peter Stephens**, VC10 XV108; **David Stevens; Nick Stone; Jon Streatfield; Sir Arthur Streeb-Greebling; Gareth Symington; Pete Tasker; Julian Temple; Dave Thomas**, Bruntingthorpe stalwart; **Stewart Toone; Nigel Towler** – *The* Cockpit Collection; **Hugh Trevor**, Lightning historian and cockpit owner; **Richard Tuck; Martin** and **Lynn Tydeman**, Gazelle XZ337; **Sam Tyler; David Underwood**, glider restorer; **Graham Vale**, East Midlands Airport Volunteers Association; **Nick Veronico; Stefanie Vincent**, Aerospace Bristol; **Adrian Vines**, British Phantom Aviation Group; **Jake Wallace**, TBAG, Buccaneers and more; **Neil Watson; Bob Wealthy**, Britten-Norman Aircraft Preservation Society; **Michael Westwood; Phil Whalley; Mark Whitnall; John Wickenden; Barry Williams**, Vulcan Restoration Trust; **David Willis; Chris Wilson**, Jet Art Aviation; **Craig Wise**, Lightning XS456; **Wodewick the Wobber; Les Woodward**.

...and Pam and Rascal

BEFORE YOU START...

From Alpha to Omicron and beyond: *Even more than ever readers need to* **check, double check and confirm** *before embarking on a visit as things may change with every Prime Minister's Questions session. W&R contributors delight in reporting in the state of catering at venues: please bear in mind that offerings may be much more basic, or even non-existent, during these uncertain times.*

Many readers will be familiar with the 'rules of engagement': **major recent changes are highlighted in bold**.

Scope: *Wrecks & Relics* serves to outline, in as much detail as possible, the status of all known PRESERVED (ie in museum or other formalised collections, under restoration etc); INSTRUCTIONAL (ie static airframes in use for training); and STORED or DERELICT (ie out of use for a long period of time, as a rescue trainer, scrapped or damaged etc) aircraft in the UK and Ireland and HM Forces airframes based on Crown Territory.

The following exceptions apply: airworthy aircraft not part of a specific collection and/or readily accessible to the public, including the happily greatly expanding number of 'warbird airlines'; aircraft that fall into any of the above categories for only a short period – generally less than a year. **The onset of Covid-19 meant that aircraft or all sizes were parked up** left, right and centre, all over the place. The vast majority of these were/are kept in 'ready-to-go' state and as such are not listed. Those that are still grounded by 2024 will appear in *W&R29*.

Airframes will only be considered if they are **at least** a cockpit or a flightdeck. The former is the full depth of the fuselage, the latter is cut at the floor, with the lower fuselage removed. Many **microlights** fall out of use at the drop of a hat and to avoid constant deletions and re-entries, **only those that have been de-registered**, and/or are part of a museum or collection, are listed. Unfinished homebuilds and/or microlights are also largely ignored: one person's long incomplete project may well be someone's well-active pride and joy! **Balloon baskets/gondolas** (envelopes on their own are *not* considered) and **civilian gliders** are included *only* if they are part of a public-accessible museum. Some discretion has been allowed to cover 'vintage' British-built and military gliders. Coverage of **drones**, UAVs, what-have-you and in general is limited to British or US military types or the the occasional 'important' type (eg Airbus Zephyr) and V-1 'doodlebugs' (real or replica). Airframes at dive sites are listed separately – see Appendix C.

Locations: Are listed by county/province and then alphabetically. County boundaries are as given by the Ordnance Survey and as defined by the Local Government Act. Entries for Scotland, Wales, Northern Ireland and Ireland are purely alphabetical, primarily to help the English! From 1st April 1996 Scotland and Wales were wholly divided into 'Single Tier' Unitary Authorities, with their 'Counties' now having little administrative meaning.

Directions are given after each place name. Readers should note that these are *to the town or village mentioned* and *not* necessarily to the actual site in question. Directions are *not* given in the following instances: where the location is a large city or town; where specific directions to the site are not fully known; or at the request of several aircraft owners – who have every right to preserve their peace and quiet – some locations have been 'generalised'.

If you find yourself frustrated locating Robin Hood Airport, turn to the Locations Index which includes alternative names. (For Robin Hood, *W&R* adopts the CAA-accepted Doncaster Sheffield Airport, while hankering for when it was Finningley!) A form of notation relating to the status of an 'aerodrome' is given: 'Aerodrome' signifies a civilian flying ground used by aircraft up to King Air, 'biz-jet' etc size. 'Airfield' is used to signify a flying ground used by the armed forces, test establishments or manufacturers. 'Airport' is used to denote a flying ground that takes 'serious' sized airliners on a regular basis. International Civil Aviation Organisation four-letter location indicators are also included. For privacy and security purposes, private strips etc are frequently *not* denoted as such.

Unless otherwise stated, *all* locations in this work are PRIVATE and entry to them *is strictly by prior permission, if at all*. A mention in this book does not imply *any* right of access.

◆ Signifies visitor and location details. This is often used to draw attention to locations that particularly *do not* allow access or where prior permission is required. No attempt is made to give GPS or Google mapping references. With a two-year publication 'span' **opening times are no longer given** and readers are urged to use the 'Contact' segment to satisfy themselves that the venue will be open when they visit. Telephone number(s), email and websites are given, where known. Note: websites, Facebook references etc are given for information only; no recommendation of content is to be implied.

Entries and Aircraft Listings: As *W&R* covers a two-year period, in this case 2020-2022, beyond the location header there is a narrative explaining the status of the entry and outlining any airframes that have moved since the last edition. Those departing are given <u>underlined</u> forwarding references, including the county, or province, where further reference can be found within the book. This allows the reader to follow the more energetic examples around! Any aircraft that fall out of any of the categories above, or are exported, will not have forwarding references. 'Ownership' or 'custodianship' of airframes within this work is not to be inferred as definitive.

Column 1: Aircraft are listed alpha-numerically, using the following rubric. British civil first (except in Ireland where EI-comes first), followed by British Gliding Association and 'B Condition' (or 'trade plate') markings. Then overseas civil registrations in alpha-numeric order.

British military serials follow (with reversal again in Ireland) followed by overseas military listed by country – ie France before Netherlands before USA. Anonymous airframes are inserted where it is thought most logical! Incorrect or fictitious registrations and serials are marked in quotes, eg 'VZ999' or 'G-BKEN'. A dash (-) is used to denote an airframe that has no confirmed primary identity. Entries new to a heading in this edition are marked *. **No attempt has been made to note if an identity is worn or not on the airframe.**

Column 2: Is devoted to individual codes, eg 'Z' or '109', *believed* worn on the airframe. Deck (eg 'O') and shore base (eg 'VL') codes for Fleet Air Arm aircraft are *not* noted.

Column 3: Type/designation, sometimes abbreviated. Design *origin* has been chosen, eg Blackburn Buccaneer, not Hawker Siddeley. (Although Column 6 contains manufacturer details, where location may differ, or for a sub-contractor, for major types, homebuilds do not get this treatment.) Reference to the *Index I Types* will provide a cross-reference. (Major rethinks of types, eg Short's extensive morphing of the Tucano and Westland's re-engineering of the Whirlwind, Wessex and Sea King is, however, acknowledged, although not the latter company's 'badge engineering' on the Gazelle and Puma.)

To acquaint readers with the nature of the types listed, some abbreviations and a symbol are used: ✈ Believed airworthy, at time of going to press. CIM: Purpose-built instructional/training airframe, not intended for flight: Classroom Instruction Model, or even Module. EMU: Purpose-built test and evaluation airframe, not intended for flight, in most cases using prototype or production jigs and tooling: Engineering Mock-up. FSM: Full-scale model, often a faithful external reproduction of an aircraft, but using construction techniques completely unrelated to the original, frequently in fibreglass. Replica or rep: Reproduction, ie a faithful, or near-faithful copy or a facsimile of a type, using construction techniques and proportions in keeping with the original. The UK MoD has dropped the full stop from its designations: the Hawk these days is a T1 not T.1. *W&R* ignores this *pointless* (geddit?!) 'innovation' and remains consistent!

Column 4: Devoted to civil registrations allocated, but not worn. Also here are *correct* identities when an incorrect or fictitious identity is presented in Column 1. Lapsed British civil registrations are also placed here.

Column 5: Year manufactured; in most cases when first flown. Dates from 1925 *onwards* are given as two digits, eg 67 = 1967, or 07 = 2007. Airframes pre-1924 have the year in full, eg 1914. In some cases, it has been possible only to give a 'stab' at the build date in which case they are given as follows: c36. With some aircraft that have never flown, if no other data is given, then the date first registered is used, eg r76. Where it is impossible to give a date a wavy dash ~ is given.

Column 6: Brief historical details are given, in a necessarily abbreviated form. In each case, units, operators, previous identities etc are listed in *reverse* order, ie the *last* location, user or identity is given *first*. Seasoned readers should have little trouble with these potted histories and the *Abbreviations* section lists the most-used alphanumeric soup. Also given here are other applicable identities, maintenance serials, heritage registers etc.

Much work has gone into showing, wherever possible, when an airframe stopped flying. This is relatively easy with UK civil registered aircraft – see the next paragraph. With British military the abbreviation SOC (struck off charge) has been used as a wide *generic* term, to avoid endless abbreviations and definitions. The date given may well be when the airframe in question *was* struck off, but it may also apply to its being sold (either intact or as scrap), transferred to display purposes, or to a museum, or similar. Occasionally, last flown dates are given.

Where a date is given prefixed 'CoA' (Certificate of Airworthiness), this is the date at which it lapsed and is given as an *indication* of how long the airframe has been flightless. The term 'CoA' is a catch-all and used for all levels of certification, eg including Permit to Fly, Ferry Permit etc. Where an airframe has suffered an accident, this is given as 'Crashed' or 'Cr', no attempt has been made to try to delineate or infer the severity, or nature, or blame (!) of the incident. 'De-reg' refers to the date when a registration was formally cancelled from the civil register. It should be borne in mind that in some cases the 'paperwork' can lag behind the reality by decades! Particularly for museum aircraft an attempt has been made to show how long a collection has had an airframe. Mostly, this is noted as 'arrived', but in some cases 'acquired' is used to signify that the airframe was taken on while the collection was based elsewhere, or similar.

Column 7: Used for footnotes – eg [7] and explained at the base of the listing.

Column 8: 'Last noted' dates are given primarily to help historians to trace the status (or demise) of an airframe and perhaps to alert readers intending a visit as to the 'currency' of the information given. The CAA seeks 'No Flight' Declarations (NFD) from registered (but *not* de-registered) aircraft. There's nothing better than a physical sighting, but where many years have gone by, to give an *indication* of continued existence dates prefixed N quote the NFD. Please note: this date does *not* *necessarily* relate to the location under which the aircraft is listed.

ENGLAND

BEDFORDSHIRE

Includes the unitary authority of Luton

BEDFORD

A Skeeter is kept at a *private* venue in the area. Although dated, the Nord is *believed* to be current at a *separate* site.

☐ G-BPMU	Nord 3202	59	ex Little Staughton, G-BIZJ, N22546, ALAT F-MAIX. De-reg 15-6-20	N4-16
☐ XL809	Saro Skeeter AOP.12 G-BLIX	58	ex PH-HOF, Moordrecht, XL809, 26 Rgt, 652, 22 Flt, 654, 652. SOC 12-12-68	12-21

BIGGLESWADE Kennet Aviation can be found under Shuttleworth, Beds

CARDINGTON east of the A600 south of Bedford

Any reader who has not made the pilgrimage to the two awesome 700ft-long airship sheds is missing out. The northern-most example, No.1, was completed in 1916. The other was dismantled at Pulham, Norfolk, in 1928 and re-erected alongside its cousin. A year later, the R-101 commercial airship first took to the air from Cardington. On 4th October 1930 it departed eastwards on its maiden voyage, only to crash in France; just six of the 54 on board survived. With this disaster, Britain's airship programme was terminated. Since then, the giant structures have been used occasionally by modern-day airships. ◆ *No access, but plenty of public vantage points.*

CRANFIELD AERODROME east of Newport Pagnell   EGTC

Cranfield University / Cranfield Aerospace: Jetstream 200 G-RAVL was passed on to the Sywell Aviation Museum and the task of dismantling began in September 2019. Of enduring Handley Page construction, it proved to be made of stern stuff. Work continued to March 2020 when Covid-19 brought things to a halt. The move to Sywell, Northants, was finally completed on 23rd March 2021. Cranfield's loyalty to the Jetstream ended in the previous year when 'flying laboratory' Series 31 G-NFLA was retired, replaced by SAAB 340B G-NFLB. The Jetstream flavour is perpetuated as the BAE Systems test-bed is held in store and the fire crews have one to play with.

In association with the university, the Farnborough-based **Air Accident Investigation Branch** (AAIB) has an enclave alongside the airfield with a couple of airframes for instruction. Last noted in July 2012, the cockpit and other sections of Nimrod MRA.4 ZJ515 have been deleted. ◆ *On an active airfield; access only by prior permission* | **www.cranfield.ac.uk**

☐ G-BWWW*	BAe Jetstream3102	83	CoA 26-6-17. First noted 4-20	[1]	8-21
☐ G-COAI	Cranfield A1 Eagle	76	ex G-BCIT. De-reg 6-2-20		1-20
☐ 'G-DHEA'	HSA HS.125-3B G-OHEA	67	ex Hatfield, G-AVRG, G-5-12. CoA 7-8-92; de-reg 23-6-94. Trailer-mounted, rescue training		4-21
☐ G-DOCB	Boeing 737-436	91	ex BA. CoA 15-2-15, de-reg 2-7-15. Flew in 23-10-14. 'Cranfield University' titles, under 'awning'		1-22
☐ G-NFLA*	BAe Jetstream 3102	84	ex G-BRGN, G-BLHC, G-31-637. Last flight 12-12-20. CoA 21-8-21		6-21
☐ G-VUEM*	Cessna Citation 501	81	ex G-FLVU, N83ND, N4246A, LV-PML, N67749. Crashed 19-11-10, de-reg 14-7-11. Fuselage, AAIB		4-21
☐ SP-KWN	BAe Jetstream 3212	89	ex LN-FAC, N856TE, N422AM, G-31-856. Flew in 2011. Rescue training		11-21
☐ XX387	Sud Gazelle AH.1	75	ex Arborfield TAD.014, Fleetlands, 651, 661, 657, 16/5 Lancers. Westland-built. Crashed 15-12-92		4-19
☐ XZ668	Westland Lynx AH.7	81	ex M Wallop, 63, 3 Rgt, 653. Ditched 18-8-95		4-19

■ [1] The registration derives from its first operator, the Edinburgh-based Distillers Company - *Triple-Whisky*! Considerably modified by BAE Systems (Operations) as the ASTREA - Autonomous Systems Technology Related Airborne Evaluation and Assessment - test-bed. Used to pioneer the integration of UAVs within airspace used by 'inhabited' aircraft. It flew a 500-mile sortie in April 2013 totally under the command of a ground-based team, with the on-board crew only monitoring proceedings for safety.

T5 Alive: Russell Carpenter and friends keep this wonderful machine 'in steam'.
◆ *Occasional open days, or only by prior arrangement* | **email** via website | **www.lightningt5.com**

☐ XS458	'T' EE Lightning T.5	65	ex Binbrook, LTF, 11, LTF, 5-11 pool, LTF, 5, 226 OCU. SOC 24-6-88	1-22

Also: Maintaining and storing HS.146s is a local speciality - only long-termers are covered. RJ100 5A-FLA departed to Cotswold, Glos on 28th May 2021 and had been reduced to produce there by October.

❑ G-BADJ*	Piper Aztec 250	72	ex N14279. CoA 2-8-08. First noted 11-20		10-21
❑ G-BFSR	Cessna F.150J	69	ex OH-CBN. Reims-built. CoA 17-7-09, de-reg 30-10-18		4-21
❑ G-BMUT	Piper Seneca 200T	75	ex EC-CUH. CoA 22-12-09		12-19
❑ G-DLAL	Beech King Air 90	75	ex N816RL, N66BP, N816EP, N900MH, N2187L. CoA 17-3-14		11-21
❑ G-OFOA	HSA HS.146-100	76	ex Biggin Hill, G-BKMN, EI-COF, SE-DRH, G-BKMN, G-ODAN.		
			Hatfield-built. CoA 13-7-17, de-reg 6-12-17. Arrived 27-6-17		12-21
❑ G-SMLA*	HSA HS.146-200	85	ex JOTA Aviation, N880PS, G-OZRH, EI-DDF, G-OZRH,		
			N188US, N364PS. Hatfield-built. Arrived 22-10-20. Inst		11-21
❑ G-TZII	Thorp T.211	03	CoA 29-8-08. AD Aerospace-built		11-21
❑ G-WEFX*	HSA HS.146 RJ100	00	ex G-ILLR, HB-IYU, G-CGAC, G-6-379. Woodford-built.		
			CoA 16-6-20	[1]	1-22

■ [1] *Fox-Xray* acquired to act as an 'electrification' test-bed for Airbus/Rolls-Royce/Siemens as the E-Fan X. the programme was axed in March 2020 with little or no work carried out on the airframe.

DUNSTABLE AERODROME Last physically noted in June 2005, Rallye G-BLGS has been deleted.

EATON BRAY west of Dunstable
David Underwood: Veteran craftsman Peter Underwood died on 21st November 2021 and with his passing the workshop of 40-odd years will be winding down. Son Peter is continuing to restore Kirby Kite BGA.310 (see under Shuttleworth, Beds), hopefully returning it to Old Warden in 2022. The status of the Martin Monoplane project has yet to be determined. Kite BGA.237 moved to Bellarena, Northern Ireland, and Dagling BGA.492 to Grantham, Lincs.
◆ *Private* location in the *general* area, *no* public access

❑ G-AEYY	Martin Monoplane	37	ex Hitchin, Bishop's Stortford, Stoke-on-Trent, Meir.		
			De-reg 3-6-98. Fuselage. Arrived 7-1-18	[1]	12-21

■ [1] Incorporated DH.53 Humming Bird components, including the wings - see J7326 at London Colney, Herts. Following a crash in late 1937 it was rebuilt with a new fuselage.

FLITWICK northwest of Luton, north of J12 of the M1
Roger Creed: Continues to progress on *Charlie-November* ◆ *By prior permission* **only** | roger.creed52@gmail.com

❑ G-AHCN	Auster J1N Alpha	46	CoA 6-12-11, de-reg 29-9-14. Fuselage, arrived 6-12	[1]	3-20

■ [1] Wings destined for G-AHCN are from J1 G-AJDW – see Spilsby, Lincs

HATCH off the B658, southwest of Sandy
Skysport Engineering: ◆ **Strictly** *by prior permission* only | www.skysportengineering.co.uk

❑ AXB	Slingsby Skylark 2	56	BGA.733, ex Lyveden. CoA 30-6-02	[1]	9-21
❑ F-ANHO	Comper Swift	33	ex France, HB-OXE, CH-352. Fuselage		1-19
❑ N5595T	Douglas C-47A-85-DL	43	ex Thruxton, Blackbushe, G-BGCG, Spanish AF T.3-27,		
	Skytrain		N49V, N50322, USAAF 43-15536. Long Beach-built		12-21

■ [1] Prototype Skylark 2, flown by Flt Lt Douglas Bridson up to 30,000ft.

HENLOW AIRFIELD on the A6007 southwest of Biggleswade
RAF Signals Museum: Centred on the collection amassed by 1 Radio School when it was at Locking, Somerset. With the closure of the station the future of the museum is uncertain: negotiations with the local council are underway.
◆ *By prior arrangement* | **email** via website | www.rafsignalsmuseum.org.uk

RAF Henlow: The base is to shut in 2023; the aerodrome closed on 12th March 2020. The Gazelle/Lynx/Typhoon are/were used by the **RAF Centre of Aviation Medicine**. Turbulents G-ARRZ and G-BGBF, and Jodel G-BHNX are unaccounted for.

❑ WT612		Hawker Hunter F.1	54	ex Halton, Credenhill, Yatesbury 7496M (29-11-57),	
				A&AEE. Displayed	6-21
❑ XZ312		Sud Gazelle AH.1	76	ex Shawbury, Wattisham, 3 Regt. Westland-built. Cockpit	12-14
❑ ZD250	'636'	Westland Lynx HAS.3S	82	ex 702, 815, 702, 815, 702, 815, 829, 702. First noted 4-12	10-19
❑ -		Eurofighter Typhoon EMU	~	cockpit. First noted 7-18	7-18

LONDON LUTON AIRPORT

EGGW

❑ G-AOVS	Bristol Britannia 312	58	ex Redcoat, 'G-BRAC', Lloyd, BOAC. CoA 31-7-79,		
			de-reg 7-5-81. Fuselage. Rescue training		12-21

| ❑ VP-BJW | Boeing 737-301 | 87 | ex Kemble, KD Avia, N563AU, N348US, N328P | |
| | | | *Mitropoht Kirvil*. Forward fuselage. Rescue training | 12-19 |

LUTON

George Clarke's Amazing Spaces television programme occasionally focuses on an airframe-based conversion. A July 2020 episode zoomed in the conversion of the cockpit of avionics test-bed HS.125 *Delta-Mike* into a 'summer house'.
◆ At *private* location in the *general* area, *no* public access

| ❑ G-AXDM* | HSA HS.125-400B | 69 | ex Pershore, Farnborough, Edinburgh, BAE Systems, | |
| | | | GEC-Marconi. CoA 7-6-03, de-reg 13-11-03. Cockpit | 1-20 |

MEPPERSHALL on minor roads southwest of Henlow

At a *private* airstrip in the general area, an S.205 is stored.

| ❑ G-BBRX | SIAI-Marchetti S.205-18 | 66 | ex Crowland, LN-VYH, OO-HAQ. CoA 15-6-10, | |
| | | | de-reg 25-8-10. First noted 7-19 | 7-19 |

SHUTTLEWORTH AERODROME or Old Warden   EGTH

Shuttleworth Collection: The scope and variety of the collection, on wings and on wheels, need not be re-iterated here. Two exhibits carry notices that convey their importance: the Blériot is 'the world's oldest flying aeroplane and engine' and the Blackburn is 'the world's oldest airworthy British aeroplane'.

Supporting in many ways is the **Shuttleworth Veteran Aeroplane Society** (SVAS - hence Super Cub G-SVAS - **www.svasweb.org**) which publishes the excellent *Prop-Swing*. Don't overlook the Swiss Garden, an enchanting 'diversion'.

Title of Avro Triplane BAPC.6 was transferred to The Aeroplane Collection, Hooton Park, Cheshire, in 2019. Blériot BAPC.9 is on loan at Coventry, Warks.

Loaned Chilton G-AESZ departed by road on 10th September 2020 for Breighton, E Yorks; Ryan SCW VH-SCW had departed by late 2020; Hurricane I P3717 (G-HITT) made the hop to Duxford, Cambs, on 22nd April 2021. By late 2020 the Me 163 Komet fuselage, '191454', built to show off an original Walter HWK 509A-2 bi-fuel rocket motor, had been taken off display, the rocket motor remaining on show. A one-off abbreviation used in this listing: OW = Old Warden.

◆ *Signed from the A1. **Access changed** during 2020: stay on the B658 and turn at the Upper Caldecote roundabout to turn westwards on to the Shuttleworth estate at the 'flagged' entrance. | Biggleswade, SG18 9EP | **01767 627927** | enquiries@shuttleworth.org | www.shuttleworth.org*
*Please note: The hangar complex in the southeast corner is **not** available for inspection. Some aircraft listed below may occasionally move to 'the other side' but are regarded as 'front-of-house' exhibits.*

❑ G-EAGA		Sopwith Dove replica ✈	90	ex 'Essex', OW, Hatch. Skysport-built. Arr 5-15	[1]	1-22
❑ G-EBHX		DH Humming Bird	1923	ex Lympne No.8. Acquired 1-9-60. *L'Oiseau Mouche*		
				Crashed 1-7-12. CoA 4-4-13. Under restoration, off-site	[2]	8-20
❑ G-EBIR		DH DH.51 ✈	1924	ex VP-KAA, G-KAA, G-EBIR. Acquired 7-65.		
				Aircraft Transport & Travel Ltd colours	[3]	1-22
❑ G-EBJI		Hawker Cygnet replica ✈	77	arrived 4-10, first flight 4-12	[4]	10-21
❑ G-EBJO		ANEC II ✈	1924	ex Radcliffe on Trent, OW, West Malling, Lympne 1924,		
				No.7. Acquired 1-37		1-22
❑ G-EBLV		DH.60 Moth ✈	1925	ex Hatfield. Arrived 1993	[5]	1-22
❑ G-EBNV	'4'	English Electric Wren II ✈	1923	BAPC.11, ex Warton, Ashton, Samlesbury, Preston,		
				Science Museum, Lympne No.4. Acquired 15-9-57	[6]	1-22
❑ G-EBWD		DH.60X Moth ✈	28	acquired 21-1-32	[7]	1-22
❑ G-AAIN		Parnall Elf II ✈	32	ex Southend, Fairoaks, Badminton. Acquired 7-51		1-22
❑ G-AANG		Blériot XI ✈	1910	BAPC.3, ex Ampthill, Blackfriars, Hendon.		
	No.13			Acquired 1935. See above		1-22
❑ G-AANH		Deperdussin ✈	1910	BAPC.4, ex *Those Magnificent Men*, Ampthill.		
	No.43			Acquired 1935		1-22
❑ G-AANI	No.9	Blackburn Monoplane ✈	1912	BAPC.5, ex Wittering. Acquired 1937		1-22
❑ G-AAPZ		Desoutter I ✈	30	ex Higher Blagdon, OW. Acquired 5-1-35		1-22
❑ G-AAYX		Southern Martlet ✈	30	ex Shoreham, Redhill, Staverton, Woodley. Acquired 1955		1-22
❑ G-ABAG		DH Gipsy Moth ✈	30	'arrived' 1-04	[1]	10-21
❑ G-ACSS	'34'	DH Comet ✈	34	ex Hatfield, Farnborough, OW, Leavesden, Hatfield,		
				London Colney, Gravesend, G-ACSS, K5084 A&AEE, RAE,		
				AA&EE, RAE, G-ACSS. *Grosvenor House*. Acquired 30-10-65		1-22
❑ G-ACTF		Comper Swift ✈	32	ex Rhos, VT-ADO. Acquired 16-8-96. *The Scarlet Angel*		10-21

☐ G-ADGP	'8'	Miles Hawk Speed Six ✈	35	ex White Waltham, OW, Southampton, USA, OW Phillips & Powis-built. Arrived 10-5-18		1-22
☐ G-ADRR		Aeronca C.3 ✈	36	ex N17423. Arrived by 12-14	[4]	10-21
☐ G-AEBB		Mignet HM.14 'Flea'	36	ex Southampton. CoA 31-5-39, de-reg 1-12-46 Acquired 1968	[8]	1-22
☐ G-AEBJ		Blackburn B-2 ✈	36	ex Brough, Warton, Blackburn, 4 EFTS, Brough, Hanworth. Arrived 3-08	[5]	1-22
☐ G-AEXF		Percival Mew Gull replica ✈	36	ex Breighton, OW, Sudbury, OW, Squires Gate, Booker, Yeadon, Blackbushe, France,ZS-AHM. Arrived 6-10-13	[9]	1-22
☐ G-AGSH		DH Dragon Rapide 6 ✈	45	ex Hurn, Lower Upham, EI-AJO, G-AGSH, Dominie NR808 n/s. Brush-built. Arr 27-2-09. BEA c/s, *Jemma Meeson*	[10]	10-21
☐ G-ARSG	'12'	Avro Triplane IV replica ✈	64	BAPC.1, ex *Those Magnificent Men...* Hampshire Aero Club-built. Acquired 1966		1-22
☐ G-ARZB		Wallis WA-116/Mc	62	ex Reymerston, XR943, G-ARZB. Beagle-built *Little Nellie*. CoA 29-6-93, de-reg 3-8-16. Arrived 4-14	[11]	1-22
☐ G-ASPP	'12A'	Bristol Boxkite replica ✈	64	BAPC.2, ex *Those Magnificent Men…* F G Miles-built. Acquired 1966		1-22
☐ G-BFIP		Wallbro Mono replica	78	ex Reymerston, Flixton, Shipdham, Swanton Morley. CoA 22-4-82, de-reg 28-3-01. Arrived 20-3-15	[11] [12]	1-22
☐ G-CAMM	'6'	Hawker Cygnet replica ✈	92	ex Hucknall, G-ERDB. Arrived 1995	[13]	3-20
☐ G-CDXU		Chilton DW.1 replica ✈	09	CoA 18-9-17	[14]	3-20
☐ G-SVAS		Piper Super Cub 150 ✈	61	ex G-BGWH, ST-ABR, G-ARSR, N10F. Acquired 13-10-08		1-22
☐ ADJ		Slingsby Kirby Kite	37	BGA.310, ex Tibenham. Acquired 2011. On overhaul at Eaton Bray, 2021-2022	[15]	10-21
☐ AQQ		EoN Primary ✈	c47	BGA.580, ex Hatch, Duxford, Henlow, Twinwood Farm,		
		G-ALPS		Cranfield, G-ALPS (de-reg 7-2-63). Acquired late 1960s		1-22
☐ –		Fauvel AV.36CR Monobloc ✈	55	BGA.1999, ex Booker, RAFGSA, F-CBSH. Wassmer-built Arrived by aero-tow from G-SVAS 16-7-14		1-22
☐ –		Dixon Ornithopter	c1912	BAPC.8, ex Dunstable. Acquired 1960s		1-22
☐ –		Lilienthal replica	06	BAPC.439, ex St Albans. Arrived 4-07	[16]	1-22
☐ –		Lilienthal biplane replica	06	BAPC.437. Donated 11-12	[17]	1-22
☐ –		Pilcher Bat Mk.3 replica	08	BAPC.337, ex St Albans. Arrived 11-08	[16]	1-22
☐ –		Pilcher Triplane replica	03	BAPC.441, arrived 2006	[18]	3-18
☐ NC8115*		Travel Air D-4000	29	Arrived 8-9-20	[19]	10-21
☐ '1611'		Bristol Scout C replica ✈	15	ex '1264'. Bristol Scout Group, Ludlow-built.		
		G-FDHB		First noted 10-15	[20]	10-21
☐ '9917'		Sopwith Pup ✈	1920	ex 'N6181', 'N5180', 'N5184', West Malling, Kingston.		
		G-EBKY		Acquired 1937	[21]	1-22
☐ 'B1162'	'F'	Bristol F.2B ✈	1918	ex Filton, Watford, D8096, 208. Acquired 2-52		
		G-AEPH		22 Sqn colours, France 3-18, by 11-20		1-22
☐ 'C1096'		Royal Aircraft Factory	03	ex F-AZBF, Le Bourget, Selby. Arrived 8-18.		
	'3'	SE.5a replica ✈ G-ERFC		Tested 19-10-18. 56 Sqn colours	[22]	1-22
☐ 'C4918'		Bristol M.1C	81	ex Dewsbury. 'C' Flight, NAW-built.		
		replica ✈ G-BWJM		Acquired 28-10-97. 72 Sqn colours	[23]	1-22
☐ 'D1851'	'X'	Sopwith Camel F1	01	ex Batley. NAW-built. Arrived 28-8-13,		
		replica G-BZSC		first flown 18-5-17. *Ikanopit*, 70 Sqn colours	[23]	1-22
☐ 'E3273'		Avro 504K ✈	1918	ex G-ACNB, 'H5199', 'E3404', *Reach for the Sky*, Woodford,		
		G-ADEV		Boscombe Down, Portsmouth, Airspeed, Avro 504N. Acquired 1936. 77 Sqn c/s, red-blue roundels	[24]	1-22
☐ F904		Royal Aircraft Factory	1918	ex 'D7000', Farnborough, Whitley, G-EBIA, F904 84 Sqn.		
		SE.5a G-EBIA		Wolseley-built. Acquired 8-59. 92 Sqn colours	[25]	1-22
☐ 'N6290'		Sopwith Triplane	80	ex Dewsbury. NAW-built. Arrived 6-90.		
		replica ✈ G-BOCK		8 Sqn RNAS colours, *Dixie II*	[23] [26]	1-22
☐ K1786		Hawker Tomtit ✈	31	ex Dunsfold, Langley, Hawker, Castle Bromwich,		
		G-AFTA		Braunstone, RAF 5 GCF, 23 GCF, 3 FTS. Acquired 5-60		1-22
☐ 'K2585'		DH Tiger Moth ✈	42	ex Mk.II T6818, Aston Down, 21 EFTS. Morris-built.		
		G-ANKT		Acquired 9-72. CFS 'sunburst' colours	[27]	1-22
☐ 'K3241'		Avro Tutor ✈	33	ex HSA, K3215, 61 OTU, 41 OTU, Hawarden SF, CFS.		
		G-AHSA		Acquired 1959. CFS 'sunburst' colours		1-22

☐ 'K5414'   Hawker Hind   37   BAPC.78. ex 'K5457', Kabul, Afghan AF. Acquired 1970.
                   (Afghan) ✈   G-AENP   'XV' - 15 Sqn colours   1-22
☐ 'K7985'   Gloster Gladiator I   37   ex '423' and '427', L8032, 'N2308', L8032, 'K8032',
                   ✈   G-AMRK   Gloster, Ansty, Hamble, 8 MU, 61 OTU, 1624F, 2 AACU.
                                                                 Acquired 7-11-60. 73 Sqn colours   [28]   1-22
☐ K8203   Hawker Demon I   37   ex Hatch, Cardington, 2292M, 9 BGS, 9 AOS, 64.
                                    G-BTVE   Boulton Paul-built. Arr 23-7-09. CoA 4-9-18, 64 Sqn c/s   [29]   1-22
☐ 'N3788'   Miles Magister I ✈   41   ex 'V1075', Shoreham, Sandown, Shoreham,
                                    G-AKPF   V1075, 16 EFTS. Phillips & Powis-built. Arrived 9-01   [30]   1-22
☐ P6382   Miles Magister I ✈   39   ex 'G-AJDR', P6382, 3 EFTS, 16 EFTS.
                   ✈   G-AJRS   Phillips & Powis-built. Acquired 3-4-70   1-22
☐ 'V9367'   Westland   42   ex 'V9441', Duxford, Strathallan, RCAF 2355.
                   'MA-B' Lysander III ✈   G-AZWT   Acquired 1997. 161 Sqn colours   1-22
☐ Z7015   '7-L' Hawker Sea   39   ex Duxford, Staverton, OW, Loughborough, Yeovilton,
                          Hurricane I ✈   G-BKTH   759, 880. CCF-built. Acq 21-2-61. 880 Sqn colours   1-22
☐ AR501   'DU-E' V-S Spitfire V ✈   42   ex Duxford, Thurleigh, Henlow, Loughborough, CGS, 61 OTU,
                                    G-AWII   1 TEU, 58 OTU, 422, 312, Culmhead Stn Flt, 504, 310.
                                                                 Westland-built. SOC 21-3-46. Arr 6-61. 312 Sqn colours   1-22
☐ 'TX176'   Avro XIX Srs 2 ✈   46   ex Woodford, Strathallan, Kemps, Treffield, Smiths.
                                    G-AHKX   Arrived 29-6-02. Coningsby SF colours   [5]   1-22
☐ XA241   JJS   Slingsby G'hopper TX.1   53   BGA.4556, ex Cambridge, Croydon. Arrived 12-95. Stored   1-14
☐ XF603   Percival Provost   55   ex Cranfield, Filton, Bristol, 27 MU, CAW, RAFC.
                   T.1 ✈   G-KAPW   SOC 12-9-67. Acquired 2-11-01. RAF grey / green camo   [31]   1-22
☐ 'S-11'*   Ryan ST-A   40   ex USA, N288Y, VH-AGZ, RAAF A50-31. Arrived 8-20
                   ✈   N7779   First flight on site 8-3-21. Dutch Naval Air Service c/s   [32]   1-22
☐ '18671'   DHC Chipmunk   52   ex G-ROYS, 7438M, WP905 CFS, 664, RAFC.
                   T.10 ✈   G-BNZC   Acquired 3-00. RCAF colours   1-22
☐ -   '28' Polikarpov Po-2   44   ex N588NB, ZK-POZ, N588NB, G-BSSY, YU-CLB,
                          Mule ✈   G-BSSY   Yugoslav AF 0094, Sov AF. Acq 31-7-03. Soviet colours   [33]   1-22

■ **[1]** Dove and Moth G-ABAG on loan from A and P A Wood. (See also Great Dunmow, Essex.) **[2]** Prototype Humming Bird, first flown 1-10-23. **[3]** DH.51 in Aircraft Transport and Travel colours (standing in for a DH.9B?) for a British Airways advert since 2011. **[4]** Cygnet *Juliet-India* and Aeronca G-ADRR owned by Colin Essex. **[5]** G-EBLV, B-2 and the 'Anson' (sorry, Avro XIX) on loan from BAE Systems, forming the **BAE Systems Heritage Flight**. **[6]** G-EBNV is substantially the unregistered Lympne trials No.4, which had been with the Science Museum until 1945, with engine parts from the original G-EBNV (Lympne No.3). **[7]** G-EBWD was bought by Richard Ormonde Shuttleworth for £300 from Brooklands School of Flying on 21-1-32. **[8]** 'Flea' built by Kenneth Owen at Southampton; Authorisation No.31 issued 2-3-36. **[9]** Most famed for the Cape Town out-and-back dash by Alex Henshaw in 2-39. This machine suffered an accident 7-8-65 and was donated to the Historic Aircraft Preservation Society - later Reflectaire - and allowed to rot at Squires Gate. Much reconfigured/rebuilt G-AEXF was restored 1972-1978 and to stress how little of the original survived, it was given a PFA project number - hence the 'replica' suffix. See under Tattershall Thorpe, Lincs, and Stafford, Staffs, for *more* 'G-AEXFs'. **[10]** Rapide on loan from Philip Meeson. **[11]** *Little Nellie* and the Wallbro - see note 12 - on loan from the Wallis family estate. See also 'off-site' below. **[12]** Replica of the original built by brothers Horace Samuel Wallis and Percival Valentine Wallis (hence Wallbro), respectively the father and uncle of the late Wg Cdr Ken Wallis, and flown at Cambridge, 4-7-1910. *India-Papa* built by Ken and his cousin Geoffrey - ie son of Percival - first flown 10-8-78. **[13]** G-CAMM, built by Don Cashmore. Don also built the Bristol M.1 replica at Cosford, Shrop. **[14]** Chilton *Xray-Uniform* on loan from Michael Gibbs. **[15]** By far and away the largest elements of BGA.310 can be found at Bellarena, N Ireland, qv. *This* BGA.310 was rebuild in 1982 using the fuselage, port wing and elevator of BGA.327 plus parts from BGA.310. **[16]** Lilienthal No.11 'Standard Flying Apparatus' circa 1894 and the Pilcher ('Standard' also referred to as 'Normal'.) Bat Mk.3 built by Eric Littledike of St Albans, Herts. **[17]** Built for Shuttleworth by Carsten Brinkmeier in Germany, a replica of the 'Kleiner Doppeldecker' (Little Biplane) of 1895. *Another* Brinkmeier replica, a 'Normalapparat' ('Normal' or 'Standard' is stored against a wall in Hangar 5. Labels describe it as 'centre section, 'fuselage' and tailfin". The Normalapparat is essentially the lower component of the Doppeldecker. **[18]** At the time Percy Pilcher was killed at Stanford Hall, Leics, on 18-9-1899 (see Stanford, Leics and Edinburgh, Scotland) he was working on a weight-shift powered triplane. A team from Cranfield University and Bill Brooks of Mainair Sports built a modern-day version for a TV film in 2003. It was flown for the first time on 29-8-03 by Bill Brooks. On 5-9-03 it managed a ¼ mile flight. It was presented to Shuttleworth by the TV company. **[19]** D-4000 owned by Mike South and Richard Seeley. **[20]** Scout on loan from Bristol Scout Group. **[21]** G-EBKY first 'surfaces' as a two-seat version of the Pup, the Sopwith Dove, registered to D L Hollis Williams 3-25. This one was part of a cache of unfinished examples stored at Kingston and acquired by DHW for £5. Stored at West Malling from 1933, it went to Richard Shuttleworth in 1937 and given Pup status. **[22]** SE.5 on loan from Tom Harris – see also Duxford, Cambs. Construction began by John Tetley of Selby in the late 1980s - see also G-BKDT at Elvington, N Yorks - completed by the French Memorial Flight at Le Bourget and first flown in France. In the colours of Canadian Henry 'Hank' Burden DSO DFC 56 Sqn. **[23]** NAW - the former Northern Aeroplane Workshops, Dewsbury. **[24]** The 504's history prior to being discovered at Portsmouth where it had been kept by Airspeed is problematical. It was converted to 504K status from what is believed to have been a glider or banner-towing 504N. The 'accepted' identity is G-ADEV, but as this ended up with an ATC unit in Windermere (as 3118M) in 1942, this is doubted. It was registered as G-ACNB in 12-82 but took up G-ADEV in 4-84. Its latest guise is as a night-fighter with 77 Home Defence Sqn, based at Turnhouse, Scotland, 1918. **[25]** As revealed in *Above the Trenches* (Shores/Franks/Guest, Grub

Street, 1990) Major Charles E M Pickthorne, CO of 84 Sqn, shot down a Fokker D.VII while flying F904 on 8-11-18. **[26]** Production of Triplanes came to 152 and as the late Sir Thomas Sopwith decreed that *Charlie-Kilo* should be considered as a late production example, it is known at Old Warden as No.153. **[27]** Tiger Moth is a composite of three acquired by the collection in 1966, making its first flight in 10-77. **[28]** Gladiator flies in the colours of Plt Off 'Cobber' Kain. **[29]** Demon was restored at Hatch, Beds and is on loan from Demon Displays Ltd. **[30]** David Bramwell's N3788 is a composite, using the centre section of G-AIUA (see Balcombe, W Sussex), rear fuselage of G-ANLT, wings of G-AHYL plus others. N3788 was 'demobbed' on 27-8-47 becoming G-ANLT; its RAF pedigree was ex 169 Sqn, 2 FIS, 2 FTS, 5 EFTS, 8 EFTS, 27 E&RFTS. **[31]** XF603 carries the markings of one delivered to the Sultan of Oman's Air Force. **[32]** Ryan owned by Arnaldo Leon. **[33]** Off-the-wall factoid: The Po-2's US registration pays homage to the Soviet all-woman 588th Night Bombing Regiment which flew nuisance raids against the Germans, earning the pilots the nickname 'Night Witches'.

Kennet Aviation and **Kennet Engineering**: Established on the 'far side' - ie strictly non-public - from mid-2016, the workshop became operational in mid-2018. Two airframes are still at the former base, North Weald, Essex: 'JP' 'XD693' (G-AOBU) and Skyraider 126922 (G-RADR). Airworthy Texan '8084' (G-KAMY) shares its time between here, North Weald and Yeovilton.
    Spitfire F.22 PK664 had moved to Sandown, Isle of Wight, by late 2020. Seafire F.17 SX336 (G-KASX) was test flown following restoration on 18th November 2021 and was ferried to Yeovilton, Somerset, on 15th December 2021.

◆ **Strictly** *by prior appointment* **only**

❏ AA810*	V-S Spitfire PR.IV	G-PRID 41	ex Norway, 1 PRU. Lost near Trondheim 5-3-42	**[1]** 1-20
❏ LA564*	V-S Seafire F.46	46	ex N Weald, Newport Pagnell, Redbourn, Newark,	
		G-FRSX	Southend, Charnock Richard, Carlisle, Anthorn, 738, 767,	
			A&AEE. SOC 29-6-51. First noted 4-17	**[2]** 10-20
❏ SR462*	V-S Seafire F.XV	45	ex Sandown, N Weald, USA, N462XV, N9413Z, Burma,	
		G-TGVP	'UB415', UB412, G-15-225, SR462 n/s. SOC 5-6-52.	
			Westland-built. Arrived by mid-2020	**[3]** 10-20
❏ SX300*	V-S Seafire F.17	46	ex N Weald, G-CDTM, Twyford, Warwick, Leamington	
		G-RIPH	Spa, Warrington, Bramcote A2054/ A646 (9-6-53), 728.	
			Westland-built. First noted 6-18	**[2]** 10-20

■ **[1]** Kennet managing this project for Spitfire AA810 Restoration Ltd. AA810 lost on its 16th 'op' and 20th flight: **www.spitfireaa810.co.uk [2]** LA564 and SX300 are registered to Seafire Displays Ltd. **[3]** SR462 registered to Dubai-based Tim Percy. His father, the late Lt Cdr Terence Gerard Vaughan 'Pablo' Percy flew this machine; its civil registration reflects his initials.

Also, off-site: The Wallis autogyros previously held at Reymerston, Norfolk, are stored in the care of the estate of the late Wg Cdr Kenneth Wallis at a site close by. Unless noted, all of these arrived on 24th September 2013. WA-116 G-ARZB and the Wallbro Monoplane are with the Shuttleworth Collection - above - on loan. WA-116 'XR944' (G-ATTB) was registered to an Oxford-based company as far back as November 2014 is believed not to have come here.

◆ **Private** *location,* **not** *open to public inspection*

❏ G-ARRT	Wallis WA-116/Mc	61	ex Reymerston. CoA 26-5-83, de-reg 3-8-16	7-19
❏ 'G-ARZB'	Wallis WA-116	67	ex London, Flixton, Reymerston, London, Reymerston.	
		G-AVDH	*Little Nellie II*. De-reg 19-2-69	**[1]** 2-20
❏ G-ASDY	Wallis WA-116/F	62	ex Rey'ton. Beagle-built. CoA 28-10-97, de-reg 3-8-16	7-19
❏ G-ATHM	Wallis WA-116/F	65	ex Rey'ton, 4R-ACK, G-ATHM. CoA 23-5-93, de-reg 3-8-16	7-19
❏ G-AVDG	Wallis WA-116/R	65	ex Reymerston. CoA 23-5-92, de-reg 3-8-16	7-19
❏ G-AVJV	Wallis WA-117 Srs 1	67	ex Reymerston. De-reg 3-8-16	**[2]** 7-19
❏ G-AVJW	Wallis WA-118/M	67	ex Reymerston. CoA 21-4-83, de-reg 3-8-16	**[3]** 7-19
❏ G-AXAS	Wallis WA-116/T/Mc	69	ex Reymerston. CoA 30-6-12, de-reg 3-8-16. *Zeus III*	**[4]** 7-19
❏ G-AYVO	Wallis WA-120 Srs 1	71	ex Reymerston, South Kensington. De-reg 3-8-16	7-19
❏ G-BAHH	Wallis WA-121/Mc	72	ex Reymerston. CoA 14-2-06, de-reg 3-8-16	7-19
❏ G-BGGU	Wallis WA-116/S	94	ex Reymerston. De-reg 3-8-16	7-19
❏ G-BGGW	Wallis WA-122/RR	78	ex Reymerston. De-reg 3-8-16	7-19
❏ G-BLIK	Wallis WA-122/F/Special	84	ex Reymerston. De-reg 3-8-16	7-19
❏ G-BMJX	Wallis WA-116/X	87	ex Reymerston. De-reg 3-8-16	**[5]** 7-19
❏ G-BNDG	Wallis WA-201 Srs 1 twin	87	ex Reymerston. De-reg 3-8-16	7-19
❏ G-SCAN	Wallis WA-116/100/R	82	ex Reymerston. CoA 4-8-10, de-reg 3-8-16	7-19
❏ G-VIEW	Wallis WA-117/L	82	ex Reymerston. De-reg 3-8-16	7-19
❏ G-VTEN	Wallis WA-117/RR	85	ex Reymerston. De-reg 12-6-89	7-19

■ **[1]** G-AVDH was turned into a clone of G-ARZB for the 1967 Bond movie *You Only Live Twice* and unofficially called *Little Nellie II*. Used for studio shots, it was later a source of spares for G-AXAS. **[2]** Built using many components from G-ATCV. **[3]** Rebuilt from G-ATPW. **[4]** *Alpha-Sierra* flew in the 1980 TV series *The Martian Chronicles*. **[5]** Rebuilt from G-ATHL.

THURLEIGH, north of Bedford, east of the A6

306th Bomb Group Museum: Sited in the wartime small arms and ammunition store, while the museum's central theme is the Flying Fortress-equipped 306th, the 'home front' and Thurleigh's Royal Aircraft Establishment days are also covered.
◆ *c/o Thurleigh Airfield Business Park, Bedford, MK44 1QU* | **@306thmuseum** | **www.306bg.co.uk**

TWINWOOD FARM near Clapham, off the A6 north of Bedford

Twinwood Museums: The tower has been turned into a Glenn Miller era 'shrine'. It was from Twinwood that the legendary band leader departed for France in a Noorduyn UC-64 Norseman on 15th December 1944, never to be seen again. Two former RAF accommodation blocks contain exhibitions: Hut 37 housing 'Under Fire' exhibition, on the wartime fire service while Hut 44 has been returned to its wartime status.
◆ **NB:** *As W&R27 closed for press the museums – but* not *other events - were closed until further notice. Keep an eye on the website* | *Twinwood Road, Clapham, MK41 6AB* | **info@twinwoodfestival.com** | **www.twinwoodevents.com**

BERKSHIRE
Includes the unitary authorities of Bracknell Forest, Reading, Slough, Windsor and Maidenhead, Wokingham

---

BINFIELD north of the B3034, northwest of Bracknell

Although the references are somewhat dated, the contents of a *private* store in the *general* area are *thought* unchanged.

❑ G-ASXF	Brantly 305	r64	ex Thruxton, Biggin Hill, CoA 16-2-79, de-reg 24-5-82	4-11
❑ G-AYNS	Airmaster H2-B1	r70	ex Redhill. CoA 13-2-73, de-reg 30-5-84. In a container	5-17
❑ G-BPCJ	Cessna 150J	69	ex Solihull, Tattershall Thorpe, N61096. *Charlie.* Damaged 25-1-90; de-reg 4-7-90	5-17

BRACKNELL

A *private* owner locally is *believed* to still have a 'JP' cockpit.

❑ XM417	'D' Hunting Jet Provost T.3	60	ex Hednesford, Fownhope, Halton 8054BM (23-10-69), Shawbury, 6 FTS, 7 FTS, 2 FTS. Cockpit	5-17

COLNBROOK south of the A4 east of the Datchet reservoir

Colnbrook Depot: Poyle Industrial Estate. A Boeing 737 cockpit is kept at the site.

❑ G-CEAF	Boeing 737-229	74	ex Hurn, European, G-BYRI, OO-SDD, EC-EEG, OO-SDD, Cockpit, trolley-mounted. DHL colours	10-21

GREENHAM COMMON east of the A339 south of Newbury

Greenham Common Tower: A combination of village centre, café, space-for-hire and museum with impressive views of the area; the tower opened to the public on 8th September 2018.
◆ *Burys Bank Road, RG19 8BZ.* | **01635 44145** | **info@greenhamtower.org.uk** | **www.greenhamtower.org.uk**

HUNGERFORD on the A4 east of Marlborough

A *private* workshop in the *general* area is at work on a Chilton and a Tiger. ◆ **Strictly** *by prior permission* **only**

❑ G-AFGH	Chilton DW.1	38	ex Billingshurst. CoA 7-7-83	N5-19
❑ G-AMCM*	DH Tiger Moth	42	ex DE249, A&AEE, 29 EFTS, 7 EFTS, 18 EFTS, Glider Pilot Exercise Unit, 296. 297. SOC 8-6-50	4-20

LAMBOURN on the B4000 north of Hungerford

A Hurricane is believed to be at a *private* workshop in the area. ◆ *By prior arrangement* **only**

❑ KZ191	Hawker Hurricane IV	43	ex N Weald, Fowlmere, Israel, 351, 1695 Flt, AFDU. SOC 26-9-46	1-15

LANGLEY on the B470 north of the junction of the M4 and A4, east of Slough

Langley Academy: Langley Road. On the site of the former Hawker flight test airfield, the aviation connection is marked by a 'Flea' on loan from the Brooklands Museum. ◆ *By prior arrangement* **only** | **www.langleyacademy.org**

❏	'G-ADRY'	Mignet HM.14 'Flea'	c67 BAPC.29, ex Brooklands, Aberdare, Swansea.	
			Suspended in foyer, on loan. Arrived 8-10	[1] 12-21

■ **[1]** Built using some original 1930s parts by P D Roberts of Swansea, circa 1967, completed by 1978.

MAIDENHEAD

Maidenhead Heritage Centre: Includes 'Grandma Flew Spitfires', a tribute to the gallantry of the men and women of the Air Transport Auxiliary. Headquartered at nearby White Waltham, ATA was nicknamed 'Anything to Anywhere' from its initials. A pre-bookable Spitfire simulator is also available.
◆ *18 Park Street, Maidenhead, SL6 1SL* | **01628 780555** | **www.maidenheadheritage.org.uk** | **www.atamuseum.org**

Also: A Harvard and a Hunter are at a *private* location in the area. At *another* venue a Bristol 170 flightdeck is kept.

❏ C-FDFC*		Bristol 170 Mk.31	54 ex Fleet, Enstone, G-BISU Instone, ZK-EPH, NZ5912, ZK-BVI,	
			G-18-194. Crashed 18-7-96. Flightdeck	6-20
❏ KF435		NAA Harvard T.2B	44 ex Swindon, Guildford, Duxford, Ottershaw, Booker,	
	'5666'		Camberley, Sandhurst, 1 FTS, 2 FTS, 22 SFTS, 20 FTS,	
			11 (P)AFU. Noorduyn-built. SOC 24-9-57. Arrived 25-9-14	8-20
❏ XL592	'Y'	Hawker Hunter T.7	58 ex Booker, Kemble, Exeter, Scampton 8836M (31-8-84),	
			1 TWU, TWU, 229 OCU. Arrived 7-14	8-20

MEMBURY Last physically noted in the area in October 2009, Dragon Rapide 'Z7258' (G-AHGD) has been deleted.

WELFORD or Welford Park, north of the M4, west of junction 13 (A34)

Ridgeway Military and Aviation Research Group: Within the former World War Two airfield, now known as Welford Park, is a *private* museum. ◆ *By prior appointment* **only** | **rmarg@hotmail.co.uk** | **www.rmarg.org.uk**

❏ 42-93510		Douglas C-47A-25-DK	43 ex -?-, Kew, Ottershaw, Kew, Cranfield, 6W-SAE, F-GEFY,	
	'CM'	Skytrain	Senegal AF, French AF, OK-WAR, USAAF 42-93510.	
			Oklahoma City-built. Cockpit. 435th TCG, 78th TCS c/s	[1] 12-19
❏ -		Airspeed Horsa replica	c76 ex *Bridge Too Far*	12-19

■ **[1]** An alternative 'back story' deserves further research. It could be 1944 and Oklahoma-built C-47A-30-DK 43-48020, which became RAF Dakota III KG737, serving with 525 Sqn and 1381 TCU until SOC 7-11-46. It then served KLM as PH-TDT, later F-OAFS, transferring to the Senegalese identity 6V-AAE. Over to you!

WHITE WALTHAM AERODROME south of the A4 southwest of Maidenhead EGLM

Shoot Aviation: Billed as "Europe's largest provider of aviation sets and content for film and TV" the company has extensive facilities, including the 'The Bond Hangar' and 'Ops Room' on the southern perimeter. Turnaround is swift on a lot of airframes: many are brought in for a particular job and leave again and others don't meet *W&R's* coverage criteria. Such items are not listed - only long-life termers are given here.

Noralpha fuselage G-BAYV had arrived from Crowland, Lincs, by April 2021. It was used in a film, perhaps about the formative years of the SAS in North Africa during World War Two, some of which was filmed at Bentwaters, Suffolk. Beyond that it was used 'on location' in Oxfordshire, before returning to Crowland, Lincs. Nord Pingouins G-ETME and G-OTME were also involved in this as was fellow F-BAOZ. (G-ETME and 'OTME had moved on to Audley End, Essex during the summer of 2021 for return to flight.)

By October 2020 a trio of de-registered helicopters were noted: JetRangers G-BPWI and G-RNBW and the fabulously registered MD600N G-THUG. By September 2021 these were joined by Agusta 109 G-BZEI and Squirrel G-CPOL. All may have lingered. Hercules forward fuselage XV221 had moved to St Athan, Wales, by May 2020.
◆ **Strictly** *by prior appointment* **only** | **www.shootaviation.com**

❏ F-BAOZ*		Nord Pingouin	82 ex Montelimar, French mil No.92	8-21
❏ N247CK		Canadair Challenger 600	82 ex *Kingsman* (2014), G-NREG, N247CK. De-reg 15-2-16.	8-21
❏ 'N247CK'		Piper Navajo 310 G-BLFZ	79 ex PH-RWS, N3538W. De-reg 27-1-17	8-21
❏ N623NP*		Grumman Gulfstream III	82 ex St Athan, Hurn, N723MM, N891MG, N802GA, N303GA.	
			Last flight 2-12. Arrived 23-9-21	11-21
❏ N2700*		Fairchild C-119G-FA	51 ex Ingatestone, Balcombe, Redhill, N Weald, Manston,	
		Flying Boxcar	3C-ABA, Belgian AF CP-9, C-119F 51-2700. Cockpit	[1] 5-21
❏ -*		Boeing 737-400	~ cockpit, first noted 9-21	9-21
❏ ZA355	'EA'	Panavia Tornado GR.1	80 ex Swansea, Selby, Lossiemouth 9310M, 15, TTTE.	
			SOC 31-5-01. Arr 9-18. Desert 'pink, *MiG Eater* colours	[2] 8-21

☐ ZB506*		Westland Sea King Mk.4X	82	ex Charlwood, Horsham, Boscombe Down, QinetiQ, DERA, DTEO, DRA, RAE. Sectioned. First noted 2-21	6-21
☐ ZF116*	'WP'	Westland Sea King HC.4	86	ex Charlwood, Colsterworth (?), Gosport, 845, 848, 772. Sectioned. Arrived 21-1-20	5-21
☐ 'ZF355'	'633'	Westland Lynx HAS.3(ICE) XZ238	77	ex Croft, Fleetlands, *Endurance* Flt, 815, HAS.2, 702, 815, 700L 815, 700L	8-21 8-21
☐ ZG889*		Westland Lynx AH.9A	91	ex Ipswich, M Wallop, Staverton. SOC 23-9-16. Arr 10-8-21	8-21

■ **[1]** A former Italian Air Force C-119 cockpit is also thought to have been used in a film project. **[2]** Painted in the colours of 40+ 'ops' Gulf War veteran ZA447, which is still extant at Cosford, Shropshire.

Aerodrome:

☐ G-AFLW		Miles Monarch	38	Phillips & Powis-built. CoA 30-7-98, de-reg 3-5-01	8-21
☐ G-BZMT		Piper Warrior III	00	ex N4147D. De-reg 28-7-15. Rescue training, f/n 2-20	2-20
☐ SE-GVH		Piper Tomahawk 112	~	ex Little Staughton, Chessington. Cockpit	**[1]** 10-17
☐ HS554		Fairey Swordfish II G-RNMZ	43	ex Canada, C-GEVS, RCAF (SOC 2-8-46), 745 Sqn FAA, RCAF. Blackburn-built. Arrived 23-7-19	**[2]** 4-21

■ **[1]** Tomahawk cockpit tours around local events with the Joystick Club. **[2]** Registered to White Waltham Airfield Ltd.

WINDSOR

Sydney Camm Memorial: In Alexandra Gardens, Barry Avenue, a Hurricane honours its Windsor-born designer.

☐ 'R4229'	'GN-J'	Hawker Hurricane FSM	12	BAPC.334, Pole-mounted, unveiled 20-7-12. 249 Sqn c/s	**[1]** 12-21

■ **[1]** Commissioned and financed by the Sir Sydney Camm Commemorative Society - **www.sirsydneycamm.org**

WOKINGHAM south of the M4 and A329(M) southeast of Reading

A1 Motor Spares: Highland Avenue

☐ G-BSGV	Rotorway Executive	90	Hythe-built. De-reg 7-4-95	10-21

WOODLEY east of Reading

Museum of Berkshire Aviation: A delight in the scope and detail of its contents, the visitor needs to be constantly reminded that all of this took place within the boundaries of the county. Add to this delicious names such as Handley Page and Miles and you are set for an engaging visit.

McBroom Arion hang-glider BAPC.248 was handed over to the British Hang-Gliding Museum (BHGM), Weston-super-Mare, Somerset, on 7th April 2021. (Also picked up was a Wasp 229 held at Woodley, but not on the museum's inventory.)

◆ *Mohawk Way, RG5 4UE.* | **0118 944 8089** | email via website | **www.museumofberkshireaviation.co.uk**

☐ G-ALMN		EoN Primary AQZ G-ALMN	c48	BGA.589, ex Farnborough, G-ALMN, BGA.589. Last flown 7-5-50, CoA 4-51. Arrived 2004	**[1]** 1-22
☐ G-APWA		HP Herald 100	59	ex Southend, BAF, PP-SDM, PP-ASV, G-APWA. CoA 6-4-82, de-reg 29-1-87. Arrived 29-8-92. BEA colours	**[2]** 1-22
☐ G-MIOO		Miles Student 2	57	ex N Weald, Bruntingthorpe, G-APLK, Cranfield, G-MIOO, Duxford, G-APLK, Glasgow, Shoreham, XS941, G-35-4. Crashed 24-8-85, de-reg 1-11-96. Arrived 1997	**[3]** 1-22
☐ –*		Goodwin-Kent GK3	~	BAPC.573, ex Turweston. Arrived 7-6-21	**[4]** 1-22
☐ BWG	'465'	EoN 460-1	65	BGA.1288, CoA 27-4-97. Arrived 27-5-09	1-22
☐ –		Broburn Wanderlust	46	BAPC.233, ex Farnborough. Arrived 28-11-92	1-22
☐ TF-SHC		Miles Martinet TT.1	43	ex Iceland, MS902, Reykjavik SF, 251. Cr 18-7-51. Arr 3-96	1-22
☐ 'L6906'		Miles Magister I G-AKKY	40	BAPC.44, ex Brooklands, Woodley, Wroughton, Frenchay, G-AKKY (de-reg 12-4-73), T9841, 11 EFTS, 16 EFTS. Phillips & Powis-built. Arrived 26-4-91	1-22
☐ XG883	'773'	Fairey Gannet T.5	57	ex Cardiff, Yeovilton, 849, Culdrose SF. SOC 8-6-70. SOC 8-6-70. Arrived 24-3-96	**[5]** 1-22
☐ XJ389		Fairey Jet Gyrodyne G-AJJP	49	ex Cosford, Southampton, G-AJJP (de-reg 9-11-50), XD759. Arrived 6-94	**[6]** 1-22
☐ 'XP849'		Westland Scout AH.1	63	ex B' Down, M Wallop. Arrived 13-10-10. ETPS colours	**[7]** 1-22

■ **[1]** EoN Primary donated by Pat Pottinger. **[2]** First production Dart-powered Herald, born at Woodley, built there by HP (Reading) Ltd and first flown 30-10-59. **[3]** Student on loan from Aces High's Mike Woodley. **[4]** Unfinished homebuild, by D Kent, based upon a racer designed by C J Goodwin in the early 1960s. **[5]** O loan from the Fleet Air Arm Museum. **[6]** RAF Museum elected to gift the Gyrodyne to the museum in early 2022. **[7]** Scout is *largely* XP895, last at Middle Wallop and crashed 10-11-66. It has the boom of XP854 - for the latter see Abridge, Essex.

BUCKINGHAMSHIRE
Includes the unitary authority of Milton Keynes

DENHAM AERODROME west of the A412, north of the town
A Squirrel, or Ecureuil if you will, is still thought to be used as a sales aid.

❑ G-TOPS	Aérospatiale Squirrel II	82	ex G-BPRH, N360E, N5794F. CoA 21-2-12, de-reg 9-3-18	11-18

HALTON AIRFIELD on the A4011 (camp) and east of the B4544 (airfield), north of Wendover　　EGWN
Trenchard Museum and **James McCudden Flight Heritage Centre**: Within the workshop a full-scale replica of a Halton Aero Club Mayfly G-EBOO biplane of 1927 is being built. Three functioning Link Trainers are within the collection.
◆ *Halton Camp, HP22 5PG* | **email** via website | **www.trenchardmuseum.org.uk**

❑ RA905		Slingsby Cadet TX.1	c45	BGA.1143. ex RAFGSA.273, RA905. CoA 14-3-00	1-22
❑ WB626		DHC Chipmunk T.10	50	ex Aylesbury, South Molton, Fownhope, Firbeck, Houghton--on-the-Hill, Southampton, Swanton Morley, Bicester, Kemble, Hendon SF, 5 FTS, 18 RFS. SOC 12-9-73. Cockpit	1-22
❑ WZ772		Slingsby Grasshopper TX.1	52	ex M Wallop, Halton, 1 MGSP, Brentwood	1-22
❑ XF522		Hawker Hunter F.6	56	ex Bletchley, Milton Keynes, Aylesbury, Halton, 92, 66, 92. SOC 8-1-63. Cockpit, trailer mounted. 92 Sqn colours	1-22
❑ XR574	'72'	Folland Gnat T.1	63	ex Cosford, Halton, Cosford 8631M (8-10-79), Kemble, 4 FTS, CFS, 4 FTS, CFS, 4 FTS, 4 FTS	1-22

RAF Halton: The station is set to close in 2025. The Hunter is with **2409 Squadron ATC** (Herts and Bucks Wing).

❑ VZ568	'C'	Gloster Meteor F.8	50	ex Sennybridge, 4 SoTT, St Athan 7261M (12-10-55), 63. Cockpit. Arrived by 3-19	[1]	7-19
❑ XF527		Hawker Hunter F.6	56	ex 1 SoTT 8680M (2-4-81), Laarbruch SF, 4 FTS, CFE, 19, Church Fenton SF, Linton SF. Displayed		1-20
❑ XW303	'127'	BAC Jet Provost T.5A	70	ex Cosford, Halton 9119M (16-9-91), 7 FTS, 1 FTS	[2]	8-21
❑ XW364	'MN'	BAC Jet Provost T.5A	71	ex Cosford 9188M (5-5-93), Shawbury, 3 FTS, RAFC, CFS, 1 FTS. Arrived 22-10-12, rescue training		8-21
❑ XZ630		Panavia Tornado GR.1	77	ex St Athan, Brüggen 8976M (24-8-88), BAe, A&AEE. Parade ground		1-22

■ **[1]** The rest of VZ568 was still to be found on the Sennybridge ranges in July 2021. **[2]** The fuselage of 'JP' XW303 serves as a jump on the equestrian course!

HIGH WYCOMBE or Walter's Ash, northwest of Naphill, north of the town
RAF High Wycombe: Headquarters, Air Command has a pair of full-scale models on display within the grounds.

❑ 'P7666'	'EB-Z'	V-S Spitfire FSM	~	BAPC.335. Gateguards UK-built. *Observer Corps*, 41 Sqn c/s	6-21
❑ 'V7467'	'LE-D'	Hawker Hurricane FSM	89	BAPC.378. Gateguards UK-built. Displayed. 242 Sqn colours	6-21

LAVENDON on the A428 west of Bedford
Tony Collins: Award-winning cockpit restorer Tony also owns and operates the **Lavendon Narrow Gauge Railway**. Canberra B(I).6 WT319 has been 'on detachment' at Doncaster, S Yorks, since mid-2021.
◆ *By prior arrangement or on railway open days*

❑ WT319		EE Canberra B(I).6	55	ex Castle Carey, Filton, Samlesbury, 213, Laarbruch SF, 213. SOC 8-12-69. Cockpit – see notes above	1-22
❑ WT684		Hawker Hunter F.1	54	ex Doncaster, Firbeck, Long Marston, Brize Norton, Reading, Halton 7422M (8-4-57), 229 OCU, DFLS. Cockpit	1-22
❑ XD235	'148'	V-S Scimitar F.1	58	ex Ingatestone, Welshpool, Southampton, Ottershaw, Foulness, FRU, 803. SOC 20-3-70. 803 Sqn colours. Cockpit	1-22
❑ XN651	'705'	DH Sea Vixen FAW.2	61	ex Bletchley, Bristol, Culdrose A2616 (29-7-71), SAH, 766, FAW.1, 893. Hatfield-built. 890 Sqn colours. Cockpit	1-22
❑ XS898	'BD'	EE Lightning F.6	66	ex Bruntingthorpe, Cranfield, Binbrook, 11, 5. SOC (24-6-88). Cockpit	1-22
❑ XW541		Blackburn Buccaneer S.2B	71	ex Welshpool, Ingatestone, Stock, Foulness, Honington 8858M (21-5-85), St Athan, 12, 16, 15. Cockpit	1-22

❏ J-1632	'V'	DH Venom FB.50		56	ex Cantley, London Colney, Cranfield, Bridgend,	
			G-VNOM		Bruntingthorpe, Cranfield, G-VNOM (de-reg 27-6-11),	
					Swiss AF. Swiss-built. Cockpit, 145 Sqn colours. Off-site	[1] 1-22

■ [1] Representing WK418 which served 145 Sqn at Celle, W Germany, as 'V' (and later 'G'), 1954-1957.

LONG CRENDON on the B4011, northwest of Thame

A 'JP' is kept at a *private* location in this area.

❏ XW432	'MX'	BAC Jet Provost T.5A	72	ex Ipswich, Cosford 9127M (14-10-91), Halton, 1 FTS,	
				Leeming SF, 3 FTS. First noted 8-14	8-20

MILTON KEYNES

Milton Keynes College: Innovation and Technology Centre. ◆ *By prior arrangement* **only | www.mkcollege.ac.uk**

❏ G-TINA	SOCATA Tobago	80	ex Little Snoring. CoA 29-10-14, de-reg 29-10-14	8-16

British Balloon Museum and Library (BBML): The *nominal* base for the huge collection of envelopes, burners, and baskets, stored across a wide range of sites, none of which are available for viewing without prior arrangement. BBML is beyond the scope of *W&R* but if such things float your boat, its extensive website is **www.bbml.org.uk**

PITSTONE between the B489 and B488 north of Tring

The Heritage Park - Pitstone Green Museum: The centre includes World War Two room and vintage radio rooms. The central feature of the former is the Lancaster forward fuselage built by Norman Groom using many original fittings. This impressive project is up for sale - details via **www.buildalanc.co.uk** ◆ *Pitstone, LU7 9EY* | **www.pitstonemuseum.co.uk**

❏ -	Avro Lancaster FSM	10	BAPC.425, forward fuselage	12-21

TURWESTON AERODROME north of the A422, east of Brackley   EGBT

Bianchi Aviation Film Services: Previously based at Booker, Bucks, the company has gathered in the machines previously on loan at Stow Maries. ◆ **Strictly** *by prior arrangement* **only | www.bianchiaviation.co.uk**

❏ G-AWXZ*		Stampe SV-4C		49	ex Booker, F-BHMZ, Fr mil, F-BCOI. SNCAN-built. CoA 8-8-14	10-21
❏ G-BAAF*		Manning-Flanders		75	ex Stow Maries, Booker, Compton Abbas, Booker,	
		MF.1 replica			Old Warden, Booker. PPS-built. CoA 6-8-96	due
❏ 'No.10'*		Blériot XI replica		99	ex Stow Maries, Booker, Compton Abbas, Booker, N1197.	
			G-BPVE		CoA 29-6-01. Arrived 16-11-21	11-21
❏ N6161*		Sopwith Pup	G-ELRT 1917	ex Booker. CoA 25-4-18		[1] 10-21
❏ 'N6377'*	'R'	Sopwith Camel		73	ex Stow Maries, 'B2458', Booker, Compton Abbas, Booker,	
		replica	G-BPOB		N8997. Tallmantz Aviation-built. CoA 2-7-19. RNAS colours	10-21
❏ 'MS824'*		MS 'N' replica		70	ex Stow Maries, Booker, Compton Abbas, Booker.	
			G-AWBU		CoA 28-4-04. PPS-built. Arrived 16-11-21	[2] 11-21
❏ '107/15'*		Fokker E.III replica		67	ex Stow Maries, '422/15', Booker, Compton Abbas,	
			G-AVJO		Booker. PPS-built. CoA 5-4-04. Arrived 16-11-21	[2] 11-21
❏ '626/18'*		Travel Air D-2000	N6268	38	ex Stow Maries, Booker, USA. Painted as a Fokker D.VIII	due
❏ -*		Fokker Dr.I replica		~	ex Stow Maries. Booker, USA. Unfinished airframe	due
❏ U-95*		Bücker Jungmeister		40	ex Booker, F-AZMN, G-BVGP, F-AZFQ, N215696, HB-MIE,	
			G-BVGP		D-EIII, HB-MIE, Swiss AF U-95. Dornier-built. CoA 22-8-18	10-21

■ [1] Registered as a 'Sopwith Scout'. [2] PPS – Personal Plane Services, the predecessor company to Bianchi Aviation Film Service.

Also: Beagle Pup prototype G-AVDF flew again on 19th May 2020; it was followed by Chipmunk WB763 (G-BBMR) on 9th December 2020. Cherokee G-BASL morphed into G-GMKA and then G-KALI and was flying by 2020. During October 2021 the Midland Aeroplane Company decamped for Oxford, Oxfordshire; taking by road: Plus D G-AHUG (first noted earlier in 2021) and Tailwind G-BDBD. Work on Jungmann G-BUCK had got to the 'paperwork' stage and it was planned to fly it out.

❏ G-AXXW*	Jodel D.117	57	ex F-BIBN. SAN-built. CoA 21-11-14	10-21
❏ G-BBLU*	Piper Seneca 200	73	ex N55984. CoA 29-6-16	10-21
❏ G-CLKX*	DHC Chipmunk T.10	50	ex Wickenby, York, Canada (?), WB555, 7924M, Lpl UAS,	
			Birm UAS, 2 SoTT Flt, Debden SF, 4 SoTT Flt, Glas UAS,	
			43 GCF, MCCF, Ox UAS. Crashed 26-4-66	5-20
❏ F-PFUG	Adam RA-14	~	ex Breighton, Boston. Cockpit. First noted 12-19	10-21
❏ 854*	Ryan PT-22 Recruit	42	ex Audley End, Chichester, N854, N50993, 41-20854.	
		G-BTBH	CoA 31-6-13. Arrived 12-20	10-21

American Air Museum (AAM): Around the north end of the building is a series of plate glass monoliths -entitled 'Counting the Cost' - each of which poignantly depicts the losses of 'Mighty Eighth' aircraft - and of course crews. The building was granted Grade II listing in late 2020.

❏ 'S4513'	'1'	SPAD XIII replica	78	ex 'S3398', Yeovilton, Land's End, Chertsey, G-BFYO	
		G-BFYO		(CoA 21-6-82, de-reg 14-10-86), D-EOWM. Arrived 17-6-96	1-22
❏ '34064'	'8U'	NAA TB-25J-30-NC	45	ex Shoreham, Dublin, Prestwick, Luton, N7614C, USAF,	
		Mitchell		TB-25J / ETB-25J / EB-25J, USAAF B-25J 44-31171.	
				Arrived 29-11-76. *Little Critter from the Moon*	1-22
❏ '46214'	'X-3'	Grumman TBM-3E	44	ex CF-KCG, RCN 326, USN 69327. General Motors-built.	
		Avenger		Arr 11-77. 'Lt George Bush' titling. *Ginny*. For disposal 9-21	9-21
❏ 155529	'114'	McD F-4J(UK)	67	ex Wattisham, 74, ZE359, US Navy 155529, VF-171, VF-31,	
		Phantom	ZE359	VF-74, VF-33. Flew in 10-7-91. USN VF-74, *America* colours	1-22
❏ '217786'	'25'	Boeing PT-17 Kaydet	42	ex Swanton Morley, Duxford, CF-EQS, Evergreen,	
				New Brunswick, Canada, 41-8169. Arrived 11-77	[1] 1-22
❏ '226413'		Republic P-47D-30-RA	45	ex USA, Chino, N47DD, Harlingen, Peru AF FAP 119	
	'UN-Z'	Thunderbolt		and 545, USAAF 45-49192. Crashed 9-2-80. Acquired 11-85.	
				56th FG c/s as 'Hub' Zemke's a/c, *Oregon's Britannia*	[2] 1-22
❏ '238133'		Boeing B-17G-95-DL	44	ex '231983', *Mary Alice*, Creil, IGN F-BDRS, N68269,	
		Flying Fortress		44-83735. Douglas-built. Last flown 1971, arrived 1975	1-22
❏ 315509		Douglas C-47A-85-DL	44	ex Aces High G-BHUB (de-reg 19-10-81), *Airline*: 'G-AGIV',	
	'W7-S'	Skytrain	G-BHUB	'FD988' and 'KG418', Spanish AF T.3-29, N51V, N9985F,	
				SAS SE-BBH, 315 TCG, 316 TCG, USAAF 43-15509.	
				Long Beach-built. Acquired 7-80. 37th TCS / 316th TCG c/s	1-22
❏ '411631'		NAA P-51D-25-NA	44	ex '472218', South Lambeth, Duxford, RCAF 9246, USAAF	
	'MX-V'	Mustang		44-73979. Inglewood-built. Acquired 12-71. *Etta Jeanne II*,	
				82nd FS, 78th FG colours. Unveiled 10-14	[3] 1-22
❏ 44-51228		Consolidated	44	ex Lackland, EZB-24M 44-51228. Ford-built.	
	'493'	B-24M-25-FO Liberator		Arrived 29-6-99. *Dugan*	1-22
❏ 461748	'Y'	Boeing TB-29A-45-BN	45	ex G-BHDK (de-reg 29-3-84), China Lake, 307th BG, Okinawa.	
		Superfortress	G-BHDK	*It's Hawg Wild* (stb). Flew in 2-3-80. 307th BG colours	1-22
❏ –		NAA Harvard II	42	ex N Weald, Dutch AF B-168, FE984, RCAF, 2 FIS, USAAF	
				42-12471. Acquired 1988	1-22
❏ 56-0689		Boeing B-52D-40-BW	57	ex 7th BW Carswell, 96th BW, 7th BW, 99th BW, 7th BW,	
		Stratofortress		96th BW, 99th BW, U-Tapao, 509th BW, 454th BW,	
				306th BW, 99th BW, 91st BW, 509th BW, 494th BW,	
				95th BW, 28th BW. Wichita-built. Flew in 8-10-83	1-22
❏ 56-6692		Lockheed U-2CT-LO	56	ex Alconbury, 9th SRW, 100th SRW, U-2C, 6515th TS, U-2F,	
				6515th TS, CIA, U-2C, 4080th SRW, CIA. Last flown 28-12-87,	
				arrived 26-6-92. Modified to single-seat configuration	1-22
❏ 61-17962		Lockheed SR-71A	66	ex Palmdale, 9th SRW, 9th SRW Det 4 Mildenhall,	
		Blackbird		9th SRW. Arrived 5-4-01	[4] 1-22
❏ 67-0120		GD F-111E-CF Aardvark	69	ex Upper Heyford, 20th TFW, 57th TTW, 442nd TFTS,	
				27th TFW. Arr 19-10-93. *The Chief*, 78th TFS, 20th TFW c/s	[5] 1-22
❏ 72-21605		Bell UH-1H Iroquois	72	ex Coleman Barracks, ATCOM, 158th Av Regt. Arr 15-7-97	1-22
❏ 76-0020		McDD F-15A-15-MC	76	ex AMARC Davis-Monthan, 102nd FIW, 5th FIS, 33rd TFW,	
		Eagle		36th TFW. Last flown 25-10-93, arrived 4-01. 5th FIS c/s	1-22
❏ 77-0259	'AR'	Fairchild A-10A-FA	79	ex Alconbury, 10th TFW, 128th TFW, 111th TASG,	
		Thunderbolt II		128th TFW, 81st TFW. Flew in 6-2-92	1-22
❏ -		GD F-111F-CF Aardvark	~	escape module	[6] 1-22
❏ -		McDD F-15 Eagle	~	ex 48th TFW, Lakenheath. Cockpit simulator, *Eagle Drivers*	1-22

■ **[1]** PT-17 is a composite, having used elements of 42-17786 during its restoration (which was carried out by Eastern Stearman). **[2]** P-47 *Oregon's Britannia* was a major reconstruction based upon large elements of P-47D 45-49192 not used in the composite that created The Fighter Collection's machine *No Guts, No Glory* (now exported). **[3]** Previously well-known as *Big Beautiful Doll*, the P-51 wears the colours of Lt Col H H Lamb's P-51K; Lamb is credited with 5½ 'kills' two of them in 'this' Mustang. **[4]** SR-71 achieved world altitude record 28-7-76 of 85,068ft. **[5]** *The Chief* carried out 19 operational missions during DESERT STORM, 1995. **[6]** Previously quoted as coming from 72-1447 but this is in private hands in The Netherlands.

Store: Some airframes are held out of public gaze at various locations on the site. Last noted in July 2015, T-33A 51-4286 and F-100D 54-2165 were 'reclaimed' by the National Museum of the USAF and are *believed* to have been 'processed'.

☐ 'AD937'* 'AF-O'	V-S Spitfire V FSM	c18	ex ARC. Acquired c2019. GB Replicas-built. AFDU colours		8-20
☐ XN239 'G'	Slingsby Cadet TX.3	59	ex Henlow 8889M (3-3-86), ACCGS, 644 GS, CGS, 644 GS.		
			For disposal 9-21		9-21
☐ XP281	Auster AOP.9	61	ex St Athan, AFWF, M Wallop. NEA 8-11-68	[1]	6-19
☐ 9893	Bristol Bolingbroke IVT	42	ex ARC, BAM, OHB, Canada, RCAF. Fairchild Canada-built	[2]	6-19
☐ 252983	Schweizer TG-3A	45	ex AAM, N66630. Arrived 8-96		6-19

■ **[1]** XP281 on loan from Army Flying Museum, Middle Wallop, Hampshire. **[2]** Bolingbroke 9893 nose along with the fuselage/centre section of G-MKIV (RCAF 10038. crashed 21-6-87) and the outer wings of 9893.

Newly arrived HS.146 CC.2 ZE701, January 2022. *Paul Middleton*

Duxford Aviation Society (DAS) **- The British Airliner Collection**: There's only so much ramp space, particularly at Duxford: choices need to be made. In December 2021 DAS announced that "due to limited space available on the current site" it was looking for a suitable museum that could take on Herald G-APWJ. The arrival of the 146 explains the eviction. DAS was optimistically hoping that relocation could be achieved by the time *W&R28* went to press and to speed the decision-making process would meet the costs of the removal. Hopes for a swift resolution were achieved when Morayvia (where the front end of G-ASVO already abides) stepped into the breach. In anticipation, G-APWJ has been propelled through the the book's pages to Kinloss, Scotland. The Preface and the Hendon section dwells on collections 'topping out' and the increasing number of airframes looking for homes... Does this one-in-one-out square dance mean that future DAS acquisitions are reliant on nifty footwork?

The following DAS airframes are within 'AirSpace' (see earlier). Hermes G-ALDG, Dove G-ALFU, York G-ANTK, Comet 4 G-APDB, Concorde G-AXDN. The cockpit of Viscount G-OPAS is on loan to the Bournemouth Aviation Museum, see Bournemouth Dorset. | **www.das.org.uk**

☐ G-ALWF	Vickers Viscount 701	52	ex Speke, Cambrian, British Eagle, Channel, BEA.		
			Last flown 12-4-72, de-reg 18-4-72, arrived 21-2-76.		
			BEA colours, *Sir John Franklin*	[1]	1-22
☐ G-ALZO	Airspeed Ambassador 2	52	ex Lasham, Dan-Air, Handley Page, Jordan AF 108, BEA.		
			CoA 14-5-72, de-reg 10-9-81. Dan-Air colours	[2]	1-22
☐ G-AOVT	Bristol Britannia 312	58	ex Luton, Monarch, British Eagle, BOAC. Flew in 29-6-75,		
			de-reg 21-9-81. Monarch c/s; repaint completed 1-17	[3]	1-22
☐ G-ASGC	Vickers Super VC10	65	ex BA, BOAC, BOAC-Cunard, BOAC. Flew in 15-4-80,		
			de-reg 22-4-80. BOAC-Cunard colours	[4]	1-22

❑ G-AVFB	HS Trident 2E	67	ex BA, Nicosia, Cyprus 5B-DAC, BEA. Flew in 13-6-82,		
			de-reg 9-7-82. BEA colours	[5]	1-22
❑ G-AVMU	BAC 111-510ED	68	ex Hurn, BA, BEA. Last flight 4-3-93, de-reg 12-7-93.		
			BA colours. *County of Dorset*	[6]	1-22
❑ G-BEVT	BN Trislander	77	ex Aurigny. CoA 13-7-17. Flew in 21-6-17	[7]	1-22
❑ ZE701*	HSA HS.146 CC.2	85	ex Northolt, 32, G-6-029, ZE701, G-6-029, ZE701, G-5-03.		
	G-CMBU		Hatfield-built. Arrived 24-1-22		1-22

■ **[1]** *Zulu-Oscar* made the last-ever flight by the type in 10-71. **[2]** *Whisky-Fox* completed 28,299 flight hours and 25,398 landings. **[3]** *Victor-Tango* factoids: completed 35,739 flight hours and 10,760 landings. **[4]** *Golf-Charlie* totted up 54,623 flight hours and 16,415 landings. **[5]** *Fox-Bravo* was damaged by ground fire at Nicosia during the Turkish invasion of Cyprus, 7-74 and remained grounded until 5-77. It completed 21,642 flying hours and 11,726 landings in 1982. **[6]** *Mike-Uniform's* stats: 45,541 landings, 40,280 hours. **[7]** *Victor-Tango* served with Aurigny throughout its career: around 86,000 flights, total time just shy of 28,000 hours.

Note: Duxford hosts a wide range of individual airworthy aircraft. The situation with some of these can be fluid and therefore difficult to cover in a book with a two-year 'life'. An increasing number of warbirds are offering flight experiences, or the opportunity to fly alongside a classic. Some are long-term residents, others frequent bases elsewhere - eg Goodwood, Lashenden, Sywell. Several of the resident 'fixed base operators' also house and maintain private owner warbirds and historic types. The status of such machines is fluid, and they are not given a formal listing here.

Aircraft Restoration Company (ARC): While specialising in Spitfires, a glance below reveals that ARC tackles a wide variety of projects. The company also operates and/or maintains aircraft on behalf of other organisations. Only the ARC 'core' fleet and long-term restoration projects are given here: unless noted all are registered to ARC or Propshop.

Reconstruction of the Fw 189 has been going on quietly for some time and by mid-2020 it had reached very substantial proportions within the main workshop. It was written out of *W&R24* (p269) as having been exported to the USA in 2009. (Its UK registration was cancelled as Stateside-bound the previous year, but it seems it never left these shores.)

By August 2020 Harvard T.2B KF183 (G-CORS) was based with Rolls-Royce at East Midlands, Leics.

The **Hawker Typhoon Preservation Group** delivered a kit-of-parts to ARC in June 2021 as fund-raising momentum for this ambitious venture reached the point where restoration/reconstruction could ramp up. The project includes the former Booker, Bucks, Typhoon cockpit and the rear fuselage of former 174 Squadron RB396 from the Netherlands (shot down 1st April 1945), a Napier Sabre and a large cache of plans. First work by ARC is centring on the cockpit section while at Sandown, Isle of Wight, Airframe Assemblies is tackling the rear fuselage. See also Northampton, Northants. More details on: **www.hawkertyphoon.com**

Myers OTW G-MOTW moved to Tibenham, Norfolk, on 24th November 2021.

◆ *ARC buildings* **not** *open to public inspection* | www.aircraftrestorationcompany.com

❑ G-DHCZ	DHC Beaver AL.1 ✈	60	ex G-BUCJ, XP772, M Wallop, Beverley, Leconfield,		
			M Wallop, 15 Flt, 667, 132 Flt, AFWF	[1]	1-22
❑ G-EDMK	Boeing A75N1	42	ex EC-AST. Stored awaiting restoration	[2]	3-20
❑ SE-BRG	Fairey Firefly TT.1	44	ex Sweden, Svensk Flygtjanst, FAA Mk.I DT989, 767, 766,		
	G-CGYD		Arr 10-2-04. Under restoration in Buildings 66 and 425		1-22
❑ 'L6739'	Bristol Bolingbroke	43	ex 'R3821', 'L8841', 'Z5722', G-BPIV, Strathallan, Canada,		
'YP-Q'	IVT ✈	G-BPIV	RCAF 10201. Fairchild Canada-built. 23 Sqn colours	[3]	1-22
❑ N3200	'QV' V-S Spitfire Ia ✈	39	ex Sandown, Duxford, Braintree, Mimoyecques, Calais, 19.		
	G-CFGJ		Shot down 26-5-40. Acquired 9-7-15. 19 Sqn colours	[4]	1-22
❑ P9373	V-S Spitfire I	39	ex 92, shot down 23-5-40, near Boulogne. CBAF-built		
	G-CFGN		Arrived 19-1-11. Stored	[5]	3-20
❑ V9312	Westland Lysander	39	ex N9309K, Canada, RCAF, RAF, 4, 613, 225. SOC 1-10-46.		
'LX-E'	TT.IIIA ✈ G-CCOM		Arrived 4-6-03 - first flown 28-8-18. 225 Sqn colours		1-22
❑ 'X9556'	'S' Supermarine	34	ex G-RNLI, Audley End, 'Sussex', Southampton,		
	Walrus I	G-WLRS	Gt Yarmouth, Winchester, Southampton, W2718, 276,		
			751, 764. Saro-built. Arrived 22-3-18	[2] [6]	1-22
❑ MB293	V-S Seafire IIc	42	ex Braintree, Malta, 879, 887, A&AEE. Crashed 31-10-44.		
	G-CFGI		Salvaged off Malta 4-94. Stored	[5]	3-20
❑ PL258	V-S Spitfire IX	44	ex Netherlands, 331 Sqn, PL258. Shot down 29-12-44.		
	G-NSFS		CBAF-built. Stored	[7]	3-20
❑ PL983	V-S Spitfire PR.XI	44	ex Sandown, Duxford, Goudhurst, N Weald, Biggin Hill,		
	✈ G-PRXI		Duxford, E Midlands, Stronebroom, Duxford, Old Warden,		
			Vickers G-15-109, N74138, PL983, 2, 4, 1 PP. Re-flown 7-5-20		1-22
❑ PS890	V-S Spitfire PR.19	44	ex France, G-CDGK, USA, N219AM, Thailand, Thai AF		
'UM-E'	F-AZJS		U14-26/97, RAF, 81, V-S. Re-flown 6-8-20. 152 Sqn c/s		8-20

☐ PT462		V-S Spitfire Tr.IX ✈		44	ex Bryngwyn Bach, N462JC, G-CTIX, Winchester, Mk.IX,		
	'SW-A'		G-CTIX		Duxford, Israel, IDFAF 4X-FOM, 20-67, Italian AF MM4100,		
					PT462, 4 SAAF, 253. CBAF-built. Arr 9-17. 253 Sqn c/s	[8]	1-22
☐ PV202		V-S Spitfire Tr.IX ✈		44	ex 'W3632', 'QV-I', 'AI-E', 'H-98', '161', G-TRIX, G-BHGH,		
	'5R-H'		G-CCCA		IAC 161, G-15-174, PV202, 412, 33. CBAF-built. 33 Sqn c/s		1-22
☐ 'RB396'*		Hawker Typhoon IB	G-TIFY	44	project arrived 24-6-21. See notes above		1-22
☐ RK858		V-S Spitfire IX		43	ex TFC, CIS, USSR, Sov AF, RK858 n/s. CBAF-built.		
			G-CGJE		Missing, Archangel region, 1947, salvaged 1992. Stored		3-20
☐ RK912		V-S Spitfire IX	G-CLCS	44	ex Italy, 93. Crashed 19-4-45. Arrived 5-10-10. Stored		3-20
☐ RN203		V-S Spitfire XIV	G-CLCT	45	ex Germany, 130. Cr 19-4-45. Salvaged 2002. Stored		3-20
☐ RX168		V-S Seafire III		45	ex Trelonk, Duxford, Swindon, Exeter, Andover, Norwich,		
			G-BWEM		Battle, Dublin, IAC 157 (SOC 27-10-53), RX168, Australia,		
					India. Westland-built. Stored	[9]	3-20
☐ '2'		Hispano HA-1112-M1L		49	ex G-BWUE, Breighton, Sandown, Breighton, Duxford,		
		Buchón ✈	G-AWHK		N9938, *Battle of Britain* (1968), G-AWHK, Spanish AF		
					C.4K-154. JG27 colours by 4-21	[10]	1-22
☐ 2100*		Focke-Wulf		c42	ex G-BZKY (de-reg 9-1-08), Sandown, Sandtoft, Lancing,		
	'V7+1H'	Fw 189A-1	G-BZKY		Murmansk USSR, Luftwaffe. Shot down 4-5-43.		
					Recovered/imported 1991. See notes above		1-22
☐ 1747		NAA Harvard IV ✈		53	ex '20385' N Weald, Port AF 1747, WGAF BF+050, AA+050,		
			G-BGPB		53-4619. CCF-built. Port AF colours. *Taz*	[9]	1-22
☐ 86690	'2-F'	Grumman FM-2		43	ex Old Warden, G-CHPN, N49JC, Seattle, Pensacola,		
		Wildcat	G-KINL		N49JC, N70637, N20HA, N68760, USN 86690. General		
					Motors-built. Arrived 27-4-16. *Hannah*	[2] [11]	1-22
☐ XX658		SAL Bulldog		74	ex local store, G-BZPS, East Low UAS, Cam UAS,		
			G-SMAT		Oxford UAS, Cam UAS, 2 FTS. Arrived 20-12-19	[12]	1-22

■ **[1]** G-DHCZ, is as close to DHC-2 as the alphabet will allow! **[2]** Registered to Tom Harris - see also Shuttleworth, Beds. **[3]** Registered to Blenheim (Duxford) Ltd. Nose from Battle of Britain veteran Mk.I L6739 (former 23 Sqn night-fighter SOC 31-12-40) to make a *representative* Mk.I. This nose was previously an electric-driven car conversion. The original nose of Mk.IVT 10201 is in store. The **Blenheim Society** works tirelessly to support the restoration of *India-Victor*: **www.blenheimsociety.com [4]** Gifted to the IWM and registered to it 1-12-15. When N3200 was shot down, 19 Sqn had applied the unit code 'QV-' but no individual letter. **[5]** UK registered to Mark One Partners LLC. *Golf-November* and *Golf-India* both cancelled as sold in the USA 11-1-16. **[6]** W2718 retired to 15 MU Wroughton 14-2-46 and acquired by Somerton Airways of Cowes, Isle of Wight. Beyond that it went to Norman Grogan who widened the fuselage and turned it into a caravan. Bless, him, he did not throw *any* of it away, leaving it as a time capsule. It was presented to the then Hall of Aviation at Southampton, Hampshire, in the mid-1980s. In 10-89 was acquired by Dick Melton who returned it to a biplane amphibian at Winchester, Hampshire, and then Great Yarmouth, Norfolk. **[7]** Registered to the Norwegian Spitfire Foundation. **[8]** There is *another* 'PT462' at Moffatt, Scotland. **[9]** Registered to Aircraft Spares and Materials. **[10]** Bf 109 with RR Merlin 500 built by Hispano. G-AWHK has the fuselage of C.4K-154 - a *Battle of Britain* non-flyer, the rest from C.4K-102. **[11]** FM-2 served in California in the 1950s as a Hardwick Special HG.1 'bug-bomber': under restoration. **[12]** Registered to Skysmart MRO.

B-17 Preservation Ltd: *Sally B* is Britain's largest privately-operated warbird. Determination keeps this magic machine going: no lottery grants, government hand-outs or other funding. Its lifeblood is the **Sally B Supporters Club**, donations from the public, the grit of its engineering team and the expertise of its operator, Elly Sallingboe.

Since 1983 *Sally B's* wellbeing was the responsibility of **Peter Brown**, an exceptionally skilled and patient engineer with a hallmark smile. Sadly, in mid-2021 Peter died; he was 88: he had devoted over 40 years to keeping *Sally B* in the skies.

◆ *PO Box 92, Bury St Edmunds, IP28 8RR* | **b-17preservation@sallyb.org.uk** | **www.sallyb.org.uk**

☐ '124485'		Boeing B-17G-105-VE ✈		44	ex N17TE, IGN F-BGSR, 44-85784.		
	'DF-A'	Flying Fortress	G-BEDF		*Sally B* (port), *Memphis Belle* (starboard)		1-22

Classic Wings / Spectrum Leisure: Maintenance base is at Clacton, Essex - which see. The fleet includes: Rapides G-AKIF, HG691 (G-AIYR) and TX310 (G-AIDL); Tiger Moths DE974 (G-ANZZ) and PG657 (G-AGPK). Please note not all will be present at any one time. ◆ *Viewable during normal museum hours and at airshows* | **www.classic-wings.co.uk**

The Fighter Collection (TFC) and the **Friends of the Fighter Collection** support group. Harvard IIB FE695 (G-BTXI) departed in June, bound for a new owner at Bicester. ◆ *Open to the public during museum hours.* | **www.fighter-collection.com**

☐ G-BRVE		Beech D.17S		45	ex N Weald, N1139V, FT475, 44-67724, 26689.		
					Acquired 2005, CoA 29-6-15		3-20
☐ N5903		Gloster Gladiator II		39	ex Yeovilton, 'N2276', 'N5226', Old Warden, Eastleigh, Ansty,		
			G-GLAD		61 OTU. Arrived 30-11-94. CoA 30-6-18. 72 Sqn colours		3-20
☐ S1581	'573'	Hawker Nimrod I ✈		32	ex St Leonards-on-Sea, St Just, Henlow, 802.		
			G-BWWK		Acquired 2004. 802 Sqn colours		1-22

☐ EP120	'AE-A'	V-S Spitfire V ✈		42	ex Audley End, Duxford, St Athan 8070M, Wattisham,
			G-LFVB		Boulmer, Wilmslow, St Athan, 5377M,53 OTU, 402, 19,
					501. CBAF-built. Arr 1-93. *City of Winnipeg* , 402 Sqn c/s [1] 1-22
☐ 'JV579'	'F'	Grumman FM-2		44	ex Monroe, USA N4845V, 86711. Arrived 25-4-93
		Wildcat ✈	G-RUMW		846 Sqn colours 1-22
☐ 'KD345'		Vought FG-1D ✈		45	ex N8297, N9154Z, USN 88297. Goodyear-built.
	'A-130'	Corsair ✈	G-FGID		Arrived 4-86. 1850 Sqn, SEAC colours 1-22
☐ PK624		V-S Spitfire F.22		45	ex St Athan, Abingdon 8072M, Northolt, Uxbridge, N Weald,
					'WP916', 9 MU, 614. CBAF-built. SOC 4-2-54. Arr 11-10-94 12-21
☐ VX281*	'120'	Hawker Sea Fury		49	ex Yeovilton G-RNHF, N Weald, VL, N Weald, USA N281L,
		T.20S	G-BCOW		N8476W, G-BCOW, DLB D-CACO, G-9-64, VX281, 738, 736.
					799 Sqn colours. Crashed 28-4-21 **due**
☐ VX653		Hawker Sea Fury		49	ex Hendon, Yeovilton, Lee-on-Solent, Lossiemouth
		FB.11	G-BUCM		'XV653', FRU, 811, 738, 736. SOC 10-3-59 1-21
☐ WG655*	'910'	Hawker Sea Fury		51	ex G-CHFP, N20MD, USA, RNHF Yeovilton (crashed 14-7-90),
		T.20S	G-INVN		Colerne, DLB D-CACU, G-9-65, Dunsfold, Chilbolton,
					FAA WG655, Eglinton SF, 781. Eglinton SF colours.
					Crashed 4-8-20, de-reg 14-4-21 [2] 4-21
☐ 'A19-144'		Bristol Beaufighter XI		45	ex Melbourne, Sydney, Drysdale, RAAF A8-324.
					DAP-built. SOC 8-8-49. Arrived 1991 [3] 1-22
☐ No.82		Curtiss Hawk 75A-1 ✈		39	ex NX80FR, Chino, France, Cazaux, GC 11/5.
			G-CCVH		Acquired 1990. French AF colours [4] 1-22
☐ 'MM6976'		Fiat CR-42 Falco		41	ex Audley End, Italy, Sweden, RSweAF (as a J11) Fv2524.
	'85-16'		G-CBLS		Acquired 1995, arrived 23-2-06. On site from 6-7-18 [5] 1-22
☐ –		Nakajima Ki-43 Hayabusa		c44	ex Australia. Stored 3-18
☐ '20'		Lavochkin La-11		c45	ex Monino, USSR. Arrived 5-93. Stored 3-18
☐ -		Curtiss P-36C Hawk ✈		38	ex N80FR, Chino - first flown there 4-15, USAAC 38-210.
			G-CIXJ		Arrived 25-6-15 1-22
☐ '160'	'10AB'	Curtiss P-40C		41	ex N80FR, Chino, Russia, Sov AF, USAAF 41-13357
		Warhawk ✈	G-CIIO		Arrived 9-6-14 1-22
☐ –	'X-17'	Curtiss P-40F-15-CU		41	ex VH-PIV, Wangaratta, Espiritu Santo, 44th FG, 347th FG,
		Warhawk ✈	G-CGZP		41-19841. Arr 7-11. 85th FS, 79th FG c/s, *Lee's Hope* 1-22
☐ 21714	'201'	Grumman F8F-2P		48	ex NX700HL, N1YY, N4995V, 121714. Acquired 3-6-81.
		Bearcat ✈	G-RUMM		VF-20 colours, Lt Cdr 'Whiff' Caldwell's aircraft 1-22

■ All registered to Patina Ltd, unless noted. **[1]** EP120 in the colours of 402 'City of Winnipeg' Sqn RCAF as flown mostly by its CO, Sqn Ldr Geoffrey W Northcott; he chalked up the bulk of his 8 'kills' in EP120: 3 x Bf 109 and 3 x Fw 190. **[2]** G-INVN was registered to Shaun Patrick. During rebuild in the USA 2002-2005, is reported to have used the centre section and wing from an Iraqi example, parts from T.20 VZ345 and the rear fuselage from an FB.11. Fitted with an 18-cylinder Pratt & Whitney R-2800 Double Wasp in place of the Bristol Centaurus 18 it was born with. Therefore using little of WG655, although the service history relates to this airframe. **[3]** 'Beau' has large elements reputed to be from Mk.XIs A19-144 (ex RAF JM135) and A-19-148 (JL946) with the cockpit from an Australian-built Department of Aircraft Production example. **[4]** G-CCVH wears GC II/5 colours to port and Lafayette Esc 'chief's head' to starboard; the latter also being TFC's logo. **[5]** In the colours of an example that force landed in Norfolk 11-11-40.

Historic Aircraft Collection of Jersey (HAC): The Hurricane and Spitfire have been operated under the **Polish Heritage Flight** banner since November 2019. See under St Leonards-on-Sea, East Sussex, for HAC's closely related Retrotec.
◆ *Viewable during normal museum opening hours and at airshows* | www.historicaircraftcollection.ltd.uk

☐ E8894		Airco DH.9 ✈		1918	ex St Leonards-on-Sea, India, 47, 30. Vulcan Motor-built.
			G-CDLI		First flown 13-5-19 [1] 1-22
☐ K3661	'562'	Hawker Nimrod II ✈		34	ex St Leonards-on-Sea, Henlow, Ashford, 802.
			G-BURZ		802 Sqn colours 1-22
☐ K5674		Hawker Fury I ✈		35	ex St Leonards-on-Sea, Duxford, St Leonards-on-Sea, SAAF
			G-CBZP		215, 13, RAF 43. *Queen of North and South*, 43 Sqn c/s [2] 1-22
☐ L7181		Hawker Hind I	G-CBLK	37	ex St Leonards on Sea, Rockliffe, Canada, Kabul,
					Afghanistan AF, RAF, 211 [1] 1-22
☐ 'R4175'	'RF-R'	Hawker Hurricane		42	ex 'P3700', 'Z5140', 'Z7381', TFC, Coningsby, Coventry,
		XII ✈	G-HURI		Canada, 71. CCF-built. New 303 Sqn colours by 8-20 1-22
☐ BM597		V-S Spitfire Vb ✈		42	ex Audley End, Fulbourne, Church Fenton, Linton-on Ouse,
	'RF-M'		G-MKVB		Church Fenton, St Athan, 5718M, 58 OTU, 317. CBAF-built.
					303 Sqn colours by 11-20 1-22
☐ -*		MS Criquet	G-BPHZ	60	ex St Leonards, 'DM+BK', 'TA+RC', Duxford, F-BJQC,
					French mil. CoA 29-4-09. Arrived 29-9-21 [1] [3] 1-22

■ **[1]** DH.9, Hind and Criquet registered to Aero Vintage, all others to HAC. **[2]** Original colours, as flown by Fg Off Frederick Rosier, OC 'B' Flight, 43 Sqn, Tangmere, 36-39. **[3]** MS.505 started as Fi 156 airframe (w/nr.1827), completed as a Criquet with a Jacobs R-755A2.

Old Flying Machine Company (OFMC): ◆ *Viewable during normal museum hours and at airshows* | **www.mh434.com**

❑ MH434	'ZD-B' V-S Spitfire IX ✈	43	ex Booker, COGEA Nouvelle OO-ARA, Belgian AF SM-41,		
	G-ASJV		Fokker B-13, Netherlands H-68, H-105 322, MH434, 349,		
			222, 350, 222. CBAF-built. 222 Sqn colours, *Mylcraine*		1-22

Plane Sailing Ltd / Catalina Aircraft Ltd: Acting in support of the Canso (PBY-5A equivalent) and uniting those interested in Catalinas wherever they may be is the **Catalina Society**, which publishes the excellent *Catalina News*.
◆ *Viewable frequently during normal museum opening hours and at airshows*

❑ '433915'	Consolidated Canso A ✈	44	ex C-FNJF, CF-NJF, F-ZBBD, CF-NJF, F-ZBAY, CF-NJF, RCAF		
	G-PBYA		11005. Canadian-Vickers built. 5th ERS colours, *Miss Pick Up*		1-22

ELY Chipmunk T.10 cockpit WG362 was written out of *W&R27* as having left by mid-2018. It moved to <u>Linton</u>, Cambs.

EVERSDEN on the A603 west of Cambridge

A Tiger is *believed* to be stored at a *private* location in the area.

❑ G-AZDY	DH Tiger Moth	44	ex F-BGDJ, French AF, PG650 n/s. Morris-built. CoA 18-8-97		N10-19

FOWLMERE AERODROME north of the A505, west of Duxford, on the B1368   EGMA

❑ G-IKAP	Cessna T.303 Crusader	83	ex N63SA, D-IKAP, N9518C. CoA 23-9-05, de-reg 7-5-13		5-21

GRANSDEN LODGE AERODROME north of the B1046 west of Longstowe

Cambridge Gliding Centre: ◆ *By prior arrangement* only | **www.www.camgliding.uk**

❑ ZE500	Grob Viking T.1	85	BGA.3005, ex Sealand. Crashed 26-8-87. Forward fuselage		8-21

GREAT ABINGTON at the junction of the A11 and A505 southeast of Cambridge

TWI Group: In Granta Park, part of the 'Cambridge Science Cluster' high-tech zone, an Eclipse is on show. The biz-jet was the first to employ the TWI-pioneered friction stir-welding technique. **www.twi-global.com**

❑ N504EA	Eclipse 500	05	ex USA. First noted 4-17. See notes above	[1]	1-22

■ **[1]** Fourth Eclipse prototype; donated by Eclipse Aerospace and prepared for display by Marshall Aviation Services.

HOUGHTON on the A1123 east of Huntingdon

Jon Wilson: Keeps his Canberra cockpit at a *private* location in the area.

❑ WJ567	EE Canberra B.2	53	ex Wyton, 100, 85, MinTech, 45, RNZAF, 45, 59, 149.		
			HP-built. Cockpit		10-21

LINTON on the A3107 east of Duxford

No.2523 Squadron Air Cadets: Within Linton College, the unit has adopted a Chipmunk cockpit.

❑ WG362*	DHC Chipmunk T.10	51	ex Ely, Newton 8630M, Swinderby, Filton 8437M (30-1-75),		
			Birm, Wales, Oxf UASs, Swanton Morley SF, Carlisle SF,		
			Mildenhall CF, 100, Edin UAS, 3 BFTS, 16 RFS, 3 BFTS, 7 RFS.		
			Cockpit, arrived by 6-18		11-20

LITTLE GRANSDEN AERODROME south of the B1046, south of Great Gransden   EGMJ

Cambridge Bomber and Fighter Society: ◆ *By prior arrangement* **only**: *annual open day* | **www.cbfs.org.uk**

❑ 'K1928'	Hawker Fury I	31	BAPC.362, fuselage, off-site	[1]	7-21
❑ L1639	Hawker Hurricane I	38	BAPC.402, ex 504, 85. Shot down 14-5-40. Composite	[2]	7-21

■ **[1]** Being built up from a variety of sections. K1928 served mostly with 43 Sqn, suffering an accident at Tangmere 19-5-37. It later became instructional airframe 2196M. **[2]** Restoration takes identity from the cockpit area and other elements salvaged from the crash site of L1639. No.504's CO, Sqn Ldr J B Parnall was killed when L1639 was shot down operating from Marcq in France.

Also: ◆ *Access to aerodrome by prior arrangement* **only**

❑ G-BOFL*	Cessna 152	80	ex Little Staughton, N5457H. CoA 30-11-11, de-reg 4-10-21		8-21
❑ G-BOFM*	Cessna 152	81	ex Little Staughton, Sibson, N6445M. De-reg 26-2-13		8-21

LITTLE STAUGHTON AERODROME south of the A45, west of Eaton Socon

With the arrival from Cranfield of International Aerospace Engineering the skyline has changed dramatically here. As well as the brand new hangars and the extensive solar farm, there has been a major clear out of the hulks that littered the aerodrome. Cessna 152s G-BOFL and G-BOFM had moved to Little Gransden, Cambs, by October 2020. The following, all last noted in March 2018, have been deleted: Cessna 150 G-AZLH, G-BPTU and 172 G-LICK.

◆ *By prior arrangement* only | www.iae.org.uk

❑ G-BHUJ	Cessna 172N	79	ex Southend, N5752E. Damaged 28-3-16, de-reg 11-7-16	7-19
❑ G-BKAS	Piper Tomahawk 112	79	CoA 6-10-17, de-reg 6-10-17. First noted 3-18	8-19
❑ G-BTZP*	SOCATA Tampico	92	de-reg 18-6-08	7-21
❑ OO-RAB	Piper Tomahawk 112	~	ex D-EKTS, N2313K. First noted 3-18	8-19

MADINGLEY at the junction of the A1303 and A14 west of Cambridge

Cambridge American Forces Cemetery: Perhaps when visiting Duxford, take a trip to Madingley and a walk through the beautifully kept grounds, amid row after row of graves and impressive memorials. | www.abmc.gov

MARCH on the A141 south of Wisbech

Ian and Gary Morton: Are hard at work returning a former CAFU Dove to 'flight checker' status.

❑ G-ANAP*	DH Dove 6	53	ex Pershore, Bristol, CAFU Stansted. CoA 6-9-73, de-reg 31-8-73. Cockpit	8-21

PETERBOROUGH

The Blue Bell Inn: By August 2020 the pub, at Werrington to the north of the city, had gained a Lynx cabin. There is an effective notice near the entrance to the 'cab': "By all means look, but don't enter! Dangerous pipes and children-eating sharks live inside!" Adding to the theme, the wall side of an outbuilding boasts an impressive mural of a Spitfire.

❑ XZ655*	'A' Westland Lynx AH.7	80	ex Weeton, Hixon, M Wallop, 671, 655, 664, 655, 664,	
	and '3'		671, 657, 651, 652, 655, 652. Cabin. First noted 8-20	12-21

PETERBOROUGH (CONINGTON) AERODROME east of the A1, south of Wansford EGSF

Duchess G-GCCL was airworthy again by mid-2020.

❑ G-BFKF	Cessna FA.150	79	Reims-built. De-reg 6-10-17	10-19
❑ XW410	'MR' BAC Jet Provost T.5A		ex 'Norfolk', Selby, Cosford 9125M, Shawbury, 1 FTS, RAFC, 3 FTS. Cockpit, first noted 3-18	10-20

RAMSEY on the B1096 west of Chatteris

No.511 Squadron Air Cadets:

❑ WK584	DHC Chipmunk T.10	52	ex Bawtry, Church Fenton, Linton-on-Ouse, 7556M (28-2-58), Edzell SF, Oxf UAS, Glas UAS, 11 RFS. Cockpit	3-19

UPWOOD southeast of Peterborough, west of Ramsey

Matt Buddle: Keeps his cockpits in the locality. ◆ *By prior arrangement* only

❑ XR754	EE Lightning F.6	65	ex Doncaster, Firbeck, Walpole, King's Lynn, Stock, Honington 8972M, Binbrook, 11, 5-11, 23, 5, A&AEE. Last flown 22-6-88. Cockpit	6-19
❑ XZ993	'M' HS Harrier GR.3	81	ex Selby, Welshpool, St Athan 9240M (25-7-94), Laarbruch, St Athan, 4, 1, 1453 Flt, 3. Cockpit. Arrived 9-11-14	6-19

Upwood Airpark: The trio of Boeing 707 cockpits – N707QJ, OD-AHD and OD-AHE – had moved on by mid-2020.

WATERBEACH on the A10 north of Cambridge

Waterbeach Military Heritage Museum: Housed in a building near the entrance to the former barracks. The museum, dedicated to the memory of Oliver Errington, covers the legacy of the airfield - including the 'round engined' Lancasters of 514 Squadron - and its final days as an Army base.

◆ *Denny End Road, CB25 9PA* | **01223 861846** | **waterbeachmilitarymuseum@waterbeach.org** | **www.waterbeachmilitarymuseum.org.uk**

WHITTLESEY on the A605 east of Peterborough

Locally, an Auster is being worked on at a *private* location.

| ☐ G-AOGV | Auster J5R Alpine | 56 | CoA 17-7-72 | N9-19 |

WITTERING AIRFIELD on the A1 south of Stamford   EGXT

RAF Wittering: Within the base is the **Harrier Heritage Centre** with *no public access.*

☐ XV279		HS Harrier GR.1	67	ex 8566M (8-2-78), WLT *The Plastic Pig*, Farnborough, Culdrose, A&AEE, BSE, Ferranti, HSA		11-21
☐ XV779		HS Harrier GR.3	70	ex 8931M (23-1-87) 'gate' 1988-2011, 233 OCU, 3, Wittering SF, 3, 20, GR.1, 20, 4, 1, 4. 4 Sqn colours	[1]	11-21
☐ XW923		HS Harrier GR.3	71	ex 8724M, 1417 Flt, 233 OCU, 1, GR.1. Crashed 26-5-81, Belize. 20 Sqn colours. Cockpit		11-21
☐ XZ146	'S'	HS Harrier T.4	76	ex North Luffenham 9281M (17-12-97), Shawbury, 20, 233 OCU, Gütersloh SF, 233 OCU, 4, 3, T.2. 20 Sqn colours		11-21
☐ ZD318		BAe/McDD Harrier GR.7A	85	ex Cottesmore, GR.7, Warton, Boscombe Down, Ferranti, Warton, GR.5. Last flown 11-7-07	[2]	11-21
☐ 162068		BAe/McDD AV-8B Harrier II	84	ex Cottesmore, 9250M, VMAT-203. Fuselage	[3]	7-15
☐ 162964		BAe/McDD AV-8B Harrier II	87	ex Boscombe Down, St Athan, Warton, USMC, VMA-542, -223, -231, -542. Cockpit in 4 Sqn colours		7-15

■ **[1]** XV779 belly-landed at Wildenrath 16-12-74; cockpit replaced by a spare. *Original* nose can be found at Selby, N Yorks. **[2]** Circa 1998 ZD318 suffered a landing accident and was fitted with the wing of ZD348. **[3]** The original fuselage of BuAer 162068 which was rebuilt as AV-8B+ 165310. Modified by the heritage centre to resemble a GR.7.

Among the resident units is **71 (Inspection and Repair) Squadron** engaged on maintenance trials. Tornado GR.4 ZA560 departed by road on 15th July 2021, bound for <u>Boscombe Down</u>, Wilts.

☐ XX351		HS Hawk T.1A	81	ex Shawbury, 4 FTS, 100, 19, 208, 234, 1 TWU. SOC 25-1-16. Arrived 12-1-16. Sectioned, 71 Sqn		5-18
☐ ZD469	'59A'	BAe/McDD Harrier GR.7A	90	ex Cottesmore, Kandahar, 3, GR.5A. Damaged 14-10-05. *Christine.* On display from 28-4-11, 1 Sqn colours	[1]	12-21
☐ ZJ810*		Eurofighter Typhoon T.3	04	ex Coningsby. SOC 21-2-19. Arrived by 8-20. Fuselage, 71 Sqn		9-20

■ **[1]** ZD469 was damaged in a mortar attack at Kandahar 14-10-05 and declared Cat 5 2-5-08 - total time 1,500.05 hours.

WYTON on the B1090 northwest of St Ives

RAF Pathfinders Archive: (Note new name.) Within the RAF enclave is an incredible volunteer-run archive, dedicated to the Pathfinder Force; including material from crash sites and a vast array of material.

◆ *By prior arrangement* only | **email** via website | **www.raf-pathfinders.com**

RAF Wyton: An enclave within the former airfield includes **Joint Force Command** and the **Joint Forces Intelligence Group**.

| ☐ XH170 | EE Canberra PR.9 | 60 | ex 8739M (27-1-82), 39, RAE, 58. Displayed | 10-21 |

Also: A Chipmunk cockpit is *believed* to still be held in the area.

| ☐ WP927 | DHC Chipmunk T.10 | 52 | ex South Molton, Ingatestone, London Colney, Ashton-under- |
| | G-ATJK | | Lyne, Woodvale, Ashton-under-Lyne, Crosby, 8216M 4-8-72), Hamble G-ATJK (1965-1968), MCS, Oxf UAS, Lon UAS, Detling SF, London UAS. Cockpit | 6-09 |

CHESHIRE

ALDFORD on the B5130 south of Chester

Eaton Hall: The late 6th Duke of Westminster, Major General G C Grosvenor, was an avid supporter of the Army Air Corps, to the extent that a Gazelle has been plinth-mounted within the grounds of the ancestral home. A board declares the Duke's opinion that the Gazelle, nicknamed 'the whistling chicken leg', is "the Maserati of the helicopter world".

◆ *North of Aldford - occasional open days, otherwise by prior arrangement* only | **www.eatonestate.co.uk**

| ☐ '316' | Sud Gazelle AH.1 | ~ | ex ????. Westland-built. Plinth mounted | 9-16 |

BURTONWOOD south of the M62, west of Warrington

RAF Burtonwood Heritage Centre: Little of the once huge USAF Burtonwood air base remains; cars that hurtle down the M62 are following the course of the main runway. The centre, to the south of the motorway and on the former domestic Site 4, has amassed an incredible collection of artefacts and images to tell the tale of this great airfield.

◆ **NB:** As W&R27 closed for press the centre was closed until further notice. Keep an eye on the website. Access from the M62 J8 or 9, 'Gulliver's World', Shackleton Close, Bewsey, WA5 9YZ | **email** via website | **www.rafburtonwood.com**

❑ N31356   Douglas DC-4-1009   46 ex '44-42914', N Weald, C-FTAW, EL-ADR, N6404.
                                                              Last flown 9-02. Forward fuselage. Arrived 8-12-15   12-21

CHESTER

Note: Airframes listed here are in the *general* area, at *separate* venues and *only* available by prior arrangement.

Air Pulford - Panavia Tornado Restorations: Simon owns Tornado F.2 cockpit ZD938 at Doncaster, S Yorks, and Sioux AH.1 XT236 which moved to Hooton Park, Cheshire, on 21st July 2021. The cockpit of Tornado GR.1 ZD710, briefly at Hawarden, Wales, has passed on to a new owner – its new permanent venue is yet to be decided. **simonpulford@btinternet.com**

Andy Blair: Andy's 'JP' will wear CFS silver and Dayglo when completed.
❑ XN549   Hunting Jet Provost T.3   61 ex Warrington, South Molton, Book, Shawbury, Halton,
                                                                       '8235M'/8335M (21-3-73), Shawbury, 1 FTS, CFS. Cockpit   1-18

Nick Foden: grummanaa5a@googlemail.com
❑ G-AXDW   Beagle Pup 100   69 ex Caterham, Cranfield. Cr 26-2-09, CoA 31-3-09, de-reg 5-8-09   1-22
❑ OO-GCO   American AA-5A   78 ex Skycraft, Belgium. Crashed 22-3-05. Fuselage, flight sim   1-22

Ian Starnes:
❑ XR654   Hunting Jet Provost T.4   63 ex Barton, Chelford, Macclesfield, Hurn, Coventry, Puckeridge,
                                                                       Hatfield, Shawbury, CAW, 3 FTS, 6 FTS. SOC 25-11-71. Cockpit   3-19
❑ -   Fieseler Fi 103 (V-1) FSM   15 BAPC.327, ex Parbold. Built by Mike Davey. Arrived 8-15   8-15

CREWE on the A51 southeast of Nantwich

Obsolete Aviation: Matt Gilbey is undertaking this challenging restoration on an 'as and when' basis.

◆ *Available for inspection* only *by prior arrangement* | **obsoleteaviation@gmail.com**
❑ ZG875   Westland Sea King HAS.6   90 ex Gosport, 819, 820, 814. Accident 12-6-99, SOC 30-10-00
                                                                        Cockpit, acquired 2015   4-21

HOOTON PARK north of Junction 6 of the M53, near Eastham Locks

Hooton Park Trust (HPT): Working hand-in-hand with **The Aeroplane Collection** (TAC), the Griffin Trust and the CH21 Home Guard Living History Group, HPT is working to create a unique visitor centre among the Grade II* 'Belfast Truss' (General Service) hangars at this famous former airfield. It is great to how well endeavours have dovetailed and a major regional treasure is being forged. Progress has been so good that, if all goes to plan, the south bay of Hangar 16 will be open to the public on full-time basis from Easter 2022 with special events also to be staged. While HPT manages the site, including a secure storage business that helps to finance the fully volunteer-operated organisation, it also has an expanding collection of aircraft and artefacts. The latest is Autocrat G-AIGP which was bought new by Wright Aviation in November 1946: one of Wright's ventures being the Liverpool Aero Club. As such G-AIGP was based at Hooton Park and just across the Mersey at Speke until January 1956: clever research, producing a five-star exhibit.

To gently remind one and all of its unique, pioneering status, The Aeroplane Collection proudly has the masthead rider 'Preserving Aviation Heritage since 1962'. Founded as the trail-blazing Northern Aircraft Preservation Society (NAPS), the current name was adopted on 7th December 1973. TAC is based at Hooton and playing a major role in the site's heritage development; all the more so with the arrival of its airframes from Manchester. The jewel is the Avian, returning to Hooton after 92 years. G-EBZM was registered to Merseyside Aero and Sports Ltd, trading as the Liverpool and District Aero Club, based at Hooton Park, in February 1929, plying the skies on that side of the Mersey for three years.

The cockpit of Chipmunk T.10 WK640 (G-BWUV) moved to Elvington, N Yorks, in December 2020, followed by the cockpit of WD387 (G-BDDD) by January 2021, bound for Westbury, Wilts. The cockpit of Hunter FGA.9 XE584 was due to move to New Brighton, Merseyside, by the time W&R went to press: this migration has been anticipated.

Please note: Not all airframes will be on show to visitors, either in workshops, or storage. Information of TAC's restoration projects can be found on the website – details below.

◆ *Airfield Way, CH65 1BQ* | HPT: **0151 327 3565** | **info@hootonparktrust.co.uk** | **www.hootonparktrust.co.uk** |
    TAC: **tac.secretary.web@gmail.com** | **www.theaeroplanecollection.org**

❑ G-EBZM*	Avro Avian IIIA	28	ex Manchester, Higher Blagdon, Peel Green, Stretford, Lymm, Speke, Huyton, Ringway, Hesketh Park. CoA 20-1-38, de-reg 1-12-46. Acquired 3-11-62. Arrived 12-21. See notes above	[1] [2]	1-22
❑ G-ADAH*	DH Dragon Rapide	35	ex Manchester, East Fortune, Peel Green, Booker, Dyce, Island Air Services, Allied AW, Northern and Scottish, British Airways, Hillman's. CoA 9-6-47, de-reg 18-2-59. Acquired 11-10-70, arrived 12-21. Allied Airways colours, *Pioneer*	[1]	1-22
❑ 'G-ADYO'* 'BHP.1'	Mignet HM.14 'Flea'	36	BAPC.12, ex Manchester, East Fortune, Chester-le-Street, Newcastle, Wigan, Stockport, Rishworth. Acquired 13-6-64. Arrived 11-21	[1] [3]	1-22
❑ G-AFIU	Luton Minor	c38	ex Barton, Wigan, Stoke, Breighton, Wigan, Peel Green, Pembroke. De-reg 31-3-99. Acquired 1971	[1] [4]	1-22
❑ 'G-AHUI'	Miles Messenger	46	ex Pulborough. Composite, under restoration	[1] [5]	1-22
❑ G-AIGP*	Auster J1 Autocrat	46	ex Spilsby .CoA 30-10-73, de-reg 31-10-73. Arrived 10-12-21. See notes above	[6]	1-22
❑ 'G-AJCL'*	DH Dragon Rapide FSM	01	BAPC.280, ex Crowne Plaza - Liverpool, 'G-ANZP', 'G-AEAJ'. Cockpit, first noted 8-21	[6] [7]	1-22
❑ G-AJEB	Auster J1N Alpha	46	ex Manchester, Hooton, Warmingham, Brize Norton, Wigan, Cosford. CoA 27-3-69, de-reg 9-6-81. Acquired 28-6-75	[1] [8]	1-22
❑ 'G-AKHZ'	Miles Gemini	47	ex Pulborough. Composite	[1] [9]	1-22
❑ G-AOUO	DHC Chipmunk T.10 WB730	50	ex Halton, RAFGSA, WB730, 11 RFS. CoA 3-4-14, de-reg 10-5-19. Arrived 3-17	[1] [10]	1-22
❑ G-APUD*	Wallis-Bensen B-7MC	59	ex Manchester, Firbeck, Nostell Priory, Wigan, Biggin Hill, CoA 27-9-60, de-reg 27-2-70. Acquired 4-72, arrived 11-21	[1] [11]	1-22
❑ -AKQ	Slingsby T.8 Tutor	46	BGA.466, ex Stamford, Tibenham. Martin Hearn-built. Arrived 31-8-14	[6] [12]	1-22
❑ -AKW	Slingsby T.8 Tutor G-ALKP	46	G-ALKP, BGA.469, ex Stamford. Martin Hearn-built. Arrived 26-7-19	[6] [12]	1-22
❑ -	Slingsby Tutor G-ALPU	47	BGA.473, ex TAC, Melton Mowbray, G-ALPU), College of Aeronautics, Cranfield, BGA.473. CoA 12-87. Martin Hearn-built. Arrived 10-6-12	[6] [12]	1-22
❑ CHQ	Slingsby Tandem Tutor XN247	59	BGA.1559, ex Selby, Bury St Edmunds, Leeds, RAFGSA.316, XN247, 622 GS. CoA 1-7-82. Arr 14-2-20	[6]	1-22
❑ '14'*	Roe Triplane replica	c53	BAPC.6, ex Manchester, London, Southend, Irlam, Peel Green, Old Warden, Woodford. Avro, Woodford-built. 'Bullseye Avroplane'. Acquired 24-10-69, arrived 11-21	[1] [13]	1-22
❑ -	Sopwith Baby replica	78	BAPC.137, ex North Stainley, Land's End, Chertsey. Arrived 12-5-18, stored	[6]	1-22
❑ -	Mignet HM.14 'Flea'	36	BAPC.201, ex TAC, Millom, Llandwrog, Talysarn. Fuselage	[14]	1-22
❑ -	McBroom hang-glider	c75	BAPC.204, ex Winthorpe, Hooton Park, Warmingham. Acquired circa 1989	[1] [8]	1-22
❑ -	Miles Wings MW.100 h-g	c77	BAPC.310, ex Warmingham. Arrived 30-8-15	[1] [8]	1-22
❑ -	UFM Easy-Riser	~	ex Manchester	[1]	1-22
❑ P9451	V-S Spitfire I	40	ex 610. Crashed 11-12-40. Cockpit. Arr by 6-15. Stored	[15]	1-22
❑ RA848	Slingsby Cadet TX.1	43	ex Wigan, Harrogate, Wigan, Handforth, Gt Hucklow. Otley Motors-built. Cockpit. Arrived 14-2-20	[6]	1-22
❑ WG303	DHC Chipmunk T.10	51	ex Stamford, Bicester 8208M (4-8-72), Shawbury, Kemble, Oxf UAS, Gatow SF, Wittering SF, Marham SF, Birm UAS, 5 RFS, 2 BFTS. Cockpit. First noted 8-16	[1]	1-22
❑ WH132 'J'	Gloster Meteor T.7	51	ex Leconfield, Chelmsford 7906M (17-7-66), Kemble, CAW, CFS, CAW, 8 FTS, 207 AFS. Arrived 5-10-17	[6]	1-22
❑ WT520	EE Canberra PR.7	55	ex Biddulph, Warton, Lytham St Annes's, Eaglescott, Burntwood, Swinderby 8184M (8-10-71), 8094M, CAW, 31, 17, 1, 17, 31, 80. Short-built. Cockpit. Arrived 7-19	[6]	1-22

Top: Avian III G-EBZM at Hooton Park, *circa* 1930. *MSI*
Bottom: Nine decades later, back at Hooton, January 2022, with the Roe Triplane replica behind. *Jonathan Howard*

❑ XA293		Slingsby Cadet TX.1	52	ex Stoke-on-Trent, Long Marston, Redditch. Forward fuselage. Arrived 14-2-20	[6]	1-22
❑ XD624	'O'	DH Vampire T.11	55	ex Haverigg, Swinton, Ringway, Macclesfield, CATCS, CNCS, Church Fenton SF, 19. SOC 15-12-70. Fairey-built. Acquired 20-3-11. Wings from XD425	[1]	1-22
❑ XT148*		Bell Sioux AH.1	65	ex Sunderland, Weston-super-Mare, Halton, Panshanger, Wroughton, ARWF. Agusta-built. Cab, no 'bubble'. Arrived 11-7-21, spares for XT236	[6]	1-22
❑ XT236*	'12'	Bell Sioux AH.1	66	ex Chester, Doncaster, Sunderland, M Wallop, MoAF, Sek Kong. Westland-built. Arrived 21-7-21	[16]	1-22
❑ –		Fairey Gannet T.2	c56	BAPC.309, ex Caernarfon, Buxton ATC, Sealand, Hooton, Park, Tangmere, Fleetlands. Cockpit. Arrived 20-7-12	[1]	1-22

■ **[1]** TAC airframe. **[2]** See narrative above. Restoration of G-EBZM included the wings tail and undercarriage of Mk.IVM G-ABEE, itself a composite with Mk.IVM G-ACKE. **[3]** 'Flea' built by S O Whiteley at Rishworth, Yorks: did not fly. It is painted as the example built by Brian Henry Park in Wigan; the link being that the Scott A.2S from the original G-ADYO is fitted to BAPC.12. **[4]** G-AFIU designated Parker CA.4 from its builder, C F Parker of Pembroke. It differed little from the LA-4 except for the rear fuselage decking. Started in 1938, it was never finished. Includes wings and tail of G-ATWS, built 1966 in Derby - de-reg 8-2-82. **[5]** Messenger is centred upon Mk.2A G-AHUI, plus elements of Mk.2 G-AILL (see also Stratford-upon-Avon, Warks), Mk.2A G-AJFF, Mk.2A G-AKDF, Mk.2A EI-AGB (G-AHFP) and Mk.4A VP-KJL (G-ALAR). *Uniform-India*, owned by E C Francis of Chester, was based at Hooton Park 1954 to 1957. Also held is the extreme forward cockpit 'slice' of Mk.2A G-AKIO, salvaged from Barton. **[6]** HPT airframe. **[7]** Built by Mike Davey as 'gate guardian' for the Crowne Plaza at the *original* Liverpool Airport - see above. Reduced to a cockpit 2019. To be hands-on exhibit alongside G-ADAH. **[8]** To be disposed of 12-21 from TAC inventory. **[9]** Gemini is centred upon: Mk.1A G-AKHZ with the rear fuselage of Mk.1A G-ALUG and bits of Mk.1 G-AKGD. **[10]** 'Supermunk' conversion with Lycoming O-360. **[11]** Built from a Bensen kit by Wg Cdr Kenneth Horatio Wallis at his then home of Southwick, Sussex, and first flown by him 23-5-59 – see also under Old W... sorry Shuttleworth, Beds - for 'PUD's' more famous siblings. **[12]** Martin Hearn Ltd of Hooton Park, no less. **[13]** Triplane was originally on loan from the Shuttleworth Trust; title was transferred to TAC on 20-11-19. **[14]** 'Flea' BAPC.201 transferred to a private owner, expected to remain on site. Built by Idwal ap Ieuan Jones at Talysarn, Wales, in 1936. Seasoned display pilot Jones was killed in Airspeed Courier G-ACSZ at Doncaster 29-5-37, along with three others. Elements from this machine - undercarriage and other metal parts - are in 'Flea' 'G-EGCK' at Caernarfon, Wales. **[15]** Spitfire cockpit, owned by Mike Davey - see also under Liverpool, Merseyside - and Graham Sparkes, is a 'space-frame' reconstruction from recovered items with no attempt to restore, merely to conserve it in a similar manner to accident investigation piece-togethers. **[16]** XT236 owned by Simon Pulford.

KNUTSFORD on the A537 west of the M6

Oliver Valves: Parkgate Industrial Estate, as well as the family business, it is the home of the incredible *private* collection established by Mark and Michael Oliver. ◆ *Available for inspection by prior arrangement* **only** | www.valves.co.uk

❑ G-BRZG		Enstrom F-28A	73	ex Ipswich, Tattershall Thorpe, N9053. CoA 20-10-13, de-reg 18-5-18. First noted 8-19		7-21
❑ –		Slingsby Tutor	47	BGA.791, ex Hooton Park, VM684, 26 GS, 49 GS. CoA 27-2-71. Arrived by 8-14		8-19
❑ 5X-UUX		Westland Scout Srs 1 *G-BKLJ*	69	ex Ipswich, East Dereham, Tattershall Thorpe, Heysham, Panshanger, G-BKLJ (de-reg 7-2-91), Uganda Police. Arrived by 5-15		6-21
❑ 'B6447'		Sopwith Camel rep	11	BAPC.385, *Susan*	[1]	8-16
❑ P8088		V-S Spitfire IIa *G-CGRM*	41	ex Brooklands, Oxford, Sleap, Ibsley, 61 OTU, CGS, 61 OTU, 19, 152, 118, 66. CBAF-built. Crashed 16-9-44. *Bette* and *Borough of Lambeth*. Cockpit, arrived 18-2-13		8-16
❑ 'W3850'	'PR-A'	V-S Spitfire V FSM	08	BAPC.304, ex Leeming. Built by Royal British Legion, Ripon branch. 609 Sqn colours. *Irene*		8-16
❑ XW330	'MJ'	BAC Jet Provost T.5A	70	ex Ipswich, Cosford, 9195M (7-6-93), 1 FTS, 7 FTS, 3 FTS, Leeming SF, CFS, RAFC, 3 FTS. Arrived by 5-15		6-21
❑ ZA399	'AJ-C'	Panavia Tornado GR.1	82	ex Selby, Cosford 9316M, St Athan, 617, 15, 20, TWCU. *Plt Off Warner Ottley DFC*		6-21
❑ ZD992	'724'	HS Harrier T.8	87	ex Ipswich, Cranfield, Yeovilton, 899. Crashed 16-11-00		7-21
❑ 13605		Messerschmitt Bf 109G-2 *G-JIMP*	42	ex Lancing, North Russia, 6/JG5 Yellow 14. Shot down 21-6-43.		4-16

■ **[1]** Camel built by Peter Grieve's Flight Engineering of Carlisle, and to quote its website is an "aluminium-framed flying replica designed by Robert Baslee in the USA. It uses original instrumentation and fittings."

LOWER KINNERTON on minor road south of the A55 Broughton

Outpost Paintball: This extensive paintball - and other forms of hostility – site includes the *cockpitless* but otherwise intact Vampire T.11 XH312. This was the victim of a reported arson attack in June 2009 and was written out of *W&R22* (p30) under Chester. The former Halfpenny Green Aztec was removed from the 25th edition (p218) as having moved on by mid-2014 – it *may* have been here since then. ◆ *By prior arrangement* only | www.outpostpaintbball.co.uk

☐ G-ATFF*   '53' Piper Aztec 250C   65 ex Halfpenny Green, N5769Y. CoA 15-5-05   9-21

NANTWICH west of Crewe

Hack Green Secret Nuclear Bunker: A 'JP' is on show in the grounds.
◆ *French Lane, Baddington, CW5 8BL* | 01270 629219 | coldwar@hackgreen.co.uk | www.hackgreen.co.uk

☐ XS179   '20' Hunting Jet Provost T.4   63 ex Manchester, Salford, Halton '8237M' (8337M - 9-8-3),
                                                   Kemble, Shawbury, CAW, RAFC. Arrived 15-1-13   1-22

RIXTON on the A57 east of Warrington

Ramswood Nurseries: Is 'guarded' by a Rallye | www.ramswoodnurseries.co.uk

☐ G-WCEI   MS Rallye Minerva   73 ex Squires Gate, G-BAOC. De-reg 11-12-14. First noted 4-15 10-21

SANDBACH on the A534 northeast of Crewe

The Andover was a regular at the Glastonbury Festival and is stored at a yard in the town.

☐ XS641   'Z'   HS Andover C.1(PR)   67 ex Cosford 9198M (10-1-94), Shawbury, 60, 115, 46,
                                                   84, SAR Flt, 84. Forward fuselage   2-20

WARRINGTON

Jonathan Howard: Jonathan keeps his Vampire in the area. ◆ *By prior arrangement* only| email@jhoward.org.uk

☐ VZ193   DH Vampire FB.5   49 ex Chelmsford, Doncaster, Firbeck, Malmesbury,
                                                   Hullavington, 229 OCU, 247. EE-built. SOC 29-5-59. Cockpit 12-21

WIDNES

Vintage Barn / Halton Reclamation: Birchfield Road | www.haltonreclamation.com

☐ G-SSWM   Short 360-100   84 ex Liverpool, Coventry, Streamline Av, SE-KCI, G-OAAS,
                                                   OY-MMB, G-14-3648. CoA 14-10-06, de-reg 6-6-07. Cockpit   10-21

WINSFORD on the A54 south of Northwich

Classic Autos: In the Woodford Park Industrial Estate has a 'gate guardian'.

☐ ZE691   '710' HS Sea Harrier F/A.2   87 ex Queensbury, Ipswich, St Athan, Yeovilton, 899, 801, 899,
                                                   800, 899, 801, 800. Crashed 4-2-98. Arrived 7-08   9-21

Also: Two Austers *should* still be at a *private* workshop in the *general* area. A long out-of-use Jodel is kept at a local airstrip.

☐ G-AGLK   Taylorcraft Auster 5D   44 ex RT475 n/s. CoA 15-7-14   6-18
☐ G-BKXP   Auster AOP.6   46 ex Thruxton, Little Gransden, Royston, Oakington, Belgian
                                                   Army A-14 (SOC 10-1-57), VT987 n/s. Arrived by mid-15   6-18
☐ G-BITO*   Jodel D.112D   63 ex F-BIUO. Ests Valladeau-built. CoA 5-9-02   9-21

CORNWALL

BODMIN AERODROME east of the A30, north of Bodmin   EGLA

To tidy up: Cessna 175 G-ARUZ (last noted in January 2012) and Aztec G-AXDC (October 2014) have been deleted.

☐ G-BMFZ   Cessna F.152 II   85 Reims-built. CoA 27-5-10, de-reg 13-12-10. Fuselage   4-19

CALLINGTON on the A390 southwest of Tavistock

A Lightning is kept at a *private* location in the area.

☐ XR755   'BN' EE Lightning F.6   65 ex Binbrook, 5, 5-11 pool. SOC 21-6-88   7-21

CULDROSE AIRFIELD on the A3083 south of Helston   EGDR

HMS Sea Hawk:

☐ WF225		Hawker Sea Hawk F.1	53	ex A2623, A2645 (4-6-58), FRU, 738, 802. AWA-built. Displayed	6-21
☐ XV673	'27'	Westland Sea King HU.5	70	ex Fleetlands, 771, 706, HAS.1, 7-6. 819, 824, 826, 706	
				Arrived mid-2015, placed on display 23-3-16	6-21
☐ XV786	'123'	HS Harrier GR.3	70	ex A2611[3], A2615 (5-6-91), St Athan, 3, 4, 1, 4.	
				Cockpit, in fire station	9-21

The **School of Flight Deck Operations** (SFDO) is the main 'user' of *W&R* airframes. 'DD' codes relate to the 'dummy deck' the trainees work on. Sea Harrier ZH798 left for Church Fenton, sorry <u>Leeds East</u>, N Yorks, on 29th January 2021, arriving on 1st February. Departing the same time, but for <u>Selby</u>, N Yorks, were fellow 'SHARS', ZH804 and ZH811.

☐ XX510	'DD69'	Westland Lynx HAS.2	73	ex A2683[2], Gosport, Lee-on-S' A2772, A2601[2] (10-10-89),		
				Foulness, Boscombe Down, A&AEE, RAE, A&AEE		9-19
☐ XZ248	'DD02'	Westland Lynx HAS.3S	78	ex A2854 (18-8-10), Yeovilton, 702, 815, 702, 815,		
				702, 815, 702, 815, 829, 815		9-18
☐ XZ440	'DD40'	HS Sea Harrier F/A.2	79	ex Yeovilton, 800, BAe, FRS.1, 801, 800, A&AEE. Arr 14-2-06		6-18
☐ ZB603	'DDT03'	HS Harrier T.8	83	ex St Athan, 899, 233 OCU. Arrived 6-3-06		6-18
☐ ZD579		HS Sea Harrier F/A.2	85	ex Shawbury, Yeovilton, 800, 801, 800, 801, 899, FRS.1, 800,		
	'DD79'			801, 800, A&AEE, 801, 899, 800, 899. Arrived 16-10-07.		7-19
☐ ZE690	'DD90'	HS Sea Harrier F/A.2	87	ex Yeovilton, 801, 899, 801, 800, 801, 800, 801, 899,		
				FRS.1, 899. Arrived 29-3-06		7-19
☐ ZE692		HS Sea Harrier F/A.2	87	ex Yeovilton, 899, 801, 899, 800, 801, 899, 801, 899,		
	'DD92'			FRS.1, 801, 899. Arrived 23-3-06		4-21
☐ ZF641		EHI EH 101 PP1	87	ex Fleetlands, Westland. Arrived 18-6-98	[1]	6-21
☐ ZH797	'DD97'	HS Sea Harrier F/A.2	95	ex Yeovilton, 801, 899. Arrived 24-6-09		9-20
☐ ZH802	'DD02'	HS Sea Harrier F/A.2	96	ex Yeovilton, 899, 800, 899, 800, 801. Arrived 21-2-06		6-18
☐ ZH813	'DD13'	HS Sea Harrier F/A.2	99	ex Culdrose, Shawbury, Yeovilton, 801, DERA. Arr 18-1-09		9-19
☐ 'AV511'	'DD511'	EHI Merlin EMU	~	ex Yeovil. Arrived 16-11-99		9-19
☐ -	'GTA-02'	Lockheed Martin F-35B	16	Gateguards UK-built. First noted 5-17	[2]	5-17
☐ -	'GTA-03'	Lockheed Martin F-35B	16	Gateguards UK-built. Delivered 10-8-16	[2]	9-19
☐ -	'GTA-04'	Lockheed Martin F-35B	16	Gateguards UK-built. First noted 9-16	[2]	6-18
☐ -		Lockheed Martin F-35B	16	Gateguards UK-built. First noted 5-17	[2]	5-17

■ **[1]** Prototype Merlin first flown 9-10-87. **[2]** A quartet of F-35B full-scale, towable mock-ups are in use. They are reported to have adapted Tornado undercarriage units and water tanks so that different weights can be set during towing training. At least one of these has an opening canopy to enable rescue procedure tuition.

DAVIDSTOW MOOR on minor road west of the A39 and Camelford

There are two aviation museums, side-by-side, on the former technical site located in the north western corner of RAF Davidstow Moor. This isn't overkill; both offer different coverage. With respect to these venues, it is the airfield that will dominate memories of a visit. Built on common land under the strict proviso that it be returned as much as practical to its former status, at 970ft above sea level it is the highest airfield ever built in Britain and it is a delight to walk on.

Davidstow Airfield and **Cornwall at War Museum:** Occupying several former RAF buildings; is dedicated to the armed services and to wartime life in the county. A display hall was erected during 2016.

◆ *Nottles Park, PL32 9YF* | **07799194918** | **hq@cornwallatwarmuseum.co.uk** | **www.cornwallatwarmuseum.co.uk**

☐ XG164		Hawker Hunter F.6	56	ex Poole, Shawbury, Halton 8681M (2-4-81), Kemble,		
				West Raynham SF, 74, 111. 111 Sqn c/s. Arrived 15-7-14	[1]	1-22
☐ XG831	'396'	Fairey Gannet ECM.6	57	ex Helston, Culdrose SAH-8, A2539 (20-5-66), 831, AS.4.		
				Arrived 16-2-08		1-22
☐ XK627		DH Vampire T.11	56	ex Hurn, Felmersham, Lavendon, Barton, Bacup, Hazel Grove,		
				Woodford, Chester, St Athan, 8 FTS, CFS. Hawarden-built.		
				SOC 3-12-68. Cockpit		1-22
☐ XW999		Northrop Chukar D.1	71	ex Culdrose, 792. Arrived 26-9-09		12-19
☐ XZ791		Northrop Shelduck D.1	c84	ex Culdrose, Portland. Arrived 26-9-09		12-19
☐ ZG347		Northrop Chukar D.2	00	ex Culdrose, 792. Arrived 26-9-09	[2]	12-19
☐ -		Fieseler Fi 103 (V-1) FSM	~	BAPC.345		12-19

■ **[1]** Hunter XG164 has the starboard wing of T.7 XL623. The port wing is at Beck Row, Suffolk. The fuselage of XL623 – with *altogether* different wings – is at Dunsfold, Surrey. **[2]** Mike Draper's exceptional *Sitting Ducks and Peeping Toms* records ZG347's first and only flight on 22-2-01 from a ship in the South West Approaches. Salvaged, it 'clocked' 16 minutes total time.

Davidstow Moor RAF Memorial Museum: Occupying what was the sergeants' shower block and within room after room of carefully presented artefacts tell the story of the personnel, units and locals that came together on the moor to do long-ranging battle. The words on the memorial sum up the mood that the airfield and its museums generate: 'They flew by day and night and gave their lives to keep forever bright that precious light of freedom'.
◆ *Davidstow, Camelford, PL32 9YF* | **01840 213266** | **www.davidstowmemorialmuseum.co.uk**

HELSTON on the A3083 north of Culdrose
The Flambards Experience: There are many attractions within, including 'Britain in the Blitz'.
◆ *Clodgey Lane, TR13 0QA* | **01326 573404** | **info@flambards.co.uk** | **www.flambards.co.uk**

❑ –	BAC/Sud Concorde EMU	c68	ex Filton, cockpit, instrument layout trials	12-21
❑ WG511	Avro Shackleton T.4	52	ex Colerne, St Mawgan, MOTU, Kinloss Wing, MOTU, 120, 42. Cockpit	3-20

LAND'S END on the A30 southwest of Penzance
Land's End: The Bölkow portrays the example that was flown by the Cornwall Air Ambulance from St Mawgan.
◆ *Sennen, TR19 7AA* | **01736 871501** | **visitorscentre@ landsend-landmark.co.uk** | **www.landsend-landmark.co.uk**

❑ 'G-CDBS'	Bölkow Bö 105D	G-BCXO 73	ex 'G-BOND', D-HDCE. CoA 23-5-94, de-reg 4-3-92	1-22

LISKEARD on the A38 northwest of Plymouth
Castle Motors / Castle Air: The dramatically-posed Lightning graces the heliport on the A38 to the southeast of the town.

❑ XS936	EE Lightning F.6	67	ex Binbrook, 5, 11, LTF, 5/11, LTF, 5, 11, 23. SOC 21-6-88	6-21

MABE BURNTHOUSE on the A39 northwest of Falmouth
A plant hire yard in the locality has taken delivery of a Lynx.

❑ XZ648*	'7' Westland Lynx AH.7	80	ex Weeton, Hixon, M Wallop, 847, 653, 656, 664, 661, 662, 671, LCF. First noted 8-21	8-21

■ [1] Fitted with the boom of XZ680 – see East Grinstead, Surrey.

NEWQUAY CORNWALL AIRPORT or St Mawgan, off the A3059, northeast of Newquay   EGDG
Cornwall Aviation Heritage Centre (CAHC): The spirited team have created a major local attraction. Several aircraft, including the BAC 111 and VC10, are open to the public. See under JARTS below for a superb co-operation scheme.
    The fuselage of an unfinished Eastbourne Monoplane replica arrived from Brooklands, Surrey, in early 2020. Construction started by Steve Green circa 2020 as a faithful replica of the Eastbourne Aviation Company's first original type, 1911. It is forming the basis of a Vintage aircraft Club/LAA project being conducted by the museum and as such does not merit a formal listing. By mid-2020 the museum had acquired three Airbus (A330?) fuselage sections, from the pax/freight floor upwards. These have been put to good use for storage and serve as exhibits in their own right.
    The light aircraft 'squadron' returned to the custody of its owner in early 2020 - possibly near Falmouth - those involved were as follows: Sonerai G-BJBM, Evans VP2s G-BKFI and G-BTSC, FREDs G-BKVF and C-GUI, Jodel D.18 G-BUAG, Cri-Cri G-MCXV. Stern ST-80 G-BWVI was registered to a Bolton, Lancashire, owner in April 2020 and had also migrated. The fuselage of Navajo ZF622, listed in *W&R27* under this heading, was last used by the JARTS team - see below.
    On 1st November 2021 four former RAF VC10s were registered to Kepler Aerospace of the USA: CAHC's ZA148 becoming N148ZA; ZA147 (N147ZA) and ZD241 (N241ZA) at Bruntingthorpe, Leics, and ZA150 (N150ZA) at Dunsfold, Surrey. According to the Kepler website - **https://kepleraerospace.com** - the Texas-based company is involved in satellite delivery systems and the Dunsfold example - a 'runner' – would appear to be the main centre of interest. Watch this aerospace!
    One-off abbreviation in the listing below: CAF = Classic Air Force, the short-lived off-shoot of Air Atlantique, based at St Mawgan, that collapsed in 2014. ◆ *Aerohub 2, TR8 4GP - off the A3059 Newquay road, south of the airport* | **01637 861962** | **info@ cornwallaviationhc.co.uk** | **www.cornwallaviationhc.co.uk**

❑ G-CCIS	Scheibe SF.28A	78	ex OE-9154. CoA 9-1-15, de-reg 12-6-20. Dismantled. Inside an Airbus fuselage section – see above	[1]	1-22
❑ G-ULPS	Everett Gyroplane Srs.1	87	ex G-BNMY. CoA 10-7-01		1-22
❑ N8205H*	Fisher Celebrity	~	first noted 9-20		9-21
❑ 'VN799'	EE Canberra T.4 G-CDSX	54	ex CAF, G-CDSX (de-reg 6-11-14), WJ874, Marham, 39, Gaydon SF, Binbrook SF, Coningsby SF, 231 OCU, FRADU, FRU, 231 OCU, Wyton SF, 231 OCU, 39. Arrived 30-7-13. Prototype colours		1-22

❑ WJ945		Vickers Varsity T.1	53	ex CAF, Duxford G-BEDV (CoA 15-10-87, de-reg 15-6-89),		
		G-BEDV		CFS, 5 FTS, AE&AEOS, CFS, 115, 116, 527. Hurn-built		1-22
❑ WN149*	'AT'	BP Balliol T.2	54	ex Cosford, Wolverhampton, Bacup, Salford, Failsworth,		
				RAFC. SOC 26-6-57. Arrived 7-1-21	[2]	1-22
❑ WT525*	'855'	EE Canberra T.22	55	ex 'Spitfire Corner', Wyton, South Woodham Ferrers,		
				Stock, St Athan, FRADU, 17, 80. Short-built. SOC 10-5-92.		
				Cockpit. First noted 7-20		6-21
❑ WT722	'873'	Hawker Hunter T.8C	55	ex CAF, G-BWGN (CoA 3-9-97, de-reg 16-3-11), Coventry,		
		G-BWGN		Kemble, Exeter, Shawbury, Yeovilton, FRADU, 764, 703,		
				26, 54. Arrived 9-7-12		1-22
❑ WV256	'D'	Hawker Hunter GA.11	54	ex CAF 'WB188', G-BZPB (CoA 17-7-03, de-reg 16-3-11),		
		G-BZPB		Coventry, Kemble, Exeter, WV256, Shawbury, Yeovilton,		
				FRADU, 738, 229 OCU, 26. Arrived 13-7-12. 26 Sqn colours		1-22
❑ WV798	'147'	Hawker Sea Hawk	54	ex CAF, Wycombe, Lasham, Chertsey, Culdrose A2557, FRU,		
		FGA.6		801, 803, 787. SOC 25-5-67. Arrived 7-12. 803 Sqn c/s		1-22
❑ WZ450*		DH Vampire T.11	52	ex Sleap, Corscombe, Lashenden, N Weald, Birmingham,		
				Sealand, Wrexham, Woodford, Hawarden, Shawbury, RAFC,		
				233 OCU, 202 AFS. SOC 7-1-69. Christchurch-built. Arr 1-22		1-22
❑ XK885		Percival Pembroke C.1	56	ex St Athan, Charlwood, N46EA, Staverton, St Athan 8452M		
		N46EA		(22-8-75), 60, 21, WCS, Seletar SF, B&TTF, Seletar SF,		
				S&TFF, 209, 267		1-22
❑ XN494	'43'	Hunting Jet Provost T.3A	60	ex Pool, Bruntingthorpe, Charlwood, Crawley, B'thorpe,		
				M Wallop, Halton 9012M (10-3-90), 1 FTS, RAFC		1-22
❑ XP642		Hunting Jet Provost T.4	62	ex Welshpool, Lavendon, Luton, Bruntingthorpe,		
				Nottingham, Finchampstead Ridges, Lasham, Shawbury,		
				2 FTS, CFS. SOC 14-8-72. Cockpit. First noted 2-17	[3]	6-21
❑ 'XR768'	'A'	EE Lightning F.53	67	ex Gateguards (UK), Samlesbury, Saudi AF 53-672		
		ZF580		G-27-42. Last flown 14-1-86. Arrived by 9-14. 74 Sqn c/s		1-22
❑ XV148*		HS Nimrod proto	67	ex Malmesbury, Guildford, Woodford, Bedford,		
				Pershore, A&AEE. Cockpit, arrived 10-4-21	[4]	1-22
❑ XV753		HS Harrier GR.3	69	ex CAF, Predannack, Culdrose A2691[2] (24-4-96), Halton,		
				Abingdon 9075M, St Athan, 233 OCU, 1, GR.1, 3, 233 OCU.		
				Arrived 19-6-13		1-22
❑ ZA148	'G'	Vickers VC10 K.3	67	ex CAF, Brize Norton, 101 Sqn, Srs 1154, Filton,		
		N148Z		East African A/W 5Y-ADA. Flew in 28-8-13. See above		1-22
❑ ZH763		BAC 111-539GL	80	ex CAF, Boscombe Down (last flown 21-12-12), QinetiQ,		
		G-BGKE		DRA, Ferranti, G-BGKE British AW. Flew in 26-4-13	[5]	1-22
❑ -*		HS Nimrod MR.2 SIM	~	ex Bridlington, 'Lincs', Kinloss. Rediffusion-built.		
				First noted 11-20	[3]	1-22
❑ -*	'AV-011'	Panavia Tornado SIM	~	ex Cosford. Forward cockpit 'emulator' procedure SIM	[3]	12-20
❑ -		Fieseler Fi 103 V-1 rep	~	BAPC.344. First noted 5-16		9-21
❑ J-1649		DH Venom FB.50	56	ex CAF, Coventry, Market Drayton, Coventry, Hurn,		
				Swiss AF. Swiss-built. Cockpit		6-21

■ [1] Scheibe registered to Cornwall Aviation Heritage Centre Ltd. [2] Balliol is described as 'half restoration, half replica' by its previous owners, the Boulton Paul Association. [3] 'JP', Nimrod SIM and Tornado SIM on loan from Geremy Britton / Aircraft Preservation Foundation - see Bridlington, E Yorks. [4] Unfinished Comet 4, became first 'full' - ie Spey-powered - Nimrod prototype; first flown by John Cunningham at Hawarden 23-5-67. Cockpit restored and on loan from Martin Painter. [5] As G-BGKE *County of West Midlands*, carried out the last British Airways 111 service on 30-3-91 and its flight into St Mawgan - as ZH763 - was the last of the type in the UK.

Defence Survival, Evasion, Resistance, Extraction Training Organisation: Operates as an RAF enclave within the airport.

❑ XV700	'ZC'	Westland Sea King	71	ex Gosport, 824, 814, 819, 814, 706, 814, 819, 814, 825,	
		HAS.6CR		706, 820, 810, 849, 846, 845. Arrived 25-9-15	9-15
❑ XZ587	'C'	Westland Sea King	78	ex Gosport, 202 'E' Flt, 22, 202, 22, 202, 1564 Flt, 202,	
		HAR.3		SKTU. Arrived 19-1-16	6-21

Joint Aircraft Recovery and Transport Squadron (JARTS): Based at Boscombe Down, Wilts, the unit uses the airport as a sub-site for training exercises. In a superb piece of co-operation, the airframes are positioned close to the CAHC and function as exhibits while JARTS personnel have access to the collection's VC10- and One-Eleven in return. Also on site is the centre section and starboard wing of Canberra TT.18 WK124, last in use with the fire school at Manston, Kent. Its cockpit is to be found at Gilberdyke, East Yorks. The fuselage of Navajo ZF622 had returned to Boscombe Down, Wilts, by April 2021.

❑ XX240	'840'	HS Hawk T.1	78 ex Shawbury 736, FRADU, 19, 74, 6 FTS, 4 FTS. Arrived 30-1-20	9-21
❑ XZ607		Westland Lynx AH.7	81 ex Manston, Arborfield, Fleetlands, 657, 847, 657, 672, 662, 663, 671, 653, 654. Cabin. First noted 12-18	9-21
❑ ZA398	'087'	Panavia Tornado GR.4	82 ex Manston, Warton, 2. SOC 14-1-14. *Second to None* [1]	9-21
❑ ZD704		HSA HS.125 CC.3	83 ex Manston, Hawarden, St Athan, 32. Damaged Kandahar 23-4-13. First noted 9-18	9-21
❑ ZH553	'RT'	Panavia Tornado F.3	93 ex Manston, Shawbury, Leuchars, 56, 11, 56, 11, 56, 29	6-21

■ **[1]** ZA398 is fitted with the fin from ZD739, hence the 'mis-matched' code.

Lancaster forward fuselage replica '976' (BAPC.553) awaiting shipment to Russia, October 2021. *Tony McCarthy*

Replica Aircraft Fabricators: As well as creating full-size replicas, refurbishing used versions for onward sale, and industrial projects, the company occasionally has *real* airframes on its books, often as the basis for moulds. The former Spitfire Corner - see below - trailer-mounted Tornado ADV FSM arrived on site by January 2020, but had moved on by September 2021.

The former Long Marston Shackleton and the *Night Flight* Lancaster forward fuselage replica were brought on to the site in 2021. They were reportedly for a movie in Russia and afterwards it is intended to create a monument to Operation PARAVANE of September 1944 when Lancasters of 9 and 617 Squadrons flew to Yagodnik, near Archangel, in order to attack the *Tirpitz* in northern Norway. Lancaster forward fuselage replica '976' (BAPC.553) arrived from East Kirkby, Lincs, by January 2021 and Shackleton MR.3/3 WR985 arrived from Long Marston, Warks, by May 2021. The combo departed in a convoy on 28th October 2021 bound for frozen Russia.

◆ Private *workshop, by prior application* only | www.gateguardsuk.com

❑ WL332*		Gloster Meteor T.7	52 ex Long Marston, Cardiff-Wales, Croston, Moston, FRU, Lossiemouth SF, Ford SF. SOC 11-3-69. Arrived 13-10-20	9-21
❑ A-125		Pilatus P.2-05	G-BLKZ 48 ex Duxford, Spanhoe, Duxford, Swiss AF A-125, U-125. Crashed 31-5-08, de-reg 22-8-08. Forward fuselage, f/n 7-20	6-21

Also: St Mawgan's well-known Shackleton is under restoration in its own compound.

❑ WL795	'T'	Avro Shackleton AEW.2	53 ex RAF side, 8753M (24-11-81), 8, 205, 38, 204, 210, 269, 204. Last flown 24-11-81. Moved 4-12-15	1-22

Former **Spitfire Corner**: By July 2020 the cockpit of Canberra T.22 WT525 moved to the CAHC, above, and the Tornado ADV FSM to Replica Aircraft Fabricators, also above. By September 2021 Spitfire FSM 'PL279' (BAPC.268) and the cockpit of Canberra B.2 WD954 had both departed – no forwarding address.

PREDANNACK AIRFIELD off the A3083 south of Helston

Fleet Air Arm School of Flight Deck Operations Fire School: There are also some complex purpose-built burning rigs here. Long-term resident Canberra B(I).6 WT308 was offered for disposal in early 2021 and the hulk was removed on 5th August 2021 bound for the scrapyard at Spey Bay, Scotland.

☐ XS738	'U'	HS Dominie T.1	66	ex Cosford 9274M, Cranwell, 3 FTS, 6 FTS. Arrived 11-12-06		6-21
☐ XV371		Sikorsky SH-3D Sea King	68	ex Culdrose, Gosport, A2699, Boscombe Down, RAE,		
	'DD261'			RRE, RAE, A&AEE. SOC 30-4-95		6-21
☐ XV654		Westland Sea King	69	ex Culdrose, Gosport, A2698, Fleetlands, 819, 820, 706,		
	'DD705'	HAS.6		824, 706. Crashed 21-7-93. Arrived by 11-14		6-21
☐ XV657		Westland Sea King	70	ex Culdrose, A2600[4], ETS, Fleetlands, Wroughton, 826,		
	'DD132'	HAS.5		824, 706,826, 824, 706, 824. Arrived 5-6-17, via Chinook	[1]	6-21
☐ XX479	'563'	HP Jetstream T.2	72	ex A2611 (19-2-97), St Athan, 750, CFS, 5 FTS, Sywell,		
		G-AXUR		Radlett, G-AXUR (de-reg 17-1-74). SAL-completed		6-21
☐ XX845	'EV'	SEPECAT Jaguar T.4	75	ex Cosford, St Athan, 6, T.2, 6, 226 OCU, 41, 226 OCU, 14,		
				17, 2, 20, 17. Last flown 1-6-05		6-21
☐ XZ570		Westland Sea King	76	ex Culdrose, Gosport, A2672, A2686 (11-10-01),		
		HAS.5(mod)		Boscombe Down, RAE Bedford, A&AEE		6-21
☐ XZ969		HS Harrier GR.3	80	ex Culdrose A2612, Manadon A2610 (24-4-91),		
				St Athan, 4, 1, 3		6-21
☐ ZA111	'565'	HP Jetstream T.2	81	ex 750, 9Q-CTC. SAL-built. Arrived 6-17, via Chinook		6-21
☐ ZD581	'124'	HS Sea Harrier F/A.2	85	ex St Athan,800, FRS.1, 800, 801, 899		6-21
☐ ZG915		Westland Lynx AH.9A	91	ex M Wallop. Arrived 19-9-17		6-21
☐ ZG919		Westland Lynx AH.9A	91	ex M Wallop. Arrived 19-9 9-17		6-21

■ [1] XV657 fitted with the tail of ZA135 - see Beckley, Oxfordshire, for the bulk of it.

ST AGNES on the B3277 southwest of Newquay
The Swift continues to be stored at a *private* location in the locality.

☐ G-ABTC	Comper Swift	32	ex Lelant. CoA 18-7-84, de-reg 22-2-99. *Spirit of Butler*		7-20

TORPOINT on the A374, west of Plymouth, across the Tamar
HMS *Raleigh*: The large initial training base is *thought* still to have a pair of instructional airframes.

☐ XZ726	'316' Westland Lynx HMA.8SRU	80	ex M Wallop, 815, HAS.3, 702, 815. Arrived 3-12-15		3-17
☐ ZF118	'O' Westland Sea King HC.4	86	ex Gosport, 845, 846, 845, 846, 845, 846, 772, 846, 707,		
			846, 845. Arrived 3-12-15		12-15

TRELONK on minor roads west of the A3078, northwest of Varyan
Parnall Engineering Advanced Ltd: Within the Trelonk Estate, the institution has the following aim: 'Finding bright young sparks in Cornwall'. The Spitfire static replica has been created to an exceptionally high spec and a Parnall Panther replica is reported to be on the cards. ◆ By *prior arrangement* only | www.parnall.net

☐ BL688	V-S Spitfire V	41	ex Twyford, 58 OTU, 41 OTU, 58 OTU, 63, 316, 501, 335th FS		
	G-CJWO		USAAF, 610, 132. CBAF-built. Cr 29-5-45, excavated 1982	[1]	9-21
☐ 'BL709'*	V-S Spitfire Vb FSM	20	*St Ives - Cornwall*. Unveiled 6-21		6-21

■ [1] Registered to Robert Parnall.

CUMBRIA

BACKBARROW on the A590 northeast of Ulverston, near Newby Bridge
Lakeland Motor Museum: As well as the aeronautical exhibits, highlights include full-size replicas of Sir Malcolm Campbell's 1935 Bluebird car and his 1939 Bluebird K4 boat, plus the Bluebird K7 in which son Donald was killed in 1967.
◆ *Old Blue Mill, LA12 8TA* | 015395 30400 | info@lakelandmotormuseum.co.uk | www.lakelandmotormuseum.co.uk

☐ 'G-ADYV'	Mignet HM.14 'Flea'	94	BAPC.243, ex Malvern Wells, 'A-FLEA', Leigh-on-Sea		1-22
			Bill Francis, Leigh-on-Sea-built.		
☐ G-BNDV	Cameron N-77	87	CoA 9-5-93, de-reg 18-3-14. *English Lake Hotels*.		
	hot-air balloon		Basket, burner, 'skirt' etc		1-22
☐ G-MBCG	Solar Wings Typhoon	r81	ex Blackburn. De-reg 6-9-94		1-22

BARROW-IN-FURNESS As predicted, Sea Hawk FGA.6 XE368 moved out: to Lubenham, Leics, by April 2021.

Hunter F.51 E-425 back in Danish Air Force plumage, November 2021. *David S Johnstone*

CARLISLE LAKE DISTRICT AIRPORT or Crosby-on-Eden

EGNC

Solway Aviation Museum: While the impressive airframe collection might draw the eye, the displays charting the incredible aviation heritage of the airport and the region are particularly pleasing. There is a workshop - available for inspection by prior arrangement. The shop and the cafe are both well stocked!

There were some positives to come out of the prolonged 'lockdowns'. Solway's David Price built a Spitfire IX FSM - 'PV144' marked as '4D-A' of 74 Squadron (BAPC.581) - locally. It was being offered for sale during the summer of 2021.

◆ *Crosby-on-Eden, CA6 4NW* | **01228 573823** | **email** via website | **www.solway-aviation-museum.co.uk**

❑ 'G-ADRX'		Mignet HM.14 'Flea'	36	BAPC.231, ex Millom, Torver, Ulverston. Arrived 7-9-10 [1]	1-22
❑ G-APLG		Auster J5L Aiglet Trainer	58	ex Maryport, Bletchley, Romsey, Southend, Rettendon, Corringham. CoA 26-10-68, de-reg 11-2-99. Arrived 4-95	1-22
❑ G-ARPP		HS Trident 1C	65	ex Dumfries, Palnackie, Glasgow, Heathrow, BA, BEA. CoA 16-2-86, de-reg 10-3-83. Arrived 19-8-09. Cockpit	1-22
❑ G-BDTT		Bede BD-5 Micro	r76	ex Haverigg, Barrow, Tattershall Thorpe, Bourne. De-reg 2-2-87. Arrived 2012	1-22
❑ G-BNNR		Cessna 152 II	81	ex N40SX, N40SU, N6121Q. CoA 15-11-08, de-reg 8-9-11. Arrived 2011. Plaything	1-22
❑ G-BRHL		Bensen B-8M	89	CoA 26-8-03, de-reg 19-10-10. Arrived 2012	1-22
❑ G-BSEG*		Ken Brock KB-2	91	ex Newcastle, Marham. CoA 2-7-02, de-reg 23-5-12. F/n 12-21	1-22
❑ WB584		DHC Chipmunk T.10	50	ex Newcastle, Morpeth, East Fortune, Manston, Kilmarnock, Edinburgh 7706M (16-1-61), Shawbury, Debden CF, 11 GCF, Tangmere SF, Glasgow UAS, 8 FTS, Bristol UAS, 12 RFS, 22 RFS. Cockpit, trailer-mounted	1-22
❑ WB670		DHC Chipmunk T.10	50	ex Newcastle, Morpeth, East Fortune, Currie, Southend, London Colney, Welwyn Garden City, 8361M (22-8-73), Hatfield, MoS, 5 FTS, LAS, 12 RFS, 5 RFS. 1 AEF colours. Cockpit. Arrived 13-12-12 [2]	1-22
❑ WE188		EE Canberra T.4	53	ex Samlesbury, 231 OCU, 360, 231 OCU, 360, 100, 56, 231 OCU, Upwood SF, 231 OCU, Upwood SF, Waddington SF, Hemswell SF. SOC 19-11-81. Arrived 4-88	1-22
❑ WP314	'573'	Percival Sea Prince T.1	53	ex Preston, Hull, Syerston, Halton 8634M (8-8-79), Kemble, 750, Sydenham SF, 750, Lossiemouth SF, Shorts FU, Brawdy SF, Lossiemouth SF, 750. Arrived 8-98	1-22
❑ WS832	'W'	Gloster Meteor NF.14	54	ex RRE Pershore, RAE Llanbedr, AWOCU. AWA-built. SOC 24-4-69. Arrived 15-1-77	1-22
❑ WV198	'72'	Sikorsky Whirlwind HAR.21	52	ex Firbeck, Warmingham, Chorley, Blackpool, Heysham, Carnforth G-BJWY (de-reg 23-2-94), Gosport, Lee-on-Solent A2576, Arbroath, 781, 848, USN 130191. Last flown 9-56. Arrived 13-11-92	1-22
		G-BJWY			
❑ WZ515		DH Vampire T.11	53	ex Duxford, Staverton, Woodford, Chester, St Athan, 4 FTS, 8 FTS, 56, 253, 16. Hawarden-built. SOC 4-12-68. Arr 5-90	1-22

☐ 'WZ784'		Slingsby Grasshopper TX.1	52	arrived 2001	[3]	1-22
☐ XA459	'E'	Fairey Gannet AS.4	56	ex White Waltham, Woodlands St Mary, Lambourn, Cirencester, Cardiff, Culdrose SAH-7 A2608, Lee-on-Solent, 831. SOC 18-11-70. Arrived 12-2-20		1-22
☐ XJ823		Avro Vulcan B.2	61	ex 50, Wadd Wing, 35, 27, 9/35, Wadd W, 230 OCU. Flew in 24-1-83		1-22
☐ XS209	'29'	Hunting Jet Provost T.4	64	ex Bruntingthorpe, Kemble, Staverton, Halton 8409M (7-10-74) St Athan, Kemble, Shawbury, CAW. Arr 24-6-06		1-22
☐ XV406	'CK'	McD Phantom FGR.2	68	ex 14 MU Longtown 9098M (14-11-91), St Athan, 228 OCU, 111, 43, 228 OCU, 56, 23, 111, 54, 41, 54, 228 OCU, HSA, A&AEE. Arrived 22-4-98. 111 colours		1-22
☐ XX477		HP Jetstream T.1 G-AXXS	73	ex Sunderland, Askern, Finningley 8462M, Little Rissington, CFS, G-AXXS (de-reg 2-5-73). SAL-completed. Crashed 1-11-74. Fuselage. Arrived 27-11-19		1-22
☐ ZF583		EE Lightning F.53	68	ex Warton, Saudi AF 53-681, G-27-51. Last flown 14-1-86. Arrived 8-1-89. 11 Sqn colours		1-22
☐ E-425		Hawker Hunter F.51	56	ex 'XG190', Coventry, Dunsfold, G-9-446, Danish AF Esk.724, E-425. SOC 28-2-76. Arrived 26-11-08. Danish c/s by 11-21		1-22

■ [1] 'Flea' built by Ronnie Jolly at Ulverston; several attempts at flight ended in damage and storage. Restoration carried out at HMP Haverigg, Millom, initial funding came from the Flying Flea Archive. [2] WB670 was used for life-extension trials at Hatfield and was SOC as tested to destruction 31-12-71. [2] Composite, with the port wing *thought* to be from WZ824 - see Bridge of Weir, Scotland. The fin fillet is marked WZ792 and the starboard wing is also marked WZ792. There is *another* 'WZ784' at Felixstowe, Suffolk.

Also:

☐ G-BBBI*	American AA-5 Traveller	73	CoA 29-6-<u>16</u>. First noted 10-20	11-21
☐ G-BHFC*	Cessna F.152	78	Reims-built. CoA 14-9-<u>16</u>	7-21
☐ G-BJMR*	Cessna 310R	79	ex N2631Z. CoA 22-6-18	7-21
☐ G-BLHJ*	Cessna F.172P	83	ex Oban. Reims-built. CoA 30-6-<u>17</u>. Arrived 2-21	7-21
☐ G-BOIO*	Cessna 152	77	ex N24445. CoA 7-10-18	11-21
☐ G-BXBZ*	PZL Wilga 80	93	ex EC-GDA, ZK-PZQ. CoA 22-11-<u>15</u>	11-21

HOLMESCALES south of the B2654, west of the M6, southeast of Kendal
The Outdoor Adventure Company: ◆ *By prior arrangement* only | www.theoutdooradventurecompany.co.uk

☐ TC-MBE	Fokker Friendship 500	81	ex Coventry, MNG Cargo, D-ACCT, G-JEAG, D-ADAP, G-JEAG. Damaged 18-1-07	6-21

KIRKBRIDE AERODROME south of the B5307, west of Carlisle
Among the active gyros is a long-out-of-use Bensen.

☐ G-BHEM	Bensen B-8MV	85	CoA 5-10-00, de-reg 8-4-16	8-21

MILLOM on the A5093 west of Ulverston
Millom Heritage and Art Centre: (Note name change.) Among the many superb displays is John Nixon's incredible section on the aviation of the area, in particular the former RAF Millom, is well worth visiting. A 'star' item is an outer wing from a Blackburn Botha, signed by Millom veterans.
◆ *Station Building, Station Road, LA18 5AA* | 01229 772555 | info@millomhac.co.uk | https://millomhac.co.uk

SPADEADAM FOREST north of the B6318, northeast of Carlisle
RAF Spadeadam / Electronic Warfare Tactics Range: The vast ranges are centred on the former ballistic missile test/launch facility. The *Hind* is alongside the helicopter operating area, known as the H-7 Complex.

☐ XW768*	'N'	HS Harrier GR.3	71	ex Manston, Gosport, Cosford, Halton 9072M (10-8-90), 4, 1, 4, 20. First noted 6-21	9-21
☐ XZ215*		Westland Lynx AH.7	79	ex Manston, M Wallop, 9 Regt. Boom of XZ607. Arr 17-6-21	9-21
☐ XZ216*		Westland Lynx AH.7	77	ex Manston, Arborfield, Fleetlands, 654, 663, 656, 671, 663, 662. Cabin. Arrived 6-21	9-21
☐ XZ966*	'G'	HS Harrier GR.3	73	ex Manston, Cottesmore 9221M (13-10-93), St Athan, 1417 Flt, 4, 1417 Flt, 233 OCU, 1, 1417, 1. First noted 6-21	9-21
☐ FT-02	'12'	Lockheed T-33A-1-LO	52	ex Prestwick, Belgian AF, 51-4043. Arrived 13-3-80	9-21

☐ FT-06	'10'	Lockheed T-33A-1-LO	52	ex Prestwick, Belgian AF, Netherlands AF M-44, 51-4231	
				Arrived 19-3-80. Also wears 'AC12'	9-21
☐ FT-07	'70'	Lockheed T-33A-1-LO	52	ex Prestwick, Belgian AF, Netherlands AF M-45, 51-4233.	
				Arrived 27-3-80. Also wears '18' and 'AC11'	9-21
☐ FT-10	'11'	Lockheed T-33A-1-LO	52	ex Prestwick, Belgian AF, 51-6664. Arrived 7-3-80.	
				Also wears '77' and 'AC6'	9-21
☐ FT-11	'01'	Lockheed T-33A-1-LO	52	ex Prestwick, Belgian AF, Netherlands AF M-47, 51-6661.	
,				Arrived 3-80. Also wears '80' and 'AC5'	9-21
☐ 61	'AC2'	Dassault Mystère IVA	c56	ex Sculthorpe, Fr AF. Last flown 27-7-81, arrived 28-2-82	9-21
☐ 64	'AC1'	Dassault Mystère IVA	c56	ex Sculthorpe, Fr AF. Last flown 27-7-81, arrived 3-82	9-21
☐ 81	'AC9'	Dassault Mystère IVA	c56	ex Sculthorpe, Fr AF. Last flown 19-1-82, arrived 17-3-82	9-21
☐ 139	'AC10'	Dassault Mystère IVA	c56	ex Sculthorpe, Fr AF. Last flown 1-7-81, arrived 3-28	9-21
☐ 180	'AC8'	Dassault Mystère IVA	c56	ex Sculthorpe, Fr AF. Last flown 1-7-81, arrived 28-2-82	9-21
☐ 184	'AC7'	Dassault Mystère IVA	c56	ex Sculthorpe, Fr AF. Last flown 19-1-82, arrived 17-3-82	9-21
☐ 207	'AC4'	Dassault Mystère IVA	c56	ex Sculthorpe, Fr AF	9-21
☐ 282	'AC3'	Dassault Mystère IVA	c56	ex Sculthorpe, Fr AF	9-21
☐ 98+10	'SU-1'	Sukhoi Su-22M-4 *Fitter*	c59	ex Farnborough, Boscombe Down, Luftwaffe,	
				LSK-LV 820. Arrived 4-95	9-21
☐ 09559	'HH1'	Mil Mi-24 *Hind-D*	c59	ex Boscombe Down (?), Iraq (?). Arrived by 5-08 [1]	9-21

■ [1] To add to the mystery of this *Hind*, it *could* be ex-Afghanistan.

SPARK BRIDGE on the A5092 north of Ulverston

Lakes Lightnings Collection: See also Lightning F.6 XS897 on loan at Coningsby, Lincs. Also on long term loan is Hunter T.7 XL618 at the Gutersloh Flugplatz Museum, Germany.
◆ *Annual open cockpits day over August Bank Holiday. Otherwise available for inspection* **strictly** *by prior permission* **only** | lakeslightnings@hotmail.co.uk

☐ WK122		EE Canberra TT.18	54	ex Chipperfield, Bruntingthorpe, Helston, Samlesbury, 7,	
				15, 61. SOC 10-11-81. Cockpit	1-22
☐ WT711	'833'	Hawker Hunter GA.11	55	ex Coventry, Culdrose A2645, A2731 (23-9-85), Shawbury,	
				Kemble, FRADU, FRU, 764, 738, F.4, 14	1-22
☐ XL609		Hawker Hunter T.7	58	ex South Molton, Yarmouth, Boscombe Down, Firbeck,	
				Elgin, Lossiemouth 8866M (24-7-85), 12, 216, 237 OCU,	
				4 FTS, 56. Cockpit. 12 Sqn colours. Arrived 4-12	1-22
☐ XM172	'B'	EE Lightning F.1A	60	ex Booker, Coltishall 8427M (10-7-74), 226 OCU, 56	1-22
☐ XS181	'F'	Hunting Jet Provost T.4	63	ex Spanhoe, Bruntingthorpe, Market Harborough, North	
				Weald, Bletchley, Desborough, Bruntingthorpe, Halton	
				9033M (15-2-90), Shawbury, CATCS, RAFC, 3 FTS. Cockpit [1]	1-22
☐ XS922	'BJ'	EE Lightning F.6	66	ex Stansted, Salisbury, Stock, Wattisham 8973M (14-6-88),	
				Binbrook, 5-11 pool, 56, 5. Cockpit	1-22
☐ ZA327		Panavia Tornado GR.1	80	ex Samlesbury, Warton, Leeming. Cockpit	1-22
☐ ZF596		EE Lightning T.55	68	ex Haverigg, Swinton, Warton, Portsmouth, Stretton,	
				Warton, Saudi AF 233, 55-715, G-27-71.	
				Last flown 22-1-86. Cockpit	1-22
☐ –		HS Harrier two-seater	~	ex Haddington, Long Marston, Dunsfold. Cockpit [2]	1-22
☐ –		Panavia Tornado F.3 EMU	~	ex Blackpool, Warton	1-22
☐ 0446		Mikoyan-Gurevich	~	ex Salisbury, East Tilbury, Farnborough, Egyptian AF.	
		MiG-21UM *Mongol*		Front cockpit. Arrived late 2019	1-22
☐ 7907		Sukhoi Su-7BMK *Fitter*	~	ex Robertsbridge, Farnborough, Egyptian AF. Cockpit	1-22

■ [1] Owned by Andrew 'Mack' Mackay. [2] A plate on the side declares it to be a Sea Harrier Mk.60 - that would be to the build spec for the Indian Navy T.60s.

WHITEHAVEN on the A595 south of Workington

Whitehaven Academy: Cleator Moor Road. *May* still have a Tomahawk-turned-sim.
◆ *By prior arrangement* **only** | www.whitehavenacademy.org.uk

| ☐ G-BJNN | | Piper Tomahawk 112 | 80 | ex Carlisle. CoA 17-8-09, de-reg 19-7-16. Simulator   [1] | 4-16 |

■ [1] Converted to a simulator by Creative Cockpits.

WINDERMERE on the A592 north of Bowness on Windermere

Windermere Jetty - Museum of Boats, Steam and Stories: A sensational venue, with views of the lake and trips along it and the unique water glider. ◆ *Rayrigg Road, LA23 1BN* | **info@windermerejetty.org** | **https://lakelandarts.org.uk/windermere-jetty-museum/** - one of the most unintelligible websites I seen in a long time

❑ –		Slingsby T.1 Falcon	36	BGA.266	[1] 12-21

■ **[1]** Modified by Capt T C Pattinson DFC as a flying-boat glider and first flown 3-2-43.

DERBYSHIRE
Includes the unitary authority of Derby City

BRAILSFORD on the A52 northwest of Derby

Wild Park Derbyshire: ◆ *By prior application* only | **www.wildparkderbyshire.com**

❑ XZ235	'630'	Westland Lynx HAS.3S	77	ex Hixon, Fleetlands, 815, *Endurance* Flt, 702, 815, 702, 815, 829, 815, HAS.2, 815. SOC 17-2-10	1-22
❑ XZ237		Westland Lynx HAS.3S	77	ex Hixon, Fleetlands, 702, 815, 702, 815, 702, 829, HAS.2, 829, 815, RAE	1-22
❑ XZ693		Westland Lynx HAS.3S	79	ex Hixon, Fleetlands, 815, 702, 815, HAS.2, 702	1-22

CHESTERFIELD on the A61 south of Sheffield

A car sales centre on the Dronfield Road, has a former Finningley 'JP'.

❑ XM480	'02'	Hunting Jet Provost T.3	60	ex Finningley, Halton 8080M (21-4-70), 6 FTS, 1 FTS	7-21

DERBY

Museum of Making: The totally rejuvenated museum is devoted to three centuries of industry in Derby and its surroundings re-opened during late 2020. Dominating the Flight Deck hall is a suspended Rolls-Royce Trent 1000 turbofan.
◆ *Silk Mill Lane, off Full Street, DE1 3AF* | **info@derbymuseums.org** | **www.derbymuseums.org**

Rolls-Royce Heritage Trust: Within the Rolls-Royce Learning and Development Centre, the Trust has established an impressive exhibition of engines. On another site, there is an extensive engine and artefact collection and restoration workshop. The company's airworthy Spitfire PR.19 PS853 (G-RRGN) and Harvard T.2B KF183 (G-CORS) are based at East Midlands Airport, Leics, and *not* available for inspection. Spitfire XIV RM689 moved to Biggin Hill, Gtr Lon, by June 2020.
◆ *Open to groups by prior arrangement* only | PO Box 31, Derby DE24 8BJ | **heritage.trust@rolls-royce.com** | **www.rolls-royce.com/about/heritage-trust**

❑ WH960		EE Canberra B.15	55	ex Willmore Road, Nottingham, Bruntingthorpe, Cosford 8344M (9-11-72), Akrotiri Wing, 32, 9, 12. Cockpit	3-20

DERBY AERODROME or Egginton, south of the A5132 between Egginton and Hilton

Comet Racer Project Group: Like many other ventures, Covid-19 has slowed down the project, but much has been achieved. Maestro Ken Fern is also working – from an off-site workshop – on a 100% replica, G-RCSR.
◆ *By prior arrangement* only | derbyaeroclub@btconnect.com | **www.cometracerproject.co.uk**

❑ G-ACSP		DH Comet	34	ex Stoke-on-Trent, Coventry / Staverton, Bodmin, Chirk, Portugal, CS-AAJ, E-1. *Black Magic*	[1] 1-22
❑ 'G-ACSS'		DH Comet FSM	97	BAPC.257, ex Sywell, London Colney, Hatfield. Acorn Scenery, Feltham-built. *Grosvenor House*. Trailer-mounted	[2] 1-22
❑ G-APNZ		Druine Turbulent	59	ex Lashenden. Dam 2-7-95, CoA 13-12-95. Rollason-built	[3] 1-22

■ **[1]** *Black Magic* was originally registered to James Allan Mollison 21-8-34 and cancelled as sold in Portugal 12-34. **[2]** Best described as *nearly* a full-scale replica! It is actually seven-eighths scale. **[3]** Registered to the Turbulent G-APNZ Preservation Society.

Also: Pup G-AZGF had departed by 2020, variously reported to 'Cheshire' or 'Shropshire'.

❑ G-ARAX	Piper Tri-Pacer 150	56	ex N2423A. CoA 3-10-11	10-21
❑ G-ARFB	Piper Caribbean 150	60	ex N3225Z. CoA 19-6-16. First noted 1-18	10-21
❑ G-ASSF	Cessna 182G	64	ex N2492R. Crashed 26-12-07, CoA 10-4-08, de-reg 12-7-11	10-21
❑ G-AVLM	Beagle Pup 160	67	ex Shenstone, Tatenhill, Tollerton, Chippenham. CoA 24-4-69	6-18
❑ G-AXSC	Beagle Pup 100	69	ex G-35-138. CoA 28-4-07	10-21
❑ G-AYPH	Cessna F.177RG	71	Reims-built. CoA 27-5-07	7-21

☐ G-BAFW	Piper Cherokee 140	65	ex PH-NLT. CoA 4-6-11. First noted 4-17	10-21
☐ G-BBJY	Cessna F.172M	73	Reims-built. CoA 30-6-11	7-21
☐ G-BDBF	Clutton FRED II	85	W T Morrell, Bures-built. CoA 18-3-98. Off-site	N1-19
☐ G-BHAV	Cessna F.152	79	Reims-built. CoA 6-12-13	6-18
☐ G-BHZS	SAL Bulldog 120	74	ex Botswana DF OD5, G-BHZS. CoA 20-2-06, de-reg 19-12-12	10-21
☐ G-BNMC	Cessna 152 II	78	ex N6921B. CoA 10-8-03, de-reg 19-1-09	8-18
☐ G-BNMD	Cessna 152 II	79	ex N5170B. Crashed 23-7-90, CoA 28-7-01. Fuselage	6-14
☐ G-BSWH	Cessna 152 II	78	ex N49861. CoA 14-3-02	6-18
☐ G-BTBJ	Cessna 190	52	ex F-AZRE, G-BTBJ, N4461C. CoA 2-5-16	5-21
☐ G-KWAX	Cessna 182E	62	ex N9902, YV-T-PTS, N2808Y. CoA 16-4-06, de-reg 27-4-10	8-18
☐ G-OFLG	SOCATA Tobago	79	ex G-JMWT, F-GBHF. Crashed 23-7-05, de-reg 15-11-05	10-21
☐ G-SACF	Cessna 152 II	79	ex G-BHSZ, N47125. Crashed 21-3-97, de-reg 11-8-97	10-21

RIPLEY on the A610 northwest of Nottingham

Iconic World War Two Aircraft: Brothers Mel and Steve Heappey's Spitfire FSM features original undercarriage and much of the cockpit has original fittings. ◆ *By prior arrangement* **only** | www.iconic-ww2aircraft.co.uk

| ☐ 'BA<u>377</u>' | 'UF-J' V-S Spitfire IX FSM | ~ | BAPC.<u>377</u>, ex 'EN398', Sleap, Cannock. 601 Sqn colours | 1-20 |
| ☐ - | '6' M'schmitt Bf 109E-4 FSM | 17 | BAPC.376, II/JG 51 colours. Gateguards UK-built | 1-20 |

DEVON

Includes the unitary authorities of Plymouth and Torbay

ABBOTSHAM The Big Sheep disposed of Whirlwind Srs 3 VR-BEU – destination/fate unknown.

BARNSTAPLE

Tim Jones: During July 2021 Tim exchanged Buccaneer S.2 cockpit XX888 for a Cadet forward fuselage, at <u>Doncaster</u>, S Yorks. During Tim's Air Cadet days he flew solo three times in Cadets at nearby Chivenor. ◆ *By prior appointment* **only**

| ☐ XN238* | Slingsby Cadet TX.3 | 59 | ex Doncaster, Firbeck, Robertsbridge, St Athan, 622 VGS, ACCGS, 1 GC, 626, 634, 614 and 662 GSs. SOC 20-10-83. Acquired 5-97. Forward fuselage. Arrived 7-21 | 1-22 |

BERE ALSTON at the end of the B3257 north of Plymouth

Tony Thorne: Keeps his rotorcraft in the area. ◆ *Viewing by prior appointment* **only**

| ☐ – | Adams-Wilson Hobbycopter | ~ | ex 'Leicestershire' | 12-21 |
| ☐ – | Bensen B-7 Gyroglider | ~ | - | 12-21 |

BIDEFORD on the A39 southwest of Barnstaple

No.20 Squadron Air Cadets:

| ☐ XR747 | EE Lightning F.6 | 65 | ex Cubert, Plymouth, Rossington, Binbrook, 5, 11, 5, 11, 5, 111. 23. SOC 24-6-88. Cockpit | 3-20 |

BRAUNTON on the A361 west of Barnstaple

A Hunter is kept on a nearby farm. ◆ *By prior arrangement* **only**

| ☐ WT744 | '868' Hawker Hunter GA.11 | 55 | ex Ilfracombe, Eaglescott, Yeovilton, FRADU, 738, F.4, 247, AFDS. Last flight 16-3-94. Arrived 15-5-16 | 2-20 |

CHIVENOR south of the A361 south of Braunton

The famous former RAF station, now a **Royal Marines** base, continued to be home to a Chipmunk cockpit despite the best efforts of W&R. The anonymous Chipmunk was kept by 722 (Devon and Somerset) Squadron Air Cadets within the base. It was written out of *W&R24* (p45), last noted in April 2009 and moving to the Exeter area. It seems it stayed put, until it travelled to <u>Stamford</u>, Lincs, in October 2021. *W&R23* was doing its best to uncover the cockpit's identity quoting a plate reading 'DHB732 26-8-52': the 'DHB' bit being de Havilland Broughton (aka Hawarden). David Burke notes that this build number applies to the upper fuselage and that the completion date would therefore be beyond late August 1952.

Once held at Exeter, WP978 - awaiting collection by the RAF on 28th February 1953 - was always in the frame for this cockpit. Rubbing down of the area ahead and below the cockpit revealed the code 'R' from its days with Hooton Park-based 663 Squadron, thereby almost certainly putting its identity to bed!

COBBATON north of the A377 / B3227 west of South Molton
Cobbaton Combat Collection: The largest private collection of military vehicles and wartime memorabilia in the southwest.
◆ *Umberleigh, EX37 9RZ* | **01769 540740** | **info@cobbatoncombat.co.uk** | **www.cobbatoncombat.co.uk**

❑ –	'5' Airspeed Horsa replica	c76	BAPC.351, ex *A Bridge Too Far* (1977)	6-16

DUNKESWELL AERODROME north of Honiton   EGTU
Dunkeswell Heritage Centre: Part of the South West Airfields Heritage Trust - see also Upottery, Devon. Dunkeswell gained fame as home to US Navy B-24 Liberators and PB4Y Privateers among other units.
◆ *Close to the Aviator restaurant* | **email** via website | **www.southwestairfields.co.uk**

Aerodrome: Vagabond OY-AVW had moved to Weston Zoyland, Somerset, by October 2020. A bit of tidying up: Thruster G-MWAR (last noted May 2016) and Norecrin OO-AJK (January 2013) have been deleted.

❑ G-AFIN	Chrislea Airguard	38	ex Bury St Edmunds, Wigan, Stoke, Warmingham, Wigan [1]	9-20
❑ G-AJON	Aeronca 7AC Champion	47	ex OO-TWH. CoA 10-5-08	7-18
❑ G-AKUL	Luscombe Silvaire 8A	46	ex Southend, N1462K. CoA 21-5-90	10-18
❑ G-APFA	Druine Turbi	57	ex Exeter area. Britten-Norman built. CoA 22-9-92	9-20
❑ G-BJIG	Slingsby T.67A Firefly	82	CoA 15-4-04	7-19
❑ G-BJNG	Slingsby T.67AM Firefly	82	CoA 23-7-01	1-19
❑ G-BPRV	Piper Warrior II	83	ex N4292G. Crashed 29-3-97, de-reg 20-6-97. Cockpit	8-19
❑ G-BTON	Piper Cherokee 140	74	ex N43193. CoA 3-1-15. First noted 7-18	8-19
❑ G-BXYU	Cessna F.152 II	80	ex Exeter, Dunkeswell, OH-CKD, SE-IFY. Reims-built. Crashed 2-8-99, de-reg 16-10-99. Cockpit	3-18
❑ I-IJMW	Mooney M.20J	87	crashed 11-1-14. First noted 12-15	9-21
❑ N21381	Piper Seneca 200	~	ex F-BUTM, F-ETAL	9-21
❑ TC-NLB	American AA-5B Tiger	93	first noted 6-14	8-19

■ **[1]** Airguard is under long-term restoration by Aerocrafting using original parts. It was withdrawn from use 2-6-45, was rescued by the Northern Aircraft Preservation Society 7-2-70.

EAGLESCOTT AERODROME west of the A377, north of Ashreigney   EGHU
Grasshopper WZ798 (BGA.5074) was exported to the Netherlands, circa 2014. Sedbergh TX.1 WB981, last noted in July 2018, had moved on by mid-2020.

❑ G-AKRP*	DH Dragon Rapide	45	ex Coventry, Eaglescott, Sywell, Little Gransden, Germany, CN-TTO, Senegal, F-DAFS, G-AKRP, Dominie RL958. Brush-built. CoA 6-1-08. First noted 7-20	7-20
❑ G-BOLD	Piper Tomahawk 112	78	ex N9740T. CoA 16-3-09	N9-19
❑ G-BTIL	Piper Tomahawk 112	80	ex N24730	N9-19
❑ WB971* FKP	Slingsby Sedbergh TX.1	50	BGA.3238, ex Aston Down	10-21
❑ WZ819* FLB	Slingsby Grasshopper TX.1	60	BGA.3498, ex Halton. Dismantled, in rafters	10-21
❑ XA295* FLB	Slingsby Cadet TX.3	62	BGA.3336, ex Aston Down	10-21

EGGESFORD AERODROME east of Winkleigh and west of the A377
Only long-term restorations and stored airframes are listed at this heavily Auster-flavoured venue.

❑ G-AFZA	Piper J4A Cub Coupe	39	ex N26198. Crashed 21-4-02, CoA 2-12-02	N1-20
❑ G-AMUI	Auster J5F Aiglet Trainer	52	ex Liverpool, Stretton, CoA 15-2-66	8-19
❑ G-AYDW	Beagle Terrier 2	46	ex King's Lynn, Little Gransden, King's Lynn, Camberley, Cranfield, Bushey, G-ARLM, Auster AOP.6 TW568, LAS, AOPS, 227 OCU, 43 OTU. CoA 1-7-73, de-reg 1-7-85	7-20
❑ G-BGKZ	Auster J5F Aiglet Trainer	53	ex Liverpool, Stretton, F-BGKZ. Crashed 30-1-93	8-18
❑ G-CKXF	Auster J5G Autocar	53	ex 'Home Counties', Saudi Arabia, AP-AHK, VP-KKO. F/n 12-17	8-19
❑ XX561	SAL Bulldog T.1	74	ex CFS, 3 FTS, St Andrews UAS, Queen's UAS, Southampton UAS, CFS. CoA 25-5-05	9-20
	G-BZEP			

Locally: Last flown on 14th July 1989, Stampe G-BKSX departed by road on 25th February 2019 bound for Antwerp, becoming OO-RTC the following month.

☐ G-ASBH   Beagle Airedale   62   CoA 19-2-99   N6-18

EXETER

Arden Family Trust: The late Bertram Arden's airframes are held in careful and *very private* store in the area.

☐ G-AALP   Surrey AL.1   r29 CoA 17-5-40, de-reg 1-12-46   12-97
☐ G-AFGC   BA Swallow II   38 ex BK893, GTS, CLE, RAE, G-AFGC. CoA 20-3-51,
                                                          de-reg 15-3-10   6-06
☐ G-AFHC   BA Swallow II   38 CoA 20-3-51, de-reg 18-2-59   12-97
☐ G-AJHJ   Taylorcraft Auster 5 Alpha   44 ex NJ676, 83 GCS, 440. CoA 27-6-49, de-reg 18-2-59   12-97

EXETER AIRPORT   EGTE

Last noted in June 2016, Cessna 152 G-BRUA has been deleted.

☐ G-ATSX*   Bölkow Junior   66 ex Kirkbride, D-EJUC. CoA 1-7-02, dam 31-3-13.
                                                          De-reg 29-10-14   10-21
☐ G-FTIN*   Robin DR.400-100   88 crashed 31-8-13, de-reg 4-6-14   10-21
☐ G-JEAT   HSA HS.146-100   87 ex JEA, N171TR, J8-VBB, G-BVUY, B-2706, G-5-071.
                                                          Hatfield-built. CoA 23-10-05, de-reg 4-8-04. Rescue training   2-22
☐ G-WYSZ*   Robin DR.400-100   88 CoA 5-6-14   10-21
☐ OO-TAQ   HSA HS.146-200   87 ex TNT Airways, G-BNPJ, I-TNTC, G-5-078.
                                                          Hatfield-built. Arrived 23-7-11   2-22

Exeter College - Future Skills Centre: The former Flybe Training Academy, on the eastern edge of the airport, became an extension of the college's multi-site campus in April 2021. A Jetstream has arrived as a teaching aid.

◆ *By prior application* **only** | https://exe-coll.ac.uk

☐ G-BLKP*   BAe Jetstream 3102   84 ex St Athan, Macclesfield, Humberside, Eastern, G-BLEX,
                                                          G-31-364. CoA 19-4-03, de-reg 7-12-06. Arrived by 5-21   5-21

NEWTON ABBOT on the A380 south of Exeter

Andrew Hawkins: Andrew is hard at work on his Firefly cache. He also holds the rear fuselages of Mk.I PP566, AS.5 VT409 and Sea Fury FB.11 VW589. Son, Ben, has joined in with the acquisition of a Widgeon forward fuselage.

◆ *By prior arrangement* **only** | griffon74@btinternet.com

☐ G-APWK*   Westland Widgeon   59 ex Harrington, Corby (?), Sywell, *Eye of the Needle*, Yeovil.
                                                          De-reg 10-7-73. Forward fuselage, arrived 4-21   1-22
☐ WB440   Fairey Firefly AS.6   50 ex Newton-le-W, Manchester, Heaton Chapel, Newton,
                                                          Salford, Failsworth, Anthorn, 737, 826, AS.5. SOC 8-3-57.
                                                          Fuselage   1-22
☐ WD889   Fairey Firefly AS.5   51 ex Haverigg, Sunderland, Failsworth, Anthorn, 771, 814.
                                                          SOC 2-3-57. Cockpit   1-22
☐ -   Fairey Firefly AS.7   ~ ex Quarrywood. Cockpit reconstruction - see above   1-22
☐ WF145   Hawker Sea Hawk F.1   52 ex Ingatestone, Welshpool, S' Molton, Salisbury, Torbay,
                                                          Brawdy, Abbotsinch, RAE, A&AEE. SOC 21-7-59. Cockpit   1-22

Trago Mills: Or the 'The Big Shop' – the Excalibur is on show within. | www.trago.co.uk

☐ G-BDDX   Whittaker Excalibur   76 ex Helston. De-reg 23-6-83   10-21
■   [1] Single seat, twin-boom ducted fan pusher, only made one flight, 1-7-76, designed and built at Bodmin, by Mike Whittaker.

UCZ Paintball Park: Poltimore ◆ *By prior arrangement* **only** | www.ucz.info

☐ G-OPNI   Bell JetRanger II   67 ex G-BXAA, F-GKYR, HB-XOR, G-BHMV, VH-SJJ, VH-FVR.
                                                          Ditched 5-4-99, de-reg 20-1-00   12-21

SOUTH MOLTON south of the A361, southeast of Barnstaple

Dave Taylor - Cockpitmania: By March 2020 an anonymous Strikemaster Mk.80 cockpit had arrived. This is believed to be the one written out of *W&R23* (p87) at Blackpool. It had been used by the Saudi Support Unit at Warton heading up a composite airframe involving the centre section from a Strikemaster engineering mock-up, the rear end of 'JP' T.3 XN634 and Jet Provost Wings - see *W&R19* for more. It moved on to Westbury, Wilts. Also thought to have departed is Auster AOP.9 XP286 – no further details. ◆ *By prior arrangement* **only** | cockpitmania@aol.com

❑ –		Bell JetRanger	~ ex Bolton, Iver Heath. 'Alaskoil' titles	3-20
❑ –		HS Harrier GR.1	~ ex Welshpool, Market Drayton, Stafford, Abingdon,	
			Hamble. Cockpit	[1] 3-20

■ **[1]** GR.1 cockpit is a 'spare', marked '4 Spare Ser 41H-769733', which falls within the 'XW' range in the production sequence.

TOPSHAM between the M5 and the A376 south of Exeter
Home to a *private* collection of fast-jets. ◆ *By prior arrangement* **only**

❑ XV359	'035'	Blackburn Buccaneer S.2B	69 ex Culdrose, A2693 [2] (20-3-94), Predannack, Lossiemouth, 208, 237 OCU, 12, 208, 12. Arrived 23-4-05. 809 Sqn c/s	7-20
❑ XZ378	'EP'	SEPECAT Jaguar GR.1A	77 ex Shawbury, 6, 41, 17, 31, 20. Arr 14-11-05. 6 Sqn colours	7-20
❑ ZA353*		Panavia Tornado GR.1	80 ex Selby, Boscombe Down, TTTE. First noted 7-20	7-20
❑ ZD612	'731'	HS Sea Harrier F/A.2	85 ex Yeovilton, St Athan, 899, 800, 899, 800, 801, 899. Arrived 2006. 899 Sqn colours	7-20

UPOTTERY east of the A30, northeast of Honiton
Upottery Heritage Centre: Part of the South West Airfields Heritage Trust - see also Dunkeswell, Devon - is well established in a wartime Nissen hut on the northeastern edge of the former home of the 439th Troop Carrier Group.
◆ *Cherry Hayes Farm, Slough Lane, EX14 9RD* | **email** via website | **www.southwestairfields.co.uk**

YARCOMBE Currie Wot G-AVEY was flying by 2020.

DORSET
Includes the unitary authorities of Bournemouth and Poole

BOURNEMOUTH
LV Streetwise Safety Centre: Within the awareness training centre is the cabin of a Twin Squirrel is *thought* to be current.
◆ *By prior arrangement* **only** | via **www.bournemouth.co.uk**

❑ 'S-WISE'	Aérospatiale Squirrel	~ ex PAS Staverton, N354E, F-GIRL	12-19

BOURNEMOUTH AIRPORT or Hurn   EGHH
Bournemouth Aviation Museum (BAM): On the southern perimeter of the airport, co-located with the Adventure Wonderland Theme Park. BAM affords good views of the activity at the airport.
◆ *Follow signs for the airport and then Adventure Wonderland. Merritown Lane, BH23 6BA* | **01202 473141** | enquiries@bamhurn.org| **www.aviation-museum.co.uk**

❑ G-AZKS*	American AA-1A Trainer	70 ex airport, N6134L. CoA 1-6-10. Fuselage, arrived 29-1-20		1-22
❑ G-BAMK*	Cameron D96 airship	72 CoA 24-4-90. de-reg 16-8-00. Gondola	[1]	1-22
❑ G-BBFC	American AA-1 Trainer	73 ex N9945L. Cr 9-6-96, de-reg 14-10-96. Arrived 6-19	[2]	1-22
❑ G-BEYF	HP Herald 401	63 ex Booker, Hurn, Channel Express, RMAF FM1022, CoA 17-3-00, de-reg 18-11-99. Cockpit. Arrived 9-7-15	[3]	1-22
❑ G-BKRL	CMC Leopard	88 ex airport, Old Sarum, Cranfield. CoA 14-12-91, de-reg 25-1-99. Arrived 18-2-05		1-22
❑ G-BOUT	Colomban Cri-Cri	83 ex Eaglescott, Stinsford, N120JN. Arrived 6-19		1-22
❑ G-BWGS	BAC Jet Provost T.5	71 ex N Weald, XW310, 3 FTS, RAFC, 1 FTS. CoA 2-9-08, de-reg 13-7-17. Arrived 8-17		1-22
❑ G-CEAH	Boeing 737-229	75 ex airport, OO-SDG. CoA 14-11-07, de-reg 6-11-13. *The Spirit of Peter Bath*. Forward fuselage. Arrived 8-12-13		1-22
❑ G-OPAS	Vickers Viscount 806	58 ex airport, Duxford, Southend, BWA, BAF, BEA G-AOYN, CoA 26-3-97, de-reg 24-2-94. Cockpit	[4]	1-22
❑ 'GO-CSE'	American AA-5B G-BFZR	79 ex airport, Fordingbridge, Oxford, EI-BJS, G-BFZR. CoA 24-5-07, de-reg 3-11-05. Travelling exhibit. Arr 9-13		1-22
❑ G-PLAH*	BAe Jetstream 31	84 ex Old Sarum, Millom, Blackpool, G-LOVA, G-OAKA, G-BUFM, G-LAKH, G-BUFM, N410MX, G-31-640. CoA 26-7-02, de-reg 22-1-08. Cockpit. Arrived -19-8-20		1-22

Harvard T.2b KF388 with Vampire T.11 XE856, BAC 111-479 ZE432, Viscount 806 G-OPAS and Victor K.2 XL164 behind.
David Willis

☐	–		Vickers Vanguard SIM	~	ex airport, Booker, 'Essex', Hunting, East Midlands. BEA c/s		1-22
☐	LX-ARS*		American AA-1 Trainer	~	ex airport, D-EHLD. Arrived 3-2-20		1-22
☐	KF388		NAA Harvard T.2b	45	ex 'KF488' airport, Hurn, Wimborne, Sandhurst, 6 FTS, 3 FTS, 1 FTS, 7 FTS. Noorduyn-built. SOC 11-2-57. Arrived 2000	[5]	1-22
☐	WS776	'K'	Gloster Meteor NF.14	54	ex airport, Armthorpe, Sandtoft, North Coates, North Luffenham, Lyneham 7716M (3-5-61), 228 OCU, 60, 72, 85, 25. AWA-built. Arrived 5-2-05		1-22
☐	WT532		EE Canberra PR.7	55	ex airport, Lovaux, Cosford, 8890M / 8728M, RAE, 13, Wyton SF, 58, 31, 13, 80. Arrived 5-7-99. Cockpit		1-22
☐	WW450	'PB'	Percival Provost T.1	53	ex 'WW421', Booker Armthorpe, Sandtoft, G-BZRE		
			G-BZRE		(de-reg 22-5-05), Binbrook, Norwich, Lowestoft, East Kirkby, Tattershall, Lytham, WW450, St Athan '7688M', 7689M (2-11-60), TCCF, 8 FTS, 2 FTS. Arrived 10-10-05	[6]	1-22
☐	XE856	'V'	DH Vampire T.11	54	ex airport, Henlow, Catfoss, Long Marston, Lasham,		
			G-DUSK		Welwyn GC, Woodford, Chester, St Athan, 219, N Weald SF, 226 OCU. Hatfield-built. SOC 30-10-67, de-reg 19-3-09. Arrived 6-9-05. 219 Sqn colours	[7]	1-22
☐	XG160	'U'	Hawker Hunter F.6A	56	ex airport, Scampton 8831M (2-9-84), 1 TWU, 229 OCU,		
			G-BWAF		111, 43. De-reg 9-12-10. 111 Sqn colours		1-22
☐	XH537		Avro Vulcan B.2MRR	59	ex airport, Bruntingthorpe, Ottershaw, Camberley, Abingdon 8749M (25-3-82), 27, 230 OCU, MoA. Arrived 29-10-91. Cockpit		1-22
☐	XL164		HP Victor K.2	61	ex Brize Norton 9215M (11-11-93), 55, 57, 55, 57, MoA. Cockpit, on loan. *Saucy Sal*. Arrived 24-5-13		1-22
☐	XM404		Hunting Jet Provost T.3	59	ex Doncaster, Nottingham, Bruntingthorpe, Moreton-in-Marsh, Halton, Newton 8055BM (21-11-69), Shawbury, 3 FTS, 2 FTS. Cockpit. Arrived 22-3-18	[8]	1-22
☐	XR346		Northrop Shelduck D.1	61	'Army' titles	[9]	1-22
☐	XT257		Westland Wessex HAS.3	67	ex airport, East Grinstead, Cosford, Halton 8719M (9-10-81), A&AEE. Arrived 20-1-05. RAF SAR colours		1-22
☐	XT431	'462'	Westland Wasp HAS.1	65	ex 'XS463' Charlwood, Crawley, Ipswich, Weston-super-M, Fleetlands, Wroughton, 829. SOC 10-12-81. Arr 21-12-13	[10]	1-22
☐	XX763	'24'	SEPECAT Jaguar GR.1	75	ex Blackstone, St Athan 9009M, Shawbury, 54, 226 OCU. Arrived 26-9-09. 226 OCU colours	[11]	1-22
☐	ZD620		HSA HS.125 CC.3	82	ex Dunsfold, 32. Last flight 25-3-15. Arrived 29-10-15	[11]	1-22

❑ ZE432	BAC 111-479	73	ex Boscombe Down, ETPS, DQ-FBV. Forward fuselage.		
			Arrived 30-4-14. QinietiQ / ETPS colours.	[12]	1-22
❑ ZF582	EE Lightning F.53	68	ex Reading. Llantrisant, Luton, Desborough, Portsmouth,		
			Stretton, Warton, Saudi AF 207, 53-676, G-27-46.		
			Last flown 22-1-86. Arrived 21-9-04. Cockpit		1-22

■ **[1]** Hot-air airship; envelope stored by the British Balloon Museum and Library. **[2]** On loan, composite airframe. **[3]** *Yankee-Fox* made the last-ever Herald flight, at Bournemouth, on 9-4-99 and was handed over to BAM on loan 26-5-99 but was scrapped 30-6-08 when the museum had to vacate the airport site. The cockpit section returned to Bournemouth in 2015. **[4]** Viscount cockpit on loan from the Duxford Aviation Society. **[5]** Harvard is a composite and carries the serial KF388, which contributed to the amalgam. That being so, it was SOC 11-2-57 and served with 7, 1, 3 and 6 FTSs respectively. **[6]** Provost T.1 has the fuselage of WW450 and the wings of WW421. This exchange occurred during its days at St Athan, when it was even painted up as 7688M (WW421's maintenance serial). **[7]** *Sierra-Kilo* owned by Dick Horsfield and Rod Robinson. **[8]** Wings marked XM404 can also be found at East Wretham, Norfolk. **[9]** Shelduck is a composite, including parts of XV383 and XW578. **[10]** Wasp has the boom of XS463. **[11]** Jaguar and HS.125 on loan from Hayward and Green Defence Ltd. **[12]** The 111 is a local product, it first flew from Hurn 16-7-73.

Airport: As noted in *W&R27*, site redevelopment work saw the demise of several long-established hulks. There is a frequent throughput of so-called 'legacy' airliners here, but only long-termers are listed. **Departures**: AA-1 G-AZKS moved to the museum (above) on 29-1-20 as a source of spares; Falcon 20 G-FRAP's time on the ground was fleeting, it was flying again by mid-20; AA-1 LX-ARS had moved to the museum - above - by 9-20; Boeing 737 fuselage N470AC moved to St Athan, Wales, 4-8-20; Gulfstream III N623NP was dismantled by early 2021, initially moving to St Athan, Wales, before settling upon White Waltham, Berks; 737s, N733UK and 'EV-RAMP' (N475EL) were freighted to China in 6-20, both destined to become instructional airframes. The fire crew trainer airframes, HS.125 G-ATPD and BAC 111 VR-BEB were both scrapped in 2-21. At the same time Canberra T.4 WJ992 was also chopped, its cockpit travelling to St Athan, Wales, 9-2-21.

Canadair CL-44-O 'Guppy' N447FT, probably not long for this world, December 2021. *Mark Presswood*

❑ G-AVLD	Piper Cherokee 140	67	CoA 11-6-06, de-reg 7-12-18	1-21
❑ G-AZDE	Piper Arrow 200	71	ex Elstree. CoA 20-4-08	1-22
❑ G-BBGI*	Fuji FA.200-160	73	CoA 30-6-17	1-21
❑ G-BFZM	Rockwell C'der 112TCA	77	ex Lambourn, N4661W. CoA 21-8-09	1-22
❑ G-BGSW	Beech Bonanza F33	70	ex OH-BDD. CoA 28-7-17	1-22
❑ G-BNSY	Piper Warrior II	80	ex Sandtoft, N4512M. CoA 6-11-09	1-22
❑ G-BPXX	Piper Seneca 200T	79	ex N923SM. Crashed 13-10-17, CoA 22-12-17	1-22
❑ G-BRPU	Beech Duchess	79	ex N6007Z. CoA 10-8-12, de-reg 29-6-12	1-22
❑ G-BTJL	Piper Tomahawk 112	79	ex N2477N. CoA 14-5-15, de-reg 9-4-21. Fuselage	1-18
❑ G-CBBF	Beech Duchess	80	ex OY-DED, EI-BHS. CoA 12-10-14	1-22
❑ G-FRAO	Dassault Falcon 20D	69	ex Cobham, N906FR, N33FE, N4400F, F-WNGO.	
			CoA 28-1-18, de-reg 5-5-20	1-22
❑ G-FRBA	Dassault Falcon 20C	70	ex FRA, OH-FFA, F-WPXF. CoA 23-9-11, de-reg 6-12-11	1-22

☐ G-GPFI	Boeing 737-229	74	ex European, VH-OZQ, G-GPFI, VH-OZQ, G-GPFI, F-GVAC, OO-SDA, LX-LGN, OO-SDA. CoA 2-4-09, de-reg 19-6-11. OzJet titles. Forward fuselage, cabin trainer	[1]	1-22
☐ G-IKOS*	Cessna 550 Citation Bravo	01	ex N957PH. CoA 9-6-<u>14</u>		1-21
☐ G-MGBG	Cessna 310Q	70	ex N727MB, G-AYND, N7610Q. First noted 8-17		1-20
☐ G-SMTH	Piper Cherokee 140	70	ex G-AYJS. De-reg 2-08-17		1-22
☐ G-TLET	Piper Cadet 161	89	ex museum, Shoreham, G-GFCF, G-RHBH, N9193Z. CoA 18-10-12, de-reg 10-6-13, crashed 21-7-12	[2]	1-22
☐ G-TWNN	Beech Duchess	80	ex N127MR, N127MB, N67161. Cr 3-5-17, de-reg 2-6-17		1-20
☐ G-VIPP	Piper Navajo 350	79	ex G-OGRV, G-BMPX, N3543D. De-reg 4-5-17		1-22
☐ D-EFUC	Cessna 172S	98	ex G-NEWI, N563ER. Crashed 2-8-12. Arrived 18-10-12		1-18
☐ M-ALUN	HSA HS.125-700A	80	ex N125AM, G-BHKF, G-5-13. Last flown 7-16		1-22
☐ N447FT	Canadair CL-44-O 'Guppy'	61	ex RP-C-8023, 9G-LCA, 4K-GUP, N447T, EI-BND, N447T, CL-44D4. Conroy 'Guppy' conversion. De-reg 4-11-19		1-22
☐ N666AW	Piper Navajo 325	84	ex Biggin Hill. Fuselage. Arrived 18-8-15		1-20
☐ 2-ESKA	Boeing 737-301F	86	ex N126WF, EC-LJI, OO-TNI, N94417, OO-TNI, N558AU, N434US, N323P. Arrived 1-8-17	[3]	1-22
☐ 2-MOVE	Boeing 737-382QC	89	ex N596BC, OY-JTF, OK-GCG, F-GIXG, F-OGSX, CS-TIA. Arrived 24-3-17	[3]	1-22
☐ 2-PSFI	Boeing 737-33	87	ex G-CKTI, OY-JTA, N371FA, N127AW. Arrived 2017	[3]	1-22
☐ XW293	'Z' BAC 'JP' T.5A G-BWCS	71	ex Tatenhill, 6 FTS, CFS. CoA 3-2-09, de-reg 18-10-19		1-22
☐ –	Hawker Hunter T.7	57	ex Biggin Hill, 'G-ERIC', Hurn, Leavesden, Elstree, Hatfield, Danish AF	[4]	1-22

■ **[1]** *Fox-India* is owned and operated on behalf of the airport management by the JARE Airline Training Partnership. **[2]** *Echo-Tango* was the test-bed for the Thielert TME 125 diesel. **[3]** If, like the author, 2- befuddles you, it is the new-fangled civil register of Guernsey. **[4]** Hunter is dedicated as a memorial. The plaque reads: 'Richard Michael Carlton - Aviator'. It is a composite with the cockpit of FGA.9 XJ690 - ex Bitteswell, G-9-451, 20, 14 - the rest is a complex story of ex-Danish T.7(s)!

BOVINGTON off the A352 near Wool, west of Wareham

Tank Museum: Home to the world's finest international collection of armoured fighting vehicles. Walking through the display halls visitors come across what appears to be a packing case with a tank in it: not a bad description of a Hamilcar! The temptation not to restore this relic is to be applauded.

◆ *Linsay Road, BH20 6JG* | **01929 405096** | **visit@tankmuseum.org** | **www.tankmuseum.org**

☐ TK718	GAL Hamilcar I	44	ex Beverley, Christian Malford	[1]	1-22
☐ XM564	Saro Skeeter AOP.12	59	ex Celle, 652, CFS, 12 Flt, 652. 2 RTR colours. Stored	[2]	1-22

■ **[1]** Birmingham Railway Carriage-built; parts of TK718 were used in the creation of the example at Middle Wallop, Hampshire. **[2]** The last Skeeter flown in BAOR; XM564 was presented to the museum by 2 RTR in 3-69.

CANFORD north of the A3049, north of Poole

An ATR 42 fuselage has. appeared in the locality.

☐ G-ISLG*	ATR 42-320	85	ex Hurn, Greenwich, Hurn, Blue Islands, F-HAAV, F-WKVB, OY-CIG, YU-ALK, VH-AQD. De-reg 3-8-16. Fuselage. Convict Airways titles, *The Cage*. Arrived 23-12-20		1-22

COMPTON ABBAS AERODROME southeast of Shaftesbury   EGHA

Last noted serving the fire crew in July 2012, Arrow G-AZRV has been deleted.

☐ G-BRIJ	Taylorcraft F19	78	ex N3863T. CoA 12-6-01		9-18
☐ G-CBRT*	Murphy Rebel	02	de-reg 4-5-21, dumped	[1]	8-21

■ **[1]** Alongside the Murphy is the *cockpitless* hulk of Tomahawk G-RVRB.

CORSCOMBE Last noted in January 2014, Vampire T.11 WZ450 arrived at <u>Sleap</u>, Shropshire, in December 2020.

FERNDOWN on the A348 north of Bournemouth

A *private* owner is *believed* to be restoring a J4 in the area; with an Alpha held in store.

☐ G-AIJS	Auster J4 Archer	46	ex France, Clothall Common	N1-18
☐ G-APRF	Auster 5 Alpha	58	ex France (?), Felixkirk, Squires Gate, VP-LAF, G-APRF. CoA 14-6-05, de-reg 14-6-05	12-15

POOLE on the A35 west of Bournemouth

A Short 330 forward fuselage is *believed* to linger at a *private* address in the area.

❑ G-BGNG	Short 330-200	79	ex Hurn, Gill, N330FL, G-BGNG. CoA 14-4-97, de-reg 16-8-96. Fuselage	8-17

PORTLAND

The Sailing Academy: Osprey Quay, displayed within the marina complex is a Lynx.

❑ XZ250	'426'	Westland Lynx HAS.3S	78	ex M Wallop, 702, 815, 702, 815, 702, Fleetlands, 702, 829, HAS.2, 702, 815, 702. SOC 13-10-10	7-21

DURHAM and CLEVELAND
The unitary authorities of Hartlepool, Middlesbrough, Redcar and Cleveland, Stockton-on-Tees and Darlington form the region

---

DURHAM

Stu-Art Aviation Furniture: Stuart Abbott up-cycles aviation components, fittings and sections into a wide variety of furniture and decorations. His workshop includes a 737 cockpit as an 'office'.

◆ *By prior arrangement* **only** | **www.stu-artaviationfurniture.co.uk**

❑ G-CELU*	Boeing 737-377	86	ex Kemble, Jet2, VH-CZE. Last flight 8-12-14, de-reg 29-6-15. Cockpit, first noted 7-21	1-22

EDMONDSLEY on the B6532 northwest of Durham

Holmside Park Arena: A Sea King is displayed. ◆ *By prior application* **only** | **www.holmsidepark.co.uk**

❑ ZE368	'R'	Westland Sea King HAR.3	85	ex Colsterworth, Gosport, Fleetlands, 202, 1564 Flt, 202	1-22

Also: The remainder of the former Mini-Moos Sea Kings are held in *private* storage and are *not* available for inspection.

❑ XV651	'824'	Westland Sea King HAS.5	69	ex Colsterworth, Gosport, Fleetlands, QinetiQ, 771, 706, 826, 814, HAS.1, RAE Thurleigh, RRE, A&AEE	1-20
❑ XZ921	'269'	Westland Sea King HAS.6	79	ex Eastleigh, Bruntingthorpe, Gosport, 820, 814, 810, HAS.5, 706, 820, Falklands, 820, HAS.2	1-20
❑ ZA291	'N'	Westland Sea King HC.4	79	ex Eastleigh, Gosport, Fleetlands, 848, 846, 845, 848, 707, 846, 707, 846, Falklands, 846	1-20
❑ ZA313	'M'	Westland Sea King HC.4	82	ex Eastleigh, Gosport, Fleetlands, 845, 846, 845, 848, 845, 846, Falklands, 846, 707	7-21
❑ ZD625	'P'	W'land Sea King HC.4	84	ex E'leigh, Gosport, F'lands 848, 846, 848, 846, 845, 846, 707	1-20
❑ ZE425	'WR'	Westland Sea King HC.4	85	ex Eastleigh, Gosport, Fleetlands, 848, 846, 845, 848, 846, 845, 772, 846, 845, 848, 846. 'Arctic' stripes	7-21
❑ ZE428	'H'	Westland Sea King HC.4	85	ex Eastleigh, Gosport, Fleetlands, 845, 846, 845, 846, 845, 846, 845, 848, 772, 845	1-20
❑ ZF121	'T'	W'land Sea King HC.4	86	ex E'leigh, Gosport, F'lands, 846, 845, 846, 845, 846, 845, 772	1-20

FISHBURN AERODROME or Morgansfield, on the B1278, north of Sedgefield

Fishburn Historic Aviation Centre: Run by the **Aircraft Restoration Group** (ARG) good progress is being made with the site and the 'fleet' is expanding. Special events are open cockpit days are staged. Having been replaced with *Tango-Alpha*, Rallye G-BBLM moved to Chessington, Gtr London, in January 2022.

◆ *Check details on Facebook for availability.* | *Aerodrome details:* **www.fishburnairfield.co.uk**

❑ G-AYTA*		MS Rallye Club	71	ex Manchester, Moston, Wickenby. CoA 7-11-88, de-reg 12-5-93. Arrived 19-11-21		1-22
❑ D-IFSB		DH Dove 6 G-AMXR	52	ex London Colney, Hatfield, BFS, D-CFSB, Panshanger, Srs 2A G-AMXR, N4280V. Last flew 24-10-78. Arr 2-2-16	[1]	1-22
❑ XG743	'798'	DH Sea Vampire T.22	54	ex Pickhill, Duxford (issued to IWM 15-6-72), Wymondham, Duxford, Brawdy SF, A&AEE, Brawdy SF, 766, 736, 764. Christchurch-built. Arrived on site 3-7-18		1-22

☐ XN458*	'19'	Hunting Jet Provost T.3	60	ex Northallerton, Ashington, 'XN594' Cardiff, St Athan,
				Halton 8334M (21-3-73), Shawbury, 1 FTS. Arrived 7-9-21 1-22
☐ J-1790		DH Venom FB.54	57	ex London Colney, 'WR410', 'Norfolk', Hurn, Bruntingthorpe,
		G-BLKA		Cranfield, G-BLKA, G-VENM, Swiss AF J-1790. CoA 14-7-95,
				de-reg 13-10-00. Swiss -built. Arrived 2-2-16. 'Gate guard' 1-22

■ **[1]** Dove is on permanent loan from the DH Aircraft Museum.

Workshop and Store: By *prior arrangement*, this can also be viewed. The Sea Vampire is a 'third-party' restoration project.

☐ 'G-ADRZ'	Mignet HM.14 'Flea'	~	ex Masham, Pickhill, South Molton, Dunstable,	
			South Molton. Arrived on site 19-10-19	[1] 1-22
☐ G-APWU	Thurston Tawney Owl	59	ex Masham, Pickhill, Leamington Spa, 'Herefordshire',	
			Stondon, Stapleford Tawney. Crashed 22-4-60, de-reg	
			15-9-86. Arrived on-site 19-10-19	[2] 1-22
☐ G-CDGT	Montgomerie-Parsons	05	ex 'Essex'. *The Flying Scotsman II / Merlin*	
	Two-Place		Arrived 19-1-20	1-22
☐ G-CHTX*	Skill Voltair 86	13	ex Sunderland, Eshott, Hartlepool, Newcastle.	
			De-reg 29-3-21. Arrived 29-5-21	[3] 1-22
☐ G-GREG*	Jodel DR.220	67	ex Northallerton, Huddersfield, Eversden, F-BOKR.	
			CEA-built. CoA 19-2-91, de-reg 1-4-97. First noted 2-20	1-22
☐ XG775*	DH Sea Vampire T.22	55	ex Llandysul, 'Norfolk', London, Southall, Lossiemouth SF,	
			Yeovilton SF, FOFT, 766, 1833, 718. Christchurch-built.	
			SOC 30-1-70. Cockpit, arrived 21-7-21	[4] 1-22

■ **[1]** Exact provenance of the 'Flea' is unknown, it is likely a 'new-build' from the 1980s. **[2]** Tawney Owl was written off on its first flight, at Stapleford Tawney. **[3]** Electric-powered microlight, designed and built by David Skill of Newcastle. "Hopped and skipped" at Eshott in 2013 but made no sustained flight (corrects *W&R27*). **[4]** Under restoration by ARG's Mike Eastman for owner Max Valk. See under Llandysul, Wales, for this machine's immediate past.

Aerodrome: The aerodrome is a thriving community, staging special events and the Aviator Bistro is rightly popular.

☐ G-AKTP*	Piper Vagabond	48	ex Swansea, N4683H. CoA 5-8-03. Arrived 9-21	1-22
☐ G-AVOD*	Beagle D5 Husky 180	67	ex Harrogate, Spilsby. Crashed 31-7-92	10-21
☐ G-DAVE*	Jodel D.112	57	ex F-BICH. Ets Valladeau-built. CoA 17-8-17	10-21
☐ G-RADA	Soko Kraguj	76	ex Linton-on-Ouse, Biggin Hill, Yugoslav AF 30140.	
			CoA 5-9-05. Arrived 22-4-17	[1] 6-21

■ **[1]** Spares for the airworthy G-BSXD.

HARTLEPOOL

Hartlepool College of Further Education: The Travel, Tourism and Aviation training centre also boasts a 'slice' of former Cathay Boeing 747 passenger cabin: this facility was inaugurated in April 2018.
◆ *By prior application* only | **www.hartlepoolfe.ac.uk**

☐ XW309	'ME'	BAC Jet Provost T.5	70	ex Cosford 9179M (11-3-93), Shawbury, 6 FTS, 1 FTS 11-21
☐ XW404	'77'	BAC Jet Provost T.5A	71	ex Exeter, St Athan 9049M (16-8-90), 1 FTS 11-21
☐ XW405		BAC Jet Provost T.5A	71	ex Exeter, Cosford 9187M (5-5-93), Shawbury, 6 FTS, 1 FTS,
				7 FTS, 6 FTS, 1 FTS, RAFC. Plinth-mounted 11-21
☐ –	TAD.002	Sud Gazelle CIM	~	ex Colsterworth, Arborfield, M Wallop. Westland-built [1] 11-21
☐ -	'AV002'	Panavia Tornado SIM	~	ex Sunderland. Cockpit. Built by Environmental Tectonics 11-21

■ **[1]** Inspection of the CIM reveals it to be a transmission, controls and fuel system rig which is labelled '341 Training Aid Unit 1'.

MIDDLESBROUGH

Teesside University: Near Albert Park. ◆ *By prior application* only | **www.tees.ac.uk**

☐ G-BAMG	Lobet Ganagobie	r73	ex Yearby. Unfinished homebuilt. De-reg 5-8-91. Arr 12-16	1-22

NEWTON AYCLIFFE on the A167 southeast of Bishop Auckland

Aviator Gin Bar: With seating from a variety of airliners and other elements of aeronautica, the venue invites participants to "Broaden your horizons"! The proprietors claim the Dauphin was acquired for six bottles of 'mother's ruin'!
◆ *Hanger [sic] 18, Northfield Way, DL5 6EJ* | **01325 589076** | **www.the aviatorginbar.co.uk**

☐ G-BLAI*	Monnett Sonerai 2L	97	T Simpson, Kirkcaldy-built. CoA 12-1-99. Fuselage, f/n 7-20	3-21
☐ G-BTNC*	Sud Dauphin II	91	De-reg 26-8-20. Gutted fuselage. Arrived 3-21	[1] 3-21

■ **[1]** Fitted with the tail of G-CEYU.

TEESSIDE INTERNATIONAL AIRPORT or Middleton St George, formerly Durham Tees Valley   EGNV
The Middleton St George Memorial Association is pledged to re-open the heritage room within the former RAF Middleton St George Officers' Mess: keep an eye on **www.middleton-st-george-memorial-association.org**

International Fire Training Centre: As well as real airframes, the school has 'synthetic' training rigs, including a 'DC-10' lookalike and the forward fuselage of an 'A380'. ◆ **Strictly** *by prior application* **only | www.iftcentre.com**

❑ G-AWZS	HS Trident 3B-101	71	ex BA, BEA. CoA 9-9-86, de-reg 18-3-86		1-22
❑ G-AZLS	Vickers Viscount 813	58	ex BMA, SAA ZS-CDV. Hurn-built. CoA 9-6-83, de-reg 19-12-86. Fuselage		1-22
❑ 'G-JON'	Short 330-100 G-BKIE	76	ex Newcastle, G-SLUG, G-METP, G-METO, G-BKIE, C-GTAS, G-14-3005. CoA 22-8-93, de-reg 16-9-97		1-22
❑ XP330	W'land Whirlwind HAR.10	61	ex Stansted, 21, 32, 230, 110, 225. SOC 26-1-76		1-22
❑ XZ360	'FN' SEPECAT Jaguar GR.3	76	ex Ipswich, St Athan, 41, GR.1, 41. Arrived 28-8-19		1-22
❑ XZ652	Westland Lynx AH.7	81	ex Ipswich, M Wallop. NEA 3-13. Red scheme, Serco logo. Arrived 7-10-14		1-22

Others:

❑ G-BNGR	Piper Tomahawk 112	79	ex N2492F. CoA 1-8-03, de-reg 18-2-05. Trolley-mounted		1-22
❑ G-CLUE	Piper Seneca 200T	79	ex N8089Z. Damaged 28-7-13, CoA 28-2-14		1-22
❑ N5039Q	ATR 42-300	94	ex Air Ukraine UR-UTA, VP-BLP, D4-CBE, F-WWEA. Arrived 7-12-13. Rescue training		1-22

THORNABY ON TEES west of the A19 and Middlesbrough
Thornaby Aerodrome Memorial: At Spitfire Roundabout on the A1045, is a tribute to the former airfield.

❑ -	V-S Spitfire V FSM	07	BAPC.301, GB-Replicas-built. Pole-mounted	[1]	1-22

■ **[1]** As Mk.V 'BM481' 'YO-T' of 401 Sqn RCAF 1943 (port), and F.22 'PK651' 'RAO-B' of 608 (North Riding) Sqn 1948-1950 (stb).

URLAY NOOK north of the A67, east of Teesside Airport
Great North Air Ambulance: Has a Dauphin fuselage in use as a training aid.
◆ *By prior application* **only | www.greatnorthairambulance.co.uk**

❑ G-BTEU	Sud Dauphin II	90	ex Teesside, Bowburn, Teesside, Newton Aycliffe, Yeadon, Durham, CoA 18-5-15, de-reg 11-6-15. Arr 18-9-19		1-22

YEARBY on the B1269 south of Redcar
A local, and *private*, airstrip. ◆ *By prior application* **only | https://acro.co.uk**

❑ G-APYB	Tipsy Nipper III	59	CoA 12-6-96. Avions Fairey-built	12-21
❑ G-BHUO	Evans VP-2	82	CoA 21-12-94, de-reg 23-8-00	7-19
❑ G-BPAA	Acro Advanced	94	CoA 20-7-17	12-21
❑ G-MYKY*	Mainair Mercury	93	de-reg 27-10-21	12-21

ESSEX
Includes the unitary authorities of Southend and Thurrock

ABRIDGE on the A113, south of the M11/M25 junction
Mayhem Paintball Games: ◆ *By prior arrangement* **only | www.mayhem-paintball.co.uk**

❑ G-AOHL	Vickers Viscount 802	57	ex Stock, Southend, BAF, BA, BEA. CoA 11-4-80, de-reg 27-3-81. Cockpit	[1]	12-17
❑ G-AREE	Piper Aztec 250	60-	ex Stapleford. De-reg 16-12-91. Fuselage		3-15
❑ G-BOIP*	Cessna 152 II	79	ex Stapleford, Tattershall Thorpe, Staverton, N49264. Damaged 11-1-90, de-reg 13-1-06. Tail of C.152 G-BOTB	[2]	9-19
❑ G-OBHD	Short 360-100	87	ex Hinstock, Blackpool, G-BNDK, G-OBHD, G-BNDK, G-14-3714. CoA 5-3-06, de-reg 27-1-11. Arrived 1-8-12		3-15
❑ G-OBPL	Embraer Bandeirante	78	ex Stock, Southend, 'G-OBWB', PH-FVB, G-OEAB, G-BKWB, G-CHEV, PT-GLR. De-reg 27-2-04. Fuselage		12-17

☐ XP854		Westland Scout AH.1	63	ex Ipswich, Bedford, Ipswich, Wattisham, M Wallop		
				TAD.043 / 7898M. Crashed 15-5-65		7-20
☐ XT455	'U'	Westland Wessex HU.5	65	ex Hixon, Gosport A2654 [2], Lee-on-Solent A2741 (3-7-86),		
				845, 707, 845, 846, 845, 707. First noted 3-15		7-20
☐ XX744		SEPECAT Jaguar GR.1	74	ex Ipswich, Coltishall 9251M, Cosford, Shawbury,		
	'DJ'			Warton, 31, 17, 31, 6, 14, 17, A&AEE. 31 Sqn colours		11-21
☐ ZD276		Westland Lynx AH.7	83	ex Yeovilton, 655, 671, 656, 661, 652. Cr 18-3-07. Cabin		7-20
☐ -		Sud Gazelle	-	with a Scout boom	[3]	6-18
☐ 776		Westland Sea King	75	ex Market Drayton, Gosport, Egyptian Air Force, G-BDMJ,		
		Mk.47 G-BDMJ		G-17-25. Cockpit plus the cabin/rear of HAS.6 ZA136. F/n 9-14		7-20

■ [1] Close to the Viscount nose is the centre section of F.27 3C-QSB, from Stock, Essex. [2] Written out of *W&R25* (p54), clearly it was capable of sustaining more splats! [3] Gazelle is *very probably* G-TURP.

ANDREWSFIELD AERODROME or Great Saling, north of the A120, west of Braintree   EGSL
The Mystère is a reminder of the Rebel Air Museum which was open to the public here 1979 to 1986.

| ☐ G-BAOB | | Cessna F.172M | 73 | Reims-built. CoA 12-5-07, de-reg 17-12-10 | | 9-21 |
| ☐ 319 | '8-ND' | Dassault Mystère IVA | c57 | ex Sculthorpe, French AF. Last flew 17-10-79, arrived 6-80 | [1] | 7-21 |

■ [1] Mystère *presumably* held on behalf of the National Museum of the USAF, USA.

AUDLEY END AERODROME off the B1383, west of Saffron Walden
Vintage Fabrics: Clive Denney and team work wonders transforming aircraft of all eras. 'Long-termers' only are listed. Chipmunk T.10 G-BAPB was flying again by 2020. PT-22 854 (G-BTBH) moved to Turweston, Bucks, in December 2020.
◆ *Private workshop, by prior permission* only | www.vintagefabrics.co.uk

☐ G-AXUA		Beagle Pup 100	69	ex G-35-150. CoA 5-6-08		1-22
☐ G-BTOG		DH Tiger Moth	44	ex France, F-BGCJ, French AF, NM192 n/s. Morris-built		1-22
☐ A2-25*		Royal Aircraft Factory	1918	ex Elmsett, Sudbury, Australia, RAAF, C8996.		
		SE.5a G-ECAE		Austin-built. Crashed 15-7-27. Arrived by 1-21	[1]	1-22

■ [1] SE.5a registered to Westh Flyg AB of Sweden - see under Elmsett, Suffolk, for the company's Hawker Hart.

Also: As noted in *W&R27* (p53) **Provost Preservation**'s Provosts WW388 and XF836 were offered for disposal in September 2019: they moved to Weston Zoyland, Somerset, by July 2020. XF597 is stored.

☐ G-ACGS*		DH Leopard Moth	33	ex ZK-AGS, G-APKH, AX858 1473 Flt, 109, Special Signals		
				School, G-ACGH, PH-ALM, G-ACGS		6-21
☐ G-AXMW*		Beagle Pup 100	69	ex G-35-101. De-reg 19-2-21. First noted 9-21		9-21
☐ XF597	'A-H'	Perc' Provost T.1 G-BKFW	55	ex Thatcham, CAW, RAFC. CoA 27-7-07. Arrived 7-18, stored		1-22

BILLERICAY on the A129 east of Brentwood
Delta Force Paintball: Heath Road. ◆ *By prior arrangement* only | www.paintballgames.co.uk

| ☐ XZ606 | 'O' | Westland Lynx AH.7 | 79 | ex Upminster, Ipswich, M Wallop. First noted 4-17 | 4-17 |

BOXTED between the A134 and the A12, north of Colchester
Boxted Airfield Museum: Run by the Boxted Airfield Historical Group, tells the story of the 386th BG, Gabreski's 56th FG, and the 354th FG. Centrepiece of the new display building is the rear fuselage of B-26C-25-MO 41-35253 *Mr Shorty* on loan from the trustees of the Marks Hall Estate at Earls Colne: it is the largest piece of Marauder extant in the UK.
◆ *Off Langham Lane, Langham, CO4 5NW* | email via website | www.boxted-airfield.com

BRADWELL ON SEA at the end of the B1021 north of Tillingham
Eastland Meadows Country Park: At the camping and caravan site the Jaguar and Lynx of the moribund Bradwell Bay Military Museum are kept. ◆ *By prior arrangement* only

☐ XX146	'GT'	SEPECAT Jaguar T.2	74	ex Bentwaters, St Athan, 54, T.2, SAOEU, 54, 16, 41,		
				Shawbury, 54, 41, 6, Coltishall SF, 6, 226 OCU, JOCU.		
				Last flown 7-3-05. Arrived 24-5-17		9-21
☐ ZD266	'673'	Westland Lynx HMA.8	83	ex Bentwaters, 815, 702, DERA, HAS.3, DERA, A&AEE		9-21

BRAINTREE north of the A120, west of Colchester
B-17 Cockpit Project: Small steps lead to great strides... Dave Littleton made a B-17 instrument panel in 1998. One thing led to another and he and his brother Paul now have an incredible B-17G cockpit recreation, complete with upper gun turret.

There are plans to expand on that, if extra space can be found. The inspiration for this was their late father, John, indefatigable crew chief to *Sally B*. The workmanship is incredible, hence the description 'recreation', this is *way beyond* a replica. The cockpit is available for film work, set-piece photo sessions etc. Dave also offers B-17 parts, component fabrication, film consultation and much more.

◆ *By prior arrangement* only | b17man@live.co.uk | **www.b-17cockpitproject.com**

❑ -*   Boeing B-17G Fortress   20   see narrative   1-22

CHELMSFORD

De Havilland Hornet Project: David Collins continues with his exceptional DH Hornet F.1 re-creation. The aim is to make as much of a Hornet as possible and it will be finished in the Medium Sea Grey over PRU Blue colours of 64 Squadron. This is a fitting scheme as some components from PX250 - which served with 64 from new - are to be incorporated into the build.

◆ *Visits* **not** *possible, but appearances at events are made.* | **www.facebook.com/dehavilland.hornet.F1/**

❑ -   DH Hornet F.1   06   BAPC.349, cockpit project   1-22

Also: A *private* collector in the locality *should* have the cockpit of a Pucará.

❑ A-533   FMA Pucará   c81 ex Boscombe Down, Salisbury, St Mary Bourne, M Wallop,
                                                          Boscombe D', Abingdon, Finningley, ZD486, Arg AF. Cockpit   2-16

CLACTON AERODROME   EGSQ

Classic Wings: Has its maintenance base here and its main site of operation at Duxford, Cambs.

❑ G-ANFV   DH Tiger Moth   42   ex DF155, 25 RFS, 28 EFTS. Morris-built. Crashed 12-8-12   3-19
❑ G-ANPE   DH Tiger Moth   40   ex Duxford, G-IESH, G-ANPE, F-BHAT, G-ANPE, T7397,
                                                          19 RFS, 18 EFTS. Morris Motors-built. CoA 9-8-12   N9-18
❑ G-BJTB   Cessna A.150M   75   ex N9818J. CoA 27-11-07   N10-18
❑ G-CFII   DH Tiger Moth   42   ex N90277, VT-DKN, Indian AF HU726, SAAF 4613, DE630.
                                                          Morris Motors-built   3-19
❑ DF112   DH Tiger Moth ✈   43   ex Duxford, 202 AFS, 1 GU, 2 GU, 11 RFS, 22 RFS, 22 EFTS,
                             G-ANRM   16 PFTS, 22 EFTS. Morris-built. Accident 30-6-18, CoA 20-5-19 2-19

CLACTON ON SEA

East Essex Aviation Museum (EEAM) **and Museum of the 1940s**: Located within a Martello tower.

◆ *Orchards Holiday Camp at Point Clear, St Osyth CO16 8NG* | via **Facebook**

❑ 44-14574   NAA P-51D-10-NA   44   ex 479th FG, 436th FS *Little Zippie*. Inglewood-built.
                             Mustang   Crashed off-shore 13-1-45. Recovered 16-8-87   6-21

Also: The Terrier project is *believed* to be under way at a *private* location. Dragon 150s G-MJUZ and G-MMAI, last recorded in October 2012, have been deleted.

❑ G-TIMG   Beagle Terrier   c47 restoration project, unused AOP.6 fuselage fame   N3-18

COGGESHALL off the A120, east of Braintree

At a *private* location, the Jungmeister owner also has Jungmann G-JMNN under restoration at Sywell, Northants.

❑ G-MEIS   Bücker Jungmeister   42   ex Rayleigh, USA, Span AF ES.1-36. CASA-built   10-21

COLCHESTER

Charleston Aviation Services ◆ *Private workshop*, **strictly** *viewable by prior application* **only**

❑ LA546   V-S Seafire F.46   46   ex Newport Pagnell, Newark, Charnock Richard, Carlisle,
                             G-CFZJ   Anthorn, Lossiemouth Stn Flight. SOC 29-6-51   [1] [2] N12-19
❑ 0854   Messerschmitt   c40 ex Russia, JG5. Shot down 19-4-42. Erla-built.
                             Bf 109E-3   G-CLBX   Salvaged 1994   [2] N11-18
❑ 8347   Messerschmitt   41   ex Hungary, Colchester, Sussex, Russia. Erla-built.
                             Bf 109E-4   G-CLFN   Force landed 13-3-42.   [3] N7-19

■ **[1]** See also Old Sarum, Wilts. **[2]** Registered to Craig Charleston. **[3]** Registered to Fighter Aviation Engineering.

Merville Barracks: The Dakota 'guards' 'the **16 Air Assault Brigade** HQ.

❑ 'KG374'   Douglas Dakota C.4   45   ex N Weald, Aldershot, Kemble, AFNE, New Delhi, AFNE,
     'YS-DM'   KP208   HCCF, 24, MEAF, USAAF C-47B-35-DK 44-77087.
                                                          Oklahoma City-built. SOC 18-5-70   1-22

No.308 Squadron Air Cadets:

❑ ZE556	Grob Viking T.1	84	ex Wethersfield, Syerston, Stapleford, Beeston, Syerston, BGA.3031, CGHF, Arbroath, 662 VGS, 636 VGS, 631 VGS, 661 VGS, 622 VGS. Crashed 12-4-02. Cockpit	3-18

Locally: A Proctor is under restoration at a *private* location in the *general* area.

❑ G-ANVY* '4-47'	Percival Proctor IV	44	ex Great Oakley, SE-CEA, RM169, 4 RS. Hills-built. F/n 6-21	6-21

DANBURY on the A414 east of Chelmsford
A *Flogger* is stored at an industrial estate locally.

❑ 20+45	Mikoyan-Gurevich	80	ex Germany, Luftwaffe, E German AF	
	MiG-23BN *Flogger*	80	Stored	6-20

EARLS COLNE south of Earls Colne, east of Halstead
A Texan project is *believed* current at a *private* location in the area. Last noted at a private house in January 2019, Rotorway Scorpion SE-HXF has been deleted.

❑ G-BRBC	NAA T-6G Texan	52	ex It AF MM54099, USAF 51-14470. Off-site	N11-18

EAST TILBURY on a minor road east of Tilbury
Whitley Project: Elliott Smock's ambitious project is based locally. The venture does not, as yet, merit a 'formal' listing. Salvaged elements of two Kinloss-based 19 OTU Whitleys, one of which is Mk.V EB384, form the bulk of the project. The centre section of Mk.V N1498, which crashed south of Inverness on 6th January 1942, was acquired from RAF Museum holdings. ◆ *Viewing by prior arrangement* **only** | **elliott1940@yahoo.com**

GREAT DUNMOW on the A120 west of Braintree
Paul and **Andy Wood**: Keep a Hunter at a *private* location in the area. See also Shuttleworth, Beds.

❑ WP185	Hawker Hunter F.5	55	ex Abingdon, Hendon, Henlow 7583M (30-10-58), 34, 1. AWA-built	9-18

GREAT OAKLEY AERODROME off the B1414 south of Harwich
Percival Aircraft: Mike Biddulph and friends have established a centre of excellence for all things Proctor. Mk.IV G-ANVY had moved to Colchester, Essex, by June 2021. ◆ *Private workshop, viewable by prior application* **only**

❑ G-AHTE	Percival Proctor V	46	ex Nayland, Clacton, Llanelli, Cardiff, Swansea, Llanelli, Hereford, Walsall. CoA 10-8-61	9-21
❑ G-AKEX	Percival Proctor III	43	ex Sweden, SE-BTR, G-AKEX, LZ791, ATA, CFE. Hills-built. Crashed 11-1-51	9-21
❑ G-ANPP	Percival Proctor III	42	ex Thruxton, HM354, BCCF, 21 EFTS, BCCF, Digby SF, 34 Wing CF. Hills-built. De-reg 3-4-89	9-21

Also:

❑ G-AWVE*	Jodel DR.1050/M1	65	ex 'Devon', Laindon, S'end, F-BMPQ. CEA-built. CoA 18-5-00	9-21
❑ G-BCMD*	Piper Super Cub 95	52	ex OO-SPF, Netherlands AF R-70, L-18C 52-2455. CoA 31-7-15	9-21

HALSTEAD on the A131 northeast of Braintree
An Auster is *believed* to be still kept in the area at a *private* location.

❑ G-AJUL	Auster J1N Alpha	47	CoA 11-9-81	N4-18

INGATESTONE on the A12 southwest of Chelmsford
Stuart Gowans: Stuart's ambitious Spitfire IX reproduction, with a Merlin and many original parts, is *believed* to be in the general area. The cockpit of C-119G N2700 moved to White Waltham, Berkshire, in 2020.

❑ –	V-S Spitfire IX rep	-	see above	10-13

LAINDON north of the A127, near Basildon
A *private* strip in the area holds a trio of homebuilds. *W&R27* (p56) noted the departure of Jodel G-AWVE for 'Devon'. This may well have been so, but by September 2021 it was to be found at Great Oakley, Essex.

☐ G-ARXP	Luton Minor	65	CoA 17-10-95	10-21
☐ G-BKCN	Currie Wot	87	CoA 7-11-08	10-21
☐ G-BKHY*	Taylor Monoplane	91	CoA 12-8-16	10-21

LAYER MARNEY south of the B1022, east of Tiptree

Gunsmoke Paintball: The aeronautical target 'fleet' has been disposed of: Jet Provost T.3 XN554 travelled to <u>Abbots Ripton</u>, Cambs, in mid-2018; 'JPs' T.3A XN579 and T.4 XP686 departed during 2021 – address unknown; Wessex HU.5 XS488 had gone to the dive centre at Cromhall, Glos, by late 2020 - see Appendix C. Scout XW796 departed to <u>Sutton</u>, Surrey, 19th June 2020; Wessex HU.5 XT467 moved by May 2020 to Wickford, Essex.

Vulcan B.2 XL426 in action, September 2021. *Barry Williams*

LONDON SOUTHEND AIRPORT once Southend Airport, or even Rochford   EGMC

Vulcan Restoration Trust (VRT): XL426 got back into the swing of things in 2021 with several fast taxis. With the delta's 60th birthday and the 70th anniversary of the maiden flight of the prototype both taking place in August 2022, a major celebration will be staged: details of this and other runs will be found on the website. Covid-19 has meant that plans to find a permanent – covered – site for XL426 have not progressed and operations continue from outside Hangar 5, with the VRT engineering team housed within. VRT remains committed to finding a roof for XL426 and maintaining it in taxying condition.
◆ *Regular open days and special events* | **info@avrovulcan.com** | **www.avrovulcan.com**

☐ XL426	Avro Vulcan B.2	62	ex Scampton, Waddington, VDF, VHF, Wadd SF, 50, 617, 27,	
	G-VJET		617, 230 OCU, 617, 230 OCU, 617, 230 OCU, 617, 230 OCU,	
			Scampton, 83. 617 Sqn colours to port, 50 Sqn to stb	[1] 1-22

■ [1] XL426 factoids: Replaced with the Vulcan Display Flight by XH558, it made its last flight 19-12-86, clocking up 6,230 flying hours.

Airport: Airliner storage these days is mostly transient: vastly so during the 'lockdown': only long-termers are given here. **Departures/demises:** HS.146 G-CKTO fuselage to <u>Biggin Hill</u>, Gtr Lon, 19-1-21. Nord Pingouin G-ETME moved to <u>White Waltham</u>, Berks, by 6-20 and was followed by fellow G-OTME by 5-21.

☐ G-ATEX	Victa Airtourer 100	65	CoA 7-3-17	1-20
☐ G-ATPN	Piper Cherokee 140	66	accident 11-2-18, de-reg 3-8-18	10-21
☐ G-ATRP	Piper Cherokee 140	66	damaged 16-10-81. De-reg 10-11-86	1-22
☐ G-AXBF	Beagle Husky 180	69	ex OE-DEW. CoA 20-9-10, de-reg 15-1-16	10-21
☐ G-BGAF	Cessna FA.152	78	Reims-built. CoA 25-6-74, accident 2-6-14, de-reg 28-3-17	10-21
☐ G-BPEL	Piper Warrior 151	74	ex C-FEYM. CoA 8-2-92, de-reg 28-2-02	1-22
☐ G-BVEV	Piper Seneca 200	72	ex N1428T, HB-LLN, D-GHSG, N1428T. CoA 1-6-14	10-21
☐ G-FLTY	Embraer Bandeirante	79	ex G-ZUSS, G-REGA, N711NH, PT-GMH. CoA 5-8-06,	
			de-reg 11-4-06. Rescue training from 24-8-18	1-22

☐ G-JOTC*	HSA HS.146-300QC		74	ex EC-MHR, OO-TAD, G-TNTM, RP-C480, G-TNTM, G-BSLZ, G-6-166. Woodford-built. Arrived 16-5-<u>18</u>	1-22
☐ D-CSAL	Swearingen Metro III		86	ex I-FSAH, N90AG, OY-BPJ, N3117K. Arrived 19-10-18	1-22
☐ VX113	'36' Beagle Terrier 1	G-ARNO	48	ex Auster AOP.6, AAC, 651, 662. CoA 4-10-16	10-21
☐ FAB-108	HSA HS.146-RJ70		96	ex Bolivian Air Force, VT-MDM, G-CDNB, TC-THJ, G-6-230. Woodford-built. Arrived 19-1-18. Engine test rig [1]	1-22

■ **[1]** The '146 has yet to make it all the way to Bolivia.

Skylark Airport Hotel: Aviation Way, opposite what was the Historic Aircraft Museum. HS.748 VH-AMQ was gutted by fire on 28th January 2021 in a suspected arson attack.

☐ VH-AHL	HS HS.748-2/228	69	ex airport, RAAF A10-606	1-22
☐ VH-AMQ	HS HS.748-2/228	68	ex airport, RAAF A10-603. Hulk, burnt 28-1-21	1-22

LONDON STANSTED AIRPORT
EGSS
Deep inside a hangar, Ryan has an instructional 737.

☐ SU-MWC	Boeing 737-683	99	ex Kemble, G-CDKT, SE-DNT. Last flight 4-5-10. Fuselage, Ryanair training school	4-21

Stansted Airport College: On the western edge, near the threshold of Runway 04, has a Challenger for 'Learning on a Jet Plane' as the publicity has it. ◆ *By prior arrangement* **only | www.stanstedairportcollege.ac.uk**

☐ G-CIAU	Canadair Challenger 600	82	ex Inflite, M-IFES, N240AK, N800AB, N50928, C-GBZE. De-reg 24-4-18, rolled in 14-11-18	12-19

NAVESTOCK west of the A128, southwest of Doddinghurst
Moth Minor G-AFOJ moved to <u>Southampton</u>, Hampshire, on 3rd February 2021. Tiger Cub G-MMKT, last noted in February 2015, has been deleted.

NORTH BENFLEET on the A130 and east of Basildon
Bonville Farm (previously Action Park): Of the stored airframes, Warrior G-BSPM had gone by January 2022.
◆ *By prior arrangement* **only**

☐ G-BODX	Beech Duchess	79	ex N67094. CoA 3-9-09, de-reg 22-10-09, fuselage	1-22
☐ XL586	Hawker Hunter T.7	58	ex Melksham, Kemble, Ipswich, Colsterworth, Shawbury, BAe Warton, 1 TWU, 2 TWU, 1 TWU, 229 OCU [1]	1-22

■ **[1]** T.7 XL586 is fitted with the rear-end of XL578 *but* carries XL586 to port and XL578 to starboard.

NORTH WEALD AERODROME off the A414, junction 7, M11 east of Harlow
EGSX
North Weald Airfield Museum: Based at 'Ad Astra' House, located at the former main gate of the station, with a very impressive memorial dedicated to all those who served at 'Weald and another to the Norwegians that were stationed there. The museum spearheaded the Hurricane 'gate guardian' - see below.
◆ *Off Hurricane Way, from North Weald village - ie the B181 -* **not** *via the aerodrome. 'Ad Astra House', 6 Hurricane Way, CM16 6AA |* **01992 523010 | email** *via website |* **www.nwamuseum.co.uk**

☐ 'V7313'	'US-F' Hawker Hurricane FSM	08	BAPC.346. 56 Sqn colours, *Spirit of North Weald* Plinth-mounted, 'guarding' the aerodrome entrance	9-21

Note: *The site is extensive: aircraft are listed below under their nominal 'keepers'. Airworthy aircraft are not listed: coverage is restricted to long-term restorations and stored types.*

Aero Legends: Stage experience flights and carry out some maintenance here but comings and goings of the fleet are fluid. The main Aero Legends operating base is Lashenden, Kent, plus the Vintage Aero restoration centre at Hythe, Kent – which see. ◆ **Private** *working fleet - by prior arrangement* **only | www.aerolegends.co.uk**

Hangar 11 Collection: Airworthy Spitfire PR.XI PL965 (G-MKXI) and P-51D G-SIJJ *Tall in the Saddle* remain based. In glorious Soviet colours, Spitfire IX PT879 (G-PTIX) returned from restoration at Biggin Hill, Gtr Lon, on 20th February 2021.
◆ **Strictly** *by prior appointment* **only | www.hangar11.co.uk**

Heritage Aircraft Trust | Gnat Display Team:. Flies Gnat T.1s XR538 (G-RORI) and 'XR992' (G-MOUR - XS102) from 'Weald.
◆ **Strictly** *by prior appointment* **only | www.gnatdisplayteam.org**

☐ N513X	Folland Gnat T.1	63	ex USA, *Hot Shots* (1991), XP513, RAE, 4 FTS. F/n 4-16	9-21

❑ XR537		Folland Gnat T.1	63	ex Hurn, Cosford 8642M (10-10-83), 'Red Arrows', 4 FTS.	
		G-NATY		CoA 13-7-16. Arrived 12-12-17	9-21
❑ XX841	'EW'	SEPECAT Jaguar T.4	75	ex Tunbridge Wells, Ipswich, Shawbury, 6, 16, T.2, 6, ETPS,	
		VH-UXB		41, 226 OCU. SOC 15-8-05. 6 Sqn colours. Arrived 27-9-18	[1] 10-21
❑ –	'PF179'	Folland Gnat T.1	63	ex Bruntingthorpe, USA (?), Humberside, Binbrook,	
		XR541		Ipswich, Worksop, St Athan 8602M (17-12-78), CFS, 4 FTS	[2] 10-21
❑ E296		Folland Gnat F.1	67	ex N296PS, USA, Indian AF E296. Hindustan-built.	
		G-SLYR		Arrived 1-5-14. Taxying by 9-18	[3] 9-21

■ **[1]** Registered to Miltek Aviation Pty, Melbourne. **[2]** 'PF179' from the Gnat's time with the Painting and Finishing School at St Athan, Wales. **[3]** Registration derived from the nickname 'Sabre Slayer', from victories in the Indo-Pakistan conflicts of 1965 and 1971.

Kennet Aviation: The move to Shuttleworth, Beds - aka Old Warden - was completed in mid-2018. Seafire SX336 (G-KASX) relocated by mid-2017. Airworthy Texan '8084' (G-KAMY) shares its time between here, Old Warden and Yeovilton. Two aircraft remain at 'Weald and are listed under the Weald Aviation 'umbrella' below: Jet Provost 'XD693' and Skyraider 126922. Scout AH.1 G-BWHU took to the air again on 24th June 2020, joining its owners, Dragonfly Aviation. Wasp NZ3909 (G-KANZ) was also transferred to Dragonfly in May 2021 and is listed under Weald Aviation.

C-54 Skymaster Trust: Allan Vogel acquired the C-54 in 2017 and gifted it to the trust in 2019. A restoration programme has been initiated and in March 2021 two of the R2000s burst into life.
◆ *By prior arrangement* only | info@C54skymaster.com | www.savetheskymaster.com

❑ 56498		Douglas C-54Q	45	ex US Navy R5D-3, USAF MAC, BuNo 56498, USAAF	
		N44914		C-54D 42-72525. Arrived 27-9-02. Air Transport Cmd colours	9-21

Weald Aviation Services (WAS): Jet warbirds, historic helicopters and others operate out of the 'Weald' hangars and ramp but as they are not part of a collection or 'fleet' as such are not individually listed; only 'long-termers' only are given here. C-54 56498 is listed under C-54 Skymaster Trust, above. Airworthy Vampire T.11 WZ507 (G-VTII) had moved based to Coventry, Warks, by 2020. As noted above, some aircraft from Tim Manna's Kennet Aviation operation lodge at WAS. See also Shuttleworth, Beds. Scout AH.1 G-BYKJ was recorded as sold in Bahrain 15th August 2019.
◆ **Strictly** *by prior appointment* only | www.wealdaviation.com

❑ G-BVSP		Hunting Jet Provost T.3A		59	ex XM370, 1 FTS, 7 FTS, 1 FTS, 2 FTS. First noted 5-18	10-21
❑ G-BWJW	'R'	Westland Scout AH.1		70	ex Thruxton, Babcary, Lee-on-Solent, Thruxton, XV130, 666.	
		XV130			CoA 25-1-06, de-reg 13-11-12. First noted 9-18	12-21
❑ WV322		Hawker Hunter T.8M		55	ex Exeter, Kemble, Cranwell 9096M, WV322, Kemble,	
		G-BZSE			237 OCU, 764, 736, 809, 764, F.4 92. CoA 19-11-11	[1] 4-21
❑ 'XD693'	'Z-Q'	Hunting Jet Provost		55	ex Cranfield, Winchester, Thatcham, Old Warden,	
		T.1	G-AOBU		Loughborough, Luton, XM129, G-42-1. CoA 13-3-07.	
					2 FTS colours	[2] 10-21
❑ XP884*		W'land Scout AH.1	G-WDST	63	ex M Wallop, Arborfield, M Wallop. Arrived 18-8-21	[3] 12-21
❑ XR759*		EE Lightning F.6		65	ex Haxey, Rossington 'TVI759', Binbrook, 5-11 pool, 56,	
					74, 5. SOC 24-6-88. Cockpit. 56 Sqn c/s. Arrived 16-9-20	[4] 1-22
❑ XT634		Westland Scout AH.1		66	ex Thruxton, M Wallop. Crashed 29-12-15. De-reg 12-7-16.	
		G-BYRX			First noted 5-18	8-19
❑ XZ179	'W'	W'land Lynx AH.7	G-NCKS	78	ex Ipswich, M Wallop, 669. Arrived 9-19	[5] 11-21
❑ XZ188*		Westland Lynx AH.7		78	ex Lyneham, Arborfield, Fleetlands, 4654, 662, 655,	
					665, 655, LCF, 651. 20-10-21	10-21
❑ XZ678*		W'land Lynx AH.7	G-NCKY	82	ex Ipswich, Fleetlands, M Wallop. Arrived 13-10-21	[5] 10-21
❑ ZF595*		EE Lightning T.55		68	ex Bruntingthorpe, USA, Portsmouth, Warrington, Warton,	
					Saudi AF 231,1317, 212, 55-714. Cockpit, arrived 7-20	[6] 10-21
❑ NZ3909		Westland Wasp		66	ex G-KANZ, Thruxton, N Weald, Cranfield, RNZN, XT782,	
		HAS.1	G-CMBE		Wroughton, 829. De-reg 17-4-19	[7] 7-21
❑ 1211		Mikoyan-Gurevich		58	ex Hurn, G-BWUF Duxford, Polish AF. PZL-Mielec-built,	
		MiG-17 *Fresco*	G-MIGG		SBLim-5. North Korean colours	10-21
❑ 126922		Douglas AD-4NA		48	ex G-RAID, F-AZED, La Ferté Alais, Gabon AF,	
	'H-503'	Skyraider ✈	G-RADR		Fr AF No.42, USN 126922. CoA 19-6-17. VA-155, colours	[2] 9-21
❑ 2100884*		Douglas C-47A-75-DL		42	ex Dunsfold, N Weald, Dunsfold, N Weald, G-DAKS	
	'L4-D'	Skytrain	N147DC		(de-reg 5-3-98), , Duxford, '10884', 'KG374', *Airline*	
					'G-AGHY', Dakota III TS423, RAE, Ferranti, Airwork,	
					Gatow SF, 436, 1 HGSU, 42-100884. Long Beach-built.	
					439th TCG, 91st TCS colours, last flown 10-19	[8] 5-21

■ **[1]** Hunter registered to Canfield Hunter Ltd. **[2]** Registered to Tim Manna. **[3]** XP884, registered to Northern Ireland-based A B Godfrey, under restoration for the Army Historic Flight at Middle Wallop, Hampshire. **[4]** Owned by Glenn Edwards – see also ZF595. **[5]** Registered to Bury St Edmunds-based Graham Hinkley, who was last recorded in *W&R17* (p163) with a former Polish MiG at Tibenham, Norfolk. **[6]** Part of a static restoration project for Glenn Edwards, including wings, belly tank, fin and tailplane, and the rear fuselage of ZF596 – see also XR759. **[7]** Wasp registered to Dragonfly Aviation. **[8]** The famous 'G-DAKS' is owned by Aviation Filming – previously Aces High – based at Dunsfold, Surrey.

Also: Yak-52 G-FLSH moved to St Athan, Wales, on 20th November 2018.

❏ G-AHUN	Globe GC-1B Swift	46	ex Thurrock, EC-AJK, OO-KAY, N77764. CoA 4-8-95	5-18
❏ G-AKUP	Luscombe Silvaire 8E	48	ex N2774K	N10-18
❏ G-APTU	Auster 5 Alpha	59	ex Leicester, Sywell, Leicester. CoA 8-6-98	N2-18
❏ G-BDXX	Nord NC.854	54	ex airfield, F-BEZQ. CoA 3-7-96. Off-site	N2-20
❏ G-BIVV	American AA-5	79	ex 'G-PRAT', Elstree, N26979. CoA 18-7-05, de-reg 3-10-08. Rescue training	6-17
❏ G-LUND	Cessna 340 II	73	ex G-LAST, G-UNDY, G-BBNR, N69452. CoA 17-9-06, de-reg 12-4-11	5-21
❏ G-SEMI	Piper Seminole	78	ex G-DENW, N21439. *Lady Gabriella II*. CoA 23-3-08	N2-19
❏ G-TINY	Zlin Z.526F	72	ex OK-CMD. CoA 1-4-09, de-reg 15-2-21	5-21
❏ G-VDIR	Cessna 310R II	75	ex N5091J. Crashed 4-9-05, de-reg 3-6-06	5-21

PURFLEET on A1090 west of the Dartford Bridge
Purfleet Heritage and Military Centre: Incorporating the **Hornchurch Wing** and housed in the incredible Royal Gunpowder Magazine 18th century arsenal, the centre holds an incredible wealth of aviation artefacts.
◆ *Just off the A1090, in Centurion Way, off Tank Hill Road* | **www.purfleet-heritage.com**

RAYLEIGH on the A1095 northwest of Southend-on-Se
The Cockpit Collection: Nigel Towler's collection was located at several sites within the region and this heading was used as 'flag of convenience'. In early 2021 Nigel announced: "It's time for me to pass on the baton. I hope someone will come along with the same passion and dedication as me." All four of the painstakingly restored V-bombers were put up for virtual auction by a Derbyshire-based auction house on 9th March 2021, but it was inconclusive. Nigel hopes to keep the V-bombers together and is also offering substantial stocks of spares.
◆ *Serious purchasers only,* **strictly** *by prior arrangement* | **info@v-bombers.org** | **www.v-bombers.org**

❏ WZ608	DH Vampire T.11	53	ex Market Harboro', Lutterworth, Bitteswell, Woodford, St Athan, 3 CAACU, 5 FTS, 266, Fassberg SF, 11, 5, Wunstorf SF, 266. Hawarden-built. SOC 17-11-67. Cockpit **[1]**	1-22
❏ XD826	Vickers Valiant BK.1	57	ex Cardiff-Wales 'WZ826', Abingdon, Stratford, Cosford, Feltwell 7872M (5-3-65), 543, 232 OCU, 138, 90, 7. Cockpit	1-22
❏ XH560	Avro Vulcan K.2	60	ex Marham, Waddington, 50, Wadd W, 27, Akrotiri Wing, Cott W, Wadd W, Cott W, 230 OCU, 12, MoA, 230 OCU. SOC 5-1-84. Cockpit	1-22
❏ XH669	HP Victor K.2	59	ex Waddington 9092M, *Black Buck* -82, 55, 57, Witt Wing, A&AEE. Written off 21-6-90. Cockpit	1-22
❏ XH670	HP Victor B.2	59	ex East Kirkby, Tattershall, Woodford, Radlett, MoA. SOC 31-10-75. Cockpit	1-22

■ **[1]** The wings of Vampire WZ608 can be found on WZ518 at Sunderland, N&T.

Also: PT-22 G-BPUD was written out of this location in *W&R27* (p59) as leaving for destination unknown in late 2019. The story can be picked up at Tranent, Scotland and it is likely to have headed north as early as 2012.

RIDGEWELL on the A1017 southeast of Haverhill
Ridgewell Airfield Memorial Museum: Run by the Ridgewell Airfield Commemorative Association and housed in USAAF Station 167's former hospital Nissen huts,. this superb museum – which includes the Tony Ince Collection – honours the 381st Bomb Group and the airfield's illustrious past.
◆ *Off the A1017 between Ridgewell and Great Yeldham* | **email** *via website* | **www.rafcamuseum.co.uk**

SHOEBURYNESS east of Thorpe Bay
Defence Science and Technology Laboratory: Last noted in January 2016, Sea King Mk.47 771 had gone by April 2021.

SOUTHEND-ON-SEA

Adventure Island: Marine Parade, Lost City Adventure Golf has a novel putting hazard, while the R22 adorns the pay-booth!

❑ G-AZRX	Gardan Horizon 160	63	ex Great Yarmouth, Tattershall Thorpe (?), F-BLIJ. Crashed 14-8-91, de-reg 21-10-91	1-22
❑ G-BOEX	Robinson R22	88	ex Rochester. Crashed 13-8-02, de-reg 11-10-02	1-22

Also: Restoration of the Brochet continues in the area. To the east of the town, a Europa is stored.

❑ G-AVKB	Brochet Pipistrelle	48	ex F-PFAL. CoA 30-10-96	10-21
❑ G-JERO*	Shaw Europa XS	02	CoA 21-5-07	1-22

STAPLEFORD AERODROME or Stapleford Tawney, on the A113 south of the M11/M25 junction   EGSG

A pair of long-termers are among the thriving light aircraft population.

❑ G-BEXO	Piper Apache 160	55	ex OO-APH, N1176P. CoA 10-10-07, de-reg 4-2-09		11-20
❑ G-BHGP	SOCATA Tobago	80	CoA 29-5-05, de-reg 4-2-07		11-20

Also: The Gazelle AH.1 cache continues to find customers. G-KEMH (XX386) was flying by mid-2020. XX394 had moved to a customer 'on the south coast' by early 2021. XX445 and ZB673 were sold to the Mozambique Air Force as FA-085 and FA-083 respectively and were shipped out by February 2021. ◆ **Not** available for public inspection.

❑ XW848*	'D' Sud Gazelle AH.1	72	ex Colsterworth, Shawbury, M Wallop, 671, 670, ARWS, AETW. Arrived by 8-12	[1] [2]	4-21
❑ XX437	Sud Gazelle AH.1	76	ex Colsterworth, Shawbury, Wattisham, 669, 664, 651, 652, 661, 663, 12 Flt, 661, 12 Flt, 669. Last flown 2-3-05. Arrived 10-12	[1]	9-21
❑ XX438	Sud Gazelle AH.1	76	ex Colsterworth, Shawbury, 666, 663, 665, 664. Last flown 26-2-09. Arrived 5-12	[1]	9-21
❑ XX455	Sud Gazelle AH.1	80	ex Colsterworth, Shawbury, Fleetlands, 652, 661, 655, 663, 669, 659. Last flown 24-1-05. Arrived 5-12	[1]	4-21
❑ XX456	Sud Gazelle AH.1	80	ex Colsterworth, Shawbury, 3 Flt, 669, 7 Flt, 659, 669, 659. Arrived 7-12	[1]	4-17
❑ XX462*	Sud Gazelle AH.1	76	ex Colsterworth, Shawbury, 658, 669, 661, 652, 661, 662, GCF. Arrived by 8-12	[1] [2]	9-12
❑ ZA776	Sud Gazelle AH.1	81	ex Colsterworth, Shawbury, Yeovilton, 847, 3 CBAS. Last flown 29-6-05. Arrived 5-12	[1]	11-17
❑ XZ344*	'Y' Sud Gazelle AH.1	78	ex Colsterworth, Shawbury, 658, 3 Flt, 658, 656, 657, 670, 3 Flt, 656, 3 Flt, 655. Arrived by 8-12	[1] [2]	4-21

■ **[1]** All Westland-built. **[2]** Written out of *W&R24* (p137) at Colsterworth as indeed coming to Stapleford!

STOW MARIES AERODROME north of the B1012 east of South Woodham Ferrers

Stow Maries Great War Aerodrome: Described as "Europe's most complete surviving Great War aerodrome" is an active aerodrome, stages regular events, has an expanding museum and an exceptional 'feel'. The 'Pilots' Mess' consistently gets votes of approval from the *W&R* cake test pilots! The site serves as a memorial to aircrew lost from 37 Squadron at Stow Maries, Rochford and Goldhanger.

An airworthy Fokker Dr.I is being built under PFA - sorry, LAA - aegis and will join the 'fleet' in due course. By March 2021 the rear fuselage of *another* Camel replica was on show; it's far too early for a formal listing. See under St Albans, Herts, for a potential new exhibit.

Former RAF Museum Robinson R22 'G-RAFM' did not migrate here – see Charlwood, Surrey. Nieuport 17 'N1977' (G-BWMJ) departed for the 'private' side of Old Warden, Beds, on 22nd March 2020. Blériot XI 'No.10 (G-BPVE), MS 'N' 'MS824' (G-AWBU) and Fokker E.III '107/15' (G-AVJO) all were roaded to Turweston, Bucks, on 16th November 2021.

◆ *Hackmans Lane, Purleigh, CM3 6RN* | **01245 322644** or **'429134** | **info@stowmaries.org.uk** | **www.stowmaries.org.uk**

❑ G-ABAA*	Avro 504K	c1918	ex Manchester, 'H2311', 9244M, Henlow, Heathrow, RAeS, Hendon, Nash, Brooklands. CoA 11-4-39, de-reg 1-1-39. Arrived 20-1-22	[1]	1-22
❑ -	American AA-5B	77	BAPC.546, ex Hendon, 'G-ROWL', Cabair, Elstree. Cockpit. Arrived 10-19		10-21
❑ '168'*	Sopwith Tabloid replica G-BFDE	80	ex Stafford, Hendon, Cardington, Hendon, Cardington, G-BFDE (CoA 4-6-83, de-reg 8-12-86)	[1]	**due**
❑ '9753'	Airco DH.2 scale rep	15	BAPC.407. Arrived 15-5-16	[2]	1-22

Avro 504K G-ABAA after
arrival from Manchester,
20th January 2022.
Terry Dann

❑ 'A673'	Sopwith Pup replica	76	BAPC.179, ex 'A7317', Northampton, Coventry,		
			Waltham Abbey, N Weald, *Wings* (1976). 37 Sqn colours	[3]	1-22
❑ 'A2943'	Royal Aircraft Factory	14	ex Old Warden, Bicester, New Zealand, ZK-TFZ.		
	BE.2e replica ✈ G-CJZO		Vintage Aviator-built. Arrived 9-9-17	[4]	1-22
❑ 'F235' 'B'	Rep' Plans SE.5a ✈ G-BMDB	88	ex Boscombe Down. Arrived 12-13		10-21
❑ ZE686	Grob Viking TX.1	85	ex Hendon, Syerston, BGA.3099. Cockpit. Arrived 10-19	[5]	10-21
❑ -	Sopwith Camel rep	14	BAPC.414, ex South Africa. Arrived 30-4-15	[6]	10-21
❑ -	'Rocking Nacelle' rep	16	Piloting/gunnery simulator, locally built	[7]	1-22
❑ 'D2263'	Albatros D.Va rep	16	ex Old Warden, ZK-ALB. Vintage Aviator-built.		
	✈ G-WAHT		Arrived 15-10-19	[4]	1-22
❑ -	Gotha G.V rep	16	BAPC.412. Cockpit. Stow Maries-built. First noted 5-16	[8]	10-21

■ **[1]** On loan from the RAF Museum. **[2]** Built by Roger Barrett, taxiable seven-eighths replica. **[3]** Built by Charles Boddington at Sywell for the TV series *Wings*. **[4]** BE.2 and Albatros on loan from Oliver Wulff. **[5]** Viking cockpit *may* be from ZE655. Whichever, it was tested to destruction in mid-1986 in a fatigue rig at Syerston. **[6]** On loan from Bianchi Aviation Film Service Ltd. **[7]** Built by local volunteers using Tiger Moth forward fuselage frames to Major Lanoe George Hawker's scheme for crew familiarisation simulator.

Locally: As *W&R* went to press, three Bianchi Aviation Film Service airframes - MF.1 replica G-BAAF, Travel Air '626/18' (N6268) and an anonymous Fokker Dr.I replica - stored off-site were expected to make the trip to <u>Turweston</u>, Bucks, and this migration has been anticipated. Last noted in July 2019, Whittaker MW-7 G-BPHK has been deleted.

WESTCLIFF-ON-SEA on the A13, south of Southend-on-Sea

Milton Hall Primary School: A Citation fuselage serves as a classroom. ◆ *By prior arrangement **only**.*

❑ G-DWJM	Cessna 550 Citation	81	ex Southend, G-BJIR, N6888C. CoA 18-10-10, de-reg 26-2-14.	
			Fuselage. Arrived 3-16	1-22

WETHERSFIELD on the B1053 west of Halstead

Wethersfield Museum: Ross Stewart has been working on this project since 2012 and has assembled an impressive collection of material on the former airfield. ◆ *Building 301, CM7 4AZ | By prior application **only** | via* **Facebook**

Locally: A 'JP' is kept at a *private* location in the area.

❑ XM473	Hunting Jet Provost T.3A	60	ex Ipswich, Bedford, Norwich Airport 'G-TINY', Halton,	
			8974M (9-6-88), 7 FTS, 1 FTS, 7 FTS, 1 FTS, CFS, 3 FTS, 1 FTS	4-21

WICKFORD on the A129 north of Basildon

Bedlam Paintball: ◆ *By prior arrangement **only*** | **www.bedlampaintball.co.uk**

❑ XT467* 'BF'	Westland Wessex HU.5	65	ex Layer Marney, Hadleigh, Ipswich, Bramley, Odiham,	
			Laarbruch, Brüggen, Gütersloh, 'XR504' 8922M (8-1-87),	
			Wroughton, 848, 771, Wroughton, 707, 781, 845. F/n 5-20	5-20
❑ XZ175*	Westland Lynx AH.7	77	ex Barby, Ipswich, Fleetlands, 25 Flt, 661, 671, LCF,	
			ARWF, 1 FTU. First noted 7-18	5-20

GLOUCESTERSHIRE

Includes the unitary authorities of Bristol and South Gloucestershire

ASTON DOWN AIRFIELD south of the A419 west of Cirencester

Cotswold Gliding Club ◆ *By prior arrangement* only | www.cotswoldgliding.co.uk

❏ WZ796	Slingsby Grasshopper TX.1	52	ex Nympsfield. SOC 27-1-88	11-18
❏ XP493	Slingsby Grasshopper TX.1	61	ex Syerston. Last flight 9-8-84	8-21

BRISTOL

Bristol's City Museum and Art Gallery: In Queen's Road, the Bristol Boxkite 'flies' within the museum.
◆ *Queen's Road, BS8 1RL* | *0117 9223571* | **email** via website | **www.bristolmuseums.org.uk**

❏ –	Bristol Boxkite replica	64	BAPC.40, ex Old Warden, Ford, *Those Magnificent Men...* F G Miles-built	1-22

M-Shed: There are buses, boats, locos and lorries that go 'on steam', an observation gallery provides panoramic views of the incredible 'Floating Harbour', and a 'Flea'. **L-Shed**, contains many treasures from the former Bristol Industrial Museum: behind-the-scenes tours can be arranged by prior application.
◆ *Princes Wharf, Wapping Road, BS1 4RN* | **0117 3526600** | **email** via website | **www.bristolmuseums.org.uk**

❏ G-AEHM	Mignet HM.14 'Flea'	36	ex Wroughton, Hayes, Sydenham (London), West Byfleet, Whitchurch, Bristol. *Blue Finch*. De-reg 12-38	[1]	1-22

■ [1] Built by Harold Dolman of Bristol – no permit issued. On loan from the Science Museum: acquired 9-38.

Bristol Activity Centre: Cribbs Causeway. See comments under Portishead, Somerset.
◆ **Only** *by prior permission* | **www.bristolactivitycentre.co.uk**

City of Bristol College: Advanced Engineering Centre at New Road, near the Parkway Centre. Despite the antiquity of the airframe noted dates, they are *believed* current. ◆ *By prior application* only | **www.cityofbristol.ac.uk**

❏ G-AVDR	Beech Queen Air B80	67	ex Hurn, Shobdon, Exeter, A40-CR, G-AVDR. CoA 30-6-86, de-reg 18-5-90.	3-16
❏ N309LJ	Learjet 25	69	ex Kemble, Staverton, N309AJ, N19FN, N17AR, N3UC, N6GC, N242WT, N954FA, N954GA. Arrived 11-2-16	3-16
❏ TY-SAM	HSA HS.125-700A	83	ex Kemble, N46WQ, N46WC. Fuselage. First noted 9-15	12-15

Pytch: On the Brislington Trading Estate, this events and PR organisation took delivery of a Boeing 727 from Kemble – sorry, Cotswold – in February 2021. ◆ *By prior application* only | **https://pytch.co.uk**

❏ VP-CMN*	Boeing 727-46	67	ex Kemble, VR-CLM, VR-CBE, N4245S, D-AHLQ, JA8325. Last flown 2011. Fuselage, arrived 27-2-21	10-21

University of Bristol, Faculty of Engineering: In the Queen's Building, University Walk, near Tyndalls Park.
◆ *By prior application* only | **www.bris.ac.uk/engineering**

❏ XZ649	Westland Lynx AH.7	80	ex Farnborough, Boscombe Down, 657	[1]	7-18

■ [1] Lynx XZ649 is fitted with the boom of XZ646.

Vanguard Storage: Dramatically mounted within the atrium of the Russell Town Avenue facility, on the A420 to the east of the city centre, is a Lightning. See also Vanguard's Greenford, Gtr Lon, premises. **www.vanguardstorage.co.uk**

❏ XP745	'H' EE Lightning F.3	64	ex Greenford, Boulmer 8453M (25-9-75), Leconfield, 29, 56. 56 Sqn colours. Arrived 5-19, unveiled 9-19	1-22

CHELTENHAM

In the area, **Nick Parker** has a Scimitar cockpit.

❏ XD215	V-S Scimitar F.1	57	ex Ottershaw, Foulness, Culdrose A2573 (9-10-67), 764B, 800, 803, A&AEE. Cockpit	1-19

CHIPPING CAMPDEN on the B4081 north of Stow on the Wold

Mike Pyment: At a *private* location, the Comet cockpit/flight sim is *believed* extant. ◆ *By prior permission* **only**

❏ XV814	DH Comet 4	58	ex Boscombe D, RAE, MSA, Air Ceylon, BOAC G-APDF.	
	G-APDF		Hatfield-built. Last flown 28-1-93, acquired 13-8-97. Cockpit	10-15

COLEFORD on the B4228 east of Monmouth

An Auster is under restoration in the locality at a *private* workshop.

☐ G-BDFX*   Taylorcraft Auster 5   45   ex Oaksey Park, Kemble, Oaksey Park, F-BGXG, TW517,
                                    661. Crashed 10-10-93. First noted 7-<u>17</u>   4-21

COTSWOLD AIRPORT or Kemble, on the A429 southwest of Cirencester   EGBP

***Note:** The site is large and aircraft are given under nominal 'keepers'.*

Bristol Britannia XM496 Restoration Society: Lockdown in 2020 provided time to carry out a refurbish to Regulus. See the website for special events. ◆ *On the airport site, follow the signs marked 'XM496'* | **email** via website | **www.XM496.com**

☐ XM496   Bristol Britannia C.1   60   ex Lanseria, EL-WXA, 9Q-CJH, CU-T120, Afrek, G-BDUP,
                             G-BDUP   Kemble, XM496 99/511. Short-built. *Regulus*, RAF c/s   [1]   1-22

■ **[1]** Factoids: First flown at Sydenham, 24-8-60, delivered to Lyneham 17-9-60; made last-ever flight by a 'Brit', into Kemble, 14-10-97 – the arrival footage on the website is incredible!

Phantom FG.1 XT597 and FGR.2 XT905 after arrival from Wymeswold, July 2021. *Ian Topham*

British Phantom Aviation Group (BPAG): Relocated from Wymeswold, Leics, during 2021 – a massive task, greatly facilitated by the warm welcome from Cotswold Airport's management. With the 'birds' safely on site, work turned to reassembly and inspection, establishing workshop and store facilities, and planning visitor premises. A successful crowd-funding campaign has enabled the first phase of building work.

F-4J(UK) ZE360 will join the fleet in due course: at present is undergoing restoration at Manston, Kent - which see.

◆ *At present* **only** *by prior arrangement – keep an eye on the website* | **contact@bpag.co.uk** | **www.bpag.co.uk**

☐ XT597*   McD Phantom FG.1   66   ex Wymeswold, Bentwaters, Boscombe, BDAC, DERA,
                               A&AEE, Bedford, NATC Patuxent River, USN.
                               Last flight 28-1-94. Arrived 21-7-21   [1]   1-22

☐ XT905*   'P'   McD Phantom FGR.2   68   ex Wymeswold, Bentwaters, North Luffenham,
                               Coningsby 9286M (7-5-00), 74, 228 OCU, 31, 17, 31, 14,
                               17, 228 OCU. Arrived 29-6-21   [2]   1-22

■ **[1]** XT597 made the last-ever flight by a British Phantom; it is owned by Mark Abbott. **[2]** Owned by BPAG's chairman, Paul Wright.

The Buccaneer Aviation Group: (TBAG, pronounced, lovingly, as Tea-Bag!) The group relocated from its previous base at Bruntingthorpe in August 2020; the moving of its two complete Buccaneers making an imposing - and expensive - convoy. As with BPAG – above – TBAG's members set to the enormous operation with determination and have settled into create workshop/store and plans for visitor events. ◆ *At present* **only** *by prior* arrangement | **michaelovers@btinternet.com** | Facebook: **Tbagbruntingthorpe** | **www.the-buccaneer-aviation-group.com**

❑ XW544*	'O'	Blackburn Buccaneer S.2B	72	ex Bruntingthorpe, Shawbury, Cosford 8857M (21-5-85), Shawbury, 16, 15. 16 Sqn c/s. Arr 21-8-20, first taxi 3-7-21	[1]	1-22
❑ XW550*		Blackburn Buccaneer S.2B	73	ex Bridgnorth, B'thorpe, West Horndon, Stock, St Athan, 16, 15. SOC 18-8-80. Cockpit. 16 Sqn c/s. Arrived by 9-21	[2]	1-22
❑ XX894*	'020'	Blackburn Buccaneer S.2B	75	ex Bruntingthorpe, Farnborough, Kemble, Bruntingthorpe, St Athan, 208, 16, 12, 208, 12. Last flown 7-4-94. 809 Sqn colours, *Norma*. Taxiable. Arrived 21-8-20	[3]	1-22

■ **[1]** XW544 owned by Rob Goldstone. **[2]** XW550 owned by Francis Wallace and TBAG. **[3]** XX894 owned by Colin Robinson; on 27-2-91 it destroyed an An-12 *Cub* on the ground at Shaykh Mazhar, Iraq.

Resource Group: Maintains a fleet of instructional airframes. ◆ *By prior arrangement* only. | **www.resourcegroup.co.uk**

❑ G-BIBG		Sikorsky S-76A II+	80	ex Aberdeen, Norwich, 5N-BCE, G-BIBG. CoA 18-8-09, de-reg 8-12-09. Arrived 13-8-13.	4-20
❑ D-ASDB		VFW 614	77	ex St Athan, Copenhagen, Muk Air OY-RRW, D-ASDB, Luftwaffe 17+03, D-BABS	4-20
❑ N19EK	'K'	HS Dominie T.1	66	ex Cranwell, XS737, 55, 6 FTS, 1 ANS, HS. Arrived 14-5-11	4-20
❑ N19UG	'H'	HS Dominie T.1	65	ex Cranwell, XS730, 55, 3 FTS, 6 FTS, 1 ANS. Arrived 14-6-11	4-20
❑ 80+55		Bölkow Bö 105M	~	ex St Athan, HEER	4-20
❑ 80+77		Bölkow Bö 105M	~	ex Hoofddorp, HEER	4-20

Also: 'Jumbo' *Victor Bravo* is owned by Kemble Air Services and is parked next to the tower on its own hardstanding. It is planned to turn it into a cinema/conference centre. Storage and parting out of airliners is Kemble's forte: most of this done by **Air Salvage International**. Much of this activity is too transitory for *W&R*; only long-term items are listed here. This process produces shed-loads of cockpit and flightdeck sections, the majority of which must go *somewhere*! See Henley-on-Thames, Oxfordshire, for a rare 'escapee' – the flight deck of 747 G-BYGB. Others held since 2020 may well be Covid-19 'refugees': any staying longer will have to await *W&R29*.

    Departures: Bandeirante 'G-FIRE' (SX-BNL) gave up the ghost in the fire pits circa mid-14; **Boeing 727** fuselage VP-CMN departed for Bristol, Glos, 27-2-21; **Cessna** 150M G-BOVS had gone by 10-21; **HS.146** cockpit G-CGYU, last noted 10-17, has been deleted; **Jet Provost** T.5A XW358 arrived from Lee-on-Solent, Hants; it was dismantled and 'cut' to a truncated fuselage - more than a cockpit section; it departed to 'Berkshire' by 6-20; **JetStar** HB-JGK was scrapped 10-20; **Premier I** G-OOMC cockpit had gone by 10-21; **Sioux** AH.1 XT140 departed 30-4-16, destination/fate unknown. Last noted in the fire pits in 4-15 Aztec 'G-ESKY' (G-BADI) has been deleted.

◆ *By prior arrangement* only | https://airsalvage.co.uk | **www.cotswoldairport.com**

❑ G-BYGA*		Boeing 747-436	98	ex Heathrow, BA. Arrived 8-9-20, de-reg 21-1-21		12-21
❑ G-CIVB*		Boeing 747-436	93	ex Heathrow, BA. 'Retro' BA colours. Arrived 8-10-20. De-reg 30-10-20 – see above	[1]	1-22
❑ G-CIVN*		Boeing 747-436	97	ex Heathrow, BA. Arrived 16-4-20, de-reg 21-1-21		12-21
❑ G-EMBC*		Embraer EMB-145EP	97	ex Exeter, PT-SYU. De-reg 13-4-17. Cockpit, first noted 9-19		12-21
❑ G-JRSL		Agusta 109E	98	CoA 22-12-01, de-reg 6-7-00. Hulk, rescue training		4-19
❑ G-MKGA		Boeing 747-2R7F	79	ex MK Airlines, 9G-MKL, N926FT, N639FE, N809FT, EI-BTQ, LX-DCV. De-reg 30-9-15		12-21
❑ G-WFFW		Piper Warrior II	81	ex N8342A. CoA 12-2-10. First noted 10-1		10-18
❑ M-FTOH		Boeing 727-269	80	ex N169KT, 9K-AFA. Arrived 29-6-16, de-reg 11-7-16		12-21
❑ 2-MMTT		Boeing 727-76	66	ex M-FAHD, VP-BAB, N682G, N10XY, N8043B, VH-TJD. Arrived 7-12-18		12-21
❑ PH-ADO*		Bombardier CRJ-900LR	07	ex S5-AAL. Arrived 15-11-19, broken up 7-20. Forward fuse		12-21
❑ N19CU	'E'	HS Dominie T.1	65	ex Cranwell, XS728, 55, 6 FTS, RAFC, 6 FTS, 1 ANS. Arr 13-6-11		7-21
❑ EZ-A107*		Boeing 717-200	05	ex Turkmenistan AL. Arr 3-10-18, broken up 3-21. Cockpit		12-21
❑ LZ844	'UP-X'	V-S Spitfire V	43	ex Australia, 'R6915', Auckland, New Guinea, cr 12-12-43, RAAF A58-213, LZ844 n/s. CBAF-built. Arr 11-7-11. Stored		8-13
❑ XE665	'876'	Hawker Hunter T.8C ⟶ G-BWGM	55	ex Exeter, G-BWGM (CoA 24-6-98, de-reg 16-3-11), Shawbury, Yeovilton, FRADU, 764, Jever SF, 118. Squires Gate-built. Displayed at the AV8 Cafe		10-21
❑ XH134		EE Canberra PR.9 ⟶ G-OMHD	59	ex Midair, Marham, 39, 1 PRU, 39, 58, MoA. Short-built. CoA 13-8-15. 'Silver' scheme	[2]	10-21
❑ XH135		EE Canberra PR.9	59	ex Marham, 39, 1 PRU, 39, 13, 58, MoA, HS. Short-built		10-21
❑ 'XR540'		Folland Gnat T.1 XP502	62	ex Ipswich, St Athan 8576M, 4 FTS. 'Red Arrows' colours. Displayed		10-21

■ **[1]** Owned by Kemble Air Services. **[2]** Registered to Kemble Airfield Estates 9-16: reported bound for Indian Air Force Vintage Flight.

DURSLEY on the A4135 southwest of Stroud

Retro Track and Air Ltd: Specialist engine overhaul and airframe company equally at home with historic Grand Prix cars.
◆ **Strictly** *by prior arrangement only* | **www.retrotrackandair.com**

❑ N5719	Gloster Gladiator II	38	ex Narvik, 263.	
	G-CBHO		Abandoned in Norway 22-5-40	[1] N7-19
❑ P8208	V-S Spitfire IIb	41	ex Oxford, Severn estuary, 52 OTU, 1 CACU, 1 CACF, 303.	
	G-RRFF		CBAF-built. Crashed 26-1-43	[1] N6-21
❑ TE566	V-S Spitfire IX	45	ex Australia, VH-IXT, South Africa ZU-SPT, cr 25-4-02,	
	VH-IXT		Duxford, G-BLCK, Audley End, Ludham, St Leonards on Sea,	
			Duxford, Israel, IDF/AF 20-32 4X-FOB, Czech AF, 312, TE566.	
			Arrived 11-7-11. Stored	3-13
❑ WP859	'E' DHC Chipmunk T.10	52	ex Kemble, 8 AEF, 4 AEF, Lpl UAS, PFS, AOTS, 1 ITS, Bri UAS,	
	G-BXCP		4 SoTT, 663, RAFC. De-reg 18-4-17	6-18
❑ GA-43	Gloster Gamecock II	28	ex Finland, Finnish AF	
	G-CGYF			[1] N6-19

■ [1] Registered to Retro Track and Air.

Chris Wiltshire: *Should* have a Vampire cockpit in the locality.

❑ XD452	'66' DH Vampire T.11	54	ex Chester, Whixhall, Whitchurch, London Colney, Shawbury,	
			7990M (19-2-68), 3 FTS, 7 FTS, 1 FTS, 8 FTS, 5 FTS.	
			Hawarden-built. Cockpit	8-12

FILTON south of the M5 at Patchway, north of Bristol

Aerospace Bristol / Bristol Aero Collection Trust: Hangar 16M, a 1916 structure last used by the Western Air Ambulance, was inaugurated as the **Conservation-in-Action Workshop** on 15th July 2021 – see below.
◆ *Hayes Way, Patchway, BS34 5BZ* | **info@aerospacebristol.org** | **www.aerospacebristol.org**

❑ 'G-EASQ'	Bristol Babe III replica	72	BAPC.87, ex Kemble, Banwell, Stoke, Hemswell, Cleethorpes,		
			Selby. Acquired 11-94, arrived by 12-12		1-22
❑ G-ALRX	Bristol Britannia 101	53	ex Kemble, Banwell, Boscombe Down, WB473 / VX447,		
			Crashed 4-2-54, de-reg 5-4-54. Cockpit.		
			Acquired 23-12-13, arrived by 12-12		1-22
❑ G-BOAF	BAC/Sud Concorde 102	79	ex BA, G-N94AF, G-BFKX. CoA 11-6-04. De-reg 11-6-04.		
			Flew in 26-11-03. Rolled in 7-2-17	[1]	1-22
❑ -	BAC/Sud Concorde EMU	~	ex Kemble, Brooklands. Test shell, nose. Acquired 1997		1-22
❑ 'A1742'	Bristol Scout replica	62	BAPC.38, ex Old W', Solihull, Norwich, Lowestoft, Duxford,		
			St Mawgan, St Athan, Colerne, Weeton. Arrived by 3-17	[2]	1-22
❑ 'A7288'	'7' Bristol F.2B replica	10	BAPC.387. Unveiled 10-7-10	[3]	1-22
❑ –	Bristol Beaufighter	c42	BAPC.463, ex Hendon, East Fortune, Hendon, Duxford,		
			Hendon, Cranfield. Cockpit. First noted 7-16	[4]	1-22
❑ XF785	Bristol 173 Srs 1	52	ex Kemble, Cosford, Henlow 7648M (10-7-60), G-ALBN		
	G-ALBN		(de-reg 21-7-60). Arrived 8-1-13	[5]	1-22
❑ XL824	Bristol Sycamore HR.14	57	ex Stafford, Manchester, Henlow 8021M (11-6-68), Wroughton, CFS, 1564 Flt, 103, 284. Arrived 2015		1-22
❑ ZD610	'000' HS Sea Harrier F/A.2	85	ex Bruntingthorpe, Dunsfold, Yeovilton, 800, 899, 801,		
	and '126'		800, 899, 801, 899. Arrived 30-9-15, airlifted on site 3-17.		
			801 Sqn colours to stb, 800 to port	[6]	1-22

■ [1] *Alpha-Fox* factoids: Last UK Concorde built, first flown at Filton 20-4-74 and made the type's last-ever flight, back to its birthplace, on 26-11-03. Withdrawn from British Airways service 24-10-03, total hours 18,257, landings 6,045. It is on long-term loan from British Airways. [2] Scout 'A1742' is a fine static replica restored by Keith Williams and Mike Thorne. [3] F.2B replica built by GKN-Aerospace and Rolls-Royce apprentices for the BAC 100 celebrations, 2010. It is *probably* BAPC.387 [4] Beaufighter cockpit on loan from RAF Museum; thought to be from a 1941-1942-built Merlin XX Mk.IIf. [5] Bristol 173 was on loan from the RAF Museum, title has been transferred to AB. [6] 'SHAR' on loan from Gary Spoors - see also his main reference at St Athan, Wales. It was airlifted across the former airfield from the Brabazon hangar storage site by an RAF Chinook 3-17. Its Dunsfold origins might seem at odds with the 'Bristol' theme, but its exceptional Bristol Siddeley Pegasus engine is 100% Filton.

Deep Store / Conservation-in-Action Workshop: As noted above, this facility was opened in July 2021: a viewing gallery allows inspection of the Bolingbroke and Freighter. Other items are 'deep stored' and not available for viewing. These airframes were reviewed in 2020-21. The cockpit of Beagle 206 G-ATDD and a Tornado F.3 SIM departed for Sunderland, N&T, arriving on 16th September 2021. Whittaker MW-4 G-MBTH was offered for disposal in February 2021 and it was returned to its donor with plans to be displayed within the workshop of a Gloucestershire-based maintenance company.

As the last aircraft designed, built and *flown* at Filton, by former BAe engineer Mike Whittaker, the removal of *Tango-Hotel* passes up an exhibit of great local significance, not to mention small – 'hangable' even – size and adding another era to the collection. Roe Biplane replica G-ROEI returned to the Brooklands Museum off-site store circa 2017, before settling upon Brooklands, Surrey. With several locally-built HS 146 'barrels' on show, the unfinished HS.146 RJX100 cockpit and sections (Set 396, c/n E3396) a refugee from the abortive Manchester museum revamp of 2007, was handed over to BAE Systems. With an example already on show, Sycamore HR.14 XJ917 made the transit to Sunderland, N&T, on 3rd June 2021 as part of the 'Sycamore Shuffle' - full details under Sunderland. Jindivik A92-708 moved to Newark, Notts, on 28th June 2021.

❑	-*		Bristol F.2B	41	BAPC.386. ex USA, Weston-on-the-Green. Fuselage frame, arrived 2-10-20		1-22
❑	9048	'YO-T'	Bristol Bolingbroke IV	41	ex Kemble, Los Angeles, Chino, RCAF, 7 BGS, 3 BGS, 8(BR). SOC 21-8-46. Fairchild Canada-built. Arrived 25-7-06, acquired 11-19. Workshop	[1]	1-22
❑	NZ5911		Bristol 170 Mk.31M	53	ex Ardmore, NZ ZK-EPG, RNZAF NZ5911, ZK-BJP,		
			G-AMPK		NZ5911, G-AMPK. Last flight 31-8-78. Arrived 28-12-17		1-22

■ **[1]** Donated by Graham Kilsby in honour of his late father W K Kilsby.

Rolls-Royce Heritage Trust - Bristol Branch: The **Sir Roy Fedden Heritage Centre** keeps an exceptional array of engines, and supportive material, large and small. As well as Bristol and Bristol Siddeley and Rolls-Royce (from 1966), de Havilland and Blackburn powerplants are also represented.
◆ *By prior arrangement* only | www.rolls-royce.com/about/heritage-trust

No.**2152 Squadron Air Cadets:** Pine Grove. The unit *should* still have a Cherokee cockpit in use as a simulator.
❑	G-BOXY	Piper Archer II	78	ex Netherthorpe, N3073D. Crashed 24-7-02, de-reg 22-10-02. Cockpit	6-16

GLOUCESTER

Gloster Aviation Club: Clive Davies and friends are hard at work on the collection of cockpits. (Clive is a part owner of Canberra WT333 at 'Brunters' – which see. *W&R27* (p65) relocated Lightning ZF590 to Bruntingthorpe, Leics, this was not the case. ◆ **Not** *available for public inspection.*
❑	XE339	'149'	Hawker Sea Hawk FGA.6	55	ex Dunsfold, Lee-on-Solent, Culdrose A2635, Halton 8156M (19-1-71), FRU, 801, 803, 800. AWA-built. Cockpit	1-22
❑	XF383		Hawker Hunter F.6	56	ex Kidlington, North Scarle, Wittering 8706M (19-1-82), Kemble, 12, 216, 237 OCU, 4 FTS, 229 OCU, 65, 111, 263. AWA-built. 65 Sqn colours. Cockpit	1-22
❑	XG331		EE Lightning F.1	59	ex Quedgeley, Staverton, Hucclecote, Barton, Chelford, Long Marston, Innsworth, Staverton, Foulness, Warton, A&AEE. Last flight 28-9-66. Cockpit	1-22
❑	ZF590		EE Lightning F.53	68	ex Upwood, Binbrook, Lewes, *Wing Commander* (1999), Portsmouth, Warrington, Warton, Saudi AF 220, 53-679, G-27-49. Last flown 22-1-86. Cockpit	1-22

Also: A Hunter cockpit is *believed* still kept at a *private* location in the general area.
❑	XX466	'830'	Hawker Hunter T.7	59	ex Guernsey, Predannack A2651 [2], Culdrose SAH A2738 (15-5-86), FRADU, 1 TWU, Jordan AF, Saudi AF 70-616, HSA, XL620, 74, 66. Cockpit. Arrived 9-6-16	9-16

GLOUCESTERSHIRE AIRPORT or Staverton   EGBJ
Jet Age Museum: Operated by the **Gloucestershire Aviation Collection**, tells the story of the jet engine, Gloster aircraft and the aerospace industry of the region. The second display hall was completed by the autumn of 2021 and fund-raising for its fitting out was ongoing: it is planned to open it to the public by the time *W&R28* is published. During October 2021 a pair of exhibits took to the air, albeit temporarily. On the 13th Javelin XA634 was manoeuvred off the airport site and into the museum compound, care of a low loader and cranes. A week later, Meteor NF.14 was suspended from a a jib – from *Ellis Crane Hire* no less – to bring it within the fold.

The McBroom Arion hang-glider was donated to the British Hang-Gliding Museum - see Weston-super-Mare, Somerset - on 10th December 2021. Meteor T.7 WF784 moved to St Athan, Wales, on 2nd September 2021 in exchange for the ownership transfer of TT.20 'WM366' - see below. Canberra TT.18 WK126 is destined for St Athan, Wales, in early 2022: this move has been anticipated.
◆ *Meteor Business Park, Cheltenham Road East, GL2 9QL* | **01452 260078** | **email** via website | **https://jetagemuseum.org**

❏ G-AWZU		HS Trident 3B-101	71	ex Basingstoke, Stansted, Heathrow, BA, BEA. CoA 3-7-85, de-reg 18-3-86. *Tina*. Forward fuselage, BEA colours to port, BA to stb. Arrived 28-11-13	[1] 1-22
❏ 'J7904'		Gloster Gamecock reproduction	97	BAPC.259, ex Staverton, Dursley, Staverton. Project unveiled 9-8-98, arrived 10-13. 43 Sqn colours	[2] 1-22
❏ N5914		Gloster Gladiator II	40	ex Dursley, Norway, 263. Shot down 2-6-40. Recovered 12-98, arrived on-site 20-11-13. Frame	[3] 1-22
❏ 'V6799'	'SD-X'	Hawker Hurricane FSM	68	BAPC.72, ex 'V7767', Hurn, Brooklands, N Weald, Baginton, Stoneleigh, *Battle of Britain* (1968). Acquired 2-7-97. 501 Sqn colours	1-22
❏ -		Airspeed Horsa replica	16	BAPC.383. Cockpit, built on site	1-22
❏ -		Hawker Typhoon I	c42	BAPC.363, ex Staverton, Twyford, Chippenham. Gloster-built. Forward fuselage, arrived 26-8-17	[4] 1-22
❏ 'W4041/G'		Gloster E28/39 FSM	05	BAPC.331, on site 2003	[5] 1-22
❏ EE425		Gloster Meteor F.3	45	ex Yatesbury, Earls Colne, Andrewsfield, PEE Foulness (16-2-56), 206 AFS, 210 AFS, 206 AFS, 63, 266, 1, 222. Cockpit. Acquired 1-00. Moved back on site 5-4-12	1-22
❏ VW453	'Z'	Gloster Meteor T.7	49	ex Innsworth 8703M, Salisbury Plain, Hullavington, Takali, 604, 226 OCU, 203 AFS. SOC 12-6-57. Arr 22-4-13	[6] 1-22
❏ WH364		Gloster Meteor F.8	52	ex Kemble 8169M (23-8-71), 85, Takali C&TTS, Idris SF, Takali SF, 601. Arrived 10-9-03. 601 Sqn colours	1-22
❏ 'WM366'		Gloster Meteor TT.20	52	ex Bruntingthorpe, Enstone, Lasham, Aborfield, FRL, NF.11, 68, 264. AWA-built. Suez stripes. Arrived 16-4-14 - see above	[7] 1-22
	WM234				
❏ WS807	'N'	Gloster Meteor NF(T).14	54	ex Kemble, Staverton, Bentham, Staverton, Yatesbury, Watton 7973M (6-7-67), Kemble, 1 ANS, 2 ANS, NF.14 n/s. AWA-built. Arrived 7-97. 46 Sqn colours	1-22
❏ XA634	'L'	Gloster Javelin FAW.4	56	ex Leeming, Shawbury, Colerne, Melksham 7641M (2-6-60), Gloster. 228 OCU colours. Arrived 25-3-15	1-22
❏ XE664		Hawker Hunter F.4	55	ex Marlborough, ?, HSA, 26. SOC 14-4-59. Squires Gate-built. Cockpit. Acquired 21-2-99. Moved on site 5-4-12	[8] 1-22
❏ XH903	'G'	Gloster Javelin FAW.9	58	ex Bentham, Staverton, Hucclecote, Innsworth 7938M (10-8-67), Shawbury, 5, 33, 29, 33, FAW.7, 23. Acquired 19-5-93. 33 Sqn colours	[9] 1-22
❏ XM569		Avro Vulcan B.2	63	ex Bentham, Staverton, Enstone, Cardiff, 44, Wadd Wing, 27, Cott Wing, 27. SOC 21-1-83. Arrived 6-2-97. Cockpit	[10] 1-22
❏ XW264		HS Harrier T.2	69	ex Hucclecote, Innsworth, Dowty, Boscombe D, HSA. Damaged 11-7-70. Acquired 28-6-94. Cockpit	[11] 1-22
❏ -*		Folland Gnat T.1 CIM	c62	ex Innsworth. Procedures trainer., forward cockpit. Folland-built. Arrived circa 2014	[12] 1-22

■ **[1]** Donated by Gary Spoors - see also St Athan, Wales. **[2]** Gamecock is fitted with a Jupiter IV, on loan from the RAF Museum. **[3]** On 2-6-40, flown by P/O J L Willkie, N5914 was shot down by a 1/ZG 76 Bf 110 flown by Lt Helmut Lent; Willkie was killed. **[4]** Typhoon salvaged from a yard in Chippenham in 1998, the Typhoon's restoration is dedicated to the memory of Michele Clarke. **[5]** E28/39 FSM used the mouldings for the Farnborough, Hampshire, and Lutterworth, Leics, examples. **[6]** VW453 acquired for JAM in 2013 by Tony Mackinnon and Martin Clarke. **[7]** A complex composite, with the centre section, wings and tailplane from ex Israeli DF/AF 1953-built NF.13 4X-FNA / 5616, ex RAF WM366, A&AEE and RRE; the cockpit from TT.20 WM234 (service history quoted above); and rear fuselage of F.8 VZ462 from Biggin Hill. Previously owned by Gary Spoors, title was transferred to Jet Age in exchange for Meteor WF784 in 8-21. **[8]** Hunter F.4 XE664, original nose, on loan from Bob Kneale. The remainder of XE664 was refurbished in 1959 as a T.8 for the FAA with a new cockpit. In 1969 it was rebuilt for the Singapore ADC as T.75 514 (G-9-293 allocated) and is preserved in New Zealand. **[9]** Javelin on loan from the RAF Museum. **[10]** Vulcan cockpit is on loan from Gary Spoors and David Price, via JAM. **[11]** The wings of XW264 are on XV798 at Hucknall, Notts. **[12]** One that got away, with thanks to Paul Griffiths. This came from 2342 (Innsworth) Sqn, Air Training Corps.

Airport: By April 2020 Taylor G-BIAX and Fournier G-BLWH had gone and Seneca G-BSGK was scrapped. Aztec G-BAUI, Duke G-IASL, Agusta 109 'G-OPAS' (D-HCKV) all with the fire crews; and Robin G-BGBA were all cleared out by November 2021.

❏ G-ATHT		Victa Airtourer 115	65	CoA 24-9-16. First noted 7-19	4-20
❏ G-TMHK		Piper Tomahawk 112	78	ex G-GALL, G-BTEV, N9315T. CoA 1-6-12	1-22
❏ N477PM		Piper Navajo	~	De-reg 31-8-13. First noted 9-19	1-22
❏ WL349	'Z'	Gloster Meteor T.7	52	ex Kemble, 1 ANS, 2 ANS, CFE, 229 OCU. SOC 22-6-76. Arrived 1992. Stored	[1] 11-21

■ **[1]** WL349 owned by Gloucestershire Airport.

MARSHFIELD on the A420 east of Bristol

A homebuild Jodel is stored at a *private* location in the *general* area.

❑ G-BMEH*	Jodel D.150 Special	87	CoA 21-5-08	1-22

MORETON-IN-MARSH on the A44 northeast of Cheltenham

Wellington Aviation Museum: The collection deals in depth with RAF Moreton-in-Marsh but its displays take in a fascinating sweep of wartime artefacts and details. ◆ *Bourton Road, GL56 0HB* | **www.wellingtonaviation.org**

The Fire Service College: Purpose-built rigs are the teaching aid of choice at the site, including a helicopter (referred to as a 'Merlin') and a jetliner (called a '737'). The facility has taken on the training of MoD fire personnel – previously carried out at Manston, Kent – hence the addition of more military hardware. Last noted in October 2014 the hulks of Cessnas 172K G-AZDZ and 320 have been deleted. ◆ *By prior arrangement* **only** | **www.fireservicecollege.ac.uk**

❑ XP680		Hunting Jet Provost T.4	62	ex St Athan 8460M (21-12-75), CAW, 6 FTS. 'Crash' scene	8-17
❑ XZ187*		Westland Lynx AH.7	78	ex Lyneham, Arborfield, Fleetlands, 655, 667, 655, 667,	
				655, 651, 654. Arrived 3-21	10-21
❑ XZ207*		Westland Lynx AH.7	79	ex Lyneham, Arborfield, Fleetlands, 652, 669, 655, 654.	
				Crashed 17-4-00. Cabin. Arrived 24-8-21	9-21
❑ ZE165*	'GE'	Panavia Tornado F.3	86	ex Manston. Shawbury, 43. Arrived 30-11-20	11-21
❑ ZG773*		Panavia Tornado GR.4	92	ex Boscombe Down, Warton, BAE Systems/BAe, GR.1.	
				Last flown 20-1-16. Arrived 2020	11-21
❑ TAD.013*	'A'	Westland Lynx	77	ex Lyneham, Arborfield, Fleetlands, Almondbank, Wroughton,	
		HC.28 G-BFDV		Qatar Police QP-30, G-BFDV, de-reg 18-7-78. Arr 24-8-21	11-21

STONEHOUSE on the A419 west of Stroud

Tile Trader: On the Reyford Industrial Estate displays an unflown VP-2. **www.tiletraderstroud.co.uk**

❑ G-BEFV*	Evans VP-2	c89	de-reg 6-12-95. First noted 6-20	8-21

TETBURY on the A433 southwest of Cirencester

Military Mementos: A military artefact specialist buying, selling and trading. The cockpits were up for sale via a virtual auction, bids closing in May 2021. ◆ *By prior arrangement* **only** | **www.militarymementos.com**

❑ XE982	DH Vampire T.11	55	ex Newbridge, Weston, Dunkeswell, Hereford, St Athan	
			7564M (15-5-58), RAFC. Hawarden-built. Cockpit.	2-20
❑ J-1573	DH Venom FB.50	55	ex Newbridge, Portarlington, Hurn, HB-RVB, G-BMOB,	
	G-VICI		Swiss AF. Swiss-built. CoA 24-11-99, de-reg 5-3-13.	
			Cockpit.	8-21

TEWKESBURY on the A38 north of Gloucester

To be found at a *private* yard in the *general* area in June 2020 were no less than eleven, tightly packed Westland WG.30s. A concentration of the UK's worst-ever helicopter programme. Exhaustive research by Mark Presswood has pinned down their pedigrees, the bulk being from the ill-fated Indian order. Previous editions of *W&R* have mentioned the possibility of former Indian machines, held at Biggin Hill, Gtr London, and a farm in the Redhill, Surrey, area. Other than an example that may still be at Biggin' - which see - eight examples languish here. These were returned to the UK in July 2000 and *may* well have spent their time in Surrey. The date that the Indian WG.30s came to Tewkesbury *could* be September 2011 when some of this cache were reliably reported to have left Biggin Hill bound for 'Gloucestershire' - reported in *W&R23*, p141.

The balance are former US-operated examples that were part of The Helicopter Museum's reserve collection at Weston-super-Mare (WSM), Somerset. These moved during 2011, also for 'Gloucestershire' - *W&R23*, p193. The plot was that they were to be converted into egress trainers, perhaps for Singapore. ◆ **Strictly private** *site - no public access.*

❑ VT-EKE*	Westland	84	ex Biggin Hill (?), Redhill, India, Pawan Hans, G-BLPR	
	WG.30-100-60 G-BLPR		First noted 6-00	6-20
❑ VT-EKG*	Westland	85	ex Biggin Hill (?), G-BLTY (31-8-04 to 2-2-11), Redhill, India,	
	WG.30-100-60 G-BLTY		Pawan Hans, G-BLTY, G-17-9. First noted 6-00	6-20
❑ VT-EKK*	W'land WG.30-100-60	86	ex Redhill, India, Pawan Hans, G-17-13. First noted 6-00	6-20
❑ VT-EKL*	W'land WG.30-100-60	86	ex Redhill, India, Pawan Hans, G-17-14. First noted 6-00	6-20
❑ VT-EKM*	W'land WG.30-100-60	86	ex Redhill, India, Pawan Hans, G-17-15. First noted 6-00	6-20
❑ VT-EKN*	W'land WG.30-100-60	86	ex Redhill, India, Pawan Hans, G-17-16. First noted 6-00	6-20

❑ VT-EKX*	W'land WG.30-100-60	87	ex Redhill, India, Pawan Hans, G-17-27. First noted 6-00	6-20
❑ VT-EKY*	Westland	87	ex Redhill, Biggin Hill (?), India, Pawan Hans, G-17-28	
	WG.30-100-60		First noted 6-00	6-20
❑ N112WG*	W'land WG.30-100-60	84	ex WSM, Yeovil (?), PanAm. De-reg 8-6-13	[1] 6-20
❑ N118WG*	W'land WG.30-100-60	84	ex WSM, Yeovil (?), PanAm. De-reg 4-1-13	[1] 6-20
❑ N5820T*	W'land WG.30-100-60	84	ex WM, Yeovil (?), Airspur. De-reg 4-11-13	[1] 6-20

■ [1] *Believed* arrived 14-6-11.

THORNBURY west of the A38, north of Bristol
Delta Force Paintball: Gloucester Road. ◆ *By prior arrangement* **only** | www.paintballgames.co.uk
❑ XZ723	'672' Westland Lynx HMA.8	80	ex Ipswich, Fleetlands, 815, 702, 815, HAS.3, 815, HAS.2.	
			First noted 6-16	2-19

TODENHAM east of the A429, south of Shipston on Stour
A Hunter is held at a *private* location in the area.
❑ WT804	'831' Hawker Hunter GA.11	55	ex Moreton-in-Marsh, Culdrose A2646, A2732 (22-10-85),	
			Shawbury, FRADU, Lossiemouth, 247. Arrived 10-17	12-21

HAMPSHIRE
Includes the unitary authorities of Portsmouth and Southampton

ALTON on the A339 southwest of Farnham
Iron Curtain Museum: With the masthead 'A trip through some of our most dangerous years', a collection of military hardware - mostly tracked - has been assembled from late 2018. The site is yet to open to the public.
◆ *Keeper's Lodge, GU34 4AB - **not yet** open to the public* | email via website | www.thecoldwarmuseum.com
❑ 7811	Mikoyan-Gurevich	68	ex Polish AF	
	MiG-21MF *Fishbed*		Arrived 26-1-20	8-21

Flying Without Fear: The One-Eleven fuselage is used as a teaching aid: 'Nothing to lose and a whole world to gain'.
◆ *On the A339 at GU34 4BH* | www.flyingwithoutfear.com
❑ G-AWYV	BAC 111-501EX	69	ex Hurn, European, BA, BCAL, Caledonian, BUA.	
			CoA 24-6-04, de-reg 17-12-04. Forward fuselage	5-21

BASINGSTOKE on the A33 southwest of Reading
Centerprise International: A former Danish Hunter is displayed outside this IT and 'solutions' specialist at the Hampshire International Business Park. ◆ www.centerprise.co.uk
❑ '349'	Hawker Hunter F.51	56	ex 'WT720', Lee-on-Solent, Caerphilly, North Scarle, Sealand,	
[٣٤٩]	E-408		Cranwell 'XF979', Brawdy 8565M, Dunsfold, G-9-436 (10-7-76),	
			Esk.724, Dan AF E-408. Iraqi Air Force c/s, arrived 5-19	5-21

Also: At a private location in the locality, an Auster is under restoration.
❑ TJ672*	'TS-D' T'craft Auster 5	G-ANIJ 44	ex Netheravon, Eggesford, Hurn, 227 OCU, 657. CoA 5-5-71	4-20

BLACKBUSHE AERODROME on the A30 west of Yateley   EGLK
The Archer cockpit is used as a simulator by disabled flying charity Aerobility.
❑ G-BDFW	Rockwell Commander 112	75	ex N1308J. CoA 22-11-08, de-reg 5-4-11. *This is it!* Spares	9-21
❑ G-KITE	Piper Archer II	84	ex N4338X. Cr 3-5-08, de-reg 12-28-08. Cockpit, SIM	9-21
❑ N9432B	Cessna 175C	58	ex Seething. Arrived 2-15	9-21

BORDON and LONGMOOR CAMP on the A325 south of Farnham
A pair of Lynx serve as targets/waypoints.
❑ XZ190	Westland Lynx AH.7	78	ex M Wallop, AH.1. Arrived 2012	7-19
❑ XZ677	Westland Lynx AH.7	82	ex M Wallop, AH.1. Arrived 2012	7-19

BRAMLEY southeast of Tadley, east of the A340

Army Training Estate Home Counties: Although mostly dated, the airframes are *thought* current.

❏ XK970		Westland Whirlwind HAR.10	56	ex Odiham 8789M, Akrotiri, 84, 230, CFS, Khormaksar SAR Flt, 228 JEHU. Poor state		9-21
❏ XZ300	'L'	Sud Gazelle AH.1	76	ex Fleetlands, M Wallop, 670, 664, 662. Crashed 14-2-97. Westland-built		4-14
❏ 'XZ654'		Westland Lynx AH.7 XZ219	79	ex M Wallop, Fleetlands, 847, 656, SFOR, 654, 669, 654, 669, 662, 653, 662	[1]	9-21
❏ XZ661	'V'	Westland Lynx AH.7	81	ex M Wallop, 671, 653, 1 Rgt, 655, 671, 652, 651		8-16
❏ -	TAD.900	Sud Gazelle AH.1 XW900	74	ex Aborfield, M Wallop SEAE, 660. Crashed 25-5-76		4-14

■ [1] XZ219 is painted as 'XZ654' or more likely wears its boom - the rest of it is at Shannon, Ireland.

CALSHOT at the end of the B3053, southeast of Fawley

Calshot Castle and Heritage Area: The former flying-boat base hosted the last Schneider Trophy races, in 1929 and 1931. The final Sunderlands flew away in October 1953 and the RAF station closed in May 1961. The massive 'H' shed, now known as the Sunderland Hangar, is 600ft long and houses the Calshot Activities Centre. There are plenty of displays on Calshot's aviation days within the castle and great views of the Solent. **www.english-heritage.org.uk**

CHILBOLTON AERODROME Last noted in April 2016, Tomahawk G-PRIM has been deleted.

DURLEY east of the B3354, between Horton Heath and Bishop's Waltham

A *private* airstrip in the *general* area holds an eclectic variety of 'retirees'.

❏ G-AXSV*	Jodel DR.340 Major	68	ex F-BRCC. CEA-built. De-reg 2-1-97	4-21
❏ G-AYDR*	Stampe SV-4C	46	ex F-BCLG. SNCAN-built	4-21
❏ G-AYDY*	Luton Minor	74	CoA 7-1-16	4-21
❏ G-BPZE*	Luscombe Silvaire	46	ex Hardwick, N1177K. Damaged 8-7-07, CoA 2-5-08	4-21
❏ G-BVMD*	Luscombe Silvaire	47	ex 9Q-CGB. Crashed 28-7-06, de-reg 6-2-07	4-21
❏ G-STMP*	Stampe SV-4A	49	ex F-BCKB. De-reg 24-9-18	4-21

FAREHAM on the A27 west of Portsmouth

No.1350 Squadron Air Cadets: Farm Road.

❏ XX745	'GV'	SEPECAT Jaguar GR.1A	74	ex Boscombe D, Shawbury St Athan 9340M, 54, 16, 6, 16, 6, 226 OCU, 54, 6, 20, 226 OCU. Dam 31-5-00. Cockpit	4-20

FARNBOROUGH

Whittle Memorial: Dramatically displayed on the roundabout to the north of the airfield, the E28/39 is a tribute to Sir Frank Whittle. This and the one at Lutterworth, Leics (qv), were financed and built by the Sir Frank Whittle Commemorative Trust.

❏ –	Gloster E28/39 FSM	03	BAPC.285, unveiled 28-8-03	7-19

Prince's Mead Shopping Centre: The SE.5a still provides 'top cover' for the shoppers.

❏ 'D276'	'A'	Royal Aircraft Factory SE.5a replica	90	BAPC.208, AJD Engineering-built. 74 Sqn, 'A' Flt, Edward 'Mick Mannock, colours	1-19

FARNBOROUGH AIRFIELD east of the A325, north of Aldershot   EGLF

Farnborough Air Sciences Trust (FAST): The mass of material on show is only the tip of the iceberg that can be displayed within The Old Balloon School, renamed as Trenchard House in honour of one of its earliest 'bosses'. The incredible Cody is housed within its own pavilion. It is a replica of the British Army Aeroplane No.1A which made the first sustained flight by a British-built aircraft on 16th October 1908, just a stone's throw from FAST's site. In a great piece of 'reverse technology' a mock-up Cody pilot's position - it can't really be called a cockpit - forms the basis of a simulator.

Andrew Lee and his dedicated team have restored *Zulu-India* as a 'live' exhibit. Autoland development with the Trident was a major occupation of Royal Aircraft Establishment, hence it's highly appropriate placing at FAST. The cockpit is opened and 'powered up' regularly. | email **lasaviation@virginmedia.com**

Scout AH.1 XT633, always a bit of an 'orphan' in the collection departed in April 2018 for refurbishment, *perhaps* at North Weald, Essex, and travelled to Bridgwater, Somerset, on 20th August 2020.

◆ *Farnborough Road, GU14 7TF* | **01252 375050** | **secretary@airsciences.org.uk** | **www.airsciences.org.uk**

☐ G-AWZI		HS Trident 3B-101	71	ex Lasham, Alton, Reigate, Heathrow, BA, BEA.	
				CoA 5-8-85, de-reg 9-7-87, arrived 15-12-04. Cockpit	[1] 1-22
☐ -		Cody Army Aeroplane No.1A replica	07	BAPC.359. Unveiled 16-10-08, in Cody pavilion. See notes above	[2] 1-22
☐ -		Airbus Zephyr 6	07	BAPC.531, handed over 6-3-17, in Cody pavilion	[3] 3-20
☐ WT309		EE Canberra B(I).6	55	ex Booker, Boscombe Down, Farnborough, B' Down, A&AEE, HS. Arrived 2-98. Cockpit	1-22
☐ WV383		Hawker Hunter T.7	55	ex Boscombe D, DERA, RAE, 28, Jever SF, Gütersloh SF, F.4, RAFFC. *Hecate–Lady of the Night*. Arrived 13-4-00	[4] 1-22
☐ XL563		Hawker Hunter T.7	57	ex South Moor, Hereford 9218M (9-6-95), Kempton, Farnborough, IAM. Last flown 9-7-93. Arrived 4-14	1-22
☐ XP516	'16'	Folland Gnat T.1	63	ex DS&TL, RAE, 8580M (8-2-78), 4 FTS. Arrived 8-6-04	[4] 1-22
☐ XP848		Westland Scout AH.1	62	ex M Wallop, Arborfield, M Wallop, Wroughton, 662, 651, A&AEE. Arrived 3-9-15	3-20
☐ XS420		EE Lightning T.5	65	ex Walpole St Andrew, West Walton Highway, Narborough, Binbrook, LTF, 5, LTF, 226 OCU. SOC 16-6-88, arrived 3-9-03. 226 OCU colours	[5] 1-22
☐ XV631		Westland Wasp HAS.1	69	ex RAE site, Wroughton, 829, *Cleopatra* Flt, *Eskimo* Flt, SOC 19-3-84, arrived 11-2-10. Cabin, off-site	3-18
☐ XW241		Sud SA.330E Puma	68	ex DS&TL, RAE Bedford, F-ZJUX. SOC 10-11-88. Arrived 29-8-07	[4] 1-22
☐ XW566		SEPECAT Jaguar B.08	71	ex DS&TL, RAE, A&AEE. Last flown 17-6-85. Arrived 8-6-04	[4] 1-22
☐ XW934	'Y'	HS Harrier T.4	73	ex DS&TL, 20, 233 OCU, 1. Arrived 29-8-09. 20 Sqn colours	1-22
☐ XZ166		Westland Lynx HAS.2	75	ex QinetiQ, RAE site, A&AEE, Rolls-Royce G-1-2, A&AEE. SOC 18-12-80, arrived 10-09. Cabin, off-site	3-18
☐ ZD280		Westland Lynx AH.7	83	ex Fleetlands, M Wallop, AH.1, 671. Last flown 31-7-15. Arrived 5-12-17	[6] 1-22
☐ ZG631		Northrop Chukar D.2	96	ex Aberporth, Fleet Target Group. Last sortie 15-5-01. Arrived 10-08. Off-site	9-19
☐ ZJ496		GAF Jindivik 104A	c83	ex Boscombe Down, Llanbedr, A92-901. Arr 10-5-05	[4] [7] 1-22
☐ -		EE Lightning	~	procedure trainer	[8] 3-20
☐ -		Short MATS-B	~	(SBAS-029)	[9] 3-20

■ **[1]** Trident cockpit is on loan from Andrew Lee - see narrative above. **[2]** The incredible Cody is housed within its own pavilion. It is a replica of the British Army Aeroplane No.1A which made the first sustained flight by a British-built aircraft on 16-10-08, just a stone's throw from FAST's site. This has *also* been allocated BAPC.394. There is also a replica of a Cody centre section used as a simulator. **[3]** This circumvents the UAV 'ruling' by virtue of its size! Zephyr 6 sub-scale development prototype of the Airbus Defence and Space Zephyr S and T 'pseudo-satellites'. (At 39ft 5in span, sub-scale is a relative phrase!) Built at the Airbus facility within the Cody Technology Park at Farnborough. In 2-08 a Zephyr 6 reached 60,000ft and stayed aloft for 82 hours on a sortie from Yuma, Arizona. **[4]** Airframes on loan from DS&TL / QinetiQ. **[5]** Lightning T.5 on loan from Richard Hall - take a look at **www.xs420.com [6]** ZD280 on loan from the Army Flying Museum, Middle Wallop, Hampshire. **[7]** Jindivik carries 12 mission markers. **[8]** Procedures trainer fitted with ejector seat marked XM171. **[9]** This was deleted during the UAV 'cull' in *W&R26*, but as it has a build number, and the hunt is on for a serial, it's back!

Royal Aircraft Establishment Heritage Quarter: Within the Farnborough Business park, which occupies much of the former RAE site, are several listed buildings reflecting the significance of the airfield. The skeletal 1911 balloon hangar has been erected close to its original location and serves as a unique symbol of the Balloon Factory and Royal Aircraft Factory days. The Grade I-listed Building Q121 is the famous wind tunnel and a local landmark. The former Weapons Testing Building, Q134, is now called **The Hub** and includes a display entitled 'The Secret Factory' and the Aviators Cafe. Also within The Hub is the **National Aerospace Library**, which is open to the public. **www.aerosociety.com**

Defence Science and Technology Laboratory / QinetiQ: *Noseless* Merlin HC.3 ZJ138 was roaded to the scrapyard at Spey Bay, Scotland, on 14th August 2021. Last noted in 2009, AV-8B 162958 cockpit has been deleted.

☐ XV344		Blackburn Buccaneer S.2C	67	ex Boscombe Down, RAE, 809, 800, 809. Withdrawn 9-94. *Night bird*. Displayed	4-21

Also: A Canberra cockpit is kept in the *general* area.

☐ WJ775		EE Canberra B.6RC	54	ex Upwood, Bodney, St Athan, Swanton Morley 8581M (5-5-74), 51, 192. Cockpit. Arrived 26-4-15	12-19

FLEET By mid-2020 the flightdeck of Bristol 170 C-FDFC had moved to Maidenhead, Berks.

FLEETLANDS on the B3334 south of Fareham

StandardAero Aviation Holdings: Rotary wing repair, maintenance and storage contractor-run facility.

❑ XS539	'435'	Westland Wasp HAS.1	64	A2640 [2], ex A2718 [2] (7-1-92), Lee-on-Solent,		
				Portland, 829, 703, 829, 848, 829. Displayed	[1]	3-18
❑ XW844	'GAZ.4'	Sud Gazelle AH.1	72	ex Wroughton. 659. Westland-built. Displayed		6-21
❑ XZ697*	'313'	Westland Lynx HMA.8SRU	80	ex 702, 815, HAS.3, 815, HAS.2, 815. Arrived 3-<u>18</u>		6-21
❑ ZD480		Westland Sea King HC.4	84	ex Gosport, 846, 845, 846, 845, 846. Arrived by 8-15.		
				'Zebra' stripe camo. Displayed by 12-15		11-21

■ **[1]** Wasp XS539 attacked the Argentine submarine *Santa Fe* with missiles off South Georgia 25-4-82.

GOSPORT on the B3333 south of Fareham

HMS *Sultan*: Defence School of Aeronautical Engineering (DSAE): The school is a sub-set of the Defence College of Technical Training at Lyneham, Wilts. Also here are the **Defence School of Marine Engineering**, the **Royal Naval Air Engineering and Survival Equipment School** and **764 Initial Training Squadron**, 'operating' the airframes here. The instructional airframe fleet continues to expand.

Departures: Sea Kings to <u>Somerton</u>, Somerset during 2020: HAR.3s XZ586, XZ590, XZ594, XZ596; HU.5s XV670, ZA134, ZA137; ASaC.7 XV656, XV664, XV671, XV697, XV714. HU.5 XV647 to <u>Higher Purtington</u>, Somerset, by 9-21; HAR.3 XZ589 to <u>Scalby</u>, N Yorks, by 3-21.

❑ XP110	'55'	Westland Wessex HAS.3	62	ex A2636, A2714, A2728 (25-4-85), Lee-on-Solent,		
				Fleetlands, 737, 706, HAS.1, 737, 706, 737. *Humphrey*	[1]	4-19
❑ XR518	'O'	Westland Wessex HC.2	64	ex Shawbury, 60, 72, 22, 18, 72, 18		4-15
❑ XS514	'YL'	Westland Wessex HU.5	64	ex A2653, Lee-on-Solent A2740 (7-7-86), 845, 847,		
				845, A&AEE, 845, 781, 845		4-15
❑ XS568	'441'	Westland Wasp HAS.1	64	ex A2637, Fleetlands A2715 (18-5-83), 829, 771		4-19
❑ XT453	'B'	Westland Wessex HU.5	65	ex Culdrose, Gosport A2666, Lee-on-Solent A2756		
				(22-7-86), Yeovilton, 845, 707, 845, 707		4-19
❑ XT484	'H'	Westland Wessex HU.5	66	ex A2655, Lee-on-Solent A2742 (3-7-86), 845, 846		4-19
❑ XT485	'621'	Westland Wessex HU.5	66	ex A2680, Lee-on-Solent A2769 (30-3-88), 772,		
				Lee SAR Flt, 772, 771, 846, 848, 847		4-15
❑ XV370	'260'	Sikorsky SH-3D	66	ex A2682, Lee-on-Solent A2771 (8-1-90), ETPS,		
		Sea King G-ATYU		A&AEE, Yeovil, G-ATYU de-reg 25-10-66		4-19
❑ XV642	'259'	Westland Sea King	69	ex A2614, ex A2613 (20-3-91), Yeovil,		
		HAS.2A		A&AEE, Yeovil, A&AEE, Yeovil		4-19
❑ XV643	'262'	Westland Sea King	69	ex Cosford 9323M, St Athan, Gosport A2657 (24-3-00)		
		HAS.6		Culdrose, 819, 849, 819, 814, 820, 819, 824, 814, A&AEE.		
				Arrived 30-3-16		4-19
❑ XV649	'85'	Westland Sea King	69	ex Culdrose, 857, 849, AEW.2, 849, HAS.2, 706, Falklands,		
		ASaC.7		824, HAS.1, 706, 737, 826, 700S. First noted 9-18		4-19
❑ XV653*	'63'	W'land Sea King HAS.6	69	ex Cosford 9326M, Gosport, 810, 706. Arrived 17-9-20		9-20
❑ XV655	'70'	Westland Sea King	69	ex A2805 (10-12-01), 814, 819, 826, 814, 824, 826, 814,		
		HAS.6		826, 819, 737, 824		4-19
❑ XV659*	'62'	Westland Sea King	70	ex Cosford, 9324M, Gosport, Fleetlands, 810, 814, 819,		
		HAS.6		706, 826, 824, 819, 814, FTU, 824. First noted 10-20		10-20
❑ XV660	'69'	Westland Sea King	70	ex A2810 (10-12-01), Culdrose, 819, 814, 810, 706, 810,		
		HAS.6		819, 810, 824, 706		4-19
❑ XV665	'507'	W'land Sea King HAS.6	70	ex A2812 (10-12-01), 810, 820, 810, 824, 706, 819, 826		4-19
❑ XV672	'87'	Westland Sea King	70	ex Culdrose, 857, 849, AEW.2, 849, HAS.2, 824, 826, HAS.1,		
		ASaC.7		814, 819. First noted 9-18		4-19
❑ XV675	'701'	Westland Sea King	71	ex A2622 (1-5-02), 819, 706, 824, A&AEE, 814, 819,		
		HAS.6		814, 819, 737, 819, A&AEE, 819		4-19
❑ XV676	'ZE'	Westland Sea King	71	ex 845, 846, Fleetlands, 771, 810, 819, A&AEE, 819, 824,		
		HAS.6CR		814, 706, 826, 706, 819, A&AEE, 819		4-19
❑ XV696	'267'	W'land Sea King HAS.6	71	ex A2813 (1-5-02), Culdrose, 814, 819, 826, 810, 825, 814, 820		4-17
❑ XV699	'823'	Westland Sea King	71	ex Gannet SAR Flt, 771, Gannet SAR Flt, 771, 819, HAS.1,		
		HU.5		Wroughton, 826, 814, 826, 846, 826, 824, A&AEE, 824		4-19
❑ XV701	'64'	Westland Sea King	71	ex Cosford, Gosport, Cosford, Gosport A2809 (10-12-01),		
		HAS.6		814, 820, 810, 819, A&AEE, 819, 706, 824. *Lulabelle*		4-19

❑ XV703	'ZD'	Westland Sea King HAS.6CR	71	ex Fleetlands, 845, 846, 771, 819, 820, 819, 826, 706, 814,826, 706, 820, 824	4-19
❑ XV706	'017'	Westland Sea King HAS.6	71	ex Culdrose, 8344M *and* A2656 (28-2-02), ex Culdrose, 810, 706, 810, 810, A&AEE, 706, 810, 706, 814, 819 [2]	4-19
❑ XV707	'84'	Westland Sea King ASaC.7	71	ex Culdrose, 849, AEW.2, 849, HAS.2, 819, 706, HAS.1, 819, 814, 819. First noted 9-18	4-19
❑ XV708	'501'	Westland Sea King HAS.6	71	ex A2643 [3], A2635 (1-5-02), 810, 819, 706, 819, 706, 820, 826, 737	4-19
❑ XV711	'515'	Westland Sea King HAS.6	72	ex A2808 (25-3-02), 810, 819, 814, 824, 814, 706, 820, 706, 824, 706, 814, 819, 814, 819	4-19
❑ XV713	'18'	Westland Sea King HAS.6	72	ex A2804 (19-5-00), Fleetlands, 820, 810, 706, 826, 824, 826, 810, 814, 820	4-19
❑ XV724	'DD41'	Westland Wessex HC.2	68	ex Shawbury, Fleetlands, 22, SARTS, 18	4-15
❑ XW852		Sud Gazelle HCC.4	73	ex Cosford 9331M, St Athan, Fleetlands, 32 [3]	4-19
❑ XX412		Sud Gazelle AH.1	75	ex Cosford, Shawbury, 847, 3 CBAS. Arr 12-18. '238 Sqn' colours [3]	4-19
❑ XX431	'43'	Sud Gazelle HT.2	75	ex M Wallop, Shawbury, 9300M, 705, FONA, 705 [3]	3-20
❑ XZ305		Sud Gazelle AH.1	76	TAD.020, ex M Wallop, Arborfield, 3 Regt, 665, 662, 654, GCF [3]	4-19
❑ XZ576		Westland Sea King HAS.6	76	ex A2806 (1-5-02), Boscombe D, A&AEE, A&AEE, 824, A&AEE, 820	4-19
❑ XZ579	'707'	Westland Sea King HAS.6	77	ex A2843 (25-7-07), Brize Norton, Gosport, 819, 820, 814, 820, 819, 826, 824, 706, 814	4-19
❑ XZ580	'ZB'	Westland Sea King HAS.6CR	77	ex Fleetlands, 846, 845, 846, Boscombe D, Gosport, 819, 814, 810, 706, 737, 706, 825, 814	4-19
❑ XZ581	'269'	Westland Sea King HAS.6	77	ex A2638, A2627 (1-5-02), Fleetlands, 814, 810, 826, 819, 824, A&AEE, 826, 706, 814	4-19
❑ XZ692	'764'	Westland Lynx HAS.8SRU	72	ex 702, 815, 702, HAS.2, 815, 702, 815. Arrived 13-8-15. Displayed. 'Black Cats' c/s to port, 764 ITS c/s to starboard	4-19
❑ XZ920	'24'	W'land Sea King HU.5	79	ex Gannet Flt, 771, HAS.2, 771, 810, Falklands, 820. F/n 8-18	4-19
❑ XZ922	'ZA'	Westland Sea King HAS.6CR	79	846, 845, 846, Boscombe Down, Gosport, 819, 810, 826, 810, 826, 814, 706	4-19
❑ XZ930	'Q'	Sud Gazelle HT.3	78	ex A2713 (17-11-00), Shawbury, 2 FTS, CFS. Displayed [3]	4-19
❑ ZA128*	'010'	Westland Sea King HAS.6	81	ex Cosford, Gosport (10-10-02), 820, 706, 820. Arr 17-9-20	9-20
❑ ZA131	'271'	Westland Sea King HAS.6	81	ex Cosford, Gosport A2639[3], Cosford, Gosport, A2628 (19-6-02), 814, 820, 826, 810, 826	4-19
❑ ZA133	'31'	Westland Sea King HU.6	81	ex Fleetlands, Gosport, 771, 820, 810, 819, 820, 826, 810, 829, 826. SOC 3-4-06	4-19
❑ ZA167		W'land Sea King HU.5	81	ex 771, QinetiQ, 771, HAS.5, 826, 814, Falkland's, 814	4-19
❑ ZA168	'830'	W'land Sea King HU.6	82	ex A2844 (12-3-09), 771, 820, 849, 820, 810, 819, 826, 814	4-19
❑ ZA169*	'515'	Westland Sea King HAS.6	82	ex Cosford, Gosport A2844 (12-3-09), 820, 771, 810, 814, 820, 819, 820, 706, 820. First noted 10-20	10-20
❑ ZA170		W'land Sea King HAS.5	82	ex A2830, A2645 (2-4-04), Fleetlands, 706, 810. Black c/s	4-15
❑ ZA323	'TAZ'	Panavia Tornado GR.1	83	ex Cosford, 9339M, St Athan, 15, TTTE. Arrived 25-4-19	9-19
❑ ZD254	'305'	Westland Lynx HAS.3S	82	ex A2840 (14-1-09), 815, 702. Recruiting airframe	3-20
❑ ZD479	'WQ'	Westland Sea King HC.4	83	ex 848, 845, 848, 707, 846, 707	4-19
❑ ZD630	'012'	W'land Sea King HAS.6	84	ex Culdrose, 820, 814, 820	4-19
❑ ZD634	'503'	W'land Sea King HAS.6	85	ex A2845 (12-3-09), 771, 810, 819, A&AEE, 819	4-17
❑ ZD636		W'land Sea King ASaC.7	85	ex Fleetlands, 857, 854, 849, AEW.2, 849, HAS.5, 771, 819	4-19
❑ ZD637	'700'	W'land Sea King HAS.6	85	ex A2811 (15-11-02), 819, 771, 819, 814, 810, A&AEE, 819	4-19
❑ ZE418	'86'	W'land Sea King ASaC.7	86	ex Culdrose, 849, 854, 849, HAS.5, 706, 819, 810, 819. First noted 9-18	4-19
❑ ZE426	'WX'	Westland Sea King HC.4	85	ex 848, 845, 848, 707, 846, 848, 845, 846	4-19
❑ ZF115	'WV'	Westland Sea King HC.4	86	ex Yeovilton, 848, 845, 848, Gosport A2815, A&AEE	9-21
❑ ZF119	'WY'	Westland Sea King HC.4	86	ex 848, 846, 707, 846	4-19
❑ ZF649		EHI EH 101 PP5	89	ex A2714 (9-4-01), Weston-super-Mare, Yeovil	4-19
❑ ZG816	'014'	Westland Sea King HAS.6	89	ex 820, 819, 820	4-19
❑ ZG817	'702'	Westland Sea King HAS.6	90	ex A2814 (19-6-02), 819, 810	4-19
❑ ZG818	'707'	Westland Sea King HAS.6	90	ex Fleetlands, 814, 819, 814	4-19

❏	ZG819	'265'	Westland Sea King HAS.6	90	ex A2654, A2641 [4] (19-6-02), 814, 820	4-19
❏	ZZ402		Westland Wildcat AH.1	10	ex Yeovil. Handed over 12-10-16	4-19

■ **[1]** Another *Humphrey*, of much greater fame, is to be found at Yeovilton, Somerset. **[2]** XV706 has a rare distinction; its 'M' number was allocated on 2nd May 2003 and was the *last ever*. For good measure, it had been given an 'A' number a year earlier... **[3]** Gazelles, of course, built by Westland.

HAMBLE southeast of Southampton

Hamble Aerostructures: Part of the Spanish-based Aernnova, is guarded by a Gnat at the former Folland plant.

❏	XM693	Folland Gnat T.1	60	ex Abingdon, Bicester 7891M (10-8-65), A&AEE	5-21

LASHAM AERODROME west of Golden Pot, northwest of Alton   EGHL

Gliding Heritage Centre: There is a bewildering list of other types that have been 'volunteered' for occasional loan: the website provides details. As befitting the world of silent flight, the emphasis is on informality and the 'best time' to visit is quoted as Sunday afternoons when 'there *might* be some flying'. The list below can be considered the 'core', a large number of others are made available from time to time.

◆ *Follow signs for the Gliding Centre. Alton, GU34 5SS* | enquiriy@glidingheritage.org.uk | www.glidingheritage.org.uk

❏	G-AEKV	DZQ	Kronfeld Drone	36	BGA.2510, ex Brooklands, CoA 6-10-60, de-reg 14-1-99.		
					Arrived 1-9-13	[1]	10-21
❏	–		Mignet HM.14 'Flea'	c05	BAPC.302, ex Shoreham. *Le Pou du Ciel- L'Autre Aviation.*		
					First noted 7-16	[2]	11-19
❏	G-ALJR	ACF	Abbott-Baynes Scud III	36	BGA.283, ex Dunstable, G-ALJR, BGA.283.		
					Donated by Laurie Woodage. Arrived 18-7-13		10-21
❏	G-ALLF	ARK	Slingsby Prefect ✈	36	BGA.599, ex PH-1, BGA.599, G-ALLF, BGA.599. *Piglet*	[3]	10-21
❏	G-ALRU	ASR	EoN Baby	49	BGA.628, ex Shoreham, Aston Down, G-ALRU.		
			G-ALRU		Crashed 28-5-71. Donated by Bob Kent		10-21
❏	G-APWL*	BRK	EoN 460 Srs 1A ✈	59	BGA.1172, ex Kidlington, Eaglescott, BGA.1172, G-APWL,		
					RAFGSA.268, G-APWL. CoA 26-4-00, de-reg 18-2-10	[4]	10-21
❏	G-CFYE*		Scheibe Zugvogel 3b	63	BGA.3624. CoA 25-2-17. Donated by Pete Purdel	]	10-21
❏	G-DBSA		Slingsby Dart 15	~	BGA.1187	[5]	10-21
❏	G-DCBP		SZD Foka C ✈	63	ex Sutton Bank. Last flown 6-00. Arrived 27-3-14.		
					Donated by Leslie Nicholson and Gwyneth Sutton		10-21
❏	G-DCKD*		PZL SZD-30 Pirat ✈	70	BGA.1596. CoA 10-9-22. Donated by John Halford		10-21
❏	G-DCXV	CXV	Yorkshire Sailplanes YS-53	74	BGA.1897. *The Beast*	[6]	10-21
❏	G-DHOC*		Scheibe Bergfalk II-55 ✈	63	BGA.4111. CoA 18-6-20. Donated by Rainer Karch		10-21
❏	G-KSIX*		Schleicher Ka.6E	63	BGA.1452. De-reg 19-8-19. Donated by Chris Sterritt		10-21
❏	–		Clarke Chanute glider	1910	BAPC.100, ex Stafford, Hendon Wyton, Hendon,		
					Cardington, Hayes, South Kensington	[7]	10-21
❏	AHU		Scott Viking 1 ✈	G-ALRD 38	BGA.416, ex G-ALRD, BGA.416. *Lou the Glue*		10-21
❏	ALR*		SlingsbyT.8 Tutor	46	BGA.485, ex Germany, G-ALPE, BGA. 485.		
			G-ALPE		Donated by Bob and Sylvia van Aalst		10-21
❏	ATH		Slingsby Gull III	39	BGA.643, ex Brooklands, TJ711. CoA 20-6-04. Arr 18-7-13	[1]	10-21
❏	AWX*		Slingsby Skylark 2 ✈	55	BGA.729. Donated by Graham Leach		10-21
❏	BAN		Slingsby Prefect ✈	58	BGA.815. Arrived 4-11-14. Donated by Sir John Allison		10-21
❏	BCV	'155'	Slingsby Skylark 3B ✈	59	BGA.870. Arrived 4-14. Donated by Jeffrey Price		10-21
❏	BGR		EoN Olympia 2B	58	BGA.962		10-21
❏	BJK		Slingsby Skylark 3F ✈	58	BGA.1004. Donated by Ron Page		10-21
❏	BZM		Slingsby Swallow ✈	67	BGA.1365, ex Arbroath. CoA 4-6-05.		
					Donated by Francis Webster		10-21
❏	BZV		EoN Olympia 463	65	BGA.1373. Arrived 2-14, donated by Bruce Cooper		10-21
❏	CSU		Manuel Hawk	69	BGA.1778, ex Fairoaks. Arrived 26-8-13.		
					Donated by Tom Coldwell		10-21
❏	DJF	'500'	Halford JSH Scorpion	77	BGA.2146, ex Doncaster, Wroot, Firbeck. Arrived 1-18	[8]	10-21
❏	DPG		München Mü 13D III	57	BGA.2267, ex D-1327. Scheibe-built.		
					Arrived 1-13, donated Geoff Moore		10-21
❏	EHB		Kaiser Ka-3	58	BGA.2689, ex RAFGGA 559. Donated by Leigh Hood		10-21
❏	ELV*		Scheibe Zugvogel 3b ✈	64	BGA.2779. Donated by Daniel Chidley	]	10-21
❏	HFS		Vogt Lo 100 Zwergreiher	53	BGA.3915. Hirth-built. Fuselage, used as simulator		10-21
❏	HFZ		Abbott-Baynes Scud I rep	31	BGA.3922, Brooklands. Arrived 18-7-13	[1]	10-21

❏	–		Colditz Cock replica	11	BAPC.347, ex *Escape from Colditz*	[9]	10-21
❏	–		Manuel Willow Wren	32	BGA.162, ex Brooklands, Bishop's Stortford.		
					The Yellow Wren. Arrived 7-13	[1]	10-21
❏	–		Abbott-Baynes Scud II	35	BGA.231, ex Old Warden, G-ALOT, BGA.231.		
		G-ALOT			Slingsby-built. CoA 1-6-06, arrived 6-10-17		10-21
❏	–		Manuel Crested Wren	86	BAPC.405, 'BGA.178'. Donated by Barbara Reed	[10]	10-21
❏	'D-11-875'		Jacobs Schweyer Weihe	43	BGA.448, ex G-ALJW, BGA.448, Luftwaffe LO+WQ.		
		'17'	G-ALJW		Damaged 20-7-79. Donated by Nick Jaffrey		10-21
❏	'D-6932'	KFW	DFS Grunau Baby IIB	52	BGA.5066, D-6932, D-1932. Hersteller Flug-built.		
					Donated by Roger Slade		10-21
❏	HB-357		Spalinger S-21h	43	'Canada Dry' titling. Donated by the David Braham estate		10-21
❏	'OE-0324'	ERZ	Oberlerchner Mg 19a ✈	55	BGA.2903, ex OE-0324. Arr 2011, donated by Chris Wills		10-21
❏	'CK-8592'		Zlin Z24 Krajanek ✈	46	BGA.655, ex 'OK-8592'. Arr 6-14, donated by John Dredge		10-21
❏	WB990*	'993'	Slingsby Sedburgh TX.1	52	BGA.3148 / FCF. Martin Hearn-built		10-21
❏	WP270		EoN Eton TX.1	51	ex Stafford, Manchester, Henlow, Hendon, 8598M,		
					27 MU, 61 GCF. First noted 5-16		10-21
❏	XA225		Slingsby Grasshopper TX.1	53	ex Odiham, Keevil, Upavon, Keevil, Petersfield.		
			TX.1 ✈		Donated by Ian Pattingale. Stored		10-21
❏	XE762		Slingsby Cadet TX.2	46	ex TX.1 VM594. Fuselage. Arrived 21-12-17		10-21
❏	XE800*	FFQ	Slingsby Cadet TX.3	46	BGA.3229		10-21
❏	XN243	FCC	Slingsby Cadet TX.1	59	BGA.3145, ex Germany, Bicester. First noted 5-18		10-21
❏	'XP463'	JBA	Slingsby Grasshopper TX.1	61	BGA.4372, ex Lasham resident, Rufforth.		
					Donated by Paul Wheatcroft and Gary Pullen	[11]	10-21
❏	'XS651'*	BYB	Slingsby Swallow	46	BGA.1211, ex Little Rissington, RNGSA 'LS33', BGA.1211		10-21
❏	42-53027		Laister-Kaufmann TG-4	42	C-FRAH, ex Canada, USAAF - no service. Arr 13-4-18	[12]	10-21

■ **[1]** On loan from Brooklands Museum, Surrey. **[2]** 'Flea' built by Tony Short circa 2005 and modelled on the example Henri Mignet brought to Shoreham 17-8-35 at the start of his British tour. **[3]** T.30A prototype, donated by John Hopkins and Kevin Fresson. **[4]** EoN 460 prototype, donated by AFE. **[5]** Prototype Dart, donated by Robin Birch. **[6]** YS-53 donated by Yvonne and Henry Stott and Alison and Paul Myers. **[7]** Chanute biplane glider on loan from the Royal Aero Club Trust via the Science Museum; acquired 1914: transferred to the RAF Museum 1983. **[8]** Scorpion is a rebuild of Holmes KH.1 BGA.1666 of 1971 and was donated by the South Yorkshire Aircraft Museum. **[9]** Cock on loan from its builder, South East Aircraft Services, used in *Escape from Colditz*. **[10]** Crested Wren an unflown replica. **[11]** Grasshopper is a complex hybrid, identity taken from one of the wings - see under Rufforth, N Yorks, for possible duplication. **[12]** TG-4 donated by Douglas Ogle of Brighton, Ontario, Canada.

Airfield: There is a healthy in-and-out of airliners here: only long-termers are listed. The fuselage of Boeing 737 'G-PIPJ' (G-GFFJ) was broken up in 2018.

❏	EI-DOO	Boeing 737-400	87	ex KD Avia, D-AGEB, N222DZ. 'Fire Trainer'	12-14
❏	VP-CMO	Boeing 727-212/RE	80	ex N31TR, VR-COJ, N310AS, 9V-SGJ	7-19
❏	VP-CZY	Boeing 727-200	78	ex A7-AAB. Arrived 27-11-11	10-21
❏	5U-BAG	Boeing 737-200	78	ex Niger Government. Arrived 1-9-14	8-21

LEE-ON-SOLENT AIRFIELD, see Solent Airport

MIDDLE WALLOP AIRFIELD on the A343 southwest of Andover   EGVP

Army Flying Museum: The multi-million extension and re-organisation of the display space was completed during 2020. As with several other museums, the hope to provide 'venue hire' has produced a huge gap in Hayward Hall, giving the impression that some of the airframes were an afterthought, crammed along the building's side, to make way for a 'dance floor'. Don't forget to visit the 'Apache Cafe' which offers views of the activity on the airfield.

Aircraft on loan: Duxford, Cambs: Auster XP281; Farnborough, Hampshire, Lynx ZD280; Southampton, Hampshire: Skeeter XL770; Flixton, Suffolk, Pucará A-528; Newark, Notts: Gazelle XW276. See under 'Headquarters', below, for a potential new exhibit. ◆ *Middle Wallop, SO20 8FB* | 01264 781086 | info@armyflying.com | www.armyflying.com

❏	G-AXKS		Bell 47G-4A	69	ex Bristow, ARWF, G-17-8. Westland-built. CoA 21-9-82,		
					de-reg 9-9-82. Acquired 22-4-82		1-22
❏	'G285'	'E'	Slingsby Kirby Kite	ACH 36	ex Ulster G/C, G-ALNH (de-reg 11-1-63), BGA.285.		
					Acquired 1989		1-22
❏	'B-415'		AFEE 10/42 replica	82	BAPC.163, ex Wimborne. Acquired 7-82	[1]	1-22
❏	P-5		Hafner Rotachute III	43	8381M, ex Henlow. Acquired 1983	[2]	1-22

☐ N5195		Sopwith Pup	G-ABOX	ex Redhill, Lincoln, RNAS War School Manston,	
			1916	3(Naval), 8(Naval), 3(Naval), 2(Naval).	
				Acquired, on loan, 1985. CoA 22-4-93	[3] 1-22
☐ 'KJ351'		Airspeed Horsa II	45	BAPC.80. Acquired 1968. Fuselage/centre section	[4] 1-22
☐ 'HH268'		GAL Hotspur II replica	95	BAPC.261. Acquired 13-12-01	[5] 1-22
☐ TJ569		Taylorcraft Auster 5	45	ex PH-NAD, PH-NEG, TJ569, 652, 660, 659.	
			G-AKOW	CoA 26-6-82, de-reg 5-8-87. Acquired 10-81	1-22
☐ TK777		GAL Hamilcar I	44	ex Christian Malford. Birmingham Railway Carriage	
				and Wagon Co-built. Forward fuselage/centre section	[6] 1-22
☐ WG432	'L'	DHC Chipmunk T.10	51	ex AFWF, LAS, Bristol UAS, 19 RFS, Cam UAS, 4 BFTS.	
				Acquired 1997	1-22
☐ WJ358		Auster 6A Tugmaster	52	ex Perth, AOP.6 WJ358, 651, 657, 1913 Flt.	
			G-ARYD	De-reg 5-8-87. Acquired 7-80	1-22
☐ WZ721		Auster AOP.9	55	ex Life Guards Air Sqn, 4 RTR, 16 Flt, 14 Flt, 7 Flt, 11 Flt,	
				6 Flt, 652. SOC 1-9-66. Acquired 1969.	
				Dragon, 4 RTR colours	1-22
☐ XG502		Bristol Sycamore HR.14	55	ex 'gate', Wroughton, MCS, CFS, 118, 72, TCCF,	
				Op *Musketeer*, JEHU. SOC 29-8-72	1-22
☐ XK776		ML Utility Mk 1	57	ex Cardington, M Wallop, A&AEE. Acquired 7-82	[7] 1-22
☐ XL813		Saro Skeeter AOP.12	59	ex ARWF, 4 Regt, 9 Flt. SOC 25-3-68	1-22
☐ XP821	'MCO'	DHC Beaver AL.1	61	ex Shawbury, Kemble, St Athan, Defence Attaché,	
				Laos, 130 Flt, 30 Flt RASC, 656. Acquired 2-10-85.	
				White/grey colours	1-22
☐ 'XP822'		DHC Beaver AL.1	61	ex Arborfield, Sharjah, 668, 13 Flt, 15 Flt, 131 Flt, 6Flt.	
			XP806	Crashed 16-9-70. Acquired 1990. Displayed outside	[8] 1-22
☐ XP847		Westland Scout AH.1	61	ex AETW, Wroughton, Yeovil. Acquired 1984	1-22
☐ XP910	'D'	Westland Scout AH.1	63	ex SEAE. Crashed 13-9-89, acquired 2002.	
				Displayed outside	1-22
☐ XR232		Sud Alouette AH.2	60	ex Historic Flight, Wroughton, A&AEE, M Wallop, EW&AU,	
				656, A&AEE, 16 Flt, 6 Flt, F-WEIP. Acquired 5-92	1-22
☐ XT108	'U'	Bell Sioux AH.1	64	ex Duxford, Yeovilton, M Wallop, D&T Flt, M Wallop.	
				Agusta-built. Acquired 6-84	1-22
☐ XV127		Westland Scout AH.1	67	ex Fleetlands, Chelsea, Wroughton, 655. Acquired 1995	1-22
☐ XX153		Westland Lynx AH.1	72	ex Yeovil, Wattisham 9320M, Foulness, Westland.	
				Acquired 28-10-03, handed over 13-11-03	1-22
☐ XZ675	'H'	Westland Lynx AH.7	81	ex Yeovilton, GDSH M Wallop, 671, 4 Rgt, 671, 652.	
				Acquired 7-8-11	1-22
☐ ZA737		Sud Gazelle AH.1	80	ex 1 Rgt, 847, Fleetlands 'hack', 670, ARWS. Westland-built.	
				Acquired 12-99	1-22
☐ ZE410		Agusta 109A	80	ex 7 Rgt, Yeovilton, M Wallop, 846, Arg Arm CAB.601,	
				AE-334. Workshop, first noted 12-14	1-22
☐ ZG993		BN Islander AL.1	88	ex Shawbury, 1 Flt, G-BOMD (de-reg 19-3-90).	
			G-BOMD	Last flight 1-7-10. Arrived 25-11-15	[9] 1-22
☐ AE-409	'656'	Bell UH-1H	72	ex Duxford, M Wallop, 656, Stanley, Argentine Army,	
		Iroquois		72-21506. Acquired 7-82	1-22
☐ 111989		Cessna L-19A Bird Dog	51	N33600, ex Fort Rucker, Alabama. Acquired 1982	1-22
☐ '243809'		Waco CG-4A Hadrian	44	BAPC.185, ex Burtonwood, Shrewsbury. Acq 1985. Fuselage	1-22
☐ 70-15990		Bell AH-1F Cobra	70	ex US Army. Acquired 2003	1-22

■ **[1]** AFEE 10/42 is centred on an original Willys Jeep and on loan from the Wessex Aviation Society. **[2]** Rotachute III on loan from the RAF Museum. **[3]** N5195, with an 80hp Le Rhone, was the second Pup restored by Lt Cdr K C D St Cyrien - G-ABOX being registered 12-9-84. Acquired by a Lincoln owner on 'demob' in 1919, the remains were apparently acquired by St Cyrien in Lincoln in 1963 for £25. See under Hendon, Gtr Lon, for his first, N5182 (G-APUP). **[4]** Largest Horsa airframe on show is 'KJ351' (a Thunderbolt II serial) which is an amalgam of TL659, LH208 and 8569M. TL659 was used until salvaged in 1969 as a sports changing room in Abingdon jail. There are two other substantial Horsa sections on display, other sections are in store. **[5]** Hotspur re-creation has adopted the identity and colours of an example that flew with the Shobdon-based 5 Glider Training School. **[6]** Hamilcar (made up of parts from NX836 and TK718 - see also Bovington, Dorset). **[7]** ML Utility inflatable had three wing options, 'Clouy', 'Delta' and 'Gadfly'; all are in store. **[8]** When XP822 left the 'gate' at Middle Wallop in 1990, XP806 was prepared to take over this duty and appeared in October 1990 marked 'XP822'. Already a composite, with the wings of XP815, XP806 took on *some* parts from XP822, the most significant being the constructor's plate (1486 - XP806 being 1455). Apparently, XP806 had lost its plate at some stage... perhaps in the accident in the UAE. **[9]** Operational sorties in Northern Ireland, the Balkans and the 1st Gulf War.

Top: Auster 5 TJ569 (G-AKOW) and L-19A Bird Dog 111989 (N33600).
Bottom: Beaver AL.1 XP821 and Alouette AH.2 XR232. Both September 2020, *Ken Ellis*

Deep Store: *Not* available for inspection.

☐ 'T9707'	Miles Magister I	T9708	40	ex Cardington, Manchester, Hendon 8378M, Gaydon,	
		G-AKKR		Henlow, G-AKKR, 'T9967', T9708, 51 MU, 16 EFTS, 239.	
				Phillips & Powis-built. CoA 10-4-65, de-reg 16-7-69.	
				Acquired 6-99	4-19
☐ 'XM819'	EP Prospector		59	ex Durrington, M Wallop, Blackbushe, Lympne.	
				Acquired 14-5-81	[1] 4-19
☐ XZ795	Northrop Shelduck D.1		84	ex Fleet Target Group. Last sortie (of just two!) 29-9-85	3-18
☐ ZA209	Short MATS-B Mk.1A	c78		-	10-21

■ **[1]** Largely G-APXW, which crashed 9-73, but also has rear fuselage of G-ARDG (see Blackburn, Lancs) and bits of G-APWZ.

Historic Aircraft Flight Trust: The flight's badge carries a Latin motto which translates as 'Let Their Glory Not Fade'; its aircraft attend a variety of events. **Departures:** Auster AOP.9 XP242 (G-BUCI) to Messingham, Lincs, 2-21; Scout AH.1 XP884 to North Weald, Essex, 18-8-21 – it is due to return upon restoration; Scout XT626 (G-CIBW) also left for North Weald (under its own steam) for onward sale.
◆ **Not** *available without prior permission* | email *via website* | **www.historicarmyaircraft.co.uk**

☐ EM840	DH Tiger Moth		43	ex Shawbury, -?-, G-ANBY (de-reg 30-4-59) Rochester,	
				21 EFTS. Morris Motors-built. SOC 25-9-53	[1] 12-19
☐ LB312*	Taylorcraft Plus D		42	ex Auster I LB312, 234 Sqn, 3 TEU, 43 OTU, 653, 651.	
		G-AHXE		Registered 8-12-20	[2] 3-21
☐ WD325	'N' DHC Chip' T.10 ✈	G-CLWK	51	ex BFWF, LAS, 12 GCF, 17 RFS	[2] 3-21
☐ XL812	Saro Skeeter AOP.12		59	ex Wattisham, Saxmundham, M Wallop.	
		G-SARO		SOC 28-5-69. CoA 30-10-06, de-reg 14-4-10	12-19
☐ XL814	Saro Skeeter AOP.12		59	ex 1 Wing, 2 Wing, 651. Stored	3-18
☐ XP820	DHC Beaver AL.1 ✈		61	ex 7 Regt, 667, 132 Flt RCT, 130 Flt RCT, 30 Flt RASC,	
		G-CICP		11 Flt, 656	[2] 8-21
☐ XR244	Auster AOP.9 ✈	G-CICR	62	ex AFWF. With AAC HAAF from 11-9-81	[2] 7-21
☐ XT131	'B' Bell Sioux AH.1 ✈	G-CICN	64	ex D&T Flight. Agusta-built. Flown again 22-5-15	[2] 7-19
☐ XT151	Bell Sioux AH.1		65	ex ARWF. Westland-built. Spares	10-20

■ **[1]** G-ANBY, this machine was last heard of, unconverted, at Rochester in April 1960 when it was said to have been scrapped! **[2]** Registered to the Historic Aircraft Flight Trust.

Headquarters, Army Air Corps (AAC): Several airframes serve in the ground instructional role in Stockwell Hall. The **Multi-Platform Support Unit** (MPSU) is working on the dwindling Gazelle fleet.

☐ WZ724	Auster AOP.9		55	ex gate 'WZ670', 7432M (22-5-57), LAS. Off-site	[1] 12-18
☐ 'XT123'	'D' Bell Sioux AH.1	XT827	67	ex Wroughton, Yeovilton, Coypool, 3 CBAS.	
				Westland-built. Displayed	[2] 9-20
☐ XT638	'N' Westland Scout AH.1		66	ex Fleetlands, 666. 666 Sqn badge. Displayed	2-20
☐ XX392	Sud Gazelle AH.1		75	ex Shawbury, 3 Flt, 670, ARWS, 3 CBAS. Travelling demo	[3] 3-20
☐ XX452	Sud Gazelle AH.1		76	Westland-built. Rescue trainer	[3] 7-21
☐ XZ181	Westland Lynx AH.7		78	ex MPSU. Fire dump	1-20
☐ XZ184	'B' Westland Lynx AH.7		78	ex MPSU. Displayed by 6-16	9-20
☐ XZ212	Westland Lynx AH.7		79	ex MPSU. Dumped by 11-19	11-21
☐ XZ298	Sud Gazelle AH.1		77	cockpit, training aid	[3] 4-15
☐ XZ327	Sud Gazelle AH.1		77	ex Fleetlands. Travelling recruiting aid	[3] 3-21
☐ XZ346	Sud Gazelle AH.1		78	ex Netheravon, Shawbury, M Wallop, 665, A&AEE,	
				Yeovil, 3 CBAS, ARWS, 656, 655. Arr by 3-14, displayed	[3] 9-20
☐ XZ672	Westland Lynx AH.7		81	ex 671, 653, 655, 656, 662, 659, 669, 659. Dump. F/n 1-13	11-21
☐ ZD265*	'302' Westland Lynx HMA.8SRU		83	ex 668 Sqn inst (12-2-16), 702, HAS.3, 815, 829, 815. Dumped	11-21
☐ ZG917*	Westland Lynx AH.9A		92	SOC 3-10-18. Held for Army Flying Museum	7-21
☐ ZG918*	Westland Lynx AH.9A		92	SOC 3-10-18. Crewman training airframe	6-21

■ **[1]** Restoration required grafting on another, unconfirmed, fuselage frame in late 2018. Frame *reported* to be the original from the airworthy XP254 (G-ASCC). **[2]** Sioux on the 'gate' has its complex side. The plate in the cockpit gives it as WA-S-179, which makes it XT827, latterly with the Historic Flight. **[3]** Gazelles all Westland-built.

NEW MILTON on the A337 east of Christchurch
Sammy Miller Motorcycle Museum: Nearly 400 'bikes' in four galleries and, obviously, a Rallye.
◆ *Bashley Cross Roads, BH25 5SZ* | **01425 620777** | **www.sammymiller.co.uk**

☐ G-EISO	MS Rallye 150		66	ex D-EISO, F-BNSO. CoA 29-10-13, de-reg 4-3-17	2-19

ODIHAM AIRFIELD on the A32 south of Odiham EGVO

RAF Odiham: Last noted in May 2012, the forward fuselage of CH-47D 82-23762 moved to <u>Benson</u>, Oxfordshire, for use by 28 Squadron, the Chinook/Puma OCU.

❑ XR453	'A'	W'land Whirlwind HAR.10	62	8873M, ex Foulness, 2 FTS, CFS, 230, 1563 Flt, CFS. Displayed	6-20
❑ ZA678	'EZ'	BV Chinook HC.1	81	9229M, ex Fleetlands, 7, N37023. Crashed 24-7-89. Inst	10-16
❑ 86-1677		BV CH-47D Chinook	86	ex US Army. Training aid	10-16
❑ 03-08003	'DT'	BV YCH-47F Chinook	02	ex US Army. Unveiled on display 9-5-12	8-21

Locally: The SIPA is *believed* to still be stored in the area.

❑ G-AWLG	SIPA 903	51	ex F-BGHG. CoA 22-8-79	N7-18

PETERSFIELD on the A3 north of Portsmouth

A *private* house in the *general* area is graced by a Harrier.

❑ ZG509	'80'	BAe/McDD Harrier GR.7A	91	ex Ipswich, Cottesmore, Wittering, St Athan.
				Damaged 31-7-01	10-21

POPHAM AERODROME Last noted in May 2017, trailer-mounted Cessna 150 G-AVNC has been deleted.

PORTSMOUTH

Royal Navy Dockyard: A Sea Harrier is displayed within the Queen Elizabeth Complex. On Whale Island, a Lynx is used as an instructional airframe. Trials unit **1710 Squadron** occasionally takes airframes, mostly on a short-term basis..

❑ ZD252	Westland Lynx HMA.8	98	ex Yeovilton, 815, Fleetlands, 702, 815, HAS.3, 815.	
			First noted 3-17	8-17
❑ ZD611	HS Sea Harrier F/A.2	85	ex Culdrose, St Athan, 899, 801, 899, 800, 899, 800, 899,	
			899, 800, 899, 801. Displayed, 899 Sqn colours. F/n 5-17	12-21
❑ ZJ177	McDD Apache AH.1	01	ex Gosport, Wattisham, M Wallop, 9 Regt. Westland-built.	
			Crashed 4-9-08. 1710 Sqn. First noted 11-17	5-18

ROMSEY or Farley, on the A27 northwest of Southampton

Delta Force Paintball: Lee Lane ◆ *By prior arrangement* only | **www.paintballgames.co.uk**

❑ XZ645	Westland Lynx AH.7	83	ex Upminster, Ipswich, M Wallop. First noted 8-17	9-21

Also: A strip in the locality *should* hold a variety of *W&R* inmates.

❑ G-ARUO	Piper Comanche 180	61	ex Bruntingthorpe, N7251P. Cr 19-3-00, de-reg 18-7-00		5-18
❑ G-ASYK	Piper Twin Comanche 160	64	ex Eshott, Bruntingthorpe, N7543Y. Crashed 11-5-96,		
			de-reg 30-10-96. Fuselage. First noted 10-17		5-18
❑ G-AVKR	Bölkow Bö 208 Junior	67	ex D-EGRA. CoA 3-9-09		5-18
❑ G-AVPS	Piper Twin Comanche B	67	ex N8393Y. Crashed 30-11-04, de-reg 6-7-05		5-18
❑ G-AZBB	Bölkow Monsun 150FF	71	ex D-EFJO. CoA 3-5-08		5-18
❑ G-AZOB	Bölkow Monsun 150FF	72	ex D-EAAZ. Crashed 21-8-83, CoA 9-7-84		5-18
❑ G-BJDO	American AA-5A Cheetah	79	ex N26936. CoA 6-8-08, de-reg 27-10-08		5-18
❑ G-BYDX	American AG-5B Tiger	91	ex N374SA. CoA 5-5-08, de-reg 29-11-05		5-18
❑ G-JNAS	American AA-5A Cheetah	78	ex SE-GEI. CoA 9-3-07, de-reg 19-10-18		5-18
❑ G-RROD	Piper Twin Comanche	66	ex Henstridge. CoA 25-8-09, de-reg 11-4-11	[1]	5-18
❑ EC-AOZ	Piper Pacer G-BXBB	52	ex N1133C. De-reg 22-4-03		5-18

■ **[1]** Registered in the USA as N7967V 4-11.

SOLENT AIRPORT, or Lee-on-Solent, east of the B3385, south of Fareham EGHF

The Hovercraft Museum: Among an incredible array of rubber-skirted exhibits is a Hunter cockpit. The estate of the late Frank Matthews donated the forward fuselage of Islander VQ-SAC to the Britten-Norman Preservation Society. Initially moving to Ryde, Isle of Wight, it arrived at <u>Northwood</u>, Isle of Wight, on 7th January 2021.

◆ *Marine Parade West, PO13 9NS* | **02392 552090** | email via website | **www.hovercraft-museum.org**

❑ WV381	'732'	Hawker Hunter GA.11	55	ex Benson, Culham, Kemble, Farnborough, FRADU, FRU,	
				FWS, 222. Crashed 2-11-72. Cockpit. First noted 7-18	[1]	8-21

■ **[1]** Loaned by David Webb - see also Bournemouth, Dorset.

Fareham College Centre for Engineering and Manufacturing Advanced Skills Training (CEMAST, no less): 'JP' T.5A XW538 departed on 16th June 2020 for Kemb... Cotswold, Glos. It was followed by Wasp XT780 - donated to the Westland Wasp Historic Flight - moving to Winchester, Hampshire, on 16th August 2020. Replacement has come in the form of a Sea King and a Cessna. ◆ *By prior arrangement* only | www.fareham.ac.uk

☐ G-CIBB*	Cessna F.172H	66	ex ex OY-EGZ, N17013, Reims-built. De-reg 14-7-21		12-21
☐ ZA296*	Westland Sea King HC.4	80	ex Fleetlands, 846, Afghanistan, 846, 845, 846, Falklands, 846. First noted 11-21		12-21

Others: Bell Ranger G-BFPP had moved to Ballinamore, Ireland, by August 2021.

☐ G-AALY	DH Moth	29	ex F-AJKM, G-AALY. CoA 15-5-05		7-17
☐ G-ACLL	DH Leopard Moth	34	ex Jurby, AW165, AFEE, 7 AACU, 6 AACU, Ringway SF. CoA 6-12-95		N2-19
☐ G-BTYY	Curtiss C-2 Robin	29	ex N348K, NC348K. CoA 1-9-97		11-17
☐ G-RLON	BN Trislander	75	ex Aurigny, G-ITEX, G-OCTA, VR-CAA, DQ-FCF, G-BCXW. Flew in 5-4-17. De-reg 9-12-19	[1]	5-21

■ [1] *Oscar-November*'s total time came to 32,604 hours with a staggering 105,130 landings. Held in store for Solent Sky, Southampton, Hampshire - which see.

Locally: David Webb's Tomahawk cockpit G-DYOU to moved briefly to Bournemouth, Dorset, by mid-2021 before migrating in January 2022 to 'North Devon'. His Hunter cockpit is at the Hovercraft Museum - see above.

SOPLEY on the B3347 north of Christchurch
New Forest Airfields Heritage Centre: (Note change of name.) Based on the former back-up generator building of post-war RAF Sopley, Southern Radar. It also covers the USAAF advanced landing ground of Winkton.
◆ *Mosquito Way, Bransgore, BH23 8AU.* | email via website | https://fonfasite.wordpress.com/the-education-centre

SOUTHAMPTON
Solent Sky: As part of the 'Romance of the Flying-Boat' exhibition the Sandringham, including the flightdeck, is available for inspection and occasionally cockpits of other exhibits are opened. BN Trislander G-RLON is stored at Lee-on-Solent, pronounced Solent, Hampshire. The museum has an excellent relationship with **424 Squadron, Air Cadets** - see below. The cockpit of Sea Vixen FAW.1 XJ476 is on loan to BDAC at Boscombe Down, Wilts.
Co-sited in the Hampshire Police and Fire Museum: **www.hampshirepolicefireheritage.co.uk**
◆ *Albert Road South, SO14 3FR* | **02380 635830** | aviation@spitfireonline.co.uk | www.solentskymuseum.org

☐ 'G-ADZW'	Mignet HM.14 'Flea'	94	BAPC.253, ex Sandown, Lake, Isle of Wight. Built by Howard Shore. Arrived 5-00		1-22
☐ G-ALZE	Britten Norman BN-1F	51	ex Cosford, Kemble, Bembridge. De-reg 12-6-89. Arr 1985		1-22
☐ G-APOI	Saro Skeeter Mk.8	57	ex M Wallop, Wattisham, Saxmundham, M Wallop, Inverness, Blackpool, East Cowes, Eastleigh. CoA 2-8-00, de-reg 14-4-10. Acquired 3-8-08		1-22
☐ –	SUMPAC man powered	61	BAPC.7, ex Old Warden, Southampton. Arrived 1984	[1]	1-22
☐ –	Airwave hang-glider	80	BAPC.215, prototype. Arrived 1987		1-22
☐ VH-BRC	Short Sandringham 4 JM715	43	ex Lee-on-Solent, N158C, VP-LVE *Southern Cross*, N158C, VH-BRC, ZK-AMH, JM715. Rochester-built. Last flown 2-2-81, arrived 2-3-83. *Beachcomber*	[2]	1-22
☐ 'C4451'	Avro 504J replica	91	BAPC.210, partially sectioned. AJD Engineering-built		1-22
☐ N248	Supermarine S.6A	29	ex Cowes, Southampton, Henlow, Southampton Pier, 'S1596', Eastleigh, Calshot, S.6, RAFHSF. Acquired 7-2-76		1-22
☐ 'N546'	Wight Quadruplane rep	87	BAPC.164, ex Wimborne. Arrived 1988		1-22
☐ - 'AL-K'	Hawker Hurricane FSM	15	volunteer-built, travelling exhibit		6-18
☐ BB807	DH Tiger Moth G-ADWO	35	ex Wimborne, Valley SF, 6 FTS, 22 EFTS, 4 FIS, Cam UAS, 510, 24, 20 EFTS, 12 EFTS, CoA. De-reg 15-9-58. Arr 1988	[3]	1-22
☐ PK683	V-S Spitfire F.24	46	ex Kingsbridge Lane, Kemble, Colerne, Changi 7150M, Singapore Aux AF. CBAF-built. Accident 29-9-52. Acquired 7-2-76	[4]	1-22
☐ TG263	Saro SR.A/1	46	ex Duxford, Staverton, Cranfield, G-12-1, TG263. Arrived 1993	[5]	1-22
☐ WK570	DHC Chipmunk T.10	52	ex Hurn, Hamble, Southampton 8211M (4-8-72), 663, Hull UAS, 663, RAFC. Cockpit	[6]	1-22

❑ XF114		V-S Swift F.7	G-SWIF	57	ex Bicester, Scampton, Hurn, Connah's Quay, Aston Down,		
					CS(A), Cranfield. De-reg 19-7-04. Acquired 2005. Fuselage		1-22
❑ XJ571	'242'	DH Sea Vixen FAW.2		60	ex Brooklands, Dunsfold, Southampton, Cosford		
					8140M (30-5-71), Halton, Sydenham, 892, FAW.1,		
					899, 893. Christchurch-built. Arr 5-2-03. 893 Sqn c/s	[7]	1-22
❑ XK740		Folland Gnat F.1		57	ex Hamble, Cosford 8396M (2-8-61), Bicester, Church		
					Fenton, MoS, Filton. SOC 13-2-61. Acquired 6-3-87	[4]	1-22
❑ XL770		Saro Skeeter AOP.12		58	ex M Wallop, Shrivenham 8046M, Wroughton, 652, 654.		
					SOC 23-5-68. Arrived 1987	[8]	1-22
❑ XV760		HS Harrier GR.3		69	ex Dunsfold, Y'ton A2605 [2] A2614 (30-5-91), Culdrose,		
					St Athan, 3, 4, GR.1, 233 OCU. Cockpit. Arr 2010	[7] [9]	1-22
❑ –		V-S Swift FR.5 CIM			forward fuselage	[10]	1-22
❑ 'U-1215'		DH Vampire T.11		55	ex Farnborough, Wisbech, Huntingdon, Horley,		
			XE998		Charlwood, Biggin Hill, Warmingham, Wigan, Woodford,		
					Chester, St Athan, 8 FTS, 4 FTS, 8 FTS. Hatfield-built.		
					SOC 11-12-67. Arrived 2005. Swiss Air Force colours	[7]	1-22

■ **[1]** SUMPAC - Southampton University Man-Powered Aircraft. **[2]** Sandringham on loan from the Science Museum, South Kensington, Gtr Lon. **[3]** Tiger Moth is a composite, with parts from G-AOAC and G-AOJJ. **[4]** Spitfire F.24 and Gnat F.1 are on loan from the RAF Museum, Hendon, Gtr Lon. **[5]** SR.A.1 is on loan from the Imperial War Museum, Duxford, Cambs. **[6]** On loan from 424 Sqn ATC - see below. **[7]** Sea Vixen, Harrier and Vampire are on loan from the Hallett Collection/MCA Aviation USA. **[8]** Skeeter on loan from the Army Flying Museum, Middle Wallop, Hants. **[9]** Much of XV760 was consumed in the Sea Harrier FRS.1 composite XZ493, see Yeovilton, Somerset. **[10]** 'Favourite' for this is FR.5 XD903 - all of its life test and trials, last reported at Wisley, 1956.

Deep Store: Cadet TX.3 XN246 handed on to the Gliding Heritage Centre at Lasham, Hampshire, on 11th March 2020. As it was a duplicate, it was passed on to a private owner. ◆ Several sites in the locality are used. *Not available for inspection*

❑ WM571		DH Sea Venom FAW.22		54	ex Wimborne, Staverton, ADS, 831, RAE, FAW.21, 891, A&AEE,	
					HS. Christchurch-built. Last flown 30-4-69. Arrived 24-12-88	6-18
❑ XD332	'194'	V-S Scimitar F.1		66	ex Helston, Culdrose SAH-19, Lee-on-Solent A2574	
					(6-10-67), 764, 736, 807, 804. Arrived 10-3-99	6-20

No.424 (City of Southampton) Squadron, Air Cadets: Has its HQ within the Blighmont Army Reserve Centre in Millbrook Road West. Some airframes are held at Solent Sky - see above. Within the HQ are several impressive, wholly synthetic, procedure trainers. ◆ *By prior application* only | www.424sqn.com

❑ XD596		DH Vampire T.11		54	ex Calmore, St Athan 7939M (14-2-67), CATCS, CNCS,	
					5 FTS, 4 FTS. Hatfield-built	4-12
❑ XP542	'42'	Folland Gnat T.1		63	ex Hamble, Southampton, Shrivenham, St Athan 8575M	
					(5-1-78), 4 FTS. 'Red Arrows' c/s stb, red/white to stb	10-21
❑ –		Hunting Jet Provost CIM		~	marked 'CRAN 22/2'	[1]	4-12

■ **[1]** 'JP' cockpit *may* be wholly 'synthetic' but *perhaps* owes its origins to a Mk.3 or Mk.4, although it is marked 'T Mk 5-A' (sic).

Aero Antiques and **AeroTech:** The classic light aircraft craftsmen continue their magic, mostly with a de Havilland flavour. Several items are long-in-the-tooth but are *believed* extant. ◆ **Strictly** *by prior application* **only**

❑ G-ABNX		Robinson Redwing 2	32	ex Redhill, Old Sarum, Shoreham. CoA 12-5-03		8-20
❑ G-ACYZ*		Miles Hawk Major	34	ex Canada, C-FAUV, CF-AUV, VH-ACC, RAAF A37-4,		
				VH-ACC, G-ACYZ. Phillips & Powis-built		8-20
❑ G-ADNL*		Miles Sparrowhawk	06	ex Hatch, Bury	[1]	8-20
❑ G-AFJA		Watkinson Dingbat	38	ex Berkswell, Headcorn. Crashed 19-5-75, de-reg 1-12-14		3-16
❑ G-AFOJ*		DH Moth Minor	39	ex Navestock, London Colney, Navestock, E-1, E-0236,		
				G-AFOJ. Arrived 3-2-21		2-21
❑ G-AFSW		Chilton DW.2	r39	ex Chilton Manor. Unflown. De-reg 1-12-46		1-10
❑ G-AJOA*		DH Tiger Moth	40	ex T5424, 16 EFTS, 18 EFTS. CoA 22-5-03. First noted 4-18		8-20
❑ G-ANOD*		DH Tiger Moth	41	ex T6121, 19 RFS, 10 RFS, Lon UAS, 24 EFTS,		
				Northolt SF, 60 OUT. Morris Motors-built. First noted 4-18		8-20
❑ G-AOBH*		DH Tiger Moth	41	ex T7997, 6 FTS, 3 EFTS, 7 RFS, 3 EFTS, 1 EFTS.		
				Morris Motors-built. First noted 4-18		8-20
❑ G-AOEX		Thruxton Jackaroo	44	ex Southampton, Tiger Moth NM175, 63 GCF, 11 RFS.		
				Morris-built, Jackaroo conversion 1957. CoA 3-2-68		3-16
❑ G-BADV		Brochet MB.50	53	ex Ludlow, Dunkeswell, F-PBRJ. CoA 9-5-79		N4-18
❑ G-ECDF*		DH Fox Moth	47	ex G-CGUO, ZK-AQM. DH Canada-built. First noted 4-18		8-20
❑ G-EUKS		Westland Widgeon III	28	ex Australia, VH-UKS		8-20

❏ G-FAGK*   DH Gipsy Moth   29 ex USA, C-FAGK, CF-AGK. Moth Aircraft Corp-built   7-20
■ [1] Much-travelled, much raced Sparrowhawk G-ADNL was morphed in 1952 into the jet-powered Sparrowjet, which was burnt out at Upavon in the summer of 1964. This is a replica of the 1935-era G-ADNL, using Magister wings and a "handful" of metal components discarded during the creation of the jet version.

Hampshire and Isle of Wight Air Ambulance: *Should* still have a Bölkow travelling fund-raiser. | **www.hiowaa.org**
❏ G-ESAM   'AM' Bölkow Bö 105DB   92 ex G-BUIB, G-BDYZ, D-HDEF. De-reg 26-6-03. Cockpit   [1]   4-11
■ [1] Original cockpit from 'DBS-4 upgrade in the early 1990s. G-ESAM, now registered as G-WAAS, flies on.

Also: Last noted in July 2013, the cockpits of Gannet AS.1 WN411, Vampire T.11 'XD614' (WZ572) and all of Vampire T.11 XH318 are *believed* to have left the locality by 2017 – no 'forwarding address'.

SOUTHAMPTON AIRPORT or Eastleigh
Gentle reminder, the Spitfire on a plinth at a roundabout is a large piece of sculpture and not an airframe or FSM.

SOUTHWICK on the B2177 north of Portsmouth
Defence College of Policing and Guarding:
❏ XZ174   Westland Lynx AH.7   77 ex Gosport, Brize Norton, 3 Regt, 655, 662, 655, 652, 651.
                                                 Cabin. First noted 12-11   3-16

STOCKBRIDGE on the A30 south of Andover
Mike Draper: Author of the brilliant *Sitting Ducks and Peeping Toms* on British UAVs has long-held a MATS-B at a *private* location in the area. With an 11ft span, this aerial target is smaller than some radio-controlled *models*.
❏ 'ZA535'   Short MATS-B   82 ex Chandler's Ford, Larkhill, Manorbier.
                                    ZB535   Last flight 9-12-82, SOC 5-6-84. Acquired 5-6-84   [1]   6-12
■ [1] Serial incorrectly painted from delivery and never amended. Conducted just six flights, total time 3 hours, 8 minutes.

SWANWICK northwest of Junction 9 of the M27, north of Locks Heath
National Air Traffic Services: Swanwick Centre, in Sopwith Way.
❏ XW917   HS Harrier GR.3   71 ex Boscombe Down, Cottesmore 8975M, Laarbruch,
                                                 3, 4, 3. SOC 3-4-88   6-20

THRUXTON AERODROME north of the A303 west of Andover   EGHO
❏ G-ANWX   Auster J5L Aiglet Trainer 54 ex Chislet. Crashed 1-8-93, de-reg24-9-93   6-14
❏ G-ASAX   Beagle Terrier 2   46 ex Chislet, Auster AOP.6 TW533, 652, LAS, AOPS, 663.
                                                 CoA 1-9-96. Off-site   N1-19
❏ G-ASEF   Auster 6A Tugmaster   48 ex Bicester, AOP.6 VW985, 664. De-reg 13-1-67   5-21
❏ G-DISK   Piper Comanche 250   59 ex Turweston, G-APZG, EI-AKW. CoA 27-10-10,
                                                 de-reg 14-6-16. Arrived 2016   8-16
❏ G-HALP*   SOCATA Tobago   78 ex Booker, G-BITD. CoA 25-9-06, de-reg 21-5-12. F/n 7-21   7-21
❏ XW799   Westland Scout   72 ex Chiseldon, M Wallop, 657, 656, 658,
                  AH.1   G-BXSL   CoA 19-8-02, crashed 19-11-01, de-reg 7-5-02. Rescue tng   1-20

WINCHESTER east of the M3, north of Southampton
Westland Wasp Historic Flight: Also owns XT434 - see Higher Purtington, Somerset.
❏ XT780*   '636' Westland Wasp HAS.1 66 ex Lee-on-Solent, Fareham, Fleetlands, A2638 [2], ex A2716
                                                 (17-8-83), Fleetlands, 703, 706, 829. Arrived 20-8-20   4-21

Army Training Regiment, Sir John Moore Barracks: A Gazelle is displayed opposite the guardroom,
❏ ZB672   Sud Gazelle AH.1   84 ex Shawbury, Fleetlands, 651, 663, 654, 672, 662, 657,
                                                 664, 3 Flt, Garrison Air Sqn. Westland-built   12-20

Others: The following, all not physically sighted for eight-plus years, have been deleted: Tri-Pacer G-ARBV, Taylorcraft BL-65 G-BVRH (*perhaps* to Devon), Stampe G-BXSV, Challis Chaffinch G-KIRC, Spezio Tuholer G-NGRM and Cub G-OINK.

HEREFORDSHIRE

BICTON west of the B4361, northwest of Leominster
Oaker Wood Leisure: ◆ *By prior arrangement* **only** | www.oakerwoodleisure.co.uk
☐ XP360   'V'   Westland Whirlwind   62 ex Upper Hill, Sunderland, Warmingham, Lasham,
                     HAR.10   Fawkham Green, CFS, 225. SOC 31-3-76. Red overall   7-21

CREDENHILL north of the A438, west of Hereford
Stirling Lines: Named after Colonel David Stirling, the man who set up the Special Air Service. See also Ewyas Harold, below.
☐ ZE412   Agusta 109A   88 ex M Wallop, Arborfield. 8 Flt. SOC 12-6-09.
                                         Displayed, first noted 10-17   8-21

EWYAS HAROLD on the A465 southwest of Hereford
Pontrilas Army Training Area: Exercise area for the Herefordshire Gun Club, sorry, SAS - see Credenhill, above.
☐ TF-AME   Boeing 747-312   94 ex Kemble, Air Atlanta, F-GSEA, SIA N121KG. Arr 7-2-15   6-17
☐ 9M-MMI   Boeing 737-4H6   92 ex Kemble, Malaysia Airlines. Fuselage. Arrived 24-2-13   6-17

KINGTON west of Leominster, on the A44
Martin Aubrey - Classic Ultralight Heritage Collection: Although dated, the fleet is *believed* current.
◆ *By prior arrangement* **only**
☐ G-ADPJ   BAC Drone II   35 ex Selby, Breighton, Wigan, Bristol, Benson, Thetford.
                                       Damaged 3-4-55. Also parts from G-AEKU   N8-18
☐ G-ARIF   Ord-Hume OH-7 Coupe   61 ex Breighton, Wigan   [1]   N8-18
☐ G-ASDF   Edwards Gyrocopter   r62 ex Innsworth, Woking, Coulsdon. De-reg 3-10-63   3-02
☐ G-BXIY   Blake Bluetit   30 ex N Weald, Old Warden, BAPC.37, Winchester   [2]   N8-18
☐ G-MBEP   Aerolights Eagle 215B   80 ex Caernarfon. CoA 8-4-96   3-18
☐ G-MBWI   Microlite Lafayette 1   r82 ex Selby, Leeds, Leigh. De-reg 13-6-90   N12-14
■ **[1]** OH-7 is a version of the Luton Minor developed and built by Arthur Ord-Hume, Chiswick. **[2]** Devised by the Blake brothers at Winchester. Cut-down wings from an Avro 504K and the rear fuselages of Simmonds Spartan Two Seater G-AAGN and Spartan Three Seater G-AAJB used in the construction. Flew, unhampered by 'paperwork' from 1930 for about two years.

Also: An Auster is under restoration at a *private* site in the locality.
☐ RT610*   Taylorcraft Auster 5A-160   44 ex 657, SOC 9-12-47. CoA 10-6-13   10-20

SHOBDON AERODROME north of the A44 west of Leominster   EGBS
Last noted in September 2010, Autocrat G-AGYK moved to Taunton, Somerset.
☐ G-AFGD*   BA Swallow II   37 ex BK897, GTS, CLE, RAE, G-AFGD. CoA 10-7-14   9-21
☐ G-ARVV   Piper Cherokee 160   62 CoA 17-3-09   7-19
☐ G-AWDU* Brantly B2B   68 CoA 3-1-14   6-21
☐ G-TGRA   Agusta 109A   82 ex D-HEED. CoA 14-5-11   4-20

HERTFORDSHIRE

BERKHAMSTED Last physically noted in December 1999, Jodel D.9 G-AVPD has been deleted.

BOVINGDON on the B4505 southwest of Hemel Hempstead
Delta Force Paintball: On part of the former airfield. ◆ *By prior arrangement* **only** | www.paintballgames.co.uk
☐ XZ612   'UDF'   Westland Lynx AH.7   79 ex Upminster, Ipswich, M Wallop. First noted 1-18   1-18

ELSTREE AERODROME north of Junction 4, M1   EGTR
Baron 55 N7219L departed in June 2019, possibly bound for the USA.
☐ G-ASFA   Cessna 172D Skyhawk   63 ex N2582U. CoA 20-7-16   7-21

☐ G-AWOE	Aero Commander 680E	59	ex N3844C. CoA 22-6-10, de-reg 21-12-15	7-21
☐ G-AWTJ	Cessna F.150J	68	Reims-built. CoA 18-12-04, de-reg 18-5-10. Cockpit	7-21
☐ G-BORH	Piper Seneca 200T	80	ex N8261V. CoA 21-3-08, de-reg 21-2-11	7-21
☐ G-BOXR*	American GA-7 Cougar	78	ex N772GA. De-reg 3-12-19. First noted 7-20	7-20
☐ G-CYMA	American GA-7 Cougar	79	CoA 9-10-13	7-21
☐ G-ENTW	Cessna F.152	78	CoA 4-5-13. Reims-built	7-21
☐ G-PIKK	Piper Cherokee 140	67	ex G-AVLA, N11C. CoA 17-12-16, de-reg 29-12-20	12-20
☐ C-FQIP	Lake LA-4-200	~	ex N1068L	7-21
☐ N23103	Cessna 150H	~	dismantled	7-21
☐ 'XX704'*	SAL Bulldog T.1 G-BCUV	75	ex Hurn, Ghana AF G-112, G-BCUV. CoA 5-8-14. F/n 12-20 [1]	12-20

■ [1] The real XX704 was exported to the USA, from storage at Shawbury, Shropshire, in 2000.

HARPENDEN on the A1081 north of St Albans
No.795 Squadron Air Cadets: The unit *should* still have a Cessna fuselage employed as a simulator.

| ☐ G-OPJC | Cessna F.152 II | 79 | ex Stapleford Tawney, N68354. Reims-built. | |
| | | | CoA 17-10-07, de-reg 25-4-08. Fuselage, simulator | 10-18 |

HATFIELD
University of Hertfordshire: The School of Engineering and Technology has a Model 23 Musketeer: its fin fillet carries the quaint title 'Beechcraft Musketeer BE XXIII'. ◆ *By prior arrangement* **only | www.herts.ac.uk**

| ☐ G-NRIA | Beech Musketeer | 63 | ex I-MIFA, N2373J. De-reg 5-7-12. First noted 5-19 | 7-19 |

HEMEL HEMPSTEAD on the A414 west of St Albans
The Vampire Collection: Alan Allen's airframes are kept in the locality.
◆ *By prior arrangement* **only | alanwz581@gmail.com**

☐ WZ581	'77' DH Vampire T.11	53	ex Ruislip, Bushey, Keevil, Exeter, 3/4 CAACU, 229 OCU,	
			233 OCU, 25. SOC 16-12-71. Hawarden-built. Cockpit	8-21
☐ XT439	'605' Westland Wasp HAS.1	65	ex King's Lynn, Bruntingthorpe, Cranfield, Wroughton,	
			829, 703, 829, 845. Crashed 25-3-86. Arrived 10-5-02	8-21

HITCHIN on the A505 northeast of Luton
Philip Leaver: *Should* still have his cockpit-cum-sims. ◆ *By prior arrangement* **only**

☐ G-KAYT	Robinson R22	88	ex G-EIST, N9081H. Crashed 31-8-94, de-reg 18-1-95. Sim	3-12
☐ XV759	'O' HS Harrier GR.3	69	ex Bruntingthorpe, South Molton, Welshpool, Llantrisant,	
			Pendine, St Athan, 233 OCU, 1417 Flt, 233 OCU, 1, 233 OCU	
			1, GR.1, 233 OCU. SOC 10-7-89. Cockpit, sim	3-12

Also: An Auster is under long term rebuild at a *private* location.

| ☐ G-AOZL | Auster J5Q Alpine | 57 | ex Earls Colne, Southend. CoA 28-5-88 | N2-20 |

KING'S LANGLEY on the A41 north of Watford and J20 of the M25
Great Westwood Equestrian Park: off Old House Lane. Within this huge woodland site are two airframes, used as jumps.
◆ *By prior permission* **only | www.windm https://greatwestwoodequestrianpark.weebly.com/**

| ☐ G-BFBB | Piper Aztec 250E | 73 | CoA 4-8-10, de-reg 6-4-17 | 11-18 |
| ☐ N519MC | Piper Cherokee 140 | ~ | ex Elstree. De-reg 24-10-17. Fuselage | 11-18 |

LONDON COLNEY south of the A414, southeast of St Albans
De Havilland Aircraft Museum: Since 1958 and the arrival of the Mosquito prototype back at the site where it was designed and built, this pioneering museum has gone from strength to strength. The £2 million-plus **Sir Geoffrey de Havilland Hangar** was opened up to the public on 16th February 2020, bringing inside such treasures as the gleaming Comet 1A fuselage.

   A DH.71 Tiger Moth – the *monoplane* of 1927 – replica began construction in September 2020; it will merit a formal listing in due course. Several airframes are in store off-site. These are listed separately and are *not* available for inspection. Dove D-IFSB is on loan at Fishburn, D&C.

◆ *Access from the B556, paralleling the M25. AL2 1BU* | **01727 826400** | **museum@dehavillandmuseum.co.uk** | **www.dehavillandmuseum.co.uk**

☐ G-ABLM		Cierva C.24	31	ex Hatfield, Sydenham (London), West Byfleet.		
				CoA 16-1-35, de-reg 12-39. DH-built. Arrived 7-80	[1]	1-22
☐ 'G-ACSR'	'19'	DH Comet FSM	90	BAPC.216, ex 'G-ACSS', St Albans, Kings Langley,		
				Wroughton, Australia. Arrived 2001	[2]	1-22
☐ G-ADOT		DH Hornet Moth	35	ex Hatfield, Old Warden, Stoke Ferry, Stapleford,		
				Houghton-on-the-Hill, X9326, 5 GCF, 23 OTU, 24 GCF,		
				6 AONS, Halton SF, 2 CPF, G-ADOT. CoA 5-10-59,		
				de-reg 18-9-63. Arrived 1977		1-22
☐ G-AKDW		DH Dragon Rapide	45	ex Amsterdam, F-BCDB, G-AKDW, YI-ABD, Dominie NR833.		
				Brush-built. Arr 1994. *City of Winchester*		1-22
☐ G-ANAV		DH Comet 1A	52	ex Wroughton, S Kensington, Farnborough, BOAC G-ANAV,		
				CPA CF-CUM, G-ALZA. Hatfield-built. De-reg 1-7-55.		
				Arrived 2016. Cockpit	[3]	1-22
☐ G-ANRX		DH Tiger Moth	39	ex Belchamp Walter, N6550, SLAW, 25 EFTS, 18 EFTS,		
				241, 14 EFTS, 56 E&RFTS. CoA 20-6-61, de-reg 8-6-67.		
				Arrived 1976. Crop duster. *Border City*		1-22
☐ G-AOTI		DH Heron 2D	56	ex Biggin Hill, Exeter, G-5-19. CoA 24-6-87, de-reg		
				17-10-95. Arrived 19-8-95		1-22
☐ G-AREA		DH Dove 8	61	ex Hatfield. CoA 8-9-87, de-reg 19-9-00. Arr 2000. BAe c/s		1-22
☐ G-ARYC		HSA HS.125 Srs 1/521	63	ex Hatfield, Filton, R-R, BSE. CoA 1-8-73, last flight 7-9-73,		
				de-reg 31-3-76. Hatfield-built. Acquired 3-76, arrived 1979		
				Rolls-Royce colours (stb), Bristol Siddeley (pt) colours		1-22
☐ G-AVFH		HS Trident 2	71	ex Heathrow, BA, BEA. Forward fuselage.		
				De-reg 12-5-82. Arrived 7-82. BEA colours		1-22
☐ G-AWZP*		HS Trident 3B-101	71	ex Manchester, Heathrow, BA, BEA. CoA 14-3-86,		
				de-reg 27-6-86. Cockpit	[4]	due
☐ G-JEAO		HSA HS.146-100	83	ex Filton, Air France Express/JEA, G-UKPC, C-GNVX,		
				N802RW, G-5-512, PT-LEP, G-BKXZ, PT-LEP. Hatfield-built.		
				CoA 4-6-05, de-reg 2-11-09. Arrived 27-7-09. Fuselage	[5]	1-22
☐ –		DH Comet 2	53	ex Wroughton, Dan-Air, BOAC, Crawley, Hatfield.		
				Arrived 14-6-96. Simulator. BOAC Comet 4 colours	[6]	1-22
☐ F-BGNX		DH Comet 1A	53	ex Farnborough, G-AOJT (de-reg 9-7-56), Air France		
		G-AOJT		F-BGNX. Hatfield-built. Last flight 27-6-56.		
				Arrived 20-3-85. Fuselage, Air France colours	[7]	1-22
☐ J7326		DH Humming Bird	24	ex Hatch, Audley End, Bishop's Stortford, Hamble,		
		G-EBQP		Henlow, Farnborough, J7326, RAE, A&AEE.		
				Crashed *and* de-reg 21-7-34. Arrived 25-3-03	[8]	1-22
☐ W4050		DH Mosquito	40	ex Hatfield, Chester, Hatfield, Panshanger, Hatfield,		
		prototype		RR, DH, A&AEE, E-0234. Last flown 12-43. Arrived 9-58	[9]	1-22
☐ LF789		DH Queen Bee	43	BAPC.186, ex 'K3584', Hadfield, Droylesden, Redhill,		
	'R2-K'			St Athan, Pilot-less Aircraft Unit, Manorbier, St Athan,		
				Scottish Aviation-built. SOC 26-11-46. Arrived 13-4-86		1-22
☐ –		Airspeed Horsa I / II	c44	BAPC.232, composite fuselage, rear of Mk.II TL615,		
				latter arrived 7-10-78		1-22
☐ TA122	'UP-G'	DH Mosquito FB.6	45	ex Soesterberg, Delft, 4, 2 GCS, 48, 4, 605. SOC 30-6-50.		
				Arrived 26-2-78. 605 Sqn and/or 4 Sqn colours	[10]	1-22
☐ TA634	'8K-K'	DH Mosquito TT.35	45	ex Speke, G-AWJV (de-reg 19-10-70) *Mosquito Squadron*		
		G-AWJV		(1968), Speke G-AWJV Aldergrove, 3 CAACU, APS		
				Schleswigland, APS Ahlorn, APS Sylt, 4 CAACU, B.35.		
				Last flown 16-7-68. Arrived 29-9-70. 571 Sqn colours		1-22
☐ WP790	'T'	DHC Chipmunk T.10	52	ex Rush Green G-BBNC (de-reg 23-9-74), WP790,		
		G-BBNC		Birm UAS, Wales UAS, PFTS, AOTS, 1 ITS, RAFC, Man, Glas,		
				Leeds UASs, 24 GCF, Binbrook SF, 5 RFS, 17 RFS.		
				SOC 5-11-73. Arrived 1976. Birmingham UAS colours		1-22
☐ XG730	'438'	DH Sea Venom FAW.22	57	ex Southwick, Portsmouth, Lee-on-Solent, ADS, Sydenham,		
				893, 894, 891. Hawarden-built. Last flight 7-7-70,		
				SOC 13-7-70. Arrived 28-10-78. 891 Sqn colours		1-22
☐ XJ565	'127'	DH Sea Vixen FAW.2	60	ex RAE, 899, 893, 766B. Christchurch-built. SOC 29-7-76.		
				Arrived 31-10-76. 899 Sqn colours		1-22

❏ XJ772	'H'	DH Vampire T.11	55	ex Brooklands, Wisley, Shawbury, CATCS, 1 FTS, 8 FTS, RAFC,
				Norway AF 15018 'PX-G'. Christchurch-built. SOC 3-2-71.
				Arrived 29-3-94 1-22
❏ XK695		DH Comet C.2(R)	56	ex Stock, Newton 9164M (10-11-92), Duxford, Wyton, 51,
		G-AMXH		216, Srs 2 G-AMXH (de-reg 2-3-55). Hatfield-built.
				Last flown 10-1-75. Arrived 17-12-95. Cockpit 1-22
❏ J-1008		DH Vampire FB.6	49	ex Hatfield, Swiss AF. Hatfield-built.
				Last flown 20-8-74. Arrived 11-5-75 1-22

■ [1] DH-built Cierva C.24 is on loan from the Science Museum, acquired 9-35. [2] DH.88 Comet FSM was built in Australia for use in the film *The Great Air Race*. Owned by Ralph Steiner. [3] Comet cockpit acquired by the Science Museum 21-5-62, gifted to DHAM upon arrival. [4] Trident cockpit courtesy of DHAM's Lee Rawlins and Kevin Bowen (see Feltham, Gtr Lon). [5] The 146 first flew at Hatfield 8-11-83 and made its last flight, into Filton, on 7-1-03. [6] Comet 2 sim was built at the same time as the cockpits for the first two prototypes and was used for structural tests. It then went to the DH Servicing School and was later converted into a simulator, fitted with Mk.4 instrumentation. It served with BOAC and then Dan-Air, retiring in 1983 with a total of 10,660 training hours. [7] Comet 1A registered as G-AOJT for the ferry flight to Farnborough 27-6-56 in the hands of John Cunningham. [8] Humming Bird has the wings of Martin Monoplane G-AEYY - see Eaton Bray, Beds - which itself used a set of DH.53 wings, probably from J7325. The project is on loan from Terry Pankhurst and Peter Kirk and is under restoration to fly. J7326, served on trials with the Airship R-33 in 1925. [9] 'Mossie' prototype W4050 was built at Salisbury Hall and first flown on 25-11-40 by Geoffrey de Havilland Junior at Hatfield. Five days after delivery to A&AEE W4050 broke its back in a taxying accident. On 24-2-41. The fuselage was replaced by the one intended for the photo-recce prototype, W4051, and fitted at Boscombe Down. (W4051 was completed with a production fuselage.) [10] FB.6 TA122 rebuilt using the wing of TR.33 TW233 acquired in Israel. The codes 'UP-G' relate to TA122's days with 605 Squadron in May 1945 and with its use with 4 Sqn in Germany 1949-1950. (And *possibly* during its time in between with 2 Group's comms unit at Evere.)

Store: Airframes *not* available for inspection.

❏ TJ118	DH Mosquito TT.35	45	ex Elstree/Borehamwood, *Mosquito Squadron* (1968), *633 Sqn*
			(1963), Exeter, 3/4 CAACU, 3 CAACU, B.35. SOC 18-9-61.
			Cockpit, arr 1973: rear fuselage arr (from Oxford) by 6-92 [1] 6-20
❏ VV217	DH Vampire FB.5	48	ex Sunderland, Barnham, Bury St Edmunds, 'VV271',
			7323M (23-3-56), Oakington, DH. EE-built. Arrived 12-8-09 6-20
❏ WM729	DH Vampire NF.10	52	ex 'Glos', London Colney, Ruislip, Bingley, Bradford, Church
			Fenton, CNCS, 2 ANS, 25, 151. Hawarden-built.
			SOC 30-11-59. Arrived 22-6-94. Cockpit, 6-20
❏ WR539	DH Venom FB.4	56	ex Staverton, London Colney, Fownhope, Rhoose, Cosford
			8399M, Kai Tak, 28, 60. Fairey-built. SOC 4-7-62. Arr 11-92 6-20
❏ WX853	DH Venom NF.3	55	ex Debden 7443M (10-7-57), Shawbury, 23.
			Hawarden-built. Arrived 1-68 6-20

■ [1] TJ118's cockpit was used for studio shots for both films, sectioned allowing unlimited access to the port side. Stripped rear fuselage displayed at the Victoria and Albert Museum, London, 2017 as part of a moulded wood exhibition

NUTHAMPSTEAD east of the village and the B1368, southeast of Royston
Nuthampstead Airfield Museum: Located alongside the 'Woodman Inn', the collection charts the history of USAAF Station 131 and the resident 55th Fighter Group and 398th Bomb Group.
◆ *South of Bell Lane and Park Farm Lane, SG8 8NB* | **01638 718427** | www.398th.org

RYE PARK Last noted in September 2017, Cessna 421 N41098 has been deleted.

ST ALBANS
The Paralyser Group (TPG): A group of largely former Handley Page employees has created a faithful replica O/400 forward fuselage in the *general* area. Known as 'TPG.2', the project is a precursor of a full-scale flying replica. (The registration G-BKMG was allocated in May 2010 for TPG.1.) ◆ **Not** *available for public inspection.*

❏ -	HP O/400 replica	20	forward fuselage, construction began 2017 - see above [1] 3-20

■ [1] Due to be presented to a museum in 2022.

Also: Last noted in February 2017, Cessna FR.172 G-BEZS has been deleted.

ISLE OF MAN

The Island is a self-governing British Crown Dependency - part of the British Isles, but not part of the UK

ANDREAS AERODROME on the A9 northwest of Ramsey

Last noted in December 2018, Hamsa G-BZBP, Demon G-MMTD and Hornet G-MRRM have been deleted.

☐ G-BMFI	SZD-45A Ogar	76	CoA 30-5-08, de-reg 22-5-19	12-18
☐ G-BSYA	Jodel D.18	93	CoA 1-10-07, de-reg 7-1-18	N9-20

DOUGLAS

A Super Skymaster is *thought* to still be kept at a *private* location in the area.

☐ G-BOYR	Cessna F.337G	74	ex RA-04147, G-BOYR, PH-RPE. Reims-built.	
			CoA 30-4-09, de-reg 18-11-11	12-17

ISLE OF MAN AIRPORT or Ronaldsway   EGNS

Manx Aviation and Military Museum: Run by the Manx Aviation Preservation Society, the superb displays chart the island's varied aviation history and occupies wartime buildings on the airport site. Part of the exhibition is the **Museum of the Manx Regiment** which has extensive displays on anti-aircraft artillery.

With the completion of the restoration of ATP 'G-MAUD' – see separate notes below – the airliner was positioned alongside the museum compound in early 2021 to become a permanent exhibit.

◆ *South of the airport on the Castletown road, IM9 2AT* | **01624 829294** | **airmuseum@manx.net** | **www.maps.org.im**

☐ G-BGYT	Embraer Bandeirante P1	79	ex Keenair, N104VA, G-BGYT, PT-SAA. CoA 12-1-06, de-reg 26-9-06. Manx Airlines colours	1-22
☐ 'G-MAUD'*	BAe ATP	89	ex airport, West Atlantic, LX-WAN, SE-LHX, LX-WAN, SE-LHX,	
	SE-LHX		N851AW, G-WISS, G-11-20, G-WISS. Last flight 19-6-15. Manx Airlines colours. See above	1-22
☐ 9019	Bristol Bolingbroke IVW	41	ex Nanton, Canada, RCAF. Fairchild Canada-built. Arrived 21-6-04. Cockpit	[1] 1-22

■ **[1]** Identity confirmed. The 'W version was powered by P&W Wasp Juniors.

ATP Preservation Project: Terry Liddiard and friends took on SE-LHX (identity amended) courtesy of the generosity of West Atlantic from 12th August 2018. Restored to Manx Airlines colours, it has been placed alongside the museum = see above.

Airport: The ATP fleet continues to contract: SE-LGX returned to service by early 2021; SE-LHX transferred to the local preservation group, see above; SE-LPT broken up in December 2020. The following met the axe during December 2020 to January 2021, with last flight dates in brackets: SE-MHC (12-10-19), SE-MHE (16-1-19) and SE-MHJ (12-8-19).

☐ G-JBAS	Lancair 200	08	CoA 11-5-11	N2-20
☐ –	Eider Duck	c66	BAPC.282, displayed within the terminal	[1] 1-20
☐ SE-MEX	BAe ATP	89	ex West Air, CS-TFJ, ES-NBB, G-MANG, G-LOGD, G-OLCD.	
	G-MANG		Arrived 30-4-18. Stored	1-20
☐ SE-MHF*	Bae ATP	89	ex West Atlantic, G-BTPF, EC-HCY, G-BTPF, N383AE. Last flight 19-9-18. Rescue training by 2-21	2-21

■ **[1]** Single-seat pusher-configured homebuild, unflown.

Also: The Spitfire FSM has been used for the 'Island at War' celebrations, held each August.

☐ 'P7966'	'D-B' V-S Spitfire FSM	88	BAPC.283, ex Jurby, Farnsfield, Newtown, Kettering, *Piece of Cake*. Feggans Brown-built	9-16

JURBY on the A14 west of Andreas

Isle of Man Motor Museum and TT Museum: On the northern perimeter of the former airfield.

◆ *Ballamenagh Road, IM7 3BD* | **01624 888333** | **isleofmanmotormuseum.com** | **www.isleofmanmotormuseum.com**

☐ XN586*	'91' Hunting Jet Provost T.3A	61	ex Ipswich, Brooklands, Weybridge, Cosford 9039M (10-5-90), 7 FTS, 1 FTS, CFS, 2 FTS, RAFC. Arrived 3-20	3-20

SURBY north of Port Erin

A *private* location in the area *should* still be home to an ATP cockpit.

☐ SE-LGV	BAe ATP	91	ex Ronaldsway, West Air Cargo, N857AW, G-11-034. Cockpit. Arrived mid-17	12-18

ISLE OF WIGHT

ARRETON on the A3056 west of Sandown
Amazon World Zoo Park: Watery Lane ◆ 01983 867122 | www.amazonworld.co.uk
❏ G-OPUS	Jabiru SK	98 ex Sandown. De-reg 30-10-15. First noted 4-19	8-19

BEMBRIDGE AERODROME southwest of Bembridge   EGHJ
Restored by the **Britten-Norman Aircraft Preservation Society**, the oldest surviving Islander, G-AVCN, departed from the workshop at Ryde on 17th December 2020 for Northwood, Isle of Wight. To recoup the 'geography' of the project: it moved from Bembridge, to Bembridge Harbour in July 2010 and restoration began the following year. As the work progressed, larger premises were sought, settling on Ryde in March 2016.

A pair of Islanders have arrived for 'deep' - and *private* - storage on behalf of Britten-Norman.
❏ ZG844*	BN Islander R.1	G-BLNE	87 ex Shawbury, 1 Flt, G-BLNE (de-reg 12-6-89). First noted 5-21	6-21
❏ ZG847*	BN Islander R.1	G-BLNV	87 ex Shawbury, 1 Flt, G-BLNV (de-reg 12-6-89). First noted 6-21	6-21

COWES on the A3020, north of the island
Sir Max Aitken Museum: An 18th century sail-maker's loft was the home of Sir Max Aitken from 1947 until his death in 1985. Most of the exhibits are maritime, but there are items from his night-fighting days and 601 Squadron.
◆ *83 High Street, PO31 7AJ* | 01983 293800 | email via website | www.sirmaxaitkenmuseum.org

Cliftongrade Ltd: The scrap dealers keep a Phantom cockpit at the yard.
❏ XT863	'AS' McD Phantom FG.1	68 ex Abingdon, 43, 111, 892, 767. SOC 24-2-89. Cockpit	5-21

ISLE OF WIGHT (SANDOWN) AERODROME north of the A3056, west of Sandown   EGHN
Wight Aviation Museum: Years of planning and much endeavour came to fruition with the opening of the collection – in an understandably restricted way – in 2020. A purpose-built museum building is planned.
   The Bulldog is part of the exceptional collection of Richard Holleyman and the museum has secured all of his artefacts for display. Other personal archives are also on show and there is a comprehensive reference library. A full-size replica of a Saro Black Arrow R3 rocket is on show. During 2020 another local product, a very low-flyer, Cushioncraft (aka Britten-Norman) hovercraft XX102, built in 1969 at Cowes, was acquired.
◆ *Hangar 2, well signed* | 07949 704052 | wightaviationmuseum@gmail.com | www.wightaviationmuseum.org.uk
❏ 'G-AXEH'	SAL Bulldog 122	75 ex Yarmouth, Ghana AF G-111, G-BCUU. Damaged	
		G-CCOA	22-8-01, de-reg 16-6-02. Fuselage. Arrived 2-18	[1] 1-22

■ **[1]** The *real* G-AXEH can be found at East Fortune, Scotland.

Airframe Assemblies (AA): The Spitfire specialists are also engaged in the early phases of the Typhoon project - see under ARC at Duxford, Cambs. AA was signed up as the build partner for the **Spitfire P8331 Restoration Project** in June 2020. This is in its early days and will resurrect Mk.II P8331, registered as G-KOSC – flown by Wg Cdr Piotr Laguna of 303 Squadron and shot down on 27th June 1941 - www.lagunasspitfirelegacy.org
   Long stored Hurricane BH238 was due to move to the craftsmen at Rochester, Kent, in early 2022 and this move has been anticipated. The fuselage of Seafire XV SR462 (G-TGVP) had moved to Shuttleworth, Beds, by mid-2020. Spitfire IX EN570 (LN-AOA) was delivered to Biggin Hill, Gtr Lon, by June 2021. ◆ *Private premises* - **strictly** *by prior permission*

❏ MJ444*	V-S Spitfire IX	43	ex 443, 403, 411. Shot down Belgium 13-1-45.	
		G-LEGD	Salvaged 2020. For completion as Tr.IX	[1] 1-21
❏ PK664*	V-S Spitfire F.22	45	ex Old Warden, N Weald, Stafford, South Kensington, Stafford, Cosford, Wyton, Cardington, St Athan, Binbrook, Waterbeach 7759M, 615. CBAF-built. SOC 4-2-54.	5-21
❏ TB382	V-S Spitfire XVI	44	ex Coningsby, EP&TU, 'MK673', 'X4277', 7244M, Abingdon, Bicester, Henlow, Ely, Middleton St George, Thornaby, 602. CBAF-built. Arrived 2002	[1] 5-21
❏ TP298	V-S Spitfire FR.XVIII	44	ex USA N41702, Duxford, India inst, IAF HS662,	
		N41702	RAF TP298 n/s. Crashed 19-5-94	12-13

■ **[1]** Registered to Aero Legends 17-3-21 – see also Hythe and Lashenden, Kent. **[2]** TB382 was written out of *W&R20* (p136) as 'consumed' as a source of spares for the rebuild to flying condition of Mk.XVI TE311 of BBMF. It passed on to Airframe Assemblies in return for the new wings for TE311.

Also: Last noted in December 2013, Rallye G-BRDN and AA-5A G-OMOG have been deleted.
❑ G-BLWW* Taylor Mini-Imp 85 ex Sleap. CoA 4-6-87 N2-21

NEWPORT on the A3054, middle of the island
Windmill Campersite: Froglands Lane, south of Carisbrooke Castle. Among the 'glamping' options is 'Galahad the Helicopter' - kip in a Falklands veteran! ◆ *By prior permission* **only** | **www.windmillcampersite.com**
❑ XT469 Westland Wessex HU.5 65 ex Weeton, Bowgreave, Kirkham, Stafford, 8920M,
Wroughton, 771, 847, 772, 846, 848, 847, 848. SOC 27-9-07 12-21

Also: Kept in *separate* and *private* locations *should* be two homebuilds.
❑ G-AZJE Gardan GY-20 Minicab 74 ex Sandown. CoA 7-7-82 N9-18
❑ G-BCMF Levi Go-Plane 74 flown only once, 16-11-74, de-reg 5-12-83 12-13

NORTHWOOD on the A3020, south of Cowes
Wight Military and Heritage Museum: Among the vehicles and set-pieces is an icon of the Island. After a painstaking, decade long, restoration by the Britten-Norman Aircraft Preservation Society, *Charlie-November* is scheduled for an official unveiling in April 2022. This is has been an epic process, the result is an exhibit of international status.
◆ *Newport Road, PO31 8QU* | **01983 632039** | **office@bunker.co.uk** | **www.wmahm.org.uk**
❑ G-AVCN* BN Islander 67 ex Ryde, Bembridge, Puerto Rico, N290VL, F-OGHG, G-AVCN,
Aurigny. De-reg 4-6-15. Aurigny c/s. Arrived 17-12-20 [1] 1-22
❑ VQ-SAC* BN Islander 71 ex Ryde, Lee-on-Solent, Bembridge, East Preston,
Shoreham, 5Y-ANU, G-51-287. Crashed 4-9-76.
Forward fuselage. Arrived 7-1-21 [2] 1-22
■ [1] *Charlie-November* is the oldest surviving Islander: first flown at Bembridge, IoW, on 24th April 1967. It carried out Aurigny's first passenger service, Alderney to Guernsey, on 1st March 1968. It was restored by, and is on loan from, the Britten-Norman Aircraft Preservation Society – **www.bnaps.org.uk** [2] Also on loan from BNAPS, under conversion to flight simulator.

RYDE Last noted in December 2012, Kitfox G-ELIZ has been deleted.

KENT
Includes the unitary authority of Medway

ASHFORD on the M20 west of Folkestone
Although the entry is long-in-the-tooth, the Buccaneer is *believed* extant at a *private* address in the locality.
❑ XV165 Blackburn Buccaneer S.2B 66 ex Spanhoe, Bruntingthorpe, Farnborough, Staverton,
Bentham, Staverton, Hucclecote, Heathrow, Stock,
Shawbury, 12. Cockpit. 12 Sqn colours 11-11

BELTRING Last noted in February 2015, the fuselage of Seneca G-BAGZ has been deleted.

BRENCHLEY Last noted in September 2006, Luton Minor G-ATKH has been deleted.

BRENZETT on the A2070 northwest of New Romney
Romney Marsh Wartime Collection: (Formerly the Brenzett Aeronautical Museum Trust.) Throughout the season the volunteers offer a range of special events and commemorations.
◆ *Ivychurch Road, TN29 0EE* | **01797 344747** | **www.rmwcollection.co.uk**
❑ G-AMSM Douglas Dakota 4 43 ex Booker, Brenzett, Duxford, Brenzett, Lydd, Skyways,
Eagle, Starways, KN274, TCDU, 77, St Eval SF, Azores SF,
C-47B-20-DK 43-49948. Damaged 17-8-78, de-reg 11-9-78.
Oklahoma City-built. Cockpit. Acquired 1979. Air Freight c/s 1-22
❑ 'R6599'* 'DW-J' V-S Spitfire I FSM c19 BAPC.539, first noted 5-21 1-22
❑ V7350 Hawker Hurricane I 40 ex Robertsbridge, 85. Cr 29-8-40. Acquired 1989. Cockpit [1] 1-22

❑ VR192		Percival Prentice	47	ex Hailsham, Lasham, G-APIT (de-reg 8-11-79,		
	G-APIT			CoA 7-9-67), Biggin Hill, Southend, VR192, 1 ASS, 6 FTS,		
				CFS, 2 FTS. Damaged in gales 18-2-22	[2]	2-22
❑ WH657		EE Canberra B.2	52	ex Godalming, Cranfield, RAE, 231 OCU. SOC 29-11-77.		
				Acquired 1987. Cockpit		1-22
❑ XH136	'W'	EE Canberra PR.9	59	ex Spanhoe, Bruntingthorpe, Cosford 8782M (8-2-83),		
				1 PRU, A&AEE, 39, 13, 58, Moa. Short-built.		
				Acquired 2014. Cockpit		1-22
❑ XK625		DH Vampire T.11	56	ex Firbeck, N Weald, Southend, Woodford, St Athan,		
				4 FTS, 1 FTS, 7 FTS. Hawarden-built. SOC 4-12-68.		
				Acquired 11-89		1-22

■ [1] Sgt Frank Walker-Smith was shot down by Bf 109s and he successfully baled out of V7350 and it crashed at Etchington, Kent. [2] Prentice on loan from David Bird - see Hailsham, E Sussex. [2]

CANTERBURY

War and Peace - Battle of Britain Experience: The organisation has replicas available for hire. Its notional headquarters is in the Canterbury area, but the airframes may well be kept elsewhere.

◆ *By prior arrangement* only | email via website | **01304 813337** | **www.warandpeace.uk.com**

❑ –	'F-4L'	Mignet HM.280	98	BAPC.260, ex Wickenby, Millom. RAF colours	[1]	9-21
❑ 'P7370'	'ZP-A'	V-S Spitfire II FSM	~	74 Sqn colours		9-21
❑ 'V6555'	'DT-A'	Hawker Hurricane I FSM	09	257 Sqn colours		9-21
❑ -		Messerschmitt Bf 109 FSM	~			9-21

■ Faithful replica of a 'Pou Maquis' built under the supervision of the South Copeland Aviation Group at HM Prison Haverigg.

CAPEL LE FERNE on the B2011 northeast of Folkestone

National Battle of Britain Memorial: The deeply moving statue of a pilot sitting, contemplating the English Channel, is set against a huge three-bladed propeller akin to the ancient chalk figures found on the South Downs. The Christopher Foxley-Norris Memorial Wall carries the names of all who took part in the Battle.

◆ *Signed from B2011* | **01303 249292** | **enquiries@battleofbritainmemorial.org** | **www.battleofbritainmemorial.org**

| ❑ 'P2970' | 'US-X' | Hawker Hurricane I FSM | 03 | BAPC.291. GB Replicas-built. 56 Sqn colours. *Little Willie* | 1-22 |
| ❑ 'R6775' | 'YT-J' | V-S Spitfire I FSM | 04 | BAPC.299. GB Replicas-built. 65 Sqn colours | 1-22 |

CHATHAM east of Rochester

The Historic Dockyard Chatham: A huge number of naval attractions await, including a Dragonfly.

◆ *North of the A231. Chatham ME7 1UR* | **01634 823800** | **info@chdt.org.uk** | **www.thedockyard.co.uk**

❑ WG751	'710'	Westland Dragonfly HR.5	52	ex Gosport, Condover, Ramsgreave, Ancoats, *The Last Caravan*,	
				Wisbech, Blackbushe, Fleetlands, RAF Handling Sqn,	
				Lossiemouth SF, HR.3, Yeovilton SF, 705. SOC 16-9-65.	
				705 Sqn colours	1-22

Royal Engineers Museum and Library: Has a superb catch-line: 'Local Heritage - Global Impact'. Among the exhibits are the medals etc of James McCudden. The former Chattenden, Kent, V-1 is in deep store here.

◆ *On the B2004. Prince Arthur Road, ME7 1UR* | email via website | **www.re-museum.co.uk**

❑ –		Military gas balloon	~	basket only. RAF Museum loan	3-12
❑ XZ964	'D'	HS Harrier GR.3	80	ex St Athan, 1417 Flt, 233 OCU, 3, 233 OCU, 1.	
				Ninja One, 1417 Flt colours	1-22
❑ –*		Fieseler Fi 103 (V-1)	c44	BAPC.158, ex Chattenden. Stored, from circa 2013	1-20

CHATTENDEN With the closure of the EOD facility, circa 2013, the V-1 moved to deep storage at Chatham, Kent.

DOVER

Dover Museum: Within the varied collection is a 'Doodlebug'.

◆ *Market Square, CT16 1PH* | **01304 201066** | **museumenquiries@dover.gov.uk** | **www.dovermuseum.co.uk**

| ❑ – | | Fieseler Fi 103 (V-1) FSM | c00 | BAPC.290 | 12-19 |

EASTCHURCH Isle of Sheppey

Eastchurch Aviation Museum: (Previously the Sheppey Aviation Centre.) Located within the HM Prison Standford Hill, to the south of the town: the site of the pioneering Eastchurch aerodrome, established in 1910. There are extensive displays and plans to restore a former hangar as a heritage centre. The memorial in the middle of the town is a 'must visit'.

◆ *Wrights Way, off Brabazon Road, ME12 4AA* | **email** via website | **https://eastchurchaviationmuseum.org.uk**

GRAVESEND on the A226 east of Dartford

A Buccaneer S.1 cockpit is *believed* to be kept by a collector at a *private* location.

☐ XN928	Blackburn Buccaneer S.1	62	ex Manston, Bruntingthorpe, Rhoose, St Athan 8179M (10-9-74), 736, 809, 801. Pink, *Glenfiddich*, *Jaws / Liz*. Cockpit	7-18
☐ -*	Blackburn Buccaneer EMU	~	test rig	7-18

HAWKINGE on the A260 north of Folkestone

Kent Battle of Britain Museum: Occupies buildings used during the Battle of Britain by the famous RAF station. The depth and intensity of the displays is exceptional, as the website says this is: "The world's largest Battle of Britain collection of memorabilia, artefacts from over 700 crashed aircraft are on display."

The He 111 is reported as Heinkel-built and exported to Spain in 1943. Thanks to Paco Rivas that can be laid to rest. Pure CASA Seville manufactured, it was initially fitted with Jumo 211Fs - as a B.2H - and first issued to service in May 1952. It was re-engineered 1957-1959 with Merlin 500s - as a B.2I. Much is made of the battle damage repair of bullet holes that are "typical of a German-style repair" and a pair of Heinkel manufacturer plates, The former stems from pot shots while patrolling the troubled secessionist skies of Spanish Sahara (Moroccan territory from 1975) in the 1950s and 1960s and given the Germanic input into Spanish military aviation and its aircraft industry, the nature of the repairs would be standard procedure. Regarding the Heinkel plates, political circumstances dictated the careful re-use of components/sub-assemblies in Franco's Spain: this parlous state began to be remedied only after the 1953 bases-for-military equipment defence agreement conducted with the USA. Be it 1940s German or 1950s Spanish – go and see this very significant exhibit.

A major milestone will be the unveiling of the 'Spirit of the Few; monument during 2022. The cockpit section of a Westland Whirlwind fighter is expected by the time *W&R* is published.

◆ *Signed off the A260 to the west of the town. Aerodrome Road, CT18 7AG* | **Note**: *Photography in any form is not permitted within the museum* | **01303 893140** | **info@kbobm.org** | **www.kbobm.org**

☐ 'G-AAAH'		DH Moth replica	81	BAPC.168, ex Croydon, Gatwick. *Jason*. Stored	[1]	1-22
☐ 'K5054'		V-S Spitfire rep	c88	BAPC.297, ex Luton, Lowestoft, Luton	[2] [3]	1-22
☐ 'K5054'		V-S Spitfire rep	84	ex Southampton, Sandown, Keevil.		
	G-BRDV			CoA 18-2-95, de-reg 19-5-00	[3] [4]	1-22
☐ 'L7005'		BP Defiant replica	02	BAPC.281, ex Cosford, Wolverhampton.		
	'PS-B'			264 Sqn colours. Arrived 28-2-15	[5]	1-22
☐ 'L9446'		Bristol Bolingbroke IVT	42	ex Duxford, BAM, OHB, Canada. Fairchild-built.		
	'LA-N'			Composite. 235 Sqn colours	[6]	1-22
☐ 'N2532'	'GZ-H'	Hawker Hurricane FSM	99	BAPC.272. 32 Sqn colours	[7]	1-22
☐ 'N3289'		V-S Spitfire FSM	68	BAPC.65, ex Chilham Castle, *Battle of Britain* (1968).		
	'DW-K'			610 Sqn colours		1-22
☐ 'N3317'*		V-S Spitfire FSM	68	BAPC.71, ex Flixton, 'N8140', Chilham Castle, 'P9390'		
				and 'N3317', *Battle of Britain* (1968)		1-22
☐ 'N3842'*		Miles Magister	c00	first noted 10-21	[8]	1-22
☐ 'N7033'	'K'	NAA Harvard T.2B	44	Hurn, Fordingbridge, B'mouth, Sandhurst, Hullavington,		
	FX442			501, 226 OCU, 203 AFS, 61 OTU. SOC 14-12-56		1-22
☐ 'N9181'		DH Tiger Moth	~	ex Bedford area	[9]	1-22
☐ 'P2921'	'GZ-L'	Hawker Hurricane FSM	99	BAPC.272, 32 Sqn colours	[7] [10]	1-22
☐ 'P3059'	'SD-N'	Hawker Hurricane FSM	99	BAPC.273, ex Chilham Castle, *Battle of Britain* (1968),		
				501 Sqn colours		1-22
☐ 'P3208'	'SD-T'	Hawker Hurricane FSM	68	BAPC.63, ex 'L1592', Higher Blagdon,		
				Battle of Britain (1968). 501 Sqn colours		1-22
☐ 'P3679'	'GZ-K'	Hawker Hurricane FSM	99	BAPC.278, 32 Sqn colours	[7]	1-22
☐ -*	'KV-H'	Hawker Hurricane FSM	68	ex *Battle of Britain* (1968). Foreshortened fuselage		1-22
☐ 'P9398'	'KL-B'	V-S Spitfire FSM	68	BAPC.69, ex 'N3313' (?), Higher Blagdon, Stoneleigh,		
				Battle of Britain (1968), 54 Sqn colours		1-22
☐ 'X4255'*	'LZ-J'	V-S Spitfire FSM	c90	fuselage. 66 Sqn colours	[7]	1-22
☐ 'X4321'	'LZ-X'	V-S Spitfire FSM	c90	fuselage. 66 Sqn colours	[7]	1-22

❑ 'MK356'	'2I-V'	V-S Spitfire IX FSM	~	on Queen Mary trailer	[11] 1-22
❑ '425/17'		Fokker Dr.I FSM	78	BAPC.133, ex Winthorpe, Higher Blagdon	[12] 1-22
❑ -		Fokker Dr.I replica	05	BAPC.565, ex Manston, Halton, *Flyboys* (2006)	1-22
❑ -		Gotha G.IV replica	05	BAPC.564, ex Manston, Halton, *Flyboys* (2006). Forward fuselage	1-22
❑ 'D-3-340'		DFS Grunau Baby	~	ex Ramsgate	1-22
❑ '14'	1480	Messerschmitt 'Bf 109'	68	BAPC.67, ex Coventry, N Weald, Newark, *Battle of Britain* (1968). JG52 colours	[13] 1-22
❑ –		Messerschmitt 'Bf 109' FSM	68	BAPC.66, ex '1480', Chilham Castle, Langley, *Battle of Britain* (1968)	[13] 1-22
❑ '6'		Messerschmitt 'Bf 109' FSM	68	BAPC.74, ex '6357', '6', Higher Blagdon, *Battle of Britain* (1968)	[13] 1-22
❑ -*	'EP'	Messerschmitt Bf 110 FSM	c02	BAPC.566, ex Aviemore, *Monarch of the Glenn*. Fuselage, first noted 6-18	1-22
❑ '3140'	'A1+DA'	Heinkel He 111	52 B.2I-103	ex Duxford, OFMC, Tablada, Spanish AF B.2I-103, B.2H-51. SOC 4-71. CASA-built C2.111. Arrived 14-3-20. Luftwaffe c/s by 5-20. See narrative above	[14] 1-22
❑ –		Fieseler Fi 103 (V-1) FSM	64	BAPC.36, ex Old Warden, Duxford, Old Warden, *Operation Crossbow* (1964)	1-22
❑ –		Fieseler Fi 103 (V-1) FSM	c90	ex Lowestoft. Stored	1-22

■ **[1]** Other 'G-AAAHs' can be found at Kingston upon Hull, E Yorks, and the *real* thing at South Kensington, Gtr Lon. **[2]** *This* 'K5054' is an unfinished project started as an all-metal reproduction by Barry Gennard in Luton. **[3]** There is *another* 'K5054' at Tangmere, W Sussex. **[4]** *This* 'K5054' is full-scale, but with wooden airframe, powered by a converted Jaguar V-12; built 1984 by Viking Wood Products. **[5]** Defiant re-creation uses an original turret and parts from salvaged remains. **[6]** Duxford components, which arrived 6-12-17, comprise the fuselage, centre section and outer wings of RCAF 9893 (the cockpit section of this machine is held in store by the IWM at Duxford). The cockpit of a Mk.IVT and other elements, arrived from Canada in 2019. **[7]** Built by Terry Arlow of Lowestoft. **[8]** Magister described as "part replica/part original". **[9]** Composite of two accident-damaged airframes. **[10]** There are *other* 'P2921s' at Bentley Priory, Gtr Lon, and *two* at Biggin Hill, Gtr Lon. **[11]** 'MK356' has a real counterpart, at Coningsby, Lincs, and there is *another* 'MK356' at Cosford, Shropshire! **[12]** Triplane built by Gp Capt A Wilson at Brixham. **[13]** Styled as Merlin-engined Hispano Buchones to match the airworthy examples used in the film, *Battle of Britain*. **[14]** See the introductory narrative. Bulk is from B2I-103, with the tail from B2I-27. Painted as a He 111H-2 of Stab/KG 53 shot down on 15-9-40, raiding London. Parts of the original 3140 are on show.

HYTHE on the A259 west of Folkestone

Vintage Aero Ltd: The restoration arm of Aero Legends was established at an airstrip in the general area during 2019. The Aero Legends operating base is at Lashenden, Kent, and its line maintenance operation is at North Weald, Essex. Aero Legends Spitfire Tr.IX project MJ444 (G-LEGD) is at Sandown, Isle of Wight. Spitfire Tr.IX BS410 (G-TCHI) had returned to Biggin Hill, Gtr Lon, by May 2021. ◆ *By prior arrangement* only | www.vintageaero.co.uk

❑ EN179	V-S Spitfire Tr.IX	G-TCHO 43	ex Exeter, 316, 306, Northolt SF, 315. FTR 19-8-43, salvaged	[1] 1-20
❑ '21' white	Yakovlev Yak-3	G-CDBJ 03	ex RA-44553. Accident 5-7-08, CoA 12-5-09	[2] 6-20

■ **[1]** Registered to Martin Phillips - see also Biggin Hill, Gtr Lon. **[2]** Allison V-1710 engined new build by Yakovlev under the Opytno-Konstruktorskoyr Byuro Imeni A S Yakovleva OAO.

Also: References here are dated but *believed* to be current.

❑ G-BECU	Bücker Jungmann	51	ex Spanish AF E.3B-384. CASA-built	8-19
❑ G-BECW	Bücker Jungmann	53	ex Spanish AF E.3B-423. CASA-built. CoA 4-11-06	6-19
❑ G-BLTW	Slingsby T.67B Firefly	85	CoA 15-9-06	N4-19
❑ G-BLUX	Slingsby T.67M Firefly	85	ex G-7-145, G-BLUX, G-7-113. CoA 27-4-07	N4-19
❑ G-BOCL	Slingsby T.67C Firefly	86	CoA 26-2-07	N10-18
❑ G-BONU	Slingsby T.67B Firefly	86	ex Hinton-in-the-Hedges. CoA 29-6-00	N4-19
❑ G-RIXA	Piper J-3C-65 Cub	48	ex 7Q-YDF, 5Y-KEV, VP-KEV, VP-NAE, ZS-AZT	N11-18

LANGLEY HEATH southeast of Maidstone

A Hunter is at a *private* location in the *general* area.

❑ 'WB188'	Hawker Hunter GA.11	55 G-BZPC	ex Melksham, Kemble, Exeter, Shawbury XF300, Yeovilton, FRADU, F.4, 130, 234, 71. Squires Gate-built. De-reg 16-3-11. Red scheme. Arrived 7-7-17	[1] 1-22

■ **[1]** See under Tangmere, W Sussex, for the *real* one.

Kent continues after the photo-spread, on page 113

BEDFORDSHIRE

Thorp T.211 G-TZII
Cranfield, Jun 2021
Paul Middleton

CAMBRIDGESHIRE

Spitfire Vb BM597 (G-MKVB)
Duxford, Dec 2020
Col Pope

Lynx AH.7 XZ655
Peterborough, Dec 2021
Nigel Price

CORNWALL

Schiebe SF.28A G-CCIS
(inside an Airbus fuselage
section)
Newquay Cornwall, Sep 2021
Ian Greenhalgh

Balliol T.2 WN149
Newquay Cornwall, Sep 2021
Ian Greenhalgh

Hawk T.1 XX240
Newquay Cornwall, Sep 2020
Richard Hall

DEVON

HS 146-200 OO-TAQ
Exeter, Jun 2021
Ian Doyle

DORSET

Lynx HAS.3S XZ250
Portland, Jul 2021
Ian Greenhalgh

DURHAM

Thurston Tawney Owl G-APWU
Fishburn, Sep 2021
John Wickenden

DURHAM

Sea Vampire T.22 XG775
Fishburn, Jul 2021
David E Thompson

Jet Provost T.5A XW405
Hartlepool, May 2021
John Wickenden

ESSEX

HS 748-2s VH-AMQ (rear)
and VH-AHL
Southend, Jun 2021
Ian Haskell

GLOUCESTERSHIRE

Boeing 727-46 VP-CMN
Bristol, Oct 2021
Tony McCarthy

Buccaneer S.2Bs XW544
(foreground) and XX894
Arriving at Cotswold
28th Aug 2020
Jake Wallace

GLOUCESTERSHIRE
Buccaneer S.2B XW544 at full power in the hands of Mike Birt
Cotswold, Sep 2021
Jake Wallace

Westland WG.30s
Tewkesbury, Jun 2020
Mark Presswood

HAMPSHIRE
MiG-21MF 7811
Alton, Aug 2020
John Wickenden

HAMPSHIRE

Hunter F.51 '349' (E-408)
Basingstoke, Aug 2020
Alexander Rankin

Beaver AL.1 'XP822' (XP806)
Middle Wallop, Sep 2020
Ken Ellis

Lynx AH.7s XZ212 and XZ672
Middle Wallop, Nov 2021
Richard Hall

ISLE OF WIGHT

BN-2A Islander G-AVCN
Northwood, Oct 2021
Bob Wealthy - BNAPS

KENT

Prentice VR192 (G-APIT)
Brenzett, Jul 2021
John Wickenden

F-4J(UK) Phantom ZE360
Moving at Manston
25th Apr 2021
*British Phantom Aviation
Group*

LANCASHIRE

Cherokee
Blackpool Zoo, May 2021
Ian Humphreys

LEICESTERSHIRE

VC10 C.1K XV108
East Midlands, Jul 2020
Peter Stephens

Boston III 'BZ264'
Hinckley, Oct 2020
Ken Ellis

LEICESTERSHIRE

The 'graveyard',
Bruntinthorpe, Nov 2021
Nigel Bailey Underwood

The 'museum' compound,
Bruntingthorpe, Sep 2021
Ian Haskell

LEICESTERSHIRE

Grob G.115A 'G-FIRE' (EI-CAE)
Leicester, May 2021
Nick Stone

Whirlwind HAR.10 XP344
North Luffenham, Nov 2020
Timothy Day

LINCOLNSHIRE

Dakota 3 ZA947
Coningsby, Jul 2021
Richard Hall

LINCOLNSHIRE

Lynx 1-03 XW838
Cranwell, Jul 2021
John Wickenden

Hunter F.1 WT680
Fleet Hargate, Sep 2021
David Willis

Jetstream 4100 G-MAJH
Humberside, Apr 2021
Geoff Eastham

LINCOLNSHIRE

Jetstream 4100 VH-XNF
Humberside, Apr 2021
Geoff Eastham

Auster AOP.9 XP242 (G-BUCI)
Messingham, Jun 2021
Andy Wood

Airco DH.2 replica '5964'
(G-BFVH)
Scampton, Jul 2021
John Wickenden

LINCOLNSHIRE

Wessex HAS.1 XS887
Tattershall Thorpe, Dec 2021
Richard Hall

Sentry AEW.1 ZH102
Waddington, Mar 2020
Ian Humphreys

Jetstream T.1 XX499
Wainfleet, Nov 2020
Richard Hall

GREATER LONDON
Lynx HAS.3S XZ727
Battersea, Sep 2020
David E Thompson

Hurricane XII two-seater
'BE505' (G-HHII)
Biggin Hill, Oct 2021
Ian Haskell

NORFOLK
HS 146 RJ85 EI-RJN
Norwich, Jul 2021
Ian Haskell

NORFOLK

Jaguar GR.3 XZ394
Sculthorpe, Aug 2020
Paul Middleton

NORTHAMPTONSHIRE

Jetstream 200 G-RAVL
Northampton, Jun 2021
Terry Dann

NORTHUMBERLAND

Brooklands Mosquito;
G-AVYW' (G-AWIF)
Sunderland, May 2021
Brian Downs

LASHENDEN AERODROME or Headcorn, on the A247 south of Headcorn   EGKH
Lashenden Air Warfare Museum (LAWM): **Trevor Matthews**, the founder and jovial powerhouse of this exceptional venue died in February 2021. The depth of presentation of the displays is breath-taking and the warmth of the welcome from volunteers is a tribute to Trevor and the team. During late 2020 Chris Samson donated the extreme nose – about 5ft, ie forward of the cockpit – of Short Sturgeon TT.3 TS482 '592'. The Fa 330 is destined to go to Rochester, Kent, in due course for painstaking MAPS 'treatment'.
◆ *Ashford, TN27 9HX. Hangar tours are available for a small additional fee, subject to staffing levels.* | **01622 891810** | lashendenairwar@gmail.com | www.lashendenairwarfaremuseum.co.uk

| ☐ 100549 | Focke Achgelis Fa 330A-1 Bachstelze | 44 | ex Manchester, Liverpool, Blackpool, Lavenham, Hullavington, Biggin Hill, Farnborough. Weser Flug-built | | 1-22 |
| ☐ 6/2080 | Fieseler Fi 103R-IV | 44 | BAPC.91, ex Germany, Lashenden, Rochester, Horsham, Farnborough, Dannenburg. Arrived 4-3-13 | [1] | 1-22 |

■ **[1]** Almost certain to have originated at Dannenberg and captured 23-4-45; this is a piloted V-1 'Reichenberg'.

Aerodrome: The aerodrome is home to **Aero Legends** offering the public flights in a growing and varied fleet of classic aircraft - full details at **www.aerolegends.co.uk** The organisation also operates from Duxford, Cambs; North Weald, Essex; Sywell, Northants, and has a workshop at Hythe, Kent. There is no public access to the Aero Legends Lashenden facility, but a public viewing area and the museum -see above - offer great vantage points.
 The contents of the Seneca 'graveyard' – G-AZVJ, G-BAKD, G-BCID - last noted in mid-2016, have been cleared. Two others to clear up: Robin R3000 G-BLYP (last noted May 2016) and Starduster G-BSZG (March 2013).

☐ G-ARNI	Auster J1N Alpha	61	CoA 15-6-98, de-reg 24-9-03. First noted 9-18	9-18
☐ G-BFMR*	Piper Pacer	50	ex N7025K. Crashed 15-7-03, CoA 6-3-06	7-21
☐ G-BJOV*	Cessna F.150K	70	ex PH-VSD. Cr 1-10-20, de-reg 4-11-20. Reims-built	7-21
☐ G-BVYK*	Team MiniMax 91A	95	ex Rochester. De-reg 19-11-14	7-21
☐ G-PVML	Robin DR.400-140B	74	ex F-BVML. CoA 27-8-12, de-reg 24-10-18	7-21

LONDON ASHFORD AIRPORT or Lydd   EGMD
Home to Priti Patel's Channel-scouring drones, the fire crews *may* still have a pair of light aircraft for exercises.

| ☐ G-BUCS | Cessna 150F | 65 | ex N3568L. CoA 1-4-04, de-reg 16-3-11. Rescue training | 7-19 |
| ☐ G-DAZY | Piper Seneca 200T | 77 | ex N953A. CoA 2-6-11, de-reg 14-12-11. Rescue training | 11-17 |

MAIDSTONE on the A229 south of Chatham and the M20
A group of owner/restorers have a Jaguar and a Harrier II in the *general* area. The latter has required the fabrication of much of the rear fuselage and the cockpit. ◆ *By prior arrangement* **only**

| ☐ XX720* | 'FL' SEPECAT Jaguar GR.3A | 74 | ex Ipswich, Shawbury, 41, 54, GR.1, 54, 6, A&AEE, 54, Indian AF JI003, G-27-319, Abingdon, A&AEE. Arrived 2018 | 1-22 |
| ☐ 163423* | BAe/McDD AV-8B Harrier II | 88 | ex Ipswich, Basingstoke(?), St Athan, USMC VMA-211, VMA-513, VMA-311. Arrived 2018. See note above | 1-22 |

■ **[1]** Cockpit removed circa 1999 when imported to UK; reported for use by QinetiQ at Boscombe Down, Wilts, or Farnborough, Hants.

MANSTON on the A253 west of Ramsgate
A plan for a new airfreight hub was quashed early in 2021, so the site remains 'Manston' and not 'Manston Airport'. The runways and extensive hard-standings were used for Brexit chaos – sorry, economic adjustment - parking in early 2021.

Spitfire and Hurricane Memorial Museum: The superb Hurricane and Spitfire are both examples of the workmanship of Medway APS, Rochester. There is a wealth of other material to see and the superb 'Merlin Cafeteria' to sample. There is a synthetic Spitfire simulator in the same colours as TB752 which is available on a pre-bookable basis.
◆ *Manston Road, CT12 5DF* | **01843 821940** | enquiries@spitfiremuseum.org.uk | www.spitfiremuseum.org.uk

☐ 'BN230'	'FT-A' Hawker Hurricane IIc	44	ex Rochester, Bentley Priory, Waterbeach 5466M		
		LF751	(21-7-45), 24 OTU, 1681 BDTF. Unveiled 22-4-88	[1] [2]	1-22
☐ TB752	'KH-Z' V-S Spitfire XVI	45	ex Rochester, 8086M, Manston 7256M / 7279M, SOC 28-9-55. Lyneham, 5 CAACU, 103 FRS, 102 FRS, 403, 66. CBAF-built. Unveiled 13-6-81. Val, 403 Sqn c/s	[2] [3]	1-22

■ **[1]** 'BN230' is a composite, with parts from Mk.II Z3687 and Mk.IIc PG593. Colours of Sqn Ldr D A R G Le Roy du Vivier, CO 43 Sqn 8-42. **[2]** Both on loan from RAF Museum. **[3]** While serving with 403 Sqn RCAF, between 21-4-45 and 3-5-45 four different pilots shot down a Bf 109, an Fw 189, a long-nosed Fw 190 and a He 111.

Tailfin/rudder and forward fuselage of Nimrod MR.2 XV229. *Richard Hall*

RAF Manston History Museum: There have been some benefits from Covid-19. The volunteers of the RAF Manston History Society used the enforced absence of visitors to introduce a series of improvements and to re-appraise the aircraft collection. The entrance area has been regenerated, the shop extended, a café introduced and new displays - including a Great War exhibition - established. See below for a restoration project that museum volunteers have taken on.

Very much an 'odd-ball' within the collection, the cockpit of Short 330 G-SSWP was disposed of in 2020, reportedly to become the basis of a burger van in the Margate area. Inspection of Whirlwind HAS.7 XN380 revealed that it was too far gone from corrosion and it was scrapped by the end of 2020.

◆ *Manston Road, CT12 5DF* | **01843 825224** | **info@rafmanston.co.uk** | **www.rafmanston.co.uk**

❏	'SE-XZS'*		Pitts S-1S FSM	~	installed 8-21, suspended in main hall	1-22
❏	–		Huntair Pathfinder	c82	BAPC.466, ex Indonesia. Arrived 2003	1-22
❏	'A213'	'A'	Nieuport 17 replica	05	ex Halton, *Flyboys* (2005). Arrived 2005 [1]	1-22
❏	-		Nieuport 17 replica	05	ex Halton, *Flyboys* (2005). Arrived 2005. Forward fuselage [1]	1-22
❏	'B619'		Sopwith 1½ Strutter rep	04	BAPC.468, ex Halton, *Flyboys* (2005). Arrived 2005	1-22
❏	RT486		Taylorcraft Auster AOP.5 G-AJGJ	44	ex Old Sarum, RT486, 43 OTU. De-reg 10-10-19 Arrived 9-1-18	1-22
❏	'VM791'		Slingsby Cadet XA312 TX.3	53	ex Kenley 8876M, 636 GS, 634 GS, 2 GC, GIS. SOC 22-4-68. Arrived 1999	1-22
❏	'WD615'	'A'	Gloster Meteor TT.20 WD646	51	ex N Weald, Elmdon, Cosford 8189M (10-12-71), 5 CAACU, 3/4 CAACU, NF.11, CSE. AWA-built. Arrived 15-11-97. 85 Sqn, NF.11 colours	1-22
❏	WP772	'4'	DHC Chipmunk T.10	52	ex Lyneham, Colerne, Abingdon, St Athan, M Wallop, BFWF, QUAS, Hull UAS, 17 RFS. Arrived 1999	1-22
❏	WT205		EE Canberra B.15	55	ex Eastwood, Foulness, MoA, 9. SOC 31-8-72. Short-built. Arrived 14-10-00. 9 Sqn colours. Cockpit	1-22
❏	XA231		Slingsby Grasshopper TX.1	53	ex Stockport, 'Sealand', Cosford 8888M, Warwick, Kimbolton, Petersfield. Arrived 1999	1-22
❏	XG226		Hawker Hunter F.6A	56	ex Faversham, Manston, Faygate, Catterick 8800M (15-2-83), 1 TWU, TWU, 229 OCU, 92, 66, 92. Arrived 23-1-03. Cockpit. 92 Sqn colours [2]	1-22
❏	XL190		HP Victor K.2	61	ex St Mawgan 9216M (27-9-93), 55, 232 OCU, Witt Wing, 139. Arrived 6-2-99. Cockpit	1-22
❏	XR658		Hunting Jet Provost T.4	63	ex Prees Heath, Connah's Quay, Hurn, Wroughton, Abingdon 8192M (29-12-71), RAEF, 6 FTS, CAW, 7 FTS. Crashed 26-10-71. Arrived 1-10-16	1-22
❏	XR770	'AA'	EE Lightning F.6	65	ex Waddington, Grainthorpe, New Waltham, Laceby, Binbrook, 11, 5-11 pool, 56, 23, 74. SOC 10-6-88. Arr 3-3-15	1-22

❑ XS482	'A-D'	Westland Wessex HU.5	63	ex DSFCTE Manston, Farnborough, A&AEE, 848.	
				SOC 20-2-86. Arrived 2000. SAR colours	1-22
❑ XV229*		HS Nimrod MR.2	69	ex DFTDC Manston, Kinloss, Kin Wing, St Mawgan Wg,	
				Kin Wg, 42, A&AEE, MR.1, Kin Wg. Flew in 26-5-10.	
				Forward fuselage.. plus fin/rudder. Arrived 17-12-20	[3] 1-22
❑ XV352		Blackburn Buccaneer	67	ex Gravesend, Manston, Stock, St Athan, Lossiemouth,	
		S.2B		237 OCU, 208. Arrived 1999. Cockpit	1-22
❑ XV864*		Blackburn Buccaneer	68	ex DFTDC Manston 9234M (28-3-94), 12, 237 OCU, 16.	
		S.2B		Arrived 14-5-20	1-22
❑ XZ106	'FD'	SEPECAT Jaguar GR.3A	76	ex Ipswich, St Athan, 2, 41, SAOEU, GR.1, 41, 16, 54.	
				SOC 3-5-05. Arrived 21-11-08. 'Snow' camouflage	1-22
❑ ZA325	'TAX'	Panavia Tornado GR.1	80	ex St Athan 9338M, Cosford, St Athan, 15, TTTE.	
				SOC 13-8-03. Arrived 2010. Cockpit	1-22
❑ -		Fieseler Fi 103 (V-1) rep	c04	BAPC.465, pole-mounted	1-22
❑ -	'4'	PZL Iskra TS-11	77	ex airfield, Shoreham, SP-DOF. De-reg 24-4-09.	
		G-BXVZ		Arrived 8-13. 'Sparks' team colours	1-22
❑ '117415'		Lockheed T-33AN	54	ex N Weald, G-BYOY (de-reg 8-6-05), N36TH, N333DV,	
	'TR-415'	Silver Star Mk.3		N134AT, N10018, RCAF 21231. Canadair-built.	
				Arrived 3-2-10. 512th FBS, 406th FBW colours	1-22

■ [1] One of these is BAPC.467, the other is BAPC.469. [2] The centre section of XG226 is at East Midlands, Leics, and a wing is at Charlwood, Surrey. [3] XV229's delivery to Manston was the last-ever Nimrod MR.2 flight.

Also: Museum volunteers are restoring the former Paull Hunter on behalf of Lyndon Davies, CEO of Margate-based Hornby Hobbies. Lyndon bought the Hunter at auction and will donate it to the company, which boasts such classic brands as Airfix, Corgi and Scalextric in its portfolio. A temporary hangar has been erected for the restoration: it will revert to its 4 FTS colours. The final venue for XF509 has yet to be announced, but Hornby's base is at nearby Margate and includes a flourishing visitor centre. ◆ *By prior arrangement* **only**

❑ XF509*	Hawker Hunter F.6	56	ex Paull, Marfleet, Chivenor 8708M (21-12-81), Thurleigh,	
			4 FTS, AFDS, 54. Arrived 18-6-21	1-22

British Phantom Aviation Group: Plans to move to Wymeswold, Leics, altered during 2020 and the group has consolidated at Kemb... Cotswold, Glos. F-4J(UK) ZE360 at the DFT&DC - below - was acquired by BPAG with assistance from the 74 Squadron Association and moved to the former airfield site for a period of restoration after which it will migrate westwards. See below regarding FGR.2 XV411's legacy.

◆ *By prior arrangement* **only** *- for more see under Cotswold, Glos* | **contact@bpag.co.uk** **wwww.bpag.co.uk**

❑ ZE360	'O'	McD F-4J(UK) Phantom	c67	ex Manston 9059M, 74, USN 155574. Last flown 22-2-91
				Arrived 25-4-21	1-22

Defence Fire Training and Development Centre: A final passing out parade was staged on 22nd October 2020 and, with the lowering of the Co's pennant on 30th June 2021, the last vestiges of the RAF's long and distinguished presence at Manston came to an end. MoD fire fighters have been trained at Moreton in Marsh, Glos, since November 2020.

Departures: Buccaneer S.2B XV864 made the short trip to the RAF Manston History Museum - above - on 14-5-20; **F-4J(UK)** ZE360, originally intended to relocate to Wymeswold, Leics, made the short road journey to the airport site 25-4-21 - see below; **Gazelle** HT.3 XW870 was roaded to Selby, N Yorks, 2-12-20; **Harrier** GR.3s XW768 and XZ966 had migrated to Spadeadam, Cumbria, by 6-21 - and, for completeness, the hulk of GR.3 XW922 - *less* cockpit - travelled to Selby, N Yorks, 2-12-20; **Jaguar** GR.3A XX116 to Selby, N Yorks, 2-12-20; **Lynx** AH.7s XZ215 and XZ216 moved to Spadeadam, Cumbria, during 6-21; **Nimrod** MR.2 XV229 was reduced to a forward fuselage and tail fin and migrated to the RAF Manston History Museum - above - on 17-12-20; **Tornado** F.3 ZE165 to Moreton-in-Marsh, Glos, 30-11-20; F.3 ZE204 left for Sunderland, N&T, on 23-6-21, arriving on 28-6-21; **Wessex** HC.2 XV725 travelled to Kinloss, Scotland, 17-12-20.

Wessex HC.2 XR503 and **Dominie** T.1 XS714 were scrapped by a Kent-based contractor in December and November 2020, respectively. **Phantom** FGR.2 XV411 was scrapped on site with the remains traveling to a scrapyard at Spey Bay, Scotland, from 30th November 2020. BPAG, see above and at Cotswold, Glos, were kindly allowed to 'plunder' the airframe prior to its demise, resulting in a useful collection of parts, including the fin.

Others: Helicopter operations continue and several long-retired rotorcraft are stored.

❑ G-SUER	Bell 206B JetRanger II	69	ex HB-ZBX, CoA 28-7-09	8-18
❑ G-SUEZ	Bell 206B JetRanger II	70	ex SU-YAE, YU-HAZ. Agusta-built. CoA 17-6-13	8-18
❑ TF-AMC	Boeing 747-2B3F	79	ex Air Atlanta, F-GBOX. Flightdeck	5-19
❑ MM80279*	Bell 204B	~	ex -?-, Hayes, Cormano, It AF. Agusta-built.	
	'18'			USMC colours. Travelling exhibition airframe	[1] 10-21

■ [1] 'Huey' written out of *W&R26* (p160) as having departed Hayes, Gtr Lon, in January 2017.

PADDOCK WOOD on the B2160 east of Tonbridge
A Super Cub 'guards' a *private* strip in the *general* area.
❑ G-PCUB   Piper Super Cub 135   52 ex PH-KER, Netherlands AF R-184, L-21B 54-2474.
                                                   CoA 28-3-98, de-reg 10-3-99. First noted 3-19   1-20

POSTLING on minor road southwest of Lyminge
No further details on the Dove at a *private* location in the locality.
❑ G-ARHW   DH Dove 8   61 ex Coventry. CoA 19-5-06, de-reg 4-1-19   7-19

Scion II G-AEZF after roll-in to the new workshop, January 2022. *Philip Cole*

ROCHESTER AERODROME on the A229 south of Rochester   EGTO
Medway Aircraft Preservation Society Ltd: Hardcore for the new workshop was laid in February 2021 and the move across the aerodrome to the new premises began in November. The Scion project moved in during January 2022 and will be completed in floatplane guise and displayed amid the workbenches. Spitfire XVI RW388 returned to Stoke-on-Trent, Staffs, in June 2021, after a four-year restoration. A Hurricane will take its place in the hands of the MAPS craftsmen. GEC-Marconi Phoenix UAV BAPC.356, on loan to BDAC at Old Sarum, Wilts, is due for return in 2022. See under Lashenden, Kent, for a project-in-waiting.
◆ *New workshop on the A229 side (east) of the aerodrome, ME5 9SD* | email via website | **www.mapsl.co.uk**
❑ G-AEZF   Short Scion II   37 ex Redhill, East Tilbury, Southend, M5. Pobjoy-built.
                                                   CoA 5-5-54, de-reg 22-1-70. Arrived 13-6-13   [1]   1-22
❑ BH238*   Hawker Hurricane IIb   42 ex Sandown, Russia, Soviet AF   [2]   due
■ **[1]** Pobjoy Airmotors-built at Rochester, first flying 9-12-37 as a floatplane from the nearby Medway. **[2]** Restoration for Peter Monk – see Biggin Hill, Gtr Lon.

Also: MiniMax G-BVYK had moved to Lashenden, Kent, by July 2021.
❑ G-BFBE*   Robin HR.100-100   74 ex PH-SRK. CoA 31-5-20   12-21
❑ G-BHOL   Jodel DR.1050   60 ex F-BJQL. CEA-built. CoA 9-3-11   12-21
❑ G-BXVC   Piper Turbo Arrow IV   79 ex Redhill, D-ELIV, N2152V. Crashed 22-8-98,
                                                   de-reg 22-1-03. Rescue training   6-16
❑ G-VYAK   Yakovlev Yak-18T   93 ex HA-HUA. CoA 8-12-12   12-21
❑ HA-JAB   Yakovlev Yak-18T G-UYAK 78 first noted 10-15   9-20

BAE Systems: The Phoenix is stored within the factory on the A229.
❑ ZJ303   GEC-Marconi Phoenix UAV c95 ex MAPS. 'Army' titles   6-19

SELLINDGE on the A20 west of Folkestone
UK Heritage Aviation Trust: With the catchline 'Try for the Sky' the organisation acquired land here in September 2021 with the intention of preserving Herald G-CEXP at Gatwick, W Sussex – which see. **www.ukhat.org**

SEVENOAKS

By August 2021 Wessex HC.2 XR502 had escaped the storage site at a *private* location in the *general* area and turned up at Ticehurst, East Sussex. Two others are *thought* to remain.

❏ XV722	'WH'	Westland Wessex HC.2	68	ex Hixon, Shawbury, 2 FTS, CATCS, 18, 72, 18	1-19
❏ XV731	'Y'	Westland Wessex HC.2	68	ex Redhill area, Fleetlands, 72, WTF, 240 OCU, 18, 78	1-19

Also: Restoration of an Auster is *believed* to continue at a separate *private* location.

❏ G-APJZ	Auster J1N Alpha	57	ex St Albans, 5N-ACY, VR-NDR, G-APJZ.	
			Crashed 10-11-75, CoA 16-7-76	9-19

SHOREHAM west of the A225 north of Sevenoaks

Shoreham Aircraft Museum (SAM): This superb museum is centred upon an extensive number of 'digs'; all beautifully researched and presented. Included in the incredible selection of artefacts is the rear fuselage skin from Bf 109 *Black 6* - which exists in the 'full' at Cosford, Shropshire. SAM is carrying out an incredible project to erect memorials to honour the RAF Battle of Britain pilots that were killed in combat in crashes within a ten-mile radius. The tea room is exceptional!

◆ High Street, TN14 7TB | 01959 524416 | geoff@aviartnutkins.com | www.shoreham-aircraft-museum.co.uk

❏ P3860	Hawker Hurricane I	c40	ex 607. Crashed 17-9-40. Acquired 1986. Cockpit	[1]	1-22
❏ -	Junkers Ju 88A-1	40	ex Norway, USSR. Acquired 2008. Cockpit.		
			Traudl, KG 54 colours		1-22

■ **[1]** Hurricane is a substantial exhibit, Merlin, firewall, forward cockpit area, windscreen, and canopy, not all from Sgt John Landsell's machine, but the majority so. The serial for Landsell's Hurricane is also quoted as P3933.

WINGHAM on the A257 west of Sandwich

Wingham Wildlife Park: ◆ North of the A257, east of the town, CT3 1JL | www.winghamwildlifepark.co.uk

❏ G-MVIO*	Noble Hardman Snowbird	89 de-reg 14-1-19. First noted 8-20	8-20

LANCASHIRE

Includes the unitary authorities of Blackburn with Darwen, and Blackpool

---

BANKS on the A565 north of Southport

A *private* workshop in the general area holds a former French Army Bell 47.

❏ F-BJDC*	Bell 47G-2	56 ex ALAT 052, F-MBDL, F-MBCS. First noted 11-19	4-21

BLACKBURN

A *private* collector *may* still have a Prospector cockpit in the locality.

❏ G-ARDG	EP Prospector	61 ex Haverhill, Redhill, Washington, Durrington, Middle		
		Wallop, Shoreham, Lympne. De-reg 28-5-82. Cockpit	[1]	9-10

■ **[1]** At least the rear end of EP.9 G-ARDG is incorporated within the composite on show at Middle Wallop, Hampshire.

BLACKPOOL

Blackpool Zoo: East Park Drive, near Stanley Park. A Cherokee, previously used by the Squires Gate airport fire crews is just one of the attractions. ◆ www.blackpoolzoo.org.uk

❏ -*	Piper Cherokee	~ ex Squires Gate. Arrived 10-20	5-21

Sea Life Blackpool: On the Promenade, north of the Central Pier. Within the 'walk through' tank is the forward fuselage, including gun turret and parts of the tail, of a Boulton Paul Defiant, complete with staggeringly pristine codes 'YL' amid a patination of barnacles etc and passing - very real - sharks. There is an information board carrying details of a Blackpool wartime disaster: the collision of 256 Squadron Defiant I N1745 (which would have been coded 'JT-') and 3 School of General Reconnaissance Blackburn Botha I L6509 on 27th August 1941. Much of the wreckage hit Reads Avenue although N1745's tail is thought to have come down offshore. Both aircraft were based at Squires Gate: five aircrew and 13 civilians perished. While it is possible that *some* original parts are within this display, it is *considered* unlikely, and this does not merit a formal listing, particularly because of the tasteless and inappropriate setting. ◆ www.visitsealife.com

BLACKPOOL AIRPORT, or Squires Gate, on the B6430, south of Garstang, west of the M6

EGNH

Spitfire Visitor Centre: Operated by the Lytham St Anne's Spitfire Ground Display Team. The Spitfire FSMs and Hurricane FSM are available for hire and regularly travel to venues far and wide. Among the exhibits are several cockpit mock-ups and the occasional 'guesting' FSM. The centre is hosting the ambitious restoration/recreation of an Airspeed Oxford based on the centre section of former Canadian Mk.V EB518 and DH-built Mk.I AT605.

◆ *Hangar 42, H2 Area, FY4 2QS* | **01253 341902** | enquiries@spitfirevisitorcentre.co.uk | https://spitfirevisitorcentre.co.uk

☐ 'V7752'		Hawker Hurricane FSM	89	BAPC.223, ex 'V7467', St Mawgan, High Wycombe,	
	'JZ-L'			Coltishall. HFL-built. 57 OTU colours. Arrived 7-15	9-21
☐ 'W3442'	'FY-D'	V-S Spitfire IX FSM	~	ex 'PL256'. First noted 2-16. 611 Sqn colours by 9-21	[1] 9-21
☐ 'X4253'	'FY-N'	V-S Spitfire II FSM	~	BAPC.326, ex 'N3290'. 611 Sqn colours, *Vicky*	9-21
☐ 'BS435'		V-S Spitfire IX FSM	~	BAPC.324, ex Lytham St Anne's, Delabole, 'RB159', Hooton	
	'FY-F'			Park. TDL Replicas-built. 611 Sqn c/s, *Lucy*. Arrived 1-16	9-21
☐ -		V-S Spitfire IX SIM	~	first noted 7-18. *Lucy*	9-21

■ **[1]** May, or may not, be BAPC.325.

Airport: The airport maintains its ability to 'unearth' long out-of-use light aircraft. An example is Cherokee G-BBEV which was written out of *W&R26* (p134). Chipmunks G-ANWB and WZ872 (G-BZGB) were roaded to Spanhoe, Northants, on 21st September 2021. Motor Cadet EI-CJJ had moved on by September 2020.

☐ G-APPA	DHC Chipmunk T.10	52	ex Exeter, Shoreham, Kemble, Wellesbourne Mountford,	
			Carlisle, Glasgow, N5703E, G-APPA, WP917, Glasgow UAS,	
			11 RFS, 8 RFS. CoA 14-7-85	8-21
☐ G-AZIB	SOCATA Diplomate	71	ex Preston, Squires Gate. CoA 17-2-07. First noted 8-20	8-20
☐ G-BBEV*	Piper Cherokee 140D	71	ex LN-MTM. CoA 8-9-01, de-reg 16-5-07. See above	6-21
☐ G-BLLP*	Slingsby T.67B Firefly	84	CoA 4-12-00. Trailer-mounted	8-21
☐ G-BRPL	Piper Cherokee 140	72	exN15771. CoA 6-11-05. Rescue trainer by 6-21	6-21
☐ G-BVGI	Pereira Osprey 2	95	CoA 25-11-03	8-19
☐ G-HMJB*	Piper Seneca III	81	ex N8356R. CoA 10-10-04. First noted 8-20	8-20
☐ G-OOGS	American GA-7 Cougar	79	ex G-BGJW, N737G. CoA 27-3-08	6-21

No.177 Squadron Air Cadets: Should still have a Tornado F.3 FSM; but also refer to King's Lynn, Norfolk.

☐ -	Panavia Tornado F.3 FSM	c85	ex Chester, Pant Glas, Hooton Park, Elvington,
			BBC *Fighter Pilot*
			8-19

BURNLEY on the M65, northeast of Blackburn

Despite the somewhat 'historic' last noted date, **David Stansfield** is *believed* to be at work on an Albemarle. The Waco Hadrian elements do not merit a formal listing. ◆ **Not** *available for public inspection*

☐ –	AW Albemarle	~	ex Bacup, Carlisle, Westnewton. Cockpit section etc
			5-08

Hardline Airsoft: The anonymous Aztec, last noted in August 2018, is thought to have given up the ghost.

COCKERHAM on the A588 between Lancaster and Fleetwood

Black Knights Parachute Centre: *Should* still have its para-trainer. ◆ *By prior arrangement* only | www.bkpc.co.uk

☐ G-BKPC	Cessna A.185F Skywagon	79	ex N4599E. CoA 11-11-07	N11-18

ECCLESTON on the B5250 south of Leyland

Bygone Times Antique Warehouse: This huge emporium occasionally offers airframes among the piles of Poole pottery. *W&R26* (p129) wrote out the SE.5a replica as not noted since April 2015; it resolutely patrols over the cash desk!
◆ *Grove Mill, The Green, PR7 5TZ* | **01257 451889** | enquiries@bygonetimes.co.uk | www.bygonetimes.co.uk

☐ 'A4850'	RAF SE.5a scale rep	c68	BAPC.176, ex Chorley, Barton, Firbeck, Pontefract	12-21

LYTHAM ST ANNE'S south of Blackpool

Lytham Motive Power Museum: (Note change of name.) An incredible museum within the grounds of **Helical Technology**'s headquarters on Dock Rock pays homage to transport technology. Drawing the eye is the working Blue Bird Project's replica of the BSE Orpheus-powered boat *Bluebird K7* in which Donald Campbell met his fate on Lake Windermere on 4th January 1967. Also on display are railway locos, a steam roller, cars, a workshop and more.
◆ *By prior application* only | www.helical-technology.com/about-us/heritage/

☐ G-BBTL		Piper Aztec 250C	68	ex Blackpool N6525Y. De-reg 7-2-03	4-21
☐ G-MMJA		Mitchell Wing B-10	83	de-reg 13-1-90	4-21
☐ G-LORT		Avid Speedwing IV	92	de-reg 18-3-13. Stored	8-19
☐ XM708		Folland Gnat T.1	61	ex Bruntingthorpe, Kings Langley, Locking, Halton 8573M (2-12-77), 4 FTS, CFS, HS [1]	4-21

■ [1] The Gnat was the donor of the engine in the Bluebird K7 replica.

Also: On the inner Promenade a Spitfire FSM is displayed at Fairhaven Lake.

☐ 'W3644'	'QV-J'	V-S Spitfire Vb FSM	12	BAPC.323, unveiled 21-6-13. *Lytham St Anne's*, 19 Sqn c/s	9-21

PRESTON

Preston's College iSTEM Centre: St Vincent's Road. Diplomate G-AZIB had gravitated to Blackpool Airport, Lancs, by August 2020. Last recorded in October 2017, Aztec 250C N6601Y is believed to have been scrapped.

Phil Elsden: Is *thought* to still have his 'JP' cockpit. ◆ *By prior arrangement* **only**

☐ XW315	BAC Jet Provost T.5A	70	ex Wolverhampton, Long Marston, 'Lincs', CFS, 3 FTS, CFS. Damaged 5-7-84. Cockpit. Arrived 27-6-12	2-14

SAMLESBURY on the A59 east of Preston

BAE Systems: The **Academy for Skills and Knowledge** (ASK) has a former Indonesian Hawk as an instructional airframe. The *proper* Lightning and the F-35B FSMs - the author refuses to call this a Lightning II, especially here! - are mounted alongside each other at the main gate on the A59.

☐ 'XS921'	'BA'	EE Lightning F.6 FSM	14	BAPC.357. Gateguards UK-built. Displayed by 2-15	6-21
☐ ZA328*		Panavia Tornado GR.1	81	ex Preston, BAe trials fleet. Last flight 12-12-02. Stored. Arrived 12-2-05. Stored	11-21
☐ ZK532*		HS Hawk T.53	c80	ex Warton, Brough, Warton, Indonesian AF LL-5315. Last flight 10-4-02. Stored	11-21
☐ ZK533		HS Hawk T.53	c80	ex Humberside, Finningley, Brough, Warton, Indonesian AF LL-5317. Arrived 14-9-18. RAF colours	11-21
☐ –		Lockheed-Martin F-35 FSM	17	BAPC.455. Gateguards UK-built. Installed 20-5-17	6-21

WARTON AIRFIELD on the A584 west of Preston   EGNO

BAE Systems: By late 2020 Hawk T.53 ZK532 had made the short journey to Samlesbury, for further storage.

☐ XS928	'AD'	EE Lightning F.6	67	ex Binbrook, 5-11, 56, 11, 56, 74, 5, 11. SOC 13-6-88. Last flown 31-3-92, unveiled 9-9-99. 5 Sqn colours	7-21
☐ ZG969		Pilatus PC-9	89	ex Brough, HB-HQE. *Percy*. Stored since at least 1-16	6-19
☐ ZJ801		Eurofighter Typhoon T.3	04	ex Coningsby. Fuselage, fatigue tests, arrived 12-6-19	6-19
☐ ZJ922	'QO-C'	Eurofighter Typhoon FGR.4	06	ex Coningsby, 3. Arrived 10-16, SOC 21-2-19	8-19
☐ ZJ951		HS Hawk Mk.120D	02	last flight 5-6-18. SOC 21-6-19	8-19

WEETON on the B5260 east of Blackpool, north of the M55

Ream Hills Holiday Park: Ream Hills Farm in Mythorp Road. Among the attractions is a Lynx that sleeps up to four.
◆ *By prior arrangement* **only** | www.reamhills.co.uk

☐ XZ676	Westland Lynx AH.7	77	ex Hixon, M Wallop, 671, 661, 656, 671, 657, 656, 652, 9 Flt, 671, LCF. F/n 4-14	11-21

Ream Salvage: An associated salvage business has a dwindling cache of Lynx 'cabs': AH.7 XZ648 to Mabe Burnthouse, Cornwall, by August 2021; AH.7 XZ655 had moved to Peterborough, Cambs, by August 2020.
◆ *By prior arrangement* **only**

☐ XZ173	'6'	Westland Lynx AH.7	77	ex Hixon, Fleetlands, 9 Rgt, 659, 4 Rgt, 3 Rgt, 1 Rgt, 669, 661, 669, 663, 656, 3 Rgt, 1 Rgt, 651, ARWF, IFTU. Cabin	7-18
☐ XZ673	'5'	Westland Lynx AH.7	80	ex Fleetlands, M Wallop, 671, 655. Cabin	7-18

LEICESTERSHIRE

Within the administrative county boundaries of Leicestershire are the unitary authorities of Leicester - and far from a county - the People's Republic of Rutland!

The compound on the southeast perimeter, September 2021. Clockwise, from the left: Victor K.2 XM715, Jet Provost T.5A XW290, Nimrod MR.2 XV226, Comet 4C XS235. *Ian Haskell*

BRUNTINGTHORPE between the M1 and the A50 south of Leicester

As outlined in *W&R27*, Cox Automotive acquired the long-term rights to operate from majority of the former airfield, resulting in major changes for the aircraft collections. Several other aircraft have left the site, as detailed below. In order to clear the main site for its new role, scrapping of some of the larger airframes began in the autumn of 2020.

Since late 1984 when airframes of the (since defunct) Loughborough and Leicestershire Aircraft Museum moved in from East Midlands, Leics, David Walton and family have been exceptional benefactors of aircraft preservation. This has been through their own endeavours culminating in the Cold War Jets Collection and crowned by the acquisition of Vulcan XH558 which paved the way for its operation as a civilian 'warbird'. Several groups were also permitted to establish and operate from the huge airfield site. This contribution to the UK's aviation heritage is seldom acknowledged, which is a great pity; the 'movement' relies on the vision and philanthropy of people such as David Walton. This generosity has been maintained, as David owns land in the northeast corner of the airfield – centred on and including the Lightning Preservation Group QRA sheds. Most of the aircraft have gravitated to this area and to a site on the southeast perimeter. While this means that a goodly number of airframes have been secured, the days of fast taxi runs are a thing of the past. That said, the Avons of the Canberra and the Lightnings have been statically run as anti-deterioration measures since the relocation. (Those in the southern 'dispersal' are marked #)

As regards the future, there is the *hope* that regular visitor Sundays can be staged but much needs to be done before this becomes a possibility. So, for this edition 'Bruntingthorpe' remains a work in progress – stay tuned!

Cold War Jets Collection (CWJC): See comments above. Super Guppy F-BTGV and 747 SX-OAD were put to the axe in December 2020, their flightdecks travelling to St Athan, Wales, on 4th February 2021. Buccaneer S.2 XX900 made the journey to Tatenhill, Staffs, on 6th November 2020, still in the ownership of David Walton.
◆ **Strictly** *by prior permission* **only.**

❑	G-BBTG*	Cessna F.172M		73	Reims-built. De-reg 29-10-14. Stored	N8-19
❑	G-PLOW	Hughes 269B		67	ex G-AVUM. Stored	N9-15
❑	XM715	HP Victor K.2		63	ex 55, 232 OCU, 543, 232 OCU, 100, 139.	
					Flew in 19-11-93. *Teasin' Tina*	[1] # 12-21
❑	XS235	DH Comet 4C		63	ex XS235, Boscombe D, DTEO, A&AEE, BLEU. Hawarden-	
			G-CPDA		built. *Canopus.* Flew in 30-10-97. De-reg 27-3-08	[2] # 12-21
❑	XV226	HS Nimrod MR.2		68	ex Kinloss, MR.1, Kinloss/St Mawgan Wing.	
					Last flew 27-4-10	# 12-21
❑	XZ382	SEPECAT Jaguar GR.1		77	ex Coltishall, Halton 8908M (29-10-86), Shawbury,	
					14, 17. Arrived 22-2-99	12-21
❑	ZD241	'N' Vickers VC10 K.4		68	ex 101, G-ASGM, BOAC. Flew in 21-3-13.	
			N241ZA		See notes under 'Other departures' below	1-22
❑	85	'8-MV' Dassault Mystère IVA		c56	ex East Midlands, Sculthorpe, French AF. Last flown	
					15-5-79. Arrived 11-84. 'Desert' colours, displayed	[3] 12-21
❑	1018	PZL Iskra 100	G-ISKA	78	ex Polish AF. Flew in 5-7-96. De-reg 24-5-10	12-21

■ **[1]** Shedloads of material on *Teasin' Tina* on **www.victorxm715.co.uk** **[2]** Made last ever Comet flight; total flying hours as at 14-3-97 came to 8,281. Details of how you can help support the Comet on Facebook: **dh cometxs235(Canopus)project** **[3]** Mystère held on behalf of the National Museum of the USAF, USA.

Classic British Jet Collection (CBCJ): Dave 'Mr Shifter' Thomas and team. See comments above. Jaguar T.2A XX145 moved to Cosford, Shropshire, on 4th August 2020. ◆ **Strictly** *by prior permission* **only** | Facebook @ClassicBritishJets

❑	WM167	Gloster Meteor		52	ex Coventry, St Mawgan, Coventry, Hurn, Blackbushe,	
		TT.20	G-LOSM		RAE Llanbedr, NF.11, 228 OCU, Colerne CS, 228 OCU.	
					SOC 9-1-76. AWA-built. Flew in 5-1-19	12-21
❑	'WR470'	DH Venom FB.50		54	ex Coventry, G-GONE, Hurn, Chester, Hurn. Swiss AF	
			G-DHVM		J-1542. Swiss-built. CoA 29-4-16, de-reg 8-2-18.	
					Little Beauty, 208 Sqn FB.4 colours. Arrived 3-9-18	12-21
❑	WT806	Hawker Hunter GA.11		55	ex Shoreham, Ipswich, Shawbury, Abingdon, Chivenor,	
					FRADU, CFS, 14. SOC 26-11-94	12-21
❑	XJ494	'121' DH Sea Vixen FAW.2		59	ex Kings Langley, Farnborough, FRL, A&AEE, HSA,	
					Sydenham, 899, Sydenham, 892. Christchurch-built.	
					SOC 4-12-83	12-21
❑	XM365	Hunting Jet Provost		60	ex N Weald, Norwich, G-BXBH (CoA 31-8-01, de-reg 10-10-02)	
		T.3A	G-BXBH		Binbrook, SOC 29-1-97, Shawbury, 1 FTS, 3 FTS, 2 FTS	12-21
❑	XP540	'62' Folland Gnat T.1		63	ex N Weald, Cambridge, Bruntingthorpe, Halton 8608M	
					(12-10-78), 4 FTS. Arrived 30-1-18	12-21
❑	XW290	'MA' BAC Jet Provost T.5A		69	ex Cosford, 9199M (6-7-93), Shawbury, 3 FTS, RAFC, CFS	12-20

Lightning Preservation Group: . See comments above.
◆ **Strictly** *by prior permission* **only** | **email** via website | **www.lightnings.org.uk**

❑	XP703	EE Lightning F.3	63	ex Norwich, Coltishall, Bruntingthorpe, Warton, MoD,	
				29, 56, 74. Last flown 23-5-75. Arrived 7-10. Cockpit	12-21
❑	XR713	'C' EE Lightning F.3	64	ex Leuchars 8935M (9-3-87), LTF, 5, 11, 5, LTF, 11, LTF, 5,	
	and 'XR718'			111, Wattisham TFF, 111. Arrived 5-15, unveiled 23-7-17.	
				111 Sqn c/s to port, 56 Sqn c/s as 'XR718' to stb	[1] 12-21
❑	XR728	'JS' EE Lightning F.6	65	ex Binbrook, 11, LTF, 5, 56, 23, 11, 23. Last flown 24-6-88	12-21
❑	XS904	'BQ' EE Lightning F.6	66	ex BAe Warton, Binbrook, 5-11 pool. Last flown 21-1-93.	
				11 Sqn colours	12-21
❑	XV328	'BZ' EE Lightning T.5	66	ex Cranfield, Binbrook, LTF, 5, LTF, 5, 29. SOC 29-6-88.	
				Cockpit. Acquired 25-5-14	12-21

■ **[1]** The real XR718 is at Dinsdale, N Yorks.

Also: As well as the organisations listed above, several private owners keep airframes at Bruntingthorpe – see comments above. The fuselage of Boeing 737 G-BVKB was scrapped in October 2020 and the forward section was moved to Appely Bridge, Gtr Man, by late 2020. Jet Provost T.3A XN582 moved to Sleap, Shropshire, on 22nd July 2021. Lightning T.55 ZF595 and a cache of surplus airframe sections from the Anglo-American Lightning Organisation, Stennis, Mississippi, moved out to North Weald, Essex, in July 2020. *W&R27* (p134) recorded the cockpit of Lightning F.53 ZF590 as coming here: it remains listed at Gloucester, Glos. ◆ **Strictly** *by prior permission* **only**

❑	WT333	EE Canberra B(I).8		56	ex Farnborough, Bedford, RAE, C(A). Flew in 28-1-95.
			G-BVXC		De-reg 22-4-03	[1] 12-21

❑ XL565	'Y' Hawker Hunter T.7	58	ex Kemble, Ipswich, Colsterworth, Shawbury, Lossiemouth, FRADU, 237 OCU, 4 FTS, 208, 8, 'W' Raynham SF, 8, 1417 Flt, 8, Hawker. SOC 10-10-93. Arrived 21-3-02 [2] 12-21
❑ 22+35	Lockheed F-104G Starfighter	62	ex Lasham, Manching, JbG34, KE+413, DD+105 Messerschmitt-built. Arrived 28-5-10 [3] 12-21
❑ '53'	Aero L29 Delfin	c66	ex Rosehill Market Drayton, Boboc, Romanian AF, 395189. Arrived 11-2-10 [4] 12-21

■ **[1]** Roger Wintle, Steve Reglar, Clive Davies and Tony Waller own WT333 – canberrawt333@aol.com Built as a B(I).8 but was later fitted with the cockpit from B.2 WK135. Clive Davies is the leading light in the Gloster Aviation Club, see under Gloucester, Glos. **[2]** XL565 acquired from Geoffrey Pool by David and Amanda Dacre on 31-10-21. **[3]** 22+35 owned by Geoffrey Pool. **[4]** Delfin owned by Jacek Beben, Mark Boffin and Graham Smith.

Other departures: Beech Restorations: Beech D.18S '43-35943' (G-BKRN) departed by road on 20th December 2020 bound for Langar, Notts. Fairey Battle L5331 and Texan 51-14700 (G-TOMC) left about the same time for a workshop in the region and is listed under 'Off-site' below. For Harvard cockpit KF532 see, initially, under Northampton, Northants. Harvard 3019 (G-CPPM) had moved to Enstone, Oxfordshire, by the spring of 2021.

The Buccaneer Aviation Group: Decamped to Kem... Cotswold, Glos, cockpit of XW550 was the first to go, initially to Bridgnorth, Shropshire, for a period of store, then XW544 and XX894 arriving on 21st August 2020.

GJD Services and **Gary Spoors:** Shackleton MR.3/3 WR974 made the journey to St Athan, Wales, by July 2020. The **VC10 Preservation Group** launched a crowd-funding venture aiming for a cool £400,000 to acquire and relocate the ZD241, but this was abandoned by August 2020. Both the VC10s were US civil registered to Kepler Aerospace in November 2021 – see narrative at Newquay, Cornwall, for more. VC10 K.3 ZA147 (N147ZA) had been scrapped by January 2022 with its cockpit very likely having been saved. By that time it was *hoped* to move ZD241 to the compound on the southeast perimeter and *in anticipation* of that, it has been listed under Cold War Jets Collection, above.

During November and December 2021 scrapping of **Boeing 747s** VP-BGX and VP-BGY commenced and all traces had gone by early January. Ever since they flew in in March 2014 the former RAF **Tristars** have been the subject of a 'will they, won't they' debate, which was enlivened when they aspired to US civil registrations, with most people opting for the latter. The mighty Lockheed trijets were being dismantled in February-March 2022: perhaps a flightdeck or two will survive. For the record they were: KC.1s ZD948 (N304CS), ZD950 (N405CS), ZD951 (N309CS), ZD953 (N705CS), **C.2s** ZE704 (N507CS) and ZE705 (N703CS).

Off-site: Adrian Marshall and the **Beech Restorations** team decamped the challenging Battle project to a ***private*** workshop in the region, which is listed here as a 'flag of convenience. (The Beech 18 is given under Langar, Notts.)
◆ *By prior arrangement* **only**

❑ 51-14700*	NA T-6G-NT Texan G-TOMC	42	ex Bruntingthorpe, Stoke-on-Trent, Eccleshall, N Weald, Coventry, *Empire of the Sun*, La Ferté Alais, FAF, USAF, USAAF 42-44514. *Texan Tomcat* [1] 1-22
❑ L5331	Fairey Battle	39	ex Bruntingthorpe, Canada, RCAF, RAF 98. Austin-built [2] 1-22

■ **[1]** Registered to Texan Restorations. In Algeria, the French called armed Texans 'Tomcats' because of their grow. **[2]** Constitutes cockpit, centre section, engine mount and 1½ wings.

Comanche G-ASCJ and Twin Comanches G-ATFK, G-ATWR, G-AVCY, G-AVVI and G-BAWN were broken up and removed during 2020. At least G-ASCJ was handled by the famous light aircraft parting-out business at Caterham, Surrey.

EAST MIDLANDS AIRPORT or Castle Donington   EGNX
Aeropark: Run by the **East Midlands Airport Volunteers Association**. There are two viewing mounds, close to the runway 09 threshold, that provide a superb vista of the comings and goings at the airport.

Restoration of the VC10 has resulted in a nearly complete flightdeck and full interior. XV108 is the only survivor wearing the classy white, grey, and blue lightning bolt cheat line of Brize Norton's 'Tens of 10' of the 1960s.
◆ *On northern perimeter, DE74 2PR | 01332 850591 | aeropark@eastmidlandsaeropark.org | www.eastmidlandsaeropark.org*

❑ G-ANUW	DH Dove 6	55	ex Long Marston, Welshpool, N Weald, Stansted, CAFU. CoA 22-7-81, de-reg 5-6-96. Arrived 31-10-09 1-22
❑ G-APES	Vickers Merchantman	61	ex Hunting, ABC, BEA. *Swiftsure*. CoA 2-10-95, de-reg 28-2-97. BEA colours. Cockpit 1-22
❑ G-ARRM	Beagle 206-1X	61	ex Brooklands, Farnborough, Shoreham, Kemble, Banwell, Brooklands, Shoreham, Brighton, Duxford, Shoreham. CoA 28-12-64, de-reg 24-1-68. Arrived 2-3-19 [1] 1-22
❑ G-ASDL	Beagle Terrier 2	50	ex Long Eaton, Eccleshall, G-ARLN, Auster AOP.6 WE558, LAS. CoA 18-5-07; de-reg 17-8-04. Frame. Arrived 1-12 [2] 1-22

❑ G-BEOZ		AW Argosy 101	60	ex ABC, N895U, N6502R, G-1-7. CoA 28-5-86,	
				de-reg 19-11-87. Arrived 6-87. Elan colours, *Fat Albert*	1-22
❑ G-CSZB		Vickers Viscount 807	57	ex Coleorton, Southend, N141RA, G-CSZB, VQ-GAB,	
				ZK-NAI, SP-LVC, G-AOXU. *Viscount Scotland.*	
				CoA 24-1-97, de-reg 19-8-98. Arrived 4-03. Cockpit [3]	1-22
❑ G-FRJB		Aircraft Designs Sheriff	82	ex Sandown. De-reg 6-2-87. Unflown. Arrived 1-7-86 [4]	1-22
❑ -		EoN Primary	~	ex Doncaster. Stored	1-22
❑ -		Schleicher K.8	~	-	1-22
❑ -		Siebert Sie-3	~	ex Camphill	1-22
❑ VR-BEP		Westland Whirlwind	55	ex Cuckfield, Bristow VR-BEP, G-BAMH, Redhill, HAR.3	
		Srs 3 G-BAMH		XG588, 705, 701, *Warrior* Flt, *Albion* Flt. SOC 10-10-69.	
				Arrived 5-86. Bristow colours by early 2022	1-22
❑ WH740	'K'	EE Canberra T.17	53	ex Cosford 8762M, 360, B.2, RNZAF, Upwood SF, 40, 18.	
				SOC 1-12-82. Arrived 8-12-91. 360 Sqn colours	1-22
❑ WL626	'P'	Vickers Varsity T.1	53	ex Coventry G-BHDD (de-reg 21-11-09), 6 FTS, 1 ANS, 2 ANS,	
		G-BHDD		201 AFS. SOC 12-4-76. Hurn-built. Last flown 14-11-79 [5]	1-22
❑ WM224	'X'	Gloster Meteor TT.20	52	ex N Weald 'WM311', E Dereham, Swanton Morley	
				8177M (15-10-71), 5 CAACU, 3 CAACU, 3/4 CAACU,	
				NF.11, 29, 228 OCU. AWA-built. Arrived 12-1-03	1-22
❑ WM367		Gloster Meteor NF.13	53	ex Long Marston, Firbeck, N Weald, Powick, Boscombe D',	
				A&AEE. SOC 17-8-72. AWA-built. Arr 11-10-08. Cockpit [5]	1-22
❑ WP266		EoN Eton TX.1	51	BAPC.423, ex Pickhill, RAFGSA.337. SOC 13-12-66	1-22
❑ WP784		DHC Chipmunk T.10	52	ex Long Marston, Hemel Hempstead, Booker, Boston,	
	'RCY-E'			Holbeach, Wellingborough, Reading, Benson, Abingdon,	
				6 AEF, Leeds UAS, Aber UAS, 8 FTS, Man UAS, QUAS,	
				Air Attaché Paris, 5 RFS, 17 RFS. SOC 21-6-72.	
				5 RFS colours. Arrived 11-10-08 [6]	1-22
❑ WS760		Gloster Meteor	54	ex Yatesbury, Loughborough, Cranfield, Bushey,	
		NF(T).14		Duxford, Brampton, Upwood 7964M (23-8-67), 1 ANS,	
				NF.14, 64, AWOCU. AWA-built. Arrived 11-11-06	1-22
❑ WT914		Slingsby Cadet TX.3	52	BGA.3194 / FED, ex Stamford, Tibenham, Kenley.	
				CoA 7-2-87. Fuselage; wings stored. Arrived 6-14 [5]	1-22
❑ WV382	'830'	Hawker Hunter GA.11	55	ex Long Marston, Smethwick, A2724, Lee-on-Solent	
				A2730 (5-2-85), Shawbury, Kemble, FRADU, FRU,	
				738, F.4, 67. Arrived 24-1-09. FRU colours	1-22
❑ WW442	'N'	Percival Provost T.1	54	ex Charlwood, Kings Langley, Leverstock Green, Cranfield,	
				Booker, St Merryn, Houghton-on-the-Hill, Kidlington,	
				Halton 7618M (10-10-59), CNCS, 3 FTS. Arr by 9-13 [2] [7]	1-22
❑ XD447	'50'	DH Vampire T.11	54	ex Long Marston, East Kirkby, Tattershall, Woodford,	
				Chester, St Athan, 8 FTS, RAFC, 5 FTS. SOC 1-12-67.	
				Arrived 3-10-09	1-22
❑ XD534	'L'	DH Vampire T.11	54	ex 'XD382', Welshpool, Barton, Chelford, Hadfield,	
				Wythenshawe, Cheadle, Woodford, Chester, Shawbury,	
				7 FTS, CFS, 9 FTS, 10 FTS. Hawarden-built. SOC 30-10-67.	
				Arrived 2004 [8]	1-22
❑ XG737	'220'	DH Sea Venom FAW.22	58	ex Long Marston, Rhoose, Yeovilton, FRU, 894, 893,	
				RAE, 891. Hawarden-built. SOC 27-3-69.	
				Arrived 31-10-09. 809 Sqn colours	1-22
❑ XL569		Hawker Hunter T.7	58	ex Abingdon, Cosford 8833M (2-9-84), 2 TWU, 1 TWU,	
				12, 216, 237 OCU, Laarbruch SF, 15, 237 OCU, 12, 2 TWU,	
				1 TWU, TWU, 229 OCU. Arrived 20-2-93	1-22
❑ XM575		Avro Vulcan B.2	63	G-BLMC ntu, ex 44, Wadd Wing, Scampton Wing, 617.	
		G-BLMC		SOC 25-1-83, last flight 21-8-83	1-22
❑ XN492		Hunting Jet Provost T.3	60	ex Linton-on-Ouse, Redhill, Haydock, Levenshulme,	
				Firbeck, Stock, Odiham, Cosford, Halton 8079M	
				(18-3-70),6 FTS, RAFC. Cockpit. Arrived 6-15	1-22
❑ XP568	'85'	Hunting Jet Provost T.4	62	ex Long Marston, Faygate, Hatfield, Shawbury, RAFC.	
				SOC 1-10-71. Arrived 25-10-08. RAFC 'silver' colours	1-22
❑ XT604		Westland Wessex HC.2	66	ex Hixon, Colsterworth, Fleetlands, 22, 103, 78,	
				Muharraq SAR Flt, 78. SOC 16-3-00. Arrived 11-7-02 [9]	1-22

☐ XV108	'Y'	Vickers VC10 C.1K	68	ex Bruntingthorpe, 10. *William Rhodes-Moorhouse VC.*		
				Last flight 7-11-12. Arrived 16-11-13. Forward fuselage.		
				Air Support Command titles and 10 Sqn colours	[10]	1-22
☐ XV350		Blackburn Buccaneer S.2B	67	ex Shawbury, Warton, RAE. Arrived 11-12-93		1-22
☐ XW664		HS Nimrod R.1	71	ex 51, Falklands (Chile) 5-82, 51. Last flown 12-7-11	[11]	1-22
☐ XX457	'Z'	Sud Gazelle AH.1	76	ex Long Marston, Arborfield TAD.001, 2 Flt, 662, 656,		
				ARWF, GCF. Arrived 11-10-08. Cab		1-22
☐ XX494	'B'	HP Jetstream T.1	75	ex Bruntingthorpe, Retford, Ipswich, Shawbury,		
				Cranwell, 45, 3 FTS, 45, 6 FTS, METS. SAL-completed.		
				Last flown 22-3-04. Arrived 2-18	[10]	1-22
☐ XZ369*	'EU'	SEPECAT Jaguar GR.3A	76	ex Brinklow, Upminster, Ipswich, St Athan, 6, GR.1, 6,		
				Shawbury, 17, 14. Arrived 18-10-20	[12]	1-22
☐ XZ721		Westland Lynx HMA.8	80	ex Hixon, Fleetlands, 815, HAS.3S, 815. Arrived 3-16	[13]	1-22
☐ ZD477	'E'	Westland Sea King HC.4	84	ex Bruntingthorpe, Gosport, 846, 845, 846, 845,		
				846, 845, 846, 845, 846. Arrived by 3-18	[10]	1-22
☐ ZF588	'L'	EE Lightning F.53	68	ex Warton, Saudi AF 53-693, G-27-63.		
				Last flown 14-1-86. Arrived 8-1-89. 74 Sqn colours		1-22
☐ '272'		Hawker Hunter 'FR.10'	56	BAPC.548, ex 'XJ714', Long Marston.		
				Arrived 23-5-09	[14]	1-22

■ **[1]** Prototype, first flown at Shoreham 15-8-61. On loan from the Brooklands Museum, Surrey. **[2]** Terrier and Provost are from Dave Warren. **[3]** Viscount owned by Colin Jacobs. **[4]** G-FRJB's initial design was carried out by Forrester Robin John Britten (he of the Islander) who was High Sheriff of the Isle of Wight at the time. **[5]** Varsity, Meteor NF.13 and Cadet on loan from Graham Vale. **[6]** WP784 is a complex composite. **[7]** Provost was fitted with the wings of IAC T.51 161. **[8]** XD534 owned by Chris Fairhall; and fitted with the wings and tail of XD382. **[9]** XT604's rear fuselage is fitted to XT760 - see Portsmouth in Appendix C. **[10]** VC10, Jetstream and Sea King on loan from Gary Spoors - see St Athan, Wales. **[11]** XW664 was the first R.1; it retired with a total flying time of 21,466 hours. It took part in Operation ACME, Elint/Sigint sorties, from St Félix island, coast of Chile during Falklands conflict. **[12]** Inspection of the build plates on XZ369 notes that it was laid down as fuselage S138 in 11-75 but was completed as S136 11-76. **[13]** Lynx owned by Mark Lindsey. **[14]** A complex beast; with an unused F.6 cockpit from Stafford, the centre section of F.6 XG226 - cockpit at Manston, Kent - the rear end of Danish T.7 ET-272 - cockpit at Flixton, Suffolk - and the wings from PH-NLH.

Airport: Rolls-Royce bases Spitfire PR.19 PS853 (G-RRGN) and Harvard T.2B KF183 (G-CORS) at 'EMA'. This facility is **not** available for public inspection here but the PR.19 is a regular at air events. See under Derby, Derbyshire, for more on RR. Last noted in January 2016, Rallye G-BBED has been deleted.

| ☐ TC-ALM | | Boeing 727-230 | 71 | ex Air Alfa, TC-IKO, TC-JUH, TC-ALB, N878UM, D-ABDI. | | |
| | | | | Rescue trainer | | 8-19 |

HINCKLEY southwest of Leicester

Steve Milnthorpe's phenomenal project has been fitted out to Boston IIIA configuration. This restoration would make many a national museum blush! Other items held include port inner mainplane, fully restored turret, landing gear, Boston-fit Wright Cyclone, etc. ◆ *By prior arrangement* **only**

| ☐ 'BZ264' | 'B' | Douglas Boston IIIA | 43 | 88 Sqn colours, *XXX Beer is Best.* Forward fuselage | [1] | 1-22 |

■ **[1]** Based upon the forward fuselage of A-20G-30-DO 43-9628 *Lady Constance* of the 388th BS, 312th BG, which crashed in New Guinea 16-4-44. The restoration includes elements of Boston IIA Z2186 ex 418 Sqn RCAF which crashed in Snowdonia 17-10-42.

HUSBANDS BOSWORTH on the A4304/A5199 west of Market Harborough

Armourgeddon Military Collection: ◆ *On the A5199 - look for the tank 'gate guardian'* | www.armourgeddon.co.uk

| ☐ G-ARXH | | Bell 47G | 47 | ex Cranfield, N120B, Model 47D-1, 47B. De-reg 3-1-84 | | 12-21 |

HUSBANDS BOSWORTH AERODROME south of the A427, south of the village

The Gliding Centre ◆ *By prior arrangement* **only** | www.theglding centre.co.uk

| ☐ G-BVYG* | | Robin DR.300-180 | 71 | ex F-BSQB. CoA 30-9-13. Fuselage | | 9-21 |
| ☐ XK790 | | Slingsby Grasshopper TX.1 | 55 | ex Halton. SOC 9-4-85. Stored | | 9-19 |

KEGWORTH east of J24 of the M1, on the A6

Delta Force Paintball ◆ *By prior arrangement* **only** | www.paintballgames.co.uk

| ☐ XZ177 | | Westland Lynx AH.7 | 77 | ex Upminster, Ipswich, Fleetlands, M Wallop. 'Marines' titles | | 4-21 |

■ **[1]** A *Gazelle* marked 'XZ177' is at Sunderland, N&T.

LEICESTER

Leicester Aircraft Restoration Workshop: (Note change of name.) Max and Ritch Blood deservedly picked up a *Spirit of CockpitFest* award at the 2021 Newark event. This challenging project, utilises some 'new-old' stock, a great boost from Alan House's Thatcham shelves and much 'scrounging'. The cockpit side carries an original 6 FTS badge and elements of XF545 are used within the self-proclaimed 'bitza' and, for the time being, that serial will serve as its 'handle'. The father and son team have also crafted the instrument facia and controls of a Brasov IS-28M2A motor glider. Beyond the remit of *W&R*, but, as it is designed for 'small people' and disabled access, is well worthy of a mention. ◆ *By prior arrangement* **only**

☐ 'XF545'	Percival Provost T.1	55	BAPC.574, ex Thatcham, Linton-on-Ouse, Swinderby, Finningley 7957M (16-6-67), Shawbury, 6 FTS, 2 FTS. Fuselage, 6 FTS badge. See notes above	8-21

Leicester College: Painter Street. The Cavalier *may* still serve serve the students.
◆ *By prior arrangement* **only** | www.leicestercollege.ac.uk

☐ G-BAJV	K&S Cavalier SA.102·5	r72	Unfinished project. De-reg 10-12-81. Handed over 12-16	12-16

Leicestershire Museums: The aircraft are stored at two venues in the locality. See Newark, Notts, for the Bobsleigh.
◆ *By prior arrangement* **only**

☐ G-AFTN	Taylorcraft Plus C2	39	ex Coalville, Heavitree, HL535, 43 OTU, 652, 651, G-AFTN. CoA 1-11-57, de-reg 31-1-99. [1]	6-19
☐ G-AGOH	Auster J1 Autocrat	45	ex C'ville, Winthorpe, Leicester. CoA 24-8-95, de-reg 7-8-08	6-19
☐ G-AIJK	Auster J4 Archer	46	ex Coalville, Leicester, Stratford, Hemswell. CoA 24-8-68, de-reg 8-8-68. Acquired 1980. Frame [2]	8-21
☐ XP280	Auster AOP.9	61	ex Coalville, Leicester, St Athan, 6 Flt, 651. SOC 6-11-74	6-19

■ [1] *Tango-November* is the oldest surviving Auster type. [2] The firewall backwards to the windscreen of a J4 is displayed at Loughborough, Leics - see below - which *may* be from *Juliet-Kilo*.

Also: The Aeronca is *believed* current at a *private* site locally. Canberra XH174 is more accurately located at Cannock, Staffs.

☐ G-BRFI	Aeronca 7DC Champion	46	ex Londonderry, Ballymoney, N1058E. CoA 19-2-91	N4-19

LEICESTER AERODROME or Leicester East or Stoughton, southeast of Leicester   EGBG

Cub G-AEXZ, held off-site for many years was acquired by a Hampshire-based owner during the spring of 2020. Husky G-ATMH is believed to have moved to the Southend area, perhaps as a source of spares. Last noted in October 2018 the Westland Wallace frame had departed by August 2020. Grob 'G-FIRE' is used for rescue exercises and carries a placard inviting purchase at £4.51 or nearest offer!

☐ G-ARDJ	Auster D6/180	60	crashed 30-5-86. CoA 7-7-88. Off-site	N5-18
☐ G-BOCM	Slingsby T.67C Firefly	86	ex Folkestone. CoA 22-7-10. First noted 9-16	4-21
☐ 'G-FIRE'*	Grob G.115A	EI-CAE 90	ex Swiftair. Trailer mounted, fire rescue trainer. First noted 9-20 – see notes above	5-21

LOUGHBOROUGH on the A6 north of Leicester

Charnwood Museum: The 1956 King's Cup-winning Auster commemorates the wonders worked at nearby Rearsby. Within a small display cabinet installed in 2016 devoted to Auster are the firewall, Perspex windscreen and a couple of inches behind that of a cockpit from a J4 Archer, *possibly* from G-AIJK - but it's more wall plaque than airframe.
◆ *Granby Street, LE11 3DU* | **01509 233754** | museum@charnwood.gov.uk | www.charnwoodmuseum.co.uk

☐ G-AJRH	'7' Auster J1N Alpha	47	ex Leicester, Harrogate, Wigan. CoA 5-6-69, de-reg 18-1-99	1-22

Loughborough University: Department of Aeronautical and Automotive Engineering
◆ *By prior arrangement* **only** | www.lboro.ac.uk

☐ ZH200	HS Hawk 200	87	ex Brough, Warton. Arrived 5-12	12-21

LUBENHAM on the A4304 west of Market Harborough

A pair of airframes have arrived at a farm in the general area.

☐ XE368*	'200' Hawker Sea Hawk FGA.6	55	ex Barrow-in-Furness, Market Drayton, Bruntingthorpe, Helston, Culdrose SAH-3, Shotley A2534 (28-5-66), 738, 806, 803, 899. AWA-built. First noted 5-21	10-21
☐ XM405*	'42' Hunting Jet Provost T.3A G-TORE	59	ex Drakelow, Bruntingthorpe, London, Ipswich, G-TORE, (CoA 5-5-95, de-reg 2-2-04), Cranfield, XM405, 1 FTS, RAFC, 1 FTS, 2 FTS. First noted 4-21	10-21

LUTTERWORTH
Lutterworth and District Museum: Includes much Sir Frank Whittle and Power Jets material and an incredible archive.
◆ *Wycliffe House, Gilmorton Road, LE17 4DY* | **07906 303643** | **email** via website | **www.lutterworthmuseum.org**

Whittle Memorial: Dramatically displayed to the south of the town, on the A426 roundabout, is a superb tribute to Sir Frank Whittle. Static tests of Whittle's engine began at the Ladywood Works, to the north of the town, in 1938. See also Farnborough, Hampshire, for another E28/39 'monument'.

| ❏ – | Gloster E28/39 FSM | 02 BAPC.284. Sir Frank Whittle Commemorative Trust- built | 1-22 |

NORTH LUFFENHAM north of the A6121, southwest of Stamford
St George's Barracks: On the southern perimeter of the former airfield, the hulk of a Whirlwind lies on its side. This was written out of *W&R24* (p135, last noted November 2012) when the EOD enclave was wound down.

| ❏ XP344* | Westland Whirlwind HAR.10 | 62 ex Cranwell 8764M (11-10-82), Finningley, Chivenor, 22, SAR Wing, CFS | 11-20 |

RATCLIFFE ON THE WREAKE Last recorded in June 2015, Spitfire FSM project 'P9503' has been deleted.

STANFORD northeast of Rugby, near Swinford
Stanford Hall and **Percy Pilcher Museum**: In the Stable Courtyard is a display to Percy Pilcher who crashed in the grounds on 30th September 1899 flying the Hawk and died of his injuries. (The original craft is on show in Edinburgh, Scotland.)
◆ *North of Stanford on Avon. LE17 6DH* | **01788 860250** | **enquiries@stanfordhall.co.uk** | **www.stanfordhall.co.uk**

| ❏ - | Pilcher Hawk replica | 58 BAPC.45, ex Coventry, Bitteswell | [1] 1-22 |
■ [1] Built by Armstrong Whitworth apprentices.

WIGSTON southeast of Leicester
Graham Smith: Is *thought* to still have his Harrier. ◆ *By prior arrangement* **only**

| ❏ XW763 | HS Harrier GR.3 | 71 ex Bruntingthorpe, Wigston, Bruntingthorpe, Duxford, St Athan 9041M, 9002M, 4, GR.1, 1453 Flt, 1, A&AEE, 1, 233 OCU. SOC 22-3-89. Cockpit | 6-10 |

WOODHOUSE Welbeck Defence College closed its doors on 3rd July 2021. Gazelle AH.1 XX381 is unaccounted for.

WYMESWOLD on the A6006 northwest of Leicester
The **British Phantom Aviation Group's** stay was relatively short and thankfully a kind offer was seized upon, although the task of roading the mighty Phantoms again – amid the pandemic – was daunting. FGR.2 XT905 arrived at Cotswold, Glos, on 29th June 2021 with FG.1 XT597 following on 21st July. For F-4J(UK) ZE360 see under Manston, Kent.

Also: A Scout is *thought* to still be kept at a *private* location in the area.

| ❏ XP883 | Westland Scout AH.1 | 63 ex Bruntingthorpe, Oaksey Park, Boscombe Down, 658, 655, 652. Arrived 8-12-16 | [1] 12-16 |
■ [1] The boom of XP883 is to be found on another Scout - see May, N Ireland.

LINCOLNSHIRE
Includes the unitary authorities of North Lincolnshire and North East Lincolnshire

---

BARKSTON HEATH AIRFIELD on the B6403 north of Grantham
EGYE
By May 2020 Canberra B(I).8 WT339 had been reduced to a centre section and wings and as such has been deleted.

BECKINGHAM north of the A17 east of Newark
After spares recovery by the Newark Air Museum, Puma XW225 was delivered to the military exercise area.

| ❏ XW225* | Sud Puma HC.1 | 72 ex Newark, Wallingford, 18, 230, 240 OCU, 230, 240 OCU, 230, 240 OCU, 230, 240 OCU, 230, 240 OCU, 230. Crashed 15-2-97. Arrived 10-12-20 | 12-20 |

BINBROOK on the B1203 northeast of Market Rasen
Charles Ross: Keeps a whole F.6 and a cockpit at a *private* location and owns F.1A XM192 at Tattershall Thorpe, Lincs.
◆ *Admission by prior arrangement* **only**

❏ XR725	'BA' EE Lightning F.6	65	ex Rossington, Binbrook, 11, F.3, 11, 5, LTF, 5, 56, 74, 5, 23. SOC 24-6-88	9-21
❏ XS899	'E' EE Lightning F.6	66	ex Norwich, Coltishall, Bruntingthorpe, Cranfield, Binbrook, 11, 5-11 pool, 23, 5. SOC 24-6-88. Cockpit. 23 Sqn c/s. Off-site	6-18

BINBROOK AIRFIELD north of the B1203, north of the village
Lightning Association: Through the LA's incredible website Lightning fans are united.
◆ *By prior permission* **only** | **email** via website | **www.lightning.org.uk** and **Facebook**

❏ XR724	EE Lightning F.6	65	ex G-BTSY (de-reg 26-5-92), Shawbury, BAe Warton, 11,	
	G-BTSY		F.3, 11, 5, 11, 5, LTF, 11. Arrived 23-7-92	1-22

Also: Several individuals also keep jets on the site. Seeing is believing - the 'Phoenix' is risen! For many years Lightning F.2A XN728 lay rotting alongside of the A1 at Balderton, attracting a barrage of brake lights from passing traffic. Darren Swinn and friends took on the daunting task of restoring the cockpit of this rare variant: the only other survivor is XN776 at East Fortune, Scotland. Eight years in, Darren chose to bring it to *CockpitFest* 2021 where he was rewarded with the 'Cockpiteers Cockpit' and hallowed 'Grand Champion' accolades - and rightly so!

Last noted in March 2019, Vampire T.11 WZ584 moved to Grimsby, Lincs, by mid-2020. By April 2020 Sea Harrier F/A.2 ZE697 had relocated to Walcott, Lincs. ◆ *For all of those given below - by prior permission* **only**

❏ XN728	'V' EE Lightning F.2A	61	ex Lincoln, Balderton, Coningsby 8546M (4-4-77), Wildenrath, 92. Cockpit. Arrived 4-14	[1]	8-21
❏ XS416*	'DU' EE Lightning T.5	64	ex Holton cum Beckering, New York, Grainthorpe, New Waltham, Rossington, Binbrook, 5, LTF, 11, 74, 226 OCU. SOC 24-6-88. First noted 8-21	[2]	10-21
❏ XS457	EE Lightning T.5	65	ex Grainthorpe, North Coates, New Waltham, Laceby, Binbrook, 5, 11, 5, LTF, 11, 226 OCU. SOC 21-9-87. Cockpit	[3]	9-21
❏ XS459*	'AW' EE Lightning T.5	65	ex West Walton Highway, Narborough, Binbrook, 5, LTF, 56, 29, 226 OCU. SOC 21-6-88. Arrived by 5-21	[4]	9-21

■ **[1]** XN728 owned by Darren Swinn – see notes above. **[2]** XS416 is held within Hangar 3, in the Brookenby Business Park element of the former RAF Binbrook and is reported owned by H I S Church – **www.hischurch.org.uk** – for eventual display. **[3]** Owned by Roy Whitleley / Lincair - **lincair@binbrook.demon.co.uk [4]** XS459 owned by well-known Lightning 'jockey' Ian Black.

BOSTON
Previously listed under Fenland, Lincs, a cache of Austers is held at *private* locations in the locality.

❏ G-AHAP	Auster J1 Autocrat	46	ex March. CoA 20-2-91	12-21
❏ G-AMRF	Auster J5F Aiglet Trainer	52	ex VT-DHA, G-AMRF. *Grey Dove*. CoA 31-3-07	12-21
❏ NJ673	T'craft Auster 5D G-AOCR	44	ex Boston, EI-AJS, G-AOCR, NJ673, 26, 174, 137, 182, 247, 430	12-21

Also: *W&R28* (p140) declared that the MB.100 held locally was unaccounted for. It remains on site, but it due to move on.

❏ F-BBGH	Brochet MB.100	~	ex F-WBGH	10-21

COLSTERWORTH on the A1 north of Stamford
Witham Specialist Vehicles Ltd: Vast numbers of military vehicles are dealt with, all with a rapid throughput. The same is true of most of the helicopters handled. Increasingly many do not travel to the yard, being 'hammered' at the point of disposal, or at storage sites in the south of England, and going direct to the purchaser.

'Stock' for 2021, including a 'virtual' auction in May, has included the following – first noted dates in brackets: **Gazelle** AH.1 XX378 (4-21); XX442 (4-21); XX447 (4-21); XZ311 (4-21); XZ325 (from Lyneham, Wilts, 8-21); TAD.017 (XW888, from Lyneham, Wilts, 8-21); HCC.4 XZ935 (from Lyneham, Wilts, 8-21). AH.1 XZ337 was sold and moved to Freiston, Lincs, 2-6-21.
◆ *By prior arrangement* **only** | **www.mod-sales.com**

CONINGSBY AIRFIELD south of the A153, southeast of Woodhall Spa — EGXC
Battle of Britain Memorial Flight (BBMF) and **Visitor Centre**: A partnership between the RAF and Lincolnshire County Council provides the public access to the Flight. The **RAF Memorial Flight Club** offers free entry to the Visitor Centre and other goodies: **www.memorialflightclub.com**

Note: As well as attending air events all over the country, BBMF aircraft are overhauled by civilian contractors, and may be away on maintenance, sometimes for lengthy periods.

◆ *South of the A153. Access to the BBMF hangar is via guided tour* **only | 01522 782040 | bbmf@lincolnshire.gov.uk | www.lincolnshire.gov.uk/history-heritage/battle-britain-memorial-flight-visitor-centre**

❑ P7350	'KL-B'	V-S Spitfire IIa ✈ G-AWIJ	40	ex *Battle of Britain* (1968), G-AWIJ (de-reg 29-2-84), Colerne, 57 OTU, CGS, 64, 616, 603, 266. CBAF-built. Joined BBMF 5-11-68. 54 Sqn colours, *Kiwi III*	1-22
❑ AB910	'SH-F'	V-S Spitfire Vb ✈ G-AISU	41	ex *Battle of Britain* (1968), BBMF, G-AISU (de-reg 22-8-55), RWE, 527, 53 OTU, 402, 242, 133, 130, 222. CBAF-built. Joined BoB Flt 16-9-65. *Peter John I*. 64 Sqn colours	1-22
❑ 'EN398'	'JE-J'	V-S Spitfire IX FSM	~	BAPC.541, ex Duxford. GB Replicas-built. Displayed	[1] 10-19
❑ LF363	'JX-B' '	Hawker Hurricane IIc ✈	44	ex Audley End, Coningsby, Biggin Hill SF, 41, 41 GCF, Waterbeach SF, Odiham SF, Thorney Island SF, FCCS, M Wallop SF, 61 OTU, 41 OTU, 62 OTU, 26, 63, 309, 63. Joined Biggin Hill Stn Flt 1951. Will have 303 Sqn colours	1-22
❑ MK356	'QJ-3'	V-S Spitfire IX ✈	44	ex St Athan, Abingdon, 5690M St Athan, Henlow, Bicester, Hawkinge, Halton, 84 GSU, 443. CBAF-built. Restored at Coningsby, first flown 7-11-97. 92 Sqn c/s	[2] 1-22
❑ PA474	'AR-L' and 'VN-T'	Avro Lancaster I ✈	45	ex 44, Wroughton, Cranfield College, RAE, FRL, 82 (as PR.1). Joined BBMF 20-11-73. 460 Sqn (AR-L) *Leader* to port, and 50 Sqn colours, stb	1-22
❑ PM631		V-S Spitfire PR.19 ✈	45	ex Martlesham Heath SF, N Weald SF, Biggin Hill SF, THUM Flt, Buckeburg SF, 206 OCU, 203 AFS. Joined Biggin Hill Stn Flt (Historic A/c Flight) 14-6-57. 541 Sqn colours	1-22
❑ PS915		V-S Spitfire PR.19 ✈	45	ex Samlesbury, Preston, Brawdy, St Athan, Coningsby, Brawdy, Leuchars 7548M/7711M, W' Malling, Biggin Hill, THUM Flt, 2, PRDU, 541. Joined Biggin Hill Stn Flt (Historic A/c Flight) 14-6-57. 81 sqn c/s. Stored	1-22
❑ PZ865	'ZY-V' ✈	Hawker Hurricane II G-AMAU	44	ex 'P2619' 'US-B' *Angels One-Five*, Hawker G-AMAU (de-reg 19-12-72). Joined BBMF 29-3-72. 247 Sqn colours by 5-21	1-22
❑ TE311	'SZ-G'	V-S Spitfire XVI ✈	45	ex EP&TU, 7241M, 'MK178' 'X4474', France, Abingdon, Henlow, Wattisham, CAACU, 103 FRS, 102 FRS, 83 GSU. CBAF-built. 131 Wing colours	[3] 1-22
❑ WG486	'E'	DHC Chipmunk T.10 ✈	51	ex Newton, Gatow SF, ARWF, 3 AEF, Bristol UAS, 3 AEF, Bristol UAS, Liv UAS, PFS, 1 FTS, ITS, AOTS, ITS, RAFC, MECS, 114, 651, 657, 2 FTS, 63 GCF, 9 RFS, 5 BFTS. Joined BBMF 1995. Grey/dayglo, Bristol UAS colours	[4] 1-22
❑ WK518	'D'	DHC Chipmunk T.10 ✈	52	ex Newton, 1 AEF, Lon, Hull, Leeds, Hull UASs, Coltishall SF, FWS, Cam, Hull, Cam, Man, L'pool UASs, 63 GCF, RAFC. Joined BBMF 4-83. London UAS colours from 9-20	[4] 1-22
❑ ZA947	'UK'	Douglas Dakota 3 ✈	42	ex DRA, RAE, Farnborough, West Freugh, 'KG661', RCAF 661, C-47A-60-DL 42-24338. Long Beach-built. Joined BBMF 6-93. *Kwicherbichen*, 233 Sqn colours	1-22

■ [1] *Other* 'EN398s' can be found at: Sleap, Shropshire, Taunton, Somerset, Pyle, Wales. **[2]** See under Cosford, Shropshire, and Hawkinge, Kent, for 'other' MK356s! **[3]** TE311's restoration consumed elements of fellow TB382 - see Sandown, Isle of Wight - as spares. **[11]** WG486 taken on charge 31-12-51, WK518 taken on charge 28-1-52: they are the last of the breed in UK military service.

RAF Coningsby: The resident Typhoon units tend to allocate weapons loading trainers - WLTs - for short periods and then rotate them back into operational service: so *W&R* will avoid them, unless they are seriously long term.

❑ 'XP765'	'A'	EE Lightning F.6	XS897 66	ex Doncaster, Firbeck, Rossington, Binbrook, 5, 11, 5, 11, 56, 74. SOC 5-2-88. 29 Squadron, displayed	[1] 12-21
❑ XR753	'XI'	EE Lightning F.6	65	ex Leeming 8969M (25-5-88), Binbrook, 11, 5-11 pool, 23, FCTU, F.3. 11 Sqn colours, displayed	[2] 12-21
❑ XT891	'Z'	McD Phantom FGR.2	68	9136M (10-6-92), ex 74, 228 OCU, 56, 228 OCU, 29, 228 OCU, 29, 228 OCU, 29, 228 OCU, 56, 228 OCU, 6, 54, 228 OCU, 54. Displayed, 41 Sqn colours by 6-14	[3] 12-21
❑ XW924	'G'	HS Harrier GR.3	71	ex Cottesmore 9073M, Laarbruch, Halton, 3, 4, 1, 233 OCU, GR.1, 4, 20, 4. 3 Squadron, displayed	12-21

☐ XX962	SEPECAT Jaguar GR.1B	75	ex Pembrey, Cosford, Cranwell 9257M (2-10-96), Coltishall,	
			6, 17, 20, 17. Arrived 4-7-19. Cockpit	12-21
☐ ZE760	'AP' Panavia Tornado F.3	88	ex St Athan, ItAF MM7206, RAF, 5. 229 OCU c/s, displayed	12-21
☐ 'DJ666'	Eurofighter Typhoon	07	SOC 11-6-19. Typhoon Training Flight	
	FGR.4 ZJ940		First noted 10-19	12-21

■ [1] XS897 is owned by the Lakes Lightnings Collection - see Spark Bridge, Cumbria. Only F.3s were flown by 23, so it has been given a small ventral tank, but retains the F.6's conical camber wings. The 12-year agreement is is due to expire 7-22 and it is likely to be offered for sale. [2] XR753 is displayed outside 11 Sqn's Typhoon HQ on the southern perimeter - see under Tangmere, W Sussex, for its doppelgänger. [3] Careful study of the fin on XT891 reveals that it is not an RWR example; this was taken from F-4J(UK) ZE354, which was scrapped at Coningsby in July 2001.

CRANWELL AIRFIELD on the A17/B1429 northwest of Sleaford   EGYD

Cranwell Aviation Heritage Centre: Located close to but *not* at, the airfield, the centre charts the history of Cranwell. Boasting a souvenir shop, 'JP' flight simulator and archive film show, it is an excellent stop-off when visiting Cranwell - the circuit is in sight. There are expansion plans for the venue.

◆ *Off the A17, near North Rauceby, NG34 8QR* | **01529 488490** | **cranwellaviation@n-kesteven.gov.uk** | **www.heartoflincs.com/cranwell**

☐ XE946	DH Vampire T.11	55	ex Cardington, Henlow, Bicester 7473M (25-9-57),	
			Habbaniya SF, Nicosia SF. Hatfield-built. Cockpit	1-22
☐ XP556	'3' Hunting Jet Provost T.4	61	ex Bruntingthorpe, Halton 9027M (15-2-90), Shawbury,	
			CATCS, SoRF, 6 FTS, RAFC. Arrived 4-97	1-22

RAF Cranwell: The Spitfire 'guards' the Selection Centre, the Dominie and 'JP' are along the B1429 through the camp. The cockpit of Harrier GR.3 XZ138 had moved to <u>Scampton</u>, Lincs, by September 2021.

☐ 'P8448'	'DO-R' V-S Spitfire FSM	90	BAPC.225, ex Swanton Morley	12-18
☐ XS710	'O' HS Dominie T.1	65	ex Cosford 9259M (7-10-96), Cranwell, 3 FTS, 6 FTS, CAW.	
			Rescue training	12-21
☐ XS727	'D' HS Dominie T.1	65	ex 55, 3 FTS, 6 FTS, 1 ANS. Displayed by 9-13	11-21
☐ XW353	'3' BAC Jet Provost T.5A	71	ex 9090M (18-7-91), 3 FTS, RAFC, CFS, 3 FTS, RAFC.	
			Displayed	11-21
☐ TAD.009*	W'land Lynx 1-03 XW838	72	ex Lyneham, Aborfield, M Wallop, Yeovil. F/n 2-21	11-21
☐ ZE378*	Westland Lynx AH.7	86	ex M Wallop. Arrived 8-20, instructional	8-20

RAF Exhibition, Production and Transportation Unit (EP&TU): The airframes are based on a former airfield close by and run by a contractor. EP&TU is 'parented' by the Cranwell-based Directorate of Recruitment and Selection and, for that reason, the 'fleet' is listed under this heading. Access to the 'detached' site is *not* possible and indeed many of the airframes spend their time in 'transit camps' elsewhere to minimise vehicle usage. EP&TU also has two Eurofighter Typhoon cockpit mock-ups, both of which include interactive segments. These, 'Chinook' 'IR808' (BAPC.361) and a 'Hercules' - the latter owing more to Crane Fruehauf than to Lockheed Georgia - are *not* considered as deserving of a 'formal' listing.

☐ 'XX226'	'74' HS Hawk T.1 FSM	78	BAPC.152, ex St Athan, 'XX262', Abingdon, 'XX162'	4-19
☐ 'XX308'	HS Hawk T.1 FSM	81	BAPC.171, ex 'XX227', 'XX253', St Athan, 'XX297',	
			Abingdon, 'XX262'. 'Red Arrows' colours	[1] 7-21
☐ 'ZA556'	'Z' Panavia Tornado	80	BAPC.155, ex St Athan, 'ZA368' 'ZA446' Abingdon,	
	GR.1 FSM		'ZA600', 'ZA322'. Grey colours, 13 Sqn colours	4-19
☐ 'IR206'	'IR' Eurofighter Typhoon FSM	c02	BAPC.360, trailer-mounted. 17 Squadron colours	6-18
☐ -	Lockheed F-35B FSM	c18	first noted 6-18	6-18

■ [1] The *real* XX308 is at East Fortune, Scotland.

CROWLAND AERODROME on the A1073 south of Spalding

Darren Speechley: By April 2021 Noralpha G-BAYV had moved to <u>White Waltham</u>, Berks, for brief 'stardom' in Suffolk and Oxfordshire, before returning. Noralpha G-ATDB was also involving in 'shooting' in Oxfordshire, before returning to store.

◆ *By prior arrangement* only | **djs1944@hotmail.co.uk**

☐ G-ATDB	Nord Noralpha	48	ex Prestwick, Edinburgh, Skelmorie, Prestwick, F-OTAN-6,	
			Fr mil 186. CoA 22-11-78, de-reg 11-10-10	1-22
☐ G-BAYV*	Nord Noralpha	48	ex White Waltham, St Mawgan, Crowland, Barton,	
			Chelford, 'F-OTAN-6', Sevenoaks, Booker, Hawkinge,	
			Maidstone, Ford, F-BLTN, French AF. Crashed 23-2-74,	
			de-reg 28-4-83. Cockpit. See notes above	1-22

❑ -		BP Sea Balliol T.21	~ ex Quarrywood. Cockpit	1-22
❑ -		BP Sea Balliol T.21	~ ex Quarrywood. Cockpit	1-22

Noralpha G-BAYV during filming at
Bentwaters, April 2021. *Tom Davis*

DIGBY east of the B1188 north of Sleaford
RAF Digby World War Two Sector Operations Room within the **Joint Service Signals Organisation Digby** site.
◆ *Guided tours only. Groups by prior arrangement* | **www.raf.mod.uk/rafdigby**

❑ 'MJ832'	'DN-Y'	V-S Spitfire FSM	89	BAPC.229, ex 'L1096', Church Fenton. *City of Oshawa*, 416 Sqn colours. Displayed	1-22

EAST KIRKBY AERODROME on the A155 west of Spilsby
Lincolnshire Aviation Heritage Centre (LAHC): A section of the former bomber airfield is run by the Panton family as a memorial to Christopher, who was killed on the horrific Nürnberg raid of 30-31st March 1944, and as a tribute to Bomber Command as a whole. The codes on either side of *Just Jane* pay tribute to the late Fred Panton and his brother, Harold, both of whom rescued NX611 and brought it to life.

The Lancaster is the subject of a long-term project to put it back into the air. To allow *Just Jane* to continue providing taxi rides - the revenue from this being vital to the venture - a unique co-operative exchange began in 2021. Across at Le Bourget in France, Les Ailes Anciennes is restoring - to static condition - Lancaster VII NX664, like NX611 *Just Jane*, this is a former Aéronavale example. Over what is estimated will be a four-year task, the outer wings of NX664 will be restored in a jig and in turn fitted to NX611. This will then allow NX611's 'outers' to be fully restored to flight worthiness condition. Eventually Les Ailes Anciennes will receive NX664's outer wings in fully restored condition.

Gracing the cover is **Tony Agar**'s exceptional Mosquito, which has joined the Lancaster in regularly making taxi runs. The story of this incredible project is exceptional. Achieving a 'live' Mosquito from such modest, yet challenging, beginnings ranks this 'Wooden Wonder' as one of the most significant 'one man' British restorations UK's of all-time. Tony began his endeavours with the purchase of Mosquito NF.II cockpit HJ711 for £7 at the auction winding down the woeful Reflectaire museum enterprise at Squires Gate on 29thApril 1972. In an amazing co-incidence the 'star' of that sale was Lancaster VII NX611, although it was sold beyond the 'gavel' and travelled to Scampton. In LAHC Tony has found kindred spirits.

Acting in support of the upwardly mobile Lancaster is the **East Kirkby Lancaster Association** – details on the website. Two other groups are based within LAHC: **Lincolnshire Aircraft Recovery Group** (LARG): 'Prize' exhibit is the very substantial Spitfire BL655. **Lincolnshire Aviation Preservation Society** (LAPS): Main project is the painstaking restoration of AE436, the Brian Nicholls Hampden Project and Proctor IV NP294.

A Halifax cockpit is being constructed on site, using as many original parts as possible. The Lancaster replica cockpit section, '976', had moved to Newquay, Cornwall, by late 2020, bound for more exotic, and colder, climes.
◆ *PE23 4DE* | **01790 763207** | **enquiries@lincsaviation.co.uk** | **www.lincsaviation.co.uk** | **www.mossie.org/HJ711**

❑ -		Druine Turbulent	62	BAPC.154, ex Tattershall, Friskney, Nottingham. Fuselage in workshop rafters. Arrived 12-85	[1]	3-20
❑ AE436	'PL-J'	HP Hampden I	41	ex Coningsby, Henlow, Sweden, 144. Crashed 4-9-42. EE-built. Arrived 11-88. Forward fuselage, etc	[2] [3]	1-22
❑ BL655		V-S Spitfire Vb	41	ex Dorrington Fen, 416, 129, 341, 164, 602, 416. Crashed 1-7-43. Arrived 1993. Substantial remains	[4]	1-22

☐	HJ711	'VI-C'	DH Mosquito NF.II		BAPC.434, ex Elvington, Huntington (York), Squires Gate, Enfield, Chingford, 169, 14. Arrived 30-7-17. Rolled out 30-7-18. 169 Sqn c/s, *Spirit of Val*. Taxying by mid-2020	[5]	1-22
☐	NP294		Percival Proctor IV	44	ex Tattershall, Friskney, Poynton, Andover, Cosford, 4 RS, 2 RS. Hills-built. SOC 22-3-55. Arrived 12-85	[2] [6]	1-22
☐	NX611 *and*	'DX-F' 'LE-H'	Avro Lancaster VII	45	ex Scampton, 8375M, Squires Gate, Hullavington, Lavenham, Biggin Hill, Aéronavale, WU-15, St Athan, Llandow. Austin Motors-built. *Just Jane*, 57 Sqn colours to stb, 630 Sqn to port. Arrived 5-88. Taxiable	[7]	1-22
					G-ASXX		
☐	WH957		EE Canberra E.15	55	ex Bruntingthorpe, Cosford 8869M, 100, 98, B.6, 98, Akrotiri Wing, 32, Hemswell SF, Upwood SF, 21, 542, 617. Short-built. Arrived 12-85. Cockpit		1-22
☐	-		Heinkel He 111 mock-up	68	BAPC.389, ex New Zealand, East Kirkby, others, *Battle of Britain* (1968). Arrived 3-93. Cockpit, blitz display		3-20

■ **[1]** Turbulent is unfinished project PFA.1654. **[2]** Hampden and Proctor with LAPS. **[3]** See fellow P1344 at Cosford, Shropshire, lost on the same night. **[4]** Spitfire Vb with LARG. **[5]** Mosquito on loan from Tony Agar is a complex composite, using the cockpit of HJ711 (and the history of HJ711 is charted above), rear fuselage of TT.35 RS715 from Elstree; centre section from Mk XVI PF498 from Leyland; and the outer wings of T.3 VA878 from St Davids. **[6]** Proctor starboard wing from Mk.IV G-ANYR. **[7]** NX611's individual codes are 'F' for Fred Panton, 'H' for Harold. NX611 was acquired by Fred and Harold 1-9-83 while it was still on the 'gate' at Scampton.

ELSHAM west of the A15, northeast of Brigg
RAF Elsham Wolds Association Memorial Garden and Memorial Room: A poignant commemoration housed in the premises of the Anglian Water Treatment Plant at the end of one of the old runways.
◆ *On minor roads to Elsham village. By prior arrangement* only | **email** via website | **www.elshamwolds.org.uk**

FENLAND AERODROME west of the B1168 and Holbeach St Johns   EGCL
By early 2021, Mooney M.20 G-BSXI had gravitated to Sandtoft, Lincs. Tidying up, the following have been deleted: Cessna 337 G-AZLO (last noted 6-13), Arrow G-AWBA, Cessna 337 G-AZLO, Tobago G-BSDL and Seneca G-BSUW (all 3-16). Austers G-AHAP, G-AMRF and NJ673 (G-AOCR) are now listed under Boston, Lincs.

☐	G-BSDL	SOCATA Tobago	80	CoA 1-11-13, de-reg 24-5-17	3-16
☐	G-BSUW	Piper Seneca 200T	77	ex N2360M. CoA 7-9-10, de-reg 30-10-18	6-21

FLEET HARGATE on the A17, east of Holbeach
Harold Payne: The Hunter is within the grounds of the 'Anglia Motel' and looked after by **2430 Squadron, Air Cadets**.

☐	WT680	Hawker Hunter F.1	54	ex Aberporth, Weeton 7533M (22-1-57), DFLS, West Raynham SF	11-21

FREISTON on minor roads east of Boston

Gazelle AH.1 XZ337, June 2021. *Martin Tydeman*

Martin and **Lynn Tydeman**: Acquired a Gazelle during June 2021 and are gathering parts to restore it. This machine was written out of *W&R26* (p67) as departing the Defence Equipment and Support facility at Abbey Wood, where it had been displayed, in 2017. It was bound for Middle Wallop and spares reclamation, prior to auction at Colsterworth in May 2021.

◆ *By prior arrangement* **only** | **martin401@btinternet.com**

❑ XZ337*   'Z'   Sud Gazelle AH.1   77   ex Colsterworth, M Wallop, Abbey Wood-Bristol, M Wallop,
                                                          Shawbury, 658, 6 Flt, 3/4 Rgt, 664, 667, 656, 657, 658, 659,
                                                          669, Aérospatiale F-WXFX. Westland-built. Arr 2-6-21   [1]   1-22

■ **[1]** Many thanks to Martyn for filling in the early history of XZ337. Along with XZ333 (see Lyneham, Wilts) it was freighted to Marignane, France, in 2-78, returning in 1-79 having best test flown with a French experimental category registration.

GRANTHAM east of the A1, south of Newark-on-Trent
A veteran glider is kept at a *private* location in the *general* area.
❑ BGA.492*   ALZ   Hawkridge Dagling   47   BAPC.81, ex Eaton Bray, Dunstable, Duxford, Warton   10-21

GRIMSBY
A Vampire is kept at a *private* location in the *general* area.
❑ WZ584*   'K'   DH Vampire T.11   53   ex Grimsby, Cantley, Armthorpe, Sandtoft, North Coates,
                       G-BZRC   G-BZRC (de-reg 22-2-05), St Albans, Hatfield, CATCS, 1 FTS,
                                                          2 CAACU, 32. Hawarden-built. SOC 11-12-70   [1]   5-20
[1] There is *another* 'WZ584' - a Meteor - at Weston Zoyland, Somerset.

HALTHAM on the A163 south of Horncastle
An Aztec is held at a *private* location in the area.
❑ G-BBTJ   Piper Aztec 250E   73   ex Wickenby, N40369. CoA 8-9-10. Arrived 4-2-17   6-20

HAXEY Lightning cockpit F.6 XR759 was moved to North Weald, Essex, on 16th September 2020.

HEMSWELL on the A631 east of Gainsborough
The famous bomber base, 'set' for much of the ground-based sequences in *The Dam Busters*, home to the Bomber County Aviation Museum 1989 to 2003 and now home to a cluster of antique centres, has gained a 'JP' at **Antiques & Retro**.
❑ XP629*   'P'   Hunting Jet Provost T.4   62   ex Market Rasen, Layer Marney, Hadleigh, Ipswich,
                                                          North Luffenham, Halton 9026M (15-2-90), Shawbury,
                                                          CATCS, SoRF, CAW, 2 FTS   [1]   11-21
■ **[1]** This machine was written out of *W&R27* (p56) at Layer Marney, Essex, as bound for the Market Rasen area. It is fitted with the wings of fellow T.4 XP686, last recorded at Layer Marney, Essex.

HIBALDSTOW AERODROME on the B1206 south of Brigg
❑ G-ANHR   Taylorcraft Auster 5   44   ex MT192, 662. CoA 20-7-86, frame   11-21
❑ G-ASDK   Beagle Terrier 2   48   ex G-ARLM, Auster AOP.6 VF631, 654, 652, 656.
                                                      CoA 4-11-10. Frame   11-21
❑ G-BWCO   Dornier Do 28D-2   79   ex EI-CJU, N5TK, 5N-AOH, D-ILIF. CoA 19-5-99, de-reg 30-1-09   5-21
❑ G-BZHL 'TM-13' NAA Harvard IIB   44   ex Wickenby, Egypt, FT118 n/s. SOC 11-7-46   5-21
❑ CC-CRI*   Dornier Do 28D-2   ~   ex WGAF 58+23. Spares - first noted 5-21   5-21
❑ 117   Dornier Do 28D-2   ~   ex Kenyan Air Force   5-21

HUMBERSIDE AIRPORT or Kirmington   EGNJ
BAE Systems R J Mitchell Academy: ◆ *By prior arrangement* **only**
❑ N19CQ   HS Dominie T.1   65   ex Kemble, Cranwell, XS712, 55, 3 FTS, 6 FTS, 1 ANS, HS   11-20
❑ N19UK   HS Dominie T.1   66   ex Kemble, Cranwell, XS739, 55, 3 FTS, 6 FTS, 1 ANS   11-20
❑ ZA549   Panavia Tornado GR.4   81   ex Marham, 15, 13. SOC 9-11-11. Arrived 30-5-18. Fuselage   11-20
❑ ZJ100   HS Hawk Mk.102D   92   ex Finningley, Warton, Brough. Last flown 13-12-12   11-20
❑ ZJ800   Eurofighter Typhoon T.3   03   ex Coningsby RTP, 29. Arrived 13-9-18   11-20
❑ ZK531   HS Hawk T.53   c80   ex Warton, Brough, Warton, Indonesian AF LL-5306,
                                                    G-9-471. First noted 3-15, displayed from 22-9-17   9-21
❑ ZK535   HS Hawk T.53   c80   ex Finningley, Brough, Warton, Indonesian AF LL-5320   11-20

❏ 1129	BAC Strikemaster Mk.80A	76	ex Global Av, Saudi AF, G-27-295. Moved across 7-17. Displayed from 22-9-17	7-21

Also: The huge Thunderbird 3 model outside the Eastern Airways facility deserves a mention! Last noted in July 2014, the fuselage of Jetstream 4100 G-JXTA had appeared in a yard at <u>Swinderby</u>, Lincs, by November 2021.

❏ G-AVMP	BAC 111-510ED	68	ex Iver Heath, Hurn, European, BA, BEA. Forward fuselage. CoA 6-4-01, de-reg 12-11-02. Rescue trainer	7-21
❏ G-CDYI	BAe Jetstream 4100	93	ex N305UE, G-4-019. De-reg 21-217. Fuselage	11-20
❏ G-GCJL	BAe Jetstream 4100	91	ex Woodford, Prestwick. CoA 29-4-95, de-reg 15-11-02. Fuselage, rescue trainer	4-21
❏ G-MAJD*	BAe Jetstream 4100	92	ex Eastern, G-WAWR, G-4-006. wfu 30-11-18, CoA 31-3-22	10-20
❏ G-MAJE*	BAe Jetstream 4100	92	ex Eastern, G-LOGK, G-4-007. wfu 29-9-16, CoA 10-2-20	4-21
❏ G-MAJF*	BAe Jetstream 4100	93	ex Eastern, G-4-008. wfu 29-8-14, de-reg 6-8-19	11-20
❏ G-MAJG*	BAe Jetstream 4100	93	ex Eastern, G-LOGL, G-4-009. wfu 5-10-18, CoA 20-9-19	10-20
❏ G-MAJH*	BAe Jetstream 4100	93	ex Eastern, G-WAYR, G-4-010. wfu 3-8-16, de-reg 10-2-20. Rescue trainer, blue colours	4-21
❏ G-MAJI*	BAe Jetstream 4100	93	ex Eastern, G-WAND, G-4-011. wfu 4-5-16, de-reg 1-7-19	11-20
❏ G-MAJJ*	BAe Jetstream 4100	93	ex Eastern, G-WAFT, G-4-024. wfu 8-12-17, CoA 21-1-19	11-20
❏ G-MAJK*	BAe Jetstream 4100	95	ex Eastern, SE-SEB, G-MAJK, G-4-070. wfu 22-2-19, CoA due 22-7-22	11-20
❏ G-MAJL*	BAe Jetstream 4100	96	ex Eastern, G-4-087. wfu 26-2-21, CoA 16-5-21	11-20
❏ VH-XNE*	BAe J'stream 4100 G-CIHD	95	ex Brindabella Airlines, ZS-NRK, G-4-065. Arrived 7-14	12-21
❏ VH-XNF*	BAe J'stream 4100 G-CIHE	95	ex Brindabella Airlines, ZS-NRL, G-4-068. Arrived 7-14	12-21
❏ 1115	BAC Strikemaster Mk.80A	73	ex Saudi AF, G-27-226. Fuselage	9-17

INGHAM also known as Cammeringham, west of the B1398, northwest of Scampton
RAF Ingham Heritage Group: Dubbed 'Home of the Polish Bomber Squadrons'. Work continues to expand the facilities, including reception area, shop and workshop. All are based on existing wartime buildings, or contemporary structures re-erected on site. There is a very moving memorial.
◆ *Middle Street, Fillingham, DN23 5BU* | **07787 805978** | **rafingham@hotmail.co.uk** | **www.rafingham.co.uk**

KIRTON IN LINDSEY on the B1206 northeast of Gainsborough
A Vampire is kept at a *private* location in the *general* area. This was written out of *W&R26* (p149) from Glenham, Lincs.

❏ XD595*	DH Vampire T.11	54	ex Glenham, Altrincham, Woodford, Chester, St Athan, 1 FTS, Oakington SF, 7 FTS, 4 FTS. Hatfield-built. SOC 6-11-67. Cockpit	5-20

LINCOLN
International Bomber Command Centre: The site is dominated by a spire as tall as the wingspan of a Lancaster. The 'Wall of Names' wraps around the spire, honouring the Bomber Command aircrew who did not return.
◆ *Canwick Hill, Lincoln, LN4 2HQ* | **01522 514755** | **info@internationalbcc.co.uk** | **www.internationalbcc.co.uk**

LOUTH on the A16 west of Mablethorpe
A *private* airstrip in the locality has two aircraft under restoration.

❏ G-AWIV*	Storey TSR.3	70	ex Wickenby. CoA 18-6-08. Arrived 5-21	5-21
❏ G-VJZZ*	Volmer Sportsman	68	ex N7508U. First noted 2-21	5-21

MESSINGHAM on the A159 south of Scunthorpe
The gathering of AOP.9s at a *private* location in the *general* area has expanded.

❏ WZ711*	Auster AOP.9(mod) G-AVHT	54	ex Doncaster, Spanhoe, AOP.9, St Athan, 656, LAS. CoA 1-7-16, de-reg 23-2-18. Arrived 13-8-21	8-21
❏ XK417	Auster AOP.9 G-AVXY	56	ex Melton Mowbray, Tattershall Thorpe, Wisbech, Henstridge, Thruxton, 652, LAS. SOC 7-11-67. CoA 9-7-00	8-21
❏ XP242*	Auster AOP.9 G-BUCI	61	ex M Wallop, AFWF, Shrivenham, 653. CoA 19-5-00, de-reg 5-3-01. Arrived 2-21	8-21

Dakota 3 KG651 (G-AMHJ) in its new home, August 2021. *Richard Hall*

METHERINGHAM on the B1191 west of Woodhall Spa

Metheringham Airfield Visitor Centre: Based in what was part of the bomber base's communal site is an excellent presentation showing life at the station and 106 Squadron.

◆ *Westmoor Farm, LN4 3WF* | **email** via website | **www.metheringhamairfield.co.uk**

❑ KG651	Douglas Dakota 3	42	ex N Weald, Shawbury, Coventry, SU-AZI, G-AMHJ, ZS-BRW,
	G-AMHJ		KG651, 1333 CU, 1383 CU, 24, 109 OTU, C-47A-25-DK
			42-108962. Oklahoma City-built. CoA 5-12-00, de-reg
			23-1-03. Arrived 16-11-15 1-22
❑ XS186	'10' Hunting Jet Provost T.4	64	ex Ipswich, N Luffenham, Halton 8408M (7-10-74), St Athan,
			Kemble, Shawbury, CAW. Arr 4-04. CAW c/s. Taxiable [1] 1-22

■ [1] The 'JP' is on loan from Paul Flynn - **https://jetprovostxs186restoration.com/about**

Locally: Dennis Staniland has his 'JP' at a *private* location in the area. The plan is to render the interior fully 'live' electrically.

❑ G-BYED	BAC Jet Provost T.5	70	ex Sleaford, Market Drayton, Chester, Londonderry,
	XW302		N166A, XW302, 6 FTS, 3 FTS, RAFC, 1 FTS. Crashed 12-2-01,
			de-reg 30-12-04. Cockpit. First noted 6-19 8-21

NEW YORK on the B1192 south of Coningsby

W&R27 (p146) declared "Lightning T.5 XS416 departed in January 2020 - destination unknown". No more, it was on its way to <u>Binbrook</u>, Lincs, via a stop-over near Wickenby, also Lincs. The owner, at this *private* location, has traded up...

❑ ZA362*	'TR' Panavia Tornado GR.1	81	ex Inverness, Lossiemouth, 15, TTTE. Arrived 14-12-20 12-20

NORTH COATES AERODROME north of the A1031, south of Humberston

North Coates Heritage Collection: Artefacts and images covering the history of the airfield 1914 to 1992 are displayed at North Coates Flying Club. A reminder of its last RAF role, a Bloodhound Mk.1 is on show. As regards residents, Messenger 2A RG333 (G-AIEK) was back in flying trim by 2021. ◆ **www.northcoatesflyingclub.co.uk**

❑ CEK	Slingsby T.21B(T)	59	BGA.1482, ex RAFGSA.369, XN147. CoA 7-5-05 [1] 1-22
❑ N259SA	Cessna F.172G	66	ex Skegness, EI-BAO, G-ATNH. Reims-built 1-22

■ [1] Motor-glider conversion.

NORTH SOMERCOTES on the A1031, north of Mablethorpe

A trio of Whirlwind HAR.10s is stored at a *private* location in the *general* area.

❑ XJ407*	Westland Whirlwind	54	ex Tattershall, G-BKHB (de-reg 15-6-88), XJ407, Northolt,
	HAR.10 N7013H		32, 103, 110, HAR.4, 22, 155. SOC 15-6-88. First noted 4-21 12-21
❑ XP328*	Westland Whirlwind	61	ex Tattershall, Northolt, 32, 21, 28, 110, 225, 110, 225.
	HAR.10 G-BKHC		Crashed 22-8-88, de-reg 4-6-90. Cabin. First noted 4-21 12-21

☐ XP329*	'V'	Westland Whirlwind HAR.10	61	ex Shawbury, Lee-on-Solent, Akrotiri 8791M (10-7-82), 84, 230, 110, 225. First noted 4-21 12-21

SANDTOFT AERODROME south of the M180, between Sandtoft and Westgate   EGCF

☐ G-BIFB	Piper Cherokee 150	65	ex 4X-AEC. CoA 29-5-09 10-21
☐ G-BIHI	Cessna 172M	76	ex Fenland, N1125U. Cr 18-9-14, CoA 15-12-15. Arrived 2-20 10-21
☐ G-BLVS	Cessna 150M	75	ex Fenland, EI-BLS, N45356. CoA 14-12-07. First noted 4-18 10-21
☐ G-BORY	Cessna 150L	71	ex Fenland, N6792G. CoA 21-7-09. First noted 4-18 10-21
☐ G-BSXI*	Mooney M.20E	70	ex Fenland, N6766V. CoA 9-6-11. First noted 5-21 10-21
☐ G-BULR	Piper Cherokee 140	68	ex Fenland, HB-OHP. CoA 4-7-08. Fuselage 3-20
☐ N131MP	Piper Navajo P	74	ex Warlingham, Shoreham, G-BWDE, G-HWKN, HB-LIR, D-IAIR, N7304L 7-21

SCAMPTON AIRFIELD on the A15 north of Lincoln   EGXP

RAF Scampton Heritage Centre: Within Hangar 2, home to 617 Squadron at the time of the 'Dams' raid, the collection extends to over 400 items plus an expanding number of airframes. Included is the remains of Hampden P1206 of 49 Squadron, which failed to return on 8th November 1941, with the loss of all four crew. This touching epitaph was donated by the Royal Netherlands Air Force. Aircraft from Hawker Hunter Aviation – see below – occasionally 'guest'.

◆ *By prior arrangement only* | rafscamptonheritagecentre@gmail.com | www.raf.mod.uk/rafscampton

☐ BRC	Slingsby Swallow 1	64	BGA.1165. ex Kirton in Lindsey. CoA 11-5-15. Fuselage 12-21
☐ '5964'	Airco DH.2 replica G-BFVH	78	ex Wickenby, Lyneham, Haverfordwest, Dorchester, Duxford, *Gunbus* 'GBH-7', Land's End, Chertsey. Westward Airways-built. Arrived 22-2-18 12-21
☐ WG477	DHC Chipmunk T.10 G-ATDP	51	ex Birkdale 8362M (22-8-73), ex G-ATDP (de-reg 15-1-68), G-ATDI, Marham SF, MECS,114, Bristol UAS, Aberdeen UAS, 11 RFS, 2 BFTS, 25 RFS, Liv UAS, 25 RFS. Cockpit 12-21
☐ XL445	Avro Vulcan K.2	62	ex Flixton, Walpole, Lyneham 8811M (5-4-84), 50, 44, 35, 230 OCU, Wadd Wing, Akrotiri Wing, Wadd Wing, 27. Arrived 12-18. Cockpit [1] 12-21
☐ XN185	Slingsby Sedbergh TX.1 HNS	56	BGA.4077, ex Stafford, Syerston 8942M, CGS, 643 VGS, 4 MGSP, 633 VGS, 635 VGS. CoA 12-4-04. Arrived 3-14 [2] 12-21
☐ XR571	Folland Gnat T.1	63	ex Cranwell, Scampton, Cosford, Kemble, Brampton 8493M (7-5-76), Kemble, 4 FTS 12-21
☐ XX266	HS Hawk T.1A	79	ex Shawbury, 'Red Arrows'. SOC 18-8-15 10-21
☐ XX320*	HS Hawk T.1A	80	ex Walcott, Scampton, Cranwell, Shawbury, 208, 100, 19, 2 TWU, 1 TWU. Cr 20-8-08. Front cockpit. 208 Sqn colours 12-21
☐ XZ138*	HS Harrier GR.3	76	ex Cranwell, 9040M (25-3-76), SIF, St Athan, 1, 233 OCU, 1453 Flt, 1, 3, 4, 3. Cockpit. First noted 9-21 12-21
☐ –	EE Canberra T.4	~	cockpit 12-21
☐ –	Avro Vulcan B.1 EMU	c58	ex Doncaster, Reigate, East Kirkby, Tattershall, Waddington. Cockpit, crew drill tnr. First noted 9-18 [3] 12-21

■ **[1]** XL445 is on loan from a private owner. **[2]** XN185 is on loan from the RAF Museum. **[3]** An 'unplumbed' B.1 with a B.2 'hood'.

RAF Scampton: The base is slated for closure in late 2022.

☐ XX253	HS Hawk T.1A	78	ex 'Red Arrows'. Accident 23-5-10. Displayed 9-21
☐ XX306	HS Hawk T.1A	80	ex Shawbury, 'Red Arrows', 4 FTS. Arrived 11-8-15, SOC 18-8-15. Displayed on gate, unveiled 12-10-15 1-22
☐ XX349	HS Hawk T.1W	81	ex Valley, 100, 208, 19, 74, 4 FTS, 100, TWU, 4 FTS. SOC 15-12-11. Minus tail end, rescue training 11-21

Hawker Hunter Aviation: HHA is a major contractor for the military and aerospace industry and while the operational fleet is beyond the terms of reference for *W&R*, it would be a crime not to mention them: Hunter F.58s ZZ190 and ZZ191 and T.72 XE688. Only airframes under major restoration or long-term store are mentioned here. Occasionally, HHA aircraft 'guest' at the the Heritage Centre, above. T.8B XF995 was written out of *W&R21* (p43) after it had been restored to flying condition at Exeter on 18th April 2007, joining HHA's active fleet. Initially on contract to ETPS at Boscombe Down, its military identity had been re-instated on 29th March 2007 and its civvie registration was cancelled on11th April, Retired to Waddington, it was struck off the military register on 11th March 2019.

◆ **Strictly** *by prior appointment only* | www.hunterteam.com

☐ XE685	'861'	Hawker Hunter	55	ex St Athan, Exeter, Yeovilton, Hurn, FRADU, FRU, 764,	
		GA.11	G-GAII	Yeovilton SF, 764, 738, F.4 98, 93. Squires Gate-built.	
				Flew in 22-5-12. CoA 15-8-12	12-21
☐ XF994	'873'	Hawker Hunter	56	ex Boscombe D, Shawbury, Yeovilton, FRADU, 759, F.4,	
		T.8C	G-CGHU	F229 OCU, AFDS, 66. Squires Gate-built. SOC 17-3-98	12-21
☐ XF995*		Hawker Hunter	56	ex Exeter, Kemble, G-BZSF, Cranwell 9237M (11-9-94), 208,	
		T.8B	G-BZSF	12, Laarbruch SF, 237 OCU, Honington SF, 237 OCU, 764,	
				F.4, 245, 247. Squires Gate-built. SOC 11-3-19. See above	12-21
☐ XL587	'Z'	Hawker Hunter T.7	58	ex Duxford, Scampton, 8807M (2-3-84), 208, 237 OCU,	
			G-HPUX	1 TWU, 229 OCU	[1] 12-21
☐ XX885		Blackburn Buccaneer	74	ex Lossiemouth 9225M (25-11-93), 12, 208, 12, 208,	
		S.2B	G-HHAA	216, 16	12-21
☐ ZZ194*		Hawker Hunter F.58	59	ex G-HHAC, Duxford G-BWIU, Swiss AF J-4021. Stored	12-21
☐ 37+89		McD F-4F Phantom	72	ex Luftwaffe, 72-1199. Arrived 13-6-15	12-21
☐ 37+91		McD F-4F Phantom	72	ex Luftwaffe, 72-1201. Arrived 6-15 - off-site	6-15
☐ 98+14		Sukhoi Su-22M-4 *Fitter*	~	ex WTD-61 Manching, Luftwaffe, East German AF	12-21
☐ J-4110		Hawker Hunter	72	ex Norway, Swiss AF, G-9-328, A2561 (17-3-63), F.4 XF318,	
		F.58A	G-CJWL	229 OCU, 130. Squires Gate-built. Arrived 15-11-16	12-21

■ [1] Registered in honour of Hawker's famous demonstrator, T.66 G-APUX, 1959-1967.

SKEGNESS (WATER LEISURE PARK) AERODROME or Ingoldmells, on the A52 north of Skegness

Craig Wise's superb Lightning T.5 dominates the horizon at the aerodrome. Restoration began in June 2015 and makes great progress. The website charts XS456's history, the work as it unfolds and the 'wants list'.
◆ *By prior appointment* only | www.xs456.co.uk

| ☐ XS456 | 'DX' | EE Lightning T.5 | 65 | ex Wainfleet, Binbrook, LTF, 11, 56. SOC 13-7-88. Arr 7-10 | 1-22 |

Also:

| ☐ G-ARCW | | Piper Apache 160 | 60 | ex N2187P. *Mockingbird IV*. CoA 24-8-07 | 7-20 |
| ☐ G-AVPI | | Cessna F.172H | 67 | Reims-built. CoA 30-5-03 | N7-18 |

SPALDING west of the A16, north of Peterborough

Skycraft Ltd: The 'Chop Shop' continues to process light aircraft for spares. Turn-around is swift.
◆ *By prior arrangement* only | www.sky-craft.co.uk

SPILSBY on the B1195 west of Skegness

The late Pat Miller's Auster cache, at a *private* store in the locality, included damaged Grumman Turbo AgCat G-DCAT (de-registered 15th January 1992) which should have been exported to the USA by the time *W&R* went to press. One of the Auster frames had been cut into sections and can be discounted: this is *very likely* G-AJDW. Husky G-AVOD was written out from this location in *W&R26* (p153) as having moved on by mid-2017. It moved initially to the Harrogate area and is now listed at Fishburn, D&C. Autocrat G-AIGP travelled to Hooton Park, Cheshire, on 10th December 2021.

☐ G-AHAR		Auster J1 Autocrat	46	ex N Weald, F-BGRZ. De-reg 31-12-50	10-21
☐ G-AHSO		Auster J1N Alpha	46	CoA 6-4-95, de-reg 6-4-09	7-13
☐ G-AIPV		Auster J1 Autocrat	46	CoA 7-2-05	N7-19

STAMFORD

Martyn and **Aiden Steele's** *CockpitFest* award-winner is *thought* to be kept locally. ◆ *By prior arrangement* only

| ☐ XP757 | | EE Lightning F.3 | 64 | ex Boston, Woodhall Spa, Keighley, Siddal, Binbrook, | |
| | | | | 29, 23. SOC 13-11-75. Cockpit | 6-15 |

Also: A Chipmunk cockpit has joined the L-18 at a *private* store in the locality. See under Chivenor, Devon, for the background on the 'Chippie'. ◆ *By prior arrangement* only

☐ WP978*		DHC Chipmunk T.10	53	ex Chivenor, Exeter, Little Rissington 7467M (19-8-59),	
				4 SoTT CF, 663. Hawarden-built. Cockpit. Arrived 10-21	1-22
☐ MM52-2420		Piper L-18C Super Cub	52	ex Spanhoe, Lakenheath, Embry-Riddle, N917CS, It AF, USAF	1-22

STURGATE AERODROME southeast of Gainsborough, near Heapham   EGCS

During April 2021 there was a clear out with FR.172 G-AWYB, F.152 G-BIUM and Rallye G-CCZA being carted off.

☐ N9372*	DH Tiger Moth	G-ANHK	39	ex F-BHIM,G-ANHK, N9372, 1 GU, 2 GS, 24 EFTS, 5 GTS,
				22 EFTS, 9 EFTS. CoA 25-5-18. First noted 10-20	10-21
☐ G-BDDG	Jodel D.112		58	ex F-BILM. Dormois-built. CoA 28-7-04	7-21
☐ G-BGVE	Piel Super Emeraude		65	ex F-BMJE. Scintex-built. CoA 4-8-15.	7-21
☐ G-BWEU	Cessna F.152		82	ex EI-BNC, N9097Y. Reims-built. CoA 27-9-16,	
				de-reg 14-7-20.	12-19

SWINDERBY south of the A46 northeast of Newark

This location last appeared in *W&R15* with the final retreat of RAF airframes in 1995: Chipmunk T.10 WG362 to Newton, Notts, and Vampire T.11 XD506 to Pyle, Wales. (Listed in this edition at Linton, Cambs, and Foxhall, Suffolk, respectively.)

Now the focus centres on the dense forest to the southwest of the former airfield at the **Lost Village Festival**. The website declares: "The woods are waiting..." Visitors are invited every August to "navigate through a network of winding pathways, derelict houses, overgrown courtyards, dilapidated streets *and an abandoned airport*"... and hear some music to boot. Among images glimpsed in a film clip is a C-47 Skytrain in Yugoslav military markings and, horror of horrors, an Austin Allegro. Physical evidence of the C-47 was lacking as *W&R* went to press, but a Jetstream fuselage was noted and at least two more cockpit/fuselage sections. Details of the event at: **https://lostvillagefestival.com/explore**

☐ G-JXTA*	BAe Jetstream 3103	83	ex Humberside, Inverness, D-CNRY, SE-KHC, OY-EDB,	
			SE-KHC, D-CONI, G-31-50. CoA 15-9-09, de-reg 17-8-16.	
			Fuselage, trailer-mounted. First noted 11-21	1-22

TATTERSHALL on the A153 southwest of Coningsby

Last noted in September 2017, Djinn FR-150 had moved on – destination unknown – by 2018. By April 2021, the trio of Whirlwind HAR.10s - XJ407, XP328 and XP329 - had migrated to North Somercotes, Lincs.

TATTERSHALL THORPE on the B1192 southeast of Woodhall Spa

Thorpe Camp Visitor Centre: The former No.1 Communal Site (or 'Thorpe Camp') of RAF Woodhall Spa is a superb venue with a warm welcome. Themes include life in Lincolnshire during World War Two, the history of Woodhall Spa, including its resident units: 97, 617, 619 and 627 Squadrons. A new display hall should be open by the time *W&R* is published. There is a small, viewable, workshop area.

Among the exhibits is the massive arrester gear salvaged from the end of one of Woodhall's runways. This was intended to stop a Lancaster, fitted with a special hook, from over-runs and the airfield prototyped the operational version. The flight training 'simulator' designed and built by Geoff Parker in 1942-1943 for the cadets of the Holbeach and Spalding-based 1406 Squadron is also impressive.

◆ *Woodhall Spa Road, LN4 4PL* | **07396 288655** | **secretary@thorpecamp.org** | **www.thorpecamp.org**

☐ 'G-AEXF'		Percival Mew Gull replica	11	BAPC.367. Built in-house, completed 2011	[1]	1-22
☐ G-ANFU*		Taylorcraft Auster 5	45	ex Doncaster, Sunderland, Newcastle, Sunderland,		
				Bristol, TW385, 663, 227 OCU, 13 OTU. Damaged 2-1-76.		
				De-reg 3-8-76, CoA 25-8-76. First noted 11-20	[2]	1-22
☐ 'G-ANNN'		DH Tiger Moth replica	11	BAPC.409. Many original parts, completed 2011	[3]	1-22
☐ 'B7270'		Sopwith Camel replica	18	locally built, completed 2020. Cpt Roy Brown's colours	[4]	1-22
☐ 'EV771'		Fairchild Argus replica	c97	BAPC.294, ex Southampton. Arrived 2005		1-22
☐ -	'D'	Avro Lancaster replica	c08	forward fuselage. First noted 7-10		1-22
☐ RT520		Taylorcraft Auster 5	44	ex Doncaster, Firbeck, Bristol, White Waltham, AOP.V		
		G-ALYB		RT520, 85 GCS, 84 GCS. CoA 26-5-63, de-reg 29-2-84		1-22
☐ XM192	'K'	EE Lightning F.1A	61	ex Hemswell, Binbrook, Wattisham 8413M (28-5-74),		
				Wattisham TFF, Binbrook TFF, 226 OCU, 111.		
				Arrived 3-12-05. 111 Sqn colours	[4]	1-22
☐ XS887*	'403'	Westland Wessex HAS.1	66	ex Doncaster, Helston, Culdrose A2690 (29-5-80),		
				Wroughton, 772, Yeovilton SAR Flt, 829.		
				First noted 12-21		1-22
☐ XX895		Blackburn Buccaneer	75	ex Kidlington, Woking, St Athan, Lossiemouth, 208, 12,		
		S.2B		237 OCU, 12, 237 OCU, 16, 15, 12. SOC 13-1-95. Cockpit		1-22
☐ -		Panavia Tornado F.3 SIM	c82	ex Chester, Leeming. 229 OCU colours. F/n 10-16		1-22

■ **[1]** Mew Gull made by a team led by John Lord. See Shuttleworth, Beds, and Hendon, Gtr Lon, for *other* G-AEXFs. **[2]** [Composite, with G-ANFU's forward fuselage, a 'spare' rear AOP.6 frame, stb wing of G-AKPH and port from an AOP.6. **[3]** See Wickenby, Lincs, for *another* G-ANNN. **[4]** There's *another* 'B7270' at Brooklands, Surrey. **[5]** XM192 loaned by Charles Ross of Binbrook, Lincs.

WADDINGTON AIRFIELD on the A607 south of Lincoln

EGXW

RAF Waddington Heritage Centre: Volunteers have created a superb exhibition in a building that in World War Two housed the catering squadron headquarters. Among the many exhibits are remains of 463 Squadron Lancaster I PD259 which crashed in Scotland on a training detail on 31st August 1944, with the loss of all seven crew.

◆ *By prior arrangement* **only** | WAD-heritagecentre@mod.gov.uk | **www.raf.mod.uk/rafwaddington**

RAF Waddington: The final Sentinel R.1 operational flight was carried out by ZJ694 on 25th February 2021, and all four were struck off the military register on 1st April and were parked out. It is highly unlikely they will last long, or that one will join the RAF Museum, but for the sake of completeness they are/were: ZJ690, ZJ691, ZJ692, ZJ693, ZJ694.

Of the wonderful Sentry AEW.1 fleet, ZH101 staged the last operational sortie on 4th August 2021. At the time of writing, the Boeing Spinning Coffee Table was still flying training sorties as two, plus one as spares, are bound for Chile. Tenders for reduction to produce (RTP) for three examples, ZH102, ZH105 and ZH107 were released in January 2021 and these are given below. ZH104 is in the US and will be transferred to the US Navy as a crew trainer for the E-6 Mercury fleet. It is likely the rest will be processed quickly, and the chances of a whole one going to the RAF Museum remote – the back-end including the 'rotodome' would make an impressive exhibit – so for completeness, they are: ZH101, ZH103, ZH106.

The based RAF Rapid Capabilities Office is custodian of the BAE Systems Tempest - Britain's sixth generation fighter hopeful - travelling mock-up.

☐	'XE620'	'B'	Hawker Hunter F.6A	56	ex Barkston Heath, 'XE673', Cottesmore, Laarbruch 8841M	
			XE606		(29-11-84), 8737M, 1 TWU, TWU, 229 OCU, 92, 74,	
					65, 54, CFE. Arrived 10-4-13. 8 Sqn colours, displayed.	[1] 11-21
☐	XM607		Avro Vulcan B.2	63	8779M (4-1-83), ex 44, 101, 35. Displayed from 19-1-83	1-22
☐	ZH102		Boeing Sentry AEW.1	90	ex 8, *Dopey*. Spares recovery from 7-19, RTP issued 1-21	12-21
☐	ZH105		Boeing Sentry AEW.1	91	ex 8, *Sneezy*. Spares recovery from 10-11 - fuselage	
					by 6-13. Escape trainer. RTP issued 1-21	[2] 12-21
☐	ZH107		Boeing Sentry AEW.1	91	ex 8, *Bashful*. Spares recovery from 7-19, RTP issued 1-21	12-21
☐	-		BAE Systems Tempest FSM	18	BAPC.529, ex Warton. Travelling demonstrator	[3] 7-21

■ **[1]** Hunter serves as the 8 Sqn 'mascot' and will migrate to Lossiemouth, Scotland, in due course. **[2]** Known as WEST - Waddington Escape Systems Trainer. **[3]** Nominally based with the RAF Rapid Capabilities Office. Fitted with modified Tornado undercarriage.

Also: Lincolnshire Fire and Rescue Service has acquired a Jaguar for exercises: it is kept in the old bomb dump site.

☐	XX818	'DE'	SEPECAT Jaguar GR.1	75	ex Cosford, Halton 8945M (4-11-87), Shawbury, 31,	
					20, 17. Arrived 8-10-19	7-21

WAINFLEET southwest of Skegness

Former **Aerial Application Collection:** ◆ *Dispersed stores, by prior arrangement* **only**

☐	G-AOGI	DH Tiger Moth	42	ex OO-SOA, G-AOGI, Mk.II DF186, 608, Valley SF, 21 EFTS.	
				Morris Motors-built. CoA 23-8-91	7-18
☐	G-AWLX	Auster J2 Arrow	46	ex Gloucester, F-BGJQ, OO-ABZ. CoA 23-4-70	7-18
☐	G-BFBP	Piper Pawnee 235D	77	ex Rush Green. Crashed 11-5-78, de-reg 21-6-78. Cockpit	7-18
☐	G-BFEY	Piper Pawnee 235D	77	ex Old Buckenham. CoA 19-1-87, de-reg 17-7-90. Frame	7-18
☐	G-NRDC	NDN Fieldmaster	81	ex Sandown, Old Sarum. CoA 17-10-87, de-reg 3-2-95. Fuselage	7-18
☐	-	NDN Fieldmaster EMU	c81	ex Sandown, Old Sarum. Fuselage	7-18

The Tower Friskney: At the range observation tower of the former RAF Wainfleet, at the end of Sea Lane, a Jetstream and a Lynx are available as holiday cottages. ◆ *By prior arrangement* **only** | https://rafwainfleet.uk

☐	XX499	'G'	HP Jetstream T.1	76	ex Ipswich, Brooklands, Ipswich, Shawbury, Cranwell,
					45, 3 FTS, 45, 6 FTS, METS. SAL-built. Arrived 10-10-19	1-22
☐	ZG914		Westland Lynx AH.9A	91	ex Ipswich, M Wallop. First noted 5-18	1-22

WALCOTT on the B1189 south of Woodhall Spa

Richard and **Kevin Scarborough:** The cockpit of Hawk T.1A XX320 had moved to <u>Scampton</u>, Lincs, by September 2021.

◆ *Private location, by prior arrangement* **only**.

☐	XS932	EE Lightning F.6	67	ex Market Drayton, Farnborough, Shoreham, Bruntingthorpe,	
				Rossington, Binbrook, 5, 11, 56, 11. SOC 24-6-88. Cockpit	6-20
☐	XV810	HS Harrier GR.3	71	ex Wigston/Bruntingthorpe, St Athan, Abingdon 9038M,	
				St Athan, 233 OCU, 4, GR.1 4, 20. SOC 16-1-89.	
				Acquired 5-13. <u>233 OCU</u> colours. Cockpit.	8-21

☐ ZD614	'122'	HS Sea Harrier F/A.2	86	ex Lymington, Hurn, Ipswich, St Athan, Yeovilton, 800, 801, 800, 801, 800, 801, FRS.1, 800, 801, 800. Crashed 8-10-01 (into the River Yeo). Acquired 18-7-18. Cockpit	6-20
☐ ZE697*	'006'	HS Sea Harrier F/A.2	88	ex Binbrook, Charlwood, St Athan, 801, 899, 800, 899, 800, 801, 899, FRS.1, 801, 800. First noted 4-20	4-20

WALTHAM on the B1203 south of Grimsby

Waltham Windmill Trust and Preservation Society: An element of the extensive site surrounding the windmill is the excellent **RAF Grimsby Exhibition**, in a Nissen hut. This is dedicated to the personnel and Lancasters of 100 Squadron and other units that flew from Waltham, or Grimsby. The A16 cuts through the former airfield's eastern perimeter.
◆ *Signed off the B1203 | Brigsley Road, DN37 0JZ | 07747 597438 | email via website | www.walthamwindmill.org.uk*

WICKENBY (LINCOLN) AERODROME north of the B1399, northeast of Lincoln   EGNW

The former wartime tower acts as both a **Visitor Centre** and the **RAF Wickenby Memorial Collection**. The Wickenby Register - 12 and 626 Squadron Association - has its archives here. ◆ **01673 885000 | wickenbymuseum@outlook.com | www.wickenbymuseum.co.uk** *– site under reconstruction as W&R went to press*

Vintage Skunk Works: The name and logo pay homage to Lockheed's famed research and development centre at Palmdale, California. Last noted in February 2007, Autocar G-AOBV moved to Taunton, Somerset. Storey TSR.3 G-AWIV moved to Louth, Lincs, in May 20201. Chipmunk T.10 G-CLKX (WB555) moved to Turweston, Bucks, by May 2020.
◆ *Visits are* **not possible**. *Occasional appearances at special events*

☐ G-ACDJ	DH Tiger Moth		33	ex BB729, Dyce SF, 28 EFTS, 1 EFTS. Crashed 18-8-05, CoA 18-8-07. See G-ANNN below		7-21
☐ G-ANKV	DH Tiger Moth		40	ex Booker, Croydon, Redhill, T7793, 1 GU, 2 GS, 14 RFS, Ox UAS, 8 RFS, 8 EFTS, 22 EFTS, Ox UAS, 3 EFTS, 21 EFTS.	[1]	6-20
☐ G-ANNN	DH Tiger Moth		45	ex Tattershall Thorpe, Eccleshall, Hatch, T5968, Wattisham SF, 61 GCF, 3 RFS, 28 EFTS, 57 OTU. Morris Motors-built. De-reg 6-11-00. Spares for G-ACDJ	[2]	6-20
☐ N6537	DH Tiger Moth	G-AOHY	39	ex Dyce SF, Ringway SF, 11 RFS, 11 EFTS, 35 ERFTS. Crashed 17-7-06, CoA 24-11-16		2-19
☐ G-BZVW	Ilyushin Il-2M3		42	ex Lancing, Russia. Stored	[3]	5-20
☐ G-BZVX	Ilyushin Il-2M3		42	ex Lancing, Russia. Stored	[3]	5-20
☐ G-CFXT	NAF N3N-3		42	ex N45299		7-21
☐ G-CJSB*	Republic Seabee		47	ex N11NW, CF-JBN, N6513K. CoA 27-3-19		8-21
☐ G-SHOW	MS Alcyon		56	ex Spanhoe, -?-, Bruntingthorpe, Cranfield, Booker, F-BMQJ, FAF 125. CoA 24-5-83		N2-16
☐ N9606H	Fairchild PT-26 Cornell	G-CRNL	42	ex Thruxton, Leicester, Martham, Earls Colne, Andrewsfield, Southend, USA, FJ662, 42-15491	[4]	7-21
☐ WK622	DHC Chipmunk T.10	G-BCZH	52	ex York, Breighton, G-BCZH, Yeovilton, 2 FTS, Wattisham TFF, Bristol UAS, 3 AEF, Bristol, Leeds UASs, 24 GCF, Oxford UAS, 18 RFS, 22 RFS. Cr 6-9-87, de-reg 8-5-19. Arr 3-19		9-19
☐ XE624	'G' Hawker Hunter FGA.9		56	ex Metheringham, Leicester, B'thorpe, Brawdy 8875M (4-10-85), 1 TWU, 2 TWU, TWU, 229 OCU, W Raynham SF, 1		8-21
☐ C-558	EKW C-3605	G-CCYZ	48	ex Spanhoe, N31624, Norwich, L' Gransden, Booker, Swiss AF		8-21

■ **[1]** G-ANKV is being configured as a 'Rumpler C' lookalike. It was not converted (at Croydon?) and cancelled in 9-56. **[2]** See also Tattershall Thorpe, Lincs, for another 'G-ANNN'. **[3]** Registered to Leeds-based Steven Swallow 2-20. **[4]** Cornell previously assumed to be ex FH678, 42-14361. Current thinking is quoted above: It is registered to CRNL Aviation.

Others: Last reported in January 2012 Tomahawk G-BGWN has been deleted; Likewise Thruster G-MZNZ (May 2019).

☐ G-LUFT	Putzer Elster C		60	ex Rufforth, Humberside, North Coates, G-BOPY, D-EDEZ. De-reg 12-7-07. Off-site	1-12

Locally: A *private* workshop hosted Lightning T.5 XS416 by June 2020. This was written out of *W&R27* (p146) as having departed New York, Lincs, in January 2020 'destination unknown'. By August 2021 it had moved 9 miles (as the crow, or indeed the Lightning) flies, to its former base, Binbrook, Lincs. A Vampire pod is held at this site.

☐ XK632*	'67'	DH Vampire T.11	56	ex Greenham, Denham, Leavesden, H' Hempstead, Bushey, Keevil, Exeter, 3/4 CAACU, CFS. Hawarden-built. SOC 6-1-72. Cockpit. First noted 7-20	1-22

WOODHALL SPA on the B1191 and B1192 southwest of Horncastle

At the junction of the B1191 and B1192 is the impressive 'Dam Busters' memorial and 617 Squadron commemoration. Another 'must' is the 'Petwood Hotel' which was the Officers' Mess for, in turn, 97, 619 and 617 Squadrons. The 'Squadron Bar' has loads of memorabilia. **www.petwood.co.uk**

Locally: At a *private* workshop in the general area Jon Davidson is at work on an Auster cache. *Tango-Charlie* utilises the fuselage of XP28<u>3</u>; the original frame having been passed on to Doncaster, S Yorks. XP283 was written out of *W&R17* (p213) at Baxterley, Warwickshire, as having moved on.

☐ G-AMJM	Taylorcraft Auster 5		45	ex F-BBSO, Newark, Taunton, G-AMJM, TW452, 62 GCF	6-20
☐ XP282	Auster AOP.9	G-BGTC	61	ex -?-, Baxterley, Cranfield, M Wallop 7895M (14-7-64),	
				XP28<u>3</u>, 654. See notes above	2-20

GREATER LONDON

Greater London constitutes the following boroughs: Barking and Dagenham, Barnet, Bexley, Brent, Bromley (including Biggin Hill!), Camden, City of Westminster, Croydon, Ealing, Enfield, Greenwich, Hackney, Hammersmith and Fulham, Haringey, Harrow, Havering, Hillingdon, Hounslow, Islington, Kensington and Chelsea, Kingston upon Thames, Lambeth, Lewisham, Livingston, Merton, Newham, Redbridge, Richmond upon Thames, Southwark, Sutton, Tower Hamlets, Waltham Forest, Wandsworth
...which leads us, of course, to Mornington Crescent

BATTERSEA on the south bank of the Thames, near Chelsea Bridge

Battersea Children's Zoo: ◆ *Chelsea Bridge Gate, SW11 4NJ* | **www.batterseaparkzoo.co.uk**

☐ XZ727*	Westland Lynx HAS.3S	80	ex Ashurst, Hixon, M Wallop, Fleetlands, 815, 702, 815, 702,	
			HAS.2, 815. All-yellow, first noted 8-19	9-21

BENTLEY PRIORY between the A409 and A4140 north of Harrow

The Bentley Priory Museum: Administered by the Bentley Priory Battle of Britain Trust, tells the story of the magnificent country house's role as the HQ of Fighter Command.

◆ *Mansion House Drive, Stanmore, HA7 3FB.* | **020 8950 5526** | **email** via website | **www.bentleyprioymuseum.org.uk**

☐ 'P2921'	Hawker Hurricane FSM		89	BAPC.218, ex 'BN230', St Mawgan, Bentley Priory, 'P3386'.	
	'GZ-L'			611 Sqn colours, pole-mounted	[1] 1-22
☐ -	'DW-O'	V-S Spitfire FSM	11	610 Sqn colours, pole-mounted	1-22

■ **[1]** There are *other* 'P2921s', at Hawkinge, Kent and *two* at Biggin Hill, Kent!

BIGGIN HILL AIRPORT

EGKB

Biggin Hill Heritage Hangar Ltd / Spitfire Company (Biggin Hill) Ltd: As well as Peter Monk's collection, other warbirds are looked after and under restoration. There are open days, hangar tours, 'sit-in-a-Spit' and flight experiences. In the listing below, all are registered to Peter Monk, Peter Monk Ltd, or Biggin Hill Heritage Hangar, unless noted.

First flown on 19th January 2020 the Icarus Foundation's Spitfire IX MJ755 (G-CLGS) departed for Greece on 25th May 2021. Spitfire Tr.IX MJ772 (G-AVAV) was ferried to Holland on 25th August 2021 and joined the Spitfires Flying Vintage Everyday Foundation. Spitfire IX PT879 (G-PTIX) was first flown on 28th October 2020 in Soviet colours, it was ferried to North Weald, Essex, on 20th February 2021. Spitfire IX RN201 (G-BSKP) moved to <u>Northampton</u>, Northants, in mid-2019 and re-flew on 9th June 2020.

◆ *Special events staged, otherwise strictly by prior arrangement* only | **01959 576767** | **office@bigginhillspitfire.com** | **www.bigginhillheritagehangar.co.uk** | **www.flyaspitfire.com**

☐ 'P2921'	Hawker Hurricane X		41	ex 'P3886', Chino, USA, N33TF, Sudbury G-TWTD,	
	'GZ-L'	✈	G-CHTK	Lancing, Se<u>a</u> Hurricane I AE977, 760, 759. CCF-built.	
				Blue Peter, 32 Sqn colours	[1] [2] 11-21
☐ P9372	V-S Spitfire I		39	ex Tonbridge, 92. Shot down 9-9-40.	
		G-CLIH		Salvaged 1996, arrived 2011	[3] 11-21
☐ X4276	V-S Spitfire I	G-CDGU	40	ex Breighton, 54. Crashed 28-12-40. Salvaged 9-87	N6-18
☐ 'BE505'*	Hawker Hurricane		40	ex Elmsett, N Weald, Sudbury, G-HRLO, RCAF 5403.	
	'XP-L'	XII two-seater ✈	G-HHII	CCF-built. 174 Sqn c/s, *Mauritius / Pegs*. Arrived by 4-20	10-21
☐ BS410*	V-S Spitfire Tr.IX	G-TCHI	42	ex Hythe, Biggin Hill, Sandown, 315. Crashed 13-5-43,	
	'PK-A'			France, excavated 2005. First noted 5-21	[4] 11-21
☐ EN570*	V-S Spitfire IX		43	ex Sandown, G-CISP, France, 611. Shot down 18-4-43,	
		LN-AOA		St Pol, France. Excavated 2012. Arrived by 6-21	11-21

☐ 'FE788'		NAA Harvard II ✈		41	ex G-BKWZ, It AF MM54137, RCAF 3064.	
			G-CTKL		Noorduyn-built. RAF colours	[5] 11-21
☐ LZ842	'EF-F'	V-S Spitfire IX		43	ex Sandown, Australia, UK, South Africa, SAAF, RAF 232.	
			G-CGZU		CBAF-built. Accident 27-4-50. Acquired 2003.	
					232 Sqn colours. Engine runs 6-21.	[6] 11-21
☐ MA764*		V-S Spitfire IX		42	ex off-site, Haverfordwest, Ipswich, 122. CBAF-built.	
			G-MCDB		Shot down 25-11-43, St Omer. Excavated 9-05. Arr 2-21	[7] 11-21
☐ MJ627	'9G-Q'	V-S Spitfire Tr.IX		43	ex Waddington, East Kirkby, Coningsby, Coventry,	
		✈	G-BMSB		Andover, G-ASOZ, IAAC 158, G-15-171, MJ627, 1, 441.	
					CBAF-built. 441 Sqn colours	[1] 11-21
☐ MK912	'SH-L'	V-S Spitfire IX		44	ex Canada CF-FLC, Duxford, Audley End, Paddock Wood,	
			G-BRRA		G-BRRA, Brussels, Belgian AF SM-29, Netherlands AF H-59,	
					H-119, MK912, 341, 312. CBAF-built. 64 Sqn c/s, Borough	
					of Bromley. Accident 1-8-15, CoA 26-9-15. Stored	10-21
☐ ML295*		V-S Spitfire IX		44	ex Bayeux, 411 Sqn. Shot down 30-7-44	
	'DB-M'		G-CLXB		For completion as Tr.IX. First noted 9-20	10-21
☐ MT818		V-S Spitfire Tr.VIII		44	ex Booker, Kemble, USA N818MT, Tillamook N58JE, G-AIDN,	
		✈	G-AIDN		Supermarine N32, MT818, RAE. Arrived 31-3-16	[8] 11-21
☐ RM689*		V-S Spitfire XIV		44	ex Castle Donington, Filton, Sandown, Filton, Hucknall,	
			G-ALGT		C' Don', 'RM619', Hucknall, 443, 350. Cr 27-6-92. F/n 6-20	6-20
☐ RM694*		V-S Spitfire XIV		44	ex High Wycombe area, Booker, Bitteswell, Southend, Henlow,	
			G-DBKL		Charnock Richard, Hoylake, Dishforth, Bicester, Hornchurch,	
					Locking 6640M (28-2-49), CFE, 402, 91. Arr 10-2-21	[9] 11-21
☐ RM927		V-S Spitfire XIV		44	ex G-JNMA, Sandown, High Wycombe, USA, Southend,	
			G-SXIV		Charnock Richard, Belgian AF SG-25, RAF, 29 MU, 403	[10] 9-20
☐ RW382		V-S Spitfire XVI ✈		45	ex Sandown, USA N382RW, Audley End, Braintree,	
	'WZ-RR'		G-PBIX		Uxbridge 8075M, Leconfield, Church Fenton 7245M,	
					C&RS, 3 CAACU, 604. CBAF-built. USAAF 309th FS c/s	[11] 11-21
☐ TA805	'FX-M'	V-S Spitfire IX ✈		44	ex Duxford, Sandown, Oxford, SAAF Museum, SAAF,	
			G-PMNF		TA805, 234, 183. CBAF-built. Spirit of Kent, 234 Sqn c/s	11-21
☐ TE184	'RY-S'	V-S Spitfire XVI ✈		45	ex Germany, Booker, Duxford, Halton, N Weald,	
			G-MXVI		St Merryn, Holywood, Aldergrove, Finningley, Cranwell,	
					Henlow, Bicester, Royton 6850M, Long Benton, CGS,	
					607, 226 OCU, 203 AFS. CBAF-built. CoA 30-5-02.	
					Arrived 10-3-12. 127 Sqn colours	[12] 11-21
☐ TE356		V-S Spitfire XVI		45	ex N356TE, N356VE, G-SXVI, B' Hill, Bitteswell, Leeming,	
					Little Rissington, Kemble, Henlow, Bicester. Arrived 1-19	11-21
☐ TE517		V-S Spitfire IX		45	ex G-JGCA, Booker, G-CCIX, Winchester, Nailsworth, G-BIXP,	
			G-RYIX		Duxford, Israel DF/AF 2046, Czech AF, RAF TE517, 313.	
					CBAF-built. Arrived 10-12-12	[13] 11-21
☐ 'A58-606'		V-S Spitfire Tr.IX		45	ex USA, N30WK, N92477, N308WK, N92477, C-FRAF,	
	'ZP-W'	✈	G-AWGB		Battle of Britain 1968, G-AWGB, IAAC 163, G-15-176,	
					TE308. Arr 21-11-19. 457 Sqn RAAF c/s, Grey Nurse	[1] 11-21
☐ 3579	'14'	Messerschmitt		39	ex Canada CF-EML, USA N81562, Colchester, Lancing,	
		Bf 109E-4	G-CIPB		Russia, JG77, shot down 2-8-42. Arado-built.	
					Arrived 6-1-15. CoA 20-11-19	11-21
☐ UB441*		V-S Spitfire IX		43	ex Booker, N94149, Sedlescombe, Rochester, USA,	
			G-SDNI		Burma AF UB441, Israeli AF/DF 20-20, Czech AF A-719,	
					ML 119, 1. CBAF-built. Arrived 9-21	[14] 11-21
☐ 42-29854		Piper L-4H Cub ✈		43	ex F-BFBA, USAAF 43-29854. Little Rock-ette	
	'44-R'		G-BMKC		First noted 2-12	10-21
☐ '47092'*		Curtiss TP-40N		42	ex USA, Evergreen, N67253, P-40K 42-104721	
		Warhawk ✈	N293FR		Arrived 10-6-21, first flown 8-6-21	[15] 10-21

■ [1] Registered to Warbird Experiences. [2] Hurricane in the colours of Flt Lt Pete Brothers, as flown from Biggin Hill in July 1940. There are other 'P2921s' - see also the Chapel, below, and Hawkinge, Kent, and Bentley Priory, Gtr Lon. [3] P9372 shot down by a Bf 109, abandoned over Biggin Hill; P/O W C Watling badly burnt. Registered to G F T van Eerd, Netherlands. [4] Registered to Martin Phillips - see also under Hythe, Kent. [5] G-CTKL registered to Simpson Marine. [6] G-CGZU registered to Mark Bennett. [7] G-MCDB registered to Mark Collenette. [8] Spitfire two-seater prototype, first flown 9-9-46. [9] RM694 was written out of W&R26 (p19) as going to 'Sussex'. [10] Registered to W AirCollection of Paris. [11] Registered to Downlock Ltd. [12] Registered to Australian-based owner 8-21. [13] Registered to 517 Ltd. [14] Registered to Paul Andrews. [15] Also quoted as 42-9749.

Also: While biz-jets and warbirds are the main 'flavour' of Biggin Hill these days, there is also a varied light aircraft population, a large number of which are sufficiently long-term flightless to merit listing. While the Prentice and Civilian Coupe (held as spares for the airworthy G-ABNT) are long-in-the-tooth, both are *believed* to still grace the airfield.

Forward fuselage of HS.146-RJ300 G-CKTO, July 2021.
John Wickenden

☐ G-AKVZ*	Miles Messenger 4B	46	ex RH427, TTC CF. Newtownards-built. CoA 21-5-16		5-21
☐ G-AMZI*	Auster J5F Aiglet Tnr	53	CoA A 30-9-16		5-21
☐ G-AOGE	Percival Proctor III	42	ex BV651, Halton SF, 2 GCS, FAA 755, 756. Hills-built		
			CoA 21-5-84, de-reg 19-1-99		5-21
☐ G-AOKH	Percival Prentice 1	48	ex VS251, 3 FTS, CFS, 2 FTS. Blackburn-built.		
			CoA 2-8-73, de-reg 17-6-92		4-01
☐ G-APPL*	Percival Prentice 1	48	ex VR189 RAE Bedford, Parachute Test Unit, Winter Exp Est		
			Flight, Canada. CoA 27-4-17		5-21
☐ G-ASOH*	Beech Baron 55	64	CoA 20-10-14. First noted 5-21		5-21
☐ G-ATXN*	Mitchell-Procter Kittiwake	69	CoA 16-6-10. First noted 9-20		5-21
☐ G-BFYA	Bölkow Bö 105DB	77	ex Norwich, D-HJET. CoA 25-5-09		9-20
☐ G-BHJA*	Cessna A152	79	ex N4954A. De-reg 8-4-02. First noted 8-20		3-21
☐ G-BHVB*	Piper Warrior II	80	ex N9638N. CoA 9-9-07. First noted 3-21		3-21
☐ G-BRCM*	Cessna 172L	71	ex N3860Q. CoA 17-9-08. First noted 3-21		10-21
☐ G-BYRC	Westland Wessex HC.2	69	ex Redhill, XT671, 60, 72		5-21
☐ G-CKTO*	HSA HS.146-RJ300	98	ex Southend, OO-DWE, G-6-327. Woodford-built.		
			De-reg 29-6-18. Forward fuselage, Arrived 21-2-21		7-21
☐ G-IFTE*	HSA HS.125-700B	78	ex G-BFVI, G-5-18. De-reg 15-5-18. First noted 9-20		5-21
☐ G-LTEE*	Cessna F.172N	78	Reims-built. De-reg 14-2-17. First noted 3-21		5-21
☐ -	Civilian Coupe	32	BAPC.404, unfinished airframe, No.7		10-95
☐ VT-EKT	W'land WG.30 100-60	87	ex Redhill, Biggin Hill, India, G-17-23. Imported to UK 7-00		9-21
☐ N114WG	Westland	84	ex Weston-super-Mare, Yeovil, G-EFIS, G-17-8.		
	WG.30-100-60	G-EFIS	Forward fuselage		9-21
☐ N181WW	Beagle Basset CC.1	75	ex G-BCJF, N181WW, G-BCJF, XS773, 26, TCCF, NCS		11-21
☐ 2-WESX	Westland Wessex HC.2	68	ex 9G-AEL, G-HANA, XV729, 22, 72, 103, 78		10-21
☐ XS674	'R' Westland Wessex HC.2	65	ex Redhill, Hixon, Ipswich, Fleetlands, 60, 72, 18, 78, 72		10-21
☐ XV726	'J' Westland Wessex HC.2	68	ex Hixon, Shawbury, 72, 60, 72, 60, 72, Queen's Flt		10-21
☐ XX414	Sud Gazelle AH.1	75	ex Sevenoaks, Hurstbourne Tarrant, Gosport, 671, Fleetlands,		
			651, 661, 662, 663, 660. Westland-built. Arr 31-1-17		11-21

St George's Chapel of Remembrance / Biggin Hill Memorial Museum: Famed for its 17 stained glass windows and a vast amount of memorabilia, the chapel was built in 1951 in the style of the original RAF Biggin Hill Station Chapel which was opened in 1943, but burned to the ground in 1946. The slab-sided museum building is right alongside the church, ruining the atmosphere that existed on the site beforehand. The 'guardians' are well cosseted, both wear cockpit covers during the winter. ◆ *Signed off the A233* | **01959 44414** | **email** via website | **www.bhmm.org.uk**

☐ 'K9998'	'QJ-K' V-S Spitfire FSM	10	BAPC.431. GB Replicas-built. Displayed, 92 Sqn colours		2-22
☐ 'P2921'	'GZ-L' Hawker Hurricane FSM	10	BAPC.477. GB Replicas-built. Displayed, 32 Sqn colours,		
			Blue Peter. Both damaged by gales 18-2-22	[1]	2-22

■ **[1]** See also Heritage Hangar - above and still *other* 'P2921s' at Hawkinge, Kent, and Bentley Priory, Gtr Lon.

No.2427 Squadron Air Cadets: Close to St George's Chapel; has a Chipmunk.

❑ WZ846	DHC Chipmunk T.10	53	ex Chatham, G-BCSC (de-reg 21-1-75), Bicester 8439M
	G-BCSC		(10-3-75), Manston, Wales UAS, AOTS, 202, 228, CFE,
			W Raynham SF, Glas UAS, Bristol UAS, 1 AEF, St Athan,
			Nott UAS, 63 GCF, Edin UAS, S'ton UAS 6-21

CATFORD south of Greenwich, on the South Circular, A205

Catford Independent Air Force: Alan Partington's collection. ◆ *By prior arrangement* only | little_fat_al@hotmail.com

❑ –	Mignet HM.14 'Flea'	33	BAPC.401, unfinished fuselage	[1] 1-22
❑ XH783	Gloster Javelin FAW.7	58	ex Booker, Sibson, Aylesbury, Halton 7798M (31-7-63),	
			64, 25, GWTS, A&AEE. Cockpit	[2] 1-22
❑ –	V-S Spitfire V FSM	~	built by Feggans Brown for *Piece of Cake*. Cockpit	1-22
❑ –	HS Harrier GR.1	~	cockpit	[3] 1-22

■ **[1]** 'Flea' has a plaque that reads 'Made at Capel'. **[2]** Javelin runs from halfway through the rear cockpit forwards. **[3]** Harrier is an unused cockpit section and *may* have come from Richmond Air Cadets. It is 41H/729048 which puts it between GR.1s XV810 and XW630. Is this the only remaining 'stock' GR.1 cockpit?

CHESSINGTON on the A243 north of J9 of the M25

World of Adventures: The Sea Life giant aquarium contains sharks, rays, parrot fish and, probably still, a Cessna. The penguin enclosure has gained a Rallye. ◆ *Off Leathergate Road, KT9 2NE* | email via website | www.chessington.com

❑ G-BBLM*	MS Rallye 100S	73	ex Fishburn, East Midlands, Sandtoft. De-reg 30-11-10. Arr1-22	1-22
❑ -	Cessna 150 / 152	~	*Azteca*, fuselage and wings	8-21

CHELSEA north bank of the Thames, near Chelsea Bridge, no less

National Army Museum: The depth of material on show here has to be experienced. A Lynx has joined the collection.
◆ *Presently pre-bookable only, Royal Hospital Road, SW3 4HT* | **020 7730 0717** | info@nam.ac.uk | www.nam.ac.uk

❑ ZG921*	Westland Lynx AH.9A	92	ex M Wallop, Odiham, AH.9. SOC 3-10-18. First noted 6-21	2-22
❑ -*	'B023' GEC-Marconi Phoenix B	c87	ex Larkhill	[1] 1-22

■ **[1]** Part of the pre-production batch; believed used only for classroom instruction and not flown.

CROYDON on the A23 in south London

Croydon Airport Visitor Centre: Within the former terminal building (Airport House) run by the **Historic Croydon Airport Trust** in association with the **Croydon Airport Society**. The pole-mounted Heron stands guard.
◆ *Purley Way. CR0 0XZ* | **020 8680 5878** | info@historiccroydonairport.org.uk | www.historiccroydonairport.org.uk

❑ 'G-AOXL'	DH Heron 2D	G-ANUO 54	ex Biggin Hill, Exeter. CoA 12-9-86, de-reg 9-8-96	[1] 1-22

■ **[1]** G-ANUO is painted as 'G-AOXL' of Morton Air Services. The *real* G-AOXL made the last passenger flight from Croydon, on 3-9-59.

DARTFORD at the southern end of *that* bridge, west of Gravesend

An Auster is thought to still be kept at a *private* location in the *general* area.

❑ XN437	Auster AOP.9	G-AXWA 59	ex Rush Green, N Weald, Lashenden, Welling, B' Hill, Luton,
			Odiham, Maghull, Hoylake, St Athan, 653, 8 Flt. SOC 28-11-67 N4-18

DENHAM Plus D G-AHUG had moved to Turweston, Bucks, in April 2021.

DULWICH on the A205 South Circular, south of Peckham

Dulwich College: The Chipmunk was due to be disposed of in 2021. ◆ *Only by prior permission* | www.dulwich.org.uk

❑ WB627	'N' DHC Chipmunk T.10	50	ex 9248M (27-3-96), Cambridge, 5 AEF, 1 AEF, Lon UAS, Camb
			UAS, 2 SoTT, 22 GCF, Debden SF, Jurby SF, 8 RFS, 18 RFS 12-20

FELTHAM on the A312 southeast of Heathrow

Heathrow Trident Collection (HTC): Kevin Bowen's incredible collection is well worth a visit. Restoration of a Rolls-Royce RB162 booster – the Trident 3B could briefly be four-engined – is complete. Along with Les Rawlins, Kevin was instrumental in the relocation of Trident 3B G-AWZP cockpit from Manchester, Gtr Man, to London Colney, Herts – qv.
◆ *By prior arrangement* only | g-awzk@msn.com

GREENFORD on the A40 west of the city

Vanguard Holdings: Appleton Lane, off the A40. See also Bristol, Glos, for the Vanguard Storage HQ. By mid-May 2021, the Scout had been mounted on the roof, having usurped a Ford Transit! The Hunter was temporarily at North Weald, Essex, in mid-2021 for a refurbish. Vampire T.11 cockpit XK632 had moved to Wickenby, Lincs, by July 2020.
◆ *By prior arrangement* **only | www.vanguardholdings.co.uk**

☐ WT555	Hawker Hunter F.1	55	ex Cosford, Locking 7499M (22-11-57), A&AEE, Dunsfold,	6-21
☐ XV123	Westland Scout AH.1	67	ex Ipswich, Shawbury, Thruxton, Ipswich, Weston-super--Mare, Fleetlands. Arrived 5-19. Displayed	7-21

GREENWICH east of the A102 Blackwall Tunnel Approach, just south of the 'Dome'

Emirates Aviation Experience: An impressive full-scale mock-up of an Airbus A380 allows access to the flightdeck; this is more a part of the building than an 'airframe' and is not listed formally. There are two A380 and a pair of Boeing 777 fixed-base simulators, all synthetic. ◆ *In East Parkside, east of the A102* | **email** via website | **www.aviation-experience.com**

Flight 338 - The Escape Plane: Well, the 'escape plane' – ATR 42 G-ISLG – absconded! It had returned to Bournemouth, Dorset, by mid-2020, but moved to storage at Canford, Dorset, on 23rd December 2020.

HENDON northwest London, near the end of the M1

Royal Air Force Museum, London: Launched in July 2020, the 'Adopt an Artefact' fund-raiser requests 'share-holders' in a series of items, from Arthur Whitten Brown's 'Twinkletoes' transatlantic mascot of 1919 to a Spitfire.

Hogging far more headlines than this initiative was the much heralded, prematurely leaked, inaccurately reported, tranche of airframe disposals outlined in late 2021 - a whopping 35 airframes. All museums, no matter what size, reassess their stock from time to time but the size of this 'reshuffle' is unprecedented; and there is good reason to believe that more will follow. Why is this process happening now?

By 2021 a perfect storm was brewing. At Manchester the National Museum of Science and Industry-run Science and Industry Museum was baling out of the long-moribund former Air and Space Museum by January 2022. Along with The Aeroplane Collection (Hooton Park, Cheshire) the RAF Museum was instrumental in 'stocking' the venue when it opened in March 1983. With no room at Cosford, Hendon or Stafford, BDAC and Avro Heritage adopted the 'strays'. The museum was lucky that Woodford could take on the Shackleton AEW.2 and the infrastructure demands it will necessitate.

At Cosford the huge Hangar 1 is destined to be the venue for a major new exhibition in 2023 and will require a complex rearrangement of airframes, made possible by the departure of - apparently - 'lesser' exhibits. Across the airfield on the southern perimeter Hangar 9, the long-held and so-called 'deep store' is showing its age and is no longer a suitable, safe environment: it needs clearing out. Tenure of the massive Stafford storage facility has been on a countdown for several years, the days of 'grace and favour' sites are long gone: the MoD and associated agencies are hard-nosed and 'heritage' is seldom on the agenda. The 'Stafford question' has been a looming headache almost since the site was occupied in 1999.

All of this meant that a review of the *entire* collection was needed. In June 2020 an 'exploratory' document charting disposal 'methodology' for airframes escaped the corridors at Hendon. It was a 'What If' expedition and *all* museums of worth should carry out such exercises: ideally storing the results within a glass case marked 'In Case of Emergency'. Some alarmist tosh has been written or sent off into the ether about the June 2020 paper and the *real* 2022 clear out, so we'll spend a little time analysing the disposal procedure as all of the 'nationals' will follow these, or similar, steps.

Included in the objectives of the RAF Museum's 'Collections Review Policy' is the need to: "Resolve issues which have arisen from historic and *unsystematic approaches to collecting*" [Author's emphasis]. All museums suffer this from time to time, some even adopt it as a policy! The museum takes into account artefacts at other 'nationals', specifically: Imperial War Museum; Museum of Army Flying; National Archives; National Army Museum; National Museum of the Royal Navy (which includes the Fleet Air Arm Museum); Science Museum. Not mentioned is the National Museum of Scotland.

Like most of the 'nationals', the options for disposing of artefacts - be it a cloth patch or a Spitfire - are limited. The RAF Museum website gives the following options: Free gift/transfer to another museum; Exchange of objects between museums; Free gift/transfer to another institution/organisation within the public domain; Return to donor; Sale (*only in extraordinary circumstances...* following consultation with donors, 'stakeholders' and the museum community); Destruction (*only* when an object is deteriorated beyond any future use or needs to be disposed of for reasons of Health and Safety).[Author's emphasis.]

In curator-speak, disposals are categorised as follows: some airframes 'scoring' in more than one category. (The definitions have been put through a jargon filter by the author.) Completeness: requiring a lot of work to make it whole, or airframe lacking a good provenance. Duplication: another of the type/sub-variant also held. Environment: kept outdoors, probably not worth devoting a roof overhead. Interpretive Potential: bearing in mind that a good curator can make *anything* have such a capability, this apparently means that it is difficult to get the public to understand the artefact. Originality: most often replica, but could also relate to a composite or poorly restored airframe. Relevance: to the core collecting policy. Significance: how important or noteworthy.

Using these parameters, in December 2021 the RAF Museum came up with the following disposals in two categories: transfer by gift – handing over legal title; or offered for outward loan – the museum has a long established track record of lending artefacts in the short, medium or long terms. In each case the recipient organisation has to meet stringent curatorial qualifications and the environment in which the airframe will be exhibited.

Transfer by gift:
Cosford: Auster C4 WE600*, Sycamore HR.14 XJ918*, SP-2H Neptune 204*; CASA 352L 'G-AFAP'*.
Cosford – deep store: Avro 707C WZ744*, Meteor T.7(mod) WA634 ejector seat test-bed; Avian hang-glider*; P-51D Mustang '413573'*; Vampire FB.5 WA346*; Gnat F.1 XK724*; Hawker P.1121 uncompleted prototype; Lakes Waterbird restoration project*; Morane-Saulnier BB A301 fuselage frame*; Slingsby Prefect TX.1 WE982*.
Hendon: TB-25N Mitchell '34037'*; EHI EH.101 ZJ116 (gifted to The Helicopter Museum, Weston-super-Mare, Somerset)*.
Stafford: DH Moth G-AAMX*; Cornell 15252*; Sedbergh TX.1 VX275*; Dragon Rapide (Dominie) G-AHED.

Offered for outward loan:
Cosford: Meteor F.8(mod) WK935 prone-pilot test-bed; Pembroke C.1 WV746; Jetstream T.1 XX496; Varsity T.1 WL679; Sea Balliol T.21 WL732*; Bristol 188 XF926; Comper Swift G-ACGL*; PBY-6A Catalina L-866*; Argosy C.1 XP411.
Cosford - deep store: Tornado P.02 XX946 prototype; Ventura II 6130; Venom FB.54 J-1704*; Valetta C.2 VX573.
Stafford; Cody Man-Lifting Kite replica*; Spitfire XVI SL674*.

Most of these reflect good reasoning while others are considered disturbing by the author. Of the above, the author has no qualms with the disposal of those marked with an asterisk (*). Let's take an example of an asterisk 'earner': the CASA 352L (Junkers Ju 52) was a government-to-government gift and was given the *original* British Airways colours to make it relevant at the time for the very much out-of-place British Airways Collection at Cosford. That said, the 'Tante Ju' is *exceptionally* important in the annals of air transport and *should* be at the Science Museum's Wroughton grouping – I wish!

Taking a major 'hit' are the decidedly 'unsexy' transports and trainers: including the heavyweight Argosy , Valetta and and Varsity which are a 'big ask' for any organisation to swallow. *If* the idea of avoiding duplication with the other 'nationals' in taken into consideration, then the ousting of Jetstream XX496, for example, makes some sense. The National Museum of Flight Scotland has Jetstream 31 G-JSSD which 'wins' on technical, industrial and national significance. See under East Fortune for specifics but it 'scores' as a Handley Page Series 1 and the *Scottish*-re-engineered Series 31 prototype, which established the Jetstream as a major type. (There are other T.1s extant; for example the Newark Air Museum, not a 'national' but well deserving that level of status, has XX492 under cover and in superb condition.)

Also worrying is the diaspora of prototype, test and trials aircraft. *Technically* most of these are not RAF machines as such, but they proudly wear the roundel and have helped to shape the RAF over the decades. We could all play who-might-get-what, eg P.1121 for Brooklands, Bristol 188 for Filton etc, but it is the *accumulation* of them at Cosford that is all the more powerful; the breaking up of this unique 'stable' is lamentable. *W&R27* noted that the variable stability Beagle 206Z2 XS743 "was almost certainly destined for the RAF Museum", thankfully it has been secured for prosperity by the wonderful BDAC at Old Sarum. Likewise, the Reid and Sigrist Bobsleigh VZ728 would have looked fantastic alongside its fellow prone-pilot Meteor F.8 WK935: the former is bound for safe hands at Newark. Yes, Hendon has a Tornado F.3 *and* a GR.4 but UK *prototype* P.02 XX946 started the ball rolling on one of the most successful warplane programmes ever. This prototype 'logic' would equally apply to Cosford's TSR.2 X0-2 XR220 – so will that be up for grabs?

Expressions of Interest for the 35 closed on 10th February 2022 - when this book was being laid out and designed; so most of this exercise will be the domain of *W&R29*. Hence this deeper than usual look at how these things are organised as this process will not be restricted to the RAF Museum. It is bound to be repeated with others in the 'national club': the Science Museum has attempted before now to come to grips with the Wroughton collection and other non-'South Ken' airframes; the Imperial War Museum has more manoeuvres to carry out at Duxford; and the inventory at Yeovilton is bound to come under the microscope.

To conclude on recent RAF retirements. A Tristar was never on the cards, impossibly expensive to bring to either museum site and would ultimately demand a phenomenal roof over its head – see Bruntingthorpe, Leics. Likewise a Sentry AWACS, although a 'rotodome' would make an impressive exhibit. The Sentinels are bound for further use with the Americans. (For both see Waddington, Lincs.) The last of the versatile HS.146s, that could 'fit' on Cosford's 3,700ft Runway 06/24 are destined for the 'private' museum sector, at Duxford (the DAS airliner collection) and St Athan, and export to Australia. On the horizon is Chinook HC.6A ZA718, the famous *Bravo-November* Falklands 'survivor', a 'must have' for the last four decades. Will a half-century-plus Puma join the ranks?
●
As noted above, the museum has long since had an active loans policy. The far-reaching review of airframes discussed above will very likely see the title of many, if not all, of the following being transferred to the hosts. For example, Bristol 173 XF785 was recently passed on to Aerospace Bristol at Filton, Glos, and it was proposed to hand on Jet Gyrodyne XJ389 to the Museum of Berkshire Aviation at Woodley, Berks, in March 2022. Present loans: **Brooklands**, Surrey: Valiant cockpit; **Chatham**, Kent: military gas balloon basket; **Duxford**, Cambs, Canberra WH725, Fi 103; **Filton**, Glos, Beaufighter cockpit; **Gloucestershire**, Glos, Javelin XH903; **Manston**, Kent, Hurricane and Spitfire: **Middle Wallop**, Hampshire, Rotachute; **Old Sarum**, Wilts Avro 707A, EE P.1A; **Scampton**, Lincs, Sedbergh XN185; **South Kensington**, Gtr Lon, P.1127;

Southampton, Hampshire, Gnat F.1, Spitfire F.24; **Stow Maries**, Essex, Avro 504K; **Tangmere**, W Sussex: Hunter, Meteor, Phantom, Swift; **Woodford**, Gtr Man, Shackleton AEW.2; **Yeovilton**, Somerset, P.1052, Dragonfly VX595, Supermarine 510. Overseas: **Munich, Germany**: a Fi 103.

As well as Hendon, there is the RAF Museum 'North' and the conservation centre at **Cosford, Shropshire**, and the storage site at **Stafford, Staffs**. There is also the **Society of Friends of the RAF Museum** - contact via the website. In the sections below, 'Rae's denotes the Royal Aeronautical Society's collection, largely based on the former Nash Collection.
◆ *Grahame Park Way, NW9 5LL* | 020 8205 2266 | london@rafmuseum.org | **www.rafmuseum.org**

'Gate guardians': The Hurricane and Spitfire, with new 'personas', are back on duty.

☐ 'P2725'	'TM-B'	Hawker Hurricane FSM	90	BAPC.205, ex 'Z3427', 'BE421'. 504 Sqn colours		1-22
☐ 'TB288'	'<u>HT</u>-H'	V-S Spitfire FSM	90	BAPC.206, ex 'MH486'. 20 Sqn colours		1-22

Hangar 1: RAF First 100 Years: This is the museum's 'Marmite' hall – you either like it or you don't!

☐ F1010		Airco DH.9A	1918	ex Cardington, Krakow, Berlin, 110. Force-landed 5-10-18 and captured. Westland-built. Acquired 15-6-77.	[1]	1-22
☐ BL614	'ZD-F'	V-S Spitfire Vb	42	ex Rochester, Manchester, St Athan, 'AB871', Colerne, Wattisham, Credenhill 4354M (6-12-43), 118, 64, 222, 242, 611. CBAF-built. Acquired 10-72. 222 Sqn colours		1-22
☐ ML824	'NS-Z'	Short Sunderland MR.5	44	ex Pembroke Dock, Aéronavale, 330, 201. Sydenham-built. Acquired 11-1-71. 201 Sqn colours		1-22
☐ XR977	'3'	Folland Gnat T.1	64	ex Cosford, Hangar 1, 2 SoTT 8640M, Red Arrows, 4 FTS. Last flown 5-10-79. Red Arrows colours. Arrived 3-12-17		1-22
☐ XZ585	'A'	Westland Sea King HAR.3	77	ex Gosport, 203, 22, 203, 202, 202, 203, 22, 202, A&AEE Last flown 23-4-15, Arrived <u>6</u>-12-17	[2]	1-22
☐ –		Fieseler Fi 103 (V-1)	45	BAPC.92, ex Cardington, St Athan		1-22
☐ –		Lockheed-Martin F-35 FSM	10	BAPC.341, installed 9-11		1-22

■ **[1]** 'Ninak' was the 13th of 18 donated to 110 Sqn and a panel reads: 'Presented by His Highness the Nizam of Hyderabad No.12A' - the potentate was clearly superstitious! The fuselage was acquired from Krakow, wings and much else created/acquired in-house. **[2]** Factoids: Total flying time 14,472 hours; undertook 533 operational winch lifts.

Hangar 2: World War One in the Air: Centred on the re-sited and re-modelled Grahame-White Factory.

☐ No.433		Blériot XXVII	1911	BAPC.107, ex Stafford, Cosford, Wyton, Hendon 9202M, Cardington, Heathrow, RAeS, Hendon, Nash, Brooklands Acquired 5-63		1-22
☐ '687'		Royal Aircraft Factory BE.2b replica	88	BAPC.181, ex Cardington. John MacKenzie-built, original fittings. Acquired 6-92		1-22
☐ '2345'		Vickers FB.5 Gunbus replica G-ATVP	66	ex Cardington, Hendon, Abingdon, Brooklands, G-ATVP. Acquired 10-6-68, last flight 14-6-68, CoA 6-5-69	[1]	1-22
☐ '3066'		Caudron G.3	1916	ex 9203M, Henlow, Stradishall, Heathrow, RAeS, Hendon, Nash, Brooklands, G-AETA, OO-ELA, O-BELA. Acq 1964		1-22
☐ 'A3930'	'B'	Royal Aircraft RE.8 replica	12	ex New Zealand, ZK-TVC. The Vintage Aviator-built. Acquired 28-8-12. 9 Sqn colours	[2]	1-22
☐ 'A6526'		Royal Aircraft Factory FE.2b	1917	BAPC.400, ex main halls, Cosford, Stafford, Wyton, Cardington, Leiston. Acquired 4-76	[3]	1-22
☐ 'C3988'		Sopwith 5F1 Dolphin	1918	BAPC.353, ex Cosford, 'D5239', Wyton, Cardington. Acquired 6-67	[4]	1-22
☐ 'E449'		Avro 504K	1918	ex 9205M, Henlow, Abingdon, Heathrow, RAeS, Nash, Brooklands. Acquired 3-63	[5]	1-22
☐ 'E2466'	'I'	Bristol F.2B	1918	BAPC.165, ex main halls, Cardington, Weston-on-the-Green. Acquired 1965. Semi-skeletal		1-22
☐ F938		Royal Aircraft Factory SE.5a G-EBIC	1918	ex Henlow 9208M, Biggin Hill, Heathrow, Brooklands, Wroughton, Brooklands, 'B4563', Colerne, RAeS, Brooklands, Hendon, Nash, Savage Skywriting, G-EBIC (CoA 3-9-30, de-reg 31-12-38), F938, 84 Sqn. Wolseley-built. Acq 12-64		1-22
☐ F6314	'B'	Sopwith F1 Camel	1918	ex 'Milestones, Cosford 9206M, Wyton, Hendon, Heathrow, Colerne, Hendon, RAeS, Hendon, Nash, Brooklands, 'H508', Tring, Waddon. Acquired 9-1-64		1-22
☐ N5912		Sopwith Triplane	1917	ex 8385M, Henlow, 49 MU, 5 MU, Cardington, School of Air Fighting, Redcar and Marske. Oakley-built. Acq 1964		1-22

☐	'D7343/17'		Albatros D.Va replica	12	ex New Zealand, ZK-TVD. Acquired 28-8-12	[7]	1-22
☐	8417/18		Fokker D.VII	1918	ex 'Milestones', Cardington, Hendon 9207M, Cardington,		
					Hendon, Cardington, Heathrow, RAeS, Hendon, Nash,		
					Brooklands, Versailles, OO- ?, Belgian AF (?), Jasta 71.		
					Ostdeutsche Albatros Werke-built. Acquired 3-66		1-22

■ **[1]** Gunbus built by the Brooklands-based Vintage Aircraft and Flying Association, first flying 14-6-66. **[2]** RE.8 fitted with a 'reverse-engineered' RAF 4a; unveiled at Old Warden 28-8-12; exchange for Farman F-HMFI (see Cosford, Shropshire) and Hanriot HD-75 (see above). Original rudder, wing and fuselage parts found in a garage in Coventry by the Northern Aircraft Preservation Society. **[3]** FE.2 is based on an unfinished nacelle built by sub-contractor Richard Garrett and Sons of Leiston and stored at their factory for close on 60 years. Much of the work creating the rest of the airframe was carried out by John MacKenzie of Aircraft and Weapon Reproductions of Southampton 1987 to 2007, with completion by Guy Black's Retrotec. **[4]** Dolphin uses many original parts. The rear fuselage comes from C3988 and this has been adopted as its identity. **[5]** Avro 504K 'E449' is a composite of G-EBJE (fuselage) and Type 548A G-EBKN (wings) - both of which used to ply their joy riding trade from Shoreham - and was originally with the Nash Collection. **[7]** D.Va built by The Vintage Aviator Ltd, fitted with original Mercedes D.III ex RAFM stocks; unveiled at Old Warden 28-8-12; exchanged for Farman F-HMFI and Hanriot HD-75.

Hangars 3, 4, and 5: War in the Air 1918-1980: Previously known as the Historic Hangars and Bomber Command Hall. By September 2021 Grasshopper TX.1 WZ791 had moved to <u>Montrose</u>, Scotland. EH.101 ZJ116 (G-OIOI) was transferred by gift and was due to move to <u>Weston-super-Mare</u>, Somerset, as W&R closed for press: this migration has been anticipated.

☐	G-FAAG		AW R.33 airship	1921	Vickers-built. Dismantled 5-28. Control gondola		1-22
☐	'E6655'	'B'	Sopwith 7FI Snipe	11	BAPC.348, ex New Zealand. Acquired 10-8-12.		
					1 Sqn colours, Hinaidi, Iraq, 1926	[1]	1-22
☐	'J9941'		Hawker Hart	35	ex HSA, 'J9933', G-ABMR. CoA 11-6-57, de-reg 2-2-59.		
			G-ABMR		Acquired 1972. 57 Sqn colours		1-22
☐	'K2227'		Bristol Bulldog IIA	30	ex Hatch, Cardington, Old Warden, Henlow, Filton, G-ABBB,		
			G-ABBB		(de-reg 22-9-61), Science Museum, R-11. Crashed 13-9-64		
					(with Shuttleworth). Acquired 31-3-99. 56 Sqn 'A' Flight c/s		1-22
☐	K4232		Cierva Rota I	34	ex Spain (96-98), Cardington, Sweden, SE-AZB, Cierva, 529,		
					1448 Flt, Cal Flight, 5 RSS, Old Warden, Cardington, SAC,		
					A&AEE, 2, SAC, K4232. Avro-built C.30A. Acquired14-6-78		1-22
☐	L5343		Fairey Battle I	39	ex Cosford, Rochester, Hendon, St Athan, Henlow, Leeming,		
					Iceland, 98, 266. Cr13-9-40. Acquired 21-11-72. 98 Sqn c/s	[2]	1-22
☐	'L8756'	'XD-E'	Bristol Bolingbroke IVT	42	ex Boscombe Down, RCAF 10001. Fairchild Canada-built.		
					Acquired 25-4-66. 139 Sqn colours as Blenheim IV		1-22
☐	N5628		Gloster Gladiator II	39	ex 263. Lost in Norway 4-40. Acq 8-68. Forward fuselage		1-22
☐	N9899		Supermarine	25	ex Cardington, Henlow, Felixstowe (as houseboat), wrecked		
			Southampton I		at moorings, Calshot, 23-11-28, 480 Flt, MAEE, 480 Flt.		
					Acquired 9-67. Fuselage		1-22
☐	P2617	'AF-F'	Hawker Hurricane I	40	ex 8373M, 71 MU, 9 FTS, 9 SFTS, 1, 607, 615.		
					Acquired 5-72. 607 Sqn colours		1-22
☐	R5868	'PO-S'	Avro Lancaster I	42	ex Scampton 7325M, 467, 83. Metropolitan-Vickers-built.		
					Acquired 3-72. 467 Sqn colours	[3]	1-22
☐	R9125	'JR-M'	Westland Lysander III	40	ex Cosford, Hendon, 8377M, Cosford, Wroughton,		
					Stanmore Park, Wroughton, 161, Mk.IIISD, School for Danger,		
					161, Mk.III, CNS, 7 OTU, CGS, 225. Arrived 22-2-22		2-22
☐	W1048	'TL-S'	HP Halifax II	42	ex 8465M, Henlow, Lake Hoklingen, Norway, 35, 102.		
					EE-built. Force-landed 27-4-42. Acquired 25-8-73. 35 Sqn c/s		1-22
☐	W2068	'68'	Avro Anson I	39	ex Duxford, 9261M, Australia, VH-ASM, W2068, 4 SFTS,		
					3 SFTS. Acquired 19-4-96. Fuselage on 'Queen Mary' trailer		1-22
☐	X4590	'PR-F'	V-S Spitfire I	40	ex Cosford 8384M, Finningley, 53 OTU, 303, 57 OTU,		
					66, 609. Acquired 1-72. 609 Sqn colours		1-22
☐	'DD931'	'L'	Bristol Beaufort VIII	44	BAPC.436, ex 9131M, Cardington, Chino, New Guinea,		
					RAAF. DAP-built. Acquired 1991. 42 Sqn colours	[4] [5]	1-22
☐	FE905		NAA Harvard IIB	43	ex Cardington, Winthorpe, Cardington, Royston, London		
					Bridge, Southend, LN-BNM, Danish AF 31-329, RCAF,		
					41 SFTS, FE905, 42-12392. Noorduyn-built. Acquired 3-85		1-22
☐	'FX760'		Curtiss Kittyhawk IV	43	ex Cosford 9150M, Stafford, Wyton, Cardington, Hendon,		
		'GA-?'			USA, Hawkins, Chino, New Guinea, 80 Sqn RAAF A29-556,		
					USAAF 42-106101. Acquired 29-5-92. 112 Sqn colours	[5] [6]	1-22

☐ 'KK995'	'E'	Sikorsky Hoverfly I	44	ex 'Milestones', Bicester, Henlow, Cranfield, 705, King's		
		KL110		Flt, TCDU, 43 OTU, USAAF 43-46596. Acquired 14-1-66	[7]	1-22
☐ 'KL216'	'RS-L'	Republic P-47D-40-RA	45	ex Cosford 9212M, Duxford, Cardington, Bittesswell, Yugo		
		Thunderbolt		AF 13064, USAAF 45-49295. Acquired 7-86. 30 Sqn SEAC c/s		1-22
☐ KN751	'F'	Consolidated	44	ex Cosford, Colerne, Ind AF 6 Sqn HE807, RAF KN751, 99.		
		Liberator VI		Ford-built. Acquired 1-7-74. 99 Sqn, Cocos Islands, c/s	[8]	1-22
☐ LB264		Taylorcraft Auster I	42	ex Cosford, Plus D G-AIXA (CoA 21-2-03, de-reg 13-12-02),		
		G-AIXA		Spanhoe, 22 EFTS, 1 EFTS, A&AEE. Acquired 23-10-02		1-22
☐ MN235		Hawker Typhoon Ib	44	ex Coningsby (7-18 to 10-18) Canada, Hendon, Shawbury,		
	'18-T'			Smithsonian, USAAF FE-491, RAF n/s. Gloster-built.		
				Acquired 19-11-68, arrived 18-10-18. 440 Sqn RCAF c/s		1-22
☐ MP425	'G'	Airspeed Oxford I	43	ex Cardington, Winthorpe, Cardington, G-AITB (CoA24-5-61,		
		G-AITB		de-reg 31-10-61), Shawbury, Perth, MP425, 7 FTS,		
				18 (P)AFU, 1536 (BAT) Flt. Standard Motors-built.		
				Acquired 3-69. 1536 Flt colours		1-22
☐ NV778		Hawker Tempest TT.5	44	ex 'Milestones' Cosford, Wyton, Cardington, Hendon,		
				8386M (5-9-73), Leeming, 'SN219', Middleton St George,		
				N Weald, Foulness, 233 OCU, Napier. Last flown 12-7-55.		
				Acquired 8-65. 233 OCU colours		1-22
☐ PK724		V-S Spitfire F.24	46	ex Finningley, Gaydon, 7288M (4-11-55) Brize Norton,		
				Lyneham, n/s. CBAF-built. Acquired 20-2-70		1-22
☐ RD253		Bristol Beaufighter	44	ex St Athan 7931M, Portuguese AF BF-13, RD253.		
		TF.10		Acquired 1965		1-22
☐ 'TB675'		V-S Spitfire XVI	45	ex Stafford, Cosford, Stafford, Cosford, St Athan, Turnhouse		
	'4D-V'	RW393		7293M (27-3-56), 602, 3, CAACU, 31, FCCS, 203 AFS.		
				CBAF-built. Arrived 9-15		1-22
☐ TJ138	'VO-L'	DH Mosquito TT.35	45	ex St Athan, Swinderby, Finningley, Colerne, Thorney Island,		
				Bicester 7607M (8-7-59), Shawbury, 5 CAACU, B.35, 98.		
				Last flight 8-5-59. Acquired 6-67. 98 Sqn colours		1-22
☐ VT812	'N'	DH Vampire F.3	47	ex Cosford, Wyton, Hendon, Cosford, Shawbury, Colerne		
				7200M, Cardington, 602, 601, 614, 32. EE-built.		
				Acquired 9-6-64. 601 Sqn colours		1-22
☐ WE139		EE Canberra PR.3	53	ex 8369M, Henlow, 231 OCU, 39, 69, 540. Acquired 23-4-69		1-22
☐ WH301		Gloster Meteor F.8	51	ex Henlow 7930M, Kemble, 85, CAW, 609, DFLS.		
				Acquired 17-2-67. 609 Squadron colours		1-22
☐ WP962	'C'	DHC Chipmunk T.10	53	ex 9287M, Newton, 3 AEF, Bristol UAS, AAC, London UAS,		
				61 GCF, 662. Acquired 5-5-00		1-22
☐ WV783		Bristol Sycamore HR.12	50	ex Rochester, Wyton, Cardington, Fleetlands, Henlow		
		G-ALSP		7841M (1-4-64), HDU Old Sarum, CFS, ASWDU,		
				G-ALSP de-reg 26-3-52. Acquired 1995. CFS colours		1-22
☐ XA302		Slingsby Cadet TX.3	52	ex Syerston, BGA.3786 / HAK, 622 GS, 661 GS, CGS, 2 GC,		
				671 GS,615 GS, 613 GS, 126 GS, 123 GS, 22 GS.		
				CoA 24-5-96, acquired 5-5-05	[9]	1-22
☐ XG154		Hawker Hunter FGA.9	56	ex 8863M, St Athan, 1 TWU, 229 OCU, 54, 43, 54.		
				AWA-built. Acquired 30-5-85. 8 *and* 43 Sqn colours		1-22
☐ XG474	'O'	Bristol Belvedere HC.1	62	ex 8367M, Henlow, 66, 26, 66. Acquired 7-8-69. 66 Sqn c/s		1-22
☐ XL318		Avro Vulcan B.2	61	ex 8733M, Scampton, 617, 230 OCU, Wadd Wing, 617, 230		
				OCU, Scamp Wing, 617. Acquired 1-1-82, arrived 12-2-82		1-22
☐ XM463	'38'	Hunting Jet Provost T.3A	60	ex 1 FTS, RAFC. Acquired 6-3-91. Fuselage, 'hands-on'		1-22
☐ XM717		HP Victor K.2	63	ex Cardington, Marham, 55, 57, 55, 543, Witt W, 100.		
				Acquired 2-3-94. *Lucky Lou*. Cockpit		1-22
☐ XP299		Westland Whirlwind	61	ex Cosford 8726M, 22, 230, 1563F, Queen's Flt, 230, CFS.		
		HAR.10		Acquired 30-11-81. 22 Sqn colours		1-22
☐ XS925	'BA'	EE Lightning F.6	67	ex 8961M, Binbrook, 11, 5-11 pool. Last flown 21-7-87.		
				Acquired 26-4-88, arrived 28-4-88. 11 Sqn colours		1-22
☐ XV424	'I'	McD Phantom FGR.2	69	ex 9152M, St Athan, Wattisham, 56, 228 OCU, 29,		
				92, 228 OCU, 29, 228 OCU, 111, 29. Acquired 12-11-92		1-22
☐ XV732		Westland Wessex HCC.4	69	ex Shawbury, 32, Queen's Flt. Last flight 31-3-98. Acq 26-3-02		1-22
☐ XW323	'86'	BAC Jet Provost T.5A	70	ex 9166M (23-10-92), Shawbury, 1 FTS, RAFC. 1 FTS c/s		1-22

☐ XW855		Sud Gazelle HCC.4	73	ex Shawbury, Fleetlands, 32. Westland-built. Acq 1-4-03		1-22
☐ ZE887	'GF'	Panavia Tornado F.3	88	ex Leuchars, 111, 43, 25, 11, 5, 11, 43, 229 OCU.		
				Last flown 4-3-10, acquired 18-10-10. 43 Sqn colours	[10]	1-22
☐ A16-199		Lockheed Hudson IIIA	42	ex Strathallan, G-BEOX (de-reg 12-12-81), VH-AGJ,		
	'SF-R'	G-BEOX		VH-SMM, 3 Comms Unit, 2 Sqn, 13 Sqn, RAAF A16-199,		
				FH174 n/s, 41-36975. Acquired 14-7-81. RAAF 13 Sqn c/s		1-22
☐ 920	'QN'	Supermarine Stranraer	40	ex Queen Charlotte Airlines CF-BXO, RCAF 920.		
				Canadian Vickers-built. Acquired 7-70		1-22
☐ 4101	'12'	Messerschmitt	40	ex St Athan 8477M, Henlow, Biggin, Fulbeck, Wroughton,		
		Bf 109E-4		Stanmore, Pengam Moors, Stafford, DG200, 1426 Flt,		
				A&AEE, DH Hatfield, Hucknall, RAE, JG51, JG52, JG51.		
				Erla-built. Force-landed 27-11-40. Acquired 9-69		1-22
☐ 120227	'2'	Heinkel He 162A-2	44	ex St Athan 8472M, Colerne, Leconfield, VN679, AM.65,		
				Farnborough, Leck, JG1. Acquired 1961. JG1 colours		1-22
☐ 494083		Junkers Ju 87G-2 'Stuka'	c44	ex St Athan 8474M, Henlow, St Athan, Biggin Hill,		
	'RI+JK'			Fulbeck, Wroughton, Stanmore, Eggebek. Acquired 9-69		1-22
☐ 584219	'38'	Focke-Wulf	44	ex St Athan 8470M, Gaydon, Henlow, Fulbeck,		
		Fw 190F-8/U1		Wroughton, Stanmore, Wroughton, Brize Norton, AM.29,		
				Farnborough, Karup. Acquired 9-70. JG54 colours.		1-22
☐ 701152		Heinkel He 111H-20/R1	44	ex St Athan 8471M, Henlow, Biggin Hill, Fulbeck, Stanmore		
	'NT+SL'			Park, RAE, 56th FG USAAF, Luftwaffe. Acquired 9-69		1-22
☐ 730301		Messerschmitt	44	ex St Athan 8479M, Biggin Hill, Stanmore Park,		
	'D5+RL'	Bf 110G-4/R6		76 MU, RAE, AM.34, Karup, I/NJG3. Acquired 8-73		1-22
☐ MM5701		Fiat CR-42 Falco	40	ex St Athan 8468M, Biggin Hill, Fulbeck, Wroughton,		
	'13-95'			Stanmore Park, AFDU, RAE, BT474, 95 SCT.		
				Force-landed Orfordness 11-11-40. Acquired 1968		1-22
☐ '34037'		NAA TB-25N-20-NC	44	ex 8838M, Blackbushe, N9115Z, *Hanover Street* (1978),		
		Mitchell		*Catch-22* (1969), USAAF 44-29366. Acquired 25-10-82		
				For transfer by gift – see narrative		1-22
☐ '413317'		NAA P-51D-30-NA	44	ex N51RT, N555BM, YV-508CP, N555BM, N4409, N6319T,		
	'VF-B'	Mustang		44-74409. Inglewood-built. Acquired 18-11-03.		
				4th FG, 336th FS colours, *The Duck*	[11]	1-22
☐ 44-83868	'N'	Boeing B-17G-95-DL	45	ex Stansted, N5237V, USN PB-1W 77233. Douglas-built		
		Flying Fortress		Acquired 13-10-83. 94th BG, 332nd BS colours		1-22

■ **[1]** Snipe reconstructed by The Vintage Aviator Ltd, with original wings, fuselage, tailplane, and Bentley; exchanged for Farman F-HMFI and Hanriot HD-75. **[2]** Original restoration of L5343 included substantial elements of the centre fuselage of a former RCAF Battle I, believed to be L5340, and other parts from P2183. **[3]** See also Woodford, Gtr Man, for a cockpit replica of 'R5868'. **[4]** Beaufort is a composite: forward fuselage A9-557, rear A9-559, centre section A9-591, all salvaged from Tadji, Papua New Guinea. **[5]** Beaufort and Kittyhawk were part of a package exchange for two 'stock' Spitfire XVIs. **[6]** Kittyhawk restored by RJ Aviation at Hawkins, Texas, and was based on the fuselage of A29-556. A replica starboard wing and tail section were constructed. **[7]** Majority of the Hoverfly is KL110 despite it wearing 'KK995'; the latter was delivered to Cranfield 5-51 and there was probably some exchange of parts. **[8]** Liberator carries 'SNAKE' alongside its serial number, denoting it was destined for Air Command South East Asia and not to be diverted to other taskings or theatres. **[9]** Cadet donated by Bill Walker. **[10]** Tornado F.3 factoids: During its first stint with 43 Sqn, it was deployed to Dhahran for Operation GRANBY, 8-90 to 1-91. ZE887's last flight was 4-3-10, total time 4,966 hours. **[11]** P-51 donated by Bob Tullius of Group 44 Inc, Sebring, Florida.

Hangar 6: The RAF in an Age of Uncertainty: Previously the Milestones of Flight hangar - aka 'The Time Tunnel'

☐ –		V-S Spitfire FSM	03	BAPC.293, built by Concepts and Innovations. Lobby		1-22
☐ XW547	'R'	Blackburn Buccaneer	72	ex Cosford 9169M, Shawbury, 9095M, Gulf Det, 12,		
		S.2B		237 OCU, 208, 12, 216, 12, 237 OCU, 12. Acquired 20-1-93		
				Guinness Girl / Pauline / The Macallan. Pink colours		1-22
☐ XX824	'AD'	SEPECAT Jaguar GR.1	75	ex Cosford, Halton 9019M (10-1-90), Shawbury, 14, 17, 14.		
				Arrived 20-2-18		1-22
☐ ZA457	'AJ-J'	Panavia Tornado GR.1	83	ex St Athan, 2, 617, RAF Gulf Det, 17, 15, 9, 617, 9, TOEU.		
				Acquired 28-7-03		1-22
☐ ZG477		BAe/McDD Harrier GR.9A	90	ex Cosford, Cottesmore, 1, 4, 800, QinetiQ, GR.7/A,		
				3, 1, 3, 4. Acquired 19-12-01, arrived 21-2-18.		
				'1969-2010' colours	[1]	1-22
☐ ZH588		Eurofighter Typhoon DA2	94	ex Brize Norton, Coningsby, Warton, BAE Systems.		
				Acquired 22-1-08	[2]	1-22

☐	64-0553	Lockheed WC-130E	64	ex Pima, Davis-Monthan 53rd WRS, 815th TAS, 53rd WRS, 54th WRS, C-130A. Cockpit. Arrived 14-6-18.	[3]	1-22
☐	83-24104	BV CH-47D Chinook	84	ex Boeing, CH-47A, 190th Av Co, Vietnam 1966-1971, US Army. Fuselage. Acquired 12-1-07. 18 Sqn, RAF c/s		1-22
	'BN'					
☐	03-33119	General Atomics MQ-1B Predator	05	ex USAF, deployments: Kuwait/Iraq (2005-2012), Djibouti (2012), 15th RS. Last flown 13-1-16. Acquired 13-4-18	[4]	1-22

■ **[1]** GR.9 factoids; Operation WARDEN, Turkey, 1993-1994; Operation ALLIED FORCE, Gioia del Colle, Italy, 1999; Operation HERRICK, Afghanistan, 2008-2009. Made final departure from HMS *Ark Royal* 24-11-10 and took part in the 'Farewell to Harrier' formation 15-12-10. Completed 4,191 flight hours and 3,969 landings. **[2]** DA2 data: First flown at Warton, Lancs, 14-8-93; last flight into Coningsby, Lincs, 29-1-07 for spares. **[3]** Herk on loan from the Pima Air and Space Museum, Tucson, Arizona. **[4]** General Atomics MQ-1B Predator, on loan from the National Museum of the USAF

Locally: The Canberra cockpit was virtually auctioned on 9th March 2021 – outcome unknown.

| ☐ | WJ731 | EE Canberra B.2T | 53 | ex Dunstable, Willington, Wyton, Wyton SF, 231 OCU, 7, 231 OCU, 50, 90. Cockpit, trailer-mounted | 1-21 |

KENLEY AIRFIELD south of Kenley, west of the A22 at Whyteleafe

Kenley Revival Project: The **Kenley Airfield Friends Group** continues to refine the site, working on the remaining blast pens, rifle range and the fuel depot. ◆ *Not yet open to the public, occasional special events.* | **www.kafg.org.uk**

KINGSTON-UPON-THAMES

Kingston University: School of Engineering, Roehampton Vale, Friars Avenue. The campus boasts the Learjet Lab and the Hawker Wing. ◆ *By prior arrangement* only | **www.kingston.ac.uk**

| ☐ | - | HSA HS.146 | ~ | cockpit, two fuselage sections | 12-14 |
| ☐ | N121EL | Learjet 25 | ~ | ex N121GL, N82UH, N10BF, N102PS, N671WM, N846HC, N846GA | 10-21 |

Also: A Hunter cockpit is *thought* to be extant in the general area.

| ☐ | XG209 | '66' Hawker Hunter F.6 | 56 | ex Chelmsford, Stock, Halton, Cranwell, Halton 8709M (17-11-81), 12 DFLS, 111, 14. Cockpit | 1-14 |

LONDON HEATHROW AIRPORT

British Airways Heritage Collection - Speedbird Centre:
◆ *By prior arrangement* only | *Waterside (HDGA), PO Box 365, Harmondsworth, UB7 0GB* | **020 8562 5777** | **email** via website | **www.britishairways.com/travel/museum-collection**

BA Engineering Base: Two decades on and still no 'plan' for what to do with the hot-rod.

| ☐ | G-BOAB | BAC/Sud Concorde 102 | 76 | ex BA, G-N94AB. CoA 19-9-01, de-reg 4-5-04 | [1] | 1-22 |

■ **[1]** *Alpha-Bravo* factoids: Withdrawn from BA service 15th August 2000, total hours 22,297, landings 7,810.

LONDON MEMORIALS

Memorials are not generally part of the remit of *W&R*, but those of national status escape that rubric. The **Bomber Command Memorial** at Green Park, Hyde Park Corner: seven statues provide a moving tribute to the 55,573 aircrew that perished during World War Two. **www.rafbf.org/bomber-command-memorial** The **Battle of Britain Memorial** on the Embankment, opposite the London 'Eye': Paul Day's dramatic - and uniquely at 'people level' - diorama **www.bbm.org.uk** The **Royal Air Force Church St Clement Danes** at Temple Bar Gate, fire-bombed by the Luftwaffe on 10th March 1941 and re-consecrated in 1958. **www.raf.mod.uk**

NORTHOLT AIRFIELD on the A4180 northwest of Northolt

RAF Northolt:

☐	'L1684'	Hawker Hurricane FSM	89	BAPC.219, ex 'L1710', Biggin Hill. Northolt Stn Flt c/s	7-19
☐	'MH314' 'SZ-G'	V-S Spitfire FSM	89	BAPC.221, ex 'EN526', 'MH777' 'RF-N'. 316 Sqn colours	9-20
☐	ZD621	HSA HS.125 CC.3	83	ex 32. Last flight 3-15, unveiled 16-7-15	1-22

PUTNEY Flight Experience London had ceased to operate at the site by mid-2020.

SHEPHERD'S BUSH south of the A40, west of the A3220
KidZania: An educational centre with the spine-chilling catch-line 'An indoor city, run by kids', has a genuine A319 cockpit; identity now confirmed. ◆ *In the Westfield Centre, Ariel Way, W12 7SL* | **www.kidzania.co.uk**

❏ EI-DFA	Airbus A319-200	00	ex Kemble, D-ANDI, F-WQQG, OO-SSJ. Hamburg-built. Last flight 15-1-13. BA c/s. Forward fuselage, arr 4-10-14 [1]	12-19

SIDCUP on the A271, southeast London
Lost Island Encounter | World of Golf: *W&R27* (p160) wrote out the Cherokee languishing on 'Manuwago Island' a in a 'crashed' pose - not so, it limps on. ◆ *Off the A20 to the south of the town* | **www.worldofgolf.co.uk**

❏ G-BOSU	Piper Cherokee 140	73	ex N55635. Crashed 6-06, de-reg 12-7-07. Zebra stripes	9-21

SOUTH KENSINGTON on the A4 west of Westminster
Science Museum: The **Flight Gallery** holds some of the UK's most iconic airframes. The engine 'stacks' are a work of art, allowing close inspection of an incredible array of powerplants, including the original Whittle unit that was fitted to W4041/G when 'Gerry' Sayer first flew it at Cranwell on 15th May 1941.

On the lower floor is the **Making of the Modern World** exhibition. Among the treasures is Stephenson's Rocket locomotive. Aircraft in this exhibition are marked #. The **Winton Gallery** is devoted to the story of mathematics and containing the long reclusive Gugnunc.

The 'large object' store is at **Wroughton**, Wilts. Other ScM airframes can be found at: **Bristol**, Glos ('Flea' G-AEHM), **Hendon**, Gtr Lon (Clarke Chanute); **London Colney**, Herts (C.24 G-ABLM), **Southampton**, Hampshire (Sandringham VH-BRC) **Yeovilton**, Somerset (Concorde G-BSST, Ohka, Vampire LZ551). The **Science and Industry Museum, Manchester**, is part of the National Museum of Science and Industry group: refer there for the dissolution of the aviation section.
◆ *Exhibition Road, SW7 2DD* | **033 0058 0058** | **email** via website | **www.sciencemuseum.org.uk**

❏ G-EBIB	Royal Aircraft Factory SE.5a	1918	ex 'F939', Hendon, Savage Skywriting G-EBIB, F937, 84 Sqn. Wolseley-built. CoA 6-6-35, de-reg 1-12-46. Acquired 24-7-39		1-22
❏ G-AAAH	DH Moth	28	CoA 23-12-30, de-reg 12-31. *Jason*. Acquired 21-1-31 Amy Johnson's Australian flight machine, 5-30	[1]	1-22
❏ G-AACN	HP Gugnunc	29	ex Wroughton, Hayes, Sydenham (London), West Byfleet, K1908 RAE. De-reg 12-30. Acquired 7-34. Unveiled 8-12-16. Winton Gallery		1-22
❏ G-ASSM	HSA HS.125-1/522	65	ex Wroughton, Chester, Southampton, 5N-AMK, G-ASSM. Acquired 16-3-89	[2]	1-22
❏ G-AZPH	Pitts S-1S	70	ex Meppershall, Chessington, N11CB. Damaged 10-5-91, de-reg 8-1-97. Acquired 10-91. *Neil Williams*	[3]	1-22
❏ DFY	Schempp-Hirth Cirrus	c75	BGA.2091, ex Army Gliding Assoc. Acquired 1992		1-22
❏ –	Frost Ornithopter	1902	wings, flapping mechanism etc. Acquired 1925	[4]	1-22
❏ –	Roe Triplane	1909	BAPC.50, ex Newton Heath. Last flown 10-09. Acq 1925	[5]	1-22
❏ –	Blériot XI	1909	BAPC.429, cockpit. Acquired 1920	[6]	1-22
❏ –	JAP-Harding Mono	1910	BAPC.54, Blériot-based, presented by JAP Ltd in 1930		1-22
❏ –	Antoinette Monoplane	1910	BAPC.55, ex Brough, Colwyn Bay. Acquired 1926. Minus starboard wing, port wing uncovered	[7]	1-22
❏ –	Vickers Vimy IV	1918	BAPC.51, Alcock and Brown's transatlantic machine Acquired 15-12-19. Starboard fuselage uncovered		1-22
❏ –	Wright Flyer replica	48	BAPC.53, Hatfield-built. Acquired 1948		1-22
❏ –	Lilienthal replica	76	BAPC.124, built for the museum	[8]	1-22
❏ NC5171N	Lockheed 10A Electra	35	ex Wroughton, G-LIOA (de-reg 26-4-02), N5171N, NC243 Boston-Maine AW, N14959 Eastern. Acquired 21-6-82	#	1-22
❏ 304	Cody Military Biplane	1912	BAPC.62, ex Farnborough, 4 Squadron, wrecked 31-3-13. Handed over to the museum 26-11-1913		1-22
❏ D7560	Avro 504K	1918	ex M Wallop, S' Kensington, Sydenham (London), West Byfleet, Hull, Waddon, 3 TDS. Acquired 22-1-20	#	1-22
❏ J8067	Hill Pterodactyl I	25	ex Yeovil, Sydenham (London), West Byfleet, Farnborough, RAE, Westland, RAE. Acquired 1951. Stbd wing uncovered		1-22
❏ L1592 'KW-Z'	Hawker Hurricane I	38	ex 9 PAFU, 5 PAFU, 9 AOS, SDF, 615, 43, 17, 43, 17, 56. Acquired 16-12-54. 615 Sqn colours		1-22
❏ P9444 'RN-D'	V-S Spitfire Ia	40	ex Sydenham (London), 53 OTU, 61 OTU, 58 OTU, 72. SOC 10-8-44. Acquired 16-12-54. 72 colours		1-22

☐ S1595	'1'	Supermarine S.6B	31	ex RAFHSF. Acquired 18-4-32. Schneider winner 1931	[9]	1-22
☐ W4041/G		Gloster E28/39	41	ex RAE, Gloster. Acquired 28-4-46	[10]	1-22
☐ AP507	'KX-P'	Cierva C.30A Rota	34	ex Halton, Sydenham (London), 76 MU, 5 MU, 529,		
				1448 Flt, Duxford Calibration Flt, RAE, G-ACWP (de-reg		
				1-6-40). Avro-built. Acquired 24-5-46. 529 Sqn colours		1-22
☐ XG900		Short SC.1	57	ex Wroughton, Yeovilton, Wroughton, Hayes,		
				S' Kensington, RAE Bedford. Acquired 22-6-71	#	1-22
☐ XJ314		R-R Thrust Measuring Rig	53	ex Wroughton, Yeovilton, East Fortune, Strathallan, Hayes,		
		'Flying Bedstead'		S' Kensington, crashed 16-9-57, RAE Bedford and F'boro,		
				Rolls-Royce. Acquired 9-1-61	# [11]	1-22
☐ XN344		Saro Skeeter AOP.12	60	ex M Wallop 8018M, 654, 652. SOC 27-5-68		1-22
☐ XP831		Hawker P.1127	60	ex Hendon 8406M, RAE Bedford, Dunsfold. Arr 31-5-92	[12]	1-22
☐ –		Short Bros gas balloon	1910	basket. Acquired c1912		1-22
☐ –		Balloon Factory Airship	1910	BAPC.430, No.17, Beta II, gondola. Acquired c1917		1-22
☐ –	'448'	Douglas Dakota 4	44	ex Ottawa, RCAF, KN448, 436, 10, USAAF C-47B-30-DK		
				44-76586. Oklahoma City-built. Acquired 1976. Cockpit		1-22
☐ 210/16		Fokker E.III	1916	BAPC.56, captured 1-4-16 and allocated XG4.		
				Acquired 27-2-18. Stripped airframe	[13]	1-22
☐ 191316	'6'	Me 163B-1a Komet	43	ex Halton, 3 MU, 47 MU, 6 MU, Farnborough, Husum,		
				II/JG.400. Acquired 1958		1-22
☐ 442795		Fieseler Fi 103A-1 (V-1)	44	BAPC.199, sectioned		1-22

■ **[1]** There are replicas of *Jason* at Hawkinge, Kent, Kingston upon Hull, E Yorks, and Dumfries, Scotland. **[2]** HS.125 wears UK markings, these were cancelled when it was exported to Nigeria, 28-5-80. Upon return to the UK, it was not restored to the UK register. **[3]** Pitts was flown by the aerobatic master, Neil Williams, and in his honour is displayed *inverted*. **[4]** Second machine built by E P Frost, 3hp engine, wings covered with artificial feathers; there is evidence of 'flight'. First example was presented to Richard Shuttleworth in 1925 - assumed broken up. **[5]** Alliott Verdun Roe made the first sustained flight by a British national in a British designed and built aeroplane 23-7-09 at Lea Marshes. **[6]** This Blériot was the first aircraft to fly the Irish Sea 22-4-12 - Denys Corbett Wilson piloting. **[7]** Almost certainly the Antoinette owned by North Wales-based Vivian Hewitt. Co-incidentally, Hewitt was *second* across the Irish Sea, on 26-4-12 in a Blériot. Robert Blackburn - aviation pioneer and founder of the company that carried his name, bought the Antoinette for £60 in 1916 and kept it at Brough until presenting it to the museum. **[8]** Lilienthal original held at Wroughton, Wilts. **[9]** S1595, piloted by Flt Lt J Boothman at Calshot, 13-9-31 secured the Schneider Trophy for the UK at 340.05mph. **[10]** First British jet, first flew at Cranwell 15-5-41, pilot P E G 'Gerry' Sayer. **[11]** The official name is the Rolls-Royce Thrust Measuring Rig, but it is universally known as the 'Flying Bedstead'. **[12]** P.1127 prototype - first tethered hover 21-10-60 - on loan from the RAF Museum. **[13]** The 'Eindecker' was being ferried from Valenciennes to Wasquehal to start its operational career when it force-landed behind the lines. It was evaluated at Upavon and retrospectively given the captured aircraft serial XG4, but probably never wore it.

Andrew Martin International: The famous Knightsbridge store. **www.andrewmartin.co.uk**

☐ XS100		Folland Gnat T.1	64	ex Fyfield, Hurn, Ipswich, Halton 8561M (14-11-77), 4 FTS.		
				Forward fuselage, stored, off-site	[1]	1-18

■ **[1]** The remainder of XS100 was at North Weald, Essex, by 3-13 and still there 2021.

SOUTH LAMBETH on the A3203 east of Lambeth Palace

Imperial War Museum London: Runs a series of sites. From a *W&R* point of view the other dominant one is Duxford, Cambs, but there is also IWM North at Manchester, Gtr Man. For completeness, there are two other London-based sites: HMS *Belfast* and the Churchill War Rooms - both brilliant venues.

◆ *Lambeth Road, SE1 6HZ* | Contacts appear to centralised... **0207 416 5000** | email via website – be warned, there's a four-section form to fill in! | **www.iwm.org.uk**

☐ N6812		Sopwith 2F1 Camel	1918	ex Duxford, South Lambeth, 'F3043', Yeovilton, Honington,		
				Cardington, South Kensington (store), South Lambeth.		
				Beardmore-built. Acquired 1920, returned by 7-14	[1]	1-22
☐ R6915		V-S Spitfire I	40	ex Duxford, South Lambeth, Cardiff, RNDU, 57 OTU,		
				61 OTU, 609. SOC 21-6-47. Arrived 15-1-14		1-22
☐ DV372		Avro Lancaster I	43	ex Duxford, South Lambeth, Croydon, 1651 CU, 467.		
	'POF'			SOC 4-1-45. Acquired 1960. Metropolitan-Vickers built.		
				Old Fred. Cockpit		1-22
☐ ZD461	'51A'	BAe/McDD Harrier GR.9A	89	ex Duxford, Cottesmore, 4, 20, GR.7, 1. Damaged 26-1-10,		
				SOC 14-12-10. Acquired 14-3-12, arrived 2-12-13		1-22
☐ 477663		Fieseler Fi 103F-1 (V-1)	44	BAPC.198, ex Duxford, South Lambeth.		
				World War Two and Holocaust gallery		1-22

☐ 3685		Mitsubishi A6M3 *Zeke*	c43	ex Duxford (arrived 1986), Boise, USA, Taroa,	
	'Y2-176'			Marshall Islands. Arrived by 7-14	1-22
☐ –		Yokosuka Ohka 11	45	BAPC.159, ex Duxford, Chattenden. Acquired 4-11.	
				Arrived 2-3-20, 'hung' 6-3-20	[2] 1-22

■ **[1]** Flown by Lt S D Culley off a lighter towed by HMS *Redoubt* on 11-8-18 to intercept, and shoot down, the Zeppelin L53. **[2]** Restoration of the Ohka revealed it to be composite, from at least two examples. The fuselage bears the number '1100' while the nose/warhead section carries '1174'.

UPMINSTER Last noted in August 2017, the anonymous Jetstream fuselage has been deleted.

UXBRIDGE on the A4020 south of the town
Battle of Britain Bunker and Visitor Centre: Guided tours of 11 Group's command bunker, 60ft below ground level and in use from 1939 to 1958, are available by prior booking *only*.
◆ **01895 238154 | bunker@hillingdon.gov.uk | www.battleofbritainbunker.co.uk**

☐ 'L1035'	'SH-D'	V-S Spitfire FSM	~	BAPC.500. GB Replicas-built. 64 Sqn colours	1-22
☐ 'P3873'	'YO-H'	Hawker Hurricane FSM	~	BAPC.499. GB Replicas-built. 401 Sqn colours	1-22
☐ 'P3901'	'RF-E'	Hawker Hurricane FSM	10	BAPC.475. GB Replicas-built. 303 Sqn colours, outside	1-22
☐ 'BS239'	'SH-V'	V-S Spitfire FSM	10	BAPC.222. GB Replica-built. 64 Sqn colours, outside	1-22

WESTMINSTER on the A202, near Vauxhall Bridge
London Film Museum: Potter, Harry Potter has usurped Bond, James Bond. Wallis 'G-ARZB' (G-AVDH) *Little Nellie* returned to Shuttleworth, Beds; the Bede BD-5J is unaccounted for.

GREATER MANCHESTER
*Includes the unitary authorities of Bolton, Bury, Manchester, Oldham, Rochdale, Salford,
Stockport, Tameside, Trafford and Wigan*

APPELY BRIDGE on a minor road north of the A5209, west of the M6
Charity Farm: Camping and glamping site. ◆ *By prior arrangement* only | www.charityfarm.co.uk

| ☐- G-BVKB* | | Boeing 737-59D | 94 | ex Bruntingthorpe, British Midland. Last flight 23-5-13, | |
| | | | | de-reg 19-7-13. Forward fuselage | 12-20 |

ASHTON-UNDER-LYNE on the A635 east of Manchester
No.247 Squadron Air Cadets: Took on a pair of 'JP' cockpits.

☐ XM474*		Hunting Jet Provost T.3	60	ex South Reddish, Levenshulme, 8121M (15-12-70),	
				Firbeck, Heaton Chapel, Warrington, Shrewsbury,	
				Shawbury, 6 FTS, CFS. Cockpit, first noted 12-18	12-18
☐ XN466*	'29'	Hunting Jet Provost T.3A	60	ex Manchester, Radcliffe, 1 FTS, 7 FTS, 1 FTS.	
				Crashed 29-1-63. Cockpit	12-18

BOLTON
Steak Out: Across the fuselage is the legend 'Steaks-on-a-Plane', a pun based on the puerile 2006 movie *Snakes on a Plane*. The steak house in Deane Road looks to be much more entertaining than the film. **Facebook** and the usual suspects

| ☐ VP-BRU | | Boeing 737-500 | 91 | ex Kemble, Yamal Airlines, F-GJNA. Last flight 6-10-14. | |
| | | | | Arrived 18-9-15. Forward fuselage | 10-21 |

LEVENSHULME on the A6 southeast of Manchester
No.1940 Squadron Air Cadets: St Oswald's Road. With nothing known to the contrary, the Chipmunk is *thought* to live on.

☐ WG418		DHC Chipmunk T.10	51	ex 8209M (4-8-72), Woodvale, Hamble, Jever SF, London	
	G-ATDY			UAS, G-ATDY (de-reg 19-1-68), 61 GCF, Queen's UAS,	
				London UAS, 3 BFTS, 16 RFS	1-06

MANCHESTER

Imperial War Museum North: The building is designed to represent a shattered globe, and three 'shards' of this 'Air', 'Earth' and 'Water'. IWM, of course, runs a series of sites: from a *W&R* point of view the two dominant ones are Duxford, Cambs, and South Lambeth, Gtr Lon.

◆ *The Quays, Trafford Wharf Road, M17 1TZ* | **0207 416 5000** | email *via website* | **www.iwm.org.uk**

❑ 159233   'CG' HS AV-8A Harrier   74 ex Yeovilton, VMA-231, USMC   1-22

Science and Industry Museum: Part of the National Museum of Science and Industry, headed by the Science Museum (ScM) - see under South Kensington, Gtr London, and Wroughton, Wiltshire. **www.scienceandindustrymuseum.org.uk**

The inevitable was announced on 14th July 2021 as the Science and Industry Museum washed its hands of the Lower Campfield market hall that served as an aviation museum since 1983. Science and Industry Museum Director, Sally Macdonald, lamented: "The decision to vacate our lease has not been easy but it's the right thing to do for our visitors, the building and the city. ...We have just completed a £5 million new Special Exhibitions Gallery... and we are investing £11.3 million in our iconic Power Hall, due to reopen in 2023. We are also undertaking repairs valued at over £3 million to the 1830 [railway] station and 1830 warehouse. As a charity we have invested significant resource [sic] to maintain and repair the Air and Space Hall since we have taken on its stewardship [in 2012] however historic buildings do have a complexity of issues that date back many decades. The repair and investment work required to bring this beautiful building back to life is substantial, the space presents real challenges in the sustainable display of historic objects and ultimately, it is the responsible thing to now pass the building back to Manchester City Council, ready for its next chapter."

Essentially the museum had inherited 'somebody else's' building full of 'other people's airframes' and could not justify the restoration costs. While the machines were of great regional significance and some of national importance, the Science Museum's contribution to aviation heritage is to be found in the 'crown jewels' at South Kensington. Hooton Park, Cheshire-based The Aeroplane Collection (TAC), a major benefactor from 1983, is reported to have had confirmation of the closure days before the press release went out. The Science Museum funded the removal of TAC's loaned airframes.

See under Hendon, Gtr Lon, for additional comments on the RAF Museum's 'Manchester' airframes.

Disposals: 'Flea' 'G-ADYO', Bensen G-APUD and Roe Triplane BAPC.6 were all repatriated to TAC, at Hooton Park, in late 11-21 and followed in December by Avian G-EBZM and Rapide G-ADAH; Avro 504K G-ABAA to Stow Maries, Essex, on 20-1-22; Trident cockpit G-AWZP to London Colney, Herts, due in 1-22; Rallye G-AYTA to Fishburn, D&C, by 12-21; Pegasus G-BYMT to St Athan, Wales, 30-10-21; EE P.1A WG763 and Avro 707A WZ736 Old Sarum, Wilts, 31-1/1-2-22; Shackleton AEW.2 WR960 to Woodford, Gtr Man, 17-1-22; Belvedere HC.1 XG454 to Weston-super-Mare, Somerset, 1-22; Ohka 11 997 moved to Cosford, Shropshire, by 10-20, ultimately bound for the USA. As *W&R* went to press the following were unaccounted for: Colt 56 G-BLKU - presumed returned to the British Balloon Museum; Mainair Tri-Flyer G-MJXE; Eon 460 BQT / BGA.1156; Volmer BAPC.175; Hiway BAPC.251; Flexiform BAPC.252; anonymous Skyhook Safari.

The cockpit of Shackleton AEW.2 WR960 departing Manchester for Woodford, 17th January 2022.
Charlotte Graham © Science Museum Group

No.**184 Squadron Air Cadets**: 'JP' XN466 moved to Ashton-under-Lyne, Gtr Man.

MANCHESTER AIRPORT or Ringway   EGCC

Runway Visitor Park: Viewing platforms allow great photographic possibilities of the airliners taxying by and the eatery has huge windows allowing all-weather eating and ogling! The RJX is open to inspection all week, the Concorde is pre-bookable.
◆ Wilmslow Old Road, WA15 8XQ | **0161 4893932** | **runwayvisitorpark.enquiries@manairport.co.uk** | **www.runwayvisitorpark.co.uk**

❑ G-AWZK	HS Trident 3B-101	71	ex Heathrow, BA, BEA. CoA 14-10-86, de-reg 29-5-90 Arrived 11-9-05. BEA colours	[1]	1-22
❑ G-BOAC	BAC/Sud Concorde 102	75	ex BA, G-N81AC. CoA 16-5-05, de-reg 4-5-04. Arr 31-10-03	[2]	1-22
❑ G-DMCA	Douglas DC-10-30	80	ex Monarch, N3016Z. CoA 11-3-03, de-reg 3-11-03. Arrived 19-12-03. Cockpit		1-22
❑ G-IRJX	HSA HS.146 RJX 100 T2	01	ex Woodford, G-6-378. de-reg 20-2-03. Arrived 6-2-03	[3]	1-22
❑ XV231	HS Nimrod MR.2	71	ex Kinloss, Kin Wing, Kin & St M Wing, 42, 203, 236 OCU. Arrived 21-4-10		1-22

■ **[1]** For details of the saving of this aircraft at Heathrow see **www.zulukilo.org.uk** **[2]** *Alpha-Charlie* factoids: Withdrawn from BA service 30-8-03, total hours 22,260, landings 7,730. It is on long-term loan from British Airways. **[3]** *Juliet-Xray* first flew 23-9-01 and last flew 6-2-03 when it arrived with a total of 198:23 hours and 135 landings.

Airport: Omitted from *W&R26* onwards, the ATP has been 'resurrected'.

❑ –	BAe ATP	~ ex Woodford, Chadderton. Arrived 8-8-11. Rescue trainer	1-20

■ **[1]** Unfinished fuselage, very likely, c/n 2071.

◆ *On the northern boundary of the airport, close to the threshold of Runway 24 Right, is the HQ of W&R's publishers,* **Crécy Publishing***, and its sister company Airplan Flight Equipment. The well-stocked shop is always well worth a visit!* ◆ *1a Ringway Trading Estate, Shadowmoss Road, Manchester, M222 5LH* | **0161 4990024** | **www.crecy.co.uk**

MANCHESTER CITY (BARTON) AERODROME   EGCB

Manchester Flight Sim: Also has a wholly synthetic A320 sim. ◆ *Prior arrangement* only | **www.manchesterflightsim.com**

❑ N9AC*	Rockwell Commander 112TC	cockpit as sim, first noted 1-21	[1]	12-21

■ **[1]** The Commander's tail has been displayed as a sign, including the legend 'Alpine Commander'.

Also: By March 2021 Tomahawk G-BXZA had moved to Eshott, N&T.

❑ G-GKFC*	Sherwood Ranger	99 CoA 7-4-15	1-22

OLDHAM

Oldham College: Rochdale Road ◆ *By prior arrangement* only | **www.oldham.ac.uk**

❑ EI-CKR	Boeing 737-2K2	95 ex Prestwick, Ryanair, PH-TVR, C-FICP, PH-TVR, D-AJAA, PH-TVR. Last flight 13-11-03. Fuselage	6-19

ROYTON on the A671 north of Oldham

No.**1855 Squadron Air Cadets**: Park Lane. The unit took delivery of Meteor NF(T).14 WS726 on 16th August 1967 and cherished this airframe for 54 years. An auction on behalf of the MoD was staged by RAMCO – "Sustainable, Compliant, Profitable" – in October 2021. WS726 was due to be moved away in December 2021 – no further details.

SALFORD southwest of Manchester

University of Salford, Faculty of Science, Engineering and Environment: Despite the website declaring "Become Unfazed, Unstoppable...." *decades* of enquiries have resulted in no reply, leaving the inevitable: Cessna FRA.150 OO-WIO (last recorded July 2005) and the anonymous Rotec Rally (October 2003) have been deleted. **www.salford.ac.uk**

SOUTH REDDISH 'JP' XM474 moved to Ashton-under-Lyne, Gr Man, by the end of 2018.

STALYBRIDGE on the A6018 east of Ashton-under-Lyne

Top Gun Flight Simulator Centre: Waterloo Court. Last noted in October 2012, stored off-site, Queen Air fuselage G-KEAB, has been deleted, believed scrapped. ◆ *By prior permission* only | **www.topgunflightsimulator.co.uk**

❑ XK637	'56'	DH Vampire T.11	56	ex Millom, Royton, Woodford, Chester, St Athan, 4 FTS, 7 FTS. Hawarden-built. SOC 30-11-67. Cockpit	1-20
❑ '47'	692147	Aero L29 Delfin	~	ex Ashton-under-Lyne, Market Drayton, Romanian AF. Cockpit, simulator	1-20

STOCKPORT on the A6 southeast of Manchester
Roger Light: The collection is *believed* unchanged. Campbell-Bensen B-8 G-ASNY is on loan to the Newark Air Museum at Newark, Notts. ◆ **Private** *collection, by prior arrangement* **only**

❑ G-ATLH	Fewsdale Tiger Mk.1	r65	ex Thornaby-on-Tees. De-reg 10-2-82	9-17
❑ G-AXIY	Bird Gyroplane	r69	de-reg 9-8-91	9-17
❑ G-AXVK	Campbell Cricket	70	CoA 27-4-05, de-reg 15-10-18	9-17
❑ G-AXYZ	WHE Airbuggy	75	CoA 22-12-92, de-reg 8-9-06	9-17
❑ G-AXZB	WHE Airbuggy	80	de-reg 8-9-06	9-17
❑ G-BIFN	Bensen B-8MR	80	de-reg 24-2-10	9-17
❑ G-BJZY	Bensen B-8MV	86	de-reg 8-11-00. D Napier & Sons-built	[1] 9-17

■ [1] The CAA gives G-BJZY's build number as 1103, built by Napier. Turning to Doug Revell's superb *Under B-Conditions* we discover possibilities. Napier assembled/licenced a trio of B-8s at Luton in 1961 under the brand name 'Agricopter'. The second, build number 1102, was G-29-3, becoming G-ATWT. *Assuming* (dangerous!) that someone at Napier was numerate, *Zulu-Yankee* began life in 1961 as G-29-4. Or, it was the first example, G-29-2. Or, for completeness, it may be something else altogether!

Peter and **Mike Rolfe**: Keep their award-winning Sea Venom cockpit in the area. ◆ *By prior permission* **only**

❑ XG692	'668'	DH Sea Venom FAW.22	57	ex Baxterley, Hatton, Alcester, Wellesbourne Mountford, Sydenham, Castlereagh, Sydenham, 750. Hawarden-built. SOC 20-8-70. Cockpit	1-20

WESTHOUGHTON Draken A-011 had left by September 2020 – destination unknown.

WOODFORD between the A5102 and A523 southwest of Poynton
Avro Heritage Museum: Negotiations with the RAF Museum have resulted in the custodianship of the Shackleton from the demise of the aviation hall of Manchester's Science and Industry Museum. This machine first took to the skies from Woodford on 5th February 1954. Initially, it will go into store on the site. There are plans to fund another building, with a maritime patrol theme, including the Nimrod. The collection has a pleasing accessibility policy: as well as the Vulcan, other cockpits can be 'sampled' - best enquire before a visit for availability.
◆ *Chester Road, Woodford, SK7 1AG* | **01625 877534** | **avroheritage@gmail.com** | **www.avroheritagemuseum.co.uk**

❑ G-AGPG		Avro XIX Srs 2	45	ex Liverpool, Market Drayton, Hooton Park, Chadderton, Brenzett, Lympne, Southend, Pye, Ekco, Skyways, Avro. CoA 13-12-71; de-reg 5-11-75. Arrived 5-12-16. Forward fuselage	[1] 1-22
❑ G-CFTF		Roe Triplane I replica	09	ex Bicester, Brooklands, Manchester. De-reg 28-8-16, arrived 16-1-19. Stored	[2] 1-22
❑ G-ORAL		HS HS.748-2A/334	77	ex Speke, Hooton Park, Blackpool, Reed, Emerald, Janes, G-BPDA, G-GLAS, 9Y-TFS, G-11-8. CoA 12-11-07, de-reg 15-6-09. *Paper Plane*. Cockpit. Arrived 8-17, stored	1-22
❑ -		Avro Type F replica	10	BAPC.328, ex Manchester. Roe Heritage Group-built. Arrived 6-3-18	[3] 1-22
❑ 'R5868'	'PO-S'	Avro Lancaster replica	15	BAPC.471, ex Scampton, North Coates. Forward fuselage. Arrived 13-11-17. 467 Sqn colours	[4] 1-22
❑ WK118	'CQ'	EE Canberra TT.18	54	ex Worcester, Stock, Wyton, 100, 7, B.2. 59, 103. Avro-built. Cockpit. Installed 11-8-16	1-22
❑ XM602		Avro Vulcan B.2	63	ex Swinton, Bruntingthorpe, Woodford, St Athan 8771M (16-3-83), 101, Wadd Wing, 35, 230 OCU, Wadd Wing, Cottesmore Wing, 12. Cockpit. Arrived 20-4-13	1-22
❑ XM603		Avro Vulcan B.2	63	ex 44, 101, Wadd Wing, Scampton Wing, 9. Flew in 12-3-82	1-22
❑ XV106		Vickers VC10 C.1K	67	ex Bruntingthorpe, 101, 10. Last flight 17-12-12. Arrived 8-9-16. Cockpit	[5] 1-22
❑ XV235		HS Nimrod MR.2	69	ex Scampton, Kinloss, Kin Wing, Kin & St M Wing, 42, Kinloss, St M, 236 OCU. Forward fuselage. Arrived 8-9-16	1-22

■ **[1]** Among other work, 'Aggie-Paggie' served as the test bed for the E320 weather radar for Concorde. Total time on retirement 1,948 hours. **[2]** Triplane on loan; built by the Roe Heritage Group, on loan from Eric Alliott Verdon-Roe, grandson of 'AV'. Fitted with a 9hp JAP, it commenced flight trials in October 2009, achieving only limited 'hops'. **[3]** On loan from Science and Industry Museum, Manchester. **[4]** Lancaster replica built by Martin Willoughby, using many original parts. It is finished in the colours of 467 Sqn colours, R5868 - see Hendon, Gtr Lon, for the original. Martin's father, Ted, worked as ground crew on the original. Previously on loan from Martin, the replica was acquired by the museum in late 2020. **[5]** On loan from Gary Spoors. The centre fuselage of XV106 is displayed at the South Wales Aviation Museum, St Athan, Wales. If the VC10 seems out of place, BAe Woodford inherited design authority for the tanker programme from Filton after the denationalisation of the consortium in 1986.

Store: *Not* available for inspection.

❏ TX235*	Avro Anson C.19/2	46	ex Hooton Park (temporary), Baginton, Caernarfon, Higher Blagdon, Andover, Shawbury, SCS, FCCS, CTFU, OCTU, 64 GCS, 2 GCS. SOC 11-10-65. Arrived 8-9-20		9-21
❏ WR960*	Avro Shackleton AEW.2	54	ex Manchester, Cosford, 8772M (28-11-82), 8, 205, A&AEE, 210, 42, 228. Arrived 17-1-22	[1]	1-22

■ **[1]** On loan from the RAF Museum.

MERSEYSIDE
Includes the unitary authorities of Knowsley, Liverpool, St Helens, Sefton, and Wirral

---

KNOWSLEY on the B5194, north of J3 on the M57
Delta Force Paintball: At the Safari Park. ◆ *By prior arrangement* **only** | www.paintballgames.co.uk

❏ ZD278	Westland Lynx AH.7	83	ex Upminster, Ipswich, M Wallop	[1]	1-20

■ **[1]** The boom of ZD278 is fitted to XZ613 - see Bedstead, Suffolk.

LIVERPOOL
Crowne Plaza Hotel: With the blessing of the hotel management, the **Speke Aerodrome Heritage Group** (SAHG) nurtures its collection. On the 'old' airport site, the superb hotel is a development of the 1930s terminal building. Sharing the apron is the **Britannia Aircraft Preservation Trust** (BAPT) which continues with the challenging restoration of *Charlie-Fox*. *W&R27* (p167) recorded Rapide FSM 'G-AJCL' as dismantled during 2019: the cockpit section moved to Hooton Park, Cheshire, by August 2021. ◆ *On the A561* | *Occasional special events, otherwise by prior arrangement* **only** | *SAHG:* www.spekeaero.org | *BAPT:* info@bristol-britannia.com | www.bristol-britannia.com

❏ G-AMLZ	Percival Prince 6E	52	ex Haverigg, Caernarfon, Coventry, VR-TBN, Shell G-AMLZ. CoA 18-6-71, de-reg 9-10-84. Arr 23-11-08. Shell c/s	[1]	1-22
❏ G-ANCF	Bristol Britannia 308F	59	ex Kemble, Banwell, Brooklands, Manston, 5Y-AZP, G-ANCF, LV-GJB, LV-PPJ, G-ANCF, G-14-1, G-18-4, N6597C, G-ANCF. CoA 12-1-81, de-reg 21-2-84. Short-built. Arrived 7-3-07. British Eagle colours, *New Frontier*	BAPT	1-22
❏ G-BEJD	HS 748-1/105	61	ex Squires Gate, Emerald, LV-HHE, LV-PUF. CoA 29-3-06, de-reg 8-4-10. Arrived 20-10-11	[2]	1-22
❏ G-JMAC	BAe Jetstream 4100	92	ex Woodford, Prestwick, G-JAMD, G-JXLI. CoA 6-10-97, de-reg 21-5-03. Arrived 29-1-03. *Spirit of Speke*		1-22
❏ G-SEXY	American AA-1 Yankee	70	ex G-AYLM. Damaged 11-2-94, de-reg 15-11-00. Arr 2006		1-22
❏ WH291	Gloster Meteor F.8	51	ex Booker, Lasham, Kemble, 229 OCU, 85, CAW, 257. SOC 10-2-76. Arrived 3-11. 79 Sqn colours	[3]	1-22

■ **[1].** *Lima-Zulu* factoids: last flown 13-11-73, total time 2,858 hours. **[2]** The only Srs 1 (15 built) surviving; so it's the oldest 748 extant; and the only complete civilian 748 preserved in the UK. **[3]** Meteor on loan from Mike Davey - see below and Newark, Notts.

Jordan and **Robbie Burgess:** Are *thought* to *still* keep the award-winning AV-8B locally ◆ *By prior arrangement* **only**

❏ 162730	BAe/McDD AV-8B Harrier II	86	ex Peterborough, Charlwood, St Athan, Wyton, St Athan, USMC VMA-231. *Lucy.* Forward fuselage, trailer-mounted	12-17

Mike Davey - F-4 Phantom Preservation Society: As well as his Meteor at the Crowne Plaza - see above - Mike has other airframes and here serves as a good place under which to list them. FGR.2 XT895 was written out of *W&R16* (p61) as having perished in ballistics trials at PEE Foulness, Essex, in 1997. Its cockpit survived and moved to an Essex-based collector and for two-and-a-bit decades existed under the *W&R* 'radar' - the disposal of Phantoms was supposedly avidly monitored by the US DoD and such possession was best kept covert. In late 2020 XT895 joined Mike's growing phabulous phleet. See also Newark, Notts, for Mike's *other* Phantom. ◆ *Airframes held at dispersed locations,* **not** *available for inspection*

❑ XT895*		McD Phantom FGR.2	68	ex 'Essex', Foulness, Valley 9171M, 74, 228 OCU, 92, 228 OCU, 111, 6, 228 OCU, 6, 228 OCU. Damaged 10-10-92. Cockpit. Arrived by 11-20	[1]	12-20
❑ ZE352	'G'	McD F-4J(UK) Phantom	67	ex Hooton Park, Haverigg, Preston, Hooton Park area, Stock, Foulness, Pendine, Laarbruch 9086M (30-8-84), 74, Wattisham, 74, USN 153783, VX-4, VMFA-333. Cockpit		12-20
❑ -		McD Phantom SIM	~	ex Leuchars. Redifon-built		12-20

■ [1] XT895 was involved in trials over Cardigan Bay, out of Valley, on 10-10-92 - the very last days of RAF Phantoms - when an errant Skyflash missile impacted the starboard intake: leaving a small hole visible to this day. That was sufficient to have it struck off charge and issued to the Valley fire crews.

Liverpool University: Within the campus a former John Lennon Tomahawk *may* still serve as a simulator.

| ❑ G-LFSD | Piper Tomahawk 112 | 82 | ex Liverpool Airport, G-BNPT, G-LFSD, N91522. Cr 9-9-06, CoA 13-7-08, de-reg 26-10-10. Fuselage, simulator | 6-13 |

LIVERPOOL (JOHN LENNON) AIRPORT or Speke - *Above Us Only Sky*   EGGP

The forward fuselage of Cessna 340 'G-ORFS' (EI-CIJ) departed on 28th July 2020.

| ❑ G-BGSH | Piper Tomahawk 112 | 79 | de-reg 31-7-17 | 6-21 |
| ❑ G-BNYK | Piper Tomahawk 112 | 82 | ex N2376V. De-reg 14-12-18. Cockpit | 7-20 |

NEW BRIGHTON on the A554 north of Birkenhead

Fort Perch Rock: Home of the **Warplane Wreck Investigation Group** since 1977. This coastal fort is amazing enough, but WWIG's recovery items, including the 'Luftwaffe over Merseyside' exhibition and a section dedicated to 610 (County of Chester) Squadron are incredible. The Hunter cockpit is expected to have arrived by the time these words are read.

◆ *Marine Promenade, CH45 2JU* | **0797 6282120** | **fortperchrock@gmail.com** | **www.fortperchrock.org**

| ❑ XE584* | | Hawker Hunter FGA.9 | 56 | ex Hooton Park, Woodford, Barton, Chelford, Macclesfield, Bitteswell, G-9-450, 208, 8, 1. SOC 12-2-76. 111 Sqn colours. Cockpit | [1] | due |
| ❑ - | | Hawker Sea Hawk | ~ | BAPC.352, ex Hooton Park, Peasedown St John, Cardiff-Wales. Red scheme. Cockpit | [1] | 1-22 |

■ [1] Both owned by Grahame Sparkes.

WOODVALE AIRFIELD on the A565 north of Formby

RAF Woodvale: A Hawk 'guards' the resident Tutor fleet.

| ❑ XX247 | HS Hawk T.1A | 78 | ex Shawbury, 19, 100, 1 TWU, 2 TWU, 1 TWU. Last flight 7-4-11. SOC 5-12-17. Arrived 27-11-17 | 7-21 |

WEST MIDLANDS

Within the administrative regional county boundaries can be found the unitary authorities of Birmingham, Coventry, Dudley, Sandwell, Solihull, Walsall and Wolverhampton

BIRMINGHAM

Thinktank - Millennium Discovery Centre, the former Birmingham Science Museum.

◆ *Curzon Street, B4 7XG* | **0121 3488000** | **email** via website | **www.thinktank.ac**

❑ 'P3395'	'JX-B'	Hawker Hurricane IV	43	ex Loughborough, 631, 1606 Flt, 137. SOC 8-3-46.	
		KX829		Acquired 1961. 1 Sqn colours	1-22
❑ ML427	'HK-A'	V-S Spitfire IX	44	ex Castle Bromwich, St Athan, South Marston, Millfield, Hucknall, 6457M (15-10-47), FLS, 3501 SU. CBAF-built. Acquired 1958. Fighter Leaders School colours	1-22

Also: A Hunter has been mounted on a plinth outside **Specialist Computer Centres Technology Campus** at the junction of Westwood Avenue and Battery Way in Tyseley.

| ❑ WT723* | '692' | Hawker Hunter | 55 | ex St Athan, 'XG164', N723WT, A2616 [3] (19-3-93) | |
| | | PR.11 | G-PRII | Culdrose, WT723, FRADU, 764, GA.11, 764, F.4 14. CoA 9-6-16, de-reg 8-2-21. Plinth-mounted by 9-21 | 1-22 |

BRIERLEY HILL on the A461 south west of Dudley

Mason Metals: ◆ _By prior arrangement_ **only** | **www.masonmetals.co.uk**

❑ XS643	HS Andover E.3A	67 ex Stock, Manston 9278M, Boscombe Down, 32, A&AEE, 115, 84. Cockpit. First noted 3-16	12-19

COVENTRY

Coventry University: The faculty of Engineering and Computing, Aerospace Workshop in Gulson Road _should_ still have its Harrier. ◆ _By prior arrangement_ **only** | **www.coventry.ac.uk**

❑ XW270	HS Harrier T.4	70 ex Ipswich, Bruntingthorpe, Cranfield, Wittering, 4, 1, 233 OCU, 1, 233 OCU. SOC 10-2-92	[1]	6-17

■ **[1]** Fitted with the wings of XV748 - which is to be found whole at Elvington, N Yorks. The cockpit is fitted out as a flight sim.

Also: The Heath Parasol is at a _private_ location in the area.

❑ G-AFZE	Heath Parasol	39 ex Reigate, Horley. De-reg 1-5-66, restored 17-7-74	8-21

HOCKLEY HEATH east of junction 4, M42, south of Solihull

Delta Force Paintball Solihull: ◆ _By prior arrangement_ **only** | **www.paintballgames.co.uk**

❑ G-SHIP		Piper Aztec 250F	76 ex -?-, Hockley Heath, Coventry, Birmingham, N62490. Crashed 4-12-83, de-reg 13-2-89	1-20
❑ XX739	'I'	SEPECAT Jaguar GR.1	74 ex Upminster, Ipswich, Syerston, Cosford 8902M (27-5-86), Halton, Shawbury, Gib Det, 6, 226 OCU. First noted 12-18	11-21

SOLIHULL

Solihull College: At Woodlands Campus, Auckland Drive, a former FAA Jetstream _should_ still serve.
◆ _By prior arrangement_ **only** | **www.solihull.ac.uk**

❑ XX478	'564'	HP Jetstream T.2	73 ex Ipswich, Culdrose, 750, RAF T.1 CFS, G-AXXT SAL-completed. De-reg 5-12-83, last flown 31-3-11. F/n 5-16	5-16

Also: A local _private_ owner may still have the cockpit of a HS.146 converted into a summerhouse.

❑ HB-IXX	HSA HS.146 RJ100	95 ex Sunderland, Kemble, Swiss, Crossair, G-6-262. Woodford-built. Cockpit	8-17

TETTENHALL south of the A41 northwest of Wolverhampton

Tettenhall Transport Heritage Centre: Based in a former Great Western Railway goods depot, the centre concentrates on the motive transport heritage of Wolverhampton and locality. ◆ _Henwood Road, WV6 9NX._ | **email** via website | **Facebook**

❑ G-MJIA		Flexiform Striker	82 ex Penkridge. CoA 20-9-96, de-reg 5-11-13. First noted 6-12	1-22
❑ G-MMFS		MBA Tiger Cub 440	83 ex Baxterley, Abbots Bromley, Wolverhampton, Otherton. _Black Adder._ CoA 27-7-01, de-reg 11-3-10. Travelling exhibit	1-22
❑ G-MVJM		Microflight Spectrum	88 de-reg 22-8-12. First noted 4-15	1-22
❑ -	'20'	S-D Demoiselle replica	64 BAPC.194, ex Stafford, Wyton, Cardington, Brooklands, Henlow, Gatow. First noted 8-16	1-22
❑ -		Breen hang-glider	~ BAPC.432, ex Stafford. First noted 8-16	[1] 1-22
❑ 'PD685'		Slingsby Cadet TX.1	~ BAPC.355, ex Penkridge, W'hampton, Stoke. Fuselage	[2] 1-22
❑ 'RG907'		Miles Martinet replica	18 BAPC.514. Cockpit	[3] 1-22
❑ WJ576		EE Canberra T.17	53 ex Baxterley, Wolverhampton, Bruntingthorpe, Cardiff, St Athan, 360, _Swifter_ Flight, 231 OCU. HP-built. SOC 9-3-83. Cockpit. Arrived 11-4-15	1-22
❑ WK576		DHC Chipmunk T.10	52 ex W'hampton, Lichfield, 8357M (10-8-73), AOTS, 3/4 CAACU, Cam, Oxf, Lon, Cam, Lon, Cam, Hull, Cam, Birm, Cam UASs, 22 RFS. Cockpit. Arrived 5-14	[4] 1-22
❑ WN516		BP Balliol T.2	53 ex Baxterley, Haverigg, Sunderland, Failsworth, RAFC. Blackburn-built. SOC 26-6-57. Forward fuselage. Arr 11-4-15	1-22
❑ WN534		BP Balliol T.2	54 ex Baxterley, Wolverhampton, Bacup, Salford, Failsworth, Silloth, RAFC. Blackburn-built. SOC 26-6-57. Cockpit	1-22
❑ WT877		Slingsby Cadet TX.3	51 ex Penkridge, W'hampton, Walsall, Swinderby, St Athan GC, Syerston, 621 GS, 625 GS, 643 GS, 22 GS. SOC 21-8-86	1-22

☐ WZ755	FSC	Slingsby Grasshopper TX.1	52	BGA.3481, ex Baxterley, Wolverhampton, Gallows Hill, Brunton, Barnstaple. CoA 30-4-93		1-22
☐ XD445	'51'	DH Vampire T.11	54	ex Baxterley, Abbots Bromley, Hemswell, Cleethorpes, Hatfield, Woodford, Chester, St Athan, 4 FTS, 5 FTS, Bückeburg SF. SOC 18-3-63. Arrived 11-4-15. Cockpit, 79 Sqn colours	[5]	1-22
☐ XP494		Slingsby Grasshopper TX.1	61	ex Baxterley, W'hampton, Rattlesden, Breighton, Stoke, Syerston, Stamford, Cosford, Ratcliffe, Syerston. Stored		1-22

■ [1] Hang-glider of original design, Gerry Breen and Sqn Ldr Dave Willis made the first-ever flights off Ben Nevis, 1973. The RAF Museum was a sponsor of early Breen ventures; hence it came into the collection. [2] Cadet restored to represent an example that served from Walsall with 43 Gliding School. [3] Wooden framed and using many original parts, including canopy. [4] WK576 on loan from 1046 Sqn Air Cadets. [5] Vampire flew in 79 Sqn colours when it served as a 'hack' with the Bückeburg Station Flight.

WILLENHALL on the A454 west of J10 of the M6
Cable and Alloys: Springvale Street. The Lansen was reported to be offered for sale in early 2021.

| ☐ G-BMSG | | SAAB Lansen | 56 | ex Cranfield, Swedish AF, Malmslatt, Fv32028. G-BMSG de-reg 20-6-14. Cockpit, wings and other parts | 1-21 |
| ☐ ZD281 | 'K' | Westland Lynx AH.1 | 83 | ex Fleetlands, M Wallop. Cabin, first noted 1-15 | 1-17 |

NORFOLK

ATTLEBOROUGH on the A11 southwest of Norwich
Dave Pope: Keeps his Raven at a *private* address in the locality.

| ☐ G-MTMK | Southdown Raven X | 87 | ex Heckington. CoA 1-8-02, de-reg 11-5-05. Arrived 19-7-18 | 1-20 |

BIRCHAM NEWTON between the B1153 and B1155 northeast of Docking
RAF Bircham Newton Heritage Centre: The former RAF station is home of the National Construction College East and, thanks to that institution, volunteers have established a tribute to the airfield (1918-1962) and its satellite at Docking.
◆ *Occasional open days: otherwise* group *tours by prior arrangement* | **email** via website | **www.rafbnmp.org.uk**

BODNEY CAMP on the B1108 west of Watton
Army Training Estate East: South of the camp is an extensive training area, centred upon Stanford Water and referred to as STANTA, for Stanford Training Area. See also East Wretham, below.

| ☐ XS872 | Westland Wessex HAS.1 | 65 | ex Wroughton, Farnborough, A2666, Leatherhead, Wroughton, *Eagle* SAR Flt, 706, 820. SOC 18-5-78 | 11-20 |

CANTLEY on the B1140 south of Acle
Great British Aircraft Spares: Bruce Gordon's treasure trove in the locality probably has the widget you've long been looking for. ◆ *Airframes within a private store, by prior application* only | Facebook **@gbspares**

☐ -*		Piper Pawnee	~	ex Enstone. Fuselage frame, stored	[1]	1-22
☐ XD547	'Z'	DH Vampire T.11	54	ex Elgin, Felixkirk, Dumfries, Aberfoyle, Strathallan, Milngavie, Glasgow, CATCS, 8 FTS, 1 RS, 263. Hawarden-built. SOC 22-3-71	[2]	1-22
☐ XH328		DH Vampire T.11	56	ex London Colney, Duxford, Hurn, Cranfield, Hemel Hempstead, Croxley Green, Bushey, Keevil, Exeter, 3 CAACU, 60. Hawarden-built. SOC 22-6-71. Cockpit		1-22

■ [1] Pawnee frame is most likely G-AWFS, crashed 27-4-73, de-reg 15-2-74. [2] XD547 has the wings of XD425 – see Kinloss, Scotland.

CLENCHWARTON on minor roads west of King's Lynn
Along with a huge anchor, the fuselage of a Robin 'guards' the entrance to a farm.

| ☐ G-OCFC* | Robin R2160 | 02 | crashed 27-5-15, de-reg 9-11-16. Fuselage. First noted 12-18 | 6-20 |

COLTISHALL or Scottow Enterprise Park, east of the B1150, north of the village

RAF Station Coltishall Heritage Trust: A project 14 years in the making, the Trust finally opened up within the main guardroom of the former and famous RAF station in the summer of 2021.
◆ *Former Main Guardroom, Building 40, NR10 5FB* | **07933396021** | **rafscht@btinternet.com** | **www.rafscht.co.uk**

Swift Aircraft: As well as developing its own light aircraft, the company supports and overhauls Slingsby T.67s. An unflown example has arrived for engineering development. ◆ *By prior arrangement* **only** | **www.swiftaircraft.com**

❑ G-BYBX*	Slingsby T.67M Firefly	98	ex Teversham, Kirbymoorside. De-reg 29-1-15. Arr 18-12-20	12-20

DEREHAM on the A47 west of Norwich

The Moth Minors are at a *private* workshop in the *general* area. At another equally *private* venue in the locality is a Pilatus.

❑ G-AFNI*	DH Moth Minor	39	ex Stalbridge, Woodley, W7972 100 GCF, Foulsham SF, 241, G-AFNI. CoA 26-5-67	6-20
❑ G-AFOB*	DH Moth Minor	39	ex Dorchester, Old Warden, Duxford, X5117 10 OAFU, St Andrews UAS, 513, G-AFOB. CoA 11-5-93	6-20
❑ A-806*	Pilatus P.3-03	G-BTLL 56	ex Lashenden, Swiss Air Force. CoA 23-6-94	9-20

EASTON on the A47 west of Norwich

Congo Rapids Crazy Golf: Within the Norwich Family Golf Centre is a zebra-striped KR-2 | **www.congorapids.co.uk**

❑ G-WYNN	Rand KR-2	95	de-reg 17-7-04	10-20

EAST WRETHAM east of the A1075 north of Thetford

Thorpe Camp: See also the 'northern' end of this area, listed under Bodney Camp, Norfolk.

❑ XM386	'08'	Hunting Jet Provost T.3	59	ex St Athan, Halton 8076M (2-2-70), Shawbury, 2 FTS, CFS [1]	5-19
❑ XT643		Westland Scout AH.1	66	ex Waterbeach, Wroughton, 660, 661	5-19

■ [1] The wings alongside the fuselage of XM386 are from XM404 - see Bournemouth, Dorset.

FORNCETT ST PETER west of the A140 and Long Stratton

Norfolk Tank Museum: Has an impressive collection of 'Cold War' era hardware; some of it 'in steam'.
◆ *Station Road, NR16 1HZ* | **01508 532650** | **info@norfolktankmuseum.co.uk** | **www.norfolktankmuseum.co.uk**

❑ XL739	Saro Skeeter AOP.12	58	ex Wattisham, Detmold, 15/19 Hussars, 1 Wing, 651, A&AEE, BATUS, AAEE. Stored. Arrived circa 2011	7-21

FRETTENHAM east of the A140, southwest of Coltishall

New Farm Aviation Heritage Group: Material held includes the remains of 458th BG, 754th BS B-24H Liberator 42-50404 *Belle of Boston* which crashed on take-off from Horsham St Faith (Norwich Airport) on 8th May 1944.
◆ *Buxton Road, NR12 7NG. Regular open days, otherwise by appointment* | Facebook: **new farm aviation heritage group**

GREAT YARMOUTH Last noted in September 2016, Cessna 150 G-BPRO has been deleted.

HARDWICK or Shelton Common, east of the A140, west of Bungay

93rd Bomb Group Museum: An incredible museum set in Nissen (sorry, Quonset) huts and the all-important Mess (sorry, that would be Chow) Hall on the former Station 104's Communal Site A. The website is a delight! ◆ *Denton Road / Topcroft Street, NR35 2BA. Regular open days, or by prior arrangement* | **email** via Facebook | **www.93rd-bg-museum.org**

HETHEL north of the B1135, east of Wymondham

389th Bomb Group Memorial Exhibition and **Home for the 466th BG Attlebridge**: As well as two recently inaugurated Nissen huts, Station 114's wartime chapel is a unique element of Eighth Air Force history.
◆ *Potash Lane, NR14 8EY. Regular open days, or by prior arrangement* | **www.hethel389th.wordpress.com**

KING'S LYNN

By December 2020 a Tornado cockpit had appeared at a *private* house. See under Blackpool, Lancs, for a candidate.

❑ -*	Panavia Tornado EMU / FSM	~	cockpit – see above	12-20

LANGHAM south of Stiffkey, between Cockthorpe and Langham

Langham Dome: Announcing itself as "small building, big story', the rare anti-aircraft gunnery trainer dome includes exhibitions on the former airfield's heritage, gunnery training and more. Please note: the Spitfire comes down off its plinth and 'hibernates' for the winter.
◆ *Langham Road, Cockthorne, NR25 7BP* | **01328 830169** | **admin@langhamdome.org** | **www.langhamdome.org**
❑ -*   V-S Spitfire FSM   ~ 'The Silver Spitfire', pole-mounted, unveiled 21-8-20   1-22

LONG STRATTON on the A140 south of Norwich

Stratton Motor Company: Over the years the company has supplied cars for the Bond, James Bond films.
◆ *By appointment* only | **www.strattonmotorcompany.com**
❑ 'F-ZWWW'   Eurocopter Tiger FSM   94   ex Leavesden, *GoldenEye* (1995). First noted 5-14   8-18

MARHAM AIRFIELD south of the A47 west of Swaffham   EGYM

Marham Aviation Heritage Centre: within the former station church. The cockpits are used for special occasions and are not generally accessible. ◆ *By appointment* only | **marham.aviation.heritage@gmail.com**
❑ WH850   EE Canberra T.4   54   ex Narborough, Winthorpe, Barton, Chelford, Samlesbury,
                                             St Athan, Laarbruch SF, Wildenrath SF, 14, 88, Marham SF.
                                             SOC 26-11-81. Cockpit. Arrived 10-2-16   11-20
❑ XD857   Vickers Valiant BK.1   57   ex Flixton, Manston, Rayleigh, Foulness, 49. SOC 6-3-65.
                                             Arrived 5-5-17. Flightdeck   [1] 11-20
❑ XL160   HP Victor K.2   61   ex Flixton, Walpole, Marham 8910M (2-7-86), 57, 55, 57,
                                             55, Witt Wing, 100, Rolls-Royce. Cockpit. Arrived 27-4-18   [1] 11-20
■ [1] On loan from Garry O'Keefe.

RAF Marham: Victor K.2 XH673 bowed to the inevitable and was scrapped during November 2020. It seems the cockpit did not survive. Tornado GR.4 ZA463 had migrated to Lossiemouth, Scotland, by March 2019.
❑ XH169   EE Canberra PR.9   60   ex 39, 1 PRU, 39, 58. Short-built. *End of an Era*.
                                             Unveiled 20-11-07, displayed   11-20
❑ ZA407   Panavia Tornado GR.1   83   ex 9336M, 617, TWCU. Last flown 22-11-01.
                                             Removed from its plinth 3-3-20   3-20
❑ ZA614   '076'   Panavia Tornado GR.4   82   ex 9, GR.1, 15.Unveiled on the 'gate' 4-8-21   11-21
❑ ZD744*   '092'   Panavia Tornado GR.4   84   ex GR.1, 14. Instructional. First noted 7-19   [1]   1-21
❑ ZG791*   '137'   Panavia Tornado GR.4   92   ex trials fleet, GR.1. Instructional. First noted 3-19   11-20
■ [1] W&R27 erroneously moved ZD744 to Honington.

NEATISHEAD east of the A1151, north of Hoveton, near Horning

RAF Radar Museum Norfolk: Dedicated to every aspect of radar, air defence and battle management and housed in the original 1942 Operations Building, exhibits include a Battle of Britain 'Ops' Filter Room, a 'Cold War' era 'Ops' Room and a ROC Field Post. Don't miss the 'Crumbs' cafe!
◆ *Off the A1062, Birds Lane, NR12 8YB* | **01692 631485** | **manager@radarmuseum.co.uk** | **www.radarmuseum.co.uk**
❑ XX979   SEPECAT Jaguar GR.1A   75   ex Coltishall 9306M, St Athan, DTEO, A&AEE. Cockpit   1-22
❑ ZE936   Panavia Tornado F.3   88   ex Church Fenton, Bedford, 229 OCU. Arrived 2-8-17
                                             Cockpit   1-22
❑ –   HP Victor SIM   ~ ex Newark, Ashby de Launde, Elvington, Marham,
                                             Warton. Arrived 5-4-17   [1]   1-22
■ [1] Victor is owned by Geremy Britton / Aircraft Preservation Foundation - see Bridlington, E Yorks

Carl Lamb: Keeps two Lightning cockpits in the locality. ◆ *By prior arrangement* only | **carl.lamb1988@gmail.com**
❑ XN795   EE Lightning F.2A   63   ex Rayleigh, Foulness, RAE, A&AEE, BAC. SOC 10-3-77.
                                             Cockpit   9-20
❑ XS421   EE Lightning T.5   65   ex Rayleigh, Foulness, RAE, 23, 111, 226 OCU.
                                             SOC 22-10-75. Cockpit   9-20

NORWICH

Second Air Division Memorial Library: Plenty of memorabilia on show, along with the amazing 'Friendly Invasion' mural, all dedicated to the division's B-24 Liberator-equipped units.
◆ *The Forum, Millennium Plain, NR2 1AW* | **01603 774747** | **americanlibrary@norfolk.gov.uk** | **www.2ndair.org.uk**

County Hall: In Martineau Lane, off the A1054 between Lakenham and Old Lakenham south of the city centre.
☐ XW563   SEPECAT Jaguar S.07   70   ex Coltishall, 8563M (26-1-78), 'XX822', Brüggen.
                                         Spirit of Coltishall. Displayed, plinth-mounted   [1]   6-21
■ **[1]** Composite, based upon the cockpit and forward fuselage of S.07 XW563 which first flew 12-6-70.

Also: Dave Higgins *should* continue to work on a Chipmunk locally; he also owns Whirlwind XJ758 at Welshpool, Wales.
☐ WB560   DHC Chipmunk T.10   50   ex South Molton, Doncaster, Firbeck, Fownhope, St Athan,
                                         Oxford UAS, 242 OCU, 2 SoTT, South Cerney SF, ITS, 7 AEF,
                                         Nott UAS, 4 AEF. Cockpit, composite. Arrived mid-2012   5-16

NORWICH AIRPORT or Horsham St Faith   EGSH

City of Norwich Aviation Museum (CNAM): A new road snaking its way across the northern perimeter has 'severed' the museum from the airport. This meant that the delivery of the RJ85 involved complex 'fence hopping', whereas in bygone years, it was a more straightforward 'roll-in'. (Note: This is the A1270 Broadland Northway: visitor access to the museum is still off the A140 through Horsham St Faith village.)

     The RAF **100 Group Association** bases its exceptional collection at CNAM and the museum has been 'adopted' by the **74 'Tiger' Squadron Association**; the unit was based at Horsham St Faith and nearby Coltishall. Other displays show the history of RAF Horsham St Faith, Bomber Command, the Eighth Air Force, the role of women in aviation and local aviation pioneers; and there is Friendship Tearoom to sample.
◆ *Off the A140, Old Norwich Road, NR10 3JF* | **01603 893080** | **admin@cnam.co.uk** | **www.cnam.org.uk**

☐ G-ASAT		MS Rallye Club	62	ex Defford. CoA 2-8-02, de-reg 18-1-11, arrived 12-6-12	[1] 1-22
☐ G-ASKK		HP Herald 211	63	ex Air UK, PP-ASU, G-ASKK, PI-C910, CF-MCK.	
				CoA 19-5-85, de-reg 29-4-85. Arrived 5-85	1-22
☐ G-AYMO		Piper Aztec 250	65	ex Wellesbourne Mountford, 5Y-ACX, N5845Y.	
				De-reg 27-11-13. Arrived 5-16	1-22
☐ G-BCDN		Fokker Friendship 200	63	ex airport, Air UK, PH-OGA, JA8615, LV-PMR, PH-FDP.	
				CoA 19-7-96, de-reg 28-1-98. Arrived 7-4-17	1-22
☐ G-BHMY		Fokker Friendship 200	62	ex KLM UK, Air UK, F-GBDK, F-GBRV, PK-PFS, JA8606,	
				PH-FDL. CoA 22-5-99, de-reg 27-2-03. Arrived 10-8-00	1-22
☐ G-BTAZ		Evans VP-2	90	ex airport, unflown project. De-reg 12-3-09. Arrived 2006	1-22
☐ G-OVNE		Cessna 401A	69	ex airport, N401XX, N171SF, N71SF, N6236Q.	
				CoA 8-10-92, de-reg 8-2-94. Arrived 2006	1-22
☐ EI-RJN*		HSA HS.146-RJ85	99	ex airport, Cityjet, N526XJ, G-6-351. Woodford-built.	
				Last flight 16-2-19. Moved on site 31-10-20	1-22
☐ –		Westland Whirlwind I rep	06	BAPC.433, forward fuselage. *Crikey!*	[2] 1-22
☐ WH984		EE Canberra B.15	55	ex Mold, Bruntingthorpe, Hinckley, B'thorpe, Cosford	
				8101M (6-8-70), Handling Sqn, B.6, 9, Binbrook SF, 9.	
				Short-built. Arrived 30-11-05. Cockpit. 32 Sqn colours	[3] 1-22
☐ WJ633	'EF'	EE Canberra T.17	54	ex Wyton, St Athan, Wyton, 360, B.2, 231 OCU, 100.	
				HP-built. Arrived 2007. Cockpit	[4] 1-22
☐ WK654	'B'	Gloster Meteor F.8	52	ex 'WL135' Neatishead 8092M, Kemble, 85, CFE, Odiham	
				SF, AWFCS, 247. SOC 9-4-70. Arr 25-11-95. 245 Sqn c/s	1-22
☐ WM267		Gloster Meteor NF.11	53	ex ?, Walpole, Firbeck, Hemswell, Misson, 151, 256, 11.	
				AWA-built. SOC 30-10-67. Arrived 11-9-06. Cockpit	1-22
☐ –		V-S Scimitar CIM	c58	arrived by 1998	1-22
☐ –		Hawker Hunter F.6	c57	ex Wymondham, Duxford. Cockpit. 74 Sqn c/s, sim	[5] 1-22
☐ 'XE683'	'G'	Hawker Hunter F.51	56	ex 'XF383' Cardiff-Wales, 'WV309', 'XF383', Dunsfold,	
				G-9-437 (9-12-75), Danish AF Esk.724 E-409.	
				Arrived 7-10-95. 74 Sqn colours	1-22
☐ 'XG168'	'10'	Hawker Hunter F.6A	56	ex N Weald, Ipswich, Scampton 8832M (2-9-84), 1 TWU,	
		XG172		229 OCU, 263, 19. Arrived 2-2-01. 79 Sqn colours	[3] 1-22
☐ XL564		Hawker Hunter T.7	58	ex Aylesbury, South Molton, Yarmouth, Boscombe Down,	
				ETPS, 229 OCU. Crashed 6-8-98. Cockpit. Arrived 7-15	[6] 7-21
☐ XM612		Avro Vulcan B.2	64	ex 44, Wadd Wing, Scampton Wing, 9.	
				SOC 19-1-83. Arrived 30-1-83	1-22
☐ XN967	'233'	Blackburn Buccaneer S.1	63	ex Coltishall, Weybourne, Fleckney, Helston, Culdrose A2627,	
				SAH-20, Lossiemouth, 736, 809. SOC 23-1-70. Arr 2006. Cockpit	1-22
☐ XP355		Westland Whirlwind HAR.10	62	ex G-BEBC (de-reg 5-12-83), Faygate, 8463M (6-2-76),	
				38 GCF, 21, CFS. Arrived 15-6-80. 22 Sqn colours	1-22

☐ XV255		HS Nimrod MR.2	70	ex Kinloss, Kinloss Wing, A&AEE, 42, Kin Wing, 42, St Mawgan Wing. *Brenda*. Arrived 24-5-10		1-22
☐ XV426	'P'	McD Phantom FGR.2	69	ex Coltishall, Coningsby, 56, 19, 56, 23, 29, 228 OCU, 56, 111, 31, 31. Arrived 2007. 56 Sqn colours. Cockpit		1-22
☐ XW268	'720' and '68'	HS Harrier T.4N	70	ex Faygate, Yeovilton, 899, 233 OCU, T.2, 233 OCU. Accident 27-6-94. Arrived 8-5-08. 899 Sqn colours	[6]	1-22
☐ XX109	'GH'	SEPECAT Jaguar GR.1	72	ex Coltishall 8918M (21-10-86), Warton, A&AEE. Arrived 1-9-04. 54 Sqn colours	[7]	1-22
☐ XX830		SEPECAT Jaguar T.2	74	ex Coltishall 9293M, Warton, Shawbury, St Athan, ETPS, A&AEE, 226 OCU. Last flown 29-9-99. Arr 2006. Cockpit	[8]	1-22
☐ XZ375		SEPECAT Jaguar GR.1	76	ex Coltishall, St Athan 9255M (20-9-96), Warden Det, 54, Gulf Det, 54, 14, 20. Arrived 2006. *The Avid Guardian Reader*. Cockpit	[8]	1-22
☐ 121	'8-MY'	Dassault Mystère IVA	c57	ex Sculthorpe, FAF. Last flown 27-7-81, arrived 31-1-82		1-22
☐ 53-686 and G-AWON	ZF592	EE Lightning F.53	68	ex Portsmouth, Luxembourg, *Wing Commander* (1999), Stretton, Warton, R Saudi AF 223, 53-686, 1305, G-AWON, G-27-56. Last flown 22-1-86, arrived 6-2-02	[3] [9]	1-22
☐ 16718	'TR-999'	Lockheed T-33A-5-LO	51	ex Sculthorpe, Turkish AF, FAF. Arrived 31-5-86. USAF colours, 47th BW		1-22

■ [1] Rallye has come 'home' having bashed the circuit with the Norfolk and Norwich Aero Club 8-63 to 11-69. [2] Built by the late Ray Wood of Thetford as a reminder of an extinct type - W E W Petter's incredible Whirlwind twin-Peregrine fighter. [3] Canberra cockpit WH984, Hunter F.6A 'XG168' and Lightning ZF592 / 53-686 are on loan from John Sheldrake. [4] Canberra cockpit WJ633 is on loan from Richy Doel. [5] Based on a real Hunter cockpit, 1986 Squadron Air Cadets superb simulator is *possibly* from F.6 XE612. That being the case it is very appropriate, serving only with 74 Squadron, it aborted take-off and hit the barrier at Horsham St Faith 17-5-60 and caught fire. [6] Hunter cockpit and Harrier on loan from Dan Lander - see also **www.xw268.net** [7] XX109 is coded 'GH' in honour of Graham Hall, who worked on its restoration. [8] Jaguar cockpits are on loan from The Coltishall Cockpit Collection. [9] ZF592 carries Saudi markings to port and G-AWON to starboard; it appeared as *Oscar-November* at Farnborough 1968. It is reportedly fitted with the wings of 53-700 (ZF589) - see Charlwood, Surrey, for its cockpit.

Airport: Is used for storage and parting-out of jetliners: most are short term; only long-termers are given. The reference to the Friendship fuselage at the **KLM UK Engineering Training School** is long-in-the-tooth: the 737 may well be a replacement.

☐ G-BCDO	Fokker Friendship 200	63	ex Air UK, PH-OGB, JA8621, PH-FEZ. *Lord Butler*. Damaged 19-7-90, de-reg 27-1-95. Fuselage	6-12
☐ G-CELS*	Boeing 737-377	86	ex Jet2, VH-CZH. De-reg 21-8-19, arrived 21-9-16	6-20
☐ VH-NUV*	Fokker F70	95	ex Alliance, OE-LFH, PH-EZN. Arrived 5-11-18	8-20
☐ P4-GIU*	HSA HS.146-RJ85	99	exYV-2767, EI-RJL, OH-SAQ, EI-RJL, N524XJ, G-6-349. Woodford-built. Arrived 2-11-11	7-21

Offshore Fire and Survival Training Centre: An extensive facility on the northern perimeter of the airport.
◆ Strictly *by prior appointment* only | **www.petans.co.uk**

☐ 'G-DRNT'	Westland WG.30-100	83	ex N5880T, Weston-super-Mare, Yeovil, Air Spur, G-17-31	7-21

OLD BUCKENHAM AERODROME south of the A11, east of the B1077 near Attleborough   EGSV

453rd Bomb Group Museum and **Eighth Air Force Heritage Gallery**: Drive into the aerodrome and the genial face of that great film actor James 'Jimmy' Stewart will greet you. Major James Maitland Stewart DFC arrived at 'Ol Buck' on 30th March 1943, becoming the resident 453rd BG's operations officer. As well as the museums, a memorial to the men of the 453rd was rededicated within a garden of remembrance in 2013. A major attraction is 'Jimmy's' cafe and there is an outside area offering views of the comings and goings at this superb aerodrome.
◆ **01953 860806** - *press for option 7* | email via website | **www.453museum.com**

Locally: The biplane cache is believed to be current at a *private* workshop.

☐ G-AOAA	DH Tiger Moth	42	ex Turweston, Lavenham, Spanhoe, Manston, Thruxton, Chilbolton, DF159, 24 GCF, 1 RS, 1 GTS, 20 PAFU, 5 GTS. Morris-built. Crashed 4-6-89. 'Super Tiger' variant	2-16
☐ G-AYCG	Stampe SV-4C	46	ex Staverton, F-BOHF, F-BBAE, French mil. Nord-built. CoA 19-12-14	7-19
☐ G-BHFG	Stampe SV-4C	46	ex Staverton, F-BJDN, French mil. Nord-built. CoA 17-4-08	7-18
☐ G-EHLT	DH Tiger Moth	41	ex G-BHLT, Turweston, Sywell, ZS-DGA, SAAF 2272, T6697, n/s. Morris Motors-built	2-16
☐ 156	Stampe SV-4A	46	ex Staverton, F-BBBL, French AF, F-BFCE, French AF 156.	
	G-NIFE		Nord-built. CoA 18-8-11. French Air Force colours	7-18

SCULTHORPE on the A148 west of Fakenham

RAF Sculthorpe Heritage Centre: Housed within the Wicken Green Rural Centre, on the northwest edge of the airfield, the centre has exceptional displays on a very distinctive air base. Among the artefacts are the remains of Douglas RB-66 Destroyer 54-433 of the resident 47th BW which was abandoned and crashed on 3rd July 1958. A former Coltishall Jaguar has been acquired; it is displayed on farmland nearby.
◆ *Chapel Street, NR21 7RR* | **07766 715548** | **rshc1955@gmail.com** | **www.rafsculthorpeheritagecentre.org**
❑ XZ394   'FG' SEPECAT Jaguar GR.3   77 ex Ipswich, Shoreham, Bentwaters, St Athan, 41, GR.1,
                                                 54, 6, Shawbury, 17, 20. 'Saint', black colours. F/n 9-19   [1]   1-22
■ [1] Jaguar on farmland at Tattersett, west of the B1454: there's an honesty box – make sure it's filled!

SEETHING AERODROME east of the B1332, north of Bungay   EGSJ

Station 146 Control Tower Museum: On the southern perimeter of the aerodrome the tower is dedicated to the Liberator-equipped 448th Bomb Group. ◆ *Toad Lane, NR35 2EQ* | **info@448bombgroup.co.uk** | **www.448bombgroup.co.uk** | also **www.storiesofthe448th.com**

Aerodrome: Rex Ford and team relocated to Fenland, Cambs, during 2021. The former Key Publishing Beagle 'FlyForce One', was written out of *W&R26* (p181) as having returned to airworthiness, but this was fleeting. Tiger Moth G-ADGT had moved to Northampton, Northants, by January 2021. ◆ **Strictly** *no access without prior arrangement*
❑ G-AFFD   Percival Q.6   38 ex Isle of Man, Sutton Coldfield, Duxford, Redhill, G-AIEY,
                                                 X9407, MCS, 510, Old Sarum SF, Halton SF, Heston SF,
                                                 Northolt SF, 6 AACU, G-AFFD. CoA 31-8-56   11-21
❑ G-FLYP*   Beagle 206 Srs 2   67 ex Cranfield, N40CJ, N97JH, G-AVHO, VQ-LAY, G-AVHO.
                                                 CoA 6-9-18   11-21

Others:
❑ G-EGUR*   Jodel D.140B   61 ex Oxenhope, D-EGUR. CoA 20-10-14   6-21

SHIPDHAM AERODROME off the A1075 southwest of East Dereham   EGSA

Slingsby T.61A G-AYUM had moved on by June 2020.
❑ WZ797   FMA Slingsby Grasshopper TX.1 52 BGA.3359, ex Upwood, Shenington, Locking, Wimborne.
                                                 CoA 17-8-89. Off-site   8-21

SWAFFHAM on the A1065, northeast of Downham Market

No.1894 Squadron Air Cadets: Keep the frame of an Auster at the TA Centre, Sporle Road.
❑ XK418   Auster AOP.9   56 ex Hardwick, South Molton, Lasham, Basingstoke, Thruxton,
                                                 Netheravon, M Wallop 7976M (24-7-57), 19 MU, 12 Flt,
                                                 M Wallop, LAS. Frame   6-21

SWANTON MORLEY east of the B1110, north of East Dereham

Two Nords are stored at a *private* location in the *general* area.
❑ No.37   Nord 3400   G-ZARA 60 ex Boston, Stixwould, Breighton, Coventry,
                                         La Ferté Alais, ALAT F-MMAB. De-reg 30-6-97   6-21
❑ No.124   Nord 3400   G-BOSJ 60 ex La Ferté Alais, ALAT F-MMAB. Damaged 12-6-94   6-21

THETFORD

Combat Paintball: On Roudham Heath. ◆ *By prior arrangement* only | **www.combatpaintball.com**
❑ G-BMVA   Scheibe SF-25B Falke   72 ex RAFGGA.512. CoA 5-6-08, de-reg 16-4-14. F/n 6-17   7-18

Also: A *private* collection of cockpits is *believed* to be extant in the locality.
❑ WW664   Hawker Hunter F.4   55 ex Spanhoe, Cottesmore, Newark, Winthorpe, Newark,
                                                Harrogate, HSA, 26. Squires Gate-built. Cockpit   [1]   3-13
❑ XG325   EE Lightning F.1   59 ex Rayleigh, Southend, Wattisham, Foulness, DH Hatfield,
                                                A&AEE. SOC 23-6-65. Cockpit   3-13
❑ XN650 '456' DH Sea Vixen FAW.2   61 ex Spanhoe, Bruntingthorpe, Newton Abbot, Welshpool,
                                                Bruntingthorpe, Cardiff, Culdrose A2639, A2620, A2612
                                                (3-3-72), RAE, 892. Christchurch-built. Cockpit. Arrived 9-10 3-13

❑ 764	Mikoyan-Gurevich		66	ex Northampton, Booker, East Germ AF.	
	MiG-21SPS *Fishbed*			Cockpit	3-13

■ [1] The rest of WW664 became the prototype T.8B in 1958 for the Fleet Air Arm and later went to Singapore as a T.75.

THORPE ABBOTTS off the A140 at Dickleburgh, north of Scole
100th Bomb Group Memorial Museum: Contents of the tower museum are exceptional (as is the website and the archive services), offering poignant insights into the life and times of the men and machines of the 'Bloody Hundredth'.
◆ *Common Rd, Dickleburgh, IP21 4PH* | **01379 740708** | **info@100bgmus.org.uk** | **www.100bgmus.org.uk**

TIBENHAM north of the B1134, north of Diss
Three *separate* restoration projects are in the *general* area. Chris Jefferson is restoring the Kensinger.

❑ G-ASSV		Kensinger KF		53	ex Deopham Green, Brenchley, Deopham Green,	
					Tonbridge, Bobbington, N23S. Crashed 2-7-69	N3-18
❑ G-MOTW*		Myers OTW-145		41	ex Duxford, Breighton, N34301, NC34301. Arr 24-11-21	11-21
❑ N6965	'FL-J'	DH Tiger Moth	G-AJTW 38		ex N6965, 13 OTU, 16 EFTS, 13 OTU, 418, Northolt SF,	
					24, 81, 613. Crashed 7-6-99, CoA 9-9-00. 81 Sqn colours	N2-20

WEST RAYNHAM north of the A1065, west of the village
In November 2016 Jon and Shell Booty acquired the control tower, fire section and immediate surrounds at the former airfield. Since then feverish activity has transformed the building, and the airfield designator and signals square have been returned to their former glory. Attention to detail is excellent including their choice of a Hunter to grace the setting: WT660 served from February 1955 for two years at 'Raynham with the Day Fighter Leaders School.
◆ *Open days planned; otherwise by prior arrangement only.* | **www.westraynhamcontroltower.co.uk**

❑ WT660*	'C'	Hawker Hunter F.1		54	ex Inverness, Cullen, New Byth, Carlisle, 71 MU 7421M	
					(11-4-57), 229 OCU, DFLS. Arrived 15-10-20	10-21

WEST WALTON HIGHWAY on the A47 northeast of Wisbech
Fenland and West Norfolk Aviation Museum: Run by the Fenland and West Norfolk Aircraft Preservation Society. Inside is a treasure trove of superbly presented artefacts, many recovered from East Anglian 'digs'. These include the remains of Stirling I BF386 of Bourn-based 15 Squadron which crashed on an air test on 29th October 1942 near Downham Market.
Last noted in August 2017, the frame of Colt G-ARNH was disposed of. The former Crowland Hurricane FSM 'Z3174' has also moved on. Lightning T.5 XS459 made the trek to Binbrook, Lincs, by May 2021.
◆ *Bambers Garden Centre, Old Lynn Road, PE14 7DA* | **01945 461771** | **info@fenlandaviationmuseum.org.uk** | **www.fenlandaviationmuseum.org.uk**

❑ -		V-S Spitfire FSM		~	BAPC.540, ex Duxford. First noted 4-19		1-22
❑ WR971	'Q'	Avro Shackleton MR.3/3		56	ex Narborough, Cosford 8119M (14-12-70), 120, Kinloss Wing,		
					201, 120, Kin' Wing, CA. Arr 2002. Cockpit and sections	[1]	1-22
❑ XD434	'25'	DH Vampire T.11		54	ex Marham, Barton, Woodford, Chester, St Athan,		
					5 FTS, 7 FTS. Hawarden-built. SOC 1-12-67. Arrived 3-89		1-22
❑ XM402	'18'	Hunting Jet Provost T.3		59	ex Narborough, West Raynham, Halton, Newton 8055AM		
					(21-11-69), Shawbury, 6 FTS, 2 FTS. Arrived 10-9-95		1-22
❑ XN983		Blackburn Buccaneer		65	ex Terrington St Clement, 12, 208, 15, 12, 809, A&AEE, RR.		
		S.2B			SOC 10-4-94. Arrived 2002. Cockpit	[2]	8-21
❑ –		Hunting Jet Provost CIM		~	procedure trainer, on loan from March Air Cadets. Arr 2000		4-19

■ [1] A 'slice' of WR971 is also held at Flixton, Suffolk. [2] On loan from the Terrington Aviation Collection.

WEYBOURNE on the A149 west of Cromer
Muckleburgh Collection: Bannered as Britain's largest working military collection, there is much to fascinate, including 'live' tank demonstrations. ◆ *Military Camp, NR25 7EH* | **01263 588210** | **info@muckleburgh.co.uk** | **www.muckleburgh.co.uk**

❑ 'XT581'		Northrop Shelduck D.1	13	BAPC.501. 'Army' titles. Suspended within the cafe	[1]	10-17
❑ XZ968	'3G'	HS Harrier GR.3	80	ex Marham 9222M (13-10-93), St Athan, 233 OCU,		
				1417 Flt, 1,4		12-21
❑ ZJ385		GEC-Marconi Phoenix UAV	c95	'Army' titles		10-17
❑ –		Fieseler Fi 103 V-1 replica	~	BAPC.550, on ramp		12-21

■ [1] The *real* XT581 is at Duxford, Cambs. This Shelduck was created by the Kelling Model Flying Club using an original wing - complete with shrapnel damage - left behind when Weybourne Camp closed in 1958.

WINFARTHING on the B1077 north of Diss
Sound Sleep: The bedding showroom in Mile Road has a 'guardian' | www.sound-sleep.co.uk

❑ G-CBCY	Beech Sierra	77 ex Goodwood, N881RS, PH-HLA. CoA 24-3-11	8-21

WISBECH off the A47 southwest of King's Lynn
At a private residence in the general area, a Boeing 737 cockpit is kept.

❑ N70353*	Boeing 737-300	87 ex Continental. Last flown 5-6-08. Cockpit, first noted 8-19	8-19

NORTHAMPTONSHIRE

AYNHO The move of Sea Harrier F/A.2 ZD582to Sunderland, N&T, in the spring of 2022 has been anticipated.

BARBY south of the M45, north of Daventry
During 2018 the trio of Lynxes left the paintball site: XZ175 bound for Wickford, Essex, in July and the other two – XZ664 and XZ665 – to destination unknown.

BARTON SEAGRAVE north of the A6633 east of Kettering
Kestrel Caravan Park: A collection of light aircraft has been gathered within the site.
◆ *By prior arrangement* only | www.kestrelcaravans.co.uk

❑ G-APWP*	Druine Turbulent	60	de-reg 20-6-18	9-21
❑ G-ATFR*	Piper Pawnee 150	60	ex OY-ADJ. De-reg 20-3-18. First noted 7-20	9-21
❑ G-OMAX*	Brantly B2B	67	ex G-AVJN. CoA 19-1-10, de-reg 13-3-12	9-21
❑ G-TAMA*	Hughes 269D	04	ex Kelham 'K-HALL', Shoreham. Schweizer-built. CoA 12-6-08, de-reg 16-6-08, crashed 4-2-08 [1]	9-21

■ **[1]** The Hughes was written out of *W&R27* (p185) as departing Kelham Hall by late 2019 bound, possibly' for 'Essex'.

CORBY
Frank and **Lee Millar**: Keep their Vampire in the area. See under Newark, Notts, for their Canberra PR.9 cockpit.

❑ XE849	'V3'	DH Vampire T.11	54 ex Barton, Shobdon, Mildenhall, Long Marston, Yatesbury, Monkton Farleigh, Conington, Ware, St Athan 7928M (13-10-66), 3 CAACU (?), CATCS, CNCS, 5 FTS, 7 FTS, 1 FTS, 4 FTS. Hatfield-built	12-19

HARRINGTON southeast of Market Harborough
'Carpetbagger' Aviation Museum: Centred upon the hardened group operations building of what was once USAAF Station 179 and home of the clandestine 492nd and 801st BGs. Exhibitions on the covert operations of the US from Harrington and by the RAF from Tempsford, Beds. Working in support of the museum is the **Harrington Aviation Museum Society**.
    The forward fuselage of Widgeon G-APWK moved to Newton Abbot, Devon, in April 2021.
◆ *Sunny Vale Farm Nursery, off Lamport Road, NN6 9PF Note: Photography, via cameras or mobile phones, not permitted within the museum.* | **01536 711556** | **enquiries @harringtonmuseum.org.uk** | **www.harringtonmuseum.org.uk**

IRTHLINGBOROUGH on the A6 northwest of Higham Ferrers and Rushden
Rock UK Frontier Centre: Within **Mission Aviation Fellowship** *should* have a Cessna 150. (See also Glasgow, Scotland.)
◆ *By prior arrangement* only | www.rockuk.org | www.maf-uk.org

❑ 'G-BMAF'	Cessna 150J	G-BOWC 69 ex Defford, N60626. De-reg 16-9-94. 'Taildragger'	7-14

KETTERING
Chariots: Kettering Venture Park | www.chariotsspecialistcars.com

❑ 'G-BGEI'	Oldfield Baby Great Lakes	85 G-BGLS, de-reg 12-12-11. Displayed [1]	12-21

■ **[1]** The Great Lakes masquerades as another of the species, G-BGEI, also out of CoA (27-6-13). One reason for this might be that *Echo-India* was tested at Samlesbury, Lancs, for PFA permit clearance 26-8-80 by none other than Wg Cdr Roland Beamont.

Tresham College: In the campus (main entrance on Windmill Avenue, near Wickstead Park) is a One-Eleven used by the Travel and Tourism courses. ◆ **Strictly** *by prior arrangement* | **www.tresham.ac.uk**

❑ G-AVMJ	BAC 111-510ED	68	ex Watford, Horton, Hurn, Farnborough, Hurn, Filton,
			BA, BEA. CoA 17-11-94, de-reg 11-5-01.
			Fuselage [1] 12-21

■ **[1]** *Mike-Juliet* factoids: First flew 15-7-68, last flew with BA 13-1-92, ferry to Hurn. Final flight Hurn-Filton 25-5-93.

NORTHAMPTON AERODROME or Sywell, northeast of Northampton, off the A43   EGBK

Sywell Aviation Museum (SAM): Charting the history of wonderful Sywell and the entire county, SAM is a landmark among 'small' museums: 2022 is the museum's 21st birthday. The Paul Morgan Hall honours a gifted local engineer and warbird owner who was killed in his Sea Fury FB.11 WH588 (G-EEMV) on 12th May 2001. There is a poignant 'missing man' memorial fountain to Paul in front of the 'Aviator Hotel'.

One of the hangars at Sywell is called the Jetstream Hangar - for a very good reason. After Handley Page collapsed in August 1969 'Bill' Bright of Terravia acquired the design rights to the type and set up Jetstream Aircraft to breathe life back into the programme. An arrangement was made with the College of Aeronautics at Cranfield, Beds, to oversee the new baseline Series 200. Premises were secured at Sywell by September 1970 and three complete airframes were moved there as well as ten or so unfinished fuselages. Originally delivered to the USA in 1969, N1035S was brought back to the UK to act as a demonstrator. Jetstream Aircraft completed five Radlett-built airframes in 1971 and 1972: three at Sywell and two more at Leavesden in 1974. Thanks to Bright the rights to the Jetstream were passed on to Scottish Aviation and the type was reborn, production ending in 1997 under the aegis of British Aerospace.

Through the generosity of Cranfield University, SAM acquired N1035S, which ended its days as a flying laboratory at Cranfield as G-RAVL. Stalled by Covid-19, *Victor-Lima* - aka 'Jenny the Jetstream' - arrived in March 2021. The plan is to finish it on one side as G-RAVL and on the other as G-AWVK during its days with Racal-Decca - 1974-1986.

Harvard cockpit KF532, previously listed under Bruntingthorpe, Leics, was passed on to Tony Dyer on 10th April 2021, see under <u>Old Sarum</u>, Wilts.

◆ *Car parking for the museum (no charge) doubles as a viewing area for the aerodrome*. NN6 0BN | **01604 670824** | sywellaviationmuseum@gmail.com | www.sywellaviationmuseum.org.uk

❑ G-RAVL*	'197'	HP Jetstream 200	69	ex Cranfield, G-AWVK, N1035S, G-AWVK. CoA 26-2-94,	
				de-reg 30-1-01. 'Jenny'. Arrived 23-3-21 – see notes above	1-22
❑ KF650		NA Harvard T.2B	45	ex Kenilworth, Henlow, 2 FTS, 22 FTS. Crashed 14-5-54.	
				Noorduyn-built. Forward cockpit. Arrived by 10-14 [1]	1-22
❑ WG419		DHC Chipmunk T.10	51	ex Armthorpe, Finningley 8206M (2-8-72), Laarbruch SF,	
				Gütersloh SF, Ahlhorn SF, Oldenburg SF, CFS, Abn UAS,	
				Birm UAS, 15 RFS, 4 BFTS, 6 RFS. Cockpit. 'Clare'. Arr 2008	1-22
❑ WH887	'847'	EE Canberra TT.18	54	ex Upwood, Basingstoke, Llanbedr St Athan, FRADU, B.2,	
				Upwood SF, 21, 542, 1323 Flt. Short-built. Cockpit.	
				'Cindy'. Arrived 25-10-14, off-site from 3-21 [2]	1-22
❑ WN904 and 'WN921'	'Q'	Hawker Hunter F.2	54	ex Waterbeach, Duxford, Newton, Melksham, Halton 7544M (31-3-58), 257. AWA-built. Arrived 2-8-12. 'Heidi'	
				257 Sqn colours to port, 263 Sqn to starboard [3]	1-22
❑ XD599	'A'	DH Vampire T.11	54	ex Ingatestone, Welshpool, Shobdon, Caernarfon,	
				Hurn, Blackbushe, Staverton, Stroud, CATCS, RAFC, 1.	
				Hatfield-built. SOC 15-12-70. Arrived 10-10-04. Cockpit	1-22

■ **[1]** KF650 on loan from the Midland Aircraft Recovery Group. **[2]** WH887 is under restoration locally, not available for inspection. **[2]** **[3]** Canberra owned solely by Andy Shemans from 2020. It is being restored and will have the electrics 'live'. While with the Wyton-based 1323 Flt, WH884 briefly served with 82 Sqn, probably on brief loan for monitoring sorties for US Bikini Atoll CASTLE nuclear 'shot' 3-54. **[3]** WN904 is dedicated to the memory of 23-year-old Fg Off Dennis R Courtney of 263 Sqn.

Store: *Not* available for public inspection.

❑ G-AOES	DH Tiger Moth	41	ex Baxterley, Redhill, Biggin Hill, Cosford, Mk.II T6056,	
			Waddington SF, Benson SF, 18 EFTS. Morris-built.	
			Crashed 26-9-99, CoA 15-6-02. Fuselage. Arrived 3-13	1-22
❑ WZ820	Slingsby Grasshopper TX.1	52	ex Shoreham, Lancing College. Arrived 2001	1-22

Air Leasing / Ultimate Warbirds: Two blister hangars, one is simply called 'The Spitfire Blister', but both inevitably known locally as 'Graceland', form the home of the Grace family's operational warbird fleet and an incredibly productive restoration centre. Sywell is base of the iconic Spitfire Tr.IX ML407 (G-LFIX), Seafire III PP972 (G-BUAR), Buchón two-seater '11' (G-AWHC), among others. As with elsewhere in the book, the active warbirds are not formally covered, *W&R* concentrating on restoration projects.

Spitfire IX MH415 (G-AVDJ) visiting Duxford in September 2021; it was last there in October 1968 for the filming of *Battle of Britain*. Col Pope

Aerial Speed Icons Spitfire IX RN201 (G-BSKP) arrived from Biggin Hill, Gtr Lon, in mid-2019; it was test flown on 9th June 2020. Spitfire IX MH415 arrived from Australia by March 2020 for Air Leasing, it returned to its British registration from 1966 of G-AVDJ. Spitfire IX PL344 (G-IXCC) was cancelled as sold in Australia – as VH-IUK – on 29th September 2020. *Delta-Juliet* made its first engine runs on 6th October 2020 and had its first flight on 8th April 1921 - joining the based fleet. A *Battle of Britain* veteran, G-AVDJ visited Duxford in September 2021: it was last there - for filming - in October 1968.

◆ *Private workshop, not available for inspection* | www.ultimatewarbirdflights.com

❏ G-HISP		Hispano HA-1112-M1L	c52	ex USA, *Battle of Britain* (1968), Pinewood and Spain,		
		Buchón		Spanish AF C.4K-111. Arrived 2-16	[1]	1-20
❏ G-NZOC*		Le Vier Cosmic Wind	48	ex N289A, N20C. Little Toni. First noted 3-21	[2]	9-21
❏ G-TMPV		Hawker Tempest V	44	ex Bentwaters, 4887M (9-10-44), JN768, 3. Spares	[3]	2-21
❏ 'V6748'*		Hawker Hurricane XII	44	ex VH-JHW, C-FDNL, N678DP 'P2970', G-ORGI, Popham,		
			G-ORGI	Sandown, Canada, SOC 29-11-44, RCAF 5481. CCF-built		
				Arrived 11-10-21	[4]	1-22
❏ EN224		V-S Spitfire XII	42	ex Bentwaters, Newport Pagnell, Redbourn, Salford,		
			G-FXII	Cranfield (4-7-46), 595, 41		1-20
❏ 'PR533'		Hawker Tempest II	45	ex N Weald, Wickenby, Sandtoft, Brooklands, Chichester,		
	'5R-V'		G-TEMT	Poona, Indian AF HA586, RAF MW763. 33 Sqn c/s		
				Rolled out 24-5-21	[5]	9-21
❏ 14798		Messerschmitt	42	ex Australia, VH-EIN, JG 5 *Black 11*, shot down Russia		
		Bf 109G-2	G-CLFI	30-3-44. WNF-built. Recovered 1981	[6]	1-20
❏ HA604		Hawker Tempest II	45	ex Wickenby, Sandtoft, Brooklands, Chichester, India,		
			G-PEST	Ind AF, RAF MW401 n/s (SOC 25-5-48). Bristol-built	[5]	6-17
❏ C.4K-30	'7'	Hispano HA-1112-M1L	58	ex USA, *Battle of Britain* (1968). Spares. First noted 7-18	[1]	7-18
❏ 22-596		Royal Aircraft Factory	1919	ex Bentwaters, Greenham Common, Duxford, M Wallop,		
		SE.5E	G-BLXT	Booker, 'B4863', Orlando, Tallmantz, N4488, *Hell's Angels*		
				(1930), USAAS 22-296. CoA 15-9-16. Arrived by 7-16	[7]	9-18
❏ 42-66841		Lockheed P-38H-5-LO	42	ex Bentwaters, Germany, Australia, Papua New Guinea.		
	'153'	Lightning		Crashed PNG 10-6-44. *Scarlet Angel*		6-17
❏ 413668*		NAA P-51D-5-NA	44	ex 338th FS, 55th FG, 44-13668. Crashed 9-10-44.		
		Mustang	G-CLRG	Inglewood-built. Restoration project. First noted 7-20		9-20
❏ 464005		NAA P-51D-20-NA	44	ex USA, N51WB, N6339T, RCAF 9561, USAAF 44-64005.		
	'E9-Z'	Mustang	N51CK	Inglewood-built. *Mary Mine*. Arrived 3-17		12-17

■ All registered to Air Leasing unless noted. **[1]** Bf 109 with RR Merlin 500 built by Hispano Aviacion, Spain, -M1L single-seater, -M4L two-seater. With thanks to Paco Rivas please note that the plural of Buchón is Buchones – *without* the accent. **[2]** Registered to Richard Grace. **[3]** Registered to the Hawker *Typhoon* Preservation Group – see main entry under Duxford, Cambs. **[4]** Registered to Warbird Experiences. **[5]** Registered to Anglia Aircraft Restorations. **[6]** Registered to Fighter Aviation Engineering. **[7]** British-built SE.5a re-engined by Eberhart Steel Products Co, at Buffalo, New York. US designation SE.5E - cap 'E'. Registered to Flying A Services.

Matthew Boddington: Both the Tiger Moth and the scale SE.5a were once flown by Matt's late father, Charles.

❑ G-ADGT*	DH Tiger Moth	35	ex Seething, Headcorn, BB697, 652, 26 EFTS, 6 EFTS.		
			CoA 25-8-12. First noted 1-21	[1]	1-21
❑ G-APVT	DH Tiger Moth	35	ex K4254, Colerne SF, 81 GCF, 60 GCF, 18 RFS, Lon UAS,		
			6 EFTS, 1 GTS, 101 OTU, 17 EFTS, 7 EFTS, 14 EFTS,		
			20 E&RFTS, 24. Crashed 29-7-73		9-21
❑ G-ARAM	Piper Super Cub 150	60	ex N10F. Crashed 4-7-01, CoA 22-6-02		1-18
❑ G-JMNN	Bücker Jungmann	50	ex SpanAF E.3B-335. CASA-built. Arrived 27-12-13	[2]	10-21
❑ 'C8846' 'M'	Slingsby SE.5a	67	ex N908AC, USA, EI-ARJ, G-AVOU.		
G-AVOU			Slingsby-built. Arrived 24-3-15	[3]	9-21

■ **[1]** *Golf-Tango* and *Fox-Delta* registered to the London Aerobatic Company. **[2]** See under Coggeshall, Essex, for the owner's Jungmeister. **[2]** SE.5a scale replica based upon a Currie Wot airframe.

Also: Widgeon G-ANLW had moved to Higher Purtington, Somerset, by November 2021.

❑ G-EGLG	Piper Navajo	78	ex N45TY. De-reg 20-6-16. Spares	1-18
❑ G-FILL	Piper Navajo C	79	ex OO-EJM, N3521. CoA 13-10-11, de-reg 25-5-11. Fuselage	1-18
❑ G-KSWI	Hughes 369E	86	CoA 18-6-12, de-reg 19-1-12. Fire training ground	1-18
❑ G-SWLL	Aero AT-3 R100	05	ex SP-KAC. CoA 23-11-17. Fire training ground	1-18

SPANHOE AERODROME southeast of Harringworth

Windmill Aviation: Restored to flying condition by Carl Tyers and his team, the Reid & Sigrist Bobsleigh VZ728 (G-AGOS) took to the air again on 22nd April 2018. Registered to Leicestershire County Council's Communities and Wellbeing Department, the project was always intended to presage to its disposal. The council elected to hand the aircraft on to the Newark Air Museum. Having got the unique machine airborne, a campaign was launched for it to as least appear in the static at some air events.: the pandemic, among other things, scotched this. As *W&R* went to press, preparation for the transfer to Newark, Notts, were in hand, so the opportunity has been taken to move VZ728 to its new home.

A team from SYAM moved Airedale EI-BBK to Doncaster, S Yorkshire, on 6th June 2020. The hulk of Robin HR.100 G-BLHN, last noted in August 2015, and Elster B G-BMWV, off-site since June 2016, have both been deleted.

◆ **Strictly** *by prior arrangement* **only**

❑ G-ANWB*	DHC Chipmunk 21	55	ex Blackpool. De-reg 5-10-17. Arrived 21-9-21	10-21
❑ G-ARNN	Globe GC-1B Swift	46	ex Tatenhill, Leicester, VP-YMJ, VP-RDA, ZS-BMX, NC3279K.	
			Crashed 1-9-73, de-reg 26-1-11. off-site	2-18
❑ G-BRZK	Stinson 108-2	47	ex N9846K. CoA 18-2-13	5-21
❑ G-CFGE	Stinson 108-1	46	ex Wickenby, Hibaldstow, Little Gransden, ZS-BHW, N97127	5-21
❑ EI-AYL	Beagle Airedale	63	ex Abbeyshrule, G-ARRO, EI-AVP, G-ARRO. CoA 1-2-86	10-21
❑ EI-BAL	Beagle Airedale	62	ex Abbeyshrule, G-ARZS. De-reg 29-6-79	10-21
❑ LB375	Taylorcraft Plus D	43	ex Coventry, Auster I LB375, 431, 43 OTU, 653.	
G-AHGW			CoA 3-5-96. First noted 7-17	7-21
❑ WZ872* 'E'	DHC Chipmunk T.10	53	ex Blackpool, 5, 3, 1, 3, 6, 3, 2 and 3 AEFs, 2 FTS, Lon, Oxf,	
G-BZGB			Cam, Oxf UASs, PFTS, AOTS, ITS, South Cerney SF, 1 FTS,	
			Wattisham SF, 12 GCF, Marham SF, 3 GCF.	
			CoA 18-8-06. Arrived 21-9-21	10-21

NORTHUMBERLAND and TYNESIDE

The five unitary authorities of Gateshead, Newcastle-upon-Tyne, Sunderland, North Tyneside and South Tyneside comprise the 'counties'

BAMBURGH on the B4130 east of Belford and northwest of Seahouses

Bamburgh Castle Aviation Artefacts Museum: In the West Ward, is the superb **Armstrong and Aviation Museum**. Among the exhibits are sections of 280 Squadron Vickers Warwick I HG136 which crashed near Wooler on 23rd July 1946.

◆ *NE69 7DF* | **01668 214208**| **administrator@bamburghcastle.com** | **www.bamburghcastle.com**

BELSAY on the A696 northwest of Newcastle
Battlezone Paintball Newcastle: The site is *believed* to have taken the KIS from previous similar duties at Rowley, D&C.
◆ *By prior application only* | **www.battlezonepaintball.co.uk**
| ☐ G-BVTA | Tri-R KIS | 95 ex Rowley. CoA 30-1-12, de-reg 30-4-15 | ?? |

BOULMER east of Alnwick
RAF Boulmer: The Air Surveillance and Control System station is guarded by a Phantom.
| ☐ XV415 | 'E' McD Phantom FGR.2 | 68 ex 9163M, 56, 74, 228 OCU, 23, 56, 92, 29, 228 OCU, 56, 228 OCU, 31, 228 OCU, 41, 228 OCU, 41, 54, A&AEE. Displayed | 8-21 |

CURROCK HILL northwest of Leadgate, south of Prudhoe
Contrary to *W&R27* the Cherokee is not at the gliding club, but at a *private* house in the locality.
| ☐ G-AWBH | Piper Cherokee 140 | 68 CoA 30-12-04, de-reg 16-3-10. First noted 8-15 | 1-22 |

ESHOTT AERODROME east of the A1 south of Fenton
Chipmunk T.10 WG458 (G-CLLI) arrived on 10th July 2020 and was flying by 2021.
☐ G-ANOK	SAAB Safir	r54 ex Morpeth, Yarrow, Strathallan, East Fortune, SE-CAH. De Schelde-built. CoA 5-2-73	7-21
☐ G-ASWW	Piper Twin Comanche 160	64 ex Skegness, N7531Y. Damaged, CoA 23-1-10, de-reg 12-8-09	6-19
☐ G-BDNC	Taylor Monoplane	84 CoA 15-7-16, de-reg 28-5-21	4-19
☐ G-BMKK	Piper Arrow 200	75 ex ZS-JNY, N9537N. CoA 17-1-13	9-19
☐ G-BWVR	'52' Yakovlev Yak-52	87 ex LY-AKQ, Sov AF 134. IAR Bacau-built. CoA 7-12-06	7-21
☐ G-BXZA*	Piper Tomahawk 112	79 ex Barton, N2480N. De-reg 26-10-16. First noted 4-21	6-21
☐ YU-DLG*	UTVA 66 G-CLJX	70 ex Morpeth, Linton-on-Ouse, Biggin Hill, Yugoslav AF 51109. First noted 6-20	7-21
☐ WP860*	'6' DHC Chipmunk T.10 G-BXDA	52 ex Ballyboy, WP860 12, 13, 6 AEFs, Abn UAS, Leeds UAS, 9 AEF, Leeds, Abn, St And, Perth, St And UASs, CNCS, 5 FTS, CNCS, RAFC. CoA 21-11-14, arrived 24-1-22	1-22

MORPETH or Tranwell, east of the A1, north of Newcastle upon Tyne
BlackStone Aviation: UTVA 66 YU-DLG (G-CLJX) relocated to Eshott, N&T, by June 2020. Isaacs Fury 'K5673' (G-BZAS) had moved to the "south country" (levelling *down*?) by the summer of 2020.
| ☐ G-APOL | Druine Turbulent | 63 ex Charterhall. Crashed 24-7-93, de-reg 13-9-00 | 3-20 |
| ☐ 42-58687 | 'IY' Taylorcraft DF-65 G-BRIY | 43 ex N59687, TG-6 42-58678. CoA 10-7-98 | N3-18 |

NEWCASTLE AIRPORT or Woolsington   EGNT
Newcastle Aviation Academy ◆ *By prior arrangement* only | **www.ncl-coll.ac.uk**
☐ G-AZMF	BAC 111-530FX	72 ex Hurn, European, 7Q-YKJ, G-AZMF, PT-TYY, G-AZMF. CoA 22-1-04, de-reg 10-3-06. Forward fuselage	7-21
☐ G-BBYM	HP Jetstream 200	69 ex Cosford, Cranfield, BAe, G-AYWR, G-8-13. Jetstream A/c, Leavesden-completed. CoA 20-9-98, de-reg 7-6-00	7-21
☐ G-CCXI	Thorp T-211	03 de-reg 18-2-10. Unfinished project, first noted 3-12	2-20
☐ C-GWJO	Boeing 737-2A3	69 ex Westjet, HR-SHO, CX-BHM, N1797B, N1787B	7-21
☐ N37LW	Piper Aztec 250	60 ex Fishburn, Kirknewton, G-EEVA, G-ASND, N4800P	1-14
☐ XM355	'D' Hunting Jet Provost T.3	59 ex Bruntingthorpe, Shobdon, Cambridge, B'thorpe, Halton 8229M (17-10-73), Shawbury, 1 FTS, 7 FTS, CFS. Blue/white colours	7-21
☐ XM419	'102' Hunting Jet Provost T.3A	60 ex St Athan 8990M (15-3-89), 7 FTS, 3 FTS, CFS, RAFC, CFS, 3 FTS, RAFC, 6 FTS, RAFC, 2 FTS	7-21

SEATON BURN east of the A1, north of Newcastle upon Tyne
Spit4Hire ◆ *By prior arrangement* only | **www.spit4hire.com**
| ☐ - | V-S Spitfire FSM | 13 cockpit/sim, travelling demo | 12-17 |

SUNDERLAND site of the former Usworth aerodrome, west of Sunderland

North East Land, Sea and Air Museums (NELSAM): Combining the exhibits and enterprise of the **North East Aircraft Museum**, the **Military Vehicle Museum** and the **North East Electrical Traction Trust** has produced a wonderful selection of exhibits. A look through the website reveals the incredible scope of this venue.

Former Tornado F.3 navigator, AVM Colin Da'Silva - with 'time' on ZE204 - officially handed over the Tornado F.3 on 13th September 2021. The aircraft was gifted to Lord Lieutenant of Tyne and Wear who accepted it on behalf of the people of the North East of England. The 'SHAR' and the Pucará will be the centrepiece of a Falklands 40th anniversary exhibition which will also remind visitors of the ships building in the region that took part in the armada.

During May and June 2021 the 'Sycamore Shuffle' took place, once again proving that the 'regionals' lead the way when it comes to rationalising collections. NELSAM took delivery of HR.14 XJ917, a duplicate airframe, from Aerospace Bristol which was taken on charge by Thornaby-based 275 Squadron on 11th January 1957, a fabulous local provenance eclipsing NELSAM's long-held Mk.3 WA577. Having served with A&AEE at Boscombe Down, WA577 travelled to the completely appropriate BDAC at Old Sarum, Wilts, on 4th June 2021. Completing the 'shuffle', BDAC's XJ380 travelled all the way to Morayvia, at Kinloss, Scotland, where it completed that collection's line-up of RAF ASR helicopters - Sycamore to Sea King. Everyone involved, take a bow!

Departures: Voltair 86 G-CHTX to Fishburn, D&C, 29-5-21; Sioux AH.1 XT148 to Hooton Park, Cheshire, 11-7-21.

◆ *Off the A1290 and A19, Old Washington Road, SR5 3HZ* | 0191 5190662 | info@nelsam.org.uk | www.nelsam.org.uk

❏ 'G-ADVU'		Mignet HM.14 'Flea'	93	BAPC.211, ex Stoke-on-Trent. Arrived 1994	[1] 1-22
❏ 'G-AFUG'		Luton Minor	44	BAPC.97, ex Stoke-on-Trent, Sunderland, Sibson,	
				Sywell, Sunderland, Stanley. Acquired 1977	1-22
❏ G-APTW		Westland Widgeon	59	ex Helston, Southend, Westland. CoA 26-9-75,	
				de-reg 24-8-72. Arrived 1993	1-22
❏ G-ARAD		Luton Major	60	ex local, Borgue. De-reg 16-10-02. Arrived 4-6-01	[2] 1-22
❏ G-ARPO		HS Trident 1C	65	ex Middleton St George, BA, BEA. CoA 12-1-86, de-reg	
				18-1-84. Arr 31-7-11, unveiled 11-6-15. Northeast c/s	[3] 1-22
❏ G-ATDD*		Beagle 206-1	65	ex Filton, Kemble, Filton, Wroughton, South Kensington,	
				Leeds. Damaged 6-73, de-reg 9-4-74. Cockpit. Arr 16-9-21	1-22
❏ 'G-AVYW'		Brooklands Mosquito	69	ex Gloucester, Clitheroe. De-reg 27-11-18.	
		G-AWIF		Unveiled 3-19	[4] 1-22
❏ G-AWRS		Avro Anson C.19	46	ex Strathallan, Kemps, TX213, WCS, 22 GCF, OCTU, 18 GCF,	
				2 TAF CS, 527, CSE, RCCF. SOC 6-9-68. CoA 10-8-73,	
				de-reg 30-5-84. Arrived 6-8-81	1-22
❏ G-BCPK		Cessna F.172M Skyhawk	74	ex Stamford, Spanhoe, Little Staughton, D-ELOB.	
				CoA 12-1-01, de-reg 18-8-14. Fuselage. First noted 7-17	1-22
❏ G-BEEX		DH Comet 4C	61	ex East Kirkby, Tattershall, Woodford, Lasham, Dan-Air,	
				Egypt Air/UAA SU-ALM. Hatfield-built. Last flight 15-10-76,	
				de-reg 19-5-83. Arrived 1989. Cockpit	1-22
❏ G-OGIL		Short 330-100	81	ex Woolsington, Gill, G-BITV, G-14-3068. Damaged 1-7-92,	
				de-reg 12-11-92. Arrived 4-93	1-22
❏ –		Brown Helicopter	62	BAPC.96, ex Stanley. Acquired 1977	1-22
❏ –		Bensen B-7	c65	BAPC.119, ex Stanley. Acquired 1977	1-22
❏ –	'AF-'	Hawker Hurricane FSM	19	BAPC.521, under construction	[5] 1-22
❏ '5191'		MS Type 'N' FSM	18	BAPC.472	[6] 1-22
❏ -		V-S Spitfire Vb FSM	94	BAPC.242, ex 'BL924', Lower Basildon, Liskeard,	
	'AZ-G'			Perranporth, Tangmere. TDL Replicas-built.	
				Arrived 24-3-19. 234 Sqn colours	[7] 1-22
❏ WG724	'932'	Westland Dragonfly	52	ex Chester-le-Street, Leyburn, Darlington, Blackbushe,	
		HR.5		Fleetlands, Lossiemouth SF, FRU, Ford SF, Eglinton SF	
				SOC 16-9-65. Acquired 3-75	1-22
❏ WJ639		EE Canberra TT.18	54	ex Samlesbury, 7, B.2, 57. HP-built. SOC 9-12-81.	
				7 Sqn colours. Arrived 8-88	1-22
❏ WL181	'X'	Gloster Meteor F.8	54	ex Chester-le-Street, Acklington, Kemble, CAW,	
				Tangmere SF, 34. SOC 3-11-71. Acquired 3-5-75. 92 Sqn c/s	1-22
❏ WT913	FGA	Slingsby Cadet TX.1	52	BGA.3239, ex Doncaster, Strubby, 614, 618, 613, 618, 671,	
				671 203 and 183 GSs. CoA 21-7-96. Arrived 2-7-19	[8] 1-22
❏ WZ518	'B'	DH Vampire T.11	53	ex Chester-le-Street, Handforth, Pomona Dock, 5 FTS,	
				Oldenburg SF, 2 TAF CF, 14. Hawarden-built. SOC 30-10-67.	
				Arrived 11-10-75. 14 Sqn colours	[9] 1-22

☐	XG680	'438'	DH Sea Venom FAW.22	56	ex Sydenham, ADS, 891, Merryfield SF. Hawarden-built. SOC 20-1-70. Arrived 7-81		1-22
☐	XJ917*	'S-H'	Bristol Sycamore HR.14	57	ex Filton, Kemble, Banwell, Helston, Wroughton, CFS, 275. SOC 12-12-72. Arrived 3-6-21		1-22
☐	XL319		Avro Vulcan B.2	61	ex 44, Wadd W, 35, 230 OCU, 617, 230 OCU, Scamp W, 617. 44 Sqn colours. Flew in 21-1-83		1-22
☐	XM555		Saro Skeeter AOP.12	59	ex Stafford, Hendon, Cosford, Shawbury 8027M, Ternhill, CFS, HQ BAOR, 654. SOC 25-7-68. Arrived 12-5-15		1-22
☐	XN258		Westland Whirlwind HAR.9	59	ex Helston, Culdrose SF, *Hermes* SAR Flt, HAS.7, Lossie' SF / SAR Flt, 705, A&AEE. SOC 27-6-74. Arr 10-93		1-22
☐	XN503		Hunting Jet Provost T.3A	60	ex Old Sarum, Boscombe D, Haverfordwest, Milford Haven, Salisbury, Firbeck, Coventry, Bicester, Kemble, RAFEF, 4 FTS, 2 FTS, 6 FTS, A&AEE. SOC 28-5-76. Cockpit. Arrived 3-11-18		1-22
☐	XN696	'751'	DH Sea Vixen FAW.2	61	ex Flixton, Wisbech area, Walpole, Farnborough, RAE, Tarrant Rushton, FRU, 899, 893, FAW.1, 899, A&AEE, 899. Christchurch-built. SOC 10-11-81. Arr 2-3-11. Cockpit	[10]	1-22
☐	XP627		Hunting Jet Provost T.4	62	ex London Colney, Hatfield, Shawbury, 6 FTS, 3 FTS, 1 FTS. SOC 1-10-71. Arrived 25-11-80.	[11]	1-22
☐	'XS933'		EE Lightning F.53 ZF594	68	ex Warton, ZF594, Saudi AF 226, 1308, 53-696, G-27-66. Last flown 14-1-86. Arrived 4-89. 11 Sqn c/s	[12]	1-22
☐	'XZ177'		Sud Gazelle 1 G-SFTA	73	ex Carlisle, 'XZ345', G-SFTA, HB-XIL, G-BAGJ, XW858. Westland-built. Crashed 7-3-84, de-reg 21-5-86. Arrived 11-86. 'ARMY' black/green camo	[13]	1-22
☐	ZD582*	'123'	HS Sea Harrier F/A.2	85	ex Aynho, Henley-on-Thames, Shawbury, Colsterworth, Shawbury, 800, 899, 800, 899, FRS.1, 801, 800		**due**
☐	ZE204*	'FC'	Panavia Tornado F.3	86	ex Manston, Shawbury, Leuchars, 25, 23. Last flown 17-3-08. Arrived 28-6-21, handed over 13-9-21. See above		1-22
☐	-*		Panavia Tornado GR.4 SIM	~	ex Filton, Boscombe Down. Arrived 16-9-21		1-22
☐	A-522		FMA Pucará	c80	ex Yeovilton, St Athan 8768M (27-9-82), Stanley, Argentine AF. Arrived 24-7-94	[14]	1-22
☐	E-419		Hawker Hunter F.51	56	ex Dunsfold, G-9-441, Dan AF Esk.724. Last flown 10-4-76. Acquired 12-7-77		1-22
☐	42157	'11-ML' and '11-ER'	NAA F-100D-16-NA Super Sabre	54	ex Sculthorpe, French AF, USAF 54-2147. Last flown 24-5-77, arrived 4-78	[15]	1-22
☐	16171		NAA F-86D-35-NA Sabre	53	ex Greek AF, USAF 51-6171. Arrived 7-87. *Sabre Knights*, 325th FIS USAF c/s to stb, 512th FIS to port		1-22
☐	26541		Republic F-84F-40-RE Thunderstreak	53	ex Greek AF, USAF 52-6541. Arrived 9-10-85		1-22
☐	–		HP C-10A Jetstream EMU	c68	ex Doncaster, Sunderland, Booker, Bushey, West Ruislip, Stanmore, St Albans, Radlett. Arr 1993. Cockpit, RAF c/s		1-22

■ **[1]** 'G-ADVU' incorporates parts from an original, built at Burns Garage, Congleton, Cheshire, 1936. **[2]** G-ARAD is an unflown project; construction started 1959 at Borgue, Scotland. **[3]** Take a look at **www.savethetrident.org** for details of the story of *Papa-Oscar* and how to help. **[4]** Mosquito is a memorial to Spennymoor-based designer/constructor/pilot Ernie Brooks, killed in the real G-AVYW 9-3-69. **[5]** Hurricane will wear 607 Sqn colours as 'P2874' 'AF-F'. **[6]** The 'N' commemorates Fulwell-born Claude Riley MM, who flew 'Ns' and other types on the Western Front and as CO of 37 Sqn at Stow Maries. Built with a grant from Heritage Lottery Fund is association with local Air Cadets and Sunderland College. **[7]** On loan from the Spitfire Society. **[8]** WT913 fitted with the wings of WT917. **[9]** WZ518 is fitted with the wings of WZ608, the cockpit is at Rayleigh, Essex. **[10]** Sea Vixen cockpit transferred to NELSAM ownership by 2021. **[11]** 'JP4' XP627 has the wings of Mk.3 XN584, see Treforest, Wales, for the fuselage. **[12]** See under Farnham, Surrey, for the real XS933. **[13]** The *real* XZ177 - a *Lynx* - is to be found at Kegworth, Leics. **[14]** Pucará is on loan from the Fleet Air Arm Museum. **[15]** On loan from the National Museum of the USAF's Loan Program.

Deep store: *Not* available for inspection.

☐	G-APKM	Auster J1N Alpha	58	ex Doncaster, Spanhoe, Newark. CoA 9-1-89. Arr by 12-18	[1]	1-22
☐	G-MBDL	AES Lone Ranger	81	de-reg 13-6-90. Arrived 1989		1-22
☐	DUC	Carmam M.100S	r78	BGA.2383, ex Carlton Moor, F-CCSA. CoA 6-5-88. Arr 2009		1-22
☐	–	Electra Flyer Olympus	c85	BAPC.228. Arrived 1989. Hang-glider, in its bag!		1-22
☐	WB685	DHC Chipmunk T.10	50	ex Leeds, Irlam, Edin UAS, Lyneham SF, 8 RFS, 1 RFS. SOC 19-7-72. Arrived 1986	[2]	1-22
☐	WZ767	Slingsby Grasshopper TX.1	52	ex Halton. Arrived 4-85. On loan		1-22

■ **[1]** *Kilo-Mike* was based at Newcastle from 1960 to 1969 and leased to the Sunderland Flying Club at Usworth. **[2]** WB685 is a composite, including the rear of WP969 (G-ATHC) and wings of WP833.

NOTTINGHAMSHIRE
Includes the unitary authority of Nottingham

BILSTHORPE east of the A614, south of Ollerton
Paintball Jungle Nottingham: ◆ *By prior application only* | **www.paintball-jungle.co.uk**

❑ XZ178	Westland Lynx AH.7	77 ex Hixon, M Wallop. Cabin. First noted 4-17	7-17
❑ XZ611	Westland Lynx AH.7	80 ex Hixon, M Wallop. Cabin. First noted 4-17	7-17

COLWICK southeast of Nottingham, south of the A612 ring road
St John the Baptist Primary School: Maintains its innovative classroom.
◆ *By prior arrangement* **only** | **www.st-johns-pri.notts.sch.uk**

❑ G-SSWO	Short 360-100	83 ex Millom, Blackpool, Emerald, SE-KLO, N343MV,	
		G-BKMY, G-14-3609. CoA 4-12-04, de-reg 6-6-07	9-21

HUCKNALL on the A611 north of Nottingham and south of Hucknall town
Hucknall Flight Test Museum: The former airfield was a famous engine flight test site. Affiliated with the Rolls-Royce Heritage Trust, the 'Wing Hangar' test-bed buildings will become the centre-piece of this museum-in-the-making.
◆ *Off the B6009, NG15 6GQ. Pre-arranged visits* **only** | **huflighttest@gmail.com** | **www.huflighttestmuseum.co.uk**

❑ XV798	HS Harrier GR.1	70 BAPC.450, ex W'-super-Mare, Kemble, Banwell, Foulness,	
		Dunsfold, 20, 233 OCU. Crashed 23-4-71. Arrived 1-2-20 [1]	2-20

■ [1] With the wing of T.2 XW264 - see Gloucestershire, Glos. XV798 was used for Pegasus plenum chamber burning (PCB) ground trials.

LANGAR AERODROME on minor roads south of the A46, north of Harby
Beech Restorations: Moved out of Bruntingthorpe during December 2020, bringing *Naval Encounter* to a private workshop here for completion. The Battle project is listed under 'Off-Site' at Bruntingthorpe, Leics. ◆ *By prior arrangement* **only**

❑ '43-35943'*	Beech D.18S		52 ex Bruntingthorpe, Cranfield, Perth, Prestwick, CF-DTN,	
		G-BKRN	RCAF inst A675, RCAF 1500. CoA 26-6-83. US Navy c/s,	
			Naval Encounter. Arrived 20-12-20	12-21

MANSFIELD on the A60 north of Nottingham
Vision West Nottinghamshire College: Derby Road. The Travel and Tourism faculty has an A321 fuselage.
◆ *By prior arrangement* **only** | **www.wnc.ac.uk**

❑ YL-LCL*	Airbus A320-214	95 ex St Athan, EI-DDL, SP-IAA, EI-DDL, F-GYFK, F-WQSY,	
		B-652L, B-2224, H-B-IJA, F-WWIF. Toulouse-built.	
		Last flight 11-10-20. Forward fuselage, arrived 26-8-21	12-21

No.384 Squadron Air Cadets: Botany Avenue. *Should* still have a Canberra cockpit.

❑ WT507	EE Canberra PR.7	54 ex Halton 8548M (11-3-71) 8131M, St Athan, 31, 17,	
		58, A&AEE, 58, 527, 58. Cockpit	1-12

NEWARK or Winthorpe, on the A46 northeast of Newark-on-Trent
Newark Air Museum: Visitors to the museum will have noticed the steady progress to GAL Monospar VH-UTH: its epic and largely unsung restoration was completed in mid-2021. This is an exceptional piece of work and a 'missing link' in charting Britain's aircraft industry. As *W&R* closed for press, Typhoon DA4 ZE590 had yet to arrive from Duxford, Cambs, as had the Reid & Sigrist Bobsleigh from Spanhoe, Northants: both are listed below in anticipation. See under Spanhoe for further comment the former prone-pilot test-bed Bobsleigh.

In Hangar 1's 'Lancaster Corner' is a Lancaster rear fuselage section, presented in March 1974, that had served for decades as a garden shed in Gainsborough. With the 9 Squadron codes 'WS-J' still evident on its sides, it was soon confirmed as Mk.I W4964 *Johnnie Walker - Still Going Strong* which took part in the raid on the German warship *Tirpitz* on 15th September 1944. That was W4964's hundredth 'op': only 36 Lancasters became 'century' bombers.

The museum has hosted the unique *CockpitFest* since its inception in 2000 - see also the Appendix section.

After spares recovery the hulk of Puma HC.1 XW225 departed a short distance east to the military exercise area at Beckingham, Lincs, on 10th December 2020.

◆ *Alongside Newark Showground, Drove Lane, NG24 2NY* | **01636 707170** | **enquire@newarkairmuseum.org** | **www.newarkairmuseum.org**

Bobsleigh VZ728 (G-AGOS) at Spanhoe, May 2021. *Ken Ellis*

☐ G-AHRI	DH Dove 1	46	ex Long Marston, East Kirkby, Tattershall, Little Staughton, 4X-ARI, G-AHRI. De-reg 18-5-72. Arrived 13-5-89. Iraq Petroleum Trans Co colours	1-22
☐ G-ANXB	DH Heron 1B	53	ex Biggin Hill, BEA, G-5-14. CoA 25-3-79, de-reg 2-11-81. Arrived 27-10-81. *Sir James Young Simpson*, BEA colours	1-22
☐ G-APRT	Taylor Monoplane	59	CoA 31-7-12, de-reg 16-4-12. Arrived 10-4-12 [1]	1-22
☐ G-APVV	Mooney M.20A	59	ex Skelmersdale, Barton, N8164E. Crashed 11-1-81, de-reg 3-4-89. Arrived 13-12-95	1-22
☐ G-ASNY	Bensen B-8	c64	ex Eccles. De-reg 17-12-91. Arrived 20-4-09 [2]	1-22
☐ G-AXMB	Slingsby Motor Cadet	71	ex Ringmer, BGA.805, VM590 (Cadet TX.1 1946). CoA 9-7-82, de-reg 9-1-92. Arrived 18-8-02	1-22
☐ G-BFTZ	MS Rallye Club	68	ex Firbeck, Hooton Park, Warmingham, Fownhope, Rhoose, F-BPAX. CoA 19-9-81, de-reg 14-11-91. Arr 27-1-96. *Kathy-S*	1-22
☐ G-BJAD	Clutton FRED Srs 2	r81	ex Retford. Unfinished project, de-reg 13-3-09. Arr 9-1-02	1-22
☐ G-BKPG	Luscombe Rattler Strike	r83	ex Egginton, Tatenhill. De-reg 31-7-91. Arrived 16-12-00	1-22
☐ G-CCLT	Powerchute Kestrel	93	ex Nantwich. De-reg 9-12-03. Arrived 27-10-03	1-22
☐ 'G-MAZY'	DH Tiger Moth	c41	BAPC.21, ex Innsworth, Staverton, Newark (1967), Thruxton. Arrived 25-6-95. Partially covered [3]	1-22
☐ G-MBBZ	Volmer VJ-24W	r81	ex Old Sarum. CoA 3-9-93, de-reg 29-11-95. Arr 16-10-98	1-22
☐ G-MBUE	MBA Tiger Cub 440	r82	ex Retford, Worksop. De-reg 6-9-94. Arrived 16-7-94. *The Dormouse Zeitgeist*	1-22
☐ G-MBVE	Hiway Skytrike	r82	de-reg 13-6-90, arrived 21-6-95	1-22
☐ G-MJCF	Maxair Hummer	r82	de-reg 24-1-95, arrived 17-1-06	1-22
☐ G-MJDW	Eipper Quicksilver MX	82	ex Horncastle. CoA 5-5-07, de-reg 13-2-08. Arrived 15-12-07	1-22
☐ G-MNRT	Aviasud Sirocco 377GB	86	ex Mansfield area. CoA 18-8-01. Arrived 28-6-05 [4]	1-22
☐ BDW	Slingsby T.8	c47	BGA.895, ex VM637. CoA 12-6-93. Stored	1-22
☐ CDX	SZD Pirat	68	BGA.1470, ex Darlton. CoA 6-1-07. Arrived 2007. Stored	1-22
☐ –	Lee-Richards Annular rep	64	BAPC.20, ex Shoreham, Winthorpe, *Those Magnificent Men...* Arrived 1975	1-22
☐ –	Mignet HM.14 'Flea'	37	BAPC.43, ex E' Kirkby, Tattershall, Wellingore. Arr 9-3-94 [5]	1-22
☐ –	Mignet HM.14 'Flea'	36	BAPC.101, ex Tumby Woodside, East Kirkby, Tattershall, Sleaford. Arrived 9-3-94. Battered fuselage [6]	1-22
☐ –	Zurowski ZP.1 helicopter	c77	BAPC.183, ex Burton-on-Trent. Unflown. Arrived 26-4-85	1-22

☐	–		Ward Gnome	c00	BAPC.330, unflown. Citroen 2CV. Arrived 11-07		1-22
☐	–		Slingsby T.67 Firefly CIM	95	ex Barkston Heath. Arrived 1-11. Cockpit procedure trainer		1-22
☐	-		Lockheed TriStar SIM	c75	ex Hendon, British Airways. Arrived 2-16	[7]	1-22
☐	VH-UTH		GAL Monospar ST-12	35	ex Innsworth, Winthorpe, Booker, Croydon, Panshanger,		
					Biggin Hill, Australia, New England Airways. Arrived 18-3-68		1-22
☐	9L-LSG*		Sud SA330L Puma	~	ex Horsham, Booker, Sierra Leone, Chilean Army H-259.		
					Arrived 1-10-20, spares source		1-22
☐	RA897		Slingsby Cadet TX.1	c44	stored. Arrived 2004		1-22
☐	TG517		HP Hastings T.5	48	ex 230 OCU, SCBS, BCBS, 202, 53, 47. Flew in 22-6-77		1-22
☐	VL348		Avro Anson C.19	46	ex Southend, G-AVVO (de-reg 16-9-72), Shawbury, 22 GCF,		
			G-AVVO		24 GCF, Colerne SF, 62 GCF, HCMSU, RCCF. SOC 15-11-67.		
					Arrived 11-72	[8]	1-22
☐	VR249	'FA-EL'	Percival Prentice T.1	48	ex G-APIY, Laarbruch Fg Club, 1 ASS, RAFC. SOC 17-8-57.		
			G-APIY		CoA 18-3-67, de-reg 19-4-73. Flew in 8-7-67. RAFC colours		1-22
☐	VZ608		Gloster Meteor FR.9	51	ex Hucknall, Shoreham, MoS, RR. RB.108 test-bed. Arr 2-70		1-22
☐	VZ634		Gloster Meteor T.7	48	ex Wattisham 8657M, 5 MU, Leeming SF, Stradishall SF,		
					41, 141, 609, 247. SOC 15-11-71. Arrived 16-12-85		1-22
☐	VZ728*		R&S Bobsleigh	G-AGOS 45	ex Spanhoe, Coalville, Perth, Strathallan, Thruxton, RAE,		
			(Desford Trainer)		Desford. CoA 28-11-80. First test flight 22-4-18	[9]	**due**
☐	WB491		Avro Ashton 2	51	ex Woodford, Rhoose, Dunsfold, Farnborough, RR, RAE,		
			G-AJJW		Tudor 2 G-AJJW (de-reg 10-4-49), TS897. SOC 13-2-62.		
					Arrived 26-2-03. Forward fuselage	[10]	1-22
☐	WB624		DHC Chipmunk T.10	50	ex Hooton Park, Firbeck, Long Marston, Warmingham,		
					East Midlands, Wigan, Dur UAS, Aberdeen UAS, Henlow,		
					St Athan, 22 GCF, Debden, Jurby SF, 8 FTS, 18 RFS.		
					SOC 14-7-72. Arrived 14-9-95		1-22
☐	WF369	'F'	Vickers Varsity T.1	51	ex 6 FTS, AE&AEOS, AES, 2 ANS, 201 AFS.		
					SOC 1-4-76, flew in same day. 6 FTS colours		1-22
☐	WH791		EE Canberra PR.7	54	ex 'WH792' Cottesmore 'WH717' 8187M (19-11-71),		
					St Athan 8176M and 8165M, 81, 58, 82, 542.		
					Arrived 29-11-98. 81 Sqn colours	[11]	1-22
☐	WH863		EE Canberra T.17	53	ex Marham 8693M, 360, A&AEE, B.2, RAE, IAM.		
					Short-built. SOC 29-5-81. Arrived 10-7-90. Cockpit	[12]	1-22
☐	WH904		EE Canberra T.19	53	ex Cambridge, 7, 85, T.11, W Raynham TFF, 228 OCU,		
					B.2 35, 207. Short-built. SOC 4-6-80. Arrived 1-10-85	[13]	1-22
☐	WK277	'N'	V-S Swift FR.5	55	ex Congresbury, Wisley, Cosford, Leconfield 7719M		
					(9-11-61), 2, F.4, RAE. Arrived 18-8-69. 2 Sqn colours		1-22
☐	WM913	'456'	Hawker Sea Hawk FB.3	54	ex Fleetwood, Sealand 8162M, Culdrose A2510 (14-7-61),		
					Abbotsinch, 736, 700, 895, 897, 806. Arr 1-7-84. 897 c/s		1-22
☐	WR977	'B'	Avro Shackleton MR.3/3	57	ex Finningley 8186M (3-11-71), 203, 42, 206, 203, 42,		
					201, 206, 201, 220. Arrived 1-5-77. 42 Sqn colours	[14]	1-22
☐	WS692	'C'	Gloster Meteor NF.12	53	ex Cranwell, Henlow 7605M (8-7-59), 72, 46. AWA-built.		
					Arrived 31-10-81. 72 Sqn colours		1-22
☐	WS739		Gloster Meteor	54	ex Misson, Church Fenton 7961M (12-10-67), Kemble, 1 ANS,		
			NF(T).14		2 ANS, NF.14, 25. AWA-built. Arrived 21-1-84. 25 Sqn c/s		1-22
☐	WT651	'C'	Hawker Hunter F.1	54	ex Lawford Heath, Halton, Credenhill, Weeton 7532M		
					(22-11-57), 229 OCU, 233 OCU, 229 OCU, 222.		
					Arrived 17-1-92. 222 Sqn colours		1-22
☐	WT933		Bristol Sycamore 3	51	ex Sutton, Strensall, Halton 7709M (18-11-60), A&AEE,		
			G-ALSW		G-ALSW (de-reg 26-3-51). Arrived 17-6-80		1-22
☐	WV606	'P-B'	Percival Provost T.1	54	ex Halton 7622M (20-11-55), 1 FTS. Arrived 2-72		1-22
☐	WV787		EE Canberra B.2/8	52	ex Abingdon 8799M (23-12-83), A&AEE, Ferranti, ASM.		
					Arrived 24-11-85. Hefner 'bunny' logo, A&AEE colours		1-22
☐	WW217	'351'	DH Sea Venom FAW.21	55	ex Cardiff, Ottershaw, Culdrose, Yeovilton, ADS, 891, 890.		
					Hawarden-built. SOC 20-8-70. Arrived 18-12-83. 890 Sqn c/s		1-22
☐	WX905		DH Venom NF.3	53	ex Henlow, Hendon, Yatesbury 7458M (14-10-57),		
					27 MU, 23. Hawarden-built. Arrived 16-5-89. 23 Sqn c/s		1-22
☐	XA239		Slingsby Grasshopper TX.1	53	ex 'Northampton'. Arrived 2004		1-22
☐	XB261		Blackburn Beverley C.1	55	ex Duxford, Southend, A&AEE. SOC 6-10-71.		
					Arrived 25-5-04. Flightdeck		1-22

❑ XD593	'50'	DH Vampire T.11	54	ex Woodford, Chester, St Athan, 8 FTS, CFS, FWS, 5 FTS, 4 FTS. Hawarden-built. SOC 12-12-68. Arr 30-3-73. CFS c/s 1-22
❑ XH992	'P'	Gloster Javelin FAW.8	59	ex Cosford 7829M (21-2-64), Shawbury, 85. Arrived 22-8-81. 85 Sqn colours 1-22
❑ XJ560		DH Sea Vixen FAW.2	59	ex RAE Bedford, Farnborough, Halton 8142M (29-6-71), 893, 899, 892, 890. Christchurch-built. Arrived 10-8-86 1-22
❑ XL764	'J'	Saro Skeeter AOP.12	58	ex Nostell Priory, Rotherham, M Wallop, Arborfield 7940M (13-3-67), Hayes, A&AEE, MoA, AAC, Saro, AAC. Arr 16-7-80 1-22
❑ XM383	'90'	Hunting Jet Provost T.3A	60	ex Crowland, Scampton, 7 FTS, 1 FTS, RAFC, 6 FTS, BSE, 2 FTS, A&AEE, 2 FTS. Arrived 12-11-94. 7 FTS colours 1-22
❑ XM594		Avro Vulcan B.2	63	ex 44, Scampton Wing, 617, 27. SOC 19-1-83. Flew in 7-2-83. 44 Sqn colours [14] 1-22
❑ XM685	'513'	Westland Whirlwind HAS.7	59	ex Panshanger, Elstree, Luton, G-AYZJ (de-reg 29-12-80), Fleetlands, Lee-on-Solent, 771, Ark Ship's Flt, 847, 848. SOC 24-3-71. Arrived 17-6-80. 771 Sqn colours 1-22
❑ XN573	'E'	Hunting Jet Provost T.3	61	ex Blackpool Airport, Kemble, 1 FTS, CFS. SOC 28-5-76. Arrived 15-4-89. Cockpit 1-22
❑ XN819		AW Argosy C.1	61	ex Finningley 8205M (10-7-72), 8198M, Shawbury, Benson Wing, 105, MoA. Arrived 2-84. Cockpit in display hall 1-22
❑ XN964	'630'	Blackburn Buccaneer S.1	63	ex Bruntingthorpe, E Midlands, Brough (10-10-76), Pershore, RRE, RAE, 803, 736, 801. Arr 26-2-88. 736 Sqn c/s 1-22
❑ XP226		Fairey Gannet AEW.3	62	ex Lee-on-Solent, Southwick, Lee-on-S', A2667 (28-3-79), Lossiemouth, Ilchester, 849. Arr 7-11-82. 849 'D' Flt colours 1-22
❑ XR534	'65'	Folland Gnat T.1	63	ex Dunholme Bridge, Valley 8578M (2-12-77), 4 FTS, CFS. Arrived 2-12-00. 4 FTS colours 1-22
❑ XR757		EE Lightning F.6	65	ex Scampton, Grainthorpe, New Waltham, Rissington, Binbrook, 5-11 pool, 23, 5. SOC 24-6-88. Cockpit. Arrived by 6-15. 11 Sqn colours [15] 1-22
❑ XS238		Auster AOP.9	62	ex M Wallop, 14/20 Air Sqn, 21 Flt 651. SOC 15-7-66. Arrived 1999. Fuselage 1-22
❑ XS417	'DZ'	EE Lightning T.5	64	ex Binbrook, LTF, 5, 11, 5, 11, LTF, 56, 23, 11, 23, 226 OCU. SOC 29-7-88. Arrived 5-9-88. LTF colours 1-22
❑ XS726	'T'	HS Dominie T.1	65	ex Ipswich, Cosford 9273M (24-6-97), Cranwell, 3 FTS, 6 FTS, CAW. Arrived 24-9-14 1-22
❑ XT200	'F'	Bell Sioux AH.1	65	ex M Wallop. Westland-built. Arrived 1978 1-22
❑ XV490		McD Phantom FGR.2	69	ex Nantwich, Bruntingthorpe, Wattisham, 74, 228 OCU, 92, 56, 22, 92, 56, 23. SOC 1-10-92. Cockpit. 92 Sqn c/s [16] 1-22
❑ XV728	'A'	Westland Wessex HC.2	68	ex Fleetlands, 72, 2 FTS, CFS, 18. Arr 18-8-98. Argonaut 1-22
❑ XW208		Sud Puma HC.1	71	ex Cranwell, Shawbury, Boscombe Down, 33, 230, 33, 72, 33, 230, 240 OCU, 1563 Flt, 33, 240 OCU, 33, 240 OCU, 33. Arrived 7-2-18. 33 Sqn colours 1-22
❑ XW276		Sud Gazelle 03	70	ex Sunderland, Wroughton, Southampton, M Wallop, Farnborough, Leatherhead, F-ZWRI. Arrived 4-99 [17] 1-22
❑ XX467		Hawker Hunter T.7 G-TVII	58	ex Bruntingthorpe, Exeter, Kemble, G-TVII (de-reg 28-7-14) Perth, SOC 13-10-83. 1 TWU, Jordan AF 836, Saudi AF 70-617, G-9-214, XL605, 66, 92. Arrived 3-5-17 [18] 1-22
❑ XX492	'A'	HP Jetstream T.1	75	ex Culdrose, Cranwell, 45, 3 FTS, 45, 6 FTS, METS. SAL-completed. Arrived 9-12-04. 45 Sqn colours 1-22
❑ XX634	'T'	SAL Bulldog T.1	74	ex Wellesbourne M', Shawbury, Liv UAS, Man UAS, E Mids UAS, CFS, 3 FTS, CFS, Cam UAS, 2 FTS. Arr 9-1-06. CFS c/s 1-22
❑ XX753		SEPECAT Jaguar GR.1	75	ex RAF EP&TU, Bottesford, 9087M, St Athan, Abingdon, Shawbury, 54, 226 OCU, 6. Arr 1-5-10. Cockpit. 16 Sqn c/s 1-22
❑ XX829	'GZ'	SEPECAT Jaguar T.2A	74	ex Ipswich, Shawbury, St Athan, 54, 16, 6, 226 OCU, 6, 54. Arrived 21-3-12. 54 Sqn colours 1-22
❑ XX899		Blackburn Buccaneer S.2B	76	ex Coventry, Kidlington, Stock, St Athan, Lossiemouth, 208, 12, Gulf Det, 12, 237 OCU, 16, 15, 208, 12. SOC 10-10-94. Arrived 26-10-18. Cockpit. 12 Sqn colours [19] 1-22
❑ ZA176	'126'	HS Sea Harrier F/A.2	81	ex Yeovilton, 801, 800, 801, 899, 801, 899, 800, 801, 899, 801, 809, 800, 809, 899. Arr 21-7-04. 800 Sqn c/s 1-22

☐	ZA717	BV Chinook HC.1	82	ex Cranwell 9238M, St Athan, Fleetlands, 78, 7, 1310 Flt, 18, N37056. Crashed 25-7-89. Arrived 22-2-18		1-22
☐	ZH590	Eurofighter Typhoon DA4	97	ex Duxford, Coningsby, Warton trials fleet	[20]	**due**
☐	–	Hunting Jet Provost CIM	c60	procedures trainer. Arrived 1998		1-22
☐	–	Folland Gnat T.1 CIM	c62	ex Melton Mowbray. Procedures trainer - forward cockpit. Folland-built. Arrived 1994		1-22
☐	'DB001'	McD Phantom CIM	69	ex Wattisham. Full-axis simulator. Arrived 1992		1-22
☐	–	EE Canberra PR.9	c52	BAPC.518, ex Corby, Stock, Rhoose, Brough, Boscombe Down, Short-built. Arrived 14-11-00. Cockpit	[21]	1-22
☐	–	SAL Bulldog T.1 CIM	~	ex Newark, Newton	[22]	1-22
☐	A92-708*	GAF Jindivik 103B	c75	ex Filton, Kemble. Llanbedr. Lost 28-8-80 on 125th sortie, salvaged. Arrived 28-6-21		1-22
☐	AR-107	SAAB S.35XD Draken	71	ex Scampton, Esk.729, Danish AF. Last flight 25-2-94. Arrived 29-6-94		1-22
☐	83 '8-MS'	Dassault Mystère IVA	56	ex Sculthorpe, French AF. Last flown 3-5-78, arrived 9-78. ET.1/8 colours	[23]	1-22
☐	QP-31	Westland Lynx HC.28	77	ex Fleetlands, Almondbank, Wroughton, Qatar Police, G-17-21. Arrived 18-12-18	[24]	1-22
☐	56321	SAAB 91B-2 Safir G-BKPY	56	ex G-BKPY (for the delivery), Norwegian AF. Flew in 14-7-82. De-reg 8-2-02		1-22
☐	Fv37918 '57'	SAAB AJSH.37 Viggen	76	ex Cranwell, Swedish AF, F21 and F10 Wings. Last flight 7-2-06, arrived 25-6-06. F21 colours		1-22
☐	'458'	Mikoyan-Gurevich MiG-23M *Flogger*	c75	ex Chester, Latvia, USSR. (024003607). Imported 1993. Arrived 22-5-02. Polish colours	[25]	1-22
☐	'71'	Mikoyan-Gurevich MiG-27K *Flogger*	c79	ex Chester, Latvia, USSR. (61912507006). Imported 1993. Arrived 22-5-02. Soviet AF colours	[25]	1-22
☐	42-12417	NAA Harvard IIB	42	ex Earls Colne, Harrington, East Tilbury, Windsor, North Weald, Dutch AF B-163 (SOC 15-11-62), RCAF FE930, 42-12417. Noorduyn-built. Arrived 24-8-10		1-22
☐	51-9036	Lockheed T-33A-1-LO	51	ex '5547', Sculthorpe, French AF. Last flown 30-5-78. Arrived 1979. 36th FBG colours for 2022	[22]	1-22
☐	'0-63008'	NAA F-100D-16-NA Super Sabre 54-2223	54	ex Sculthorpe, French AF, USAAF 54-2223. Last flown 24-5-77, arrived 5-78. 4 494th TFS colours by 8-21. *Spirit of Liberty*	[22]	1-22
☐	'82127' and G-APNJ	Cessna 310 G-APNJ	56	ex Shoreham, EI-AJY, N3635D. CoA 28-11-74, de-reg 5-12-83. Arrived 4-3-04. USAF L-27 / U-3A colours, *Blue Canoe*		1-22

■ **[1]** G-APRT is the prototype JT.1 Monoplane, designed and built by John Taylor and first flown at White Waltham 4-7-59. **[2]** *November-Yankee* is on loan from Roger Light - see Stockport, Gtr Man. **[3]** Tiger Moth 'G-MAZY' is a composite; mostly G-AMBB, ex T6801, in which case it is: ex Scampton SF, 6 FTS, 18 EFTS. **[4]** Sirocco was built by Midland Ultralights at Bitteswell, Leics. **[5]** Built by Alan Troop at Wellingore, Lincs - made a few hops in 1938. **[6]** Built by 'Bobby' Earl at Carlight Motors, Sleaford; believed unfinished. **[7]** Simulator built by Atkins and Merrill, Tulsa, Oklahoma. **[8]** Anson has the outer wings of Mk.XI G-ALIH (ex NL229) which was delivered to the museum on 3-9-69 from Southend, but destroyed by fire on 11-5-71. **[9]** Built by Reid and Sigrist at Desford as the RS.3 Desford advanced trainer, first flown 9-7-45. Converted to RS.4 Bobsleigh prone-pilot test-bed VZ728, first flown 13-6-51. Civilianised for aerial survey work in 1958 as Desford Trainer. **[10]** Laid down at Woodford as Tudor 2 G-AJJW, TS850, but completed as an Ashton. **[11]** PR.7 WH791 on loan from 81 Squadron Association. **[12]** T.17 cockpit is on loan from Aaron Braid. **[13]** T.19 WH904 was built by Shorts Brothers and Harland as a B.2 and therefore the forward fuselage *should* have a plate reading SHB-0-2388. Inspection found the cockpit to have the plate EEP71123, which would make it WH651. The logic works out like this... WH651 was issued to English Electric for conversion from a B.2 to a T.4 on 5-7-56 and in this process it would have been fitted with a new-build T.4 cockpit. It looks as though the old cockpit passed on to Boulton Paul for use in the B.2 to T.11 conversions. WH904 was issued to BP on 17-10-57 for T.11 fit. It received the cockpit of WH651. (And later was further converted to T.19 status.) **[14]** Shackleton and the Vulcan were transferred from ownership by Lincolnshire's Lancaster Association to the museum 15-12-21. **[15]** XR757 on loan from Trevor Garrod. **[16]** Phantom cockpit on loan from Mike Davey - see also Liverpool, Merseyside. **[17]** Gazelle on loan from the Army Flying Museum, Middle Wallop, Hampshire. **[18]** T.7 on loan from Colin Savill. **[19]** Buccaneer cockpit, a 1991 Gulf War veteran - 19 missions - on loan from Robin Phipps - see also under Steventon, Oxfordshire. **[20]** DA4 made its first flight on 3-3-97 and its last on 13-12-06. **[21]** PR.9 cockpit, owned by Frank and Lee Millar (also ex Corby, Northants), is the first of two unflown 'boiler plate' cockpits for development and/or installations trials. It was last used for miniature detonation cord trials at Brough. **[22]** Bulldog CIM is on loan from Higgins Aviation, Newark, Notts. **[23]** From the National Museum of the USAF's Loan Program. **[24]** Lynx donated by Andy Rawdon, see South Clifton, Notts. **[25]** *Floggers* on loan from Hawarden Aviation Services, Hawarden, Wales: both briefly away from the site in September 2019 for use in a film.

NEWARK-ON-TRENT

Cliff and **David Baker**: The famous Auster workshop and store. Airedale G-ARXC moved to 'Kent' for restoration by 2020.

◆ Strictly *by prior permission* **only**

❑ G-AHHK	Auster J1 Autocrat	46	ex Shobdon, Cranfield. Damaged 3-86, CoA 22-3-70, de-reg 3-4-89. Frame	[1]	1-15
❑ G-ALNV	Taylorcraft Auster 5	44	ex Nottingham, Leicester, AOP.V RT578, 341, 329. CoA 4-7-50, de-reg 1-5-59		1-15
❑ 'G-AMKL'	Auster 'B.4'	~	nearing completion	[2]	11-19
❑ G-ANHW	Taylorcraft Auster 5D	45	ex Shipdham, AOP.V TJ320, 664. CoA 9-3-70, de-reg 15-12-71		1-20
❑ G-AOCP	Taylorcraft Auster 5	45	ex AOP.V TW462, 666. Damaged 4-70, de-reg 24-6-71	[3]	1-15
❑ G-ARGB	Auster 6A Tugmaster	46	ex Waddington, AOP.6 VF635, 662, 1901 Flt. CoA 21-6-74, de-reg 30-5-84		1-20
❑ G-AROJ	Beagle Airedale	62	ex Leicester, Thorney, HB-EUC, G-AROJ. CoA 8-1-76, de-reg 21-1-80		1-15
❑ G-ARTM	Beagle Terrier 1	50	ex Chirk, Auster T.7 WE536, 651, 657, Schwechat SF. Crashed 28-5-70, de-reg 12-9-73		1-15
❑ EI-AMF	Taylorcraft Plus D	42	ex Abbeyshrule, G-ARRK, G-AHUM, Auster I LB286, Coltishall SF, 309, 70 GCF, 84 GCF, 22 EFTS, 43 OTU, 653		1-20
❑ –	c/n 3705 Auster D6/180	~	ex White Waltham, Rearsby. Frame		1-15
❑ –	c/n B.648 Beagle Terrier 3	~	ex White Waltham, Rearsby. Frame		1-15

■ **[1]** This J1N frame, originally thought to be the second fuselage used by G-AIGR, is *believed* to be from J/1 G-AHHK. **[2]** A reproduction of the Auster rear-loading ambulance one-off, the B.4, it will wear the original's identity of G-AMKL. It is based on an as yet unidentified 'donor' airframe. **[3]** Auster 5 G-AOCP is a composite, including parts from G-AKOT.

NOTTINGHAM

University of Nottingham Aerospace Technology Centre: Innovation Park, Triumph Road.

◆ By prior arrangement **only** | www.nottingham.ac.uk/aerospace

❑ –*	Robinson R22	~	first noted 3-21	3-21

Also: The Archaeopteryx is at a *private* location in the *general* area. It is held by the descendants of the Granger brothers, Richard Francis and Richard John, who designed and built light aircraft in the 1920s and 1930s: including G-ABXL.

❑ G-ABXL	Granger Archaeopteryx	30	ex Old Warden, Radcliffe on Trent, Old Warden, Chilwell. Arrived 28-4-67. CoA 22-9-82	N10-18

NOTTINGHAM CITY AERODROME or Tollerton, south of the A52, east of the city   EGBN

❑ G-BGGF	Piper Tomahawk	78	CoA 15-10-94, de-reg 4-12-02. Fuselage	9-21
❑ G-GRAY	Cessna 172N		ex N4859D. Ditched 2-4-93, de-reg 27-9-00. Fuselage, dumped	9-21

SOUTH CLIFTON south of the A57 and west of the A1133, west of Lincoln

Andy Rawden: Airframes are kept at a *private* location in the area.

❑ 5N-AAN	'K'	HSA HS.125-3B/RA	67	ex Newark, Sunderland, Woolsington, Biggin Hill, F-GFMP, G-AVAI, LN-NPA, G-AVAI. Cockpit. Dominie colours	8-20
❑ XT640*		Westland Scout AH.1	64	ex Westbury, Ipswich, Arborfield, Lee-on-Solent, M Wallop, 654, 666, 663. Arrived by 7-21	8-21
❑ XZ694		Westland Lynx HAS.3	79	ex Ipswich, Fleetlands, Yeovilton, 815, Gulf War, 815, HAS.2, 815, 702. Arrived by 6-18	[1] 8-20

■ **[1]** Took out an Iraqi tug 15-2-91 care of a Sea Skua missile.

SYERSTON AIRFIELD off the A46 southwest of Newark-on-Trent   EGXY

RAF Syerston: Home of the **Air Cadet STEM College**'s Tornados and Tucano, and the **Central Glider Maintenance Flight**.

❑ ZA267	'FA'	Panavia Tornado F.2	80	ex Marham 9284M, Boscombe Down. First noted 8-18	10-21
❑ ZA357	'TTV'	Panavia Tornado GR.1	81	ex Cosford, 9341M, St Athan, 15, TTTE. Arrived 25-4-19	10-21
❑ ZF202*		Short Tucano T.1	89	ex Linton-on-Ouse, Shawbury, 72, 1 FTS, 3 FTS, CFS. Arrived 18-8-20	10-21
❑ ZH185*		Grob Vigilant T.1	90	ex D-KGRO, D-KMSN	9-19

WORKSOP on the A57/A60 east of Sheffield
Phil Jarvis: Phil also has two cockpits at Doncaster, S Yorks: Harvard FX322 and Harrier XV806.
☐ ZH655   BAe/McDD Harrier T.12   94   ex Doncaster, Ipswich, Cottesmore, Wittering.
                                                Crashed 26-7-95. Cockpit   4-18

OXFORDSHIRE

ABINGDON
Lodge Hill Garage: West of the A4183, close to its junction with the A34, has a plinth-mounted Spitfire.
☐ 'N3310'   'AI-A' V-S Spitfire FSM   ~   BAPC.393, ex Wellesbourne Mountford, Winthorpe   3-19

Also: A Chipmunk should still be at a *private* location in the *general* area.
☐ WP977   DHC Chipmunk T.10   52   ex South Molton, Cambridge, Yateley, Crowland, Doncaster,
                 G-BHRD   Stamford, Burford, 9M-ANA, VR-SEK, WP977, Malayan
                                              Aux AF, Rufforth SF, Man UAS, Liv UAS, 63 GCF, Queen's UAS,
                                              Man UAS. Crashed 21-1-97, de-reg 19-1-98   6-17

ARNCOTT south of the A41 southeast of Bicester
St George's Barracks: Within is the **Defence Explosive Ordnance Disposal, Munitions and Search School.**
☐ XP855   Westland Scout AH.1   63   ex Arborfield, Wroughton, 652, 651, 655. First noted 6-17   12-19
☐ XW430   'MW' BAC Jet Provost T.5A   72   ex Cosford, 9176M (20-1-93), 1 FTS, CFS, 3 FTS, Leeming SF,
                                              3 FTS. First noted 6-17   12-19
☐ XX396   'N'   Sud Gazelle HT.3   75   ex Cranwell, 8718M, EPTT, St Athan, Abingdon, Henlow,
                                              2 FTS. Westland-built. Crashed 30-6-81. First noted 6-17   12-19
☐ ZD607   HS Sea Harrier F/A.2   85   ex Gosport, St Athan 9328M, Warton, St Athan, 800,
                                              FRS.1, 801, 800, 801, 800, 801, 800, 899. Crashed 2-7-00.
                                              Arrived 23-8-12   12-19

BECKLEY north of the B4027, northeast of Oxford
The Sea King has been joined by a JetRanger at a private location.
☐ N260A*   Bell JetRanger III   ~   gutted cab, first noted 4-21   8-21
☐ ZA135   '705' Westland Sea King HAS.6   81   ex Hixon, Fleetlands, Gosport, 771, 849, 820, *Gannet* SAR Flt,
                                                  819, 820, 819, 810, 706, 820. SOC 7-10-09. Arrived 12-13   [1] 8-21
■ **[1]** The tail end of ZA135 is fitted to XV657 at Culdrose, Cornwall.

BENSON AIRFIELD east of the A4074, east of Wallingford   EGUB
RAF Benson: With the venerable Puma due to leave service in December 2022, several examples are entering long-term
storage. If – and it's a big MoD-type 'if' – the stand down date holds, this will not require formal listing. For the record, the
following were in 'deep' store here in late 2021: XW217, XW219, XW232, ZA935 and ZA936. Puma HC.1 XW201, used for
BDRT training, is believed to have been scrapped.
☐ 'PL904'   V-S Spitfire FSM   89   BAPC.226, ex 'EN343', displayed, 541 Sqn colours   1-22
☐ XW223   Sud Puma HC.1   71   ex 33, 230. Westland-built. SOC 31-12-12. Instructional   4-16
☐ ZA937*   Sud Puma HC.2   80   ex 230, 33, 230. Westland-built. SOC 31-12-12. For display 8-20
☐ 82-23762*   BV CH-47D Chinook   66   ex Odiham, US Army, Fort Rucker, CH-47A 66-0122.
                                              Arrived UK 1-07. Forward fuselage, procedures trainer   1-22

BICESTER Tornado GR.1 ZA319 had moved to Old Sarum, Wilts, by November 2021.

BRIZE NORTON AIRFIELD on the A4095 southwest of Witney   EGVN
RAF Brize Norton: The **Defence Movements Training Squadron** (DMTS) and the **Joint Air Delivery Test and Evaluation Unit**
(JADT&EU) keep airframes for instruction and trials. Several mock-ups are employed, including the rear end of an A400M.
The fuselage of Hercules C.3 XV304 had left JADT&EU by October 2021, very likely scrapped as the venerable 'Herk' nears
the end of its service life. The Dakota is displayed outside the **47 Air Despatch Squadron** hangar.

❏ 'FZ626'	Douglas Dakota 4	44	ex Lyneham, Coventry, Air Atlantique, G-AMPO, LN-RTO,	
	'YS-DH'		G-AMPO, KN566, Oakington SF, 77, 62, Waterbeach SF,	
			1381 CU, 133 CU, 238, USAAF C-47B-30-DK 44-76853.	
			Oklahoma City-built. CoA 29-3-97. de-reg 18-10-01.	
			Arrived 16-9-12. 271 Sqn colours	10-21
❏ XW236	Sud Puma HC.1	73	ex Benson, 33, 230, 27, 33, 230, 1563 Flt, 33. Westland-	
			built. Forward fuselage. Arr 16-6-14. DMTS. Dumped by 9-20	12-21
❏ ZB684	Sud Gazelle AH.1	83	ex 9330M, Fleetlands, 667, 665, 655. Westland-built.	
			JADT&EU. First noted 9-15	10-21

CHALGROVE AIRFIELD on the B480 northwest of Watlington   EGLJ
Martin-Baker: Meteor T.7s WL419 (G-JSMA) *Asterix* and WA638 (G-JWMA) act as flying test-beds for M-B. A pair of Danish Air Force GD F-16 cockpits – E-196 and ET-626 - arrived via air freight at Brize Norton on 18th March 2021 destined for tests/trials here. They may merit a formal listing come *W&R29*.

❏ EE416	Gloster Meteor III	46	ex Wroughton, South Kensington, M-B. Cockpit	[1] 12-20

■ **[1]** With a Martin-Baker ejection seat squeezed in behind the pilot, EE416 carried out the first airborne use of a British 'bang seat' on a sortie out of Chalgrove on 24-7-46. The 'ejectee' was Bernard 'Benny' Lynch, a volunteer.

CULHAM on the A415 east of Abingdon
Lasergaming Oxford: Located within the former airfield. ◆ **Strictly** *by prior permission* | www.outdoorlaser.com

❏ XV720	Westland Wessex HC.2	68	ex Hixon, Gosport A2701 [2], Fleetlands, SARTU, 22, 18.	
			First noted 5-14	5-21
❏ XZ643	'C' Westland Lynx AH.7	80	ex Croft, Middle Wallop. First noted 11-13	5-21

ENSTONE AERODROME on the B4030 east of Chipping Norton   EGTN
Bit of tidying up: the following have been deleted Cessna 172 G-ARYI (last noted June 2018), Horizon G-BFAA (July 2017), Jodel G-BMKF (March2018) and Horizon F-WREI (March 2018). The anonymous Pawnee frame moved to Cantley, Norfolk, by late 2021. Chipmunk T.10 WK620, last recorded in September 2015, moved to Hawarden, Wales.

❏ G-ARET	Piper Tri-Pacer 160	60	ex North Moreton. CoA 20-5-83	6-21
❏ G-AXPF	Cessna F.150K	69	CoA 22-4-02, Reims-built	7-21
❏ G-BHRW*	Jodel DR.221 Dauphin	67	ex F-BPCP. CEA-built. De-reg 7-7-17	7-21
❏ G-BNCG*	QAC Quickie	91	crashed 21-8-97, de-reg 12-1-98, CoA 29-5-98. F/n 7-20	7-20
❏ G-BODS	Piper Tomahawk 112	79	ex N2379F. CoA 30-3-15, fuselage	7-20
❏ G-BTET	Piper J-3C-65	46	ex N98141. Damaged 31-8-13, CoA 4-12-13	7-20
❏ G-JIMB*	Beagle Pup 100	69	ex G-AWWF, G-35-033. CoA 10-5-12. First noted 11-20	12-21
❏ G-RORY	Piaggio P.149D	58	ex Marshall, G-TOWN, D-EFFY, Luftwaffe 90+06, BB+394.	
			Focke-Wulf-built. CoA 7-1-08. First noted 6-14	12-21
❏ G-SION	Piper Tomahawk 112	81	ex N32661. Crashed 2-7-97, CoA 28-12-00, de-reg 9-9-02	12-21
❏ F-GDNR*	SOCATA Trinidad	~	de-reg 12-5-11. First noted 8-20	12-21
❏ D-ECFE	Oberlerchner JOB 15	60	ex OE-CAO. First noted 11-12	6-21
❏ N66576	Boeing PT-17 Kaydet	~	ex USA. Fuselage, first noted 8-16	8-21
❏ LB369*	Taylorcraft Plus D	42	ex South Africa ZU-MGM, VP-YPX, G-AHHY, Auster I	
	G-AHHY		LB369, 655, 657, 1 'hack'. Arrived 7-20	12-21
❏ XX764	'13' SEPECAT Jaguar GR.1	75	ex Woodmancote, Small Dole, St Athan 9010M, Shawbury,	
			226 OCU, 6, 226 OCU, 14. Last flown 3-9-84.	
			Arrived 22-9-17, displayed	[1] 1-22
❏ 3019*	NA Harvard II G-CPPM	41	ex Bruntingthorpe, Canada, Trenton, Uxbridge (Ontario),	
			RCAF 3019, 1 FTS, 1 SFTS, 8 SFTS. RCAF colours	[2] 6-21

■ **[1]** Jaguar under restoration by Neil Atterbury - www.jaguarxx764.co.uk **[2]** Two other Harvards also reported present 4-21

GROVE on the A417 northwest of Wantage
Grove Business Park: Located on the western edge of the former airfield. | www.grovebusinesspark.com

❏ J-1758	DH Venom FB.54	57	ex Lambourn, N Weald, N203DM, Cranfield, G-BLSD (de-reg	
	G-BLSD		(5-6-96), Swiss AF. Swiss-built. 145 Sqn colours.	
			Badly damaged in gales 18-2-22	2-22

HENLEY-ON-THAMES on the A4155 north of Reading

Bremont Manufacturing and Technology Centre: The high-tech company headquarters in Reading Road for the famous watch maker, opened in 2021. The building is called 'The Wing' and appropriately boasts a 747 flightdeck.
◆ *By prior arrangement* **only** | **www.bremont.com**

❑ G-BYGB*	Boeing 747-436	99	ex Kemble, St Athan, BA. Last flown 2-9-20. De-reg 5-5-21. Flightdeck	11-21

No.447 Squadron Air Cadets: Friday Street

❑ XS218	Hunting Jet Provost T.4	64	ex Woodley, Halton 8508M (23-2-77), Shawbury, 3 FTS. Cockpit	1-19

Also: At separate sites in the *general* area, the Aero and Vampire are at *private* locations.

❑ G-ATBH*	Aero 145	65	ex Redhill. LET-built. CoA 26-10-81	9-18
❑ J-1169	DH Vampire FB.6	~	ex Samedan, Swiss AF. Swiss-built	6-20

OXFORD AIRPORT or Kidlington

EGTK

Midland Aeroplane Company relocated from Turweston, Bucks, during October 2021: the Plus D and the Tailwind merit a listing. Classic *W&R...* fire trainer Warrior G-BYKR was written out of Edition 27 as bound to have expired, unrecorded since 2015: not so, it 'lives' on. Previously 'flown' inside the business centre opposite the airfield, in the summer of 2020 EoN 460 G-APWL moved to Lasham, Hampshire.

❑ G-AHUG*	Taylorcraft Plus D	42	ex Turweston, Thame, Panshanger, Auster I LB282, Turnhouse SF, 43 OTU, 653. First noted 11-21	11-21
❑ G-BDBD*	Wittman Tailwind	63	ex Turweston, N1198S. Hamilton Tool-built. Crashed 2-8-11, CoA 22-2-12	11-21
❑ G-BYKR*	Piper Warrior 161	88	ex HB-PLM. Crashed 30-8-06, CoA 11-8-08, de-reg 22-8-07. Rescue trainer, trailer mounted	6-21

SHRIVENHAM east of Swindon, south of the A420

Defence Academy of the United Kingdom: Part of Joint Services Command.

❑ XT621		Westland Scout AH.1	66	ex Wroughton, 655, 656, 666, 664, 666	7-14
❑ XV122	'A'	Westland Scout AH.1	68	ex Almondbank, Wroughton. Displayed	5-14
❑ ZA556	'047'	Panavia Tornado GR.4	81	ex Marham, 9, GR.1, Warton. Arrived 2-4-19	5-19
❑ ZJ369		GEC-Marconi Phoenix UAV	c95	'Army' titles	5-19
❑ 69-16445		Bell AH-1F Cobra	69	ex US Army, 1/1 CAV, Budingen. Arrived 2-7-96 Technology School. 'IFOR' (Bosnia) markings.	9-19

STEVENTON on the B4017 south of Abingdon

Robin Phipps: Keeps his Gannet and Sea Vixen cockpits at *private* locations in the general area. His Buccaneer cockpit is at Newark, Notts. ◆ *By prior arrangement* **only**

❑ XL449	'044'	Fairey Gannet AEW.3	58	ex Booker, Camberley, Booker, Camberley, Cardiff, Yeovilton, Lossiemouth, GSU, 849, A&AEE. SOC 2-10-78. Cockpit	6-19
❑ XN647	'707'	DH Sea Vixen FAW.2	61	ex B'thorpe, Helston, Culdrose SAH-10, A2610 (25-2-71), 766, 892, FAW.1, 766, 899. Christchurch-built. Cockpit	6-19

UPPER HEYFORD or Heyford Park, north of the B4030, north of Oxford

Heyford Park: A small museum has been established in what was the base commander's building at the former USAF base.
◆ *By prior arrangement* **only** | **www.raf-upper-heyford.org**

WALLINGFORD on the A4130 east of Didcot

The scrapyard was cleared during 2020; Wessex HC.2 XT681 is reported to have moved elsewhere in the locality.

SHROPSHIRE
Includes the unitary authority of Telford and Wrekin

BRIDGNORTH
Millington Racing Engines: Roy Millington and friends have lovingly restored a Harrier to 'running' condition.
◆ *By prior arrangement* **only** | **www.millingtonengines.com**

❑ XV808	HS Harrier GR.3	71	ex Gosport, Culdrose, A2687[2] (11-7-94), 9076M, 233 OCU,	
	'DD08'		3, GR.1 20, 4. Arrived 13-9-12. Engine runs 5-19	6-21

COSFORD AIRFIELD south of Junction 3 of the M54
EGWC

Royal Air Force Museum: The ongoing review of exhibits is dealt with in detail under Hendon, Gtr Lon. Expressions of interest were due on 10th February 2022 for the first tranche of airframes. Apart from a few exceptions departures were unlikely to have been realised by the time *W&R* went to press. Those offered for **transfer by gift** are marked: ●: those offered for **outward loan** are marked ❖.

As well as the display halls and the external exhibits, there is a superb cafe within the visitor centre, with views over the active airfield. The **Aerospace Museum Society** provides a vital link in both the restoration of exhibits and the running of the museum and special events. (Royal Air Force Museum 'South' is, of course, Hendon, Gtr Lon. See also under Stafford, Staffs.) See under Hendon for comments relating to the present round of disposals.

◆ *Off Junction 3 of the M54. Cosford, TF11 8UP* | **01902 376200** | **cosford@rafmuseum.org** | **www.rafmuseum.org**

Hangar 1:

❑ G-EBMB		Hawker Cygnet	25	ex Hendon, Cardington, Henlow, Lympne No.14. De-reg 30-11-61, acquired 1968		1-22
❑ G-ACGL	'6'	Comper Swift	33	ex Hatch, Stafford, Timperley, Wigan, Stockport, Kinver. CoA 22-3-40, de-reg 1-12-46, arrived 3-11-11	❖	1-22
❑ G-AEEH		Mignet HM.14 'Flea'	36	ex St Athan, Colerne, Bath, Whitchurch. CoA 15-5-38. Acquired 1966	[1]	1-22
❑ 'G-AFAP'		Junkers Ju 52/3m	54	ex Spanish AF, CASA 352L T.2B-272, CASA 352A T.2-272. CASA-built. Last flew 31-5-78. British Airways colours	●	1-22
❑ G-APAS		DH Comet 1XB	53	ex Shawbury 8351M, XM823, G-APAS, G-5-23, Air France F-BGNZ. Hatfield-built. De-reg 22-10-58, last flown 8-4-68, arrived 17-9-78. BOAC colours		1-22
❑ K4972		Hawker Hart Trainer	35	ex Hendon, Cosford, Cardington, Hendon, St Athan, 1546 ATC, Carlisle, Wigton 1764M, 2 FTS. AWA-built. Acquired 16-10-63. Arrived 20-4-17		1-22
❑ T6296		DH Tiger Moth	41	ex Hendon, 8387M, Yeovilton SF, BRNC, RNEC, Stretton, 7 EFTS, 1 EFTS. Morris-built. Acquired 15-3-72. Arr11-16		1-22
❑ 'FS628'		Fairchild Argus II	43	ex Rochester, G-AIZE, Cosford, Henlow, Hanwell, G-AIZE,		
		G-AIZE		N9996F, 43-14601. CoA 6-8-66, de-reg 6-3-73, acquired 2-73. SEAC colours		1-22
❑ 'RG904'		V-S Spitfire FSM	12	BAPC.333, *Haldane Place*, 441 Sqn colours	[2]	1-14
❑ TX214		Avro Anson C.19	46	ex Henlow 7817M, HCCS, MCS, RCCF, Staff College CF, 1 FU, 16 FU. Acquired 29-8-63		1-22
❑ VP952		DH Devon C.2/2	47	ex St Athan 8820M, 207, 21, WCS, SCS, Upavon SF, TCCF, MCS, BCCS, HCCS, A&AEE, MCCF, AAFCE, Hendon SF, HS. Last flown 5-7-84		1-22
❑ WE600		Auster C4 'Antarctic'	51	ex St Athan, Swinderby, Finningley 7602M, Trans-Antarctic Expedition 1956-1957, 663. Acq 10-64. Skis	● [3]	1-22
❑ WL679		Vickers Varsity T.1	53	ex 9155M, Farnborough, RAE, BLEU, RAE. Hurn-built. Last flown 27-7-92	❖ [4]	1-22
❑ WL732		BP Sea Balliol T.21	54	ex store, Henlow, A&AEE, Lossiemouth, Anthorn. Acquired 7-2-69. On show by 7-14	❖	1-22
❑ WP912		DHC Chipmunk T.10	52	ex Hendon 8467M, Man UAS, RAFC, ITS, Cam UAS, CFS, 2 FTS, Lon UAS, FTCCS, HCCS, 8 FTS. Acquired 14-12-76	[5]	1-22
❑ WV562		Percival Provost T.1	54	ex MBCC, 'XF688' Oman c/s, Hendon, Cosford, Cranwell,		
	'P-C'			Henlow 7606M (30-6-59), 22 FTS. Acquired 9-79		1-22
❑ WV746		Percival Pembroke C.1	55	ex 8938M, 60, 207, 21, WCS, TCCF, FTCCS, BCCS, Handling Sqn, 2 TAFCF. Acquired 13-4-87. 60 Sqn colours	❖	1-22

☐ XD674	Hunting Jet Provost T.1	54	ex store, St Athan, Swinderby, Finningley, Bicester 7570M, 71 MU, A&AEE, AS Bitteswell, Hunting. Last flown 4-6-57	1-22
☐ XJ918 *and* 8190M	Bristol Sycamore HR.14	56	ex 2 SoTT 8190M, 32, MCS, Kemble, Wroughton, 110, Seletar, A&AEE, 275. Acquired 1983	● 1-22
☐ XP411	AW Argosy C.1	62	ex 2 SoTT 8442M (22-5-75), 6 FTS, Kemble, 70. Acquired 4-88	❖ 1-22
☐ XR525 'G'	Westland Wessex HC.2	64	ex Shawbury, 72, 60, 72, Benson SF, SAR Wing, Benson SF, 72. Acquired 13-5-04. *Sunshine*, 72 Sqn colours	1-22
☐ XS639	HS Andover E.3A	67	ex 9241M, Northolt, 32, 115, C.1, 32, 46. Last flown 13-7-94. 32 Sqn colours	1-22
☐ 418947	Fieseler Fi 103 (V-1)	c44	BAPC.94, ex 8583M, Westcott	1-22

■ **[1]** 'Flea' built by Edgar George Davis in Bath, first flew 5-11-36, Authorisation No.68. **[2]** Spitfire, claimed to be the only 1:1 'Airfix' 'kit', was assembled during a James May TV programme called *Toy Story* at Cosford in 2009. It was removed during 2010, going to Gateguards (UK) Ltd at Newquay, Cornwall, for what was termed "maintenance and strengthening". It returned in October 2010 and occupies space that could be taken up by a *real* exhibit. **[3]** WE600 is one of two specially-modified Auster T.7s. **[4]** WL679 made the last-ever flight by the type, into Cosford, on 27-7-92. **[5]** Chipmunk was used by the Duke of Edinburgh during his flying training.

Hangar 2 - Test Flight:

☐ WG760	EE P.1A	54	ex Binbrook, Henlow, Bicester 7755M, St Athan, Warton, A&AEE. Acquired 1-86	1-22
☐ WG768	Short SB.5	52	ex Topcliffe, Finningley 8005M, ETPS, RAE Bedford, RAE Farnboro', A&AEE, RAE Bedford, A&AEE. Last flown 7-3-68 [1]	1-22
☐ WG777	Fairey FD.2	56	ex Topcliffe, Finningley 7986M, RAE Bedford. Acq 8-9-67	1-22
☐ WK935	Gloster Meteor F.8(mod)	53	ex St Athan, Colerne 7869M, Lyneham, Kirkbride, RAE. AWA-built. Last flown 12-6-59. Acquired 12-1-65. Prone-pilot test-bed	❖ [2] 1-22
☐ XD145	Saro SR.53	56	ex Brize Norton, Henlow, Westcott, A&AEE. Last flown 20-10-59, arrived 2-3-82	[3] 1-22
☐ XF926	Bristol 188	63	ex 8368M, Foulness, RAE. Last flown 12-1-64. Arr 3-9-72	❖ [4] 1-22
☐ XM351 'Y'	Hunting Jet Provost T.3	58	ex 2 SoTT, Halton 8078M (25-2-70), Shawbury, 3 FTS, 7 FTS, 2 FTS. Acquired 6-96. Education area	1-22
☐ XN714	Hunting 126/50	63	ex RAE Bedford, NASA Ames and Moffett, Holme-on-Spalding Moor, RAE. Last flown 9-11-67, arrived 30-4-74	1-22
☐ XR220	BAC TSR.2 XO-2	64	ex Henlow 7933M, Boscombe Down, A&AEE. Never flown. Acquired 20-6-67, arrived 4-5-75	1-22
☐ XS695	HS Kestrel FGA.1	65	ex Wyton, Cardington, Yeovilton, Culdrose 'SAH-6', Manadon A2619 (10-5-73), A&AEE, RAE, CFE, Tri-Partite Eval Sqn, A&AEE, RAE. Crashed 1-3-67	[5] 1-22
☐ XX765	SEPECAT Jaguar GR.1(mod)	75	ex Loughborough, Warton, BAe, GR.1, 226 OCU, 17, 14. Last flown as GR.1 4-8-78, as ACT 11-84. Arr 10-11-99	[6] 1-22
☐ ZF534	BAe EAP	85	ex Loughborough, Warton. Last flown 1-5-91, Arr 27-3-12	[7] 1-22

■ **[1]** The T-tail rear fuselage is displayed alongside WG768. **[2]** Last Meteor to be built by AWA at Coventry; converted as prone pilot test-bed, first flown 10-2-54. Issued to RAE Farnborough 31-8-54. **[3]** SR.53 first flew on 16-5-57 and last flew 20-10-59 with a total time of just under 18 hours in 46 sorties. **[4]** Only Bristol turbojet-powered design to fly: total flying time came to a mere 26 hours, 11 minutes. **[5]** Kestrel was placed on RAF Museum charge 10-5-74 but went to Manadon on extended loan, before coming back into the fold. **[6]** XX765 is much-modified Active Control Technology (ACT) test-bed. It was the world's first to fly with an all-digital quadruplex 'fly-by-wire' control system, on 21-10-81. **[5]** EAP factoids: first flown at Warton 8-8-86, total time 191 hrs, 21 mins.

Hangar 3 - 'War in the Air': Spitfire PM651 had moved to the conservation centre by August 2020.

☐ 'A8226'	Sopwith 1½ Strutter replica G-BIDW	80	ex Hendon, Cardington, Land's End, '9382', G-BIDW Westward Airways-built. (CoA 29-12-80, de-reg 4-2-87). Acquired 1-81. Arrived 15-7-14	1-22
☐ 'C4994'	Bristol M.1C replica G-BLWM	87	ex Hendon, Cardington, 'C4912', Hucknall, G-BLWM (CoA 12-8-87, de-reg 12-5-88). Don Cashmore-built. Acquired 8-87. Arrived 15-7-14	[1] 1-22
☐ 'N5182'	Sopwith Pup G-APUP	16	ex 9213M (31-8-93), Hendon, Blackbushe, Old Warden, G-APUP (CoA 28-6-78, de-reg 4-10-84), Musée de l'Air, Dover Defence Flt, Walmer DF, 9, 3, 8 Sqns RNAS, 1 Wing, A8736. Acquired 6-82. Arrived 15-7-14. *Shelia*	[2] 1-22
☐ K8042	Gloster Gladiator II	37	ex Hendon, 8372M, Biggin Hill 'K8442', 61 OTU, 5 (P)AFU, A&AEE. Acquired 11-65. 87 Sqn colours. Arrived by 11-16	1-22

Two from the RAF Museum's disposals list: prone-pilot test-bed Meteor F.8 WK935 (*Les Woodward*) and SP-2H Neptune 204.
Ian Humphreys

☐ K9942	'SD-D'	V-S Spitfire I	39	ex Hendon 8383M, Rochester, Hendon, 71 MU Bicester, Fulbeck, Wroughton, Newark, Cardiff, 53 OTU, 57 OTU, 72. Acquired 9-11-71. 72 Sqn colours		1-22
☐ N1671		Boulton Paul Defiant I	38	ex Hendon, Rochester, Hendon 8370M, Finningley, 285, 307.		
	'EW-D'			307 Sqn colours. Acquired 23-7-68, arrived by 11-16		1-22
☐ LF738	'UH-A'	Hawker Hurricane II	44	ex Rochester, Biggin Hill, Wellesbourne M', 5405M, 22 OTU, 1682 BDTF. Acquired 8-2-84. 1682 BDTF colours		1-22
☐ 'PR536'*		Hawker Tempest II	46	ex MBCC, Hendon, Duxford, Cardington, Chichester,		
	'OQ-H'			Indian AF HA457, RAF 5. Acquired 13-11-91, arrived by 10-20. 5 Sqn colours	[3]	1-22
☐ RF398		Avro Lincoln B.2/4A	45	ex 8376M, Henlow, Abingdon, 151, CSE, BCBS. AWA-built. Last flown, and acquired, 30-4-63		1-22
☐ TA639	'AZ-E'	DH Mosquito TT.35	45	ex Henlow, CFS, *633 Squadron* (1963), 'HJ682', CFS 7806M (6-5-63), 3 CAACU, Aldergrove TT Flt, Ballykelly SF, B.35. Last flight 3-10-65. Acquired 5-7-67. 627 Sqn colours	[4]	1-22
☐ XX654	'3'	SAL Bulldog T.1	74	ex Shawbury Newton, CFS, 3 FTS, CFS, 3 FTS, Bristol UAS, 2 FTS. Acquired 1993		1-22
☐ XZ997	'V'	HS Harrier GR.3	82	ex Hendon 9122M, 233 OCU, 1453 Flt, 4, 1, 4. Acquired 4-12-91, arrived 10-18. 4 Sqn colours		1-22
☐ 10639	'6'	Messerschmitt Bf 109G-2 G-USTV	40	ex Hendon, Duxford G-USTV (de-reg 24-9-98), Benson, Northolt, Lyneham 8478M, Henlow, Wattisham, Stanmore Park, Sealand, CFE-EAF, 1426 Flt, RN228, Lydda, 3 Sqn Gambut, III/JG77. Erla-built. Crashed 12-10-97. Acquired 10-3-02, arrived 11-16		1-22
☐ 112372	'4'	Messerschmitt Me 262A-2a	45	ex Hendon, Cosford 8482M, St Athan, Cosford, Finningley, Gaydon, '110880', Cranwell, Farnborough, VK893, Twenthe. Acquired 1972, arrived 5-17	[5]	1-22
☐ 191614	'14'	Messerschmitt Me 163B-1 Komet	44	ex 8481M, Biggin Hill, Westcott, Brize Norton, Farnborough, Hussum, II/JG400. Acquired 1975	[6]	1-22
☐ 360043	'D5+EV'	Junkers Ju 88R-1	43	ex Hendon, St Athan 8475M, Henlow, St Athan, Biggin H', Fulbeck, Wroughton, Stanmore, PJ876, 47 MU, CFE, 1426 Flt, RAE. Defected 9-5-43. Acquired 9-69. Arrived by 2-17		1-22
☐ 420430*	'3U+CC'	Messerschmitt Me 410A-1/U2	43	ex MBCC, museum, St Athan 8483M, Cosford, Fulbeck, Wroughton, Stanmore Park, Brize Norton, Farnborough, AM.72, Vaerlose. First noted 11-19		1-22
☐ 475081	'GM+AK'	Fieseler Fi 156C-7 Storch	44	ex St Athan, Coltishall, Bircham Newton, Finningley, Fulbeck, Halton 7362M (3-8-56), VP546, RAE, AM.101, Farnborough. Mraz-built. Arrived 6-4-89		1-22
☐ 733682		Focke-Wulf Fw 190A-8/R6	43	ex South Lambeth, 9211M, ex Duxford, South Lambeth, Biggin Hill, Cranwell, Brize Norton, Farnborough AM.75. Arrived 20-12-12	[7]	1-22
☐ –		Focke Achgelis Fa 330A-1 Bachstelze	44	ex 8469M, Henlow, Farnborough. Weser Flug-built. Acquired 9-67		1-22
☐ 16336	'24'	Kawasaki Ki-100-1b	c44	BAPC.83, ex MBCC, Hendon, Cosford, St Athan 8476M, Cosford, Henlow, Biggin Hill, Fulbeck, Wroughton, Stanmore, Sealand, Japanese Army		1-22
☐ 5439		Mitsubishi Ki-46-III *Dinah*	44	BAPC.84, ex St Athan 8484M, Biggin Hill, Fulbeck, Wroughton, Stanmore, Sealand, ATAIU-SEA. Arr UK 8-46, Cosford 3-89. 3 Sqn, 81st HQ Rec Group, c/s		1-22
☐ '10461'		Yokosuka Ohka 11	c45	BAPC.99, ex St Athan 8486M, Cosford, Westcott		1-22

■ **[1]** Don Cashmore also built Hawker Cygnet G-CAMM at Shuttleworth, Beds. **[2]** The story goes that Lt Cdr K C D St Cyrien was permitted to bring this out of museum storage for return to flight and that he did it piece by piece over a series of years! In 2-59 he registered G-APUP as a Pup *replica*, but in 1973 changed this to an *original*. Cyrien was also responsible for G-ABOX, currently at the Army Flying Museum, Middle Wallop, Hampshire. **[3]** 'PR536' fitted with wings of an IAF Mk.II and Centaurus donated by IAF 11-7 and rear fuselage of Mk.II 'KB418' from RNEC Manadon 4-87. **[4]** 'M' number nominal as TA639 retained for display flying 30-5-63 to -10-65 when total time was 607 hours. *Loaned* for use in *633 Squadron*, 1963. Last 'Mossie' to fly under RAF aegis. Portrays Mk.XX KB627 in which Wg Cdr Guy Gibson was killed 19/20-9-44. **[5]** History track revised to reflect recent thinking on the Me 262; it is most likely 112372. **[6]** Komet is marked '191461' on the port fin. **[7]** Fw 190A was modified to be the upper component of a Mistel S3B flying-bomb combination and was mounted on a Ju 88H when captured. It joined the collection at Cranwell from 18-9-46 and remained on loan from the RAF Museum during its time at IWM.

National 'Cold War' Exhibition:

☐ N9050T*	Douglas Dakota 3	44	ex Stafford, Hendon, Rochester, Cosford, Fleet, Thruxton, Hal Safi, 5N-ATA, PH-MAG, G-AGYX, KG437, USAAF C-47A-10-DK 42-92648. Oklahoma City-built. Cockpit	1-22
☐ KN645	Douglas Dakota C.4	44	ex 'KG374', 8355M, Colerne, AFN CF, MinTech, AFN CF, MinTech, AFN HQ, SHAPE CF, Malta CF, BAFO CS, 2nd TAF CS, USAAF C-47B-35-DK 44-77003. Oklahoma City-built. Acquired 1-5-74. Transport Command colours	1-22
☐ TG511	HP Hastings T.5	48	ex 8554M, 230 OCU Radar Tng Flt, SCBS, BCBS, Met.1, 202, C.1 Lyneham Wing, Topcliffe Wing, 47. Acquired 16-8-77	1-22
☐ TS798	Avro York C.1	45	ex 'MW100', Shawbury, Brize Norton, Staverton, 'LV633', G-AGNV, Skyways, BOAC, TS798. CoA 6-3-65, last flight 9-10-64. De-reg 7-5-65. Acquired 16-5-72 [1]	1-22
☐ WS843	'J' Gloster Meteor NF(T).14	54	ex Hendon, St Athan, Henlow 7937M, St Athan, Kemble, 1 ANS, NF.14, A&AEE, 228 OCU. AWA-built. SOC 8-3-66. Acquired 13-3-67. 264 Sqn colours	1-22
☐ XA564	Gloster Javelin FAW.1	54	ex 2 SoTT, Locking 7464M, Filton. Acquired 9-75	1-22
☐ XB812	'U' NAA Sabre F.4	53	ex Hendon, 9227M, Duxford, Rome, Italian AF MM19666, XB812, 93, 112, RCAF (n/s) 19666. Acq 31-1-94. 93 Sqn c/s	1-22
☐ XD818	Vickers Valiant BK.1	56	ex Hendon, Marham 7894M, 49 'A' Flt. Acquired 25-5-65, arrived 8-05. 49 Sqn colours [2]	1-22
☐ XE670	Hawker Hunter F.4	55	ex deep store, St Athan 8585M / 7762M, Abingdon, Bicester, 93, 26. Squires Gate-built. Cockpit	1-22
☐ XG337	EE Lightning F.1	59	ex 2 SoTT 8056M, Warton, A&AEE, Warton. Acquired 10-83	1-22
☐ XH171	'U' EE Canberra PR.9	60	ex 2 SoTT 8746M, 39, 13, 39 MoA, 58. Short-built. Last flight 13-7-82. 39 Sqn colours	1-22
☐ XH672	HP Victor K.2	60	ex 9242M (26-3-94), Shawbury, 55, 57, 543, MoA. Last flown 30-11-93. *Maid Marion*. 55 Sqn colours [3]	1-22
☐ XL568	'X' Hawker Hunter T.7A	58	ex Cranwell 9224M (19-11-93), Lossiemouth, 12, 74, MoA, 74, HS. Acquired 12-2-02. 74 Sqn colours	1-22
☐ XL993	SAL Twin Pioneer CC.1	58	ex Henlow 8388M (6-2-69), Shawbury, 21, 78	1-22
☐ XM598	Avro Vulcan B.2	63	ex 8778M, 44, Waddington Wing, Cottesmore Wing, 12. Arrived 20-1-83. 44 Sqn colours	1-22
☐ 'XN972'	Blackburn Buccaneer S.1 XN962	63	ex Hendon, Cosford, St Athan, 'XN972', Abingdon 8183M, Foulness, 736, 800, 809. Acquired 7-95. Cockpit	1-22
☐ XR371	Short Belfast C.1	67	ex Hucknall, Kemble, 53. Arrived 6-10-78. *Enceladus*. 53 Sqn colours	1-22
☐ XV591	'013' McD Phantom FG.1	69	ex St Athan, 111, 43, 892. 892 Sqn Trans-Atlantic air race colours. Cockpit	1-22
☐ 503	Mikoyan-G'vich G-BRAM MiG-21PF *Fishbed*	66	ex Farnborough, Hurn, G-BRAM (de-reg 16-4-99), N610DM, N Weald, Hungarian AF. Acq 18-10-06. Hungarian AF colours	1-22
☐ 1120 red	Mikoyan-Gurevich MiG-15bis *Fagot*	55	ex Hendon, Cardington, South Lambeth, Hendon, Middlesbrough, Polish AF. WSK-built Lim-2. Acquired 29-10-86. Polish AF c/s	1-22
☐ 68-8284	Sikorsky MH-53M Pave Low	68	ex Brize Norton, Baghdad, *Desert Thunder*, 20th SOS, 67th ARRS, SEA. Acquired 17-12-08	1-22
☐ 74-0177	GD F-111F Aardvark	64	ex Mildenhall, AMARC, 27th TFW, 48th TFW, 366th TFW, 347th TFW. Last flown 10-95, arr 3-11-05. 492nd TFS c/s	1-22

■ **[1]** York made its and the type's last-ever flight on delivery to the Skyfame Museum at Staverton 9-10-64. **[2]** On 15-5-57 XD818 dropped a 'Short Granite' thermonuclear fusion bomb over Christmas Island, SW Pacific. **[3]** Victor XH672 flew during the Falklands conflict, including the BLACK BUCK raids and had the highest sortie score during Operation GRANBY - 52 'ops'. When it landed at Shawbury (for roading to Cosford) on 30-11-93 it made the last flight by a Victor.

External Exhibits: The 'Brit', VC10, Dominie and Nimrod are hopefully long-term candidates for a roof over them. Airframes offered for **transfer by gift** are marked: ●: those offered for **outward loan** are marked ❖.

☐ XG225	Hawker Hunter F.6A	56	ex 8713M (15-2-82), Weapons School, 2 SoTT, Kemble, 229 OCU, 92, 74, 20. Acquired 1988. 237 Sqn colours	1-22
☐ 'XM497'	Bristol Britannia 312F G-AOVF	57	ex Southend, 9Q-CAZ, G-AOVF (de-reg 21-11-84), Stansted, British Eagle, BOAC. Last flown 2-5-84. RAF c/s, *Schedar*	1-22

❏ XR808	'R'	Vickers VC10 C.1K	66	ex Bruntingthorpe, 101, 10. *Kenneth Campbell VC.*		
				Last flew 29-7-13. Arrived 21-6-15, on display by 11-15		1-22
❏ XS709	'M'	HS Dominie T.1	64	ex Cranwell, 55, 3 FTS, 6 FTS, 1 ANS, CAW, 1 ANS, A&AEE,		
				G-37-6S Rolls-Royce. Last flight 11-2-11		1-22
❏ XV202		Lockheed Hercules C.3	67	ex Brize Norton, 47, Lyneham TW, C.1, Lyneham TW, 48,		
				USAF 66-8552. Last flown 12-8-11		1-22
❏ XV249		HS Nimrod R.1	70	ex Kemble, Waddington, 51, MR.2 Kinloss Wing, St Mawgan		
				Wing, 42, MR.1, Kin W, 203, Kin W. 'Nimrod R.1 1974-2011'		
				titles. Last flown 29-7-11, arrived 3-12, unveiled 28-9-12	[1]	1-22
❏ XX496	'D'	HP Jetstream T.1	75	ex 'Cold War', Cranwell, 45, 6 FTS, 3 FTS. SAL-built.		
				Arrived 22-3-04. 45 Sqn colours. Outside by 11-17	❖	1-22
❏ L-866		Consolidated PBY-6A	45	ex 8466M, Colerne, Danish AF Esk.721, 82-866,		
		Catalina		BuNo 63993. Acquired 29-5-74, moved outside 9-16	❖	1-22
❏ 204		Lockheed SP-2H Neptune	61	ex Dutch Navy, 320 Sqn, Valkenburg, 5 Sqn, 321 Sqn.		
				Last flight 22-7-82. 320 Sqn colours	●	1-22

■ **[1]** Nimrod made the last-ever flight by the breed (into Kemble) on 29-7-11, completing 18,488 flying hours.

Michael Beetham Conservation Centre (MBCC): Always a challenging restoration, the decision has been made not to restore the wings of Hampden P1344. (The wings will, of course, be stored for posterity.) *W&R27* moved Lysander R9125 to Hendon, Gtr Lon, as it was due there. As of January 2022 it was still in Shropshire, but remains listed at Hendon in hope! Me 410 4320430 had returned to Hangar 3, and Tempest II 'PR536' moved there, both by October 2021. The cockpit of Dakota N9050T moved to the Cold War hall by October 2021. The Ohka is destined for the Pima Air and Space Museum, Tucson, Arizona, USA. A pair of Spitfire cockpits were under construction in later 2021 for use as 'sit-ins' at Hendon and here.
◆ *Annual open event - see website for details. Otherwise by prior arrangement* **only.**

❏ P1344	'PL-K'	HP Hampden TB.I	42	ex 9175M, Wyton, Cardington, Hatch, Petsamo, USSR,		
				144, 1 OTU. Forced down 4-9-42. Salvaged 1990.		
				Arrived UK 4-9-91. See narrative above	[1]	1-22
❏ MF628		Vickers Wellington T.10	44	ex Hendon 9210M, Abingdon, St Athan, Biggin Hill, Hendon,		
				Heathrow, Wisley, Vickers, *Dam Busters* photo-ship, 1 ANS.		
				Acquired 1964, arrived 1-7-10	[2]	1-22
❏ PM651	'X'	V-S Spitfire PR.19	45	ex museum, Stafford, Middle East 'tour' *Bahrain*, Stafford,		
				Cosford, Wyton, Cardington, St Athan, Hendon, Benson,		
				Bicester, Andover, Hucknall, Leconfield, Church Fenton		
				7758M, THUM Flt, 6 MU. First noted 8-20		1-22
❏ 7198/18		LVG C.VI	1918	ex Old Warden, 9239M, G-AANJ (CoA 8-5-04, de-reg 11-12-03)		
				Stanmore, Colerne, Fulbeck. Last flown 20-9-03, arr 12-11-03		1-22
❏ 1160		Dornier Do 17Z-2	40	ex Goodwin Sands, 7/KG3. Shot down 26-8-40.		
	'5K+AR'			Hulk, salvaged from sea. Arrived 6-13		1-22
❏ 997*		Yokosuka Ohka 11	c44	BAPC.98, ex Manchester, 8485M, Henlow, Cottesmore,		
				Cranwell. Arrived by 10-20. See notes above		1-22
❏ 853		Hawker Hunter FR.10	57	ex Hendon, Oman, SOAF, Jordan AF 853, XF426,		
				229 OCU, 2, 208. AWA-built. Acquired 6-9-03.		
				First noted 12-16, outside by 11-19	[3]	1-22

■ **[1]** Hampden is being restored 'half-and-half' - one side fully restored, the other allowing inspection of the interior. The wings will not be restored, but will be stored. At some stage in its career P1344 was fitted with the tailboom of Short-built Hereford I L6012. This was SOC on 20-10-41 while serving with the Jurby-based 5 BGS following a collision with an Anson. The Hereford was a Hampden powered by Napier Daggers. See fellow AE436 at East Kirkby, Lincs, lost on the same night. **[2]** Made almost certainly the last-ever Wellington flight 24-1-55, St Athan-Wisley **[3]** Hunter FR.10 was a gift from the Sultan of Oman.

Deep Stores: **Not** available for inspection. The Boulton Paul Association's Balliol T.2 WN149 moved to <u>Newquay</u>, Cornwall, on 7th January 2021.

❏ -*	'33'	Avian hang-glider	~	ex Stafford, Hendon. First noted 6-18	●	1-22
❏ DG202/G		Gloster F9/40 Meteor	42	ex Hendon, Cosford, Colerne, Yatesbury, Locking 5758M,		
				Moreton Valance. Acquired 1965. Arrived 5-17	[1]	1-22
❏ 'MK356'		V-S Spitfire IX FSM	03	BAPC.298, ex display on parade ground	[2]	11-16
❏ RH746		Bristol Brigand TF.1	46	ex Kemble, Sunderland, Failsworth, CS(A), ATDU Gosport,		
				Bristol, ATDU, A&AEE, Bristol. Fuselage; tail at MBCC		1-22
❏ VX573		Vickers Valetta C.2	50	ex 8389M, Henlow, Wildenrath CF, Buckeburg CF.		
				Acquired 7-11-68. *Lorelei*	❖	1-22

☐ WA346		DH Vampire FB.5	51	ex Cardington, Cosford, Henlow, Hendon, 3/4 CAACU, 1 FTS, 7 FTS, 130, 98, 102 FRS. EE-built. SOC 10-10-60	● [3]	1-22
☐ WA634		Gloster Meteor T.7(mod)	49	ex St Athan, Martin-Baker. Acquired 8-74	●	1-22
☐ WE982		Slingsby Prefect TX.1	50	ex 8781M, Cardington, Henlow, Syerston, Manston, ACCGS, CGS, 1 GC, 621, 612, 644, 643, 166 and 143 GSs	●	1-22
☐ WZ744		Avro 707C	53	ex museum, Topcliffe, Finningley, Colerne 7932M, RAE. Last flown 7-6-66, acquired 17-4-67. First noted 4-17	●	1-22
☐ XA893		Avro Vulcan B.1	56	ex Abingdon, Bicester 8591M (10-6-63), A&AEE. Cockpit		1-22
☐ XD515		DH Vampire T.11	54	ex Rugeley, Winthorpe, Misson, Linton-on-O' 7998M (5-1-68), 3 FTS, 7 FTS, 1 FTS, 5 FTS, 206 AFS. Christchurch-built		2-18
☐ XK724		Folland Gnat F.1	56	ex museum, Cranwell, Bicester, Henlow 7715M. Acquired 14-8-85. First noted 4-17	●	1-22
☐ 'XL554'	'Z' SAL Pioneer CC.1		56	ex MBCC, Henlow, Cosford, Manchester, Henlow		
	XL703			8034M (1-10-68), 209, 230. SOAF colours.		1-22
☐ XT903	'X' McD Phantom FGR.2		68	ex Wyton, Leuchars, 56, 228 OCU, 92, 228 OCU, 23, 228 OCU, 2, 228 OCU. Cockpit		1-22
☐ XX946	'WT' Panavia Tornado P.02		74	ex MBCC, museum, Hendon, Honington 8883M (5-2-86), Laarbruch, Honington, Warton. Acquired 16-11-94	❖	1-22
☐ -		Hawker P.1121	58	ex Henlow, Cranfield. Fuselage sections	●	1-22
☐ A-515		FMA Pucará	78	ex museum, 9245M, ZD485, A&AEE, Yeovilton, Stanley, Arg AF, Mauritania AF M4 / 5T-MAB. Last flown (as ZD485) 9-9-83. Gr 3 de Ataque colours. F/n 4-17		1-22
☐ 6130		Lockheed Ventura II	42	ex SAAF Museum, Ysterplaat, SAAF, 17, BGANS, 21, 29 OTU, RAF AJ469, n/s. Acquired 1983		1-22
☐ J-1704		DH Venom FB.54	56	ex museum, Greenham Common. Swiss AF. Swiss-built. Acquired 8-6-79. First noted 4-17	❖	1-22
☐ '413573'		NAA P-51D-25-NA	44	ex museum, Hendon 9133M, Halton, N6526D,		
	'B6-V'	Mustang		RCAF 9289, 44-73415. Inglewood-built. Acquired 1991. _Isabel III_, 361st FS, 357th FG colours. First noted 4-17	●	1-22

■ [1] Prototype Meteor, first flown 24-7-43; Rolls-Royce-built W2B/23 turbojets. [2] The _real_ MK356 can be found at Coningsby, Lincs, while _another_ 'MK356' is at Hawkinge, Kent. [3] Vampire FB.5 has the booms of VX461.

Defence School of Aeronautical Engineering (DSAE): This facility and DSAE Sultan at Gosport, Hampshire, are sub-sets of the Defence College of Technical Training at Lyneham, Wilts. No.**1 School of Technical Training** is split into squadrons and flights: **Avionics Training Flight**; **Aerosystems Training Wing** - comprising the **Avionics Training Flight** and the **Weapons Training Flight**; the **Airfield Squadron**; and a **Battle Damage Repair Flight**. No attempt has been made to delineate which airframes are with which elements in the listing below. Also here is **1 Radio School**, which does not use the airframes and the **Mechanical Training School** in Building 146, which does.

Several airframes on DSAE charge are referred to as 'Non-effective ground display' and are marked #. A number of Jaguars are believed to have been allocated to India, almost certainly for spares, as far back as 27th October 2016, but have yet to depart: these are marked @.

Departures: Jet Provost **T.5As** XW320, XW375 and XW436 to St Athan, Wales, 16-10-20; XW375 did not remain in Wales long, travelling north to Inverness, Scotland, on 25-2-21; **Sea King** HAS.6 XV653 to Gosport, Hants, 17-9-20; HAS.6 XV659 to Gosport, Hants, by 10-20; HAS.6 ZA128 to Gosport, Hants, 17-9-20; HAS.6 ZA169 to Gosport, Hants, by 10-20; **Tornado** F.2 ZD939 last recorded in 4-19 as a 'cockpit', is more accurately described as a forward fuselage skeletal frame and is not recognisable as a cockpit so was.

☐ XM362		Hunting Jet Provost T.3	59	ex 8230M, Halton, Kemble, Shawbury, 3 FTS, 2 FTS. Arrived 21-3-73. 'Cutaway' and camouflaged	4-19
☐ XR498	'X' Westland Wessex HC.2		63	ex St Mawgan, Gosport, Cosford 9342M, Shawbury, 72, 60, 72, A&AEE. Arrived 17-5-17	# 10-21
☐ XW327	'62' BAC Jet Provost T.5A		70	ex Halton 9130M (9-12-91), CFS, 7 FTS, 6 FTS, 7 FTS, 1 FTS, CFS, RAFC. Parked outside by 10-19, rescue trainer	10-21
☐ XX110	'EP' SEPECAT Jaguar GR.1		74	ex 8955M (3-12-87), Shawbury, 6, A&AEE, BAC. _Baghdad or Bust_ (stb). Outside SHQ	10-21
☐ XX112	'EA' SEPECAT Jaguar GR.3A		73	ex Coltishall, 6, GR.1, 6, A&AEE. Arrived 13-6-07	10-21
☐ XX117	'ES' SEPECAT Jaguar GR.3A		73	ex St Athan, 16, GR.1, 16, 6, SAOEU, 226 OCU, 16, Indian AF JI004, G-27-317, A&AEE, 6, 226 OCU, JOCU. Last flown 1-7-05	10-21
☐ XX119	'AI' SEPECAT Jaguar GR.3A		73	ex Coningsby, 6, GR.1, 54, 16, 226 OCU, 8898M, 226 OCU, A&AEE, 54, 226 OCU, JOCU. Last flown 29-3-06. 'Tiger' colours. Retired ground-runner	10-21

❑ XX141	'T'	SEPECAT Jaguar T.2A	74	ex Cranwell 9297M, 6, 16, 226 OCU, 6, 226 OCU, JOCU. Arrived 23-4-13	@ 10-21
❑ XX145*		SEPECAT Jaguar T.2A	74	ex Bruntingthorpe, Woodhouse, Cranwell, Boscombe D, ETPS, 226 OCU, JOCU. ETPS colours. Arrived 4-8-20	8-20
❑ XX168		HS Hawk T.1	77	ex Shawbury, Valley, FRADU, 208, 100, 6 FTS, 74, 4 FTS. NEA 12-19. Arrived 3-3-20	10-21
❑ XX178		HS Hawk T.1	77	ex Shawbury, 208, 19, 92, 234, 4 FTS. NEA 12-19. Arrived 27-2-20	10-21
❑ XX181*		HS Hawk T.1	77	ex Shawbury, 208, 19, 208, 100, TWU, 4 FTS. SOC 18-11-20. Arrived 28-10-20	10-21
❑ XX185*		HS Hawk T.1	77	ex Shawbury, Marham, 208, 6 FTS, 19, 4 FTS. SOC 18-11-20. Arrived 18-11-20	10-21
❑ XX187*	'CO'	HS Hawk T.1A	77	ex 100, 74, 6 FTS, CFS, 4 FTS, 1 TWU, 2 TWU, TWU. Arrived 26-11-21	11-21
❑ XX218		HS Hawk T.1A	78	ex Shawbury, 208, 19, 208, 74, 234, TWU. NEA 12-19. Arrived 10-3-20	10-21
❑ XX224*		HS Hawk T.1	78	ex Shawbury, 208, 19, CFS, 4 FTS, CFS, 4 FTS. SOC 18-11-20. Arrived 19-11-20	10-21
❑ XX227		HS Hawk T.1A	78	ex Shawbury, 'Red Arrows', CFS. Arrived 25-2-20	10-21
❑ XX235*		HS Hawk T.1	78	ex Shawbury, 208, 19, 208, 19, 74, CFS, 4 FTS. Accident 28-5-09, SOC 18-11-20. Arrived 17-11-20	11-21
❑ XX236		HS Hawk T.1W	78	ex Shawbury, 208, 19, CFS, 234, CFS, 4 FTS. Arrived 19-3-19	10-21
❑ XX244*		HS Hawk T.1	78	ex Shawbury, 'Red Arrows', 208, 74, 208, 234, 4 FTS. Arrived 13-10-21	10-20
❑ XX283		HS Hawk T.1W	79	ex 208, 100, TWU. NEA 12-19. Arrived 5-3-20	10-21
❑ XX335		HS Hawk T.1A	80	ex Shawbury, 208, 100, 19, 2 TWU. Arrived 27-2-18	10-21
❑ XX723	'EU'	SEPECAT Jaguar GR.3A	74	ex Shawbury, 6, 41, 54, DERA, GR.1, 54, 6, 54, 226 OCU. Arrived 24-4-07	10-21
❑ XX724	'EC'	SEPECAT Jaguar GR.3A	74	ex Coltishall, 6, T.2, 54, Shawbury, 54, 226 OCU, A&AEE. *Ecoops* (pt), *Egleno* (stb). Last flown 12-6-07. Retired ground-runner	10-21
❑ XX725	'T'	SEPECAT Jaguar GR.3A	74	ex Coningsby, 41, 54, SAOEU, GR.1, 54, SAOEU, 54, 6, Indian JI010, G-27-235, 54, 226 OCU. Last flown 2-7-07. Desert pink colours. Retired ground-runner	10-21
❑ XX726	'EB'	SEPECAT Jaguar GR.1	74	ex Halton 8947M (9-12-87), Shawbury, 6	10-21
❑ XX727	'ER'	SEPECAT Jaguar GR.1	74	ex 8951M, Shawbury, 6, 54, 6, JOCU. Last flown 26-7-84	@ 10-21
❑ XX729	'EL'	SEPECAT Jaguar GR.3A	74	ex Coltishall, 6, GR.1, SAOEU, 6, 54, 226 OCU, 6, 54, Indian JI012, G-27-326, 6, 226 OCU. *Eliam*. Arrived 18-5-07	10-21
❑ XX738	'ED'	SEPECAT Jaguar GR.3A	74	ex Coltishall, 6, GR.1, SAOEU, 54, 6, Shawbury, 54, Indian AF JI016, G-27-329, 6. Arrived 13-5-07	10-21
❑ XX743	'EG'	SEPECAT Jaguar GR.1	74	ex Halton 8949M (3-12-87), Shawbury, 6. Stored	10-21
❑ XX746	'S'	SEPECAT Jaguar GR.1A	74	ex Halton 8895M (23-5-86), Shawbury, 226 OCU, 14, 17, 6, 31, 226 OCU. Stored	@ 10-21
❑ XX748	'EG'	SEPECAT Jaguar GR.3A	74	ex Coltishall, 6, GR.1, 54, 14, 226 OCU. *Egaz*. Last flown 18-5-07. Retired ground-runner	10-21
❑ XX752	'EK'	SEPECAT Jaguar GR.3A	75	ex Coltishall, 6, 41, 16, GR.1, 6, Shawbury, 54, 226 OCU, 54. Arrived 16-6-07	10-21
❑ XX756	'W'	SEPECAT Jaguar GR.1	75	ex 8899M (23-5-86), 14, 20, 226 OCU, 14	10-21
❑ XX766	'EF'	SEPECAT Jaguar GR.3A	75	ex 9257M, St Athan, 6, 16, GR.1, 6, 54, 226 OCU, 17. Arrived 31-1-06	10-21
❑ XX767	'FK'	SEPECAT Jaguar GR.3A	75	ex Shawbury, 41, 54, GR.1, 54, 17, 31, 14, 226 OCU, 14. Last flown 11-4-06	10-21
❑ XX819	'CE'	SEPECAT Jaguar GR.1	75	ex 8923M (19-12-86), Shawbury, 226 OCU, 20, 17	@ 10-21
❑ XX821	'P'	SEPECAT Jaguar GR.1	75	ex 8896M (23-5-86), Cranwell, Coltishall, 41, 14, 17. Black colours. Arrived 4-4-12. Retired ground-runner	10-21
❑ XX825	'BN'	SEPECAT Jaguar GR.1	75	ex 9020M, Halton, Shawbury, 17, 31, 14. Stored	@ 10-21
❑ XX833		SEPECAT Jaguar T.2A	75	ex Boscombe Down, QinetiQ, DERA, RAE, 41, 14, 20, 226 OCU. QinetiQ titles. Stored	[1] 10-21
❑ XX835	'EX'	SEPECAT Jaguar T.4	75	ex Coningsby, 6, 41, T.2, 41, 6, 54, RAE, 226 OCU. Last flown 1-7-07. Retired ground-runner, 'RAF 100' colours	10-21

☐ XX837	'Z'	SEPECAT Jaguar T.2	75	ex Cranwell, Cosford, Halton 8978M (29-9-88), Shawbury, 226 OCU. Black colours. Arrived 7-8-12	@ 10-21
☐ XX840	'T'	SEPECAT Jaguar T.4	75	ex Coltishall, 6, 16, T.2, St Athan, Shawbury, 41, 2, 226 OCU, 17. Last flown 12-6-07. Retired ground-runner	10-21
☐ XX847	'EZ'	SEPECAT Jaguar T.4	76	ex Coltishall, 6, 16, T.2, St Athan, 41, Shawbury, 226 OCU, 31, 20, 14, 2, 226 OCU. Last flown 18-5-07. Retired ground-runner	10-21
☐ XX959	'CJ'	SEPECAT Jaguar GR.1	75	ex 8953M, Shawbury, 20, 14. Last flown 4-7-84. Stored	@ 10-21
☐ XX965	'C'	SEPECAT Jaguar GR.1A	75	ex Cranwell 9254M (18-9-96), Coltishall, 16, 226 OCU, 54, 14. 16 Sqn colours. Arrived 17-10-12	10-21
☐ XX967	'AC'	SEPECAT Jaguar GR.1	75	ex 9006M, Shawbury, 14, 31. Arrived 2-11-89. Stored	@ 10-21
☐ XX968	'AJ'	SEPECAT Jaguar GR.1	75	ex 9007M, Shawbury, 14, 31. Arrived 1-11-89	10-21
☐ XX969	'01'	SEPECAT Jaguar GR.1	75	ex 8897M (23-5-86), 226 OCU, 31	10-21
☐ XX970	'EH'	SEPECAT Jaguar GR.3A	75	ex Coltishall, 6, 16, 6, 226 OCU, 17, 31. Arrived 13-6-07	10-21
☐ XX975	'07'	SEPECAT Jaguar GR.1A	76	ex Halton 8905M (23-9-86), Shawbury, 226 OCU, 17, 31. Was with '238 Sqn', stored	10-21
☐ XX976	'BD'	SEPECAT Jaguar GR.1	76	ex Halton 8906M (22-10-86), Shawbury, 17, 31. Was with '238 Sqn', stored	10-21
☐ XZ103	'EF'	SEPECAT Jaguar GR.3A	76	ex Coltishall, 41, SAOEU, GR.1, 41, Shawbury, 2. *Exfoxy 2004-2009*. Arrived 12-6-07	10-21
☐ XZ104	'FM'	SEPECAT Jaguar GR.3A	76	ex St Athan, 41, 6, 2. Arrived 27-10-05	10-21
☐ XZ109	'EN'	SEPECAT Jaguar GR.3A	76	ex Shawbury, 6, SAOEU, GR.1, 6, 54, 2. Arrived 29-8-07	10-21
☐ XZ112	'GW'	SEPECAT Jaguar GR.3A	76	ex Shawbury, 41, 54, GR.1, 54, Shawbury, 2. Last flown 12-4-06	10-21
☐ XZ114	'EO'	SEPECAT Jaguar GR.3A	76	ex Shawbury, 6, 41, GR.1, Shawbury, 41. Last flown 11-4-06	102-1
☐ XZ115	'ER'	SEPECAT Jaguar GR.3A	76	ex Shawbury, 6, 16, GR.1, SAOEU, 41, Shawbury, Gulf Det, 41, 2, 41. Arrived 24-10-06	10-21
☐ XZ117	'ES'	SEPECAT Jaguar GR.3A	76	ex Shawbury, 41, 6, GR.1, Warden Det, 54, 41. Arrived 17-11-09. Retired ground-runner	10-21
☐ XZ358	'L'	SEPECAT Jaguar GR.1A	76	ex Cranwell, 9262M (18-10-96), ex Coltishall, 41, Warden Det, 41, Gulf Det, 41. 41 Sqn colours	10-21
☐ XZ367	'EE' and 'GP'	SEPECAT Jaguar GR.3	76	ex Ipswich, Coltishall 9321M, Shawbury, Warden Det, GR.1, 54, Gulf Det, 54, 2, 226 OCU, 2	[2] 10-21
☐ XZ368	'E'	SEPECAT Jaguar GR.1	76	ex 8900M (23-5-86), Coltishall, 14, 6, 14	10-21
☐ XZ370	'JB'	SEPECAT Jaguar GR.1	76	ex 9004M, Shawbury, 14, 17. Arrived 18-10-89. Stored	@ 10-21
☐ XZ371	'AP'	SEPECAT Jaguar GR.1	76	ex 8907M (23-5-86), Shawbury, 14, 17	10-21
☐ XZ374	'JC'	SEPECAT Jaguar GR.1	76	ex 9005M, Shawbury, 14, 20. Last flown 13-8-85. Was with '238 Sqn', stored	10-21
☐ XZ377	'EP'	SEPECAT Jaguar GR.3A	77	ex St Athan, 6, GR.1, 6, 16, 6, 54, 226 OCU, 2, 31, 20. Arrived 6-7-07	10-21
☐ XZ383	'AF'	SEPECAT Jaguar GR.1	77	ex 8901M (23-5-86), Coltishall, 14, 17. Was with '238 Sqn', stored	10-21
☐ XZ384	'BC'	SEPECAT Jaguar GR.1	77	ex 8954M (3-12-87), Shawbury, 17, 31, 20. Stored	10-21
☐ XZ389	'BL'	SEPECAT Jaguar GR.1	77	ex Halton 8946M (13-11-87), Shawbury, 17, 31, 20 Was with '238 Sqn', stored	10-21
☐ XZ390	'DM'	SEPECAT Jaguar GR.1	77	ex 9003M, Shawbury, 2, 20, 31. Last flown 25-4-85	10-21
☐ XZ391	'ET'	SEPECAT Jaguar GR.3A	77	ex Coltishall, 6, GR.1, 6, 16, 54, 226 OCU, 54, 31. Last flown 12-4-06	10-21
☐ XZ392	'EM'	SEPECAT Jaguar GR.3A	77	ex Coltishall, 16, GR.1, Shawbury, 54, 20, 31. Arr 12-6-07	10-21
☐ XZ398	'EQ'	SEPECAT Jaguar GR.3A	77	ex Coltishall, 6, 41, GR.1, 41, 54, 41, 6, Indian AF J1007, G-27-323, Warton. Arrived 18-5-07	10-21
☐ XZ399	'EJ'	SEPECAT Jaguar GR.3A	76	ex Coltishall, 6, GR.1, 226 OCU, 6, 226 OCU, 6, 14, 6. *Ejordan 2004-2007 - Sleep Well Mighty Cat!* Arr 12-6-07	10-21
☐ XZ941	'B'	Sud Gazelle HT.2	78	ex 9301M, St Athan, Shawbury, 2 FTS, Odiham hack, CFS. Westland-built. Battle damage repair airframe	10-21
☐ XZ991	'3A'	HS Harrier GR.3	81	ex 9162M, St Athan 9162M, 233 OCU, 4, 1417 Flt, 233 OCU, 1, R-R, 1, 3, 1	# 10-21
☐ ZA320	'TAW'	Panavia Tornado GR.1	79	ex 9314M (8-4-02), St Athan, 15, TTTE. Stored	# 10-21
☐ ZA356		Panavia Tornado GR.1	80	ex Marham, St Athan, 15. Cockpit. First noted 4-19	4-19

☐ ZA447	'019'	Panavia Tornado GR.4	83	ex Marham, 12, GR.1, 12. Arrived 14-3-18	[3]	10-21
☐ ZA450	'TH'	Panavia Tornado GR.1	83	ex 9317M, St Athan, 15, 12, 617, 12, 27, 20, 15.		
				Arrived 14-5-02		10-21
☐ ZA459	'025'	Panavia Tornado GR.4	83	ex Marham, 617, GR.1, 617. Arrived 7-3-18		10-21
☐ ZA585	'054'	Panavia Tornado GR.4	81	ex Marham, 9, GR.1, 9. Arrived 16-10-18		10-21
☐ ZB615		SEPECAT Jaguar T.2	82	ex Cranwell, Boscombe Down, ETPS. F/n 8-13. Stored		10-21
☐ ZD465	'55'	BAe/McDD Harrier GR.9	90	ex Gosport, Cosford, Gosport, Wittering, Cottesmore,		
				BAE Warton. Arrived 29-5-18	#	6-20
☐ ZD715	'083'	Panavia Tornado GR.4	84	ex Marham, 617. Arrived 7-9-16		10-21
☐ ZD793	'101'	Panavia Tornado GR.4	84	ex Lossiemouth, Marham, 15. *100 Not Out*. Arrived 4-3-17		10-21
☐ ZD849	'110'	Panavia Tornado GR.4	85	ex Marham, 12. Arrived 8-10-18		10-21
☐ ZE340	'GO'	Panavia Tornado F.3	87	ex 9298M, Coningsby, 56. Rear fuselage of ZE758.		
				Arrived 4-9-01. 43 Sqn colours	#	10-21
☐ ZH796	'001'	HS Sea Harrier F/A.2	95	ex Culdrose, Shawbury, Yeovilton, 801, 899. Arr 4-14	#	10-21
☐ ZJ619		Eurofighter Typhoon CIM	~	fuselage, in classroom. First noted 5-18	[4]	3-20
☐ ZJ695	001	GenFly Mk.2	c02	Typhoon training rig	[5]	4-19
☐ ZJ696	002	GenFly Mk.2	c02	Typhoon training rig	[5]	4-19
☐ ZJ697	003	GenFly Mk.2	c02	Typhoon training rig	[5]	4-19
☐ ZJ698	004	GenFly Mk.2	c02	Typhoon training rig	[5]	4-19
☐ ZK006		Eurofighter Typhoon CIM	c02	cabin conditioner training rig	[6]	4-19
☐ ZK007		Eurofighter Typhoon CIM	c02	unspecified training rig	[6]	10-13
☐ ZK008		Eurofighter Typhoon CIM	c02	pressure refuelling training rig	[6]	4-19
☐ TAD.018		Sud Gazelle AH.1	74	ex Aborfield, M Wallop, ARWF, GCF. Westland-built		
	XW889			Corrosion control instruction		10-21

■ **[1]** Jaguar XX833 factoids: total flying time 5,335 hours - 1,070 of these since arriving at Boscombe in April 1994; it has had five bird strikes, one lightning strike and nine different engines. **[2]** XZ367 was supplied in response to a tender issued in 2009, it seems DCAE mis-calculated how many GR.3s it would need. **[3]** See also White Waltham, Berks, for an 'imposter' ZA447. **[4]** Two-seat fuselage resting on its undercarriage, stub wings, canards, stub fin/rudder. Sophisticated training airframe, *perhaps* taken from the production line and modded. See also note [5] regarding serial allocation. **[5]** Four sophisticated Typhoon purpose-built training rigs, called GenFlies. These have the capacity to generate over 100 different faults, to really annoy the trainees. They have been allocated serials not because they are intended to fly, but because they have a full maintenance schedule, just like a live airframe. **[6]** Cockpit-based CIMs. Other 'sims' in use include a barrage of so-called Emulator Test Rigs, AV001 to AV018.

Also: Buccaneer S.2B XX889 was due to move to St Athan, Wales, in early 2022: this move has been anticipated.

Midlands Air Ambulance choppers are based at Cosford and use a trusty Bölkow Bö 105 as a travelling demonstrator/fund-raiser. This heading will suffice as a 'base' for same. **www.midlandsairambulance.com**

| ☐ - | | Bölkow Bö 105 | ~ | travelling airframe | | 4-19 |

Warped Sports: In a field near Junction 3 of the M54. The 'cab' of Robinson R22 G-HERA (lasted noted May 2012) has expired, the Gazelle may be made of tougher stuff. ◆ *By prior arrangement* only | **www.warpedsports.com**

☐ XZ318		Sud Gazelle AH.1	77	ex Shawbury, Fleetlands, Yeovil, Fleetlands, 656,		
				664, 657, 664, 656, 670, ARWS, A&AEE. Westland-built.		
				Damaged 2-1-97. Cockpit		9-15

DONNINGTON south of the A518, northeast of Telford
Defence Fulfilment Centre: This huge logistics base has a Harrier on show.

| ☐ XZ971 | 'U' | HS Harrier GR.3 | 81 | ex Shawbury, Benson 9219M (13-10-93), HOCU, 1417 Flt, | | |
| | | | | 233 OCU. Displayed | | 4-21 |

NEWPORT
W&R27 (p204) deleted the An-2 at this *general* and *private* location. Its owner is still hard at work on it, intending to return it to ground-running status. ◆ *By prior arrangement* only

| ☐ RA-01641 | '3' | Antonov An-2 Colt | ~ | ex Baxterley, Wolverhampton. Crashed 9-99. Fuselage | | 7-20 |

REDNAL east of the A5 and Oswestry
Rednal Karting: Centred around the former watch tower. ◆ *By prior arrangement* only | **www.rednalkarting.co.uk**

| ☐ XT480 | '468' | Westland Wessex HU.5 | 66 | ex Hixon, Fleetlands, A2617[2] (13-12-90), A2603[2], | | |
| | | | | Wroughton, 771, 847, 772, 846, 707 | | 8-21 |

SHAWBURY AIRFIELD on the B5063 north of Shawbury   EGOS

Aircraft Maintenance and Storage Unit (AM&SU) operated on behalf of the Defence Aviation Repair Agency by FB Services. Hawk T.1 sustainment work has ended and AMRO at Valley, Wales, will handle the reduce to produce programme. Other than the 'Red Arrows', T.1s are due to be phased out at the end of March 2022. Hawks held as spares/replacements for the 'Reds' under the RAFAT-2030 programme; are marked #. Aircraft marked NEA - non-effective airframe - have embarked upon the disposal process and are likely to depart. The first of the Tucanos have fled the nest; the Gazelle fleet is winding down, due for replacement in 2024; the venerable Puma is due to leave service in 2025.

Departures: Gazelle AH.1s XX460, XZ294, XZ328, XZ341, XZ343 and ZB667 all departed 8-9-20 to join the reduced to produce programme, but do not *appear* to have gone to the usual suspect, Middle Wallop, Hants; **Hawk** T.1A XX157 to Valley, Wales, 10-21 for return to service, with the 'Reds'; T.1 XX173 to Boscombe Down, Wilts, 11-3-20; T.1 XX244 to Cosford, Shropshire, 13-10-21; T.1 XX295 to Valley, Wales, 8-12-20 for return to service, with the 'Reds'; T.1W XX312 to Norwich Airport, Norfolk, by 8-19 for a brief period of display before relocating to St Athan, Wales, by 7-20. Transferred to Cosford, Shropshire: T.1 XX181 28-10-20; XX185 17-11-20; XX224 19-11-20; XX235 17-11-20. Islander R.1s ZG844 and ZG847 to Bembridge, Isle of Wight, by 6-21; **Puma** HC.1s XW206 and XW207 were scrapped in 5-14 as spares for the programme sustainment programme; **Tucano** T.1s ZF166, ZF211 and ZF380 were struck off charge 30-3-16 as disposed of via the Defence Sales Agency, perhaps as spares; fuselage of **Typhoon** FGR.2 ZJ943 departed 7-6-21 for an unspecified scrapyard.

☐ WV908	'188'	Hawker Sea Hawk FGA.6	G-CMFB	55	ex Yeovilton, Dunsfold, Yeovilton, Dunsfold, Yeovilton, Culdrose SF, Halton 8154M, Sydenham A2660, 738, 806, 898, 807. AW-built. Last flown 2010, 806 Sqn colours.	[1]	6-21
☐ XW198		Sud Puma HC.1		70	ex Benson, 33, 230, 72. 230, 33, 240 OCU, Benson. Westland-built. SOC 31-12-12. Arrived 23-8-17		8-17
☐ XW200		Sud Puma HC.1		71	ex 33, 240 OCU, HOCF. Crashed 9-4-01. Westland-built. Arrived 2-7-01		12-15
☐ XW210		Sud Puma HC.1		71	ex Benson, 33, Boscombe Down, 1563 Flt, 33, 240 OCU, 33, 230, 33, 240 OCU, 33. Westland-built. Arrived 12-8-14		12-15
☐ XW218		Sud Puma HC.1		71	ex 1563 Flt, 33. 230, 72, 33, 72, 18, 230, 33, 18, 230, 33, 230, 240 OCU, 230. Westland-built. Crashed 15-4-07, arrived 5-3-08		12-15
☐ XW226		Sud Puma HC.1		71	ex Benson, 33, 230, 72, 320, 33, 72, 33, 72, 27, 230, 33, 18, 230. Westland-built. Arrived 12-8-14		12-15
☐ XX158		HS Hawk T.1A		76	ex 208, CFS, 208, 19, 2 TWU. Arrived 9-5-16. NEA 12-19		10-21
☐ XX159		HS Hawk T.1A		76	ex 736, FRADU, 208, 19, CFS, 74, 4 FTS, TWU, A&AEE. Arrived 24-7-18	#	10-21
☐ XX160		HS Hawk T.1		77	ex 208, 19, 208, DERA, TEE, RAE. Arr 18-6-07. NEA 12-19		10-21
☐ XX167		HS Hawk T.1		77	ex 208, 4 FTS, TWU, 4 FTS. Arrived 27-2-12. NEA 12-19		10-21
☐ XX169		HS Hawk T.1W		77	ex 19, 92, FRADU, 19, 74, 6 FTS, 234, 4 FTS. Arrived 17-5-11. NEA 12-19		10-21
☐ XX170		HS Hawk T.1		77	ex 100, 736, Llanbedr, 234, CFS, 4 FTS. Arrived 25-5-16. NEA 12-19		10-21
☐ XX171		HS Hawk T.1		77	ex 208, 19, 208, 74, CFS, 4 FTS. Arr 20-5-11. NEA 12-19		10-21
☐ XX174		HS Hawk T.1		77	ex 208, 19, 6 FTS, 19, 74, 4 FTS. Arrived 14-1-13. NEA 12-19		10-21
☐ XX176		HS Hawk T.1W		77	ex 208, 100, 92, 19, CFS, 4 FTS. Arrived 14-1-13. NEA 12-19		10-21
☐ XX190*	'CN'	HS Hawk T.1A		77	ex 100, 208, 74, 4 FTS, 1 TWU, 2 TWU, 1 TWU, TWU. Arrived 30-6-08	#	10-21
☐ XX194	'CP'	HS Hawk T.1A		78	ex 100, 74, TWU. Arrived 8-5-13. NEA 12-19		10-21
☐ XX195		HS Hawk T.1W		78	ex 208, 4 FTS, 19, 208, 100, 2 TWU, 1 TWU, TWU. Arrived 2-2-10	#	10-21
☐ XX199		HS Hawk T.1A		78	ex 208, 74, 1 TWU, 2 TWU, 1 TWU, TWU. Arrived 3-2-16. NEA 12-19		10-21
☐ XX201	'CQ'	HS Hawk T.1A		78	ex 100, 92, 2 TWU, TWU. Arrived 17-11-16. Fleet spare		10-21
☐ XX217		HS Hawk T.1A		78	ex 736, 100, 19, 2 TWU, 1 TWU, A&AEE, TWU. Arr 6-18	#	10-21
☐ XX220		HS Hawk T.1A		78	ex 208, FRADU, St Athan, FRADU, TWU, CFS, TWU. Arrived 4-11-11. NEA 12-19	#	10-21
☐ XX222	'CI'	HS Hawk T.1A		78	ex 100, 208, 74, TWU. Arrived 15-7-11	#	10-21
☐ XX225		HS Hawk T.1		78	ex 208, FRADU, 208, 19, 4 FTS. Arrived 3-8-07. NEA 12-19		10-20
☐ XX228		HS Hawk T.1		78	ex 208, 100, 2 TWU, 1 TWU. Arrived 8-11-07. NEA 12-19		10-21
☐ XX230	'CM'	HS Hawk T.1A		76	ex 100, 74, 19, TWU. Arrived 2-11-17	#	10-21

☐ XX231		HS Hawk T.1W	78	ex 208, 74, 92, 19, 4 FTS, RAE, 4 FTS. Arr 27-9-11. NEA 12-19	10-21
☐ XX234		HS Hawk T.1	78	ex 208, FRADU, 234, 74, 4 FTS. Arrived 21-7-11. NEA 12-19	10-21
☐ XX238		HS Hawk T.1	78	ex 208, 19, 74, 19, 6 FTS, CFS, 4 FTS. Arr 11-6-08. NEA 12-19	10-21
☐ XX248	'CJ'	HS Hawk T.1A	78	ex 100, 1 TWU, 2 TWU, 1 TWU. Arrived 4-10-07. NEA 12-19	10-21
☐ XX250		HS Hawk T.1W	79	ex 208, 100, 208, 100, 6 FTS, 4 FTS, CFS, 4 FTS, CFS. First noted 6-18.	# 10-21
☐ XX258	'CE'	HS Hawk T.1A	79	ex 100, 74, 19, CFS, TWU. Arrived 2-5-19	10-21
☐ XX260		HS Hawk T.1A	79	ex 'Red Arrows'. Bird strike 7-8-11. Arr 24-8-11. NEA 12-19	10-21
☐ XX264		HS Hawk T.1A	79	ex 'Red Arrows'. Arrived 6-14. NEA 12-19	10-21
☐ XX265	'CP'	HS Hawk T.1A	79	ex 19, 100, 92, 2 TWU, 1 TWU. Arrived 6-10-10	# 10-21
☐ XX284	'CN'	HS Hawk T.1A	79	ex 100, Shawbury, 100, 208, 100, TWU. Arrived 5-12-17	# 10-21
☐ XX286		HS Hawk T.1A	79	ex 208, 234, 19, TWU. Arrived 5-9-12. NEA 12-19. Fleet spare	10-21
☐ XX287		HS Hawk T.1A	79	ex 208, 92, 2 TWU, 1 TWU. Arrived 20-4-16. NEA 12-19	10-21
☐ XX289	'CO'	HS Hawk T.1A	79	ex 100, 19, TWU. Arrived 4-7-12	# 10-21
☐ XX294		HS Hawk T.1	79	ex 'Red Arrows', 4 FTS. Arrived 2-6-11. NEA 12-19	10-21
☐ XX296		HS Hawk T.1	79	ex 208, 74, 4 FTS. Arrived 21-1-04. NEA 12-19	10-21
☐ XX299		HS Hawk T.1W	79	ex 208, 100, 19, 208, 74, 92, 4 FTS. Arr 2-4-08. NEA 12-19	10-21
☐ XX301		HS Hawk T.1A	80	ex 100, 19, 92, TWU. First noted 6-18	# 10-21
☐ XX307		HS Hawk T.1	80	ex 208, 'Red Arrows', 4 FTS. Arr 17-10-12. NEA 12-19	# 10-21
☐ XX309		HS Hawk T.1	80	ex St Athan 'hack', 208, 19, 6 FTS, 234, 4 FTS. Arrived 15-2-06. Welsh dragon colours	# 10-21
☐ XX313		HS Hawk T.1W	80	ex 208, 74, 19, CFS, 19, 4 FTS. Arrived 16-8-12. NEA 12-19	10-21
☐ XX314		HS Hawk T.1W	80	ex Valley, 19, 100, 208, 4, 4 FTS, 2 TWU, 4 FTS. Arrived 18-10-11. NEA 12-19	10-21
☐ XX315		HS Hawk T.1A	80	ex 208, 234, 1TWU. Arrived 19-1-16. NEA 12-19	10-21
☐ XX330		HS Hawk T.1A	80	ex 100, 19, 208, 92, 1 TWU, 2 TWU. First noted 6-18	# 10-21
☐ XX331		HS Hawk T.1A	80	ex 100, 2 TWU. Arrived 29-6-11	# 10-21
☐ XX338		HS Hawk T.1W	81	ex 208, 19, 208, 19, 4 FTS. Arrived 12-9-13. NEA 12-19	10-21
☐ XX345	'CB'	HS Hawk T.1A	81	ex 100, 19, 92, TWU. Arrived 3-12-08	# 10-21
☐ XX350	'D'	HS Hawk T.1A	81	ex 100, 74, 1 TWU. First noted 6-18	# 10-21
☐ ZA773	'F'	Sud Gazelle AH.1	80	ex 666, 665, 655, 665, 655. Westland-built. Arr 31-10-05	12-15
☐ ZB677*		Sud Gazelle AH.1	81	ex 29 Flt BATUS Canada. Westland-built. Arrived 27-7-20	7-20
☐ ZB683*		Sud Gazelle AH.1	82	ex M Wallop, 7 Regt. Westland-built. Arr 14-9-20	9-20
☐ ZB683*		Sud Gazelle AH.1	82	ex Aldergrove. Westland-built. Arrived 7-10-20	10-20
☐ ZF163		Short Tucano T.1	89	ex 1 FTS, CFS, 1 FTS, 7 FTS. Arrived 19-7-01	1-17
☐ ZF263		Short Tucano T.1	90	ex 1 FTS, 3 FTS, 7 FTS. Arrived 4-7-02	1-17
☐ ZF268		Short Tucano T.1	90	ex 1 FTS, CFS. Arrived 15-2-06	1-17
☐ ZF286		Short Tucano T.1	91	ex 1 FTS, CFS. Arrived 11-5-06	1-17
☐ ZF288		Short Tucano T.1	91	ex 1 FTS, CFS. Arrived 4-7-02. Spares recovery 1-17	11-17
☐ ZF315		Short Tucano T.1	91	ex 1 FTS, 3 FTS. Arrived 22-3-06	1-18
☐ ZF318		Short Tucano T.1	91	ex 1 FTS, CFS. Arrived 28-11-01	1-17
☐ ZF350		Short Tucano T.1	91	ex 1 FTS, RAFC. Arrived 25-5-02. Spares recovery 1-17	11-17
☐ ZF372		Short Tucano T.1	91	ex 1 FTS, CFS. Arrived 24-8-00. Spares recovery 1-17	11-17
☐ ZF376		Short Tucano T.1	92	ex 1 FTS. Arrived 2-7-01. Spares recovery 1-17	11-17
☐ ZF405		Short Tucano T.1	92	ex 1 FTS, 6 FTS. Arrived 21-6-06	1-17
☐ ZF408		Short Tucano T.1	92	ex 1 FTS. Arrived 7-8-01	1-17
☐ ZF414		Short Tucano T.1	92	ex 1 FTS, CFS, 1 FTS, RAFC. Arrived 14-4-00. Spares recovery 1-17	11-17
☐ ZF416		Short Tucano T.1	92	ex 1 FTS, CFS, 1 FTS. Arrived 22-3-06	1-17
☐ ZF418		Short Tucano T.1	92	ex 1 FTS, 6 FTS. Arrived 6-3-06	1-17
☐ ZF446		Short Tucano T.1	92	ex 1 FTS, 6 FTS. Arrived 15-3-06	1-17
☐ ZF449		Short Tucano T.1	92	ex 1 FTS, CFS, 1 FTS. Arrived 2-7-02. Spares recovery 1-17	11-17
☐ ZF486		Short Tucano T.1	92	ex 1 FTS. Arrived 4-9-03	1-17
☐ ZF487		Short Tucano T.1	92	ex 1 FTS. Arrived 27-2-06	1-17
☐ ZF488		Short Tucano T.1	92	ex 1 FTS. Arrived 15-2-00	1-17
☐ ZF490		Short Tucano T.1	92	ex 1 FTS. Arrived 30-9-03	1-17
☐ ZF492		Short Tucano T.1	92	ex 1 FTS. Arrived 24-8-06	1-17
☐ ZF513		Short Tucano T.1	92	ex 72, CFS, 1 FTS. *Basuto*. Arrived 9-3-06	1-17
☐ ZJ910	'DO'	E'fighter Typhoon FGR.4	07	ex Coningsby, 11. Arrived 24-6-16	6-16

☐ ZJ911	'QO-Z'	E'fighter Typhoon FGR.4	05	ex Coningsby, 11. Arrived 24-8-16	8-16
☐ ZJ912		E'fighter Typhoon FGR.4	05	ex Coningsby. Arrived 12-2-18	6-18
☐ ZJ918		E'fighter Typhoon FGR.4	05	ex Coningsby, 3. Arrived 11-1-18	1-18
☐ ZJ925	'DXI'	E'fighter Typhoon FGR.4	06	ex Coningsby, 11. Arrived 26-5-16	5-16
☐ ZJ927		E'fighter Typhoon FGR.4	06	ex Coningsby, 29. Arrived 11-1-18	1-18
☐ ZJ930		E'fighter Typhoon FGR.4	06	ex Coningsby. Arrived 22-1-18	6-18
☐ ZJ932	'DB'	E'fighter Typhoon FGR.4	06	ex Coningsby, 11. Arrived 26-5-16	5-16
☐ ZJ934		E'fighter Typhoon FGR.4	06	ex Coningsby. Arrived 18-12-17	6-18
☐ ZJ936	'QO-C'	E'fighter Typhoon FGR.4	07	ex Coningsby, 3. Arrived 23-5-16	5-16
☐ ZJ942		E'fighter Typhoon FGR.4	07	ex Coningsby, 29. Arrived 22-1-18	1-18

■ [1] Sea Hawk held on behalf of the Fly Navy Heritage Trust – see Yeovilton, Somerset.

Also: Dominie XS713 was roaded out to Kinloss, Scotland, arriving on 18th November 2020. Wessex HU.5 XT773 was scrapped during November 2020, handled by a scrapyard at Spey Bay, Scotland.

☐ XR516   'V'   Westland Wessex HC.2   64   ex Gosport, 9319M, A2709 [2], Shawbury, 2 FTS, 18. Gate   [1]   9-21

■ [1] Wessex XR516 has been 'adopted' by the resident 60 Squadron.

SHREWSBURY

Roger Marley: Has made exceptional progress with his static Demon project which includes an RR Kestrel. This is a painstaking tribute to Falklands-born Flt Lt Donald Eric Turner who flew Demons from Hal Far with 74 Squadron 1935-36. While serving with 238 Squadron, Turner was shot down and killed in Hurricane P3823 off the Isle of Wight on 8th August 1940: Roger has Turner's uniform and Demon items from his time on Malta. Other elements of the project are parts from Audax K73776 from a Shrewsbury scrapyard and Hind K6666, which was issued to the RNZAF as NZ1529 in September 1940.

◆ *Available* **only** *by prior permission* | roger.marley@btinternet.com

☐ 'K4540'   Hawker Demon I   34   Fuselage – see notes above   1-22

Also: Last noted in October 2018, Tiger Cub G-MJXL has been deleted.

The fuselage of Demon 'K4540', January 2022.
Roger Marley

SLEAP AERODROME southwest of Wem   EGCV

Wartime Aircraft Recovery Group Aviation Museum: Courtesy of Shropshire Aero Club, the group runs a small exhibition, including artefacts from 'digs' including WAG's 'founder', 61 OTU Spitfire IIa P7304 involved in a mid-air collision near High Ercall on 22nd August 1943, recovered in 1977. A recent recovery is a substantially complete under fuselage/bomb bay pannier from a Halifax/Halton. The 'Johnnie Johnson' Spitfire FSM, 'EN398' what else, departed as far back as mid-2015 to Ripley, Derbyshire. ◆ Metasphere, sorry, **Facebook** | **www.shropshireaeroclub.com/heritage**

☐ 'K7271'   Hawker Fury II replica   79   BAPC.148, ex Market Drayton, Cosford. Stored   4-21

Shropshire Aero Club Vintage Jet Group: By December 2020, Vampire T.11 WZ450 had arrived from Corscombe, Dorset: it decamped to Newquay, Cornwall, in January 2022. Jet Provost T.3A XN582 was roaded in from Bruntingthorpe, Leics, on 22nd July 2021 and it was up and taxiing almost immediately. Like the Vampire, its tenure in Shropshire was fleeting, moving to Elvington, N Yorks, on 9th December 2021.

Also: Last noted in February 2018 Mini-Imp G-BLWW had gravitated to <u>Sandown</u>, Isle of Wight, by November 2020. Also last recorded in February 2018, Pazmany PL-1 G-BDHJ has been deleted.

Locally: Bob Mitchell's former PT Flight is *believed* to be held in store. ◆ *Available* **only** *by prior permission*

❑ G-AEUJ	Miles Whitney Straight	37	ex Cosford, Sutton Coldfield, Marple, East Midlands, Hurn.	
			Phillips & Powis-built. CoA 4-6-70	N10-17
❑ G-AFRZ	Miles Monarch	38	ex Cosford, Sutton Coldfield, Shipdham, G-AIDE,	
			W6463, Kemble, 10 GCF, FTCCF, 13 EFTS, G-AFRZ.	
			Phillips & Powis-built. CoA 29-6-70	N10-17
❑ G-AWIW	Stampe SV-4B	47	ex Cosford, Colerne, F-BDCC. Nord-built. CoA 6-5-73	N10-17
❑ G-AYKZ	SAI KZ-VIII	49	ex Coventry, HB-EPB, OY-ACB. CoA 17-7-81	N10-17
❑ G-RIDE	Stephens Akro	76	ex N81AC, N55NM. CoA 13-8-92	N10-17
❑ N1344	Ryan PT-22 Recruit	41	ex Cosford, 41-20877	10-11
❑ N49272	'23' Fairchild PT-23-HO	42	ex Cosford, USAAF 42-49413	10-11
❑ N56421	'855' Ryan PT-22 Recruit	41	ex Cosford, 41-15510	10-11
❑ N58566	Vultee BT-15 Valiant	42	ex Cosford, USAAF 42-41882	10-11

SOMERSET
Includes the unitary authorities of North Somerset and Bath and North East Somerset

BRIDGWATER south of Weston-super-Mare, on the B3140
Bridgwater and Taunton College: Bath Road. Took on a Scout in 2020. ◆ *By prior permission* **only** | www.btc.ac.uk

❑ XT633*	Westland Scout AH.1	66	ex Farnborough, M Wallop, Arborfield, Wroughton, 659,	
			653, 661, 660, Wroughton. Arrived 20-8-20	8-20

BRISTOL AIRPORT or Lulsgate   EGGD
Delta Force South Bristol: West of the airport. ◆ *Available* **only** *by prior permission* | www.paintballgames.co.uk

❑ G-AWOX	Westland Wessex 60	68	ex Weston-super-Mare, Hurn, W-s-M, G-17-2, G-AWOX,	
			5N-AJO, G-AWOX, 9Y-TFB, G-AWOX, VH-BHE, G-AWOX,	
			VR-BCV, G-AWOX, G-17-1. CoA 13-1-83, de-reg 23-11-82	2-10

BURNHAM ON SEA on the A38 north of Taunton
Grahame Cox: Cherishes his superbly restored Britannia cockpit and has added an Adams-Wilson to his collection.
◆ *Available* **only** *by prior permission* - see **Facebook**

❑ -*	Adams-Wilson Hobbycopter	~	ex 'West Sussex'. Arrived 8-21	12-21
❑ 5Y-AYR	Bristol Britannia 307F	57	ex Hurn, African Cargo, G-ANCD, Gemini, Lloyd, BUA, Air	
			Charter, 4X-AGE El Al, N6595C, G-ANCD, G-18-3. Cockpit	12-21

FELTON west of the A38, east of Bristol Airport
Park Farm: A 'JP' is kept at the off-airport parking site. www.parkfarmbristol.co.uk

❑ XN551	'100' Hunting Jet Provost T.3A	61	ex St Athan 8984M (6-2-89), 7 FTS, RAFC, 1 FTS, 3 FTS,	
			6 FTS, RAFC	12-21

HENSTRIDGE AERODROME south of the A30, east of Henstridge Marsh   EGHS
By early 2020 the five unfinished Norman Freelances had left, with no more detailed forwarding address than "up north".

❑ G-AANO	DH Moth	30	ex Cambridge, S'ton, N590N. Moth Corp-built. Arr 18-12-16	10-19
❑ G-AYLP	American AA-1 Yankee	70	ex EI-AVV, G-AYLP. CoA 15-6-11, de-reg 24-5-21 [1]	10-19
❑ G-BBDO	Piper Aztec 250	73	ex N40361. CoA 4-6-16. First noted 9-18	9-18
❑ G-BIBB	Mooney M.20C	64	ex OH-MOD. CoA 23-6-08, de-reg 16-12-10	5-21
❑ G-BJLC*	Monnet Sonerai 2L	90	ex Netheravon. CoA 11-5-98. First noted 8-20	8-20
❑ G-LTFC	Piper Cherokee 140	69	ex G-AXTI, N11C. CoA 4-2-08	10-19
❑ G-SPUT	Yakovlev Yak-52	91	ex RA-01325. Aerostar-built. CoA 12-5-17. F/n 10-18	3-19
❑ G-STNR	Yakovlev Yak-52	83	ex LY-ALY. IAR Bacau-built. De-reg 23-11-18. F/n 10-18 [2]	3-19

■ **[1]** AA-1 used as a training aid for the local air ambulance. **[2]** See under Swansea, Wales, for *another* 'G-STNR'.

Sea King HAR.3 XZ597 (G-SKNG) and Wessex HU.5 XT761 (G-WSEX) performing at Abingdon, September 2021. *Richard Hall*

HIGHER PURTINGTON south of the A30 between Chard and Crewkerne

Historic Helicopters: Andrew Whitehouse and friends have made great strides with the helicopter collection. A second Sea King is airworthy, joining XZ597, the 'star' of the BBC TV thriller *Vigil*. It is planned to open a visitor centre and museum in due course, but for now regular open days are staged and the team have a policy of displaying their machines at as many airshows and events as possible.

Wessex XS507 moved to St Athan, Wales, on 18th May 2021.

◆ *See website for open days, otherwise* **only** *by prior permission* | www.historichelicopters.com

❑ G-ANLW*		Westland Widgeon 2	54	ex Sywell, Flixton, Sywell, Squires Gate, 'MD497', Wellingborough, Little Staughton, Tattershall Thorpe, *When Eight Bells Toll, Eye of the Needle*, Southend. CoA 27-5-81, de-reg 15-11-02. first noted 11-21		1-22
❑ XJ729		Westland Whirlwind HAR.10 ✈	56	ex Mullingar, Finningley 8732M (1-8-84), SARTU, 22, 202, 228, 22, HAR.2, 22. Acquired 2013		1-22
				G-BVGE		
❑ XT434*	'455'	Westland Wasp HAS.1	65	ex Breighton, Ipswich, Fleetlands, A2643 [2], A2723 Lee-on-Solent, 829, 703. *Dobbin*. Arrived 25-10-21	[1]	1-22
				G-CGGK		
❑ XT761		Westland Wessex HU.5 ✈	66	ex Culdrose, Gosport, Lee-on-Solent, A2678 [2], A2767 (12-4-88), Wroughton, 845, 771, 846, 848, 847, 848, 707. First noted 6-17, first flown 15-2-19		1-22
				G-WSEX		
❑ XT771	'620'	Westland Wessex HU.5	67	ex Culdrose, Gosport A2673 [2], Lee-on-Solent A2761 (11-4-88), 772, 845, 848, 707. First noted 6-17		1-22
❑ XV647*	'28'	Westland Sea King HU.5	69	ex Gosport, 771, Gannet Flt, 771, HAS.5, 771, 814, 826, HAS.2, 826, 820, HAS.1, 706, 826, 737, 700S. F/n 9-21		1-22
❑ XZ220*		Westland Lynx AH.7	80	ex South Clifton, Weeton, Hixon, M Wallop, 671, 667, 657, 3 Rgt/662, 653,1 Rgt, 651, 661, 651, 654, 669, 657, 659, 669, 654. Cabin. First noted 7-20		8-21
❑ XZ588		Westland Sea King HAR.3 ✈	77	ex Fleetlands, 202, 22, 202, SKTF, 202, SKTF, 202. Arrived 30-4-20; first flown 20-6-21		1-22
				G-SEAK		
❑ XZ597	'M'	Westland Sea King HAR.3 ✈	78	ex Colsterworth, 203, 202, 78, 202, SKTU, 202. Arrived 6-12-17, first flown 20-3-20		1-22
				G-SKNG		

☐	XZ616		Westland Lynx AH.7		80	ex M Wallop, AH.1. Arrived 30-4-20.	
			✈	G-LNKX		First flown 18-11-21	1-22
☐	ZA314	'WT'	Westland Sea King		82	ex Gosport, 846, 848, 845, 846, 845, 846, Bosnia, 846,	
			HC.4	G-CMDO		845, 707, 846, A&AEE. Arrived 7-1-20	1-22
☐	ZF122	'V'	Westland Sea King		87	ex Colsterworth, 846, 845, 846, 845, 846, 845, 846, 772,	
			HC.4			848, 772. Arrived 6-12-17	1-22
☐	RS-02*		Westland Sea King		76	ex Koksijde, Belgian Air Force, G-BDNI, G-17-2.	
			Mk.48	OO-SEE		Acquired mid-2020, arrived 20-10-21	1-22
☐	RS-02*		Westland Sea King		76	ex Koksijde, Belgian Air Force, G-BDNK, G-17-4.	
			Mk.48	OO-KNG		Acquired mid-2020, arrived 20-10-21	1-22

■ [1] Owned by the Westland Wasp Historic Flight – see Winchester, Hampshire.

MARKSBURY on the A39 west of Bath

Hamburger Hill: ◆ **Only** *by prior permission* **only** | **www.hamburgerhill.co.uk**

☐	XE668	'832'	Hawker Hunter GA.11	55	ex Predannack, A2647 [2], Culdrose SAH A2733 (8-2-85),	
					Yeovilton, FRADU, 738, F.4, 26, 4. Squires Gate-built	7-21
☐	XT762		Westland Wessex HU.5	66	ex Predannack, A2661 [2], Culdrose A2751 (28-7-87),	
					Lee-on-Solent, Wroughton, RAE Bedford, A&AEE, 848	7-21
☐	S-886		Sikorsky S-55C	~	ex Weston-super-Mare, Panshanger, Elstree, Danish AF	7-21

PORTISHEAD west of the M5, Junction 19

Bristol Activity Centre: Portishead. There are *two* Bristol Activity Centres; Cribbs Causeway is the 'Urban' site and this one is the 'Woodland' version. See under Bristol. Glos, for comments as to what might be here, or there! The two quoted below, have long since been associated with this site. ◆ **Only** *by prior permission* | **www.bristolactivitycentre.co.uk**

| ☐ | - | | Bölkow Bö 105 | ~ | camouflaged | 6-17 |
| ☐ | S-882 | | Sikorsky S-55C | ~ | ex Weston-super-Mare, Panshanger, Elstree, Dan AF Esk.722 | 2-15 |

SOMERTON on the B3153 northwest of Yeovil

HeliOperations: While flying from Portland, Dorset and Culdrose, Cornwall, the company has established a maintenance and storage site here. ◆ **Strictly** *by prior application* **only** | **www.helioperations.co**

☐	XV656*	'85'	Westland Sea King	70	ex Gosport, Culdrose, 854, 857, 849, AEW.2, 849, HAS.2,	
			ASaC.7		706, Falklands, 825, 819, HAS.1, 819, 824. F/n 12-20	6-21
☐	XV664*	'90'	Westland Sea King	70	ex Gosport, Culdrose, 857, 854, 849, AEW.2, 819, 824,	
			ASaC.7		826, HAS.1, 826. First noted 12-20	6-21
☐	XV670*	'17'	Westland Sea King	70	ex Gosport, Culdrose, 771, 845, 706, HAS.2, 814, 737, HAS.1,	
			HU.5		819. Arrived 3-9-20	3-21
☐	XV671*	'90'	Westland Sea King	70	ex Gosport, Culdrose, 857, 854, 857, 849, AEW.2, 849, HAS.2,	
			ASaC.7		HAS.1, 814, 820, 819. First noted 12-20	6-21
☐	XV697*	'81'	Westland Sea King	71	ex Gosport, Culdrose, 849, AEW.2, 849, HAS.1, Falklands,	
			ASaC.7		819, 706. First noted 12-20	6-21
☐	XV714*	'88'	Westland Sea King	70	ex Gosport, 849, AEW.2, 857, 849, HAS.2, 826, 824, Falklands,	
			ASaC.7		825, 706, 826, 819, HAS.1, 706, 820. Arrived by 10-20	3-21
☐	XZ586*		W'land Sea King HAR.3	78	ex Gosport, 22, 78, SKTU, 22, 202, 1564 Flt, 202. F/ 12-20	6-21
☐	XZ590*	'F'	W'land Sea King HAR.3	78	ex Gosport, 202, 78, 202, 22, 202. First noted 12-20	6-21
☐	XZ594*		Westland Sea King HAR.3	76	ex Gosport, SKTU, 202, 22, 202. Arrived 23-7-20	3-21
☐	XZ596*	'L'	Westland Sea King HAR.3	76	ex Gosport, 202, 203, SKTU, 22, 202. Arrived 23-7-20	3-21
☐	ZA105*	'Q'	Westland Sea King HAR.3	80	ex Gosport, 22, 20	3-21
☐	ZA126*	'191'	Westland Sea King	80	ex Gosport, 849, 854, 8499, HAS.6, 810, HAS.5, 706,	
			ASaC.7		820, 706, 820	3-21
☐	ZA134*	'25'	Westland Sea King	79	ex Gosport, Culdrose, 771, Gannet Flt, 771, 706, 819,	
			HU.5		Falklands -82. Arrived 3-9-20	3-21
☐	ZA137*		Westland Sea King HU.5	81	ex Gosport, QinetiQ, 771, HAS.5, 706, 826, 706, 826,	
					Falklands, 706. First noted 12-20	6-21
☐	ZE420*	'189'	Westland Sea King	86	ex Portland, Gosport, 849, 857, AEW.2, 849, HAS.5, 706,	
			ASaC.7		826, 819, 820	7-20
☐	ZE422*	'92'	Westland Sea King	86	ex Gosport, 854, 857, HAS.6, 771, 820, 810, 819, 814, 706,	
			ASaC.7		HAS.5, 826, 814. SOC 26-9-18	3-21

TAUNTON

Army Reserve Centre: Mountway Road, Bishops Hull on the western side of the town.

☐ ZB670 Sud Gazelle AH.1 84 ex Dishforth, Arborfield, 665. Westland-built. Displayed 8-21

Spitfire Spares: Specialising in trading in World War Two artefacts, spares etc, the organisation has a taxiable Spitfire IX, powered by a Rolls-Meteor V-12 tank engine and available for hire. A travelling Typhoon FSM is being created.

◆ *Available* **only** *by prior permission* | **www.spitfirespares.com**

☐ 'A1452' 'Vickers Gunbus' 85 BAPC.234, ex Sywell, 'GBH-7', Swindon, Sleap, High Halden, Hawkinge, Manston, Chelford, Coventry, Old Warden, White Waltham, *Sky Bandits, Gunbus. Bombay 3* [1] 3-12

☐ 'EN398' 'JE-J' V-S Spitfire IX FSM ~ BAPC.555, see notes above [2] 12-19
☐ 'JP8xx' 'T' Hawker Typhoon I FSM 18 BAPC.556, *Tally Ho*, under construction, see notes above 12-19
☐ - Hawker Hurricane FSM 68 ex Hooton Park, Coventry, N Weald, Coventry, Great Bridge, Wembley, *Battle of Britain* (1968). Off-site 4-17

■ **[1]** 'Vickers Gunbus' film mock-up is more DH.2 than FB.5, having been based upon G-BFVH which is at Scampton, Lincs. **[2]** Other 'EN398s' can be found at Coningsby, Lincs, and Pyle, Wales.

Also: A cache of Austers has been gathered at a *private* airstrip in the *general* area.

☐ G-AGYK* Auster J1 Autocrat 46 ex Shobdon. CoA 17-8-07, de-reg 11-2-13 12-21
☐ G-AOBV* Auster J5P Autocar 55 ex Wickenby, Cheshunt, Laindon, Stapleford Tawney, Benington. CoA 7-4-71, de-reg 14-11-91 12-21
☐ G-ASOC* Auster 6A Tugmaster 46 ex AOP.6 VF603, 227 OCU, 1958 Flt, 661. CoA 18-5-02, de-reg 22-5-09 12-21
☐ G-AXMN* Auster J5B Autocar 52 ex F-BGPN. De-reg 9-11-10 12-21

WEDMORE on the B3139 west of Wells

Castle Farm Camping and Caravanning: Neil Banwell, site owner, keeps a SHAR. It is displayed outside during the summer.

◆ *By prior permission* **only** | **www.castlefarmcampsite.co.uk**

☐ XZ494 '128' HS Sea Harrier F/A.2 80 ex St Athan, 800, FRS.1, 899, 801, 899, 800, 899, 801, 800, 899. 800 Sqn colours 7-21

WESTON-SUPER-MARE AERODROME on the A371 east of Weston-super-Mare

The Helicopter Museum (THM): Custodianship of the EH 101 from the RAF Museum is a feather in the cap for this world-class collection. Civil, passenger configured, it will contrast with the similarly intended Sud Frelon. Acquired in 2017, Belvedere HC.1 XG454 has arrived from the collapsed Manchester museum.

After inevitable Covid-induced delays, construction of a new hangar began in late 2021 alongside a campaign to raise £300,000 to finish the work. The museum has acquired around 10 acres of land, including a 500m grass strip. The helipad is a much-used facility: subject to operational conditions, there are frequent helicopter experience flight days. Regular 'open cockpit' days and loads of special events are staged. Catering is excellent - kick off with a THM breakfast!

A 'JetRanger' space frame used by Barrett Homes for publicity and display at developments and described by the museum as a sculpture is mounted on stilts and 'guards' the entrance. It is far from an 'airframe' and as such does not appear in the 'formal' listing below. Another item falls into this category, even though it is bigger than some of the complete rotorcraft at IHM. Boeing XCH-62 73-22012 prototype heavy-lift helicopter it was cancelled before it could fly. The nose wheels and main landing gear were acquired from Fort Rucker, Alabama, in 2009.

A one-off abbreviation in the listing below should cause no headaches: WSM = Weston-super-Mare. The **Reserve Collection** is listed separately – below -and the restoration centre can also be viewed.

◆ *Locking Moor Road, BS24 8PP* | **01934 635227** | **email** *via website* | **www.helicoptermuseum.co.uk**

☐ G-ALSX Bristol Sycamore 3 51 ex Duxford, Staverton, G-48/1, G-ALSX, VR-TBS (1958-1959), G-ALSX. CoA 24-9-65, de-reg 31-1-66 [1] 1-22
☐ G-AODA Westland Whirlwind Srs 3 55 ex Redhill, Bristow, 9Y-TDA, EP-HAC, G-AODA. *Dorado*. CoA 23-8-91, de-reg 23-9-93. Arrived 7-8-93 1-22
☐ G-AOUJ Fairey Ultra-Light Helicopter 56 ex Staverton, Innsworth, WSM, Harlow, White Waltham, XJ928. CoA 29-3-59, de-reg 26-2-69. Arrived 2010 1-22
☐ G-AOZE Westland Widgeon 2 57 ex Cuckfield, Shoreham, 5N-ABW, G-AOZE (de-reg 20-6-62). Arrived 1986 [1] 1-22
☐ G-ASTP Hiller UH-12C 61 ex Biggin Hill, Thornicombe, 'Wales', Thornicombe, Redhill, N9750C. CoA 3-7-82, de-reg 24-1-90. Arr 12-10-89 1-22

☐	G-ATFG	Brantly B2B		65	ex East Fortune, Newport Pagnell. CoA 25-3-85, de-reg 25-9-87. Arrived 21-1-04	[1]	1-22
☐	G-AVNE and G-17-3	Westland Wessex 60 Srs 1		67	ex Hurn, WSM, Redhill, G-17-3, 5N-AJL, G-AVNE, 9M-ASS, VH-BHC, PK-HBQ, G-AVNE. CoA 7-2-83, de-reg 23-11-82. Arrived 1987		1-22
☐	G-AWRP	Cierva Grasshopper Srs.3		69	ex Blackpool, Heysham, Shoreham, Redhill. Servotec-built. CoA 12-5-72, de-reg 5-12-83. Arrived 1993	[2]	1-22
☐	G-AXRA	Campbell Cricket		69	de-reg 25-10-90. Arrived 10-13. Inside the cafe		1-22
☐	G-BAPS	Campbell Cougar		73	CoA 20-5-74, de-reg 21-1-87. Acquired 5-76		1-22
☐	G-BGHF	Westland WG.30-100		79	ex Yeovil, Westland. CoA 1-8-86, de-reg 29-3-89. Acquired 22-12-88	[3]	1-22
☐	G-BIGP	Bensen B-8M		81	ex Shrewsbury. CoA 20-10-07, de-reg 27-11-08		1-22
☐	G-BKGD	Westland WG.30-100		82	ex Bristol, WSM, Yeovil, Penzance, G-BKBJ. CoA 6-7-93, de-reg 15-4-93. Arrived by 4-18		1-22
☐	G-BVWL	Air and Space 18A		66	ex East Fortune, Kinnetties, SE-HIE, N90588, N6152S. De-reg 18-10-00. Arrived 22-11-07		1-22
☐	G-BWCW	Barnett J4B		95	de-reg 3-3-05. Arrived 29-10-15		1-22
☐	G-BXZN	ATI CH.1		87	ex Horsted Keynes, Brentwood, Southend, N8186E, Switzerland. De-reg 28-10-05. Arrived 19-7-17	[4]	1-22
☐	G-BYMP	Campbell Cricket		99	ex Cheshire, Newtownards. Arrived 16-1-14		1-22
☐	G-EHIL	EHI EH 101 PP3		88	ex Yeovil, ZH647. De-reg 28-4-99. Arrived 26-11-99	[5]	1-22
☐	G-ELEC	Westland WG.30-200		83	ex Westland, WSM, Yeovil, G-BKNV. CoA 28-6-85, de-reg 27-2-98. Arrived 7-12-01		1-22
☐	G-HAUL	Westland WG.30 TT300		86	ex G-17-22, Yeovil. CoA 27-10-86, de-reg 22-4-92. Arr 1991		1-22
☐	G-LYNX	Westland Lynx Srs.1(mod)		79	ex Yeovil, WSM, Yeovil, ZB500, ZA500 , G-LYNX, De-reg 27-2-98. Arrived 18-1-95	[6]	1-22
☐	G-OAPR	Brantly B2B		65	ex G-BPST, N2280U. CoA 1-10-15	[1]	1-22
☐	G-ORVB	McCulloch J-2	G-HEKY	71	ex G-ORVB, G-BLGI, G-BKKL, Bahrain Public Security BPS-3, N4329G. De-reg 30-1-09. Arrived 21-12-08		1-22
☐	G-OTED	Robinson R22		81	ex Elstree, G-BMYR, ZS-HLG. CoA 17-2-02, de-reg 26-3-02		1-22
☐	G-TIGE	Aérospatiale Super Puma		82	ex Gosport, Norwich, Aberdeen, G-BJYJ, F-WTNM. De-reg 8-12-15. Arrived 30-11-15		1-22
☐	G-WBAT	Julian CD Wombat		90	ex Breeqhou, St Merryn, G-BSID. De-reg 29-4-09. Arr 9-7-13		1-22
☐	–	Slingsby T.8 Tutor		~	BGA.1759, ex Keevil, Wolverhampton, Dowty G/C, Pershore, RAFGSA.178. Arr 27-10-16. Fuselage, in Pilot Block		1-22
☐	–	Hafner R-II Revoplane		30	BAPC.10, ex M Wallop, Locking, WSM, Higher Blagdon, Old Warden, WSM, Heston, Austria. Arrived 1979, donated 1996	[7]	1-22
☐	–	Murray M-1 Helicopter		54	BAPC.60, ex Wigan, Salford. Arrived 10-95		1-22
☐	–	Watkinson CG-4		77	BAPC.128, ex Horley, Bexhill. Arrived 1978.	[8]	1-22
☐	–	Westland WG.33 EMU		78	BAPC.153, ex Yeovil. Arrived 1980	[9]	1-22
☐	–	Bensen B-8M		84	BAPC.264, ex Westbury-on-Trym. Unflown		1-22
☐	–	Bensen B-8M Gyro-Boat		c65	BAPC.289, ex Brooklands, Glasgow. Arrived 11-10-03		1-22
☐	–	Husband Modac Hornet		02	BAPC.339, ex Sheffield. 'Hopped' only. Arrived 13-11-04		1-22
☐	D-HMQV	Bölkow Bö 102		60	ex Bückeburg, Germany	[1] [10]	1-22
☐	DDR-SPY	Kamov Ka-26 Hoodlum		73	ex D-HOAY, Germany, Interflug DDR-SPY. Arrived 12-6-95		1-22
☐	F-OCMF	'335' Sud Super Frelon		67	ex Aérospatiale, Olympic, F-BTRP, F-WKQC, F-OCZV, F-RAFR, F-OCMF, F-BMHC, F-WMHC. Arrived 28-4-93. Olympic colours, Hermes	[11]	1-22
☐	F-WGTX	Intora-Firebird Atlas		c98	ex Horsted Keynes, Brentwood, Southend, France. Arrived 19-7-17	[12]	1-22
☐	F-WQAP	Sud Dauphin 2		79	ex Eurocopter, Marignane, F-WZJJ. Acquired 19-3-03	[13]	1-22
☐	N5840T	Westland WG.30-100		82	ex Yeovil, Air Spur, G-BKFF. Arrived 10-1-97. Play area		1-22
☐	OO-SHW	Bell 47H-1	G-AZYB	56	ex Thruxton, G-AZYB, LN-OQG, SE-HBE, SABENA OO-SHW. Crashed 21-4-84, de-reg 22-4-85	[1]	1-22
☐	SP-SAY	Mil Mi-2 Hoplite		85	ex Hiscso, ZEUS. PZL-Swidnik-built. Arrived 24-11-97		1-22
☐	AP506	Cierva C.30A	G-ACWM	34	ex Staverton, Tewksbury, AP506, 529, 1448 Flt, 5 RSS, G-ACWM, Autogiro Fg Club, Hanworth. Avro-built. De-reg 17-3-59. Arrived 1986. Frame	[1]	1-22

❑ WG719		Westland Dragonfly HR.5 G-BRMA	52	ex G-BRMA (de-reg 30-3-89), 'WG718', Shawbury, WSM, Yeovilton, Southampton, Fleetlands, Britannia Flt, FRU, Yeovilton SF, HR.3, 705, Hal Far SF. SOC 5-5-70. Acq 4-76 [1] 1-22
❑ XD163	'X'	Westland Whirlwind HAR.10	54	ex Wroughton, 8645M, CFS, Akrotiri SAR Flt, MoA, 228, 275, 155, MoA. SOC 20-3-80 [1] 1-22
❑ XE521		Fairey Rotodyne Y	57	ex Cranfield, W' Waltham. Sections, acquired 1981 [1] [14] 1-22
❑ XG452		Bristol Belvedere HC.1 G-BRMB	60	ex G-BRMB (de-reg 3-7-96), Ternhill, Cosford 7997M (8-12-67), RR, A&AEE, RR, A&AEE. Arrived 5-11-74 1-22
❑ XG454*		Bristol Belvedere HC.1	60	ex Manchester, Henlow, 8366M, Abingdon, A&AEE, Bristol, Old Sarum, Belvedere Trials Unit. Accident 30-8-61. Acquired 2017, arrived 1-22 1-22
❑ XG462		Bristol Belvedere HC.1	61	ex Henlow, WSM, 72, 66. Cr 5-10-63. Cockpit. Arr 1989 [1] 1-22
❑ XK940	'911'	Westland Whirlwind HAS.7 G-AYXT	57	ex G-AYXT (CoA 4-2-99, de-reg 8-8-00), Tibenham, Redhill, Northampton, Heysham, Carnforth, Panshanger, Elstree, Luton, Blackpool, Fleetlands, 771, Culdrose SF, 705, 825, 824, 845. SOC 24-3-71. Arrived 6-6-00 [1] [15] 1-22
❑ XL811		Saro Skeeter AOP.12	59	ex Stoke-on-Trent, Warmingham, Southend, Peel Green, Wroughton, 17F, 656, 651. SOC 27-5-68. Arrived 1993 [1] 1-22
❑ XL829		Bristol Sycamore HR.14	57	ex Bristol, 32, MCS, Khormaksar SAR Flight. SOC 18-12-71. Arrived 17-10-07 1-22
❑ XM328	'653'	Westland Wessex HAS.3	60	ex Culdrose, A2644 [2], A2727 (9-5-85), Wroughton, Culdrose SAR Flt, 772, 737, A&AEE, HAS.1, A&AEE. Arrived 3-04. *The Sow* 1-22
❑ XM330		Westland Wessex HAS.1	59	ex Farnborough, RAE, ATDU, ETPS, RAE Farnborough, A&AEE, HS. SOC 16-6-83. Arrived 16-5-94 1-22
❑ XP165		Saro P.531-2	60	ex HAM Southend, ETPS, A&AEE, RAE, A&AEE. Last flown 28-5-71. SOC 26-8-71. Acquired 10-5-83 1-22
❑ XR486		Westland Whirlwind HCC.12 G-RWWW	64	ex G-RWWW (CoA 25-8-96, de-reg 10-7-00), Redhill, Tattershall Thorpe, St Athan 8727M (9-12-81), 32, Queen's Flt, HAR.10 Arrived 8-6-00 [1] 1-22
❑ XT190		Bell Sioux AH.1	65	ex Wattisham, Soest, M Wallop, UNFICYP. Westland-built. Arrived 8-6-95 1-22
❑ XT443	'422'	Westland Wasp HAS.1	66	ex Oldmixon, Sherborne, 703. SOC 7-5-87. Arrived 18-1-95. HMS *Aurora* titles 1-22
❑ XV733		Westland Wessex HCC.4	69	ex Shawbury, Queen's Flight. Last Royal sortie 11-3-98, last flight 13-3-98. Arrived 15-11-01 [16] 1-22
❑ XW839		Westland WG.13 00-05	74	ex Yeovilton, A2624 [2], A2657 (1-11-88), A2710, Manadon, BS Eng. Arr 11-1-96. 'HMS *Thunderer*' titles [17] 1-22
❑ XX910		Westland Lynx HAS.2	74	ex Yeovilton, DERA/RAE Farnborough, Aberporth, A&AEE. Arrived 5-12-00 [18] 1-22
❑ ZB686		Sud Gazelle AH.1	83	ex M Wallop, 9322M, ex Fleetlands, 665, 655. Westland-built. Cockpit, trailer mounted, travelling exhibit 1-22
❑ ZE477		Westland Lynx 3	84	ex G-17-24, Yeovil, Westland. Arrived 1989 1-22
❑ ZJ116*	'IOI'	EHI EH.101 PP8 G-OIOI	90	ex Hendon, Brize Norton, Yeovil, G-OIOI (CoA 5-5-94, de-reg 1-4-96), G-17-01. Last flight 23-10-01 [19] **due**
❑ 'ZS782'		W'land WG.25 Sharpeye	81	ex Yeovil. RPV, Full-scale EMU/wind tunnel model 1-22
❑ A-41	ACB	Sud Alouette II	67	ex Belgian Army. Arrived 19-2-08 1-22
❑ 622		Piasecki HUP-3 Retriever	54	ex Philadelphia, N6699D, RCN, 51-16622. Arrived 1991 1-22
❑ 09147		Mil Mi-4 *Hound*	c57	ex Prague, Sechov, Tabor, Czech AF. Arrived 1-94 1-22
❑ FR-41	'ARB'	Piasecki H-21C Shawnee	57	ex ALAT F-MARB, F-MBEE, Marine Nationale F-XCAF, ALAT F-MAAY, 56-2025. SOC 4-70. Arrived 27-1-16 [20]
❑ FR-108	'CDL'	Sud-Ouest Djinn	59	ex ALAT F-MCDL. Arrived 1991 1-22
❑ 81+00		Bölkow Bö 105M	84	ex Heer, D-HZYR. Arrived 3-5-07 [21] 1-22
❑ 96+26		Mil Mi-24 *Hind-D*	81	ex Luftwaffe, East German A21. Arrived 20-2-95 1-22
❑ MM80927		Bell 206C-1 'CC-49'	74	Carabinieri. Agusta-built. Arrived late 2012 1-22
❑ MM81205		Agusta 109A II 'GF-128'	86	ex Guardia di Finanza GdiF-128. Arrived 6-10-10 1-22
❑ 1005	'05'	PZL-Swidnik SM-2	c65	ex Polish Air Force. Arrived 10-6-91 [22] 1-22
❑ 2007	'07'	Mil Mi-1 *Hare*	59	ex Poland. WSK-Swidnik-built SM-1. Soviet c/s. Arr 2-9-93 1-22
❑ '07' red		Mil Mi-8PS *Hip* 618	c79	ex Polish AF, 37 PST, 36 SPLT. Arr 5-2-10. Soviet c/s [23] 1-22

❑	DS-1482		Gyrodyne QH-50D	66	ex USA, Lenwood, Fort Irwin, White Sands. Arr 2-10-14	[24]	1-22
❑	66-16579		Bell UH-1H Iroquois	67	ex US Army, UH-1D. Arrived 29-8-92		1-22
❑	67-16506		Hughes OH-6A Cayuse	68	ex US Army. Arrived 8-99		1-22

■ **[1]** Airframes on loan from Elfan ap Rees. **[2]** As well as this, the Grasshopper 3 prototype, substantial elements of the unflown second and third examples are held: G-AXFM used as a ground-running rig and the centre section, floor pan and dynamics of G-AZAU. **[3]** WG.30 prototype, first flown 10-4-79. **[4]** Also known as Dragonfly DF.1, single-seat, ultra-light tip-jet-driven helicopter. Powered by the now-banned hydrogen peroxide (H_2O_2), effectively making it steam-driven! Built in the USA by Advanced Technologies Inc for Liteco Helicopter Systems of Switzerland. To the UK by 1998 and marketed by Intora-Firebird. See also **[11]**. **[5]** EH 101 factoids: First flown at Yeovil 30-9-88, retired 2-99 with 653 hours in 581 flights. **[6]** G-LYNX established a world air speed record in 8-86 of 249.1mph. **[7]** Not a cliché, a truism, this is a national - no, *international* - treasure. The oldest surviving helicopter in Britain, the R-II was designed by Raoul Hafner in association with Bruno Nagler and built and flown at Aspern, near Vienna. It was brought to the UK by 1933 and used by Hafner as a rotor test-bed at Heston before being put into store at Filton. Hafner went on to design the Bristol Sycamore. Initially on loan to the museum, Hafner's widow, Eileen, donated the R-II in 1996. **[8]** CG-4 is a man-powered rotorcraft. **[9]** WG.33 - engineering mock-up of a single-seat ultra-light observation helicopter. **[10]** Although bolted firmly down on to a base-plate, the Helitrainer was capable of flight, but intended as a fully-functioning procedure and flight trainer. **[11]** Frelon started life as SA.321 c/n 116. It is in Olympic Airways colours as worn at the 1969 Paris Salon. **[12]** Two-seat tip-jet helicopter developed from the CH.1 - see **[3]**. Third airframe, fitted with boom from prototype, F-WGTX. **[13]** First production SA.365N, modified to fly-by-wire test-bed; retired in 2001. **[14]** Rotodyne project was cancelled in February 1962 and XE521 stored at White Waltham and eventually broken up. A couple of times in *W&R* the rules are broken and although there is no cockpit, the fuselage sections and rotor pylon are substantial enough to be formally listed. **[15]** G-AYXT was also allocated to XK907, but not taken up - see Coventry, Warks. **[16]** Last Wessex built for British armed forces, first flew Yeovil 13-5-69. **[17]** Fifth prototype, 'pre-Lynx', first flown 19-6-74. **[18]** During refurbishing at Yeovilton XX910 was fitted with the boom of Danish MK.80 S-142. **[19]** 8th Yeovil-built example; civil variant, to have been marketed as the Heliliner. On RAF Museum loan. **[20]** Supplied direct to France, served in Algeria from delivery 5-57, it was loaned to the Marines mid-1958 to 4-60. Based in France from 10-62. **[21]** Bö 105M donated by Eurocopter. **[22]** SM-2 re-engineered Mi-1/SM-1. **[23]** *Hip* is a VIP version - square, not round, windows, delivered to Poland in the 1970s, serving until retirement in 2005. It flew with 37 Air Assault Regiment (PST), Leznica Wielka, Lodz. **[24]** QH-50 a pioneering rotorcraft UAV used mostly by the US Navy.

Reserve Collection: Available for inspection *only* by special arrangement - check with the contacts above.

❑	G-ANFH		Westland Whirlwind Srs 1	54	ex Redhill, Great Yarmouth, Bristow, Autair, BEAH,		
					BEA HEU. CoA 17-7-71, de-reg 2-9-77, acquired 1978	[1] [2]	10-21
❑	G-ANJV		Westland Whirlwind Srs 3	54	ex Redhill, Bristow, VR-BET. De-reg 1-8-74		10-21
❑	G-ARVN		Cierva Grasshopper 1	61	ex Shoreham, Redhill. Servotec-built		
					CoA 18-5-63, de-reg 14-3-77	[3]	3-20
❑	G-ASCT		Bensen B-8M	r62	ex Hungerford. CoA 11-11-66, de-reg 20-9-73.		
					Arrived 1993. Major components		3-20
❑	G-ATBZ		Westland Wessex 60 Srs 1	65	ex Austria, Hurn, G-17-4, WSM. CoA 15-12-81,		
					de-reg 23-11-82. Arrived 1988		3-20
❑	G-AVKE		Gadfly HDW-1	67	ex Southend, Thruxton. De-reg 12-10-81. Arrived 1978	[1]	10-21
❑	–		Bensen B-6 gyroglider	c60	BAPC.212. Major components		3-20
❑	–		Cranfield Vertigo	c82	BAPC.213, ex Yeovil, Cardington, Yeovil	[4]	10-21
❑	XG596	'66'	W'land Whirlwind HAS.7	57	ex Wroughton A2651 (7-1-76), 705, 829, 771, 705, 737	[1]	3-20
❑	XL736		Saro Skeeter AOP.12	58	ex Saxmundham, Stuttgart, Moordrecht, 1 Flt, 655,		
					M Wallop. Ground accident 25-9-68. Less boom		3-20
❑	XM557		Saro Skeeter AOP.12	59	ex Saxmundham, Stuttgart, Moordrecht, 5 Flt, 652,		
					17Flt, 652, 4 Flt, 654, 652, 1 Wing. Less boom		3-20
❑	XN345		Saro Skeeter AOP.12	60	ex Saxmundham, Stuttgart, Moordrecht, 26 Regt, 17 Flt,		
					652, 17 Flt, 654, 655, 1 Wing. SOC 20-10-69		3-20
❑	XP404		Westland Whirlwind	62	ex Finningley, Benson 8682M (10-10-82), 22, SAR Wing,		
			HAR.10		202, 228. Arrived 1991		10-21
❑	XP886		Westland Scout AH.1	63	ex Yeovil Tech, Arborfield, Wroughton, 652, 660, 651		3-20
❑	XR526		Westland Wessex HC.2	64	ex Yeovil, Sherborne, Farnborough, Odiham 8147M, 72.		
					Damaged 27-5-70. Arrived 26-8-99		10-21
❑	XS149	'61'	Westland Wessex HAS.3	63	ex Manadon, Wroughton, Templecombe, Lee-on-Solent,		
					737, HAS.1, 819, 845, 706. Arrived 1987	[5]	10-21
❑	XS486	'F'	Westland Wessex HU.5	64	ex Colerne 9272M (31-5-91), Wroughton, 772, 771,		
	and '524'				707, 848, 707, A&AEE, 707, 848, 707, 848.		
					'Union Jack'-nose		8-21
❑	XT472	'XC'	Westland Wessex HU.5	66	ex Hullavington, Netheravon, Middle Wallop,		
					Lyneham, Wroughton, 845, 847, 845. SOC 10-9-82.		
					Arrived 1987		10-21
❑	-		Westland WG.30-300 EMU	~	ex Yeovil. Transmission rig, based on unfinished c/n 022		10-21

■ **[1]** Airframes on loan from Elfan ap Rees. **[2]** Thanks to Jon Horswell for reminding the author of the vital role played by this machine, in its BEA days, in the final sequence of the 1964 film *A Hard Day's Night* - when the logo on the access door was altered to read 'BEA TLES'. It also appeared in *The Damned* (1961), *Where the Bullets Fly* and *Murderer's Row* (both 1966). **[3]** *Victor-November* is Britain's first co-axial helicopter, first flown 1962. **[4]** Vertigo, a man-powered rotorcraft and nothing to do with Cranfield, Beds; the project was led by Andrew *Cranfield*. **[5]** Wessex HAS.3 XS149 is fitted with the rear fuselage of Srs 60 G-17-6.

British Hang-Gliding Museum (BHGM): The *nominal* base for the 80-plus 'airframes' held across a series of sites. BHGM is beyond the scope of *W&R* but for those so inclined, its amazing website is **www.british-hang-gliding-museum.co.uk**

WESTON ZOYLAND AERODROME, or Middle Zoy, on the A372 east of Bridgwater
The southern element of the former RAF airfield has been substantially developed as the thriving **Middle Zoy** general aviation centre. (The element north of the A372 is a microlight strip.) The intention is to mount the Meteor on a plinth as a reminder of the heady days of 209 AFS and 12 FTS, 1952 to 1955.

❏ OY-AVW*		Piper Vagabond	~	ex Dunkeswell, D-EEMM, N4665H. First noted 10-20	10-20
❏ 'WZ584'	'54'	Gloster Meteor T.7	52	ex Booker, Malta, Yatesbury, Staverton, Hucclecote,	
			WL360	Locking 7920M (13-9-66), 229 OCU, 1, Wattisham SF,	
				211 AFS, 210 AFS, 215 AFS. Arrived 16-11-19 [1]	8-21

■ **[1]** WL360 / 'WZ584' has the wings, tail etc of T.7 WL345 (ex Booker, Hollington, Hastings, Kemble, CAW, etc SOC 1-11-74), its cockpit having been exported to Malta. The *real* WZ584 - a Vampire T.11 - is at Binbrook, Lincs.

Paul Childs makes good progress on Provost *Romeo-Fox* which carries a dedication to his late father: 'Feet on the ground - Head in the clouds - in loving memory of Bernie Childs.' ◆ *By prior application* **only**

❏ WV499	'P3'	Percival Provost T.1	53	ex Exeter, Booker, Armthorpe, Sandtoft, N Weald, St Athan,	
		G-BZRF		Weeton 7698M, 6 FTS	8-21
❏ WW388*		Percival Provost T.1	54	ex Audley End, Newport, Sleap, Hemswell, Firbeck,	
	'O-F'			Long Marston, Rhoose, Llanelli, Chinnor, Chertsey,	
				Cuxwold, Chessington, Halton 7616M (13-10-59), 2 FTS.	
				First noted 7-20	8-21
❏ WW453		Percival Provost T.1	55	ex Clevedon, Cranfield, Thatcham, Strathallan,	
		G-TMKI		Perth, Hunting, 1 FTS, 2 FTS. De-reg 3-10-11. Spares	8-21
❏ XF836*		Percival Provost T.1	55	ex Audley End, Thatcham, Popham, Old Warden, 8043M,	
	'J-G'	G-AWRY		27 MU, CATCS, CNCS, RAFC, Man UAS. Damaged 28-7-87.	
				CoA 22-8-88. First noted 7-20	7-20

YEOVIL AIRFIELD to the west of Yeovil   EGHG
Leonardo Airborne and Space Systems: Pronounced 'Westland'. Last noted in early 2015, WG.30 G-BKKI has been deleted.

❏ ZD560*	Westland Lynx AH.7	87	ex Eastleigh, Boscombe Down. Last flown 28-3-12.	
			Displayed by 10-21	11-21
❏ ZH822	EHI Merlin HM.1	97	ex Shawbury, Culdrose, Fleetlands, DERA.	
			NEA 28-11-18. Arrived 27-7-19. Stored	10-21
❏ ZH825*	EHI Merlin HM.1	97	ex Shawbury, Culdrose, Fleetlands, DERA.	
			NEA 28-11-18. Arrived 20-11-19. Stored	10-21

Yeovil College: Mudford Road ◆ *By prior application* **only** | **www.yeovil.ac.uk**

❏ ZT800	Westland Super Lynx 300	99	ex Yeovil. Handed over, on loan, 12-16	7-19

YEOVILTON AIRFIELD on the B5131, south of the A303, north of Yeovil   EGDY
A one-off abbreviation used throughout the listings below: VL = Yeovilton (from the shore station code worn on the tail).

Fleet Air Arm Museum (FAAM): Part of the **National Museum of the Royal Navy** which encompasses several venues, including Portsmouth Historic Dockyard and HMS *Victory*, among others. Yeovilton is a sure-fire all-absorbing visit, with 'Carrier' representing the best of innovation. An observation window allows visitors to see progress in the conservation workshop and another that overlooks the ramp giving views of activity on the base. The 'Swordfish' restaurant is excellent. There is an active **Friends of the FAAM** - enquiries via the museum website.

FAAM aircraft can be found on loan at: Coventry, Warks, Gannet XA508; Sunderland, Tyneside, Pucará A-522; Woodley, Berks, Gannet XG883, Scimitar F.1 XD220 with the Empire State Aerosciences Museum, New York, USA.

◆ *RNAS Yeovilton, BA22 8HT, sat-nav junkies use BA22 8HW* | **01935 840565** | **fleetairarmenquiries@nmrn.org.uk** | **www.fleetairarm.com**

Main Halls (1 and 2):

❑ –		Short S.27 replica	79	BAPC.149, ex Lee-on-Solent. Acquired 1980	1-22
❑ 8359		Short 184	1915	ex Duxford, South Lambeth, Crystal Palace, Buncrana, Rosyth, Dundee, Killingholme. Westland-built. Damaged 31-1-41. Arrived 28-1-76. Forward fuselage [1]	1-22
❑ L2301		Supermarine Walrus I	39	ex Arbroath, Thame, G-AIZG (de-reg 5-1-49), EI-ACC,	
		G-AIZG		IAC N18, L2301 - no service. Acquired 6-12-66	1-22
❑ L2940		Blackburn Skua II	40	ex Lake Grotli, Norway, 800. Crashed 27-4-40. Substantial wreckage, arrived 1974	1-22
❑ N1854		Fairey Fulmar II	40	ex Lossiemouth, Fairey G-AIBE (CoA 6-7-59,	
		G-AIBE		de-reg 30-4-59), A&AEE. Acquired 1962	1-22
❑ 'N2078'		Sopwith Baby floatplane	1916	BAPC.442, ex Cobham, Fleetlands, Heathrow, RAeS, Nash, Brooklands. Acquired 5-70. *The Jabberwock* [2]	1-22
❑ 'P4139'		Fairey Swordfish II	43	ex 'V6105', 'W5984', Manadon A2001, Donibristle, 834.	
		HS618		SOC on HMS *Hunter* 5-8-43. Blackburn-built. Acquired 1962	1-22
❑ AL246		Grumman Martlet I	40	ex Loughborough, 768, RAE, 882, 802. Acquired 1963	1-22
❑ EX976		NAA Harvard III	41	ex Portuguese AF 1657, n/s FAA, EX976, 41-33949. Acquired 30-9-80	1-22
❑ KD431	'E2-M'	Vought Corsair IV	44	ex Cranfield, 768, 1835, BuNo 14862. Acq 1964. 768 Sqn c/s	1-22
❑ KE209		Grumman Hellcat II	45	ex Lossiemouth SF, Stretton, Anthorn, BuNo 79779. Last flown 7-54. Acquired 1970	1-22
❑ LZ551/G		DH Vampire 1	44	ex Waddon (Science Museum), DH, RAE, 778, A&AEE, RAE. Hatfield-built. SOC 13-8-47. Acquired 1966 [3]	1-22
❑ SX137		V-S Seafire F.17	45	ex Culdrose, 'W9132', VL SF, 764, 759, 1831, Culham. Last flown 16-7-60, acquired 1964	1-22
❑ VX595		Westland Dragonfly HR.5	49	ex Portland, Gosport, Fleetlands, Henlow, F'lands, ETPS, RAE, ETPS, A&AEE, AFEE, A&AEE, AFEE. Acquired 23-11-98 [4]	1-22
❑ WJ231	'115'	Hawker Sea Fury FB.11	51	ex Wroughton, VL 'WE726', VL SF, FRU. Acquired 1965	1-22
❑ WN493		Westland Dragonfly HR.5	53	ex Culdrose, Culdrose SF, 705, 701, A&AEE. Acq 19-10-66	1-22
❑ XA127		DH Sea Vampire T.22	54	ex CIFE, 736. Christchurch-built. SOC 12-8-65. Cockpit	1-22
❑ XB446		Grumman Avenger ECM.6	45	ex Culdrose SF, 831, 751, 820, USN 69502, VC-11, VT-87. Acquired 9-4-68. 'Invasion stripes' and 1944 camouflage	1-22
❑ XS508		Westland Wessex HU.5	64	ex Cobham, A2677, A2766 (14-4-88), Lee-on-Solent, Wroughton, Acquired 28-6-93; on show from 8-7-15	1-22
❑ XV663	'18'	Westland Sea King HAS.6	70	ex Gosport, Falmouth, Gosport A2807 (10-12-01), Fleetlands, 819, 810, 820, 819, 737, 706, 825, 706, 706, 826. Arrived 21-5-15 [5]	1-22
❑ XZ699		Westland Lynx HAS.3	80	ex Cobham, VL, Fleetlands, 815, 702. Acquired 11-06	1-22
❑ 100545		Focke Achgelis Fa 330A-1 Bachstelgze	44	ex Wroughton, VL, Higher Blagdon, Cranfield, Farnborough. Weser Flug-built. Acquired 25-8-93	1-22
❑ 01420		Mikoyan-Gurevich MiG-15*bis* Fagot G-BMZF	64	ex N Weald, Gamston, Retford, G-BMZF (de-reg 23-2-90), Polish AF. Aero-built SBLim-2A. Acquired 14-5-87. North Korean colours	1-22

■ **[1]** Short 184 on loan from the Imperial War Museum. It was damaged in a bombing raid while stored at South Lambeth 31-1-41. **[2]** Sopwith Baby 'N2078' is a composite, using parts from the sequential 8214 and 8215. Both, ordered in 1915, were passed on to the Italian government to act as patterns in July 1916, for production by Ansaldo. This would go a long way to explaining the Italian tricolour on the rudder of the components acquired by R G J Nash. **[3]** Sea Vampire prototype on loan from the Science Museum. Piloted by Lt Cdr Eric 'Winkle' Brown, it made the world's first-ever landing by a pure-jet on a carrier - HMS *Ocean* - 3-12-45. **[4]** VX595 on loan from RAF Museum. **[5]** XV663 is painted in Royal Navy colours to port and RAF SAR rescue yellow to starboard; because of this it is nicknamed 'Banana Split'.

'Carrier' (Hall 3): Technically, Wessex XT769 is in Hall 2 - but as the method of 'travel' to 'Carrier', it really belongs here.

❑ WA473	'102'	V-S Attacker F.1	51	ex Abbotsinch, 736, 702, 800. SOC 16-6-58, acquired 1964	1-22
❑ WV856	'163'	Hawker Sea Hawk FGA.6	54	ex RAE, 781, 806.AWA-built. Acquired 7-67	1-22
❑ WW138	'227'	DH Sea Venom FAW.22	55	ex Cobham, AWS, 831, 809. Christchurch-built. Acquired 9-69. Installed 11-7-17. Suez stripes	1-22
❑ XA466	'777'	Fairey Gannet COD.4	57	ex Wroughton, VL, Lee-on-Solent, Lossiemouth, 849. Acquired 12-12-78	1-22
❑ XD317	'112'	V-S Scimitar F.1	59	ex FRU, RAE, 800, 736, 807. Acquired 18-9-69	1-22
❑ XN957	'630'	Blackburn Buccaneer S.1	63	ex 736, 809, 801. SOC 10-11-72. Acquired 1974	1-22

❑ XS590	'131'	DH Sea Vixen FAW.2	66	ex 899, 892. Hawarden-built. Acquired 26-11-70. 899 Sqn c/s	1-22
❑ XT482	'ZM'	Westland Wessex HU.5	66	A2656, ex A2745, Lee-on-Solent, Wroughton, 707,	
				845, 847, 707, 771, 707. Acquired 24-2-94 [1]	1-22
❑ XT596		McD Phantom FG.1	66	ex Scampton, Holme-on-Spalding-Moor, RAE Thurleigh,	
				H-o-S-M, Hucknall, Patuxent River, Edwards. Arr 19-1-88 [2]	1-22
❑ XT769		Westland Wessex HU.5	67	ex Lee-on-Solent, Wroughton, Culdrose, 771, 772,	
				771, 846, 848. Acquired 3-11 [1]	1-22
❑ XV333	'234'	Blackburn Buccaneer S.2B	66	ex 208, 12, 15, 16, FAA, 237 OCU, 12.	
				Arrived 23-3-94. 801 Sqn colours	1-22

■ [1] Visitors to 'Carrier' exhibition travel to the flight deck 'on board' Wessex XT769 and disembark from XT482! [2] The second YF-4K development airframe, first flown at St Louis, USA, 31-8-66.

Hall 4: Sea Vampire T.22 cockpit XA127 has moved to the Main Halls - see above.

❑ G-BSST		BAC/Sud Concorde 002	69	CoA 30-10-74, de-reg 21-1-87. Flew in 4-3-76 [1]	1-22
❑ N5419		Bristol Scout D replica	90	ex Kemble, Banwell, Cardington, USA.	
				Skeletal airframe. Arrived 30-11-98 [2]	1-22
❑ WG774		BAC 221	64	ex East Fortune, RAE Bedford, Filton, Fairey Delta 2.	
				Last flight 9-6-73. Arrived 1-80 [3]	1-22
❑ XP841		Handley Page HP.115	61	ex Cosford, Colerne, RAE Bedford. Last flown 1-2-74.	
				Acquired 6-6-79	1-22
❑ XP980		Hawker P.1127	63	A2700, ex Culdrose, Tarrant Rushton, RAE Bedford,	
				Cranwell, A&AEE. Acquired 6-3-89	1-22
❑ XZ493	'001'	HS Sea Harrier FRS.1	80	ex Dunsfold, Yeovilton, Lee-on-Solent, 899, 801.	
				Ditched 15-12-94, acquired 1-3-95. 801 Sqn colours [4]	1-22
❑ XZ720	'410'	Westland Lynx	80	ex Cobham Hall, Fleetlands, 815, 829, 815. Handed over	
		HAS.3GMS		26-4-12. 815 Sqn, 216 Flt c/s, HMS *Gloucester* titles. [5]	1-22
❑ ZA298	'Y'	Westland Sea King	81	ex Cobham, Fleetlands, Camp Bastion, 846, Basrah, 845,	
		HC.4 G-BJNM		846, 848, 845, Split, 846, 848, 846, Falklands, 846,	
				G-BJNM (de-reg 14-12-81), Westland, 846. Arr 31-3-16 [6]	1-22
❑ ZD433	'45A'	BAe/McDD Harrier	89	ex Cobham Hall, Cottesmore, 800. Acquired 20-12-11	
		GR.9A		On show from 13-6-17 [7]	1-22

■ [1] UK prototype Concorde G-BSST is on loan from the Science Museum; it first flew on 9-4-69 and clocked 836 flight hours and 438 landings. [2] Scout D is on loan from Sir George White; its 'serial' is actually its US civil registration. [3] Build date given is that of its second guise as ogival wing test-bed for Concorde, prior to that is was the first FD.2, first flying 6-10-55 and achieving the world air speed record of 1,132mph on 10-3-56. [4] FRS.1 is a composite. Rebuilt for museum purposes by BAe at Dunsfold, the forward fuselage of XZ493 was grafted on to the wings and rear fuselage of Harrier GR.3 XV760. The cockpit of XV760 can be found at Southampton, Hampshire. [5] XZ720 served almost from new during the Falklands, but came to fame in the first Gulf War when it attacked - and 'killed' - five Iraqi Navy ships with Sea Skua missiles. [6] ZA298 is known as the 'King of Kings' because of its incredible history: *four* combat theatres, Falklands, Croatia, Iraq, Afghanistan. It took part in the rescue operation of the burning HMS *Coventry*, off Pebble Island, 25-2-82. ZA298 was shot at by an Argentine A-4 Skyhawk, a cannon shell hitting a rotor blade on 13-6-82. After a forced landing, it was back in the fray just over 120 minutes later. Two days later, it ferried General Menendez and his entourage of HMS *Fearless* for the surrender. Another war, another country: it was hit by an RPG round which exited - leaving no casualties and some on the spot BDR - in Afghanistan 21-5-10. And it was briefly a civilian for a sales tour to Algeria in late 1981. [7] GR.9 is kept in its battle-weary condition and as such has been nicknamed *Dirty Harry*!

Restoration Workshop: At the end of the 'Carrier' tour can be found the workshop area, which is glass-walled to provide visitors with a great view of what's going on without delaying the technicians. During June 2019 elements of Barracuda II BV739 were salvaged from waters off Gosport. It ditched while serving with 822 Squadron on 29th September 1943.

❑ DP872		Fairey Barracuda II	43	ex Wroughton, VL, Enagh Lough, 769. Boulton	
				Paul-built. Crashed 18-1-44. Remains recovered 5-71 [1]	1-22

■ [1] The long-term restoration of Barracuda II DP872 will use the substantial wreckage of Mk.II LS931 from its crash site on the Scottish Isle of Jura 2-1-45, plus other parts from Mk.III MD953 (crashed 20-9-45) and Mk.II PM870 (crashed 14-7-45). In June 2014, the centre section of Mk.II DR306 (crashed 15-12-45) joined the cache.

Cobham Hall: Named after FAAM Trustee Sir Michael Cobham, the building is home of the FAAM's reserve collection and archive. Wasp HAS.1 XT778 was on show at Portsmouth Historic Dockyard, Hampshire, during the summer of 2018.
◆ *Occasional open days, otherwise only by prior appointment. Contact details as given above*

❑ 'G-ABUL'		DH Tiger Moth XL717	40	ex G-AOXG, Mk.II T7291, 24 EFTS, 19 EFTS. Morris-built.	
		G-AOXG		De-reg 31-10-56. Acquired 1972	1-22
❑ G-AZAZ		Bensen B-8M	71	ex Wroughton, Houndstone, VL, Manadon.	
				De-reg 19-9-75. Acquired2-12-99	1-18

☐ G-BGWZ		Eclipse Super Eagle h-g	79	ex Wroughton, Houndstone, VL. De-reg 5-12-83	1-18
☐ 'B6401'		Sopwith Camel	69	ex 'C1701', N1917H, G-AWYY. CoA 1-9-85,	
		replica G-AWYY		de-reg 25-11-91. Acquired 1985	[1] 1-22
☐ 'N4389'	'4M'	Fairey Albacore	41	ex museum, Land's End, VL, Wroughton, 828.	
		N4172		Crashed 1-4-41. Acquired 1983	1-22
☐ 'N5459'		Sopwith Triplane	76	BAPC.111, ex 'N5492', Chertsey. *Black Maria*.	
		replica		Acquired 25-3-87. 10 (Naval) Sqn, 'B' Flight colours	1-22
☐ 'N5579'		Gloster Sea Gladiator II	39	ex workshop, 'N5579', Dursley, Cardington, Norway.	
				Acquired 17-7-02. Frame. Arrived 28-6-17	1-22
☐ 'N6452'		Sopwith Pup	83	ex museum, Whitehall, G-BIAU. CoA 13-9-89,	
		replica		de-reg 10-3-97. Acquired 10-6-85	1-22
☐ 'S1287'		Fairey Flycatcher	79	ex Andover, M Wallop, Duxford, M Wallop, VL, G-BEYB	
		replica G-BEYB		de-reg 12-7-96. Acquired 5-6-96. 405 Flt colours	[2] 1-22
☐ Z2033	'275'	Fairey Firefly TT.1	44	ex museum, Duxford, Staverton, G-ASTL de-reg 2-3-82,	
		G-ASTL		TT.1 SE-BRD, White Waltham, Ringway, Hamble, G-6-3,	
				F.I Z2033, 731. Acq 25-7-00. 1771 Sqn c/s, *Evelyn Tentions*	[3] 1-22
☐ VH127	'200'	Fairey Firefly TT.4	47	ex Wroughton, VL, Culdrose, FRU, 700, 737, 812.	
				Acquired 29-11-72	1-22
☐ VR137		Westland Wyvern TF.1	49	ex Cranfield, Yeovil. Acquired 2-66. Moved 22-7-16	[4] 1-22
☐ VV106		V-S 517	48	ex Wroughton, Lee-on-Solent, Cosford, St Athan, Colerne,	
				Cardington, Halton 7175M, RAE. Acquired 2-90	[5] [6] 1-22
☐ VX272		Hawker P.1052	48	ex Wroughton, Lee-on-Solent, Cosford, St Athan, Colerne,	
				Cardington, Halton 7174M, RAE. Acquired 2-90	[5] 1-22
☐ WM292	'841'	Gloster Meteor TT.20	53	ex Bruntingthorpe, Cardiff, Yeovilton, FRU, Kemble,	
				NF.11 527. AWA-built. Acquired 4-6-69	1-22
☐ WP313	'568'	Percival Sea Prince T.1	53	ex Wroughton, Kemble, 750, Sydenham SF, 750,	
				Lossiemouth SF, 750. Acquired 1-87	1-22
☐ WS103	'709'	Gloster Meteor T.7	52	ex Wroughton, Crawley, Wroughton, Lee-on-S', FRU, Kemble,	
				VL Standards Sqn, Anthorn. SOC 19-1-71. Acquired 8-1-71	1-22
☐ WT121	'415'	Douglas Skyraider	51	ex Culdrose, 849, USN VC-12, VC-11 124121.	
		AEW.1		SOC 22-9-60. Acquired 1962	[7] 1-20
☐ WV106	'427'	Douglas Skyraider	50	ex Culdrose, Helston, Culdrose, 849, Donibristle,	
		AEW.1		Abbotsinch, US Navy VC-12 124086. SOC 23-9-60.	
				Acquired 1964. 849 Sqn colours. External store	1-20
☐ XA129		DH Sea Vampire T.22	54	ex Wroughton, VL, CIFE, 736. Christchurch-built. Acq 14-7-70	1-20
☐ XA864		Westland Whirlwind HAR.1	53	ex Wroughton, VL, RAE, A&AEE, RAE, G-17-1. Acquired 10-3-70	1-20
☐ XB480	'537'	Hiller HT.1	53	ex Wroughton, VL, Manadon, A2577, 705. Acquired 5-10-71	1-20
☐ XE340	'131'	Hawker Sea Hawk FGA.6	55	ex Montrose, Strathallan, Wroughton, Staverton, Brawdy,	
				801, 898, 897, 800. Acquired 21-10-70. External store	1-20
☐ XG574	'752'	Westland Whirlwind	55	ex museum, Portland, Wroughton, VL, Wroughton,	
		HAR.3		Lee-on-Solent, A2575, 771, 705, 701. Acquired 12-3-75	1-20
☐ XG594	'517'	Westland Whirlwind	57	ex E' Fortune, Strathallan, Wroughton, Lee-on-S', 771, A&AEE,	
		HAR.3		Fleetlands, 705, 846, 737, 701, RAE Bedford, 700. Acq 23-5-70	1-20
☐ XJ481		DH Sea Vixen FAW.1	58	ex Fleetlands, Southampton, Ilkeston, VL, Portland, VL,	
				Boscombe D', LRWE. Christchurch-built. Acquired 7-3-74	1-20
☐ XK488		Blackburn NA.39	58	ex Filton, BSE, DHE, Blackburn, RAE, DHE, Blackburn.	
				Acquired 22-7-67	[8] 1-22
☐ XL503	'070'	Fairey Gannet AEW.3	61	ex RRE, 849, A&AEE, RAE, 849, A&AEE. Acquired 26-4-73.	
				849 Sqn 'D' Flt colours	1-22
☐ XL580	'723'	Hawker Hunter T.8M	66	ex Cobham Hall, FRADU, FOFT, 764. Acquired 26-11-94.	
				Moved 13-6-17. 899 Sqn colours	1-22
☐ XL853		Westland Whirlwind	58	ex Portland, Fleetlands, Southampton, M Wallop, Lee-	
		HAS.7		on-Solent, A2630, Wroughton, VL SF, 824. Acquired 7-12-98	1-22
☐ XN332		Saro P.531	58	ex Portland, Wroughton, VL, Wroughton, VL, Manadon	
		G-APNV		A2579 (6-5-63), 771, RAE, 700, RAE, 700, A&AEE,	
				G-APNV (de-reg 1-10-59). Acquired 7-10-71	1-22
☐ XN334		Saro P.531	58	ex Wroughton, Crawley, Weston-super-Mare, VL, Arbroath,	
				A2525 (13-9-62), RAE, 771, 700, RAE, 700. Ditched 4-3-62.	
				Acquired 22-7-83	1-22

❑ XN462	'17'	Hunting Jet Provost T.3A	60	ex Wroughton, Sharnford, Shawbury, 1 FTS, 2 FTS, CFS,		
				3 FTS, 7 FTS, 1 FTS. Acquired 25-3-98	[9]	1-22
❑ XP142		Westland Wessex HAS.3	62	ex Wroughton, VL A2720, 737, 706, 814, 706, 845.		
				Acquired 26-7-82. _Humphrey_	[10]	1-22
❑ XS527		Westland Wasp HAS.1	63	ex Wroughton, 829, 703, A&AEE. Acquired 31-7-86.		
				Endurance colours	[11]	1-22
❑ XS574		Northrop Shelduck D.1	~	dismantled		1-18
❑ XT176	'U'	Bell Sioux AH.1	65	ex Wroughton, 3 CBAS. Acquired 6-6-94		1-22
❑ XT427	'606'	Westland Wasp HAS.1	65	ex Helston, VL, Wroughton, Lee-on-Solent, 829, 703, 829.		
				Acquired 28-3-84		1-22
❑ XT765	'J'	Westland Wessex HU.5	66	ex Gosport A2665, A2755, Lee-on-Solent, 845,		
				Lee SAR Flt, 772, 846, 845. Acquired 3-11		1-22
❑ XT778	'430'	Westland Wasp HAS.1	66	ex A2642, A2722 (23-3-88), ex Portland, West Moors,		
				Lee-on-Solent, 829, VL, Wroughton, Lee-on-S', A&AEE.		
				Acquired 15-2-99. _Achilles_ Flt c/s.		1-22
❑ XW864	'54'	Sud Gazelle HT.2	73	ex Shawbury, 705, Wroughton. Westland-built. Acq 21-10-02		1-22
❑ XW994		Northrop Chukar D.1	71	ex Wroughton, VL, Wroughton		1-18
❑ XZ499	'003'	HS Sea Harrier F/A.2	81	ex museum, St Athan, 801, 800, 801, 899, 800, 801,		
				800, 809, 801. Arrived 13-11-02	[12]	1-22
❑ XZ574		Westland Sea King	76	ex Gosport, 771, 810, 820, 819, 810, 820, 826.		
		HAS.6		Acquired 9-6-08, arrived 8-7-15	[13]	1-22
❑ XZ691	'310'	Westland Lynx	79	ex Fleetlands, 702, HAS.3, 815, 702, 815, HAS.2,		
		HMA.8SRU		Falklands, 815, 702. SOC 3-10-18. Arrived 3-4-19		1-22
❑ XZ725	'415'	Westland Lynx	80	ex Fleetlands, 815, 702, HAS.3, 702, HAS.2, 702,		
		HMA.8SRU		Falklands, 702. SOC 23-9-18. Arrived 3-4-19		1-22
❑ ZB604	'722'	HS Harrier T.8	83	ex Wittering, Shawbury, VL, 899, T.4, 899. 899 Sqn colours		1-22
❑ -		Fairey IIIF	~	fuselage frame		1-18
❑ AE-331		Agusta 109A ZE411	80	ex 7 Rgt, M Wallop, VL, M Wallop, 846, Arg Army CAB.601,		
				AE-331. Acquired 10-10. Argentine colours		1-22
❑ AE-422		Bell UH-1H Iroquois	74	ex Wroughton, VL, Stanley, Arg Army, 74-22520.		
				Acquired 6-6-89		1-22
❑ 0729	'411'	Beech T-34C-1	78	ex Wroughton, VL, Stanley, Pebble Island, Arg Navy		
		Turbo-Mentor		Acquired 7-7-83		1-22
❑ '102/17'		Fokker Dr.I replica	68	BAPC.88. Acquired 1975	[14]	6-19
❑ 15-1585		Yokosuka Ohka 11	c45	BAPC.58, ex Hayes, South Kensington. Acquired 1977	[15]	6-19

■ **[1]** Camel built by Slingsby. **[2]** Flycatcher built by Westward Airways (aka Viv and Rod Bellamy). **[3]** Firefly served as the aerodynamic prototype for the T.1 trainer from 5-46, eventually adopting a 'B Condition' identity. **[4]** Wyvern from a pre-production batch of 20 TF.1s, powered by the 24-cylinder RR Eagle 22: this one did not fly. **[5]** Supermarine 517 and P.1052 are on loan from the RAF Museum. **[6]** On 14-12-52 Supermarine _510_ VV106 suffered a wheels-up landing at Farnborough. It was returned to Supermarine on 10-7-53 for repair and to have a hinged rear fuselage fitted. This substantial modification was given the design number 517. **[7]** For reasons best known to someone, Skyraider WT983 was painted correctly as 'WT' but given the 'last-three' of its US Navy serial number and this stuck throughout its career. **[8]** Third prototype Buccaneer - also designated NR/A.39 - with non-folding wings; first flown 10-31-58. **[9]** Jet Provost was donated by a former RN pilot who earned his wings on this very aircraft while with 1 FTS – where a large number of Navy pilots received their training. **[10]** _Humphrey_ attacked the Argentine submarine _Santa Fe_ with depth charges 25-4-82 off South Georgia. There is another _Humphrey_, see Gosport, Hampshire. **[11]** XS527 also let rip at the _Santa Fe_, with SS.12 missiles. **[12]** XZ499 is fitted with the tail fin of ZA195. **[13]** XZ574 factoids: entered service 6-10-76; detached to HMS _Invincible_ for Operation 'Corporate' 4-82 to 9-82 and flown by - among others - HRH Prince Andrew; total time upon retirement 9,168 hours. **[14]** Triplane based on a Lawrence Parasol, making it a five-eighths scale replica. **[15]** Ohka on loan from the Science Museum.

Navy Wings Heritage Flight: The official transfer of aircraft was made on 23rd April 2021 from the Fly Navy Heritage Trust – the charity behind Navy Wings - but was sadly overshadowed by the force landing of the Sea Fury five days later. The Navy Wings Associate Collection comprises private owner aircraft working to help and support the aims of the Trust. These include some based with Navy Wings and others such as Historic Helicopters at Higher Purtington, Somerset, and Kennet Aviation at Old Warden, Beds.

In a similar manner to the Historic Army Aircraft Flight at Middle Wallop, Hampshire, the fleet has adopted civilian registrations to reflect the new status. The pandemic was sufficient to put an end to the already challenging project to put the Sea Vixen back in the air: it is however, maintained in 'live' status. Sea Fury T.20S VX281 (G-BCOW) force landed near Yeovilton on 28th April 2021, thankfully without serious injury. It was put up for disposal in July and the search is on for a replacement. It was registered to The Fighter Collection in November and is now listed under <u>Duxford</u>, Cambs. Sea Hawk WV908 is stored at Shawbury, Shropshire, for potential future use by the Flight.

◆ _Frequently attend airshows, otherwise by prior arrangement_ only | office@navywings.org.uk | www.navywings.org.uk

☐	N9328*	'69'	DH Tiger Moth ✈ G-ALWS	39	ex Henstridge, Welshpool, Bromsgrove, Rothesay, Strathallan, Perth, N9328, Upwood SF, 6 FTS, 15 EFTS, 17 EFTS 15 EFTS, 19 EFTS, Duxford SF, Farnborough SF	[1]	1-22
☐	W5856	'4A'	Fairey Swordfish I ✈ G-BMGC	41	ex Brough, Strathallan G-BMGC, Alabama, RCN, Wroughton. Blackburn-built. 820 Sqn c/s, City of Leeds	[2] [3]	1-22
☐	LS326	'L2'	Fairey Swordfish II ✈ G-AJVH	43	ex Westland, White Waltham, G-AJVH, Worthy Down, 836, Blackburn-built. 836 Sqn c/s, City of Liverpool	[2]	1-22
☐	NF389		Fairey Swordfish III	44	ex Brough, VL, Brough, Lee-on-Solent, 781, ATDU, 4 Ferry Flt. Blackburn-built. Spares use		1-22
☐	SX336*	'105'	V-S Seafire F.17 ✈ G-KASX	46	ex Old Warden, N Weald, Nottingham, G-BRMG, Cranfield, Twyford, Newark, Warrington, Stretton A2055, Bramcote, 728. Westland-built. 766 Sqn colours. Arrived 15-21-21	[4]	1-22
☐	VR930	'110'	Hawker Sea Fury FB.11 G-CLNJ	48	ex Brough, VL, Boscombe Down, Lee-on-Solent, Wroughton, VL, 8382M, Colerne, Dunsfold, FRU, Lossiemouth, Anthorn, 801, Anthorn, 802. 802 Sqn c/s	[2]	1-22
☐	WB657		DHC Chipmunk T.10 G-CNVH	49	ex BRNC, Leeds UAS, 16 RFS, 25 RFS, Leeds UAS, 25 RFS. SOC 1-4-19	[5]	1-22
☐	WK608	'906'	DHC Chipmunk T.10 ✈ G-CLNI	50	ex BRNC, Bristol UAS, 7 FTS, 3 FTS, Edinburgh UAS, 11 RFS	[2]	1-22
☐	XF690*		Percival Provost T.1 G-MOOS	55	ex N Weald, Cranfield, Thatcham, Wymeswold, Leicester, Hendon 8041M, CATCS, CNCS, 64 GCF, QUAS. CoA 14-9-19	[6]	10-21
☐	XP924	'134'	DH Sea Vixen D.3 G-CVIX	63	ex Hurn, Swansea, Llanbedr, RAE, FAW.2, FRL, RAE, Sydenham, 899, RAFHS. Hawarden-built. Arrived 12-9-14. Accident 27-5-17, CoA 27-6-17. 899 Sqn colours	[5]	1-22
☐	XT420	'422'	Westland Wasp HAS.1 ✈ G-CBUI	50	ex N Weald, Fleetlands, Wroughton, 829, Falklands, 829, 706, 829. SOC 18-4-94. Aurora Flt colours	[2]	1-22
☐	XV586	'010'	McD Phantom FG.1	69	ex airfield, Leuchars 9067M, 43, 892. Arrived 16-5-12. 892 Sqn colours, stored		8-21
☐	42-46703*		Stinson AT-19 Reliant ✈ N69745	43	ex USN 11442, FAA FK877, 703, 740. Arrived 19-12-20	[7]	1-22
☐	52-8562*	' ✈	NAA T-6J Texan G-NWHF	52	ex G-BSBG, Mozambique AF 1753, Port AF 1753, WGAF BF+053, AA+053, USAF 52-8562. CCF-built. Acq 22-3-21	[2]	1-22

■ [1] Tiger registered to Jim Norris. This was written out of W&R25 (p204) at Henstridge having re-flown in 2014 following restoration. [2] Registered to Fly Navy Heritage Trust. [3] W5856 in the colours of Lt Hugh de Graaf Hunter, awarded a DSC for the attack on the Bismarck, launched from the Ark Royal, 5-41. [4] Seafire registered to Tim Manna of Kennet Aviation – see Shuttleworth, Beds, and North Weald, Essex. [5] Registered to Naval Aviation. [6] Registered to the nicely named Yeo Pro Group. [7] Owned by Paul Kehoe.

Others: A variety of airframes are used for technical instruction, rescue training, display purposes or are stored. By October 2021 Phantom XV586 had taken up residence in the Navy Wings hangar, above.

☐	WV911	'115'	Hawker Sea Hawk FGA.6	55	ex RNHF store, Dunsfold, Lee-on-Solent A2622, A2626, Fleetlands, Lee-on-Solent A2526 (31-10-62), 700, 804. AW-built. Rescue training by 7-19		8-21
☐	XS513		Westland Wessex HU.5	64	ex A2681, Gosport, A2770 (14-3-87), Lee-on-S', 772, 845, 772, 845, 707, 846, 845, 846, 845, 707, 846, 848, 845, 848. Dump		8-21
☐	XT458	'P'	Westland Wessex HU.5	65	ex Gosport, A2679, A2768 (15-3-88), Lee-on-Solent, 772, 845, 772, 845, 846, 845, 707, A&AEE, 781. 845 Sqn c/s. Displayed outside Command HQ from 14-8-12		8-21
☐	XW630		HS Harrier GR.3	71	ex A2671, Gosport, A2759 (15-5-91) Lee-on-Solent, 3, 4, 3, 20. FAA colours. Dump		8-21
☐	XW784		M-P Kittiwake I G-BBRN	71	ex G-BBRN, CoA 15-3-08		8-21
☐	XW890		Sud Gazelle HT.2	74	ex Fleetlands, Wroughton, 705. SOC 17-3-95. Displayed outside Gazelle House	[1]	8-21
☐	XZ230*		Westland Lynx HAS.3GMS	76	ex Fleetlands, Hixon, 815, 829, HAS.2, 815, 702. SOC 17-5-04. Wildcat avionics trainer, 'WAvT' lettering	[2]	4-21
☐	XZ257		Westland Lynx HAS.3	79	ex Hixon, VL, M Wallop, 815, 702, 815, 702, HAS.2, 815, 702. SOC 13-7-09. Wildcat training aid, 'AST' lettering	[3]	9-21

Somerset, and Yeovilton, conclude beyond the photo-spread, on page 225

NORTHUMBERLAND
Short 330-100 G-OGIL
Sunderland, May 2021
Brian Downs

MS Type 'N' replica '5191'
Sunderland, May 2021
Brian Downs

NOTTINGHAMSHIRE
Monospar ST-12 VH-UTH
Newark, Aug 2020
Howard Heeley

SHROPSHIRE
BAe EAP ZF534
Cosford, Mar 2020
Ian Haskell

SOMERSET
Britannia 307F 5Y-AYR
Burnham on Sea, Oct 2021
Both *Paul Middleton*

SOMERSET

Campbell Cricket G-AXRA
Weston-super-Mare, Aug
2021
Ian Humphreys

Slingsby Tutor BGA.1759
Weston-super-Mare, Aug 2021
Ian Humphreys

Provost T.1 WW388
Weston Zoyland, Apr 2021
Tony McCarthy

SOMERSET

Stinson Reliant 42-46703
(N69745)
Yeovilton, Oct 2021
Ian Haskell

STAFFORDSHIRE

Spitfire XVI RW388
Stoke-on-Trent, Sep 2021
Dave Murray

SUFFOLK

F-84F Thunderstreak '6771'
(FU-6)
Bentwaters, Sep 2020
Paul Middleton

SURREY

Boeing 747-436 G-BNLY
Arriving at Dunsfold
5th Dec 2020
Phil Whalley

BN-2A Island G-NOIL
Redhill, Jul 2021
John Wickenden

WEST SUSSEX

Chipmunk T.10 WD377 and
Beaufort VIII
Balcombe, Mar 2020
David Willis

WEST SUSSEX

Hurricane I P3179
Tangmere, Jul 2021
Les Woodward

Provost T.1 XF840 and
Lysander III FSM 'V9822'
Tangmere, Oct 2021
Tom Davis

Phantom FGR.2 XV408
Tangmere, Dec 2021
Hugh Trevor

WARWICKSHIRE

BAe ATP SE-LPU
Coventry, Aug 2021
Dave Peace

WILTSHIRE

Typhoon T.3 ZJ807
Boscombe Down, Jul 2021
Ian Greenhalgh

Tornado GR.1 ZA319
Old Sarum, Nov 2021
Hugh Trevor

WILTSHIRE
GEC-Marconi Phoenix ZJ477
Old Sarum, May 2021
Les Woodward

EAST YORKSHIRE
L29 Delfin '51'
Breighton, Nov 2021
Andy Wood

Beverley C.1 XB259
Paull, Sep 2020
Andy Wood

NORTH YORKSHIRE

Cessna TU.206 G-CCRC
Arriving Bagby, 23rd Jun 2021
David E Thompson

Sea Harrier FA.2 ZH798
Leeds East, Aug 2021
Andy Wood

Pawnee 260 G-BFRY
Sutton Bank, Sep 2021
Andy Wood

SOUTH YORKSHIRE
'Canberra Street'
Doncaster, Jun 2021
John Wickenden

SCOTLAND
Convair CV-400 G-CONV
Carluke, Nov 2021
David S Johnstone

Bolingbroke IVT 9940
East Fortune, Aug 2021
Jim Simpson

SCOTLAND

Buccaneer S.2B XW530
Departing Elgin 11th Dec 2021
Jim Simpson

Boeing 737-528 VP-BRV
Glasgow, Sep 2021
David S Johnstone

Dominie T.1 XS713
Arriving at Kinloss, 18th Nov
2020
Jim Simpson

SCOTLAND

Sea King HAR.3 XZ592,
Wessex HC.2 XR528,
Sycamore HR.14 XJ380
Kinloss, Jul 2021
Jim Simpson

Tornado GR.4 ZA463
Lossiemouth, May 2020
Jim Simpson

Agusta A109As MM81335
and MM81220
Perth, Nov 2021
David S Johnstone

WALES

Sukhoi Su-17s '54' and '35'
Hawarden, Jun 2021
David Willis

Sherry Buzzard G-MMNN
St Athan, Oct 2021
Tom Davis

Boeing 747-436 G-BYGC
Touching down St Athan,
11th Dec 2020
Jake Wallace

WALES
Shackleton MR.3 WR974
St Athan, Aug 2020
Les Woodward

CHANNEL ISLANDS
Trislander G-JOEY
Guernsey, Sep 2021
Dave Murray

NORTHERN IRELAND
Europa XS G-TAGR
Belfast, Dec 2021
Ian Thompson

NORTHERN IRELAND
Ferguson replica G-CJEN
Long Kesh, May 2021
John Wickenden

Short Sherpa G-14-1
Long Kesh, May 2021
John Wickenden

IRELAND
Duchess G-WACI
Celbridge, Oct 2021
Ian Thompson

IRELAND

Weston line-up
Weston, Oct 2021
Ian Thompson

Goose N4575C
Weston, Oct 2021
Ian Thompson

Buccaneer S.2B XV863
Weston, Oct 2021
Ian Thompson

❑ XZ670	'A'	Westland Lynx AH.7		81	ex M Wallop, Fleetlands, 847, 4 Regt, 849, AAC
					Arrived 20-10-16. 1 Regt AAC. At Senior Rates Mess [4] 10-21
❑ XZ674	'T'	Westland Lynx AH.7		81	ex M Wallop. SOC 3-3-14. Rescue training 8-21
❑ -*		Westland Lynx AH.7		~	paint bay, first noted 2019 4-21
❑ XZ719		Westland Lynx HMA.8		80	ex Fleetlands, 815, HAS.3, 702, 815, 702, HAS.2.
					SOC 3-11-14. Arrived 27-2-15. Rescue training 8-21
❑ XZ728	'326'	Westland Lynx		80	ex A2852, Fleetlands, 815, HAS.3, 702, 815, HAS.2, 815.
		HMA.8DSP			Crashed 25-2-97. SOC 20-9-04. At Senior Rates Mess 10-21
❑ XZ736*		Westland Lynx		81	ex M Wallop, 815, 702, HAS.3, 815, HAS,2,
		HMA.8SRU			Falklands -82. Stored [5] 4-21
❑ ZD578	'122'	HS Sea Harrier F/A.2		85	ex St Athan 9329M, 801, 899, 801, 899, 801, FRS.1, 800,
	and '000'				801, 899, 801, 800, A&AEE, 800, 899. SOC 4-12-02
					Displayed, 800 Sqn colours (port), 801 (stb) 10-21
❑ 'ZH800'	'123'	HS S' Harrier F/A.2	ZH801	96	ex Cottesmore, VL, 800, 899, 801, 899 [6] 8-21
❑ 'ZH801'	'001'	HS S' Harrier F/A.2	ZH800	96	ex Cottesmore, Greenwich, VL, 899, 801, 800 [6] 8-21
❑ ZZ400		Westland Wildcat AH.1		10	ex Lyneham, Yeovil. Handed over 10-10-16 [7] 8-21
❑ -		Westland Lynx CIM		77	purpose-built at Almondbank 6-12
❑ 773		Westland Sea King		75	ex Gosport, Egyptian Air Force, G-BDMH, G-17-17.
		Mk.47	G-BDMH		Dump, on side 7-20

■ [1] XW890 has the boom of AH.1 ZB668 and is Westland-built. [2] XZ230 scored multiple ASM strikes, Iraq 1/2-91. [3] Training airframe, created from a Lynx HAS.3 by Pennant International. [4] While serving with the Royal Marines, 847 Sqn XZ670 hit an Iraqi T55 tank and then destroyed another two on 24-3-03. [5] Converted into a mobile bar for the Lynx decommissioning ceremonies, 2017. [6] Serials were transposed during repainting at Cottesmore: ZH801 was ready before the other but numerical sequence was employed! [7] With Leonard-run Wildcat Training Centre.

STAFFORDSHIRE
Includes the unitary authority of Stoke-on-Trent

ALREWAS on the A513 east of the town, midway between Lichfield and Burton
National Memorial Arboretum: The scope of the commemorations and landscaping within the 150-acre site is breath-taking. The extensive Remembrance Centre was opened during 2017. Memorials of an aeronautical nature include: Berlin Airlift, Coastal Command, Operation 'Market-Garden' etc.
◆ *Off the A513 and the A38, Croxall Road, DE13 7AR* | **01283 245100** | **info@thenma.org.uk** | **www.thenma.org.uk**

BASSETT'S POLE at the junction of the A38 and A453, northeast of Sutton Coldfield
NPF Bassett's Pole: Mult-pursuit site. ◆ *By prior arrangement* only | **www.npfbassettspole.com**

❑ XP350	Westland Whirlwind	62	ex Bruntingthorpe, Helston, Chivenor, 22, 225.	
	HAR.10		SOC 3-3-82. With boom of XK969	8-21

BIDDULPH on the A527 south of Congleton
A Jaguar cockpit is kept at a *private* location in the *general* area.

❑ XZ385*	SEPECAT Jaguar GR.3A	77	ex Selby, Ipswich, St Athan, 41, 16, GR.1, 16, 6, 16, 54, 6,	
			Gib Det, 41, 17, 14. Cockpit. First noted 9-20	9-20

BUCKNALL on the A52 east of Stoke-on-Trent
Kingsland Academy: Eaves Lane ◆ *By prior arrangement* only

❑ G-SSWE	Short 360-100	86	ex Market Drayton, Coventry, SE-IXE, G-BNBA,	
			G-14-3705. CoA 22-8-05, de-reg 6-6-07. *The King's Wings*	5-17

BURSLEM on the A50 northwest of Stoke-on-Trent
Supermarine Aero Engineering: Spitfire components and structures specialists at the appropriately-named Mitchell Works.
◆ *By prior arrangement* only | **https://supermarine.net**

❑ SL611	V-S Spitfire XVI	45	ex Scafell, 603, 111 OTU. CBAF-built. Crashed 20-11-47.	
		G-SAEA	Remains recovered 5-4-97	N5-19
❑ RW389	'E' V-S Spitfire XVI	G-SAEB 45	ex 5 CAACU, 20. CBAF-built. SOC 13-6-56	N7-19

CANNOCK

Previously listed under Leicester, Leics, XH174 is *believed* held at a *private* location in the *general* area.

| ❑ XH174* | EE Canberra PR.9 | 60 | ex South Molton, Welshpool, Staffordshire, Basingstoke, Shawbury, St Athan,1 PRU, 39, 13, 39, MoS, 39, 58. Cockpit. Arrived 7-10-12 | 10-12 |

FROGHALL Sea King HAS.3 ZE370 moved to Scalby, N Yorks, in November 2021.

LICHFIELD northwest of Tamworth

Defence Medical Services: Whittington Barracks.

| ❑ ZE449 | Sud Puma HC.1 | c75 | ex Shawbury, Boscombe Down, 230, Weston-super-Mare, 9017M, Port Stanley, Argentine Prefectura Naval PA-12. Crashed 9-7-09. Arrived 8-4-14 | 12-19 |

LONGTON on the A50 south of Stoke-on-Trent

Motor Clinic: Trentham Road, has a 'JP' on show and is known as 'The Place with the Plane' | **www.motorclinicltd .co.uk**

| ❑ XM425 | '88' Hunting Jet Provost T.3A | 60 | ex King's Lynn, Bruntingthorpe, Halton 8995M (10-4-89), 7 FTS, 1 FTS, RAFC, 3 FTS, CFS | 10-20 |

RUGELEY Last noted in June 2011, Provost T.1 WW444 has been deleted.

STAFFORD

Royal Air Force Museum Reserve Collection: 'Lodges' with the Defence Electronics and Components Agency, on a sub-site to the north of the huge Stafford storage complex - see below. The museum's tenure on this otherwise commercially managed site has got to be on a countdown. The ongoing review of exhibits is dealt with in detail under Hendon, Gtr Lon. Expressions of interest were due on 10th February 2022 for the first tranche of airframes. Apart from a few exceptions departures were unlikely to have been realised by the time *W&R* went to press. Those offered for **transfer by gift** are marked: ●: those offered for **outward loan** are marked ❖.

As well as the airframes and countless smaller artefacts, the following provide a taste of what is held here: the centre section, float and other parts from the 1911 Avro-built Lakes Waterbird; offered for transfer by gift; the pilot's seat and immediate surroundings of HP Halifax II R9371 of 10 Squadron, crashed 9th March 1942 and restored by the Cotswold Aircraft Restoration Group; tail section of a Handley Page V/1500 (and parts from an O/400); a float from a Fairey Seafox; Short Stirling III LK488 of 1651 CU, crashed 19th October 1944 and recovered from Mickle Fell, Yorks, 31st August 1977.

Last noted in August 2018, the Avian hang-glider moved to 'deep store' at Cosford, Shropshire, by 2020. Sopwith Tabloid replica '168' (G-BFDE) was due to be moved to Stow Maries, Essex; this has been anticipated.

◆ *Viewing is possible* **only** *via prior arrangement - occasional, strictly pre-booked, open days.*

❑ G-AAMX	DH Moth		29	ex Hendon, Cosford, Shoreham, N926M. Moth Corp-built CoA 7-5-94, de-reg 19-8-96. Arrived 15-5-12		●	1-22
❑ G-AEKW	Miles Mohawk		36	ex Hendon, Cosford, Hatch, Cosford, Hatch, Wyton, USA, Spain, HM503, MCCS, Turnhouse SF, G-AEKW. P&P-built			9-18
❑ 'G-AEXF'	Percival Mew Gull replica		08	BAPC.366, ex Hendon, Sudbury. Acquired 17-4-08		[1]	1-22
❑ G-AHED	DH Dragon Rapide		46	ex Cosford, Wyton, Cardington, Henlow, Dominie II RL962, Witney. Brush-built. CoA 17-4-68, de-reg 3-3-69		●	1-22
❑ 'F8614'	Vickers Vimy replica	G-AWAU	69	ex Hendon, 'H651', Wisley, Brooklands, G-AWAU. Damaged 14-6-69, de-reg 19-7-73, acquired 12-70 *Triple First*		[2]	9-18
❑ A301	Morane BB		16	ex Wyton, Cardington, Hendon. Fuselage		●	1-22
❑ K6035	Westland Wallace II		35	ex Henlow, Hatch, Henlow, Newark, Cranwell, 2361M, EWS, 502. Acquired 4-77. Fuselage		[3]	1-22
❑ P3175	Hawker Hurricane I		40	ex Hendon, 257. Shot down 31-8-40. Acquired 1978. Forward fuselage, wreck			1-22
❑ Z7197	Percival Proctor III	G-AKZN	40	ex Hendon 8380M, St Athan, Swinderby, Finningley, G-AKZN, (CoA 29-11-63), AST, 18 EFTS, 1 RS, 2 SS. Hills-built			1-22
❑ HS503	Fairey Swordfish IV		43	BAPC.108, ex Cosford, Wyton, Cardington, Cosford, Henlow, Canada, RCAF (SOC 21-8-46), 754, 745. Blackburn-built. Acquired 10-70			9-18

☐ LA226	V-S Spitfire F.21	45	ex Cosford, Wyton, Cardington, St Athan, Shawbury, Abingdon, Biggin Hill, South Marston, London, S Marston, Little Rissington, 7119M (18-1-54), 3 CAACU, 122		9-18
☐ SL674	V-S Spitfire XVI	45	ex Cosford, Wyton, Cardington, St Athan, 8392M, Biggin Hill, Little Rissington, 501, 17 OTU. CBAF-built	❖	1-22
☐ VS618	Percival Prentice T.1 G-AOLK	49	ex Hendon, G-AOLK, Southend, Southend, VS618, 9 MU, 22 FTS. CoA 17-9-10, de-reg 9-2-10. Acquired 9-10-09		1-22
☐ VX275	Slingsby Sedbergh TX.1	48	ex Cosford, Wyton, Cardington, St Athan 8884M, 612 GS, 613 GS, 623 GS, 123 GS, BGA.572	●	1-22
☐ XK781	ML Utility Mk.1	57	ex Cardington, M Wallop. Nacelle and other bits		8-13
☐ ZJ493	GAF Jindivik Mk.104AL	c98	ex Llanbedr, QinetiQ/DERA, ATA, RAAF A92-814. End of an Era. Last flight UK Jindivik flight, 26-10-04		1-22
☐ -*	Cody Man-Lifting Kite rep	~	BAPC.428. ex Manchester	❖	1-22
☐ –	Balloon Factory Airship replica	~	BAPC.296, ex Hendon. Nulli Secundus I. Gondola First noted 10-17	[4]	9-18
☐ No.164	Blériot XI	c1910	BAPC.106, ex Hendon, Cosford 9209M, Cardington, Hendon, Colerne, Hendon, Heathrow, RAeS, Hendon, Nash, Brooklands. Acquired 1964, first noted 10-17		1-22
☐ –	Blériot XI	c1910	fuselage frame	[5]	9-18
☐ –	Curtiss JN-4 'Jenny'	c22	fuselage frame		1-22
☐ –	Fairchild Cornell II	c42	ex Cosford, Wyton, Cardington, Henlow, Canada. Fleet-built	●[6]	1-22
☐ –	Hawker Hind (Afghan)	37	BAPC.82, ex Cosford, Hendon, Kabul, Afghan AF, RAF. Acquired 10-1-68, arrived by 10-16		1-22
☐ –	Eurofighter Typhoon FSM	03	BAPC.292, ex Hendon, BAE Systems		10-13
☐ –	BAE Systems HERTI-1	c06	ex BAE Systems, Afghan deployment 2007	[7]	9-18
☐ A2-4	Supermarine Seagull V	35	ex Hendon, Cardington, Wyton, VH-ALB, RAAF A2-4. Acquired 5-72. First noted 10-17		1-22
☐ E.3B-521 '781-3'	Bücker Jungmann	56	ex Hendon, Spanish AF. CASA-built. Acquired 23-1-97		9-18
☐ –	Fieseler Fi 103 (V-1)	c44	BAPC.237, ex Soesterberg. Arrived 11-13		9-18
☐ J-1172	DH Vampire FB.6	52	ex Cosford, Wyton, Cardington, Manchester, Cosford, 8487M, Colerne, Swiss AF. Swiss-built	[8]	9-18

■ **[1]** See under Shuttleworth, Beds, for the flying G-AEXF and Tattershall Thorpe, Lincs, for another replica. **[2]** Vimy built by the Vintage Aircraft and Flying Association, first flying 3-6-69 at Brooklands. Badly damaged by fire at Manchester Airport 14-6-69; it was rebuilt and handed over to the RAFM in June 1972. The name *Triple First* denotes the first Atlantic, Australia and South Africa flights undertaken by Vimys. **[3]** Other Wallace fuselage and wing parts are also held. **[4]** Replica of 1907 airship, built by the Army Balloon Factory, under the supervision of Samuel Franklin Cody. **[5]** Believed part of the Nash Collection cache. Fuselage frame appears to have been lengthened - two-seater? Set of wings also to hand, and short span, leading to the notion that this *may* have been a 'Penguin', a taxi-only 'trainer'. **[6]** PT-26A Cornell II has parts from at least three machines. Port wing is RCAF 15195, starboard from 14590. Fuselage had a plate stamped 'FAL Ser No FV351, BAC Ser No FV351, Eng No R007174'. The RAF serial FV351 corresponds to RCAF 15252. These and several other Cornell 'elements' were acquired from/via Canadian Warplane Heritage as part of an exchange. **[7]** HERTI - High Endurance Rapid Technology Insertion UAV, based on J&S Aero Fregata motor glider.

Beacon Barracks: West of the city and Littleworth. Within, the **Staffordshire Wing, Air Cadets** with a Phantom cockpit.

☐ XT672	'WE' Westland Wessex HC.2	66	ex Shawbury, Hixon, Shawbury, 2 FTS, Benson SF, 72. SOC 12-5-99. *Aries*, displayed	[1]	1-19
☐ XV581	McD Phantom FG.1	69	ex Aberdeen, Buchan, 8070M (12-9-91), Wattisham, 43, 111, 43. Cockpit, 43 Sqn colours		9-17
☐ XZ987	'C' HS Harrier GR.3	81	9185M, ex St Athan, 1417 Flt, 3, 4. 1417 Flt c/s, displayed		4-21

■ **[1]** XT672 is on loan from Air and Ground Aviation.

Also: *W&R27* (p223) 'wrote out' Cessna 421C G-FTAX last noted lying in a scrapyard here in September 2019: it was pounced upon by the SYAM crew and the forward fuselage moved to <u>Doncaster</u>, South Yorkshire.

STOKE-ON-TRENT

Potteries Museum and Art Gallery: The newly completed **Spitfire Galley** was unveiled on 17th September 2021. Spitfire XVI RW388 is the centre piece of many artefacts honouring Reginald Joseph Mitchell – Stoke being his birthplace. The Spitfire is not just a tribute to its designer, but to the craftsmen of the Medway Aircraft Preservation Society.

Without seeming to be *very* food and drink obsessed, alongside RW388 is Violet's Cafe which is well worth sampling. There is purpose in this other than the pursuit of calories, the eatery honours Canadian-born Violet Milstead who flew Spitfires and other types with the Air Transport Auxiliary. She *may well* have been the pilot that delivered RW388 from the Castle Bromwich factory to Brize Norton on 18th July 1945.

◆ *Bethesda Street, Cultural Quarter, Hanley, ST1 3DW* | **01782 232323** | **email** via website | **www.stokemuseums.org.uk**

❑ RW388*	V-S Spitfire XVI	45	ex Rochester, Stoke-on-Trent (acquired 15-2-72), Kemble,	
	'U4-U'		'AB917', 71 MU 6946M (30-9-52), 19 MU, 5 MU, Andover,	
			Benson, Colerne, FC&RS, 612, 667. CBAF-built.	
			Arrived 6-21. 667 Sqn colours	1-22

STONE on the A34 north of Stafford

Alan Simpson: Still cherishes his Sea Venom.

❑ XG629	'668'	DH Sea Venom FAW.22	56	ex Long Marston, Fleetlands, Higher Blagdon, Culdrose, ADS,
				831, Yeovilton SF, 893, FAW.21, 893. Hawarden-built.
				SOC 3-9-70 3-20

TATENHILL AERODROME south of the B5234, west of Burton-on-Trent   EGBM

A wholesale deletion of airframes last noted in January 2017: Comanche G-ARBO; Apache G-BICY; Cessna 152 G-BXGE; Cessna 152 G-BZAE; Arrow G-RUBY; Bonanza N7205T. Citation G-BWFL had moved on by May 2021. Balancing all this was the arrival of a heavyweight.

❑ G-RHHT	Piper Lance 300	78	ex N36476. De-reg 13-3-12, CoA 2-6-12, crashed 3-6-11.	
			Rescue trainer, poor state	1-17
❑ XX900*	Blackburn Buccaneer	76	ex Bruntingthorpe, St Athan, 208, 12, 208, 216, 12, 208.	
	S.2B		Arrived 6-11-20	[1] 11-21

■ **[1]** Owned by David Walton.

WOLVERHAMPTON AERODROME or Halfpenny Green, east of Bridgnorth   EGBO

The 'JP' 'guards' the flying centre.

❑ G-BSDN	Piper Seneca 200T	79	ex N2893A. CoA 11-10-11, de-reg 25-3-20	8-21
❑ G-PLAJ	BAe Jetstream 3102	87	ex N2274C, C-GJPH, N331QB, G-31-738.	
			CoA 30-11-10, de-reg 16-6-16	8-21
❑ G-XBLD	Bölkow Bö 105DB	79	ex EI-BLD, D-HDLQ. CoA 19-11-13	9-19
❑ RA-01274	Yakovlev Yak-55	~	ex Sov AF '03'. First noted 4-13	10-19
❑ XW434	'MY' BAC Jet Provost T.5A	72	ex Selby, Cosford 9091M (1-3-91), Halton, 1 FTS, 7 FTS,	
			3 FTS, CFS. Arrived 29-5-13, displayed	8-21

SUFFOLK

BAWDSEY at the end of the B1083, on a minor road south of Bawdsey village

Bawdsey Radar: Billed as the world's first operational radar site, the transmitter block at the Manor is the centre of a fascinating museum. ◆ *Bawdsey, IP12 3BA* | **07821 162879** | **info@bawdseyradar.org.uk** | **www.bawdseyradar.org.uk**

BECCLES AERODROME south of the A146 west of Lowestoft   EGSM

❑ G-ASMY	Piper Apache 160H	62	ex N4309Y. CoA 25-11-95	11-21
❑ G-ATHZ	Cessna 150F	65	ex N6286R. CoA 27-3-98	11-20
❑ G-ATMM*	Cessna F.150F	66	Reims-built. CoA 7-7-18	11-20
❑ G-AVPH	Cessna F.150G	67	ex Blackpool, Woodvale. Reims-built. CoA 9-4-86,	
			de-reg 26-3-02. Fuselage	11-20
❑ G-AVZU*	Cessna F.150H	67	Reims-built. CoA 30-7-17	11-20
❑ G-AWTX*	Cessna F.150J	68	Reims-built. CoA 2-7-19	11-20
❑ G-BAOP	Cessna FRA.150L	73	Reims-built. Crashed 22-6-01, CoA 11-4-02, de-reg 1-5-14	1-18
❑ G-BEIG*	Cessna F.150M	76	Reims-built. CoA 1-11-17	11-20
❑ G-BWSC*	Piper Tomahawk 112	81	ex N23203. De-reg 3-9-<u>14</u>	5-21

BECK ROW on the A1101 north of Mildenhall
Cross Country RV: A Hunter guards the premises on the Mildenhall Industrial Estate.
☐ XG210   Hawker Hunter F.6   56 ex DRA Bedford, Hatfield, CFE, 19, 14. SOC 11-9-85. RAE c/s   8-21
■ **[1]** XG210 has the starboard wing of XL572 (most of it is at Elvington, N Yorks) and XL623 (Dunsfold, Surrey) to port.

BELSTEAD south of the A14 south of Ipswich
Hillside Primary School and Nursery: ◆ **Strictly** *by prior arrangement* | **www.hillsidecp.net**
☐ XZ613   Westland Lynx AH.7   80 ex Ipswich, Gosport, Wallop, Arborfield, 655, 665, A&AEE,
                                                 Yeovil, 657, 654. First noted 9-17   [1]   1-20
■ **[1]** Fitted with the boom of ZD278 - see Knowsley, Merseyside.

BENTWATERS AIRFIELD south of the A1152, northeast of Woodbridge
Bentwaters Cold War Museum: Run by the **Bentwaters Aviation Society**. Centred on the Wing Command Post this incredible museum includes the 'Battle Cabin' and the War Operations rooms. Delivered on 7th December 2021 was a complete Bloodhound SAM on transportation trolley, courtesy of the RAF Museum Cosford.
    Some airframes are being worked on in a HAS on the airfield and are *not* available for public inspection.
◆ *Off the A1152 | Building 134, Bentwaters Park, IP12 2TW* | **07588 877020** | **info@bcwm.org.uk** | **www.bcwm.org.uk**

☐ WH453   'L' Gloster Meteor D.16   51 ex Llanbedr, Tarrant Rushton, West Freugh, F.8,
                                              5 CAACU, 72, 222. SOC 10-10-90. Arrived 18-1-05   [1]   1-22
☐ XE707   '865' Hawker Hunter GA.11   55 ex Ashbourne, N707XE, USA, Exeter, G-BVHY, FRADU,
              G-BVHY   764, 738, RAF F.4, 118, 98, 93. Squires Gate-built.
                                              Last flown 21-4-94. Arrived 1-7-10   [2]   1-22
☐ XV401   'I' McD Phantom FGR.2   68 ex Boscombe D', BDAC, DERA, Wattisham, 74, 228 OCU,
                                              19, 56, 23, 56, 29, 228 OCU, 56, 111, 41, 228 OCU. Arr 8-13 [3] 1-22
☐ XX741   'EJ' SEPECAT Jaguar GR.1A   74 ex Ipswich, Shawbury. 226 OCU, 6, 54, 226 OCU.
                                              Acquired 16-8-09. 6 Sqn c/s. First fast taxi 15-3-20   [4]   1-22
☐ ZD667   HS Harrier GR.3   86 ex Predannack, Culdrose 'DD67', A2684[2], 9201M,
                                              1417 Flt, 233 OCU. Arrived 2-13. 4 Sqn colours   [3]   1-22
☐ ZF581   EE Lightning F.53   67 ex Rochester, Portsmouth, *Wing Commander* (1999),
                                              Portsmouth, Warton, Saudi AF 206, 53-675, G-27-45.
                                              Last flown 14-1-86, arrived 22-5-11. 56 Sqn colours   1-22
☐ '6771'   Republic F-84F-51-RE   52 ex Cosford, Rochester, Southend, Belgian AF FU-6,
                 Thunderstreak   52-7133. Arrived 25-9-19. Will have 81st FBW colours   1-22
☐ 51-9252   Lockheed T-33A-1-LO   51 ex Tangmere, Hailsham, Sculthorpe, French AF.
                                              Last flown 25-1-78. Arr 11-7-18. Will have 81st TFW c/s   1-22
☐ 80-0219   Fairchild GA-10A   81 ex Alconbury, 509th TFS, 10th TFW, 81st TFW.
                 Thunderbolt II   Accident4-4-89. 10th TFW, 509th TFS. Arrived 24-5-16.
                                              511th TFS colours, *Phoenix*   [5]   1-22
■ **[1]** Meteor was donated to BCWM in 2012 and will appear in 72 Sqn colours and F.8 guise. **[2]** GA.11 exported to the USA and flown there in 1995, it returned in 2005. **[3]** XV401 and ZD667 acquired from Everett Aero using donation from Brian Smee. **[4]** Jaguar, first flown 4-10-74, taken on charge 18-11-74; last flight 31-1-94; total flying time 4,260 hours; disposed of 18-11-05; joined BCWM 16-8-09 thanks to a donation from Brian Smee. **[5]** 'Warthog' on loan from the National Museum of the USAF.

BROME on the A140 south of Diss
A 'JP' is kept at a *private* location in the area.
☐ XW304   'MD' BAC Jet Provost T.5   70 ex Colsterworth, Cosford 9172M (17-12-92), 6 FTS, CFS, 1 FTS   10-20

BURY ST EDMUNDS on the A140 south of Diss
Blenheim Camp: TA Centre in Newmarket Road should house a Lynx cab'.
☐ -   Westland Lynx AH.7   80 cab. First noted 10-17   8-19

DEBACH south of the B1078, west of Wickham Market
493rd Bomb Group 'Helton's Hellcats' Museum: Centred on USAAF Station 152's former control tower, the museum has been painstakingly put together – restoration of the barracks building is a current project. As has the website, which includes a vast amount of material: for example, the locals pronounce it 'Deb-idge', while Americans call it 'Dee-bark'.
◆ *Grove Farm, Clopton, IP13 6QS* | **493bgdebach@gmail.com** | **www.493bgdebach.co.uk**

ELMSETT AERODROME on minor roads northeast of Hadleigh

AJD Engineering / Hawker Restorations Ltd: Hurricane two-seater 'BE505' (G-HHII) had migrated to Biggin Hill, Gtr Lon, by June 2020. SE.5a A2-25 (G-ECAE) moved to Audley End, Essex, by January 2021.

◆ **Strictly** *by prior arrangement* | **www.hawkerrestorations.co.uk**

❏	-	Hawker Hart	G-CIAJ 37	ex St Leonards-on-Sea, Sweden, RSwAF B4A F17 Kallinge.		
				AB Gotaverken-built. Arrived by 7-16	[1] [2]	12-20
❏	L2005	Hawker Hurricane I	39	ex Sudbury, 151, 56. Shot down 28-8-40	[3]	8-18

■ **[1]** Hart registered to Westh Flyg AB of Sweden - see under Audley End, Essex, for the company's SE.5. **[2]** Substantial wreckage discovered in Sweden in the late 1980s One of 42 licence-built and originally fitted with a Nohab-built Bristol Mercury radial. **[3]** Intended restoration as a two-seater.

FELIXSTOWE at the end of the A14, southeast of Ipswich

Glenn Cattermole: XT284 makes good progress. ◆ *By prior arrangement* **only**

❏	XT284	'H'	Blackburn Buccaneer S.2A	65	ex Stock, St Athan, Abingdon 8855M (21-5-85), St Athan, 237 OCU, 15, 208, 809, 803, 736. Cockpit		1-19

Steve Williams: Has a Motor Cadet and Grasshopper in the area.

❏	G-BVFS	Slingsby Motor Cadet III	93	ex Southend. Unflown, stored		N11-18
❏	'WZ784'	Slingsby Grasshopper TX.1	c52	ex Southend, Thurrock. Composite	[1]	2-10

■ **[1]** There is another 'WZ784' at Carlisle, Cumbria.

FLIXTON on the B1062 west of Bungay

Norfolk and Suffolk Aviation Museum (N&SAM): Within are airframes from the former Boulton Paul Aircraft Heritage Project: the company started its aviation activities at Mousehold, Norwich. As well as aircraft, the company also built industrial buildings and hangars and one of the display halls in based on a B&P structure of 1937. Don't forget to take time to amble down to the River Waveney on the Adair Walk. The remains of the former airfield, home of the B-24s of the 446th BG, lie to the east. Neighbouring is the 'Flixton Buck' public house, dating from the 16th century.

Three substantial items do not merit a 'formal' listing as such: a replica Mosquito night-fighter which was started in 2016 and is essentially an instrument cluster and windscreen; a project to create a Hurricane I fuselage, using many elements from former 257 Squadron P3708, shot down on 18th August 1940; and sections from 9 Squadron Wellington I L4288 which crashed near Honington on 30th October 1939.

Spitfire FSM 'N3317' moved to Hawkinge, Kent, by late 2021.

◆ *The Street, NR35 1NZ* | **01986 896644** | **nsam.flixton@gmail.com** | **www.aviationmuseum.net**

❏	G-APUG	Luton Major	64	ex Wattisham. De-reg 5-8-87. Arrived 17-10-06		1-22
❏	G-ARLP	Beagle Terrier	48	ex Felthorpe, Fakenham, Terrier (61), AAC College, T.10 (conversion 1960), AOP.6 VX123, 19 MU,663, 661. Arr 5-7-16		1-22
❏	G-ASRF	Gowland Jenny Wren	66	ex Brookmans Park, Panshanger, Brookmans Park. CoA 4-6-71, de-reg 11-12-96. Arrived 11-9-04	[1]	1-22
❏	G-BABY	Taylor Titch	75	CoA 10-10-91, de-reg 4-12-96. Arrived 28-7-03		1-22
❏	G-BDVS	Fokker Friendship 200	63	ex Norwich, Air UK, S2-ABK, PH-FEX, PH-EXC, 9M-AMM, PH-EXC, PH-FEX. *Eric Gander Dower*. CoA 5-6-00, de-reg 19-12-96. Arrived 17-12-96. Cockpit		1-22
❏	G-BJZC	Thunder Ax7-65Z HAB	82	ex Lancing. CoA 17-6-94, de-reg 8-7-98. *Greenpeace Trinity*	[2]	1-22
❏	G-CDFL*	Zenair CH-601UL	19	ex Spalding. De-reg 4-10-19. Arr 12-21. Fuselage, simulator		1-22
❏	G-CDFW	Lovegrove Sheffy gyro	04	ex Didcot. De-reg 17-5-10. Arrived 3-4-10. *Sheffy*	[3]	1-22
❏	G-MBUD	Skycraft Super Scout 250	82	de-reg 6-9-94. Arrived 11-11-07		1-22
❏	G-MJSU	MBA Tiger Cub	r83	ex Swanton Morley. CoA 31-1-86, de-reg 23-6-93. Arr 8-8-02		1-22
❏	G-MJVI	Lightwing Rooster 1	r83	ex Littlehampton. De-reg 13-6-90. Arrived 24-2-04	[4]	1-22
❏	G-MMWL	Eurowing Goldwing	83	CoA 20-11-06, de-reg 19-4-10. Arrived 15-7-07		1-22
❏	G-MTFK	Flexiform Striker	r87	de-reg 13-6-90. Last taxi 3-7-94. Arrived 7-94	[2] [5]	1-22
❏	CDN	EoN Primary	c48	BGA.1461, ex Tibenham. CoA 29-5-69. Arr 27-4-97. Stored		1-22
❏	DUD	DFS Grunau Baby III	54	BGA.2384, ex Bristol, BGA.2074, RAFGSA.374, D-9142. CoA 29-3-92. Arrived 2002		1-22
❏	HCG	Maupin Woodstock	92	BGA.3833, ex Happisburgh. CoA 23-3-11. Arrived 25-9-10		1-22
❏	HKJ	Penrose Pegasus 2 rep	93	BGA.4002, ex Littlehampton. CoA 15-9-98. Arr 24-2-02	[4] [6]	1-22
❏	JTA	Colditz Cock replica	00	BGA.4757, ex Duxford. *Spirit of Colditz*. CoA 20-2-00	[7]	1-22
❏	'X-25'	B&P P.6 replica	01	BAPC.274, ex Cosford, Wolverhampton. Arrived 19-1-15		1-22

❑	–	'LHS-1'	Bensen B-7	66	BAPC.147, ex Loddon, Marham, Coltishall. Arrived 1978	1-22
❑	–		Mignet HM.14 'Flea'	c36	BAPC.115, ex Earls Colne, Andrewsfield, Duxford, London, Porthcawl [8] [9]	1-22
❑	–		Goldfinch Amphibian 161	96	BAPC.303, ex Old Sarum. Arrived 23-9-08 [8] [10]	1-22
❑	–		Wasp Falcon 4 hang-glider	76	BAPC.372	1-22
❑	–		Antonov C.14 hang-glider	92	BAPC.374	1-22
❑	–		UFM Icarus II	74	BAPC.364, arrived 6-11-05. Biplane, tail-less, hang-glider	1-22
❑	–		Lovegrove Discord gyro	96	BAPC.306, ex Didcot. Arrived 4-10. *The Discord* [3]	1-22
❑	NC16676		Fairchild 24C8F	36	ex Tibenham, USA, CAP. Arrived 18-3-03. CAP colours [11]	1-22
❑	–		Felixstowe F.5	18	BAPC.390, ex Felixstowe. Nose section [12]	1-22
❑	'K4556'	'F'	B&P Overstrand replica	11	BAPC.358, ex Cosford, Wolverhampton. Forward fuselage, 101 Sqn colours. Arrived 19-1-15	1-22
❑	'FJ801'		Boeing PT-27 Kaydet	42	BAPC.375, ex Tibenham, USA. Arrived 26-6-12 [13]	1-22
❑	'TD248'	'8Q-T'	V-S Spitfire XVI	45	BAPC.368, fuselage re-creation. 695 Sqn colours [8] [14]	1-22
❑	VL349 'V7-Q'		Avro Anson C.19 G-AWSA	47	ex Norwich, N5054, G-AWSA (de-reg 18-8-69), SCS, NCS, North Coates SF, WSF, FCCS, HCCS, HCEU, 116, CSE, 1 FU. SOC 5-3-68. Arrived 1-74. Central Sig Est colours	1-22
❑	VX580		Vickers Valetta C.2	50	ex Norwich, MCS, MEAF CS, Aden SF, 114, Malta CS, HS. Last flight 12-12-68. Arrived (via Chinook) 27-5-83	1-22
❑	'WE168'		EE Canberra PR.3	00	cockpit re-creation. Arrived 2002 [15]	1-22
❑	WF128	'676'	Percival Sea Prince T.1	52	ex Honington 8611M (5-2-79), Kemble, Sydenham SF, A&AEE, 750. Arrived 25-9-81. 750 Sqn colours	1-22
❑	WF643	'F'	Gloster Meteor F(TT).8	51	ex Coltishall, Kemble, 29, Nicosia SF, 611, 1, 56. AWA-built. SOC 29-11-71. Arrived 10-5-75. 611 Sqn colours	1-22
❑	WG789		EE Canberra B.2/6	52	ex Mendlesham, Booker, Kew, Burgess Hill, RAE Bedford, RRE, 231 OCU. SOC 23-2-82. Arrived 6-3-02. Cockpit [2]	1-22
❑	WH840		EE Canberra T.4	54	ex Seighford, Locking 8350M, St Athan, Geilenkirchen SF, A&AEE, 97, 151, 245, 88, 231 OCU, CFS. SOC 3-4-74. Arrived 3-94 [8]	1-22
❑	WV605	'T-B'	Percival Provost T.1	54	ex Henlow, Higher Blagdon, Macclesfield, 6 FTS, 3 FTS, 22 FTS. SOC 31-10-66. Arrived 14-9-78	1-22
❑	WV838	'182'	Hawker Sea Hawk FGA.6	54	ex Warrington, Liverpool, Bruntingthorpe, Chippenham, Fleetlands, 736, 738, 806, 802. Crashed 9-2-59. Arrived 23-8-11. 806 Sqn colours. Cockpit [2]	1-22
❑	XA226		Slingsby G'hopper TX.1	53	ex M' Keynes, Turweston, Ipswich, Halton. Arr 21-4-04, stored	1-22
❑	'XE531'		Hawker Hunter T.53	58	ex Cosford, Wolverhampton, N Weald, Bruntingthorpe, Hurn, B'thorpe, Bitteswell, Hatfield, G-9-430 (1-12-75), Danish AF Esk.724, ET-272, 35-272. Cockpit. Arr 19-1-15 [16]	1-22
❑	XG254	'A'	Hawker Hunter FGA.9	56	ex Clacton, Coltishall, Weybourne, Coltishall 8881M (9-12-85), St Athan, 1 TWU, 2 TWU, TWU, 229 OCU, 54, Handling Sqn, 54. Arrived 19-2-02. 54 Sqn colours [8]	1-22
❑	XG329		EE Lightning F.1	59	ex Swinderby, Cranwell 8050M (8-7-69), A&AEE, Warton. Arrived 1993 [8]	1-22
❑	XG518		Bristol Sycamore HR.14	55	ex Sunderland, Balloch, Halton 8009M (7-5-68), Wroughton, Khormaksar SF, El Adem SF, Habbiniya SF, CFS, Amman SF. Arrived 24-2-97 [8]	1-22
❑	XG523	'V'	Bristol Sycamore HR.14	55	ex Sunderland, Hayes, M Wallop, Ternhill 7793M, CFS, JEHU. Crashed 25-9-62. Arrived 25-1-97. Cockpit [8]	1-22
❑	XH892	'J'	Gloster Javelin FAW.9R	57	ex Duxford, Colerne 7982M, Shawbury, 29, 64, 23. AWA-built	1-22
❑	XJ482	'713'	DH Sea Vixen FAW.1	58	ex Wimborne Minster, Tarrant Rushton, Lee-on-Solent A2598 (3-8-69), 766, Thurleigh, 700Y. Christchurch-built. Arrived 25-11-79. 766 Sqn colours	1-22
❑	XK624	'32'	DH Vampire T.11	56	ex Lytham St A', Blackpool, CFS, 3 FTS, 7 FTS, 1 FTS, 23 GCF, CFS, 7 FTS. Hawarden-built. SOC 14-12-71. Arr 11-4-80	1-22
❑	XM279		EE Canberra B(I).8	59	ex Doncaster, Flixton, Firbeck, Nostell Priory, Cambridge, 16, 3. SOC 19-3-74. Acquired 3-94. Cockpit. 16 Sqn, Shark's mouth colours [8] [17]	1-22
❑	XN304	'W'	Westland Whirlwind HAS.7	59	ex Bedford, Henlow, Wroughton, Shrivenham, W'ton, 705, JHDU, 848. SOC 7-1-76. Arrived 19-7-82. 848 Sqn c/s	1-22

☐	XN500		Hunting Jet Provost T.3A	60	ex Southampton, Farnborough, East Midlands, Ipswich, Oxford, 7 FTS, RAFC, 3 FTS, RAFC, 3 FTS, RAFC. SOC 26-1-93. Arrived 7-10-07. CSE logo	[8]	1-22
☐	XR485	'Q'	W'land Whirlwind HAR.10	63	ex Wroughton, 2 FTS, CFS. SOC 29-1-81. Arrived 19-2-81		1-22
☐	XV497*	'D'	McD Phantom FGR.2	69	ex Bentwaters, Waddington, Coningsby 9295M, 74, 1435 Flt, 23, 228 OCU, 92, 19, 92, 29, 19, 228 OCU, 92, 23, 56, 228 OCU, 17, 228 OCU, 41, 6. 23 Sqn / Falklands c/s. Arrived 28-7-20	[2]	1-22
☐	ZA175		HS Sea Harrier F/A.2	81	ex Yeovilton, 899, 800, 899, 800, 899, 801, 800, 899, 800, 801, 899. Arrived 27-7-04. 899 Sqn colours	[2]	1-22
☐	-		Folland Gnat T.1 CIM	65	ex Cosford, Wolverhampton. Procedures trainer, forward cockpit. Folland-built. Arrived 19-1-15		1-22
☐	A-528		FMA Pucará	79	ex Sunderland, M Wallop, Cosford, Abingdon 8769M, Stanley, Argentine AF. Arrived 24-7-94. *Toto Juan*	[18]	1-22
☐	79	'2-EG'	Dassault Mystère IVA	54	ex Sculthorpe, FAF, ET.2/8, 314 GE, EC.1/5. Last flown 3-5-78, arrived 18-11-78. Suez stripes	[19]	1-22
☐	'157/18'		Fokker D.VIII scale rep	84	BAPC.239, ex '694', Lowestoft. Arrived 1991, stored		1-22
☐	'1972' *and* '3794'		Mikoyan-Gurevich MiG-15*bis Fagot*	56 3794	ex Duxford, Czech AF. Letov-built S-103. Czech AF colours to stb, Polish to pt. Arrived 14-8-07		1-22
☐	42196		NAA F-100D-11-NA Super Sabre	54	ex Sculthorpe, French AF, 54-2196 USAF 48th FBW, 45th FS. Last flown 22-2-77, arrived 18-3-78. 'Skyblazers' colours	[19]	1-22
☐	55-4433 '433'		Lockheed T-33A-5-LO	55	ex Sculthorpe, French AF 803rd ABG. Last flown 25-1-78, arrived 21-7-78. 20th FBG colours	[19]	1-22
☐	6289 *and* FG-289	'2W'	NAA T-28C Trojan N99153	57	ex East Ham, France, N99153, Zaire AF FG-289, Congo AF FA-289, USN 146289. Crashed 14-12-77. Arrived 28-5-81. Fuselage. Zaire AF colours to port, USN VT-3 to stb	[20]	1-22

■ **[1]** Jenny Wren built using the wings of Luton Minor G-AGEP. **[2]** Airframes on loan: Thunder balloon G-BJZC (Mobberley Balloon Collection); Striker G-MTFK; Canberra WG789 (Steve Pickup); Sea Hawk WV838, Sea Harrier ZA175 (IWM, Duxford); Phantom XV497 **[3]** Designed and built by Peter Lovegrove. **[4]** Rooster and Pegasus donated by the widow of the late John M Lee, who also built the wings of the museum's Colditz Cock. **[5]** Striker was the last aircraft to fly from Flixton before the runways were broken up. **[6]** Penrose Pegasus 2 is a reproduction of the original Harald Penrose example. **[7]** See comments under Note [10]. **[8]** Airframes on loan from Ian Hancock. **[9]** Built by, or for, George Pine, proprietor of Pine's Airways of Porthcawl – operators of Fox Moth G-ACEX and Porthcawl's Rest Bay Aerodrome. It appeared at annual displays at Rest Bay, up to 1938, but it's believed not to have flown. Skeletal remains substantially rebuilt by Stan Brett at Andrewsfield 1980-81. **[10]** Goldfinch Amphibian 161 was built by the late Flt Lt Leslie 'Bill' Goldfinch at his home in Wiltshire. His illustrious career included the designing of the Colditz Cock glider during his time 'banged up' - the museum has a replica on show. Unfinished, the Goldfinch was intended as a scale taxiable aircraft, inspired by the Loening OA-1 Air Yacht, using Jodel D.11 wings and other components. The '161' bit comes from the plans number for the D.11 that 'donated' its wings. **[11]** Fairchild 24 (pre-Argus) was the second C8F built and served with the Civil Air Patrol, fitted with bomb racks and flare chutes as a sub 'scarer'. **[12]** The extreme nose section (10ft long) of a Felixstowe flying-boat, once a potting shed, while not fitting our criteria totally, represents a singular survivor. It would be great if it were found to be B&P-built. Another section of Felixstowe, about 8ft long, is on hand from the RAF Museum. **[13]** PT-27 is a composite donated by Tibenham-based Black Barn Aviation. **[14]** Spitfire XVI fuselage is centred on the original skin of TD248 acquired from Historic Flying. The skin, coupled with an original frame No.19, and a fibreglass tail section has created a fuselage containing many original fittings. (TD248 is airworthy as G-OXVI.) After much thought, this is best termed a 're-creation'. **[15]** WE168 was vandalised during its time with its previous owner. Exceptionally well equipped inside, it was stripped out and the battered 'outer' airframe disposed of. N&SAM purchased all of the 'innards' and a completely new 'cutaway' cockpit, including outer skin, was created in wood and metal. Like TD248, it is best termed a 're-creation'. **[16]** Hunter T.53 cockpit is painted as the one-off RAE test-bed T.12 XE531, which was written off 17-3-82. The rear fuselage of ET-272 is at East Midlands, Leics. **[17]** XM279 returned from refurbish at Doncaster by 10-20. **[18]** On loan from the Army Flying Museum, Middle Wallop, Hampshire. **[19]** Airframes from the National Museum of the USAF's Loan Program. **[20]** First use of N99153, registration re-allocated to former Zaire FG-576 (140576) after the crash of 14-12-77.

FOXHALL west of the A12, south of Kesgrave

Suffolk Aviation Heritage Museum: On the southern edge of the former Martlesham Heath airfield, close to what was the Runway 04 threshold, the venue is run by the **Suffolk Aviation Heritage Group**. The cavernous building, used by the USAF for communications and known as 'The Roc', was last used by the 2164th Comms Squadron up to the early 1990s.
◆ *Off the A12, Foxhall Road, IP10 0AH* | Facebook **@suffolkaviationheritagegroup**

☐	G-BAXX	Cessna F.150L	73	ex Monewden, Bruntingthorpe, Cambridge, Shobdon, Barnstaple. Reims-built. Damaged 21-9-78, de-reg 8-10-80. Fuselage, arrived 8-7-18		1-22
☐	–	Woodhams Sprite	60	BAPC.17, ex Canterbury, Manchester, Hooton Park, Wigan, Irlam, Wigan, Liverpool, Leamington Spa. Unfinished	[1]	1-22

☐ –		Blériot XI replica	18	BAPC.479. Built by Telford 'Tom' Thompson locally	[2]	1-22
☐ WH798		EE Canberra PR.7	54	ex Canterbury, Cardiff-Wales, WAM, CTTS St Athan 8130M, 31, 17, 13, 80, 17, 100, 542. SOC 30-11-81. Cockpit		1-22
☐ XD506		DH Vampire T.11	54	ex Staverton, Bentham, Staverton, Thrupp, Staverton, Swinderby, Finningley 7983M (7-9-67), CATCS, CNCS, 5 FTS, 206 AFS. Hawarden-built. Arrived 7-10-17		1-22
☐ XD616		DH Vampire T.11	55	ex Staverton, Bentham, Staverton, London Colney, Hoddesdon, Old Warden, Woodford, Chester, St Athan, 8 FTS, 1 FTS, 8 FTS, 65. SOC 6-11-67. Fairey-built. Cockpit. Arrived 7-10-17		1-22
☐ XG274*	'71'	Hawker Hunter F.6	56	ex Newmarket, Ipswich, Halton 8710M (30-11-81), 4 FTS, 229 OCU, 66, 14. Arrived 11-21		1-22
☐ XN629	'49'	Hunting Jet Provost T.3A G-KNOT	61	ex Bentwaters, N Weald, G-BVEG (re-reg 9-6-99), XN629, 1 FTS, 7 FTS, 1 FTS, CFS, RAFC, 3 FTS. CoA 10-10-07, de-reg 21-6-07. Forward fuselage		1-22

■ [1] All-wood, single-seat twin-boom pusher, designed and built by a team led by Bill Woodhams. Work stopped in 1965 and it joined the Northern Aircraft Preservation Society (today's TAC) on 25-5-69. [2] Blériot honours Ipswich-born Edith Maud Cook, Britain's first female pilot. She took instruction at the Blériot School at Pau, France, in late 1909.

FRAMLINGHAM AERODROME or Parham, on the B1116 north of Woodbridge
Parham Airfield Museum: incorporating the **390th Bomb Group Memorial Air Museum** and the **Museum of British Resistance**. The tower houses a superb museum dedicated to the 390th and USAAF Station No.153. The Resistance Museum is dedicated to the work of the Auxiliary Units - the so-called 'Stay Behind' cells in the event of an invasion.
◆ *Off the A12, IP13 9AF* | **01728 621373** | **parhamairfield@yahoo.co.uk** | **www.parhamairfieldmuseum.co.uk**

HALESWORTH on the A144 south of Bungay
Halesworth Airfield Station 365 Memorial Museum: Established on the former Eighth Air Force airfield (also known as Holton); this museum includes an exceptional range of exhibits.
◆ *Sparrowhawk Way, Upper Holton, IP19 8NH* | **01986 875084** | **halesworthairfieldmuseum@outlook.com** | **www.halesworthairfieldmuseum.co.uk**

John Flanagan: On 19th September 2020 the Carvair departed to elsewhere in the county for restoration. It will return.

☐ CF-EPV		ATEL Carvair	43	ex Beccles, Thorpe Abbotts, Fritton Lake, Woodbridge, Southend, EI-AMR, N88819, C-54D 42-72343. Cockpit. Off-site - see notes above	[1]	9-20

■ [1] C-54 N88819 re-flew as a Carvair on 19-4-63.

HONINGTON AIRFIELD on the A1088 southeast of Thetford   EGXH
RAF Regiment: The Tornado 'squadron' provides training for airfield defence and patrol. *W&R27* (p261) moved Tornado ZD744 here from Marham, Norfolk; it tenaciously remained in Norfolk.

☐ XK526		Blackburn Buccaneer S.2	60	8648M (10-3-80), ex RAE Bedford, RRE, A&AEE, RAE, A&AEE, RAE, A&AEE. Displayed		4-21
☐ ZA553	'045'	Panavia Tornado GR.4	81	ex Marham, GR.1, 31. First noted 7-19		7-21
☐ ZA587	'055'	Panavia Tornado GR.4	81	ex Marham, GR.1, 15. SOC 25-6-19		7-21
☐ ZA613	'076'	Panavia Tornado GR.4	81	ex Marham, GR.1, 15. First noted 7-19		7-21
☐ ZD711	'079'	Panavia Tornado GR.4	84	ex Marham, St Athan, GR.1, DARA. Arrived 10-4-18		7-19
☐ ZG752	'129'	Panavia Tornado GR.4	91	ex Marham, GR.1, 13. SOC 25-6-19		7-21

HORHAM on the B1117 east of Eye
The Red Feather Club: The official museum of 95th Bomb Group, operated and managed by the **95th Bomb Group Heritage Association**, has brought back to life the former NCOs' club at USAAF Station 119, once home to the B-17s of the 95th. Included in the exhibits are the famous murals painted by S/Sgt Nathan Bindler.
◆ *Horham Road, IP21 5DG* | **email** via website | **www.95thbg-horham.com** |

IPSWICH

Everett Aero: There are several storage sites, including a former airfield, and 'Ipswich' is a generic label.
Departures: Dominie T.1 XS734 had moved on by 4-20; **Harrier** GR.3 XZ996 exported to Germany for the museum at Gutersloh by 10-20; **Hawk** T.1W XX292 exported to the Pima Air and Space Museum, USA, in mid-2020; **Jaguar** GR.3A XX720 to Maidstone, Kent, in 2018; **Jet Provost** T.3A XN586 to Jurby, Isle of Man, 3-20; as predicted in *W&R27*; T.5A XW370 had moved on by 4-20; **Lynx** AH.7 XZ208 had gone by 4-20; AH.7 XZ678 to North Weald, Essex, 13-10-21; AH.7 XZ680 to East Grinstead, Surrey, 9-19; AH.9 ZG889 to White Waltham, Berks, 10-8-21; **Phantom** FGR.2 XT907 cockpit departed to become a simulator in the 'Coventry' area; FGR.2 XV497 moved, to Flixton, Suffolk, on 28-7-20; **Scout** AH.1 XP905 to Doncaster, S Yorks, by 7-21; XR601 had gone by 4-20. *W&R27* (p262) noted Lynx AH.9 ZF539 as departing to the 'Southend area' – not bad, it moved to Kessingland, Suffolk. ◆ **Strictly** *private locations - by prior arrangement* **only | www.everettaero.com**

❑ G-OBYT		Bell JetRanger	70	ex G-BNRC, SOAF 601. Agusta-built. CoA 12-7-03	N6-21
❑ XG196	'31'	Hawker Hunter F.6A	56	ex Mytchett, Bracknell 8702M (24-11-81), Kemble, 1 TWU, TWU, 229 OCU, 19. 234 Sqn colours. Arrived 27-3-14	9-21
❑ XT624		W'land Scout AH.1 G-NOTY	66	ex N Weald, Plymouth. CoA 28-10-10, de-reg 15-11-18	5-19
❑ XV460	'R'	McD Phantom FGR.2	69	ex BCWM - Bentwaters, Ipswich, Sunderland, Coningsby, Wattisham, 74, 56, 19, 92, 29, 228 OCU, 92, 228 OCU, 19, 56, 228 OCU, 31. Arrived 4-5-16. Cockpit	9-21
❑ XW267	'SA'	HS Harrier T.4	70	ex Toton 9263M (23-10-96), Boscombe D, SAOEU, RAE, A&AEE, RAE, 233 OCU, 1, 233 OCU, T.2, 233 OCU. Arrived 12-3-14	12-19
❑ XW321	'MH' and '62'	BAC Jet Provost T.5A	70	ex Cosford, 9154M (8-7-92), Shawbury, 1 FTS, 7 FTS, RAFC, 3 FTS. Arrived 10-13	9-15
❑ XW418	'MT'	BAC Jet Provost T.5A	72	ex Cosford, DSAE, 9173M (17-12-92), Shawbury, 1 FTS, 7 FTS, CFS, 3 FTS, Leeming SF, 3 FTS. First noted 4-17	9-21
❑ XX139		SEPECAT Jaguar T.4	73	ex St Athan, 16, T.2, 226 OCU, 6, 226 OCU, JOCU. Arr 27-10-05	11-21
❑ XX144	'U'	SEPECAT Jaguar T.2A	74	ex Shawbury, 16, 226 OCU, 6, 54, 226 OCU, JOCU	11-21
❑ XX836	'ER'	SEPECAT Jaguar T.2A	75	ex Shawbury, 6, 17, 14, 54	11-21
❑ XX838	'FZ'	SEPECAT Jaguar T.4	75	ex St Athan, 41, 16, T.2, Shawbury, 226 OCU, 17, 226 OCU	11-21
❑ XX842		SEPECAT Jaguar T.2A	75	ex St Athan, 41, 16, Warton, T.2, 16, 41, Shawbury, ETPS/RAE, 6, 2, 41, 54, 226 OCU. Arrived 10-8-06	8-17
❑ XZ213		Westland Lynx AH.1	79	ex Fleetlands, Wroughton, M Wallop TAD.213, Wroughton, 659. Accident 20-3-86. First noted 5-19	5-19
❑ XZ234	'630'	Westland Lynx HAS.3S	77	ex Staverton, M Wallop, 702, 815, 702, 815, HAS.2, 815, 702, 700L, Westland. SOC 20-12-10. First noted 9-17	11-21
❑ XZ366	'FC'	SEPECAT Jaguar GR.3A	76	ex St Athan, 41, GR.1, 41, Shawbury, 2	8-18
❑ XZ735		Westland Lynx HAS.3GMS	81	ex Fleetlands, M Wallop, 815, 829, 815, HAS.2, 815. Cabin	11-21
❑ ZD249	'635'	Westland Lynx HAS.3S	82	ex Fleetlands, SOC 20-4-10, 815, 702. A&AEE	11-21
❑ ZD258	'365'	W'land Lynx HMA.8SRU	83	ex 815, 702, 815, HAS.3, 702, Gib Flt. NEA 8-14. XZ689's boom	1-20
❑ ZD274*	'M'	Westland Lynx AH.7	83	ex M Wallop	11-21
❑ ZD566	'305'	Westland Lynx HMA.8	85	ex Fleetlands, 702, HAS.3, 702. First noted 5-19	11-21
❑ ZE375		Westland Lynx AH.9A	85	ex M Wallop. SOC 23-9-16. Arrived 18-11-16	8-18
❑ ZE379		Westland Lynx AH.7	86	ex Dishforth, Arborfield, 655, 657, 655. Cabin - boom of ZD283	11-21
❑ ZG478		BAe/McDD Harrier GR.9	90	ex Yeovilton, Cottesmore. Crashed Khandahar 14-5-09	11-21
❑ ZG884		Westland Lynx AH.9A	90	ex M Wallop. SOC 23-9-16	8-18
❑ ZG885*		Westland Lynx AH.9A	91	ex M Wallop. Arrived 24-9-19	11-21
❑ ZG886		Westland Lynx AH.9A	91	ex M Wallop. SOC 23-9-16	9-18
❑ ZG887		Westland Lynx AH.9A	91	ex M Wallop. SOC 23-9-16. First noted 9-17	11-21
❑ ZG888		Westland Lynx AH.9A	91	ex M Wallop. SOC 23-9-16. First noted 9-17	11-21
❑ ZG916		Westland Lynx AH.9A	91	ex M Wallop	11-21
❑ ZH658		BAe/McDD Harrier T.10	94	ex Cottesmore, St Athan, Wittering, 20. Cr 16-4-03. Cockpit	11-21
❑ ZH665		BAe/McDD Harrier T.12	95	ex Marham, Cottesmore, T.10. Cockpit, first noted 12-14 [1]	9-15
❑ ZH806	'730'	HS Sea Harrier F/A.2	98	ex Shawbury, 899, 800, 801, 899. SOC 28-7-05. Arr 2-2-06	8-17
❑ ZH812	'005'	HS Sea Harrier F/A.2	98	ex Marham, Yeovilton, 801, 899, 801. SOC 29-3-06. Arrived 22-6-10	8-17
❑ -		BAe/McDD Harrier GR.5	~	test rig	5-19
❑ -	'TR001'	Eurofighter Typhoon	~	ex Brough. Fatigue rig. First noted 9-15 [2]	9-15
❑ H-07		Agusta 109BA	92	ex Woodmancote, France, Belgian Army. First noted 9-17	1-18

■ **[1]** ZH665 was handed over to the US for storage and spares reclamation at AMARC, Arizona 3-4-12: it possibly went noseless – comments? **[2]** Rig based on the 7th UK-built Typhoon airframe and is known as 'P-MAFT' - Production Major Airframe Fatigue Test.

KESGRAVE on the A12 east of Ipswich
The long-derelict L-21B *may well* remain as a landmark.

☐ MM54-2372	Piper L-21B	54	ex Woodbridge, Italian Army 'EI-184', I-EIXM, USAF 54-2372	5-18

KESSINGLAND on the A12 south of Lowestoft
Kessingland Beach Holiday Park: Offers 'Helibus Glamping' in a Lynx and promises an 'Airbus A320 pod', that will sleep four.
◆ *By prior arrangement* **only**

☐ ZF539*	Westland Lynx AH.9	87	ex Ipswich, M Wallop. First noted 5-20	8-21

LAKENHEATH AIRFIELD on the A1065 south of Brandon
EGUL

USAF Lakenheath, 48th FW – Wings of Liberty Memorial Park ◆ *By prior permission* **only**

☐ 'BM361' 'XR-C'	V-S Spitfire V FSM	99	BAPC.269, 71 'Eagle' Sqn, Chesley Peterson colours	3-20
☐ '65-777'	McD F-4C-15-MC 63-7419	63	ex Alconbury, Texas ANG. 48th TFW colours	6-21
☐ 74-0131	McDD F-15A-12-MC Eagle	74	ex 122 TFS / Louisiana ANG	6-21
☐ 68-011	GD F-111E-CF Aardvark	68	ex Upper Heyford, 20 TFW. 48th TFW colours, *Miss Liberty*	6-21

Airfield: Classic announcement in *W&R27* (p263): "Last noted in October 2014, F-15B 76-0124 has been deleted." Not so...

☐ '63319'	NAA F-100D-16-NA	54	ex '54048', French AF. Displayed	
	'FW-319' Super Sabre 54-2269		Marked 'A2' on the fin	10-21
☐ 76-0124	McDD F-15B-15-MC Eagle	76	BDR. See note above	10-21

LAVENHAM AERODROME on the A1141 north of Sudbury
Stampe G-BHYI was flying by mid-2020, with the Tiger next. ◆ *By prior permission* **only**

☐ G-AIRK	DH Tiger Moth	39	ex N9241, 8 EFTS, 10 FIS, TTU, 2 CPF, 224. CoA 1-8-07	N2-19

LOWESTOFT on the A12 south of Great Yarmouth
Simply Spitfire: The Spitfire is available for hire. ◆ *By prior arrangement* **only** | **www.simplyspitfire.com**

☐ 'MK805' 'SH-B'	V-S Spitfire IX FSM	10	BAPC.426, 64 Sqn colours, *Peter John III*	[1] 12-19

■ [1] The *real* MK805 (once MM4084) is preserved in Italy.

MARTLESHAM HEATH southeast of Woodbridge, the A12 runs through the site
Martlesham Heath Control Tower Museum: The vista of a control tower amid a housing estate is quite surreal. Run by the **Martlesham Heath Aviation Society**, the museum contains a vast amount of material on an exceptional airfield with an incredible heritage. The car park for the museum was once revetments where the P-47s and P-51s of the USAAF's 356th FG used to park. Concrete sandbags that made the walls of one of these have been preserved.
◆ *Parkers Place, off Eagle Way, IP5 3UZ* | **secretary@mhas.org.uk** | **www.mhas.org.uk**

MILDENHALL on the A1304 east of Cambridge
Sim2do Flight Simulation Centre: In Gregory Road has a 'synthetic' Boeing 737 and F-35B and a *real* Lynx.
◆ *By prior arrangement* **only** | **www.sim2do.com**

☐ XZ195	Westland Lynx AH.7	79	ex Hixon, Fleetlands, M Wallop, 672. Cockpit	12-21

MILDENHALL AIRFIELD on the A1304 east of Cambridge
USAF Mildenhall: The plan to close the base was cancelled during 2020. The Cayuse that was issued to the 352nd SOG for loading training is *thought* to be still held, despite an ancient 'last noted' date.

☐ 69-15979	Hughes OH-6A Cayuse	69	ex Hurlburt Field, USA. Training aid	10-14

NEWMARKET Hunter F.6 XG274 moved to Foxhall, Suffolk, in late November 2021.

ROUGHAM, or Bury St Edmunds, north of the A14 east of Bury St Edmunds
Rougham Tower Association: Much of the former B-17 airfield survives, including the superbly-preserved tower. Displays are dedicated to the men and the memories of the 322nd and 94th BGs and there are poignant memorials.
◆ *Off A14 east of 'Bury, Rougham Industrial Estate, IP33 7QB* | **07931 971771** | **email** via website | **www.rctam94th.co.uk**

STOWMARKET on the A14 east of Bury St Edmunds

Giles Howell: The EE P.1B is *believed* to still be in the area for restoration and eventual display.

❑ XA847	EE P.1B	57	ex Portsmouth, Southampton, Hendon 8371M,
			Farnborough, A&AEE, EE. Last flight 21-4-66

8-15

WALPOLE on the B1117 southeast of Halesworth

Former **Blyth Valley Aviation Collection** cockpits: **not** available for public inspection.

❑ WE122	'845' EE Canberra TT.18	52	ex N Weald, Stock, Llanbedr, St Athan, Llanbedr, FRADU, 7, B.2, 98, 245, 231 OCU. Cockpit	2-16
❑ WE192	EE Canberra T.4	54	ex Long Marston, Firbeck, Winsford, Samlesbury, St Athan, 231 OCU, 360, 231 OCU, 39, 231 OCU, 3, 231 OCU. SOC 26-11-81. Cockpit	2-16
❑ WH953	EE Canberra B.6(mod)	55	ex Lowestoft, Stock, Farnborough, RAE. Short-built. Cockpit	2-16
❑ XH165	EE Canberra PR.9	60	ex Stock, St Athan, 1 PRU, 39, 13, 58. Short-built. SOC 10-4-94. Cockpit	2-16

WATTISHAM AIRFIELD north of the B1078, south of Stowmarket

Wattisham Station Heritage Museum: Run by the **Wattisham Museum Society**. Situated in the former Station Chapel during the airfield's USAAF days, the displays are dedicated to the airfield's incredible history from 1937 to date. The team has the use of a 'Cold War' hardened aircraft shelter which serves both as a workshop and storage site. Visitors can visit this as well as the museum on special occasions.

◆ **Note:** *Remained closed throughout 2020 and 2021, hopes to open again in the spring of 2022 – check with the website. Within an Army base,* **visits must be pre-booked.** | wshmuseum@gmail.com | www.wattishamstationheritage.org

❑ XG194	'N' Hawker Hunter FGA.9	56	ex North Luffenham, Cosford 8839M (25-10-84), 1 TWU, TWU, 229 OCU, 1, F.6, 92, 111, 43. Arrived 28-11-09 111 Sqn 'Black Arrows' colours	[1]	1-22
❑ XP743	EE Lightning F.3	64	ex Burton-upon-Trent, Stafford, Pendine, Leconfield, 29, 56, 29, 56, Wattisham TFF, 56. SOC 16-10-75. Arrived 6-09. 56 Sqn colours. Cockpit	[2]	1-22
❑ XT617	Westland Scout AH.1	65	ex airfield, Almondbank, Wroughton, 653, 660. F/n 6-15		1-20
❑ XT914	'Z' McD Phantom FGR.2	68	ex Brampton, Leeming 9269M (5-10-92), 74, 228 OCU, 92, 56, 228 OCU, 92, 228 OCU, 56, 228 OCU, 17, 14, 228 OCU. Damaged 22-5-92. Arrived 8-3-12. 74 Sqn colours		1-22
❑ XX444	Sud Gazelle AH.1	76	ex airfield, Fleetlands, 25 Flt, 662, 663, 656, 663, 656, 658, 656, 658, ARWS, ARWF. Westland-built		1-20
❑ XZ605	'L' Westland Lynx AH.7	79	ex M Wallop. NEA 8-13, arrived 28-4-14		1-22

■ **[1]** Restored to F.6 status and 'Black Arrows' colours when it was flown by Sqn Ldr Roger Topp, callsign *Blackjack Red 1*, from the famed 22-ship formations flown at Farnborough and Odiham in 1958. **[2]** XP743 owned by Ken Hayward.

No.3 Regiment, Army Air Corps / 24 Air Mobile Brigade / 7 Battalion, REME:

❑ XP907	W'land Scout AH.1 G-SROE	63	ex Ipswich, M Wallop, BSE Filton. CoA 20-3-06	[1] N2-19
❑ XX380	Sud Gazelle AH.1	74	ex Sunderland, Shawbury, Fleetlands. Westland-built. Displayed, at Gate 1	4-20
❑ XZ330	Sud Gazelle AH.1	77	ex M Wallop. Westland-built. Training aid	8-16
❑ ZA729	Sud Gazelle AH.1	80	ex Gütersloh, Shawbury, Fleetlands, 658, 1 Regt. 4 Regt, 661, 652. Westland-built. Training aid	12-17

■ **[1]** Registered to Saunders-Roe Helicopter Ltd – the Scout being a much developed SARO P.531.

SURREY

ASH on the A323 east of Aldershot

A Jaguar *should* still be kept at a *private* location in the area.

❑ XX751	'10' SEPECAT Jaguar GR.1	74	ex Ipswich, Syerston, Cosford 8937M (29-5-87), Abingdon, 226 OCU, 14. Arrived 12-5-16

5-16

BROOKLANDS or Weybridge, on the B374 south of Weybridge

Brooklands Museum: The 'Aircraft Factory' and 'Flight Shed' are a drop of museum fresh air. Beneath 'Flight Shed' are a workshop, store and archive. The repositioning of the Bellman hangar - the 'Factory' - has allowed the transformation of the other 'side' of Brooklands; that of the pioneer motor racing circuit: 'petrol heads' can bask in nearly 1,000ft of race circuit returned to its heyday. The clubhouse, the hill climb, the cars, motorcycles and push-bikes all add to the magic.

Within the site is the **London Bus Museum** - entry is included with the site ticket - **www.londonbusmuseum.com** There is a very active **Brooklands Members** organisation with plenty of benefits for regular visitors.

See under Dunsfold, Surrey, for the 'VC10; Langley, Berks, for the 'Flea'; the Gliding Heritage Centre at Lasham, Hampshire, for the Gull III, Kronfeld Drone, Scud I and Willow Wren; and East Midlands, Leics, for Beagle 206 G-ARRM.

◆ *Brooklands Road, KT13 0SL* | **01932 857381** | **info@brooklandsmuseum.com** | **www.brooklandsmuseum.com**

Aircraft Factory and Flight Shed:

❑	'G-EBED'		Vickers Viking replica	74	BAPC.114, ex 'R4', Chertsey, *Land Time Forgot*. Arr 27-10-87	1-22
❑	'G-AACA'		Avro 504K replica	68	BAPC.177, ex 'G1381', Henlow. Arrived 29-1-87	1-22
❑	G-AZLP		Vickers Viscount 813	58	ex Sunderland, Middleton St George, BMA, SAA ZS-CDT. Hurn-built. CoA 3-4-82; de-reg 19-12-86. Arr 14-11-13. Cockpit, partially sectioned, in primer	1-22
❑	G-CHOI		White 'Baby' Canard rep	13	1912 replica, ground runs. Arrived 2013 [1]	1-22
❑	G-CJAU		White Sports Mono rep	16	1912 replica, ground runs. Arrived 2016. Workshop [1]	1-22
❑	G-LOTI	'2'	Blériot XI replica	82	ex Bicester, Halton, Brooklands. CoA 19-7-82, de-reg 6-3-09. Arrived 1984, acquired 12-12-89 [2]	1-22
❑	G-VTOL		HS Harrier T.52 ZA250	71	ex ZA250, Dunsfold. CoA 2-11-86, de-reg 13-3-90. Arrived 6-4-89. Skyhook markings [3]	1-22
❑	–		S-D Demoiselle XX rep	99	BAPC.256. Arrived 1-99. Ground runs [1] [4]	3-20
❑	–		Vickers Vanguard EMU	59	ex East Fortune, South Kensington. Flightdeck mock-up, Trans Canada colours [5]	1-22
❑		'3'	Sopwith Tabloid rep	13	BAPC.354, floatplane, partially covered. Handed over 27-11-13 [6]	1-22
❑	'B7270'		Sopwith Camel F1 replica	77	ex Land's End, Duxford, Chertsey, G-BFCZ (CoA 23-2-89, de-reg 23-1-03), Westward Airways-built. Arrived 14-4-88. 209 Sqn colours. Ground-runs [7]	1-22
❑	'F5475'	'A'	Royal Aircraft Factory SE.5a replica	94	BAPC.250. Arrived 1996. *1st Battalion Honourable Artillery Company* [8]	1-22
❑	'K5673'		Hawker Fury I replica	94	BAPC.249. Arrived 1996. 1 Sqn 'A' Flt colours [9]	1-22
❑	N2980	'R'	Vickers Wellington Ia	39	ex 20 OTU, 37, 149. Ditched in Loch Ness 31-12-40. Arrived 27-9-85 [10]	1-22
❑	-		Vickers Wellington	11	BAPC.421. Arrived 2000. Forward fuselage [11]	1-22
❑	Z2389	'XR-T'	Hawker Hurricane II	40	ex Murmansk, Sov AF, RAF 253, 136, 247, 71, 249. Shot down 20-6-42. Arrived 14-10-97. 71 Sqn colours [12]	1-22
❑	WK198		V-S Swift F.4	53	ex Millom, Sunderland, Failsworth, Kirkham 7428M (23-7-57), Aldergrove, MoS. Arr 3-2-11. Fuselage, primer [13]	1-22
❑	XD816		Vickers Valiant BK.1	56	ex Henlow, Abingdon, BAC, 214, 148. Last flown 23-4-68, SOC 26-8-70. Arrived 9-88. Cockpit, 'silver' colours [14]	1-22
❑	'XF314'	'N'	Hawker Hunter F.51	56	ex Booker, Sandown, Tangmere, Dunsfold, G-9-439 (27-3-76), Danish AF E-412, Esk.724. Arrived 10-9-05. Stb primer / port 4 Sqn	1-22
❑	XP984		Hawker P.1127	64	ex Dunsfold, Lee-on-Solent, Manadon A2658 (12-2-76), RAE Thurleigh, (accident 31-10-75), RAE F'borough. Arrived 28-9-00 [15]	1-22
❑	XV741		HS Harrier GR.3	69	ex Selby, Gosport, Culdrose, A2608[3], A2607 (25-4-91), Cosford, 233 OCU, 3, 233 OCU, 3. Arrived 2-4-19. 1969 Transatlantic air race colours [16]	1-22
❑	ZA101		HS Hawk Mk.50 G-HAWK	76	ex Samlesbury, Warton, G-HAWK (de-reg 13-3-90), ZA101, XX155. Last flown 3-2-05, arrived 23-1-19	1-22
❑	–		BAC TSR.2 EMU	63	ex Newark, Farnborough. Arr 13-8-92. Cockpit, primer [17]	1-22

■ **[1]** Canard Pusher, Sports Monoplane and Demoiselle built by Julian Aubert. **[2]** Blériot built by Mike Beach. The company L Blériot (Aeronuatics) Ltd was set up at Brooklands, becoming Blériot and Spad Ltd at nearby Addlestone, Surrey. In turn it became the Air Navigation and Engineering Co (ANEC) in 1919. **[3]** G-VTOL on loan from BAE Systems. **[4]** Demoiselle built on site 1996-1999 and based on the 1909 version with wing-warping and the original method of construction, bamboo.

[5] Wooden mock-up, built in the very same hangar it is now displayed in. [6] Tabloid built under the leadership of Steve Green; representing the Schneider Trophy winner, flown by Howard 'Picky' Pixton at Monaco, April 1914, at 86mph. [7] There's *another* 'B7270' at Tattershall Thorpe, Lincs. [8] SE.5a built on site. [9] Fury built on site. There is *another* 'K5673' - see Morpeth, N&T. [10] *R-for-Robert* factoids: First flown, at Brooklands, by 'Mutt' Summers 16-11-39; with 149 Sqn took part in the ill-fated 'Battle of Heligoland Bight' 18-12-39; total time 330:20. [11] Wellington based on an unidentified Hawarden-built centre section acquired from a site in Shropshire, circa 1986 - and best classified as a recreation. [12] Hurricane was shot down by a Bf 109F of JG5, near Murmansk. [13] Swift is on loan from Unimetals Industries Ltd. Piloted by Mike Lithgow in Libya, WK198 took the world speed record to 735.7mph on 25-9-53; sadly an F4D-1 Skyray raised it to 752.9mph just 48 hours later! [14] Valiant on loan from RAF Museum. XD816 was the last of the type to fly. [15] P.1127 - the 6th prototype - on loan from BAE Systems and fitted with an unidentified Harrier GR.3 wing. [16] On loan from Paul Griffith. Returned to GR.1 status, including nose profile. XV741 was flown by Sqn Ldr Tom Lecky-Thompson out of a yard near St Pancras railway station on 5-5-69 as the RAF entrant in the *Daily Mail* transatlantic air race, landing in New York 5 hours and 57 mins later. [17] TSR.2 a 'boiler plate' built for ejection seat trials.

Aircraft Park and other areas:

☐ G-AGRU		Vickers Viking 1	46	ex Cosford, Soesterberg, Channel, Kuwait Oil, BWIA, VP-TAX, G-AGRU, BEA. CoA 9-1-64, de-reg 9-6-64. Arr 27-6-91		1-22
☐ G-APEJ		Vickers Merchantman	61	ex Hunting, ABC, BEA. *Ajax*. CoA 29-1-93, de-reg 15-11-96. Arrived 26-8-95. Cockpit, in 'Strat Chamber'		1-22
☐ G-APEP		Vickers Merchantman	61	ex Hunting, ABC, BEA. *Superb*. CoA 1-10-98, de-reg 28-3-97. Flew in 17-10-96		1-22
☐ G-APIM		Vickers Viscount 806	58	ex Southend, BAF, BA, BEA. Damaged 11-1-88, de-reg 1-3-91. Arrived 11-2-90. *Viscount Stephen Piercey*		1-22
☐ G-ARVM		Vickers VC10 Srs 1101	64	ex Cosford, BA, BOAC. CoA 5-8-80, de-reg 9-11-79. Arrived 19-10-06. BA colours. Fuselage		1-22
☐ G-ASYD		BAC 111-475AM	65	ex Filton, BAe, BAC. CoA 13-7-94, de-reg 25-7-94. Flew in 14-7-94. 'Fly By Light Technology'.		1-22
☐ G-BBDG		BAC/Sud Concorde 202	74	ex Filton. CoA 1-3-82, de-reg 10-8-84. Last flight 24-12-81. Arrived 5-6-04	[1]	1-22
☐ –		Roe I Biplane replica	85	BAPC.187. Unveiled 5-6-88. In 'Avro' shed	[2]	1-22
☐ –		Vickers Vimy replica	97	BAPC.420. Arrived 2008. Cockpit, centre section, engine nacelles, displayed as 'mural'. Vickers building		1-22
☐ –		Vickers VC10 EMU	~	test shell, cockpit. BOAC colours		1-22
☐ –		BAC/Sud Concorde SIM	72	ex Filton; in its own building		1-22
☐ A40-AB		Vickers VC10 1103	64	ex Sultan of Oman, G-ASIX, BCAL, BUA. Flew in 6-7-87		1-22
☐ NX71MY		Vickers Vimy replica	94	ex Dunsfold. Flew in 15-11-09. Vimy pavilion. Ground runs	[3]	1-22
☐ WF372	'A'	Vickers Varsity T.1	52	ex Sibson, 6 FTS, 1 ANS, RAFC, 201 AFS. SOC 25-3-76. Arrived 7-11-88		1-22
☐ XT575		Vickers Viscount 837	60	ex Bruntingthorpe, DRA Bedford, OE-LAG. SOC 1-7-93. Arrived 14-1-96. Cockpit		1-22
☐ E-421		Hawker Hunter F.51	56	ex Brooklands Tech, Kingston, Dunsfold, G-9-443 (16-5-76), Aalborg, Esk.724, Danish AF. Arrived 18-3-89		1-22

■ [1] *Delta-Golf* factoids: total hours 1,282, landings 633. [2] Roe Biplane largely built on-site by Mike Beach. [3] Vimy was officially handed over to the museum by Peter McMillan on 26-8-06.

Deep Store: Until mid-2020 the museum had an off-site store in Oxfordshire. This heading is a catch-all for all out-of-public view airframes, no matter how near or far they may be. A replica of the Eastbourne Monoplane of 1912 was commenced circa 2010 to perfect construction methods for the superb Sopwith Tabloid replica -see above. Only the fuselage was completed and it was put in store. It was transferred early in 2020 to Newquay, Cornwall. Ladybird G-MJPB departed to 'the locality' on 13th July 2021. ◆ **Not** *available for inspection.*

☐ G-BJHV		Voisin scale replica	r81	ex Redhill, Brooklands, Old Warden. De-reg 4-7-91. Arr 1987		3-20
☐ G-ROEI		Roe I Biplane replica	08	ex off-site, Filton, Brooklands. Built on site. Arr 2017	[1]	3-20
☐ –		Rogallo hang-glider	73	*Aerial.* On loan		3-18
☐ –		hang-glider	~	-	[2]	3-18
☐ –		BAC 111 EMU	~	flightdeck mock-up		1-21
☐ F-BGEQ		DH Tiger Moth	44	ex Hungerford, Brooklands, Chessington, Brooklands, French mil, Mk.I NL846, n/s. Morris-built	[3]	3-18
☐ WP921		DHC Chipmunk T.10	52	ex Croydon, Henley-on-Thames, Benson, G-ATJJ (de-reg		
	G-ATJJ			19-1-68), WP921, Colerne SF, Oxford UAS, HCMSU, 10 RFS, 10 RFS. SOC 16-7-73. Cockpit. Arrived 1995.	[4]	3-20

■ [1] Roe registered to Brooklands Museum. [2] Unidentified hang-glider, previously in the 'Balloon' Hangar. [3] Tiger stored off-site from 30-1-14 by BAE Systems. [4] Chipmunk on loan from Peter Smith.

CATERHAM west of the A22, north of Junction 6 on the M25

Nalson Aviation: The long established business continues to process light aircraft types for spares. Turn-around is swift.

◆ *By prior arrangement* **only | www.nalsonaviation.com**

CHARLWOOD west of the A23/A217 junction, north of Gatwick Airport

Gatwick Aviation Museum: Mostly housed in an impressive, purpose-built, display hall. Several aircraft are maintained in ground running condition. The team have embarked upon on an ambitious development plan that will include a cafe and expanded external displays. For those of such a mind, the grounds offer great views of Gatwick's traffic!

◆ *Lowfield Heath Road, Charlwood, RH6 0BT* | **01293 862294 | hello@gamc.org.uk | www.gamc.org.uk**

☐ 'G-RAFM'	Robinson R22	G-OTHL 87	ex Hendon, Redhill. CoA 2-3-00, de-reg 8-2-00	**due**
☐ -	BN Islander	~	ex Crawley, Bristow. Cockpit. First noted 8-17 [1]	1-22
☐ VZ638	Gloster Meteor T.7	49	ex N Weald, Hurn Southampton, G-JETM (de-reg 15-12-09),	
		G-JETM	Southend, Kemble, CAW, RAFC, 237 OCU, 501, Biggin Hill SF,	
			FCCS, 85, 54, 25, 500. SOC 12-1-72. Arrived 7-88. Black c/s	1-22
☐ WK146	EE Canberra B.2	54	ex Hull, Wroughton, Abingdon, Bicester, 59, 102.	
			Avro-built. SOC 12-5-67. Arr 2001. Cockpit, sectioned	1-22
☐ WP308	Percival Sea Prince T.1	52	ex Staverton, G-GACA (de-reg 15-12-09), Kemble, 750,	
	'572'	G-GACA	Sydenham, 750, Lossiemouth, 750. SOC 16-9-80.	
			Arrived 12-11-89. 750 Sqn colours	1-22
☐ WR982	'J' Avro Shackleton MR.3/3	58	ex Cosford 8106M (28-9-70), 201, 206, MoA, 205, 203, 206.	
			Arrived 7-89	1-22
☐ 'XE489'	Hawker Sea Hawk FB.3	54	ex Jet Heritage, Hurn G-JETH (de-reg 15-12-09), WM983,	
	'485'	G-JETH	Chilton Cantelo, Culdrose, 'SAH-6', A2511, FRU, 806, 811.	
			SOC 1-9-61. Arrived 10-10-87. 899 Sqn colours [2]	1-22
☐ XL591	'82' Hawker Hunter T.7B	58	ex Kemble, Ipswich, Colsterworth, Shawbury, 237 OCU,	
			208, 237 OCU, 208, 237 OCU, 4 FTS, RAE, 4 FTS,	
			229 OCU, FCS. SOC 11-10-93. Arrived 2002. 4 FTS colours	1-22
☐ XN923	Blackburn Buccaneer	62	ex Boscombe Down, West Freugh, A&AEE, RAE, A&AEE,	
	S.1		RAE, A&AEE, RAE, A&AEE, 700Z. SOC 17-5-54.	
			Arrived 23-3-90	1-22
☐ XS587	DH Sea Vixen	65	ex Hurn G-VIXN (de-reg 15-12-09), FRL, 8828M, RAE, FRADU,	
	FAW.2(TT)	G-VIXN	FRU, 899, 893. Hawarden-built. Last flown 6-6-84,	
			SOC 4-2-85. Arrived 9-90	1-22
☐ XV751	'AU' HS Harrier GR.3	69	ex Bruntingthorpe, Charlwood, Lee-on-Solent A2672,	
			A2760, 3, 1, 3, 20, 233 OCU. Arrived 4-10-95. 3 Sqn c/s	1-22
☐ ZF589	EE Lightning F.53	72	ex Bricket Wood, Portsmouth, Luxembourg, *Wing C'der*	
			(1999), Stretton, Warton, Saudi AF 218, 53-700, G-27-223.	
			Last flown 14-1-86. Cockpit. Arrived mid-2016 [3]	8-21
☐ -	Hawker Hunter F.51	56	ex Charlwood, Faygate, Chertsey, Dunsfold, G-9-448,	
		E-430	Esk.724, Dan AF. FAA colours, GA.11-style [4]	1-22
☐ 53-671	EE Lightning F.53	67	ex Portsmouth, Luxembourg, *Wing Commander* (1999),	
		ZF579	Stretton, Warton, Saudi AF 203, 53-671, G-27-41. Last	
			flown 14-1-86. Arr 18-4-00. Saudi AF colours	1-22
☐ J-1605	DH Venom FB.50	G-BLID 52	ex Duxford, G-BLID (de-reg 15-12-09), Swiss AF.	
			Swiss built. Arrived 27-10-89	1-22

■ **[1]** The Islander is a full-motion simulator created by Thales. The museum salvaged the cockpit; the remainder was scrapped. **[2]** When Jet Heritage was restoring FGA.6 XE489 (G-JETH) to flight it was found that the spar attachments had been cut - very probably when it was moved by road to Southend, Essex, 5-67. To get around this FB.3 WM983 was borrowed from the Sea Scouts at Chilton Cantelo, Somerset, 8-85 and its *entire* fuselage was used in G-JETH, along with the wings of XE489. By 3-87 the Sea Scouts got 'their' Sea Hawk back. It constituted the fuselage of XE489 plus the wings of 'WM983', which came from FGA.4 WV909 which had been fitted as far back as the mid-1960s when it was in service on the 'deck' at SAH Culdrose. Chilton Cantelo disposed of 'WM983' (but in the majority XE489) on 8-8-89 when it was sold in the Netherlands. **[3]** A long-lost cockpit, last in use at a paintball site at Bricket Wood, Herts. First flown on 29-6-72 this was the last production Lightning. **[4]** Presented by Adrian Wright of Aerospace Logistics - see below. Fitted with wings of XF418 and XG226 - for the latter see also East Midlands, Leics, and Manston, Kent.

Aerospace Logistics: Has a storage site here, while the main base is Horsham, W Sussex: there is some 'shuffling' of stock between the two. Sea King HC.4 ZF116 moved to <u>White Waltham</u>, Berks, on 21st January 2020 and was later followed by Mk.4X ZB506. Sea Kings HAS.5 XZ575 and HC.4 ZD476 had moved on by November 2021.

◆ **Strictly** *by prior arrangement* **only | www.asl-uk.com**

☐	XZ497	'126'	HS Sea Harrier F/A.2	82	ex St Athan, 801, A&AEE, FRS.1, 899, 801	11-21
☐	XZ595		Westland Sea King HAR.3	78	ex 202, 22, 202. First noted 7-18	11-21
☐	ZA130	'19'	Westland Sea King HU.5SAR	81	ex Gosport, 771, *Gannet* Flt, 706, 819, 824, Falklands, 826. First noted 7-18	11-21
☐	ZA312		Westland Sea King HC.4	81	ex Gosport, QinetiQ, 848, 707, 845, 846, 707, 846. F/n 7-18	11-21
☐	ZE369	'S'	Westland Sea King HAR.3	85	ex Horsham, Fleetlands, 22	8-20
☐	ZE698	'123'	HS Sea Harrier F/A.2	88	ex St Athan, 800, FRS.1, 800, 801,899, 801	11-21

CHERTSEY northeast of Junction 12 of the M25 and Junction 2 of the M3

Thorpe Park: Within this adventure wonderland *should* still be an Agusta A.109. | **www.thorpepark.com**

| ☐ | 'G-SARD' | Agusta 109A | 79 | ex Alton Towers, Redhill, N754AM. Crashed 9-10-06, | |
| | | G-DNHI | | CoA 13-6-08, de-reg 7-6-07. 'Coast Guard' colours | 8-14 |

COBHAM north of the M25, east of Woking

Delta Force Paintball: Surrey: ◆ *By prior arrangement* only | **www.paintballgames.co.uk**

| ☐ | - | Westland WG.30 | ~ | Displayed at site entrance | [1] | 1-20 |
| ☐ | XZ217 | Westland Lynx AH.7 | 79 | ex *Edge of Tomorrow*, Barby, Ipswich, Fleetlands, 655 | [2] | 6-21 |

■ **[1]** Believed to be WG.30-100 G-BIWY which was last noted at Weston-super-Mare, Somerset, in *W&R18* (p190) as being exported to Italy for Agusta in November 2000. **[2]** Identity confirmed.

DUNSFOLD AERODROME or even Dunsfold Park, on the A281 south of Guildford   EGTD

The clock is ticking: planning approval for 'Dunsfold Park - A New Surrey Village' with up to 1,800 houses was approved on 29th March 2018. See under Balcombe, W Sussex, for other plans for some of the site.
See under Balcombe, West Sussex, for a plan for a museum at Dunsfold Park.

Brooklands Museum: The last of 54 VC10s built has been maintained in taxiable condition by the museum. It was US registered in November 2021 - see under Newquay, Cornwall for more. In co-operation with the museum the **Hawker Association** is restoring the last Kingston-built Hunter T.7, XL623. When completed it will be displayed on a pole near to the former Hawker plant at Kingston. ◆ *By prior arrangement* only | **www.brooklandsmuseum.com**

☐	ZA150	'J'	Vickers VC10 K.3	70	ex Brize Norton, 101, 5H-MOG East African AW.	
		N150ZA			Arrived 24-9-13. Taxiable – see above, and page 342	1-22
☐	XL623		Hawker Hunter T.7	59	ex Woking, Newton, Cosford 8770M (31-12-82), 1 TWU, 74,19, 1, 43, 92, 208, 65. Arrived 22-7-18	1-22

Reg Day Memorial Museum: (Also known as the Dunsfold Airfield Museum): A volunteer crew maintains a fascinating museum devoted to the airfield's wartime and Hawker heritage. ◆ **Note**: *By prior arrangement* **only**. *Within the security compound:* **no** *access to other areas is permitted* | **info@regdaymemorialmuseum.co.uk**

Aviation Filming Ltd (previously Aces High): Having pioneered using a 'Jumbo' for film and advertising filming, a second example arrived in October 2020 (yet another one dropping two months later, for a separate organisation). Much of the hardware used in filming is transitory and only long-term 'stars' are included here. C-47A N147DC has been kept at North Weald, Essex, since late 2019. ◆ **Strictly** *by prior arrangement* **only** | **www.aviationfilming.com**

☐	G-BDXJ	Boeing 747-236B	80	ex *Casino Royale*, Air Atlanta Europe, BA G-BDXJ	
		N88892		(de-reg 12-1-11), N1792B. Flew in 25-5-05	1-22
☐	G-CIVW*	Boeing 747-436	98	ex Rhoose, Hurn, BA. CoA 18-4-21, de-reg 30-10-20 Arrived 22-10-20. . See also page 342	[1]	1-22
☐	'HB-VEM'	BAe Jetstream T.3	85	ex Manston, Cranwell, ZE441, Culdrose, 750, *Heron* Flt,	
		N437TH		750, *Heron* Flt, 750, G-31-667. Swiss Air Ambulance c/s	9-21
☐	N797EL	Boeing 737-500	93	ex Hurn, European, Braathens LN-BRX. Last flown 21-1-15. Arrived 16-9-18. Fuselage	5-19
☐	WV795	Hawker Sea Hawk FGA.6	54	ex Farnborough, Bruntingthorpe, Cranfield, B'thorpe, Hurn, Rhoose, Culdrose A2661, Halton 8151M, Sydenham, 738, 806, 700. SOC 17-3-71. 806 'Ace of Diamonds' colours	9-21
☐	XL621	Hawker Hunter T.7	59	ex Brooklands, Hurn, G-BNCX (de-reg-1-3-93), RAE,	
		G-BNCX		238 OCU, RAE. SOC 10-12-86. ETPS colours	9-21
☐	ZE395	HSA HS.125 CC.3	93	ex Northolt, 32. Flew in 25-3-15	9-21
☐	72+59	Bell UH-1D Iroquois	70	ex HEER. Dornier-built. First noted 12-18	[2]	9-21

❑ '335'	Mil Mi-24 *Hind-D*	~ ex Leavesden, '03 red', N Weald, Chester, Latvia, USSR	
		(3532461715415) Hungarian colours. Off-site	5-19
❑ 'RA-914B11'*	Mil Mi-8 *Hip*	~ first noted 8-20	9-21
❑ SL-01	W'land Commando Mk.2C	76 ex Sierra Leone, Qatar QA-23. First noted 8-15	9-21

■ **[1]** *Victor-Whisky* joined BA on 15-5-98; last service 17-7-20, amassing 90,617 hours. **[2]** Composite, includes elements of 73+01.

Others: *Lima-Yankee* brings to three the number of 'Jumbos'.

| ❑ G-BNLY* | Boeing 747-436 | 93 ex Rhoose, BA, N60659. De-reg 16-12-20. *City of Swansea.* | |
| | | Arrived 5-12-20 | [1] 1-22 |

■ **[1]** *Lima-Yankee* joined BA on 1-2-93 and carried out its last service 22-3-20, amassing 122,358 hours.

EAST GRINSTEAD on the A22 east of Crawley
A Lynx has arrived in the *general* area.

| ❑ XZ680* | 'N' Westland Lynx AH.7 | 80 ex Ipswich, Weeton, Hixon, M Wallop, 671, 653, 669, 671, 657, | |
| | | 656, 657, 656, 665, Garrison Air Sqn. Cabin, boom of XZ608 | 9-19 |

EGHAM on the A30 west of Staines
Air Forces Memorial - Commonwealth War Graves Commission: "He is not missing, he is here." This is a quote from Field Marshal Lord Plumer when he opened the memorial at Ypres in 1927, but it sums up beautifully the role of the famed Runnymede memorial. Here is a tribute to the aircrew of RAF, Commonwealth and allied forces that have no known grave. Currently 20,291 souls are commemorated. ◆ *Cooper's Hill Lane, TW20 0LB | www.cwgc.org*

Jeremy Hall: Using as many original parts as possible, Jeremy has created the forward fuselage (all 21ft of it) of a Lancaster. It 'does the rounds' of shows and events. See also Cornwall Newquay for another of Jeremey's creations.

| ❑ – | Avro Lancaster replica | ~ ex Woodford. *Hi Ho!, Hi Ho!* to port and *Maggie's* | |
| | | *Murderous Mission* to stb. Forward fuselage | 11-19 |

FARNHAM on the A31 southwest of Aldershot
At two separate *private* locations in the area are a Terrier and a Lightning: both are *believed* extant.

❑ G-ASYN	Beagle Terrier 2	47 ex Doncaster, Bruntingthorpe, Derby, Southend, Sibson,	
		Auster AOP.6 VF519, 661. Damaged 2-1-76, de-reg 26-10-78	2-12
❑ XS933	EE Lightning F.6	67 ex Langport, Terrington St Clement, Narborough,	
		Binbrook, 5, 11, BAC, 5, 56, 11. SOC 21-6-88. Cockpit	[1] 2-10

■ **[1]** See under Sunderland, T&W, for *another* 'XS933'.

FRENSHAM By mid-2021 Jodel DR.1050 G-ATAG had moved to 'Oxfordshire'.

GODALMING on the A3100, southwest of Guildford
Restoration of a former Soviet Spitfire is *believed* to make progress in the area.

| ❑ SM639 | V-S Spitfire IX | 44 ex Norwich, Colchester, Milden, Russia, USSR, Sov AF, | |
| | G-CKYM | RAF no service. CBAF-built. Recovered 1993. Arrived 5-05 | N1-19 |

GODSTONE junction of the A22/A25 east of Redhill
A *private* collector *should* have a Scout in the locality.

| ❑ XV124 | 'W' Westland Scout AH.1 | 67 ex Tattershall, Ipswich, Arborfield, M Wallop, Arborfield, | |
| | | M Wallop, Wroughton, 656, 653, 654 | 2-13 |

PIRBRIGHT on the A324 west of Woking
Army Training Centre, Pirbright Camp:

| ❑ XZ651* | 'O' Westland Lynx AH.7 | 80 ex M Wallop, AH.1. Arrived 24-6-20 | 6-20 |
| ❑ ZE380 | Westland Lynx AH.9A | 86 ex M Wallop. SOC 1-2-18. Arrived 9-12-19 | 6-20 |

REDHILL AERODROME south of South Nutfield, southeast of Redhill   EGKR
Last noted in September 2011, Aero 45 G-ATBH had moved to the Henley-on-Thames, Oxfordshire, area by 2018. Warrior G-BVIH was re-registered as G-GFCE and moved to 'Scotland' for completion. Last noted in January 2016, the hulk of Cessna F.152 G-BLWV has been deleted.

❑ G-BRNE	Cessna 152	80	ex N4082L. Crashed 13-6-09, CoA 15-2-10	N2-21
❑ G-BRUM	Cessna A.152	79	ex N4693A. CoA 15-6-08	N9-16
❑ G-NOIL*	BN Islander	73	ex 4X-AYR, G-BJWO, 4X-AYR, SX-BBX, 4X-AYR, G-BAXC. FBN-built. CoA 116-1-16, arrived 29-6-21	7-21

SUTTON
Simon Balch: ◆ *By prior arrangement* only

❑ XP853		Westland Scout AH.1	61	ex Dunkeswell, Bramley, Arborfield, M Wallop, 655		6-20
❑ XW796*	'X'	Westland Scout AH.1	65	ex Layer Marney, Hadleigh, Ipswich, Wattisham, M Wallop, Wroughton, 660, 659. Arrived 19-6-20		6-20
❑ ZH766		Northrop Chukar D.2	c94	ex Hemel Hempstead, Aberporth	[1]	5-18

■ [1] Not deployed until 2001; one and only launch failed 29-1-01. With parts from ZJ481, ex Culdrose and Manorbier.

WALTON ON THAMES
Adrian Windsor: *Should* have a Hunter cockpit in the area.

| ❑ E-420 | Hawker Hunter F.51 | 56 | ex Marlow, Ascot, Dunsfold G-9-442 (1-5-76), Danish AF E-421. Cockpit | 1-14 |

WHYTELEAFE on the A22 southeast of Croydon
Gary Brown: The Buchón project will appear in the guise of a *Battle of Britain* film 'extra', using as many original parts, including Bf 109, as possible. ◆ *By prior application* only

| ❑ - | Hispano Buchón FSM | ~ | ex Lingfield, Bf 109G 'FM+BB', Germany | 7-17 |

EAST SUSSEX
Includes the unitary authority of Brighton and Hove

BEXHILL on the A259 west of Hastings
A Swallow is under restoration at a *private* address in the locality.

| ❑ G-ACXE | Klemm L25cl Swallow | 34 | ex 'Hastings', Bagshot, Birmingham. CoA 7-4-40 | N2-18 |

BRIGHTON
No.225 Squadron Air Cadets: Lewes Road.

| ❑ WD370 | DHC Chipmunk T.10 | 51 | ex Hove, 3 AEF, 2 SoTT, 1 AEF, Hull UAS, 2 BTFS. SOC 12-3-75. Cockpit | 7-18 |

CHAILEY on the A275 north of Lewes
A pair of cockpits *should* still be with a *private* collector in the area.

| ❑ WH964 | EE Canberra E.15 | 55 | ex Bruntingthorpe, Cosford 8870M, St Athan, 100, 98. B.15, 98, Akrotiri Wing, 32, B.6, 12. Short-built. Cockpit | 12-11 |
| ❑ XG195 | Hawker Hunter FGA.9 | 56 | ex Sleap, Seighford, Macclesfield, Bitteswell, G-9-453 (12-2-76), 208, F.6, 1, 19. Cockpit | 12-11 |

CROWBOROUGH W&R27 (p271) recorded Wessex XS510 as bound for Scotland on 6th February 2019 - see Kinloss.

DITCHLING on the B2112 east of Hassocks
Blackberry Wood: Among a variety of 'dwellings' offered at the venue is a two-berth Wessex.
◆ *By prior arrangement* only | www.blackberrywood.com

| ❑ XS886 | '27' | Westland Wessex HAS.1 | 66 | ex Ipswich, Evesham, Birmingham, Lee-on-Solent A2685 (2-4-80), Wroughton, 771, 706, *Hermes* SAR Flt, 706, 826 | 12-21 |

FOREST ROW on the A22 south of East Grinstead

Bullswood Skirmish Paintball Centre: Within the extensive woodland site is a Cherokee Six. *Tango-Victor* was written out of *W&R25* (p79) at Popham. ◆ *By prior application* **only** | **www.bullswood.com**

| ❑ G-BSTV* | Piper Cherokee Six | 67 | ex Popham, N4069R. De-reg 10-5-10 | 5-20 |

HAILSHAM on the A22 north of Eastbourne

David Bird: Is restoring a Prentice. Fellow VR192 (G-APIT) is on loan at Brenzett, Kent. ◆ *By prior arrangement* **only**

| ❑ ZS-EUS | Percival Prentice | 49 | ex South Africa, SAAF Museum, ZS-EUS, G-AOPL, VS609, 7 FTS. Arrived 2010 | 9-20 |

HASTINGS

The former Afghan Hawker Hinds are *believed* stored in the locality. ◆ **Strictly private, not** *available for inspection*

❑ K5409	Hawker Hind	36	ex Kabul, Afghan AF, RAF, 211, 218, 57, 52	7-10
❑ K5462	Hawker Hind	36	ex Kabul, Afghan AF, India, RAF 113, 15	7-10
❑ K5554	Hawker Hind	36	ex Kabul, Afghan AF, RAF 211, 113, 12	7-10
❑ K6618	Hawker Hind	36	ex Kabul, Afghan AF, India, RAF 211, 98	7-10
❑ K6833	Hawker Hind	37	ex Kabul, Afghan AF, India, RAF 211, 82	7-10
❑ L7191	Hawker Hind	37	ex Kabul, Afghan AF, RAF ME, 21	7-10

LEWES Last physically noted in August 2000, Jodel D.112 G-AYMU has been deleted.

NEWHAVEN east of Brighton on the A259

Newhaven Fort: Robertsbridge Aviation Society (see below) has a display here. Also within the Fort (but not RAS originated) is a feature on the Royal Observer Corps and much else on World War Two.
◆ *Fort Road, BN9 9DS* | **01273 517622** | **fortinfo@waveleisure.co.uk** | **www.newhavenfort.org.uk**

ROBERTSBRIDGE on the A21 northwest of Hastings

Robertsbridge Aviation Centre: Run by the **Robertsbridge Aviation Society** (RAS), the museum is a barrage of artefacts covering many aspects of aviation. RAS has a close relationship with Newhaven Fort, East Sussex - qv.
◆ **Note**: *Due to the pandemic the centre remained closed throughout 2020 and 2021, with hopes to open again in the spring of 2022. Bush Barn, Silver Hill, TN32 5PA* | email *via website* | **www.robertsbridgeaviationsociety.com**

❑ WA630	Gloster Meteor T.7	49	ex Newhaven, Robertsbridge, Sevenoaks, Oakington SF, 4 FTS, 205 AFS, RAFC. SOC 16-11-62. Arrived 1991. Cockpit	1-22
❑ WE173	EE Canberra PR.3	53	ex Stock, Coltishall, Farnborough, RAE, 39, 69, Upwood SF, 58, 82. SOC 31-3-81. Arrived 1996. Cockpit	1-22
❑ WN907	Hawker Hunter F.2	54	ex Walpole, Ascot, St Athan, Colerne, Melksham 7416M (1-8-57), 257. AWA-built. Arrived 17-3-02. Cockpit	1-22
❑ XJ488	DH Sea Vixen FAW.1	58	ex Nottingham, New Milton, Portsmouth, Boscombe Down, A&AEE, 22 JSTU, A&AEE, DH, RRE, A&AEE, RAE, DH. Christchurch-built. SOC 23-3-72. Arrived 1997. Cockpit	1-22
❑ XP701	EE Lightning F.3	63	ex High Halden, Hawkinge, Binbrook 8924M (9-2-86), LTF, 5, 11, 56, 29, 111, 29, A&AEE. Arrived 1991. Cockpit	1-22
❑ XR681	Hunting Jet Provost T.4	63	ex Newhaven, Odiham, Abingdon 8588M, RAFEF, CATCS, 6 FTS, RAFC. SOC 1-10-71. Arrived 2002. Cockpit	1-22

ST LEONARDS-ON-SEA west of Hastings

Retrotec / Aero Vintage: See under Duxford, Cambs, for the associated **Historic Aircraft Collection of Jersey**. Retrotec is involved in The People's Mosquito project, which is in its early stages - **www.peoplesmosquito.org.uk**
   MS Criquet G-BPHZ returned to Duxford, Cambs, on 29-9-21.
◆ **Strictly private** *location*, **not** *available for inspection* | **www.retrotec-ltd.co.uk**

❑ K5600	Hawker Audax I	G-BVVI 37	ex Kirkham 2015M (18-6-40), SAC, 226. Westland-built. Off-site	[1]	5-19
❑ EF545	V-S Spitfire V	43	ex New Zealand, ZK-MKV, New Guinea, RAAF A58-149,		
		G-CDGY	EF545 n/s. Westland-built. Off-site	[2]	5-19

☐ 1342	Yakovlev Yak-1	G-BTZD	41	ex Sudbury, Audley End, Paddock Wood, USSR	[3]	1-20
☐ 4034	Messerschmitt		39	ex India, JG53, force-landed Kent 11-2-40.		
	Bf 109E-1	G-CDTI		Focke-Wulf-built. Salvaged 2002	[1]	5-19

■ **[1]** Registered to Aero Vintage Ltd. **[2]** Registered to Warbird Experiences 8-21. **[3]** Yak registered to HAC.

SEDLESCOMBE AERODROME on the B2244 north of Hastings

The HM.293 may be bound for 'the Midlands' for refurbishment and potential static display.

| ☐ G-AWFT | Jodel D.9 Bebe | 68 | CoA 22-7-69 | 9-21 |
| ☐ G-AXPG | Mignet HM.293 | 71 | CoA 20-1-77 | 9-21 |

In the locality a Spitfire restoration project is *believed* to be still current.

| ☐ BM539 | V-S Spitfire V | 42 | ex G-CGBI, BM539, 19, 485, 610, 411, 242. CBAF-built. | |
| | G-SSVB | | Crashed 9-7-43, excavated 8-07 | N12-21 |

TICEHURST on the B2099 west of Hawkhurst

A *private* site in the *general* area has gained a Wessex. The Lightning cockpit was previously listed under Wadhurst, below.

☐ XR502*	'Z'	Westland Wessex HC.2	63	ex Sevenoaks, G-CCUP (de-reg 7-1-13), Colsterworth,	
	N486KA			Fleetlands, 60, 72, WTF, 18, 1 FTU. SOC 16-3-00. F/n 8-21	8-21
☐ ZF587*		EE Lightning F.53	68	ex Headcorn, Reading, Portsmouth, *Wing Commander* (1997),	
				Portsmouth, Stretton, Warton, Saudi AF 215, 53-691,	
				G-27-61. Cockpit. Arrived 1-2-20	8-21

UCKFIELD

The **Hawker Typhoon Preservation Group** handed over a kit-of-parts to the Aircraft Restoration Company on 24th June 2021. Details of this project can now be found under the ARC section at Duxford, Cambs.

WADHURST The Lightning cockpit is now to be found listed under Ticehurst, above.

WEST SUSSEX

BALCOMBE on the B2036, south of Crawley

Wings World War Two Remembrance Museum: Run by Daniel and Kevin Hunt and friends. The quality of displays is excellent, including elements of Hampden I P1273 'PL-Q' salvaged from the Russo-Finnish border; the substantial remains of A-20G Havoc 43-21664, also acquired from Russia (and previously formally listed, but it lacks the cockpit). Other crash-site relics are a 51 Squadron Halifax; Hurricane II BD731 salvaged from Murmansk; two Mount Farm-based USAAF F-5B Lightnings and a pair of Nakajima Ki-43 Hayabushas from the Kurile Isles.

In January 2019 a new venture was announced, a museum at **Dunsfold**, Surrey, dedicated to the former airfield's prolific time as a Hawker/HSA facility and its wartime activity as a Mitchell haven: the acquisition of B-25 *Bedsheet* Bomber and a HS Kestrel forming part of the plot. Planning permission applications are understood to be in hand; for now potential exhibits will be listed below.

◆ Note: *Not all airframes listed will be on public display. Brantridge Lane, off High Beeches Lane, RH17 6JT* | **07769 688064** | info@wingsmuseum.co.uk | www.wingsmuseum.co.uk | www.facebook.com/wingskestrel

☐ G-AIUA	Miles Hawk Trainer III	40	ex Redhill, King's Lynn, West Chiltington, Benington,		
			Bushey, Old Warden, Duxford, Felthorpe, T9768, 10 AGS,		
			7 FIS, 15 EFTS, Wyton SF. Phillips & Powis-built.		
			CoA 13-7-67. Acquired 2003. Fuselage	[1]	1-22
☐ G-OJAS	Auster J1U Workmaster	52	ex Redhill, F-BJAS, F-WJAS, F-OBHT. Acquired 2003		1-22
☐ -	Bristol Beaufighter If	~	ex Australia, South Africa. Cockpit. Arrived 9-15	[2]	1-22
☐ -	Bristol Beaufort VIII	~	ex Australia, Papua New Guinea. Cockpit, arrived 3-20	[3]	1-22
☐ WD377	DHC Chipmunk T.10	51	ex Blackburn, Haverhill, Dumfries, 12 AEF, Glasgow UAS,		
			HCEU, 11 RFS, 2 BFTS. Crashed 29-7-66. Cockpit	[4]	1-22
☐ -	DHC Chipmunk T.10	51	ex South Molton, Firbeck, Salisbury, Stamford,		
			Blackburn, Radley. Forward cockpit	[5]	1-22

❑ WK127	'FO'	EE Canberra TT.18	54	ex Peterborough, Bassingbourn, Wyton 8985M, 100, 7, B.2, 10. Damaged 13-12-88. Avro-built. Arr 26-1-16. Cockpit	1-22
❑ XM468		Hunting Jet Provost T.3	60	ex Terrington St Clement, King's Lynn, Stock, St Athan, Halton 8081M (6-5-70), Shawbury, 6 FTS, RAFC. Cockpit	1-22
❑ 339		Nakajima B5N2 *Kate*	c44	ex Redhill, Kurile Island. Acquired 2003. Front fuselage	1-22
❑ '2100766'		Douglas C-47A-65-DL	42	ex N Weald, Woodley, Kew, Cranfield, 6W-SAF, F-GEFU,	
	'4U-D'	Skytrain		Senegalese AF, USAF MAAG Brussels, USAAF 42-100611. Long Beach-built. *Lilly Bell II*. Acquired 9-07. Cockpit and fuselage section	[6] 1-22
❑ 43-11137	'17'	Bell P-63C Kingcobra	43	ex Redhill, Kurile Island. Acquired 2003. *Little Toots*	[7] 1-22
❑ 43-36140		NAA B-25J Mitchell	43	ex Redhill, Kurile Island. Acquired 2003. Front fuselage	1-22
❑ 64-17657		Douglas B-26K Invader	64	ex Redhill, South Molton, Canterbury, Norwich, Ludham,	
		N99218		Booker, Canterbury, Southend, Chino, USAF, USAAF 43-22649. Arrived 2-10. *Victory Belle*. Cockpit	[8] 1-22

■ **[1]** See under Magister N3788 at Shuttleworth, Beds. **[2]** Beaufighter discovered in a scrapyard in Cape Town and restored by Peter Sledge, Warbird Restorations Downunder. **[3]** Beaufort is believed to be A9-555, which served with 100 Sqn RAAF. **[4]** Rear fuselage of WD377 can be found under Upper Ballinderry, N Ireland. **[5]** *Likely* bloodline of the Chipmunk that it is WG319 SOC 18-7-61 at Valley. **[6]** Cockpit of C-47A 6W-SAF has been grafted to the fuselage of C-47B 'FL586' (ex OO-SMA, N99346, Belgian AF K-1 / OT-CWA, 43-49240. **[7]** Also substantial remains of 44-4315, from the same source. **[8]** Heavily re-engineered B-26 Invader by On Mark Engineering at Van Nuys, California, given new USAF serial.

Dunsfold airframes: Held off-site, in different locations: inspection *not* possible.

❑ XS694	HS Kestrel FGA.1	64	ex Florida, NASA 520, Langley, USAF 64-18267, TES-CFE XS694. Crashed 27-8-67. Acquired 7-18	1-22
❑ 44-30861	NAA VB-25N-NC Mitchell	45	ex Crowland, Booker, N Weald, Duxford, 'HD368', Southend, Biggin Hill, N9089Z, B-25J 44-30861. *Bedsheet Bomber*. Acquired 7-19	1-22

BOGNOR REGIS on the A27 southeast of Chichester
Aviator Bar and Grill: At the Carlton Hotel on the Esplanade, has a Bandeirante cockpit above the bar.

❑ G-OHIG	Embraer Bandeirante	79	ex Stock, Alton, G-OPPP, XC-DAI, PT-SAB. CoA 30-4-96, de-reg 11-4-01. Cockpit	1-22

BRIGHTON CITY AIRPORT or Shoreham   EGKA
Airport Visitor Centre: Offers a wide array of archives and artefacts, and tours, on the incredible history of this aerodrome.
◆ *Pre-bookable tours only* | **01273 441061** | **https://flybrighton.com/visit-the-airport/airport-tours/**

Greater Brighton Metropolitan College: Motor and aero engineering campus. Two airframes, both last noted in December 2017, have been deleted: Tobago G-BOIU and Cessna 172 G-TOBY. ◆ *By prior arrangement* only | **www.gbmc.ac.uk**

❑ G-AVKL		Piper Twin Comanche	66	ex OY-DHL, G-AVKL, N8284Y. CoA 27-6-08, de-reg 28-9-07	7-21
❑ G-AWKX		Beech Queen Air A65	68	CoA 25-10-89, de-reg 19-12-90. Forward fuselage	7-21
❑ G-AWVJ		HP Jetstream T.2	68	ex Boscombe Down, 750, A&AEE, XX475, N1036S, G-AWVJ. Arrived 20-11-05	7-21
❑ G-SACD		Cessna F.172H	67	ex G-AVCD. Reims-built. CoA 27-7-00, de-reg 29-11-10	7-21
❑ XX491	'K'	HP Jetstream T.1	76	ex Ipswich, Culdrose, Cranwell, 45, 3 FTS, 45, 6 FTS, METS. SAL-completed. Arrived 10-11-05	7-21

Also:

❑ G-APAJ		Thruxton Jackaroo	40	ex Winchester, VH-KRK, G-APAJ, T5616, 63 GCF, 5 RFS, 12 RFS, 23 RFS, 25 RFS, 28 EFTS, 24 EFTS, Church Fenton SF, 10 FIS, 5 FIS. Jackaroo conversion 1958. De-reg 21-1-19	10-21
❑ 'WV514'	'CN'	P' Provost T.1 G-BLIW	54	ex Irish Air Corps 177. CoA 16-5-05	5-21
❑ WW447		Percival Provost T.1	55	ex Reading, Exeter, CATCS, CNCS, RAFC. SOC 24-1-69	5-21

Locally: 'SHAR' XZ459 moved to Tangmere, W Sussex, on 24th August 2020.

CHICHESTER
Chichester College: Westgate Fields ◆ *By prior arrangement* only | **www.chichester.ac.uk**

❑ F-GCSL	Boeing 737-222	68	ex Air Mediterrane, Euralair, United N9028U. Forward fuselage. 'Chichester Airways' titles: *Spirit of Chichester*	9-21

Jungle Paradise Adventure Golf Course: ◆ *By prior arrangement* only | www.chichestergolf.com
❑ OO-MHB   Piper Dakota 236   80 ex Squires Gate, Southend. Accident 20-10-90. F/n 2-15   6-21

Locally: An Airedale and a Safir are kept in the *general* area at a *private* location.
❑ G-AVKP*   Beagle Airedale   63 ex Peplow, SE-EGA. CoA 26-9-03   3-21
❑ G-BCFW*   SAAB Safir   62 ex Peplow, PH-RLZ. CoA 24-7-06   3-21

CHICHESTER AERODROME or Goodwood   EGHR
Boultbee Flight Academy: Experience flights and training operations, which are also staged from Solent Airport - Lee-on-Solent, Hampshire, have expanded considerably. The fleet includes Spitfire Tr.IX SM520 (G-ILDA), T-6G Texan 'KF402' (G-TEXN) and round-the-world Spitfire IX G-IRTY is also based.
◆ **Private** *working fleet: by prior arrangement* **only** | www.boultbeeflightacademy.co.uk
❑ 'MK392'   V-S Spitfire IX FSM   85 BAPC.184, ex 'EN398', Derby, N Weald, Duxford.
       'JE-J'   Specialised Mouldings-built. Displayed   9-21

Also: Last noted in July 2017, Cherokee G-ATJG has been deleted.

COPTHORNE on the A264 east of Crawley
Driver Wood Activity Centre: Old Hollow. ◆ *By prior arrangement* **only** | https//driverwoodactivitycentre.co.uk
❑ XZ205*   Westland Lynx AH.7   79 ex High Bradfield, *Edge of Tomorrow* (2014), Hixon,
                                                    M Wallop. First noted 4-20   6-21

CRAWLEY
Central Sussex College: Aeronautical Engineering department, College Road *should* still have its Traveler.
◆ *By prior arrangement* **only** | www.crawley.ac.uk
❑ G-BBCZ   American AA-5 Traveler   73 ex Redhill, N5482L. CoA 20-8-11, de-reg 30-7-20. Arr 1-17   1-17

Also: A Scout is under restoration in the *general* area.
❑ XT630   'X' Westland Scout AH.1   66 ex Wymeswold, Bruntingthorpe, Burbage, G-BXRL.
                 G-BXRL   Crashed 16-10-99, de-reg 20-3-00. First noted 4-18   7-19

FAYGATE on the A264 between Horsham and Crawley
Holmbush Paintball Centre ◆ *By prior arrangement* **only** | www.holmbushpaintball.co.uk
❑ H255   Sud SA.330L Puma   ~ ex Billingshurst (?), Horsham, Chilean Army. Arrived 19-11-14   3-21

FORD north of the A259 west of Littlehampton
Atop a lofty plinth on the *Hunter*ford site on the edge of the former airfield is Peter Hague's Hunter.
❑ WW654   '834' Hawker Hunter GA.11   55 ex Oving, Portsmouth, Culdrose A2664, A2753, (11-2-87), FRADU,
                                                          738, F.4, 229 OCU, 98, 4, 98. Squires Gate-built. SOC 11-2-87   1-22

HAYWARD'S HEATH on the A272 north of Brighton
No.172 Squadron, Air Cadets: Inside the TAVR centre in Eastern Road *should* be a Bulldog.
❑ XX520   'A' SAL Bulldog T.1   73 ex Newton 9288M (1-9-00), EM UAS, CFS, RNEFTS, 2 FTS   9-15

HORSHAM on the A264 southwest of Crawley
Aerospace Logistics: The company has a sub-site at Charlwood, Surrey. Puma 9L-LSG was acquired by May 2019, moving to Newark, Notts, on 1st October 2020. ◆ **Strictly** *by prior arrangement* **only** | www.asl-uk.com

❑ XV674   Westland Sea King   70 ex RAN spares, FAA Gosport A2669, 820, 819, 826,
                 HAS.6   HAS.5, 819, HAS.2, 819, HAS.1 819. First noted 10-16   8-21
❑ N16-114   '05' Westland Sea King   74 ex RAN, G-BCIA (de-reg 4-10-74), G-17-5.
                 Mk.50   G-BCIA   Arrived 6-14   8-21
❑ N16-125   W'land Sea King Mk.50   75 ex RAN, G-17-10. Arrived 6-14   8-21
❑ N16-238   '20' W'land Sea King Mk.50A   83 ex RAN, G-17-12. Arrived 6-14   8-21
❑ N16-239   '21' W'land Sea King Mk.50A   83 ex RAN, G-17-03. Arrived 6-14   8-21
❑ N16-918   W'land Sea King Mk.50B   79 ex RAN, FAA HAS.2 XZ918, 706, 820, 706, 814. Arrived 6-14   8-21

LONDON GATWICK AIRPORT

The UK Heritage Aviation Trust announced plans in September 2021 to move the Herald to a site at Sellinge, Kent.

☐ G-CEXP	HP Herald 209	68	ex Skyview, Channel Express, I-ZERC, G-BFRJ, 4X-AHO.	
			CoA 7-11-96, de-reg 22-3-96. Skyview colours	1-22
☐ I-DAVA	McDD MD82	86	ex ItAli Airlines. Last flight 21-10-10. Trygon Aviation titles	1-22

STORRINGTON on the A283 north of Worthing

A Luton Minor is stored at a *private* venue in the locality.

☐ G-AFIR	Luton Minor	38	ex Aylesbury, Cobham, Rearsby. CoA 30-7-71, de-reg 22-11-21	11-21

TANGMERE south of the A27, east of Chichester

Tangmere Military Aviation Museum: As well as the aircraft and a staggering collection of memorabilia, there are several simulators, including a modified Link trainer and a fully-fledged Lightning simulator. The Lysander FSM is an impressive commission, commemorating 161 Squadron's association with Tangmere as its forward base.

◆ *Gamecock Terrace, PO20 2ES* | **01243 790090** | **info@tangmere-museum.org.uk** | **www.tangmere-museum.org.uk**

☐ -		Royal A/c Factory SE.5a rep	17	built on site by volunteers. Cockpit and centre sections			1-22
☐ 'K5054'		V-S Spitfire prototype FSM	92	BAPC.214, ex Southampton, Hendon, Thruxton, M Wallop, Thruxton, Andover. Arrived 1997			1-22
☐ 'L1679'	'JX-G'	Hawker Hurricane I FSM	92	BAPC.241, ex Chilbolton, M Wallop, Thruxton. AeroFab-built. Arrived 8-94. 1 Sqn colours			1-22
☐ P3179		Hawker Hurricane I	40	ex Hove, 43. Shot down 30-8-40. Arrived 1999. Cockpit			1-22
☐ 'V9822'	'MA-E'	Westland Lysander III(SD) FSM	15	BAPC.371, ex 'V9875'. Gate Guardians UK-built. 161 Sqn colours. Arrived 16-6-18	[1]		1-22
☐ -*		V-S Spitfire IX SIM	~	cockpit, in use by 6-21			1-22
☐ EE549		Gloster Meteor IV Special	46	ex Cosford, St Athan, Abingdon, Hendon, St Athan, Innsworth, Fulbeck 7008M, Cranwell, CFE, FCCS, RAFHSF. SOC 10-6-52. Arrived 19-9-92	[2] [3]		1-22
☐ 'VZ440'	'X'	Gloster Meteor F.8 WA984	51	ex 'WA829', Southampton, Wimborne, Tarrant Rushton, 211 AFS, 19. SOC 4-12-61. Arrived 12-90	[4]		1-22
☐ WB188		Hawker Hunter Mk.3	51	ex Cosford, St Athan, Colerne, Melksham, Halton 7154M (10-11-54), Hawker P.1067. Arrived 19-9-92	[2] [5]		1-22
☐ WE113		EE Canberra B.2	52	ex Woodhurst, Wyton, 231 OCU, 100, 85, 98, 231 OCU. Arrived 6-11. Cockpit	[6]		1-22
☐ WK281	'S'	V-S Swift FR.5	56	ex Hendon, St Athan, Swinderby, Finningley, Colerne, Northolt 7712M (7-3-61), 79. Arrived 1995. 79 Sqn c/s	[2]		1-22
☐ WP190	'K'	Hawker Hunter F.5	55	ex Quedgeley, Hucclecote, Stanbridge 8473M, Upwood, Finningley, Bircham Newton 7582M (10-9-58), Nicosia, 1. AWA-built. Arrived 2-6-02. 1 Sqn c/s, Suez stripes	[7]		1-22
☐ WV332		Hawker Hunter F.4	55	ex Godalming, Dunsfold G-9-406, Halton 7673M (17-1-61), 234, 112, 67. Arr 2003. 234 Sqn c/s. Cockpit	[8]		1-22
☐ WZ876		DHC Chipmunk T.10 G-BBWN	53	ex Goodwood, Yateley, Twyford, G-BBWN (CoA 13-7-96, de-reg 13-3-96), Tattershall Thorpe, Lon UAS, 1 AEF, Lon UAS, Biggin Hill SF, Lon, Oxf, Birm UASs, MCS, 31. Cockpit. Arrived by 10-14			1-22
☐ XF840		Percival Provost T.1	55	ex Waltham Abbey, -?-, Shawbury, CNCS, RAFC. SOC 29-5-61. . Arrived 2014. Cockpit			1-22
☐ XH313	'E'	DH Vampire T.11 G-BZRD	56	ex Godstone, Booker, Sandtoft, North Coates, St Albans, Hatfield, CATCS, Wattisham SF, 111. Hawarden-built. SOC 17-12-70. De-reg 22-2-05. Arrived 22-10-08			1-22
☐ XJ580	'131'	DH Sea Vixen FAW.2	60	ex Christchurch, Hurn FRL, RAE Farnborough, Llanbedr, 899, 766, FAW.1, 899, 893, 892. Christchurch-built. SOC 17-12-84. Arrived 27-6-00. 899 Sqn colours			1-22
☐ 'XR753'	'A'	EE Lightning F.53 ZF578	67	ex Quedgeley, Rhoose, Warton, Saudi AF 53-670, G-27-40. Last flown 14-1-86. Arr 6-02. 23 Sqn c/s	[7] [9]		1-22
☐ XS511	'M'	Westland Wessex HU.5	64	ex Gosport, A2660 [2], A2750 (18-9-86), Lee-on-Solent, 845. Arrived 2004	[10]		1-22

☐ XV408	'P'	McD Phantom FGR.2	68	ex Fairford, Halton 9165M, Cranwell, Wattisham, 19, 92,		
				19, 92, 29, 23, 228 OCU, 54, 228 OCU, 6. Arr 30-11-05		
				Repainting to camouflage from 7-21	[2] [11]	1-22
☐ XV744		HS Harrier GR.3	69	ex Shrivenham, St Athan 9167M (10-4-93), 233 OCU,		
				GR.1, 1, 233 OCU. Arrived 14-3-13		1-22
☐ XZ459*	'25'	HS Sea Harrier F/A.2	80	ex Shoreham area, Queensbury, Charlwood, St Athan, 809,		
				800, 801, 899, 800, 801, 800, 801, 800, A&AEE, 801, 899,		
				801, 899. Arrived 24-8-20	[12]	1-22
☐ -		EE Lightning CIM	~	ex Haslemere, Farnborough. Arrived 12-08. Cockpit		1-22

■ **[1]** As flown by Fg Off Jimmy 'Mac' McCairns of 'A' Flight 161 Sqn - 25 'ops', many from Tangmere. **[2]** On loan from the RAF Museum. **[3]** Flown by Gp Capt E M Donaldson, operating from Tangmere, set world airspeed record of 616mph on 7-9-46. **[4]** F.8 is a composite, including items from VZ530. **[5]** Hunter prototype and, as the one-off Mk.3, world speed record breaker - Neville Duke, operating from Tangmere, took record to 727mph on 7-9-53. See under Langley Heath, for another 'WB188'. **[6]** WE113 is on loan from S/L Joe and Pam Marsden. **[7]** Hunter F.5 and Lightning were donated by Raymond and Meryl Hansed and located in the Meryl Hansed Memorial Hall. **[8]** F.4 cockpit is on loan from 1254 Sqn ATC, Godalming, Surrey. The rest became Swiss T.68 J-4201 and is still extant. **[9]** Lightning is in the markings of F.6 XR753 'A', 23 Squadron. The *real* XR753 can be found at Coningsby, Lincs. **[10]** XS511 is on loan from 2464 Sqn ATC, Storrington, W Sussex. **[11]** During 2021 XV408 was being returned to 6 Sqn markings in honour of Gp Capt David Baron, late Chair of Trustees who flew it in those colours. **[12]** Completed 54 combat sorties during the Falklands conflict.

TURNER'S HILL
Tulleys Farm: Among the attractions *should* be a Diplomate | **www.tulleysfarm.com**

☐ G-AYKG	SOCATA ST-10 Diplomate	70	ex Somerford, Turner's Hill. Crashed 4-3-75, de-reg 27-6-75	12-17

WOODMANCOTE on the A281 east of Henfield
Hayward and Green Defence: See also the Bournemouth Aviation Museum, Bournemouth, Dorset. Sea King HAS.2 XV705 made the trek to <u>Strathblane</u>, Scotland, in 2020. ◆ *By prior arrangement* only | **www.haywardandgreendefence.com**

☐ 272	Westland Lynx SH-14D	~	ex Gilze-Rijen, Netherlands Navy. On display from 11-19	7-20

WORTHING on the A281 east of Henfield
Saywell International: At the well-known spares and product support specialist's impressive Aviation Centre is a 'heritage area' with a Taylorcraft Plus D centre stage as a reminder of the organisation's Auster pedigree.
◆ *By prior arrangement only*. | **www.saywell.co.uk**

☐ G-AHWJ	Taylorcraft Plus D	42	ex Auster I LB294, West Raynham SF, Milfield SF,	
			43 OTU, 653. De-reg 11-11-11	11-17

WARWICKSHIRE

BIDFORD AERODROME west of Stratford-upon-Avon
Restoration of the Auster T.10-based Terrier continues at a private location.

☐ WJ404	Beagle Terrier 2	G-ASOI 53	ex Auster T.10, 662, 665. CoA 30-9-16	6-21

BRINKLOW on the B4027 east of Coventry
Delta Force Paintball: On 18th October 2020 driving along the M6 westbound near Junction 2 got safer: Jaguar XZ369 was transported to <u>East Midlands</u>, Leics. There has been no replacement to induce mass brake light applications!

CORLEY MOOR on minor roads southwest of the M6's Corley Services
A *private* collection of airframes in the area is *thought* unchanged. ◆ *By prior arrangement only*.

☐ XR506	'V'	Westland Wessex HC.2	63	ex Selby, Greatham, Gosport, Cosford 9343M, Shawbury,	
				72, 60, 72, 18	5-19
☐ XV783		HS Harrier GR.3	70	ex Ipswich, Predannack, Culdrose A2609[3] (16-3-90),	
	'DD83'			Lee-on-Solent, Culdrose SAH, Cosford, 233 OCU, 4, 3, 233	
				OCU, 1, 233 OCU, 1, 233 OCU, 1417 Flt, 233 OCU, 4, 20, 4	10-13
☐ ZD284	'K'	Westland Lynx AH.7	84	ex Ipswich, M Wallop. Arrived by 12-14	12-14

COVENTRY AIRPORT or Baginton

In May 2021 **West Midlands Gigafactory**, a joint venture between Coventry City Council and Coventry Airport Ltd, announced a proposal for a vast electric vehicle battery plant sited on Runway 05/23 and – obviously – spelling the death-knell for the airport. A play on the word 'gigawatt', the Gigafactory would be the "largest industrial facility of any kind in the UK", potentially employing 20,000 on site and in the supply chain – if they can get the lorry drivers. Outline planning permission was granted on 13th January 2022 and work could start in 2025.

Midland Air Museum (MAM), incorporating the **Sir Frank Whittle Jet Heritage Centre**: In *theory*, the Gigafactory plans will not impinge on the museum site. Airframes held in deep store are listed separately - see below.

◆ *Rowley Road, CV3 4FR* | **02476 301033** | **enquiries@midlandairmuseum.co.uk** | **www.midlandairmuseum.co.uk**

☐	'G-AEGV'	Mignet HM.14 'Flea'	c69	ex Coventry, Knowle, Northampton, Sywell	[1]	1-22
☐	'G-ALVD'	DH Dove 2	47	ex airfield, VT-CEH. CoA 16-3-73, de-reg 8-9-78.		
		G-ALCU		Acquired 28-3-80. Dunlop colours		1-22
☐	G-APJJ	Fairey Ultra-Light Helicopter	57	ex Heaton Chapel, Coventry, Cranfield, White Waltham, RAE Bedford, CoA 1-4-59, de-reg 2-3-73. Arrived 1975	[2]	1-22
☐	G-APRL	AW Argosy 101	59	ex ABC/Elan, N890U, N602Z, N6507R, G-APRL. *Edna*. CoA 23-3-87, de-reg 19-11-87, flew in 20-2-87		1-22
☐	G-APWN	Westland Whirlwind Srs 3	59	ex Cranfield, Redhill, VR-BER, G-APWN, 5N-AGI, G-APWN. CoA 17-5-78, de-reg 25-6-81, arrived 1984. Bristow colours		1-22
☐	G-ARYB	HSA HS.125 Srs 1	62	ex Hatfield. CoA 22-1-68, de-reg 4-3-69. Hatfield-built. Arrived 2-12-93		1-22
☐	G-BRNM	CMC Leopard	89	ex Hurn, Old Sarum. De-reg 31-1-05, arrived 26-3-08		1-22
☐	G-CHNX	Lockheed Electra 188AF	59	ex Pershore, Hurn, Channel Express, EI-CHO, G-CHNX, N5535. CoA 31-10-01, de-reg 12-5-03. Cockpit		1-22
☐	G-MJWH	Chargus Vortex 120 h-g	r83	former microlight. Arrived 1989		1-18
☐	ANW	EoN Olympia 2 G-ALNE	47	ex BGA.538, G-ALNE, BGA.538. CoA 9-3-04. Frame		1-18
☐	–	Humber-Blériot Monoplane replica	5̲3̲	BAPC.9, ex B'ham, Yeovilton, Wroughton, Y'ton, Coventry, *Those Magnificent Men*, Old Warden, Honington. Arr 12-91	[3]	1-22
☐	–	Slingsby Cadet TX.1	c54	'BGA.804', ex Perranporth. Arrived 12-6-68		1-18
☐	–	Druine Turbulent	c58	BAPC.126, ex Shoreham, Croydon. Rollason-built non-flyer. Acquired 13-9-78		1-22
☐	F-BGNR	Vickers Viscount 708	54	ex Hatch, Perth, Air Inter. Hurn-built. Last flown 8-10-73. Arrived 6-9-07, acquired 10-7-08		1-22
☐	EE531	Gloster Meteor F.4	46	ex Bentham, Coventry , Birmingham, Weston Park, B'ham, 7090M, RAE Lasham, A&AEE. SOC 25-8-53. Acquired 26-6-73		1-22
☐	VF301	DH Vampire F.1	46	ex Stoneleigh, Debden 7060M (10-8-53), 208 AFS, 595,		
	'RAL-G'			226 OCU. EE-built. Acquired 11-72. 605 Sqn colours		1-22
☐	VS623	Percival Prentice T.1	49	ex Shoreham, Redhill, Southend, VS623, CFS, 2 FTS,		
		G-AOKZ		22 FTS. SOC 11-5-56. De-reg 4-10-61, arrived 26-7-82	[4]	1-22
☐	VT935	Boulton Paul P.111A	50	ex Cranfield, RAE Bedford. Arrived 13-7-75	[2]	1-22
☐	VZ477	Gloster Meteor F.8	50	ex Kimbolton 7741M, APS, 245. SOC 22-6-62. Arrived 4-6-92. Cockpit		1-22
☐	WF922	EE Canberra PR.3	52	ex Cambridge, A&AEE, RRE, A&AEE, Wroughton, BP, 39, 69, 58, 1323 Flt, 82. SOC 23-5-75, arrived 24-6-84. *Stevenson's Rocket*		1-22
☐	WH646	EE Canberra T.17A	52	ex Wyton, 360, B.2 45, RNZAF, 45, 10, 50. Arr 1995. Cockpit		1-22
☐	WS838	'D' Gloster Meteor NF.14	54	ex Cosford, Manchester, Cosford, Shawbury, Colerne, SOC (to RAF Museum) 9-2-72, RAE Bedford, A&AEE, RRE Pershore, 64, AW OCU. AWA-built. Arr 15-3-86	[5]	1-22
☐	WV797	'491' Hawker Sea Hawk FGA.6	54	ex Perth, Culdrose A2627, Halton 8155M (12-3-71), Sydenham, 738, 898, 899, Fleetlands, 787. AWA-built. Arrived 6-2-86		1-22
☐	XA508	'627' Fairey Gannet T.2	55	ex Yeovilton, Manadon A2472 (12-4-57), 737. Arrived 26-9-82. 737 Sqn colours	[6]	1-22
☐	XA699	Gloster Javelin FAW.5	57	ex Cosford, Locking 7809M (14-2-64), Shawbury, Kemble, Shawbury, 5, 151. AWA-built. Arr 19-9-81. 5 Sqn colours		1-22

☐ XF382	'15'	Hawker Hunter F.6A	56	ex Brawdy, 1 TWU, TWU, 229 OCU, FCS, 65, 63, 92.		
				AWA-built. SOC 10-7-84. Arrived 1-12-86	[7]	1-22
☐ XH592	'L'	HP Victor B.1A	58	ex B'thorpe, Cosford 8429M (17-10-74), St Athan, 232 OCU,		
				TTF, 232 OCU, Honington Wing, 15. Cockpit. Arr by 10-15		1-22
☐ XJ579	'121'	DH Sea Vixen FAW.2	60	ex Farnborough, A&AEE, Llanbedr, 899, 766.		
				Christchurch-built. Arrived 18-8-92. Cockpit		1-22
☐ XK789		Slingsby Grasshopper TX.1	55	ex Warwick, Cosford, Stamford		1-22
☐ XL360		Avro Vulcan B.2	62	ex 44, 101, 35, 617, 230 OCU, Wadd Wing, 230 OCU,		
				Scamp W, 617. Flew in 4-2-83. *City of Coventry*. 617 Sqn c/s		1-22
☐ XN685	'703'	DH Sea Vixen FAW.2	61	ex Chester, Cosford, Cranwell 8173M (3-8-71), 890, 766,		
				893, HSA. Christchurch-built. Arrived 14-9-92. 890 Sqn c/s		1-22
☐ XR635		Westland Scout AH.1	65	ex Coventry, Ipswich, Arborfield, Yeovilton, M Wallop,		
				653, 660. Arrived 10-9-12	[8]	1-22
☐ XR771	'AN'	EE Lightning F.6	66	ex Binbrook, 5, 11, 5, 56, 74. SOC 21-6-88, arrived 15-7-88		1-22
☐ ZA452	'021'	Panavia Tornado GR.4	83	ex Leeming, 12, GR.1, 20, A&AEE. Arrived 9-13. 2 Sqn c/s	[9]	1-22
☐ ZE694	'004'	HS Sea Harrier F/A.2	88	ex Yeovilton, 801, 800, 801, 800, 801, 899, 800, 801, 800.		
				Arrived 16-2-05		1-22
☐ –		Bristol Beaufighter	42	BAPC.398, ex Birmingham, Coventry. Arr 10-89. Cockpit	[10]	1-22
☐ –		Hunting Jet Provost SIM	c60	procedure trainer		1-22
☐ –		BAe/McDD Harrier GR.5	90	procedure trainer		3-18
☐ 8449M		Beagle 206-1	65	ex Bristol, Halton 8449M (9-8-76), G-ASWJ Rolls-Royce,		
		G-ASWJ		CoA 30-1-75, de-reg 9-9-75. Acquired 1-93. arrived by 2-13		1-22
☐ '117529'		Lockheed T-33A-1-LO	51	ex Cosford, Sculthorpe, French AF, USAF 51-7473.		
	'TR-529'		51-7473	Last flown 30-5-78, arrived 26-10-93. Italian colours	[7]	1-22
☐ R-756		Lockheed F-104G S'fighter	64	ex Aalborg, Danish AF, 64-17756. Arrived 30-4-87	[7]	1-22
☐ 'GN-101'		Folland Gnat F.1　XK741	57	ex Leamington Spa, Fordhouses, Dunsfold, Hamble,		
				Boscombe Down, Dunsfold. SOC 10-11-61. *Kreivi von*		
				Rosen, Finnish AF colours. Acquired 7-6-75. Fuselage	[11]	1-22
☐ 70	'8-NV'	Dassault Mystère IVA	c56	ex Sculthorpe, French AF. Arrived 1/2-6-79	[7]	1-22
☐ 280020		Flettner Fl 282B V-20	44	ex Coventry, Cranfield, Brize Norton,		
		Kolibri		Travemünde 'CJ+SN'. Arrived 5-75. Frame	[2]	1-22
☐ 959		Mikoyan-Gurevich	c66	ex Duxford, Cottbus, East German AF.		
		MiG-21SPS *Fishbed*		Arrived 25-6-01		1-22
☐ '1706'		PZL Iskra 100	c77	ex airfield, Scampton, Duxford, Polish AF 408. On loan		1-22
☐ 55-713	'C'	EE Lightning T.55	67	ex Warton, ZF598, Saudi AF 55-713, G-27-72.		
			ZF598	Last flown 14-1-86. Arrived 14-1-89. Saudi colours		1-22
☐ '17447'		McD F-101B-80	56	ex Alconbury, Davis-Monthan, Kentucky ANG, USAF.		
		Voodoo	56-0312	Arrived 7/8-3-92. RCAF colours	[7]	1-22
☐ 29640	'08'	SAAB J29F 'Tunnen'	c54	ex Southend, F20 R Swedish AF. Arrived 27-4-85		1-22
☐ 0-82062		DHC U-6A Beaver	58	ex Mannheim, US Army, 58-2062. Arrived 10-7-81	[7]	1-22
☐ 48-0242		NAA F-86A-5-NA Sabre	48	N196B, ex Duxford, Chino, 48-0242.		
	'FU-242'		N196B	Arrived 22-4-05		1-22
☐ 51-4419		Lockheed T-33A-1-LO	51	ex Sculthorpe, French AF. Last flown 25-1-78,		
				arrived 1979. 57th FIS colours	[7]	1-22
☐ 54-2174		NAA F-100D-16-NA	54	ex Sculthorpe, French AF, USAF 54-2174. Last flown		
	'SM'	Super Sabre		22-2-77. Arrived 29-3-78. *Carol Anne*. USAF colours	[7]	1-22
☐ 63-7699		McD F-4C-21-MC	63	ex Upper Heyford, Fairford, 55th TFS, 356th TFS, 480th		
	'CG'	Phantom		TFS, USAF 63-7699. Arrived 7-10-93. 366th TFW c/s	[7] [12]	1-22
☐ 62-4535		Kaman HH-43B Huskie	52	ex Woodbridge, 40 ARRS, Det 2. Arrived 7-3-81	[13]	1-22
☐ -	'	Mil Mi-24 *Hind-D*	c77	ex Rochester, Chester, Latvia, USSR.		
		3532464505029		Arrived 15-9-05. BAE Systems colours	[14]	1-22

■ **[1]** 'Flea' has the original wings from G-AEGV coupled with new-build fuselage etc, circa 1969. Original built by East Midlands Aviation Co at Sywell and first flew 24-5-36. **[2]** Airframes on loan from Cranfield University, Beds. **[3]** Thanks to John Berkeley, this machine likely was assembled (or 'created') at 94 MU Honington in 1953 (although 58 MU was also at the base at the time); earliest sighting at Old Warden 1959. Goldsmith provenance *possibly* in doubt... At Coventry, it was fitted with an original Humber engine, loaned from Coventry Museum, to represent a 1911 Humber-Blériot. **[4]** VS623 is fitted with the wings from G-AONB (VR244). **[5]** WS838, ownership transferred from the RAF Museum to MAM. **[6]** Gannet T.2 is on loan from FAAM, Yeovilton. **[7]** Airframes from the National Museum of the USAF's Loan Program: a large number of RAF Hunters were MDAP funded. **[8]** Scout is on loan from Coventry University (see Coventry, W Mids) and used as a teaching aid. **[9]** Tornado credited with 32 'ops' during the 1st Gulf War, deployed to Tabuk, Saudi Arabia, from 8-90; carrying the code 'GK', this gave rise to one of the two names it carried on the nose, *Gulf Killer*; the other being *I Luv Gaynor XX*. **[10]** Beaufighter cockpit is *possibly* Mk.I T5298. In which case it was previously 4552M and TFU Defford.

[11] Gnat fuselage is a composite, rear from XK539, w/o 15-7-58. [13] Sabre is on loan from the IWM, Duxford. [12] F-4 37699 crewed by Major Samuel O Bakkel and WSO Capt Robert W Lambery shot down a NVN MiG-17 *Fresco* on 14-5-67. [13] HH-43B uses parts from 24538, including the fins. [14] *Hind* on loan from BAE Systems.

Deep store: The following are *not* available for public inspection.

❑ G-EBJG	Parnall Pixie III	24	ex Coventry, Stratford, Horley, Dorking, Carlisle (?), Heston,		
			CoA 2-10-36, de-reg 1-12-46. Remains, acquired 8-67		1-14
❑ G-ABOI	Wheeler Slymph	r31	ex Coventry, Old Warden. De-reg 1-12-46. Arrived 4-68	[1]	1-14
❑ –	Crossley Tom Thumb	37	BAPC.32, ex Coventry, Bewdley, Coventry, Banbury.		
			Arrived 29-7-69	[2]	1-14
❑ XD626	DH Vampire T.11	54	ex Bitteswell, Shawbury, CATCS, CNCS, 5 FTS, RAFC, CFS.		
			SOC 19-7-67. Christchurch-built. Arrived 10-8-82. Spares		9-21
❑ XE855	DH Vampire T.11	54	ex Upton-by-Chester, Woodford, Chester, 27 MU, 22 MU,		
			10 MU, AWOCU. Hatfield-built. SOC 30-10-67.		
			Arrived 28-8-82. Cockpit		9-21
❑ XK907	Westland Whirlwind	57	ex Bubbenhall, Panshanger, Elstree, G-AYXT (de-reg 8-8-00),		
	HAS.7	G-AYXT	Luton, ETPS, RRE Pershore, Alvis. Last flown 30-10-68.		
			Arrived 8-3-81. Cockpit, spares recovered	[3]	9-21
❑ 57-0270	McD F-101B-80-MC	57	ex fire crews, MAM, Woodbridge, Davis-Monthan,		
	Voodoo		Texas ANG, USAF 57-0270. Arrived 4-92. Forward fuselage		9-21
❑ 63-7414	McD F-4C-15-MC	63	ex Woodbridge, New York ANG, USAF 63-7414.		
	Phantom		Arrived 5-92	[4]	9-21

◾ [1] On loan from the estate of the late Air Cdre Alan Wheeler. [2] Crossley is an unfinished 1930s homebuild, from Banbury. [3] See Weston-super-Mare, Somerset, for the *real* G-AYXT. [4] F-4C from the National Museum of the USAF's Loan Program.

Former **Classic Air Force Airbase / Air Atlantique**: By mid-2020 Rapide G-AKRP had moved to Eaglescott, Devon. Anson C.19 TX235 departed on 25th August 2020, initially for Hooton Park, Cheshire, before settling upon Woodford, Gtr Man. Pembroke XL929 (G-BNPU) and Twin Pioneer G-AZHJ, both long stored off-site, arrived at St Athan, Wales, 11th November 2020. DC-6A G-APSA made the move to St Athan, Wales, by September 2021. Hornet Moth G-AESE and Dragon Rapide G-AGTM, with Ben Cox, are now listed in the 'Also' category below. ◆ *Not* available for inspection

❑ KK116	Douglas Dakota 4 ✈	43	ex EI-BKJ, East Midlands, EI-BKJ, G-AMPY, N15751, G-AMPY,		
		G-AMPY	TF-FIO, G-AMPY, JY-ABE, G-AMPY, KK116, 43-49308.		
			CoA 9-7-16. Spray bars *and* RAF Transport Cmd colours	[1]	1-22
❑ VP959	'L' DH Devon C.2	48	ex Wellesbourne, Biggin Hill, N959VP, G-BWFB,		
			VP959, RAE. Stored, off-site		9-19
❑ XM223	'J' DH Dove 7	57	ex Cumbernauld, West Freugh, DGTE, T&EE, RAE.		
		G-BWWC	De-reg 10-1-19. Stored, off-site	[2]	9-19

◾ [1] Registered to Heritage Air Services of Rugby, 5-21. [2] XM223 is fitted with the wings of G-APSO.

Nimrod Preservation Group: The group works to keep XV232 live. ◆ *Occasional special events* | www.xv232.com

❑ XV232	HS Nimrod MR.2	69	ex Kinloss, Kin Wing, Kin & St M Wing, Kinloss, 203	
			Flew in 11-5-10	1-22

Shackleton Preservation Group: (SPT): WR963, nicknamed 'Growler', is kept 'in steam'.
◆ *Occasional special events and open days* | email *via website* | www.avroshackleton.co.uk

❑ VP293	'X' Avro Shackleton T.4	51	ex Duxford, Coltishall, Winthorpe, Coventry, Woodford,		
			Coventry, East Kirkby, Strathallan, RAE, MOTU, A&AEE,		
			MR.1, 206, 42, 224, 236 OCU. SOC 23-5-75, last flown		
			3-5-76. *Zebedee*. Cockpit, trailer-mounted	[1]	1-22
❑ WR963	'B-M' Avro Shackleton AEW.2	54	ex N963WR, Waddington, Lossiemouth, 8 *Ermintrude*,		
		G-SKTN	205, 28, 210, 224. Gp Capt Dave Hencken. Arrived 9-7-91		1-22

◾ [1] VP293 is on loan from Norman Thelwell.

Also: DC-6A/B G-SIXC moved St Athan, Wales, on 5th August 2021. ATP G-OBWP was scrapped by August 2018.

❑ G-ACGT	Avro Avian IIIA	28	ex Yeadon, Linthwaite, EI-AAB. CoA 21-7-39. Off-site	[1]	5-19
❑ G-AESE	DH Hornet Moth	37	ex Air Atlantique, W5775, 526, 72 Wing CF, 6 RSS,		
			4 CPF, G-AESE. *Sheena*. CoA 8-6-16	[1]	5-19
❑ G-AGTM	DH Dragon Rapide	44	ex Air Atlantique, St Mawgan, Coventry, JY-ACL,		
			OD-ABP, G-AGTM, Dominie NF875 n/s. Brush-built.		
			Sybille. CoA 30-9-16	[1]	5-19
❑ G-BXJA*	Cessna 402B	73	ex N5753M. CoA 17-10-07, de-reg 13-10-20. F/n 8-20		8-20

☐ G-LOFB	Lockheed L.188CF Electra	61	ex Atlantic, N667F, N133AJ, CF-IJW, N131US.		
			Damaged 28-1-10. CoA 8-2-11, de-reg 29-9-16		1-22
☐ -*	'Cherokee'	~	cockpit in Coventry Aeroplane Club building	[2]	1-22
☐ SE-LPU	BAe ATP	98	ex West Air, LX-WAM, SE-LPU, LX-WAM, SE-LPU, G-OBWO,		
			G-11-060. Arrived 9-9-15. Rescue trainer		1-22
☐ N308SF	Douglas C-47A-65-DL	43	ex N98BF, Aéronavale '18984', N45V, N65384, 42-100521,		
	Skytrain		436th TCG USAAF. Long Beach-built. *Night Fright*. F/n 9-16	[3]	1-22
☐ N8041B*	Douglas C-47A-50-DL	42	ex USA, Span AF, EC-ADR, G-AJAZ, Dakota III FL517,		
	Skytrain G-AJAZ		1381 CU, 511, 512, USAAF 42-24238. Cockpit, off-site	[4]	5-19

■ **[1]** Registered to Ben Cox. **[2]** This *may* be the cockpit of Cessna 310L G-AVDB which was used as the basis of a sim. Last noted in 11-08, it was written out of *W&R26* (p287). **[3]** Served with 436th's 79th TCS initially from Bottesford, then Membury - D-Day through to end of war. Plan is to operate it from Membury. **www.night-fright.com** **[4]** Cockpit, imported into the UK in 2006, to be used as a travelling exhibit for the Night-Fright project.

LONG MARSTON on the B4632, southwest of Stratford-upon-Avon
Meteor WL332 moved to <u>Newquay</u>, Cornwall, on 13th October 2020. It was followed by Shackleton WR985 by May 2021.

RED HILL on the A46 between Alcester and Stratford-upon-Avon
The fuselage of the former Long Marston Sea Prince is at a *private* location here.

☐ G-RACA	'571' Percival Sea Prince T.1	52	ex Long Marston, Staverton, Kemble, WM735, 750,	
			BTU, A&AEE. SOC 16-9-80, de-reg 28-11-95. Shark's mouth.	
			Fuselage, first noted 2-20	5-21

RUGBY Agusta 109 G-HIMJ, converted into a caravan and last noted in June 2014, has been deleted.

STOCKTON east of the A426 north of Southam
Richard Adams: Has, or *had*, a Vampire T.11 cockpit for conversion to a simulator.

☐ WZ553	'40' DH Vampire T.11	53	ex Coventry, G-DHYY (de-reg 7-11-02), Hurn, Bruntingthorpe,	
	G-DHYY		Cranfield, Lichfield, Winthorpe, S' Wigston, B'thorpe,	
			Loughborough, E Midlands, Speke, Woodford, Chester, St Athan,	
			4 FTS, 7 FTS, 202 AFS. Hawarden-built. SOC 2-12-68, Cockpit	3-10

STRATFORD-UPON-AVON
Peter Turner: Peter has many other Messenger and Gemini sections and elements; plus other Miles material.
◆ *By prior appointment* **only** - *situated on private estate*

☐ G-AKDK	Miles Gemini 1A	47	ex Coventry, Seaton Ross, 'Stratford', Denmark, G-AKDK	12-19
☐ G-ALAH	Miles Gemini 4A	45	ex Sabadell, Spain, Henlow, NAPS (1967), CoA 18-4-65,	
			de-reg 21-5-70, RH377 n/s. Arrived 22-9-14	12-19
☐ VH-GBB	Miles Gemini 1A G-AKEN	47	ex Australia, VH-BTP, G-AKEN. Fuselage	12-19
☐ VP-KJL	Miles Messenger 4A	48	ex Redhill, Woodley, Stoke-on-Trent, Coventry, G-ALAR,	
	G-ALAR		RH371, BAFO CW, AEAF CS. Fuselage and tail	12-19

WARWICK
A *private* airstrip in the locality. Chilton G-AFSV departed by road to <u>Breighton</u>, E Yorks, on 3rd September 2020. Also moving on was Isaacs Fury G-PFAR, decamping to 'Oxfordshire' in early 2020.

☐ G-AAOR	DH Moth	29	ex EC-AAO. CoA 17-11-05, de-reg 1-3-19	7-19

WELLESBOURNE MOUNTFORD AERODROME south of the B4086, E of Stratford   EBBW
Wellesbourne Wartime Museum: Operated by the **Wellesbourne Aviation Group**, the museum charts the history of the airfield centred on the restored underground Battle Headquarters. ◆ *via* **Facebook**

☐ RA-01378	'14' Yakovlev Yak-52	83	ex Sov AF	1-22
☐ WV679	'O-J' Percival Provost T.1	54	ex Dunkeswell, H' Blagdon, Halton 7615M (13-10-59), 2 FTS	1-22
☐ XJ575	DH Sea Vixen FAW.2	60	ex Long Marston, Helston, Culdrose SAH, A2611, 766, 890,	
	'SAH-13'		893, FAW.1, 766. Christchurch-built. SOC 24-3-71. Cockpit	1-22
☐ XK590	'V' DH Vampire T.11	56	ex Witney, Brize Norton, CATCS, 4 FTS, 7 FTS.	
			Hawarden-built. SOC 6-2-70	1-22

Vulcan B.2 XM655 (G-VULC), June 2021. *Ian Doyle*

XM655 Maintenance and Preservation Society: The team keep XM655 'in steam'.
◆ *Occasional ground-running days* | **email** via website | **www.xm655.com**
❑ XM655   Avro Vulcan B.2   64   ex N655AV, 44, 101, 50, 12, 35, 9.
                                G-VULC   Flew in 11-2-84, de-reg 25-3-02   [1]   1-22
■ **[1]** XM655 is owned by John Littler of Radarmoor.

WILTSHIRE
Includes the unitary authority of Swindon

AMESBURY on the A303 west of Andover
Gary Dean: Gary's exceptional P-51D cockpit procedure trainer is kept in the area. It is a tribute to Gp Capt John Francis
Xavier 'Sam' McKenna AFC, second commandant of the Empire Test Pilots' School, who was killed while testing Mustang IV
KH648 on 19th January 1945. ◆ *By prior arrangement* only | geeede@ntlworld.com
❑ '44-11175'   NAA P-51D Mustang SIM   04   BAPC.512, *One More Time*. Unveiled 14-6-14   8-21

BOSCOMBE DOWN AIRFIELD south of the A303 at Amesbury   EGDM
MoD Boscombe Down: Home of the **Aircraft Test and Evaluation Centre** and defence technology and security specialists
QinetiQ Group plc. Within Hangar 104 is the **Apprentice Training Centre** (ATC). An RAF 'lodger' unit, the **Joint Aircraft
Recovery and Transport Squadron** (JARTS), moves airframes by road and loads-in-transit can be found 'over-nighting' or
staying for longer periods; only long-termers are given here. JARTS has an 'out-station' at Newquay, Cornwall - which see.
     The Merlin store, mentioned in *W&R27* as potentially transitory, has proved to be more permanent.
     Departures: **Alpha Jet**s sold in Canada between 12-19 and 2-20, as follows: ZJ649 - C-GMBU, ZJ650 - C-GYMT, ZJ651 - C-
GLZW, ZJ652 - C-GKFN, ZJ653 as yet unregistered, ZJ654 - C-GHZH,ZJ655 0 C-GXNB, ZJ656 - C-GZEH; **Tornado** GR.4 ZG773
moved to Moreton-in-Marsh, Glos, during 2020; **Tucano** T.1s ZF510 and ZF511 registered in the USA as N889KT and N511ZF
respectively, 6-20. In December 2021 it was announced that **Beagle 206Z2** XS743 was to go to **Old Sarum**, Wilts, and this
move has been anticipated.

❑ XL629   EE Lightning T.4   59   ex ETPS, A&AEE. Last flight 3-11-75. Displayed   1-22
❑ XS180   '21' Hunting Jet Provost T.4   63   ex '8238M', St Athan 8338M (6-8-73), Lyneham, St Athan,
                                             Halton, Kemble, CAW, 6 FTS. JARTS   10-20
❑ XS646   HS Andover C.1   68   ex DERA etc, RAE, 84, 46. Forward fuselage   10-21

❑ XS765		Beagle Basset CC.1	64	ex Cranfield, G-BSET (CoA 28-7-98, de-reg 25-3-04),	
		G-BSET		ETPS, 26, 207, 32, MCS, SCS, NCS, HS. Fuselage, ATC	12-17
❑ XW906	'J'	Sud Gazelle HT.3	74	ex Shawbury, 2 FTS, CFS. Westland-built. Cockpit, ATC	[1] 12-17
❑ XX165		HS Hawk T.1A	77	ex Wittering, Boscombe Down, Shawbury, 208, FRADU,	
				4 FTS, CFS, 74, CFS, 4 FTS, CFS. SOC 7-8-17. Fuselage	5-20
❑ XX172		HS Hawk T.1	77	ex Shawbury, Yeovilton, FRADU, 19, 4 FTS, 234, 4 FTS.	
				Bird strike 15-12-06, SOC 7-8-17. ATC	12-17
❑ XX173*		HS Hawk T.1	77	ex Shawbury, FRADU, 6 FTS, 4 FTS. NEA 12-19.	
				Arrived 11-3-20. JARTS	10-20
❑ XX379	'Y'	Sud Gazelle AH.1	75	ex Shawbury, 6 Flt, 658, 3/4 Rgt, 8 Flt, 658, 656, 2 Flt.	
				Westland-built. Arrived by 5-15	6-17
❑ XX956*	'BE'	SEPECAT Jaguar GR.1	75	ex Gibraltar, Ipswich, Halton 8950M (3-12-87), Shawbury,	
				17, 31, 17, 14, 17. First noted 10-21, stored, off-site	10-21
❑ XZ183		Westland Lynx AH.7	78	ex Wittering, St Athan, M Wallop, Fleetlands. JARTS	6-20
❑ 'XZ615'		Westland Lynx AH.7	79	ex St Athan, Fleetlands, Middle Wallop, 655, 656, 662,	
		XZ209		659. JARTS	10-20
❑ XZ646		Westland Lynx AH.7	80	ex St Athan, Fleetlands, Yeovilton, 847, 657, 656, 664, 656,	
				669, 654, 654. Crashed 21-2-05. Cabin, JARTS	10-20
❑ ZA560*		Panavia Tornado GR.4	81	ex Wittering, Marham, 617, GR.1, DERA, SAOEU.	
	'EB-Q'			SOC 20-3-18. Fuselage. JARTS. Arrived 15-7-21	10-21
❑ ZD285		Westland Lynx AH.5X	85	ex A&AEE, RAE Farnborough. ATC	[2] 12-17
❑ ZD559		Westland Lynx AH.7	85	ex AH.5X, ETPS, RAE Bedford. Retired by 2-13. ATC	12-17
❑ ZF622*		Piper Navajo 350	~	ex St Mawgan, Boscombe Down, DERA, RAE, N35487.	
				SOC 25-1-16. Fuselage. First noted 4-21	4-21
❑ ZH830*	'88'	EHI Merlin HM.1	98	ex QinetiQ, Yeovil, QinetiQ, DERA	7-19
❑ ZH838*	'70'	EHI Merlin HM.1	99	ex Culdrose, 824, 700M, 824	1-17
❑ ZH848*		EHI Merlin HM.1	00	ex 820, 829, 824, DERA	7-19
❑ ZH849*	'14'	EHI Merlin HM.1	00	ex 829, 824, 814	7-19
❑ ZH852*		EHI Merlin HM.1	01	ex Cerebus (ie AEW) test-bed, Culdrose, 829, 824	7-19
❑ ZH855*	'68'	EHI Merlin HM.1	01	ex Culdrose, 814, 824	3-16
❑ ZH863*	'67'	EHI Merlin HM.1	02	ex Culdrose, 820, 814, 700M. First noted 3-16	2-19
❑ ZJ117*	'A'	EHI Merlin HC.2	98	ex QinetiQ	7-20
❑ ZJ135*	'R'	EHI Merlin HM.1	01	ex Culdrose	7-17
❑ ZJ807		Eurofighter Typhoon T.3	04	ex Coningsby. Arrived 5-2-20. JARTS, fuselage	10-21
❑ 162737		BAe/McDD AV-8B Harrier II	86	ex VMAT-203. JARTS Fuselage, first noted 4-17	7-21

■ [1] XW906 is fitted with the boom of ZA804 - see below. [3] Lynx AH.5Xs were interim airframes prior to the AH.7. ZD285 has a substantially modified nose section..

Solstice Business Park: Just off the A303, at the end of the westbound slip road to the services, within sight of the airfield, a Gazelle 'sculpture' which is almost lost within the sprawl of building development.

❑ ZA804	'I'	Sud Gazelle HT.3		ex airfield, Shawbury, 2 FTS, CFS. Westland-built	[1] 10-21

■ [1] Much-altered, the Gazelle forms a 'sculpture' that is part helicopter, part dragonfly. It was officially unveiled 11-6-07. The original boom of ZA804 is fitted to XW906 - see above.

CHIPPENHAM

Maria Merry: Maria and son Freddie converted an Agusta 109 into a 'Heli-Party Pad' complete with cocktail bar and a widescreen TV. ◆ *By prior appointment* only

❑ G-GBCA		Agusta 109A	84	ex Weston-super-Mare, Denham, Helicopter Film Services.	
				De-reg 3-9-85. Cab. Arrived by 7-18	10-19

CRICKLADE south of the A419 between Cirencester and Swindon

A Dove and and a Devon are stored at an industrial yard in the *general* area.

❑ G-ARJB		DH Dove 8	60	ex Little Rissington, Kemble, Cumbernauld, Carlisle,	
				Rocester, East Midlands. CoA 10-12-73. *Exporter*	3-21
❑ VP955		DH Devon C.2/2		ex Little Rissington, Kemble, Little Staughton,	
		G-DVON	48	Cranfield, G-BLPD, VP955, 207, 21, C.1 WCS, MCS, 31,	
				Upavon SF, Hendon SF, MEAF, Malta CF. CoA 29-5-96	3-21

LARKHILL north of the A303, northwest of Amesbury.

Royal Artillery Barracks / Institution: Elements of the base are to relocate and the Phoenix *may* be on the move.

❏ ZJ469	GEC-Marconi Phoenix UAV c95	BAPC.408. Stored	[1]	9-17

■ **[1]** Apparently merits a heritage identity.

LYNEHAM west of the A3102, southwest of Royal Wootton Bassett

REME Museum: Devoted to the story of REME, its predecessors and a presentation on the legacy of Lyneham.

◆ *Prince Philip Barracks, SN15 4XX* | 01249 894869 | **enquiries@rememuseum.org.uk** | **www.rememuseum.org.uk**

❏ XV141	Westland Scout AH.1	68	ex Arborfield, Wroughton, 657, 659, 654, 661. Arrived 11-15. In the 'World Gallery'	1-20
❏ ZJ449	GEC-Marconi Phoenix UAV c95		ex Arborfield. Acquired 7-10-08, arrived 11-15. Stored	7-17
❏ TAD.016	Westland Lynx HC.28	77	ex Arborfield, M Wallop, Almondbank, Wroughton, Qatar Police QP-32. First noted 4-16. Displayed outside	1-20

Defence College of Technical Training (DCTT): A one-off abbreviation is used in the listing below: MW = Middle Wallop.
   Disposals: Gazelle AH.1s XZ325 (8-21) and TAD.017 (XW888 22-6-21) and HCC.4 XZ935 (22-6-21) all to <u>Colsterworth</u>, Lincs: **Lynx** 1-03 TAD.009 (XW838) moved to <u>Cranwell</u>, Lincs, by 2-21; AH.7 XZ187 to <u>Moreton-in-Marsh</u>, Glos, 3-21; AH.7 XZ188 to <u>North Weald</u>, Essex, 20-10-21; AH.7 XZ207 and HC.28 TAD.013 to <u>Moreton-in-Marsh</u>, Glos, 24-8-21.

❏ XT623		Westland Scout AH.1	66	ex Arborfield, Wroughton, 655, 659, 655. First noted 4-16	7-17
❏ XZ170		Westland Lynx AH.9	77	ex Arborfield, Yeovil, A&AEE. Arrived 1-9-15	7-17
❏ XZ172		Westland Lynx AH.7	77	ex Arborfield, 653, 655, Yeovil, LCF/671, IPTU. F/n 7-17	7-17
❏ XZ180		Westland Lynx AH.7	78	ex MW. SOC 11-4-15. Arrived 9-11-15	7-17
❏ XZ191	'R'	Westland Lynx AH.7	78	ex Fleetlands. SOC 4-9-13. Arrived 25-6-15	7-17
❏ XZ214		Westland Lynx AH.7	79	ex MW. SOC 11-4-15. Arrived 9-11-15	7-17
❏ XZ222		Westland Lynx AH.7	79	ex MW. SOC 9-5-15. Arrived 10-11-15	7-17
❏ XZ316	'B'	Sud Gazelle AH.1	77	ex Arborfield, Cosford, Shawbury, 666, 670, ARWS, ARWF	[1] 11-17
❏ XZ332		Sud Gazelle AH.1	77	ex Aborfield, MW, 670, ARWF, 656, 664. Arrived 26-8-15	[1] 7-17
❏ XZ333		Sud Gazelle AH.1	77	ex Arborfield, MW, 670, ARWF, F-Wxxx. SOC 18-4-19	[1] 9-20
❏ XZ345	'W'	Sud Gazelle AH.1	78	ex B' Down (trials 9-20), Fleetlands, MW. SOC 18-4-19	[1] 9-20
❏ XZ617		Westland Lynx AH.7	80	ex MW. SOC 11-4-15. Arrived 3-9-15	7-17
❏ XZ642		Westland Lynx AH.7	80	ex MW. SOC 11-4-15. Arrived 10-11-15	7-17
❏ XZ653		Westland Lynx AH.7	80	ex Fleetlands. SOC 11-4-15. Arrived 17-6-15	7-17
❏ XZ666		Westland Lynx AH.7	81	ex Arborfield, 669, 655, 665, 655, LCF, 651. F/n 7-17	7-17
❏ XZ679		Westland Lynx AH.7	82	ex MW. SOC 11-4-15. Arrived 3-9-15	7-17
❏ XZ731*	'311'	Westland Lynx HMA.8SRU	80	ex St Athan, MW, Boscombe Down, 815, HAS.3, 702, HAS.2, 815. SOC 23-9-16. Arrived 24-7-19	3-21
❏ XZ732*	'315'	Westland Lynx HMA.8SRU	81	ex St Athan, MW, 815, 702, 815, HAS.3, 702, 815, HAS.2, 829, 702, 815	3-21
❏ XZ732*	'315'	Westland Lynx HMA.8SRU	81	ex St Athan, MW, 815, 702, 815, HAS.3, 702, 815, HAS.2, 829, 702, 815	3-21
❏ ZA735		Sud Gazelle AH.1	80	ex Aborfield, 25 Flt. Arrived 26-8-15	[1] 7-17
❏ ZA769	'K'	Sud Gazelle AH.1	80	ex Arborfield, MW, 670, ARWF. F/n 7-17	[1] 7-17
❏ ZD259*	'474'	W'land Lynx HMA.8SRU	83	ex St Athan, MW, 815, HAS.3, 702, 815	3-21
❏ ZD260*	'313'	W'land Lynx HMA.8SRU	83	ex St Athan, MW, 815, HAS.3, 815, 829, 815. SOC 23-9-16	3-21
❏ ZD261*	'314'	W'land Lynx HMA.8SRU	83	ex St Athan, MW, 815, 702,815, HAS.3, 702, 829, 815	3-21
❏ ZD262*	'316'	W'land Lynx HMA.8SRU	83	ex St Athan, MW, 815, 702, 815, HAS.3, 702, 815	3-21
❏ ZD268*	'366'	W'land Lynx HMA.8SRU	83	ex St Athan, MW, 702, 815, HAS.3, 815	3-21
❏ ZE381	'X'	Westland Lynx AH.7	84	ex Arborfield, Yeovil, 671, 25 Flt, 657, 655, 659, 655, 665. First noted 4-16	7-17
❏ TAD.001		Sud Gazelle CIM	~	ex Arborfield, MW. Cabin. First noted 4-16	[1] 4-16
❏ TAD.007		Westland Lynx CIM	~	ex Arborfield, MW. Fuselage number TO.42	4-16
❏ TAD.011		Westland Lynx CIM	~	ex Arborfield, MW. First noted 4-16	4-16
❏ TAD.012		Westland Lynx CIM	~	ex Arborfield, MW. First noted 4-16	4-16
❏ TAD.015		Sud Gazelle AH.1 ZB668	92	ex Arborfield, MW, Arborfield, Fleetlands, UNFICYP, Crashed 30-11-92. First noted 4-16	[1] 7-17
❏ TAD.019		Sud Gazelle AH.1 XW912	74	ex Boscombe D (JARTS trials 12-20 to 1-21), Arborfield, Fleetlands, 655, 3 CBAS, 656, 655, 3 CBAS. F/n 4-16	[1] 1-21

☐ TAD.021	Sud Gazelle HT.2	XW860	75	ex MW, Fleetlands, Wroughton, 705. First noted 4-16	[1]	7-17
☐ TAD.023	Sud Gazelle AH.1		76	ex Arborfield, Waddington, MW, 663, 662, 656, 657,		
		XX454		659, 669, 664, 654, 669, 659	[1]	7-17

■ [1] All Westland-built.

MALMESBURY

Dyson Campus and Institute of Engineering: ◆ Private *location, by prior arrangement* only | www.dyson.co.uk

| ☐ XM173 | 'A' EE Lightning F.1A | | 60 | ex Old Sodbury, Preston, Bentley Priory, Binbrook 8414M (28-5-74), Binbrook TFF, Leuchars TFF, 226 OCU, 56. Arrived 11-2-13, 'flies' in the canteen | 7-20 |
| ☐ ZD462 | BAe/McDD Harrier GR.7 | | 89 | ex Ipswich, Cosford, St Athan, Cosford 9302M, St Athan, 1. Ditched 25-1-97. First noted 4-12 | 7-20 |

Martin Painter: Lovingly restored Nimrod XV148 cockpit moved on loan to Newquay, Cornwall, on 10th April 2021.

MARLBOROUGH on the A346 south of Swindon

A Dominie is believed to be at a *private* location in the *general* area.

| ☐ N19XY | 'J' HS Dominie T.1 | 66 | ex Kemble, Cranwell, XS731, 55, 3 FTS, 6 FTS, 1 ANS. First noted 2-15 | 5-15 |

MELKSHAM on the A350 south of Chippenham

Adrian Brimson and **John Phillips**: Restoration of the Skeeter is complete and it awaits a new home.
◆ *Viewing by prior permission* only | john.sandie723@yahoo.co.uk

| ☐ XL765 | Saro Skeeter AOP.12 | | 58 | ex 'Northants', Clapham, Leverstock Green, Leamington Spa, Leeds, Rotherham, Wroughton, 17F, 654, 651, Saro. SOC 27-5-68 | 1-22 |

No.**2385 Squadron Air Cadets**: Lancaster Road, Bowerhill.

| ☐ WP863 | DHC Chipmunk T.10 | | 55 | ex Boscombe Down, Hurn, Marlborough, Chippenham | | |
| | | G-ATJI | | 8360M, Shawbury, G-ATJI (de-reg 3-1-68), RAFC, 664, RAFC. SOC 4-4-73. Cockpit | | 1-22 |

NETHERAVON AIRFIELD Restoration of Auster 5 TJ672 (G-ANIJ) continues in the Basingstoke, Hants, area.

OAKSEY PARK AERODROME south of Cirencester, east of the A429   EGTW

Auster 5 G-BDFX had moved to Coleford, Glos, as far back as mid-2017. Cherokee G-BDGY was flying by 2020. The German-based owner of Jungmann G-BHSL is believed to have taken it to his homeland, via a Hampshire workshop, in 2019.

☐ G-ANJK	DH Tiger Moth		41	ex Yarcombe, T6066, 1 GU, 2 GS, 2 RFS, 25 RFS, L'pool UAS, 28 EFTS, 24 EFTS		N11-21
☐ G-ATCL	Victa Airtourer 100		64	CoA 25-7-05		12-18
☐ NL985	DH Tiger Moth		44	ex G-BWIK, Thruxton, Sywell, Cranfield, Leighton Buzzard,		
		G-DHBZ		Bushey, Hendon, Finningley, Colerne, Cwmfelinfach 7015M, 9 AFTS, 2 GS, Lon UAS, Queen's UAS, 11 RFS, 5 RFS, Birm UAS, 16 EFTS, 14 EFTS. Morris-built. Damaged 23-5-71	[1]	5-21

■ [1] Once on charge with the RAF Museum, *India-Kilo* was badly damaged by fire at Hendon 23-5-71 and was replaced by T6296 from Fleet Air Arm stocks (on show at Hendon, Gtr Lon).

OLD SARUM AERODROME east of the A345 north of Salisbury   EGLS

Boscombe Down Aviation Collection (BDAC): The status of this superb museum has been further underlined by its being entrusted with former RAF Museum airframes, another airframe from QinetiQ and a Tornado. The collection charts trials and test aviation in general as well as the activities at nearby Boscombe Down and the incredible heritage of Old Sarum.

BDAC has always had a policy of extra access and the website proudly declares: "Sit in more aircraft cockpits than anywhere else in the UK" - no idle boast. A marvellous detail is an 'ops' room-like blackboard showing exhibit status, including what's new, what's being restored, and which cockpits are open. Visitors enter the display hall through a fuselage 'slice' of Hercules C.1 XV176, acquired in July 2017.

_W&R27_ (p285) jumped the gun with the Old Sarum end of the innovative 'Sycamore Shuffle' - the full story of 'grass roots' common sense is written up at Sunderland, N&T. HR.14 XJ380 remained firmly here until the long hike to <u>Kinloss</u>, Scotland, arriving there on 19th May 2021.

Meteor NF.11 WD686 remains on loan at Defford, Worcs. The cockpit of Jetstream 31 G-PLAH moved to <u>Bournemouth</u>, Dorset, on 19th August 2020. From 7th August 2020 the collection looked after a Spitfire FSM destined for display in Salisbury but delayed due to the Boris-19 Pandemonium. It made the move to <u>Salisbury</u>, Wilts, in July 2021.

A one-off abbreviation is used in the listing below, Boscombe Down = BD: the collection's former home.

◆ _Hangar 1 South, SP4 6DZ_ | **01722 323636** | email via website | **www.boscombedownaviationcollection.co.uk**

❑	G-VIVM*	BAC Jet Provost T.5	65	ex N Weald, G-BVWF, XS230 ETPS, T.5 prototype, 27 MU,		
		XS230		BAC, T.4. Luton-built. Cr 21-6-21, CoA 8-8-21.		
				'Fly Aviation UK' titles. Arrived 7-10-21	[1]	1-22
❑	'2783'	Royal A/c Factory BE.2c rep	07	BAPC.332, ex BD. BDAC-built. _Virgo Intacta_	[2]	1-22
❑	MS968	Taylorcraft Auster 5	44	ex Henstridge, Charlton Mackrell, Heathrow, Irby, AOP.5		
		G-ALYG		MS968, 661, 653. CoA 19-1-70, de-reg 15-10-14.		
				Arrived 10-4-15. Restoration to AOP.V status	[3]	1-22
❑	'PD130'*	Avro Lancaster I FSM	20	forward fuselage, construction well advanced 12-21	[4]	1-22
❑	WA577*	Bristol Sycamore 3	r49	ex Sunderland, King's Heath, Shirley, St Athan 7718M		
		G-ALST		(12-4-61), A&AEE, G-ALST (de-reg 17-10-50). Arrived <u>4-6-21</u>		1-22
❑	WD321	DHC Chipmunk T.10	51	ex BD, Husbands Bosworth, G-BDCC (crashed 29-8-99,		
		G-BDCC		de-reg 8-4-04) WD321, A&AEE, DH. Acquired 12-07		1-22
❑	WD790	Gloster Meteor NF.11	52	ex Usworth, Darlington, Leeming, 8743M (30-10-81), RAE		
				Llanbedr, RRE, Ferranti, TRE. Arrived 3--11-18. Cockpit		1-22
❑	WG763*	EE P.1A	55	ex Manchester, Henlow 7816M, RAE. Last flight 7-12-59.		
				Arrived 31-1 _and_ 1-2-22	[5]	2-22
❑	WH876	EE Canberra B.2(mod)	53	ex BD, Aberporth, BD, Chalgrove, Martin Baker, B.2(mod),		
				A&AEE, U.10, B.2(mod), A&AEE, Pershore, 728, U.14, 73,		
				207, 11. Short-built. Acquired 22-5-01. Cockpit		1-22
❑	WJ865	EE Canberra T.4	54	ex BD, Bromsgrove, Stamford, Stock, Farnborough, ETPS,		
				A&AEE. SOC 6-1-82. Acquired 7-07. Cockpit		1-22
❑	WK800	Gloster Meteor D.16	52	ex BD, Llanbedr, DS&TL, RAE, RAAF A77-876, U.21A, 23,		
				77 RAAF, F.8, RAF. Last flown 11-10-04.		
				Acquired 1-09, arrived 23-7-12	[6]	1-22
❑	WN890	Hawker Hunter F.2	54	ex BD, Doncaster, Firbeck, Robertsbridge, Stamford,		
				Hedge End, BD, A&AEE, AWA. AWA-built. SOC 21-1-63.		
				Acquired 6-05. Cockpit	[7]	1-22
❑	WT648	Hawker Hunter F.1	54	ex BD, Salisbury, Kexborough, Stock, St Athan, Weeton		
				7530M (22-11-57), DFLS. Acquired 4-02. Cockpit	[7]	1-22
❑	WT859	V-S 544	56	ex BD, Long Marston, Brooklands, Ruislip, Foulness,		
				Culdrose, Fleetlands, Culdrose, Lee-on-Solent A2499,		
				RAE, A&AEE. SOC 29-11-60. Acquired 7-02. Cockpit		1-22
❑	WV910	Hawker Sea Hawk	55	ex BD, DERA, DRA, ETPS, 806. Damaged 2-5-58.		
		FGA.4		Acquired 2000. ETPS colours. Cockpit		1-22
❑	WZ736*	Avro 707A	53	ex Manchester, Waddington, Cosford, Finningley, Colerne,		
				868M, RAE Bedford, A&AEE. Arrived 31-1 _and_ 1-2-22	[5]	2-22
❑	WZ753	Slingsby Grasshopper TX.1	52	ex Southampton, Halton, London. Arrived 7-4-19		1-22
❑	XF113	V-S Swift F.7	56	ex BD, Salisbury, Bath, Frome, Farnborough, ETPS, A&AEE,		
				Handling Sqn. SOC 31-10-61. Acquired 2000. Cockpit	[3]	1-22
❑	XF375	'6' Hawker Hunter F.6A	55	ex BD, Spanhoe, Duxford, G-BUEZ (de-reg 28-8-01),		
		G-BUEZ		Cranwell 8736M, (10-1-82), ETPS, EE, RR. AWA-built.		
				Acquired 4-07. ETPS colours		1-22
❑	XG290	Hawker Hunter F.6	56	ex BD, Salisbury, Hurn, Bruntingthorpe, Swanton Morley,		
				Bentley Priory, Halton 8711M (20-10-81), Laarbruch SF,		
				A&AEE. Acquired 6-11. Cockpit	[3]	1-22
❑	XJ476	DH Sea Vixen FAW.1	57	ex BD, Southampton, BD, A&AEE, HSD, ATU Woomera,		
				DH, A&AEE, RRE. Christchurch-built. Acq 6-06. Cockpit	[8]	1-22
❑	XK699	DH Comet C.2	57	ex Lyneham, Henlow 7971M (last flight 13-6-67), 216.		
				Hatfield-built. _Sagittarius_. Forward fuselage. Arr 12-11-13		1-22
❑	'XN149'	Slingsby T.21B	62	ex North Coates, East Kirkby, 9G-ABD, BGA.1085.		
		BMU		_Spruce Goose_. Cr 22-9-97, CoA 27-9-97. Arr 30-11-14	[3] [9]	1-22

❑	XN726		EE Lightning F.2A	61	ex BD, Rayleigh, Foulness, Farnborough, 8545M, Gütersloh,
					92, 19. Cockpit. SOC 1-4-77. Acquired 1-4-00 [10] 1-22
❑	XP899	'D'	Westland Scout AH.1	63	ex M Wallop, Arborfield, M Wallop, ARWF.
					Crashed 1-11-79. Arrived 14-9-15 [11] 1-22
❑	XR650	'28'	Hunting Jet Provost T.4	63	ex BD, DERA, Halton 8459M (19-12-75), SoRF, CAW,
					CATCS, 3 FTS, CAW, 7 FTS. Acquired 4-02 1-22
❑	XS231		BAC Jet Provost T.5	65	ex BD, South Molton, Barnstaple, Ipswich, Bruntingthorpe,
			G-ATAJ		Bruntingthorpe, Hurn, Scampton, Shawbury, A&AEE,
					G-ATAJ, de-reg 10-3-65. Acquired 9-09. Cockpit [12] 1-22
❑	XS743*		Beagle 206Z2	64	ex QinetiQ, ETPS, A&AEE. Last flight 7-11-14 [13] **due**
❑	XS790		HS Andover CC.2	64	ex BD, DERA, DRA, RAE, Queen's Flight. Acquired 11-98.
					Much-modified nose. Cockpit 1-22
❑	XR898		Northrop Shelduck D.1	62	BAPC.365, ex 'XT005', Rochester, Chatham. Gillingham.
					Arrived 5-3-18, acquired 13-6-19 1-22
❑	XT437	'423'	Westland Wasp HAS.1	65	ex BD, Lee-on-Solent A2721[2] (23-3-88), A2641[2]. 829,
					Diomede Flt, 829. Acquired 2001. *Del Boy* 1-22
❑	XV784		HS Harrier GR.3	70	ex BD, DS&TL, Wittering 8909M (10-6-86), 233 OCU, 4, 1, 4.
					Damaged 2-4-86. Acquired 2002. Cockpit [14] 1-22
❑	XW560		SEPECAT Jaguar S.06	69	ex BD, East Grinstead, Farnborough, A&AEE.
					Damaged 11-8-72. Acquired 2004. Cockpit [3] [15] 1-22
❑	XX154		HS Hawk T.1	74	ex BD, ETPS, Llanbedr, DRA, RAE, HSA. Last flight
					19-12-18, arrived 21-8-19. ETPS colours [16] 1-22
❑	XX343		HS Hawk T.1	81	ex BD, DERA, ETPS. Crashed 8-4-97. Acquired 2000.
					ETPS colours. Cockpit [3] 1-22
❑	XX734		SEPECAT Jaguar GR.1	74	ex Charlwood, Abingdon, Coltishall 8816M (21-11-84),
					Farnborough, Shawbury, Warton, Indian AF JI014,
					G-27-328, 6, JOCU. Arrived 5-5-13 [14] [17] 1-22
❑	XX761		SEPECAT Jaguar GR.1A	75	ex BD, DERA, DRA, Warton, 226 OCU, 14. *Pudsey*.
					Damaged 6-6-78. Acquired 2002. Cockpit [14] 1-22
❑	XX919		BAC 111-402	66	ex BD, DERA, RAE, D-AFWC, PI-C-1121. Acq 2001. Cockpit 1-22
❑	XZ335		Sud Gazelle AH.1	77	ex Doncaster Sunderland, Shawbury, 6 Flt.
					Westland-built. Pod. Arrived 7-19 1-22
❑	XZ457	'104'	HS Sea Harrier F/A.2	79	ex BD, Yeovilton, 899, 800, 801, 800, 899, 800, 899, 700A.
					Crashed 20-10-95. Acquired 5-03. *The Sharp End* [18] 1-22
❑	'ZA220'		Short MATS-B	82	ex Nether Wallop, Chandler's Ford, Larkhill, Manorbier.
			Mk.1A UAV ZA242		Last flight 5-2-83. Arrived 20-7-16 [19] 1-22
❑	ZA319*		Panavia Tornado GR.1T	79	ex Bicester 9315M (19-3-02), St Athan, 15, TTTE,
					Warton, A&AEE. Arrived 4-11-21 1-22
❑	ZD936	'AO'	Panavia Tornado F.2	85	ex BD, 'Manchester', Bedford, St Athan, 229 OCU.
					Acquired 2002. 229 OCU colours. Cockpit 1-22
❑	ZJ477*		GEC-Marconi Phoenix UAV	98	ex Larkhill. Arrived 15-9-20. Displayed in 'folded' form 1-22
❑	3150		Target Tech TT-3 Banshee	~	ex Swansea, Manorbier. Acquired 11-13 1-22
❑	-		GEC-Marconi Phoenix UAV	~	BAPC.356, ex Rochester. Arrived 5-3-18, stored [20] 1-22
❑	A92-466		GAF Jindivik 103B	c75	BAPC.485, ex BD, Welshpool, Llanbedr, DRA, RAE.
					Acquired 11-06 [21] 1-22

■ **[1]** Built at Luton as a T.4, converted to T.5 aerodynamic prototype and first flown at Warton 28-2-67. **[2]** BE.2b was built by a BDAC team at Boscombe Down over a 4½ year period, it represents one built by Joncques Aviation in 1914 that served with 66 and 58 Sqns, and 52 Reserve Sqn which came to Boscombe Down in 11-17 and is known to have also operated from Old Sarum. **[3]** Airframes co-owned by John Sharpe and BDAC. **[4]** Lancaster will portray Mk.I Special (Grand Slam) PD130. **[5]** On loan from the RAF Museum. **[6]** WK800 is on loan from Trevor Stone. **[7]** WN890 and WT648 on loan from the Air Defence Collection / Tony Dyer - see below. **[8]** Sea Vixen on loan from Solent Sky - see Southampton, Hampshire. **[9]** T.21 was regularly flown by former Luftwaffe test-pilot Hanna Reitsch when she was CFI of Ghana's Accra Gliding Club in the 1960s. As BGA.1085 it was converted to - or intended to be converted - to a motor glider. Restored to represent a Sedbergh TX.1 flown from Old Sarum by 622 GS. **[10]** XN726 on loan from Hugh Trevor. **[11]** Scout on long term loan from MoD. **[12]** XS231 built at Luton as a T.4, first flown 16-3-65 as T.5 engine development airframe then brought up to full T.5 aerodynamic status. **[13]** Strictly not a Basset CC.1; this was the second pre-production example for the RAF, and as such the 206Z2. Fitted with a variable-stability system at Cranfield 71-72. **[14]** XV784, XX734, XX761 co-owned by Ron Fulton and BDAC. **[15]** UK prototype Jaguar, first flown by Jimmy Dell 12-10-69. **[16]** Prototype Hawk, first flown at Dunsfold 21-8-74 by Duncan Simpson, delivered courtesy of 27 Sqn Chinook HC.6A ZH892 exactly 45 years later! Owned Chris Hodson. **[17]** XX734 is fitted with the wing of XX731. **[18]** XZ457 is a Falklands veteran: operating from *Hermes* two separate pilots accounted for two A-4 Skyhawks on 21-5-82 and two Daggers on 24-5-82: the 'kill tallies' are painted on the nose. **[19]** MATS-B donated by UAV guru Mike Draper - see Stockbridge, Hampshire. When it was built at Castlereagh it should have become ZA242 but it was painted in error as

ZA220 and it was never altered. **[20]** Phoenix is a composite, based upon an engineering trials installation fuselage, with wings etc from surplus stocks. On loan from Medway APS, Rochester and due to return in 2022. **[21]** Jindivik is a composite, including parts from A92-244, -442, -466 and -490. It was believed to be A92-664 which was lost after its 133rd and last sortie, out of Llanbedr, 1-3-83. It has been restored as A92-466 which was discovered under layers of paint on the rear fuselage.

Aerodrome: Resident light aircraft in the North Hangar can be viewed from the BDAC main hall: these are long-termers:

☐ G-AZTV	Stolp Starlet	73	CoA 7-2-12	10-21
☐ G-RENE	Renegade Spirit	91	CoA 12-6-07, de-reg 4-10-06. *Spirit of Adventure* [1]	10-21
☐ G-ROME*	Italiane Sky Arrow	99	CoA 228-6-11	10-21
☐ G-SGNT*	Townsend Skylark	15	CoA 26-2-20	10-21
☐ DE524*	DH Tiger Moth G-ANNG	42	ex Farnborough, 15 EFTS. Morris-built. CoA 8-6-19	10-21
☐ NJ633	Taylorcraft Auster 5	44	ex 29 ETFS, 22 EFTS, 659, Handling Sqn.	
	G-AKXP		CoA 21-2-17	10-21

■ **[1]** G-ANNG is no stranger to *W&R*, it was noted in *W&R* all the way through to *W&R15* as a denizen of the former 'Bagley's Barn' at Farnborough. It flew following a lengthy restoration 24-11-94. **[2]** Cancelled as sold in Thailand.

Air Defence Collection (ADC): Two of Wiltshire-based **Tony Dyer**'s cockpits (Hunters F.1 WT648 and F.2 WN890) are on loan to BDAC - see above - so this is an ideal 'port of convenience' under which to feature the remainder of his collection. Other projects include: a Sopwith Camel cockpit including a large amount of original fittings; *Aurora* (Tony likes naming his creations!) a Spitfire I that he refers to as a "slice through cockpit"; a substantial chunk of the cockpit of Seafire F.46 LA546 *Bea* (acquired in 2006, see also Colchester, Essex); and many recovered parts - around 85% of the fuselage - from P-51D Mustang 44-13835 *Dam Yankee* (crashed 8th February 1945).

◆ *Not open to the public, some airframes with BDAC - see above* | rocketeer1940@aol.com

☐ P3554	Hawker Hurricane I	40	ex Salisbury, Swanage, 607, 213, 56, 32. Shot down 5-10-40. *Jessamy*	[1]	1-22
☐ -	Supermarine Spitfire V	~	fuselage. *Valerie*	[2]	1-22
☐ KF532*	NAA Harvard T.2B	44	ex Sywell, Winthorpe, Lossiemouth, 781, 799, 727, 799, 733, 758. SOC 9-4-54. Noorduyn-built. Cockpit. Arr 10-4-21		1-22
☐ ZD264	Westland Lynx HAS.3	83	ex Hixon, Portsmouth, Fleetlands, 815, 702, 815. SOC 5-8-10. Cockpit, acquired 7-15		3-20

■ **[1]** Started in 1978 with the intention is to create an airframe 85% composed of wartime Hurricane material. To date over *100* Hurricanes have 'provided' parts. Main cockpit items come from P3554 - Plt Off D Evans of 607 Sqn baled out from it over Swanage after combat with a Bf 109. **[2]** Follows the same lines as the Hurricane; now extends from Frame 5 (the firewall) to Frame 13.

SALISBURY

Secret Spitfires Memorial: A Spitfire FSM is displayed at Hudson's Field, Castle Road - the A345 south of the Old Sarum Iron Age Fort - to commemorate the local dispersed Spitfire assembly site. ◆ www.secretspitfiresmemorial.org.uk

☐ -*	Supermarine Spitfire IX	20	BAPC.580, ex Old Sarum. GB Replicas (Norwich)-built.	
	'JE-J' FSM		Plinth-mounted 7-2-1	7-21

Also: A private strip in the area includes two long-termers.

☐ G-ASHT*	Druine Turbulent	63	CoA 28-9-17. Rollason-built. First noted 6-20	6-20
☐ G-BANV*	Currie Wot	77	first noted 6-20	6-20

SALISBURY PLAIN

Ultimately a location in this sprawling site will be the venue for the new **Royal Artillery Museum**, previously at Woolwich, Gtr Lon, and closed in June 2016. Previous exhibits Auster AOP.9 XR271, Shelduck XT583 and Phoenix ZJ356 are held at Wroughton, Wilts. Keep an eye on: https://royalartillerymuseum.com
    Within the vast Copehill Down exercise zone - known as the FIBUA, Fighting In Built-Up Areas - are two Lynx cabins.

☐ XZ171	Westland Lynx AH.1	77	ex 664, 671, RR, A&AEE	5-19
☐ XZ203	'F' Westland Lynx AH.7	79	ex M Wallop, 671, LCF	5-19

SWINDON

Restoration of a Currie Wot continues in the *general* area.

☐ G-AYMP	Currie Wot	72	CoA 4-10-94	9-20

WARMINSTER

Warminster Airsoft: Bath Road. ◆ *By prior arrangement* **only** | www.warminsterairsoft.co.uk

☐ G-BOZU	AAI Sparrow Hawk II	r88	de-reg 9-6-10	5-10

WESTBURY on the A350 between Trowbridge and Warminster

Nigel Coward: Has a collection in the *general* area. Jet Provost T.4 XS177 moved to Selby, N Yorks, during late 2021. Scout AH.1 XT640 moved to South Clifton, Notts, by mid-2021. By March 2020 Nigel had acquired an anonymous Strikemaster cockpit from South Molton, Devon, but he passed this one to an owner on the 'South Coast' during the year.
◆ *Viewing by prior permission only* | nigelcoward@gmail.com

❑ WD387*	DHC Chipmunk T.10	51	ex Hooton Park, Farnborough, WD387, Bristol UAS, 2 FTS,	
	G-BDDD		51, Wadd SF, Edin UAS, 12 AEF, Edin UAS, 11 RFS, 2 BFTS.	
			De-reg 31-7-12. Arrived 9-17. Cockpit	1-22
❑ WT486	EE Canberra T.4	55	ex Newtownards, Gilnahirk, Belfast, Aldergrove 8102M	
			(20-8-70), Wildenrath, 14, 17, 88, Wildenrath SF.	
			Short-built. Cockpit. Arrived 3-19	1-22

WINTERBOURNE GUNNER east of the A338 northeast of Salisbury

Defence Chemical, Biological, Radiological and Nuclear [Event] **Centre** and the **Defence Science and Technology Laboratory**-run the Porton Down 'Danger Area'. The Dominie is used by the Health Authority Response Team. Tornado GR.4 ZA612 moved to St Athan, Wales, in June 2021.

❑ XS736	'S' HS Dominie T.1	66	ex Ipswich, Cranwell, 55, 3 FTS, 6 FTS, RAFC, CAW	4-21
❑ ZG920	Westland Lynx AH.9A	92	ex M Wallop. SOC 3-10-18. First noted 7-18	4-19

WROUGHTON on the A4361 south of Swindon

National Collections Centre (NCR) / **Science Museum Group**: The publicly accessible, vast artefacts and documents facility is on course for a grand opening in 2024: the first items began to arrive in June 2021. Managed by the Science Museum, ten former RAF hangars are held: four 'L' type, four 'D' type and a pair of 'Cs': three of which are not in use. All national museums will keep artefacts - large and small - at the site.

Unlike the NCR, it seems the Science Museum airliner collection and airframe store remains a closed book. The wildly optimistic request made in April 2019 for 'partners' to display the Constellation, Comet and Trident appears to have failed to find any 'takers'. ◆ *By prior arrangement only* | www.sciencemuseum.org.uk

❑ G-ACIT	DH Dragon	33	ex Southend, Beagle, ANT Blackpool, BEA, Scottish,		
			Highland. Last flight 19-9-71, de-reg 26-4-02. Acquired 8-83		1-22
❑ G-ALXT	DH Dragon Rapide	43	ex Strathallan, Staverton, 4R-AAI, CY-AAI, G-ALXT,		
			Dominie NF865, 5 MU, 18 MU, MCS. Brush-built.		
			Arrived 12-81. Railway Air Services colours, *Star of Scotia*		1-22
❑ G-APWY	Piaggio P.166	59	ex Southend, Marconi. CoA 14-3-81, last flown 1-6-83,		
			de-reg 20-10-00		1-22
❑ G-APYD	DH Comet 4B	60	ex Dan-Air, Channel G-APYD, Olympic SX-DAL, BEA, G-APYD.		
			Hatfield-built. CoA 3-8-79, last flown 1-11-79, de-reg 23-11-79		1-22
❑ G-ATTN	Piccard hot-air balloon	66	ex South Kensington, Hayes, South Ken'. De-reg 5-12-77.		
			Acquired circa 1978		1-20
❑ G-AVZB	LET Z37 Cmelak	67	ex Southend, OK-WKQ. CoA 5-4-84, last flew 25-6-88,		
			de-reg 21-12-88		1-22
❑ G-AWZM	HS Trident 3B-101	71	ex Heathrow, BA, BEA. CoA 13-12-85, last flew 28-2-86,		
			de-reg 18-3-86		1-22
❑ G-BBGN	Cameron A-375	74	ex South Kensington, Hayes, South Ken'. *Daffodil II*.		
	hot-air balloon		De-reg 22-8-89. Gondola, acquired 1989		2-18
❑ G-BGLB	Bede BD-5B Micro	c79	ex Booker. CoA 4-8-81, de-reg 21-11-91. Arrived 11-93		2-18
❑ G-BXXR	Lovegrove Four-Runner	98	de-reg 3-11-09		2-18
❑ G-IPSY	Rutan Vari-Eze	82	CoA 6-8-09, de-reg 16-7-09		2-18
❑ G-MMCB	Huntair Pathfinder II	r83	de-reg 23-11-88. Acquired 9-85		2-18
❑ G-RBOS	Colt AS-105 hot air airship	82	CoA 6-3-87, de-reg 3-4-97. Acquired 9-87		2-18
❑ –	Lilienthal Glider	c1894	BAPC.52. ex South Kensington, Hayes, South Kensington,		
			Oxford, Berlin. Acquired 1920	[1]	1-22
❑ –	Newbury Manflier MPA	76	BAPC.162. Major elements, acquired 9-81		2-18
❑ –	Chargus Midas	78	BAPC.172. Acquired 1981		2-18
❑ –	Birdman Grasshopper hg-g	77	BAPC.173. Acquired 1980		2-18
❑ –	Bensen B-7 gyroglider	c74	BAPC.174. Acquired 1980		2-18
❑ –	Wood Ornithopter	c63	BAPC.182, ex Manchester, Hale. Incomplete, stored	[2]	12-18
❑ –	McBroom Cobra 88 h-g	76	BAPC.188. Acquired 10-85		2-18

☐	–	Hartman Ornithopter	59	BAPC.276. Ex Cranfield. Acquired 1993			2-18
☐	EI-AYO	Douglas DC-3A-197	36	ex Shannon, N655GP, N65556, N225JB, N8695SE, N333H, N16071. Last flown 25-12-78			1-22
☐	N18E	Boeing 247	33	ex Wings and Wheels, Orlando, Sky Tours, N18E, N18, N13340 CAA, United/National A/T. Last flown 3-8-82			1-22
☐	N7777G	Lockheed L-749A-79 Constellation	47	ex G-CONI (de-reg 13-6-84), Dublin, Lanzair, KLM PH-LDT, PH-TET. Arrived 12-8-83			1-22
☐	OO-BFH	Piccard gas balloon	32	ex South Kensington, Hayes, South Kensington. Gondola, acquired circa 1937			2-18
☐	VP975 'M'	DH Devon C.2/2	49	ex RAE Farnboro', A&AEE, CCCF, 19 GCF, CPE. Last flew 2-86			1-22
☐	XP505	Folland Gnat T.1	62	ex South Kensington, RAE, MinTech, Dunsfold, CFS. Last flew 18-11-84			1-22
☐	XR271	Auster AOP.9	62	ex Woolwich, Larkhill, St Athan, M Wallop. NEA 8-11-68	[3]		10-16
☐	XT583	Northrop Shelduck D.1	65	ex Woolwich. 'Army' titles	[3]		10-16
☐	ZJ356	GEC-Marconi Phoenix UAV	c95	ex Woolwich. 'Army' titles	[3]		10-16
☐	ZJ452	GEC-Marconi Phoenix UAV	c95	'Army' titles			2-18
☐	100509	Focke Achgelis Fa 330A-1 Bachstelze	44	ex South Kensington, Farnborough. Weser Flug-built. Acquired 2-46			2-18

■ **[1]** No.11 'Normalapparat' hang-glider built by Otto Lilienthal and brought to the UK in March 1895. **[2]** Built by Benjamin Graham Wood of Bowdon, Gtr Man, a hopeful Kremer Prize chaser... **[3]** Stored on behalf of the Royal Artillery Museum.

WORCESTERSHIRE

BEWDLEY on the A456, west of Kidderminster
Ross McNeill ◆ *By prior arrangement* only | rossmcneill@btinternet.com

☐	'Z5663'	Hawker Hurricane II	~	fuselage, complex composite	1-22
☐	-	Avro Anson II	~	ex Canada, RCAF. Cockpit	1-22
☐	XH175 'AR'	EE Canberra PR.9	60	ex Stock, St Athan, 1 PRU, 39, 58. Short-built. Cockpit	1-22

BIRLINGHAM on the A4104, east of the B4080 to the west of Evesham
◆ **Private** *collection, by prior appointment* only

☐	WF299	Hawker Sea Hawk FB.3	54	ex 'WN105', Helston, St Agnes, Topcliffe, Catterick 8164M, Lee-on-Solent, Culdrose SAH-8 A2662, A2509 (21-7-61), 802, 738, 736. AWA-built	10-21
☐	WH166	Gloster Meteor T.7	51	ex Digby 8052M (9-9-69), CFS, 5 CAACU, CAW, 4 FTS, 205 AFS, 210 AFS, 208 AFS	10-21
☐	WZ425	DH Vampire T.11	52	ex Cardiff-Wales, Woodford, Chester, St Athan, 5 FTS, RAFC, 229 OCU, CGS. Christchurch-built. SOC 24-11-67	10-21
☐	XF526 '78' and 'E'	Hawker Hunter F.6	56	ex St Athan, Halton 8679M (9-11-81), Laarbruch SF, 4 FTS, 229 OCU, 56, 43, 56, 63, 66	10-21
☐	'XN623' XN632	Hunting Jet Provost T.3	61	ex Eaglescott, Chivenor, St Athan 8352M (16-7-73), Kemble, Shawbury, 3 FTS	10-21

BROMSGROVE on the A448 northwest of Redditch
Jason Allen, Brian Barrett and Bob Dunn of the **Wolverhampton Aviation Group** keep their Hunter cockpit locally.

☐	XE597	Hawker Hunter FGA.9	56	ex Moreton-in-Marsh, Halton, Bentley P' 8874M (4-10-85), Brawdy, 1 TWU, 2 TWU, TWU, 229 OCU, W Raynham SF, 1, 54, MoA, 208, 56, 63, 66. Cockpit. 1 Squadron colours	6-21

DEFFORD on the A4104 southwest of Pershore
RAF Defford Museum: Established and run by the **Defford Airfield Heritage Group** in association with the National Trust. Visitors pay Croome Park's admission charge; there is no additional charge to visit this fascinating museum.
◆ *Within Croome Park, WR8 9DW* | **email** *via website* | **http://deffordairfield heritagegroup.wordpress.com** – superbly detailed site | also **www.nationaltrust.org.uk/croome**

| ❏ WD686 | 'S' | Gloster Meteor NF.11 | 52 | ex Old Sarum, Weybourne, Duxford, RAE Bedford, RRE Defford, Wroughton, A&AEE, CFE, TRE Defford. AWA-built. SOC 2-11-67. Entire airframe on site by 8-19 | [1] | 1-22 |
| ❏ WD956 | | EE Canberra B.2 | 51 | ex Cosford, Aldridge, Pershore, RRE, RAE, Vickers. SOC 30-12-64. Cockpit | [2] | 1-22 |

■ **[1]** On loan from BDAC, Old Sarum. Last aircraft to fly out of Defford, on 28-3-58. **[2]** WD956 served with Vickers, Wisley, and tested the huge RED DEAN missile. It later joined RAE/RRE and the cockpit *may* have been grafted to WD931.

DRAKELOW By April 2021 'JP' T.4 XM405 had moved to Lubenham, Leics.

EVESHAM on the A46 northeast of Cheltenham
Holdair: Martyn Holder has a *private* workshop in the area.
| ❏ XX665 | | SAL Bulldog T.1 | 74 | ex Selby, Wellesbourne M', Halton, Newton 9289M, E Low, Abn, E Low UASs. Crashed 20-9-97. Cockpit. Arrived by 4-18 | 5-18 |

HONEYBOURNE north of the village, on a minor road between Bretforton and Mickleton
All Things Wild: 'Hands on' animals and other attractions. ◆ www.allthingswild.co.uk
| ❏ XP346 | | Westland Whirlwind HAR.10 | 62 | ex Long Marston, Tattershall Thorpe, Shawbury, Lee-on-Solent, Akrotiri 8793M (2-9-83), 84, 22, 225. F/n 12-14 | 6-21 |

KIDDERMINSTER
Paintball Park Kidderminster: Blakedown. ◆ *By prior arrangement* only | www.paintballpark.co.uk
| ❏ XZ193 | '4' | Westland Lynx AH.7 | 78 | ex Weeton, Hixon, Fleetlands, 671, 656, 665,656, 653, ARWF. Cabin. Arrived 2-18 | 8-21 |

PERSHORE on the A44 west of Evesham
W&R27 (p291) declared that the cockpit of Dove G-ANAP moved to 'Lincolnshire'; it ended up at March, Cambs. **No.233 Squadron Air Cadets**: Last noted in February 2014, the anonymous Tomahawk cockpit has been deleted.

WORCESTER
Jungle Safari Adventure Golf: Within the Ravenmeadow Golf Centre. ◆ www.adventuregolfworcester.com
| ❏ G-AVWN | | Piper Arrow 180 | 67 | CoA 10-4-09, de-reg 13-3-09. First noted 7-19 | 7-21 |

EAST YORKSHIRE
Includes the unitary authority of Kingston upon Hull

Mower hazard Cherokee 140 G-BEYT, July 2020. *Andy Wood*

BEVERLEY AERODROME or Linley Hill, on minor roads north of Beverley
Hull Aero Club: A Cherokee acts as a mowing hazard.
☐ G-BEYT*   Piper Cherokee 140   64 ex D-EBWO, N6280W. CoA 13-8-<u>15</u>   7-20

BREIGHTON AERODROME in between Bubwith and Breighton, east of Selby
Real Aeroplane Company (RAC): Aircraft operated by Tony 'Taff' Smith, Rob Fleming and friends including, Aeronca 100 G-AEVS, Dart Kitten G-AEXT, Magister T9738 (G-AKAT), Argus HB751 (G-BCBL) etc are based at this delightful former bomber airfield. Listed below are non-flyers, stored, or long-term restoration projects. Elements of Nigel Ponsford's collection are also kept here - see also under Selby, N Yorks. _W&R27_ (p292) recorded Chipmunk T.10 WG458 as bound for an Essex-based owner: it moved via Wickenby. Lincs, to settle at <u>Eshott</u>, N&T. Dragonfly 250 G-MJLK had departed by late 2021. Wasp HAS.1 XT434 (G-CGGK) departed to <u>Higher Purtington</u>, Somerset, on 25th October 2021.
◆ _Entry restricted to RAC members **only** but rates very reasonable | Selby, YO8 6DS | www.realaero.com_

☐ G-ADXS		Mignet HM.14 'Flea'	35	ex Cambridge, East Tilbury, Andrewsfield, Southend, Staverton, Southend. CoA 1-12-36, de-reg 1-12-46. _The Fleeing Flea_	[1] 1-22
☐ G-AESZ*	'29'	Chilton DW.1	37	ex Old Warden. CoA 28-8-18. Arrived 10-9-20	1-22
☐ G-AFSV*		Chilton DW.1A	39	ex Warwick, 'Coventry'. CoA 12-7-72. Arrived 3-9-20	1-22
☐ G-AMAW		Luton Minor	48	ex Batley, Old Warden, Hitchin. CoA 6-8-88	[2] 1-22
☐ G-AXEI		Ward Gnome	67	ex East Kirkby, Tattershall. De-reg 30-5-84	[3] [4] 1-22
☐ G-AYDV		Coates Swalesong SA.2	74	CoA 8-8-07	[2] 1-22
☐ G-BAAD		Evans VP-1	73	CoA 20-9-11	1-22
☐ G-BAHL		Robin DR.400-160	72	ex F-OCSR. CEA-built. CoA 16-5-11	1-22
☐ G-BDDF		Jodel D.120 Paris-Nice	57	ex F-BIKZ. Wassmer-built. CoA 10-11-03	1-22
☐ G-BDJD*		Jodel D.112	77	CoA 2-7-<u>17</u>	1-22
☐ G-BJVS*		Piel Super Emeraude	62	ex F-BJVS. Scintex-built. CoA 28-8-18	1-22
☐ G-JUNG		Bücker Jungmann	52	ex Spanish AF E.3B-143. CASA-built. CoA 30-6-<u>09</u>. Arr 10-19	1-22
☐ G-MMUL		Ward Elf	r84	ex Newark area. De-reg 12-4-89	[3] [4] 1-22
☐ G-OMIC*		Bücker Jungmeister	40	ex HB-MIC, USA, Swiss AF U-86. Last flown 1967. Arr 21-9-20	1-22
☐ G-TYAK		Yakovlev Yak-52	89	ex RA-01038. IAR Bacau-built. CoA 29-4-16	1-22
☐ N102L		Bücker Jungmann	39	ex HB-UTT, Swiss AF A-77. Dornier-built. Off-site	1-22
☐ 'F50'		Mignet HM.14 'Flea'	89	BAPC.329, ex Harrogate	[4] 1-22
☐ 491273	'51'	Aero L29 Delfin	~	ex Chester, YL-PAG, Soviet AF. Displayed	1-22

■ [1] 'Flea' built by Christopher Storey at Southend, it first flew 15-11-35 and gained Authorisation No.20. [2] G-AMAW was built by J A Coates and was also known as the Coates SA.1 Swalesong. Original design G-AYDV was also built by John. [3] On loan from Nigel Ponsford - see also Selby, N Yorks. [4] Gnome, Elf designed and built by Mick Ward, 'Flea' built by Mick.

Tony Brier: Has a workshop in the area.
☐ 356   Kader Gomhouria Mk.6   ~ ex Gainsborough, Egyptian AF   [1] 1-22
■ [1] Gomhouria is a licence-built Zlin Z.381. The Z.381 was itself a version of the Bücker Bü 181 Bestmann. Gomhourias were built by the Heliopolis Aircraft Works / Kader Industries.

BRIDLINGTON on the A165, south of Scarborough
Aircraft Preservation Foundation: Run by <u>G</u>eremy Britton and Sarah Thorpe, a workshop has been established in the _general_ area. During 2020 an exceptional restoration of a Nimrod MR.2 simulator was completed: this, 'JP' XP642 and a Tornado SIM are on loan at Newquay Cornwall, Cornwall. The Victor procedure trainer at Neatishead, Norfolk, is also part of the collection. Present projects are an Airbus A300B and a Boeing 737-100 simulator.
◆ _By prior arrangement **only** | info@aircraftpreservation.co.uk | www.aircraftpreservation.co.uk_

BROUGH AIRFIELD south of the A63 west of Hull
BAE Systems Military Air Solutions:
☐ -		HS Hawk T.53	c80	ex Hurn, Indonesian AF LL-5313. Displayed	[1] 12-20
☐ -	TR002	Eurofighter Typhoon	~	cockpit and centre fuselage	[2] 2-15
☐ -	AJ-1	Lockheed F-35A EMU	c09	arrived 2009. 'Lifetime' fatigue testing airframe	11-17

■ [1] Composite, based upon T.53 L-5313 but with a Srs 100 nose and other mods. [2] Referred to as SIFT - Single Seat Fatigue Test.

DRIFFIELD on the A614 north of Beverley
A Pup is at a _private_ workshop to the north of the town.

| ☐ G-AXSD | Beagle Pup 100 | 69 | ex Turweston, Bagby, Prestwick, G-35-139. CoA 10-5-08, de-reg 2-2-11. Arrived 3-1-18 | | 1-22 |

FULL SUTTON AERODROME south of the A166, east of Stamford Bridge
Famous last words; *W&R27* (p292) 'wrote off' the Cessna and Cherokee: five years after their last sighting, they live on!

☐ G-BARV	Cessna 310Q	73	ex Elstree. CoA 18-8-09, de-reg 3-3-11. First noted 5-16	9-21
☐ G-COLH	Piper Cherokee 140	67	ex G-AVRT. De-reg 13-9-16	9-21
☐ G-LAKE*	Lake LA-250	88	ex Biggin Hill, N8415B. CoA 20-11-13	9-21
☐ N315P*	Cessna 310Q	73	ex G-REDB, G-BBIC, N69600	9-21
☐ N421CA*	Cessna 421C	~	ex Elstree	9-21

GILBERDYKE on the B1230 east of Goole
Joe and Lyndon Blackburne - The Provost Boys: The Canberra cockpit is being restored to represent a former Pershore B.6(mod) test bed. ◆ *Viewable by prior arrangement* only | lyndon.blackburne@everquip.co.uk

☐ WK124	'CR' EE Canberra TT.18	54	ex Binbrook, South Clifton, Manston, Wyton 9093M, 100, 7, FRU, B.2, 213, 59, 103. Avro-built. Last flew 26-3-91. Cockpit. Arrived 26-10-17	[1]	1-22
☐ XD377	DH Vampire T.11	53	ex Doncaster, Firbeck, Barton, Thornaby, Elvington, Cosford, Birmingham, Shawbury 8203M (28-7-72), Hawarden, 66. Hawarden-built. Cockpit		1-22
☐ XR662	'25' Hunting Jet Provost T.4	63	ex Shrewsbury, Tettenhall, Baxterley, Wolverhampton, Bicester, Kemble, Finningley, Halton 8410M (6-6-74), SoRF, CAW, CATCS, RAFC, CAW, 6 FTS, CAW. F/n 10-17		1-22

■ [1] Centre section and starboard wing were in use at the fire school at Manston, Kent, relocated to the JARTS enclave at Newquay, Cornwall, in 2020.

KINGSTON UPON HULL
St Stephen's Shopping Centre: Ferensway, off the A1079. **www.ststephens-hull.com**

| ☐ 'G-AAAH' | DH Moth FSM | 17 | BAPC.470. Ex railway station. *Jason* | [1] | 12-19 |

■ [1] There is another replica at Hawkinge, Kent and - of course - the real thing at South Kensington, Gtr Lon.

Streetlife Museum of Transport: Five extensive galleries ranging between bicycles, cars, carriages and railways.
◆ *High Street, Hull, HU1 1PS* | 01482 300300 | www.hcandl.co.uk

| ☐ 'G-EBVO' | Blackburn Lincock FSM | 99 | BAPC.287, ex Brough | 10-21 |

Also: The Miles types are at a *private* location in the *general* area.

| ☐ G-AGOY | Miles Messenger 3 | 43 | ex West Chiltington, Hatch, Southill, Castletown, EI-AGE, HB-EIP, G-AGOY, U-0247. CoA 25-11-53 | 12-21 |
| ☐ G-AHAA | Miles Mercury 6 | 46 | ex OY-ALW, D-EHAB, G-AHAA. First noted 1-19 | 12-21 |

LITTLE WEIGHTON west of the A164 and Cottingham
The former Pocklington Short 330 is *thought* to remain at a *private* location here.

| ☐ OY-MUB | Short 330-200 | 81 | ex Pocklington, Alton, Hurn, G-BITX, G-14-3069. Fuselage. First noted 6-17 | 6-17 |

OTTRINGHAM on the A1033 east of Hedon
A long out-of-use Cessna 120 is stored at a *private* location in the *general* area.

| ☐ G-BRPG* | Cessna 120 | 46 | ex N7203. CoA 29-8-94 | 8-20 |

PATRINGTON on the A1033 east of Hedon
A Vampire is kept at a *private* venue in the *general* area.

| ☐ XD542 | 'N' DH Vampire T.11 | 53 | ex Beverley, Montrose, Edzell, Cranwell, 'XD429', Colerne, Melksham 7604M (22-6-59), FWS, CGS. Hawarden-built | [1] | 6-21 |

■ [1] The booms of XD542 can be found at Birkin, N Yorks.

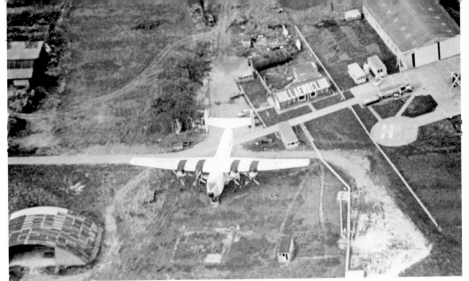

Beverley C.1 XB259 in use as a clubroom/control tower at the former Hull Aero Club at Paull – only a short distance from Fort Paull – in September 1977. It was moved to the Museum of Army Transport at Beverley by road in 1983. On the collapse of that museum, it was dismantled yet again, arriving at Fort Paull in 2004. *Author's collection*

PAULL on minor road south of Hedon
Former **Fort Paull Armouries and Visitors Centre**: The contents of the site - 1,048 lots - were auctioned on 19th September 2020. Hunter XF509 was hammered at £13,000 but was re-auctioned on 27th February 2021. It departed bound for Manston, Kent, on 18th June 2021. Blackburn Triplane replica BAPC.380 and Bulldog T.1 XX557 are reported to have both reached £850 – no further details for either.

Beverley C.1 XB259 was 'hammered' for £21,000, plus a reported £13,000 for associated 'extras', to Martyn Wiseman of North Duffield, North Yorks. Dismantling began almost immediately with help from Fort Paull volunteers, but this assistance was withdrawn in early October 2020 when the plans to turn XB259 into accommodation at North Duffield were revealed. A crowd-funding account – Save-the-Blackburn-Beverley-Aircraft – was launched in January 2021 and dismantling began again from August 2021. Many readers have expressed horror at the 'fate' awaiting XB259, but with respect to Martyn and his team, the airlifter was bought as a business venture and not as a heritage project. (There are plans that displays relating to XB259's history, and that of the Beverley in general, will be included in the 're-born' airframe-cum-holiday home.) No 'established' museums, or heritage organisations, made anything other than noise about the plight of XB259. Charismatic, last-of-the-line, the RAF's first real tactical airlifter, the Beverley was too large, a logistical nightmare and not easy to 'attribute' to a museum, even if it was wanted. (The RAF Museum has clear and present relevance, but the recent 'policy' on disposals has put serious doubt among 'experimental' airframes it already holds: XB259 was never an operational RAF airframe, spending its life on test and trials work.) The task of moving the giant was still going on as W&R went to press: but it has been listed under North Duffield, N Yorks.

POCKLINGTON AERODROME east of the A1079, west of the village

A Delfin is kept locally.

☐	'29'	Aero L29 Delfin	893046	~ ex '142', Market Drayton, Romanian AF	[1] 3-19

■ [1] L29 is a composite, with outer wings and tailplane from another, or other, aircraft.

PRESTON on the B1239 north of Hedon

Wright's Garage: Staithes Road.

☐	WL627	Vickers Varsity T.1	53	ex Hull, Newton 8488M (3-3-76), 6 FTS, 2 ANS, 1 ANS, BCBS. Hurn-built. Cockpit

9-21

SEWERBEY off the B1255 northeast of Bridlington

Sewerby Hall and Gardens: Amy Johnson opened the house in 1936 and to celebrate this there is a permanent exhibition dedicated to the locally born aviator. ◆ Church Lane, Sewerby, YO15 1EA | www.sewerbyhall.co.uk

SOUTH CAVE off the A1034, north of Brough
A *private* strip in the *general* area.

☐ G-BAXE*	Hughes 269A	64	ex N8931F. CoA 21-12,93, de-reg 17-10-19. Cab	8-21
☐ G-BLPI*	Slingsby T.67B Firefly	84	de-reg 13-3-19. Cockpit	8-21
☐ G-SHPP*	Hughes 269A	68	ex N80559. Cr 28-7-08, e-reg 9-12-08, CoA 3-6-09. Cab	8-21

STORWOOD on a minor road south of Elvington
At the *private* store in the locality, Skeeter AOP.12 XL763 was inspected in the summer of 2021 and, as little more than a cabin floor, has been deleted. ◆ *By prior arrangement* only I www.melbourneautos.co.uk

☐ G-VOCE*	Robinson R22 Beta	89	ex Doncaster, G-BSCL. De-reg 16-5-19	10-21
☐ XM565	Saro Skeeter AOP.12	59	ex Leeds, Ivybridge, M Wallop, Fleetlands, M Wallop, Southampton, M Wallop 7861M (17-9-64), 651	10-21
☐ XR627	'X' Westland Scout AH.1	64	ex Townhill, Ipswich, Wattisham, Arborfield, Dishforth, M Wallop, Wroughton, Garrison Air Sqn, 3 CBAS	10-21
☐ XT788	'316' Westland Wasp HAS.1 G-BMIR	67	ex Dunkeswell, Faygate, Tattershall Thorpe, Wroughton, 829. SOC 19-12-85. De-reg 22-12-95	10-21

NORTH YORKSHIRE
Includes the unitary authority of York

BAGBY AERODROME, or Thirsk, on the A19 southeast of Thirsk   EGNG
Tomahawk G-BPHI was flying again by 2020.

☐ G-ARLR	Beagle Terrier 2	48	ex Auster AOP.6, VW996, AAC, 663. CoA 9-9-01	1-22
☐ G-AZSW	Beagle Pup 100	69	ex PH-VRT, G-35-140. Cr 3-9-06, CoA 15-6-09, de-reg 15-2-11	1-22
☐ G-BSOK	Piper Warrior II	79	ex N9749K. CoA 9-9-13	1-22
☐ G-CCRC*	Cessna TU.206G	86	ex Movenis, 9A-DLC, YU-DLC, N9960R. CoA 24-9-11. Arrived 23-6-21	1-22
☐ G-SIMY*	Piper Cherokee Six 300	76	ex G-OCPF, G-BOCH, N9292K. CoA 17-4-19	1-22
☐ G-THMK*	Piper Tomahawk	78	ex G-GALL, G-BTEV, N9315T. CoA 1-6-12	1-22
☐ N88NA*	Piper Cherokee Arrow	~	dismantled. First noted 2-21	1-22

BIRKIN east of the A162 and north of the A645, northeast of Knottingley
Paintball Commando: ◆ *By prior arrangement* only

☐ -	Westland Lynx EMU	84	ex -?-, Weston-super-Mare, Yeovil. Zebra-striped	[1] 12-19
☐ XE874	'61' DH Vampire T.11	54	ex Montrose, New Byth, Valley 8582M, Woodford, Chester, Shawbury,1 FTS, 4 FTS, 8 FTS, 4 FTS, 1 FTS, 4 FTS, 7 FTS. Christchurch-built. SOC 30-10-67	[2] 11-21

■ [1] Built at Yeovil in 1984 using Lynx and WG.30 parts. [2] XE874 was fitted with the booms of XD528. These lie nearby, semi-submerged in a small lake. XE974 has booms fitted which *may* come from XD542.

CARTHORPE Norecrin G-BHXJ had moved on from the upmarket glamping site by June 2019.

CROFT south of Darlington, Croft-on-Tees and the A167
Point Blank Paintball: On the former No.2 Communal Site of the wartime airfield.
◆ *By prior arrangement* only | www.pointblank-paintball.co.uk

☐ G-ATSY	Wassmer Baladou IV	66	ex Rufforth, CoA 23-11-91, de-reg 6-3-15. Arr 26-3-15	9-21
☐ OY-XGP	'K6' Scheibe SF.25B	70	ex D-KOSC	9-21

DINSDALE on a minor road south of Middleton St George
Anthony Harker: Keeps a Lightning at a *private* location in the area.

☐ XR718	'DA' EE Lightning F.3	64	ex Walpole, Wattisham 8932M (9-2-87), ABDR, LTF, 11, LTF, 11, 5, LTF, 5, 11, LTF, 5, LTF, 5, 226 OCU, 29, 56	10-21

■ [1] There is a partial 'imposter' of XR718 at Bruntingthorpe, Leics.

ELVINGTON off the B1228 southeast of York

Yorkshire Air Museum and Allied Air Forces Memorial: As well as the aircraft, the watch tower and other World War Two buildings, the famed 'NAAFI' remains a 'must do' at this atmospheric site. A walk through the many wartime huts is a fascinating tour through the history of the region and there are memorials across the site. There are regular special events, including 'Night Shoots' and 'Thunder Day' runs. Pre-bookable tours of the Halifax re-creation are proving popular.

◆ *Off the A64, YO41 4AU* | **01904 608595** | **museum@yorkshireairmuseum.org** | **www.yorkshireairmuseum.org**

❑ 'G-AFFI'		Mignet HM.14 'Flea'	75	BAPC.76, ex Hemswell, Cleethorpes, Nostell, Rawdon. Yeadon Aeroplanes-built. Arrived 1989	[1]	1-22
❑ G-AVPN		HP Herald 213	64	ex Channel Express, I-TIVB, G-AVPN, D-BIBI, HB-AAK. CoA 14-12-99, de-reg 8-12-97. Flew in 20-10-97. Cockpit		1-22
❑ G-MJRA		Mainair Tri-Flyer	r82	ex Wetherby. (Demon 175 wing) De-reg 24-1-95. Arr 2001		7-21
❑ G-TFRB		Air Command 532	90	ex Hartlepool. CoA 6-8-98, de-reg 7-6-01. Arrived 11-01		1-22
❑ G-YURO		Shaw Europa 001	92	ex Wombleton. CoA 9-6-95, de-reg 22-4-98. Arrived 1997		7-21
❑ –		Wright Flyer replica	66	BAPC.28, ex Leeds, Eccleston, Cardington, Finningley. Arrived 11-99	[2]	1-22
❑ –		Cayley glider replica	72	BAPC.89, ex Manchester, Hendon, Lasham. Southdown Aero Services-built. Unveiled 12-8-99	[3]	1-22
❑ –		Blackburn 1911 replica	78	BAPC.130, ex Stoke, Helston, *Flambards*. Arrived 10-1-95		1-22
❑ '9970'		Royal Aircraft Factory BE.2c replica	62	BAPC.41, ex '6232', St Athan, Halton. 1 SoTT, Halton-built. Arrived 10-94		1-22
❑ '9828'		Avro 504K replica	68	BAPC.42, ex 'H1968', St Athan, 1 SoTT, Halton-built. Arr 10-94		1-22
❑ 'F943'	'S'	Royal Aircraft Factory SE.5a replica G-BKDT	r82	ex Selby, Elvington, Selby, G-BKDT. De-reg 11-7-91. Arrived 1987. Taxiable	[4]	1-22
❑ 'N540'		Port Victoria Kitten rep	c80	ex Selby. Arrived 1996. Taxiable	[5]	3-20
❑ 'P3873'	'YO-H'	Hawker Hurricane I FSM	99	BAPC.265. Arrived 10-00. 401 Sqn RCAF colours		1-22
❑ 'R6690'	'PR-A'	V-S Spitfire I FSM	96	BAPC.254. TDL Replicas-built. Unveiled 9-96. 609 Sqn c/s		1-22
❑ FK338		Fairchild Argus II G-AJOZ	42	ex Woodhall Spa, Tattershall, Wigan, Mkt Drayton, Wigan, Southend, Sywell, G-AJOZ, FK338, Kemble, ATA 2 FP, 42-32142. Cr 16-8-62, de-reg 27-2-67. Arrived 2000		1-22
❑ KN353		Douglas Dakota 4 G-AMYJ	44	ex 'KG427', Coventry, SU-AZF, G-AMYJ, XF747, G-AMYJ, KN353, KN353, 110, 96, 243, USAAF C-47B-25-DK 44-76384. CoA 4-4-97, de-reg 12-12-01. Arrived 10-12-01. Taxiable		1-22
❑ 'LV907' and 'NP763'		HP Halifax recreation	44	BAPC.449, *Friday 13th*, 158 Sqn colours, Mk.III 'NP-F', to port, Mk.VI 'H7-N', 346 Sqn colours to starboard	[6]	1-22
❑ RA854		Slingsby Cadet TX.1	43	ex Wigan, Woodford, RAFGSA, 186 GS, 41 GS. Otley Motors-built. Arrived 6-4-00		7-21
❑ VP967		DH Devon C.2/2 G-KOOL	48	ex Redhill, Goodwood, Redhill, East Surrey Tech G-KOOL (de-reg 13-1-12), 'G-DOVE', Biggin Hill, VP967, Kemble, Culdrose SF, 21, 207, SCCS, SCS, WCS, SCS, NCS, SCS, MCS, MCS, CCCF, 38 GCF, TTCCF, FCCS, 2 TAF CS, MCCS, RAFG CS, 2 TAF CS, Wahn SF, RCCF. SOC 1-4-82. Arrived 6-10-10. 207 Sqn c/s, taxiable		1-22
❑ VV901		Avro Anson T.21	49	ex Bacup, Burtonwood, Cosford, Irton Holme, Leconfield, CFCCU, Dur UAS, 1 RFS. Arrived 8-6-93		7-21
❑ VW993		Beagle Terrier 2 G-ASCD	48	ex 'TJ704', Holme-on Spalding Moor, Nympsfield, Blackbushe, PH-SFT, G-ASCD (CoA 26-9-71, de-reg 5-10-89), Auster AOP.6 VW993, 651, 663. Arrived 1988		1-22
❑ WH846		EE Canberra T.4	54	ex Samlesbury, St Athan, Laarbruch SF, 231 OCU. SOC 29-1-82. Arrived 19-5-88		1-22
❑ WH903		EE Canberra B.2	54	ex 102, 617. Arrived 1992. Short-built, cockpit	[7]	1-22
❑ WH991		Westland Dragonfly HR.5	53	ex Storwood, Tattershall Thorpe, Tattershall, Wisbech, Taunton, Fleetlands, Culdrose SF, 705, 700, Eglinton SF, *Centaur* Flt, 705, *Illustrious* Flt. SOC 8-6-70. Arrived 10-94		1-22
❑ WK640*	'C'	DHC Chipmunk T.10 G-BWUV	52	ex Halton, FSS, East Mids UAS, 7 AEF, RAFC, QUAS, St Andrews UAS, 1 FTS, St And UAS, 1 RFS, 17 RFS. Crashed 20-2-09. CoA 24-2-11. Cockpit. Arrived 12-20	[8]	1-21
❑ 'WK864'	'C'	Gloster Meteor F.8 WL168	54	ex Finningley, 'WH456', St Athan, Swinderby, Finningley, Heywood 7750M (10-5-62), Sylt, 604, 111. Arr 12-4-96. 616 c/s		1-22

❏ WS788	'Z'	Gloster Meteor NF(T).14	54	ex Leeming 'WS844', Patrington 7967M (5-9-67), 1 ANS, 2 ANS, NF.14, 152. AWA-built. Acquired 6-89, arrived16-3-92		1-22
❏ XH278	'42'	DH Vampire T.11	55	ex Felton, Henlow 8595M, Upwood 7866M (9-11-64), 27 MU, RAFC. Hawarden-built. Arrived 10-2-02. RAFC c/s		1-22
❏ XH767	'L'	Gloster Javelin FAW.9	57	ex Leeming, Norwich, Monkton Farleigh, Worcester 7955M (10-7-67), Shawbury, 228 OCU, 11, 25, FAW.7. Arr 4-2-01		1-22
❏ XL231		HP Victor K.2	62	ex 55, 57, Witt Wing, Victor TF, Witt Wing, 139. Flew in 25-11-93. *Lusty Lindy*. Taxiable	[9]	1-22
❏ XL502		Fairey Gannet AEW.3 G-BMYP	61	ex Sandtoft, Carlisle, G-BMYP (CoA 29-9-89, de-reg 22-2-05), Leuchars 8610M (1-12-78), 849, Pershore, 849. Arr 11-3-05		1-22
❏ 'XL571'	'V'	Hawker Hunter T.7 XL572	58	ex Brough, Hurn G-HNTR (de-reg 11-10-91), Cosford 8834M (23-8-84), XL572, 1 TWU, 2 TWU, TWU, 229 OCU. Arrived 12-1-95. 92 Sqn, 'Blue Diamonds' colours		1-22
❏ XM553		Saro Skeeter AOP.12 G-AWSV	59	ex Wattisham, Saxmundham, M Wallop, G-AWSV (de-reg 23-5-95), 15 MU, 5 Flt, 1 Wg. SOC 25-11-68. Arr 2009		1-22
❏ XN582*	'95'	Hunting Jet Provost T.3A	61	ex Sleap, Bruntingthorpe, Teversham, Cambridge, Teversham, Cosford 8957M (11-3-88), 7 FTS, 1 FTS, 3 FTS, RAFC. *Spirit of Shropshire*. Arrived 9-12-21		1-22
❏ XN589	'46'	Hunting Jet Provost T.3A	61	Linton-on-O' 9143M, 1 FTS, RAFC. Arr 31-10-19. 1 FTS c/s		1-22
❏ XN974		Blackburn Buccaneer S.2A	64	ex Warton, Holme on Spalding Moor, RAE Bedford, HoSM, A&AEE, Driffield, HoSM, A&AEE, RAE Bedford, A&AEE, HoSM. Flew in 19-8-91. Taxiable		1-22
❏ XP640	'M'	Hunting Jet Provost T.4	62	ex Halton 8501M (13-9-76), CATCS, 6 FTS, CAW, CFS, 3 FTS. Arrived 10-93		1-22
❏ XS903	'BA'	EE Lightning F.6	66	ex Binbrook, 11, 5-11 pool. Flew in 8-5-88. 11 Sqn colours	[1]	1-22
❏ XV168	'AF'	Blackburn Buccaneer S.2B	66	ex Brough, Lossiemouth, 12, 208, 12, 801. SOC 15-10-93. Arrived 18-8-13. 12 Sqn colours	[10]	1-22
❏ XV250		HS Nimrod MR.2	71	ex Kinloss, Kin Wing, Kin & St M Wing, MR.1, 42, Kinloss, 202, Kinloss. Flew in 13-4-10. Taxiable		1-22
❏ XV748	'3D'	HS Harrier GR.3	69	ex Cranfield, Bedford, 233 OCU, 1, GR.1, 233 OCU, 1. Arrived 21-10-00	[11]	1-22
❏ XX901		Blackburn Buccaneer S.2B	77	ex Kemble, St Athan, Lossiemouth, 208, 12, 237 OCU. 208. SOC 10-1-95. Arrived 26-5-96. *Kathryn - The Flying Mermaid / Glen Elgin*. Pink scheme	[1]	1-22
❏ XZ631		Panavia Tornado GR.4	78	ex Warton, Panavia, A&AEE. Arrived 22-3-05. 2 Sqn c/s		1-22
❏ ZA354		Panavia Tornado GR.1	82	ex Warton. Arrived 29-4-05		
❏ –	'1'	Hunting Jet Provost T.3	c62	ex Linton-on-Ouse. Procedure trainer. Arrived 10-92		3-20
❏ –	'2'	Hunting Jet Provost T.3	c62	ex Linton-on-Ouse. Procedure trainer, 1 FTS badge	[12]	3-20
❏ 21417		Lockheed CT-133 Silver Star	54	ex Germany, 414 Sqn, CAF 133417, RCAF 21417. Arrived 25-6-93. Canadair-built		1-22
❏ 45	'BR'	Dassault Mirage IVA	66	ex Paris, French AF. Last flight 11-9-91. Arrived 30-3-17	[13]	1-22
❏ 538	'3-QH'	Dassault Mirage IIIE	68	ex 3 Esc, French AF. Arrived 1995		1-22
❏ '15919'	'1'	M'schmitt Bf 109G FSM	94	BAPC.240, ex Garforth. Arrived 5-94	[14]	7-21
❏ QA-10		Hawker Hunter FGA.78	68	ex 'N-2' Hurn, Qatar AF QA-10, G-9-286, Dutch AF N-268. Arrived 25-4-92		1-22
❏ '319764'	'329'	Waco CG-4A Hadrian	~	BAPC.157, ex '237123', Bacup, Ormskirk. *Bonjour Julie*		7-21

■ **[1]** Airframes on loan: the 'Flea' from Dave Allan; Lightning from Peter Chambers; Buccaneer XX901 from Buccaneer Aircrew Association. **[2]** Built by RAF Finningley Vintage Aircraft Group; its first and only(?) 'hop' there 11-9-66. **[3]** Cayley test flown at Lasham 1972, also flown - and damaged -at Brompton Hall, Scarborough - Cayley's ancestral home. **[4]** Built by John Ketley and Bill Sneesby, Selby. Not flown... see John's other SE.5a G-ERFC at Old Warden, Beds **[5]** Kitten was built by Bill Sneesby; fitted with a Citroen 2CV. **[6]** Halifax re-creation is a complex composite: rear fuselage section from former 58 Squadron Mk.II HR792 which crashed Stornoway on 13-1-45; centre section and inner wings from Hastings C.1 TG536 from Catterick; unused outer wings from a Hastings C.1; myriad Halifax detail parts; Hercules engines courtesy of the French Air Force and ex-Noratlas, plus new-build cockpit and rear section. **[7]** Original nose, airframe converted to T.11 in 1964 and T.19 in 1966 as 8584M to fire pits at Marham 21-12-77. The 'back end' post-conversion served with 228 OCU, West Raynham TFF, 85, RAE, 85 and 100. **[8]** Airworthy OGMA-built Chipmunk G-CERD wears 'WK640'. **[9]** Victor acquired on behalf of YAM by André Tempest and his late father, Gerry, it regularly taxies. **[10]** XV168 donated by BAE Systems and dedicated 18-8-13 to the company aircrew who gave their lives during the development of the Buccaneer. **[11]** Harrier XV748 - see also Coventry, W Mids, for at least one set of its wings. **[12]** 'JP' '2' is *very likely* XM373, ex Cranwell 7726M, crashed 29-6-61 with 2 FTS. **[13]** Mirage IV first flown 6-5-66; last flight was also the final ever flight of a IVA; total time 6,309 hours. **[14]** Bf 109G *Black 1* was built by Danny Thornton of Garforth, W Yorks.

FELIXKIRK AERODROME between the A19 and A170 northeast of Thirsk
❑ G-AIPR   Auster J4 Archer   47 ex Popham. CoA 27-9-07   N2-19

INGLETON on the A65 southeast of Kirkby Lonsdale
Brian's Used Tractors: Well known local landmark, specialising in – well – tractors, but also 'interesting' military vehicles. The Microlight ousted the Cessna 210 G-OWAN on display. **www.briansusedtractors.co.uk**
❑ G-MBWF*   Flexiform Solo Striker   82 CoA 29-6-95, de-reg 6-11-00   7-21

LEEDS EAST AIRPORT or Church Fenton
Jet Art Aviation (JAA - see Selby, N Yorks) keeps its Tornado F.2A at the airport. It has been joined by a 'SHAR' and JAA's wonderful website outlines the recovery in microscopic detail, a little of which includes: "800-miles round trip, four lorries, one speeding ticket..." On 27th September 2021 a JAA working party succeeded in ZH798's first engine runs and taxis.
    Also of note is the centre section, complete with undercarriage, of Avro XIX G-AGPG – see Woodford, Gtr Man – stored on behalf of its Greece-based owner. ◆ **Not** available for inspection without prior arrangement
❑ N250DM   Bell UH-1H Iroquois   66 ex Sparkford, 66-16114   12-21
❑ N338CB   Bell UH-1H Iroquois   66 ex Sparkford, N312RB, 66-16118   12-21
❑ ZD902*   Panavia Tornado F.2A   84 ex Boscombe Down, DERA, 229 OCU. Arr 11-12-15   [1][2] 12-21
❑ ZH798*   HS Sea Harrier F/A.2   96 ex Culdrose, Shawbury, Yeovilton, 801, 800, 899, 801, 800.
        '002'   801 Sqn colours. Arrived 1-2-21. See notes above   [1] 12-21
■ **[1]** Held by JAA. **[2]** One-off F.2A was heavily modified to TIARA status - Tornado Integrated Avionics Research Aircraft.

LEEMING AIRFIELD east of the A1, west of Bedale
RAF Leeming:
❑ ZH552   Panavia Tornado F.3   92 ex QinetiQ, 56, F3 OCU. SOC 5-7-12. Displayed   [1] 1-22
■ **[1]** Tornado carries a trio of unit badges on the fin: 11, 23 and 25 Squadrons, each one-time based at Leeming on the type. It also carries 5 cine-camera 'zaps' denoting its role as a camera-ship during MBDA Meteor missile trials out of Boscombe Down.

MALTON northeast of York
Eden Camp Modern History Museum: Each hut in this former prisoner of war camp has a different theme and the level of presentation is breath-taking. There is a Link trainer display, a plotting room and items on 617 Squadron.
◆ Off the A64 north of Malton, YO17 6RT | 01653 697777 | admin@edencamp.co.uk | www.edencamp.co.uk
❑ 'P2793' 'SD-M' Hawker Hurricane FSM   93 BAPC.236, G B Mouldings-built. 501 Sqn c/s   [1] 3-20
❑ 'V7357' 'SD-F' Hawker Hurricane FSM   93 BAPC.399, ex 'P2793', 501 Sqn colours   3-20
❑ 'RK838' 'GE-J' V-S Spitfire FSM   91 BAPC.230, ex 'AB550', 'AA908'. TDL-built. 349 Sqn c/s 3-20
❑ –   Fieseler Fi 103 (V-1) FSM 93 BAPC.235, TDL Replicas-built   3-20
■ **[1]** After gale damage to the original 'P2793' another was commissioned for display. The first lies dismantled in a Queen Mary trailer.

NEWBY WISKE northwest of Thirsk, near South Otterington
_W&R27_ (p298) did its best to write these two out, but they are extant.
❑ G-BBBW   Clutton FRED 2   78 CoA 19-6-08   7-21
❑ G-BGFK   Evans VP-1   r92 de-reg 7-4-99   7-21

NORTHALLERTON on the A168/A684 east of Leeming Bar
By February 2020 Jodel G-GREG had moved to Fishburn, D&C and it was followed by 'JP' XN458 on 7th September 2021.

NORTH DUFFIELD AERODROME on the A163 northeast of Selby
Condor Aviation: See comments under Fort Paul, E Yorks. ◆ By prior arrangement **only**. | **www.condoraviation.co.uk**
❑ OE-KDW   Prescott Pusher   ~   pole-mounted as 'windsock' (!), first noted 10-16 12-21
❑ VP-CFI   HSA HS.125-700B   ~   ex Hurn. Fuselage, used as dwelling   12-21
❑ XB259*   Blackburn Beverley C.1   55 ex Fort Paull, Beverley, Paull, Luton, RAE, G-AOAI (15-3-55
        G-AOAI   to 30-3-55). Last flown 30-3-74   due

PICTON on a minor road west of the A19, south of Yarm
Battlezone Paintball ◆ By prior permission **only** | **www.battlezonepaintball.co.uk**

❏ G-BFGS	MS Rallye 180GT	75	ex Spalding, F-BXYK. CoA 23-12-11, de-reg 24-1-12	9-21
❏ XN385	Westland Whirlwind	60	ex Bolton, Chorley, B'thorpe, Hurn, Wroughton, Culdrose,	
	HAS.7		Wroughton, HS, A&AEE, 771, 824, 825, 824. SOC 18-9-92	9-21

RUFFORTH AERODROME south of the A1237, west of York

Gyrocopter Experience and Academy: On the 'East' site. The visitor centre had been wound down by early 2021. Five gyros departed by road on 3rd February 2021 bound for Inverness, Scotland: Bensen G-ARTJ, Cricket G-BXCJ, Bensen G-CDBE PFA Rotaglider 'PCL-132' and an anonymous 'gyroglider', first noted in March 2019. That leaves Rotorsport MT-03s G-CEUI and G-CFCG unaccounted for. Cavalier G-BWSI was flying by 2020.

McLean's Sailplanes: On the 'West' site. ◆ *When conditions permit, a charity donation allows a glimpse inside.*

❏ G-BCHX	Scheibe SF-23A Sperling	59	ex Netherthorpe, D-EGIZ. Damaged 7-8-82, de-reg 22-3-02		2-19
❏ G-BUFN	Slingsby Venture T.2	77	ex ZA631. Wrecked 5-1-12, de-reg 12-1-12		6-19
❏ XK819	Slingsby Grasshopper TX.1	55	ex Selby, Breighton, Warmingham, Stoke-on-Trent,		
			Cosford, Malvern, 2 MGSP, Kimbolton. Arrived by 4-14		12-19
❏ XP463	Slingsby Grasshopper TX.1	61	SOC 4-2-88	[1]	2-19

■ **[1]** See under Lasham, Hampshire, for *another - or this* - 'XP463'.

York Gliding Centre: On the 'West' site. Pawnee G-BLDG moved to Talgarth, Wales, on 30th October 2019.
◆ *By prior arrangement* only | www.yorkglidingcentre.co.uk

| ❏ XZ553* | Slingsby Venture T.2 | 77 | G-BUJX. CoA 4-9-14. Frame | 8-21 |

SCALBY on the A171 north of Scarborough

Sea King Cafe: Under 'Scarborough', *W&R27* (p299) recorded the disposal of Sea King HAR.3 XZ598 to Slovakia after the plan to open a themed eatery was shelved. During 2021 the plan was re-instated with the arrival of another pair: XZ589 having an almost palindromic serial of its predecessor. In December 2021 the website declared that the venture had been refused planning permission. ◆ info@seakingcafe.co.uk | www.seakingcafe.co.uk

❏ XZ589*	'E'	Westland Sea King HAR.3	78	ex Gosport, Fleetlands, 22, 202, SKTU, 22, 202, SKTU.	
				'Royal Air Farce' and 'RAF Rescued'. First noted 3-21	12-21
❏ ZE370*	'E'	Westland Sea King HAR.3	85	ex Froghall, Gosport, 202, 22. Arrived 11-21	12-21

SCARBOROUGH

Restoration of the Austers at a *private* workshop continues.

| ❏ G-AHCK | Auster J1N Alpha | 46 | ex Thwing, Spilsby, Croft, Skegness. De-reg 22-4-94 | 6-21 |
| ❏ G-AJRC | Auster J1 Autocrat | 47 | ex Thwing. CoA 14-7-02, de-reg 22-2-08 | 6-21 |

SELBY on the A19 south of York

Jet Art Aviation Ltd (JAA): With a passion for Harriers and all other things fast jet, Chris and Melanie Wilson's family-run business specialises in the restoration, supply and transportation of static display or museum airframes. The repertoire extends to cockpits, engines, Martin-Baker seats, spares and collectibles.

Sea Harrier F/A.2 ZH798 was delivered direct from Culdrose to Leeds East, N Yorks (aka Church Fenton – which see) joining Tornado F.2A ZD902, previously listed under this heading. Arriving from Manston, Kent, on 2nd December 2020 was the *cockpitless* (since at least 2005) Harrier GR.3 XW922, hence it does not get a formal entry below.

Departures: Bulldog T.1 XX705 moved on to an owner in 'Norfolk' circa 2017; **Harrier** GR.3 XZ130 exported to the USA in April 2020; **Jaguar** GR.3A XZ385 moved to Biddulph, Staffs, in September 2020.; **Super Puma** G-REDU had moved on by late 2020; **Tornado** GR.1 ZA353 had moved to Topsham, Devon, by July 2020.
◆ *Strictly private* location, **NO** public access | www.jetartaviation.co.uk

❏ XM191	EE Lightning F.1A	61	ex North Scarle, EP&TU Cranwell 8590M, St Athan,		
			Abingdon 7854M, Wattisham, 111. Crashed 9-6-64.		
			Arrived 10-13. Shark's mouth. Cockpit		1-21
❏ XR751	EE Lightning F.3	65	ex Queensbury, Ipswich, Tremar, Binbrook, 11, LTF, 29,		
			226 OCU, EE. SOC 21-6-88. Arrived 7-11. Cockpit		1-16
❏ XS177*	'N' Hunting Jet Provost T.4	63	ex Westbury, Gilberdyke, Binbrook, Metheringham,		
			Ipswich, Cosford, Valley 9044M (24-4-90), Shawbury,		
			CATCS, 3 FTS, 2 FTS. First noted 8-21		8-21
❏ XV779	HS Harrier GR.3	70	ex Hitchin, Llantrisant, Welshpool, Stafford, Abingdon,		
			Hamble, 3, Wittering SF, 3, 20, GR.1, 20, 4, 1. Cockpit	[1]	1-16

☐ XW175		HS Harrier T.2/4	69	ex Cosford, Boscombe Down, QinetiQ, RAE, HSA. Last flown 19-11-08. _John Farley OBE AFC._ Arr 17-7 -19 [2]	7-21
☐ XW870*	'F'	Sud Gazelle HT.3	73	ex Manston 9299M, Shawbury, 2 FTS, CFS. Westland-built. Crashed 8-8-95. Arrived 2-12-20	12-20
☐ XX116*		SEPECAT Jaguar GR.3A	73	ex Manston, St Athan, 16, 226 OCU, 6, Indian AF JI-008, G-27-316, GR.1, 226 OCU, JOCU. Arr 2-12-20. Black c/s	7-21
☐ XX121	'EQ'	SEPECAT Jaguar GR.1	73	ex Charlwood, Cosford, Shawbury, Warton, Shawbury, 6, 54, 226 OCU	1-16
☐ XX140		SEPECAT Jaguar T.2	73	ex Charlwood, Faygate, Brough, Cosford 9008M, 226 OCU, 54, 226 OCU, JOCU. Cockpit	11-18
☐ XX175*		HS Hawk T.1	77	ex St Athan, Shawbury, Valley, Shawbury, 208, FRADU, 208, 19, CFS, 4 FTS. SOC 7-8-17. Arrived 14-10-20	7-21
☐ XX226*		HS Hawk T.1	78	ex St Athan, Shawbury, Yeovilton, 100, 74, CFS, 74, 4 FTS. Accident 20-4-07, SOC 7-8-17. Arrived 14-10-20	7-21
☐ XX257		HS Hawk T.1A	79	ex Charlwood, St Athan, Red Arrows. Cr 31-8-84. Arr 15-1-15	7-18
☐ XX290*	'U'	HS Hawk T.1W	79	ex St Athan, Shawbury, 100, FRADU, 208, 100, 234, 4 FTS, 'Red Arrows', 4 FTS. SOC 7-8-17. Arrived 14-10-20	7-21
☐ XX341		HS Hawk T.1	81	ex Woodmancote, Boscombe Down, ETPS, A&AEE, ETPS. SOC 8-1-18. Arrived by 12-19 [3]	1-22
☐ XX747	'08'	SEPECAT Jaguar GR.1	74	ex Boscombe Down, Cranwell, Halton 8903M (23-5-86), Shawbury, Gibraltar Det, 6, 20, 31, 226 OCU. Arrived 14-3-19. 226 OCU (1977) colours by mid-2021	1-22
☐ XZ107	'FH'	SEPECAT Jaguar GR.3A	76	ex Ipswich, St Athan, 41, GR.1, 41, 6, 2	4-19
☐ XZ233*		Westland Lynx HAS.3S	77	ex Ipswich, M Wallop, St Athan, 702, Fleetlands, Yeovilton, HAS.2, 815, Falklands, 700L. Arrived 19-11-20	12-21
☐ XZ364	'FS'	SEPECAT Jaguar GR.3A	76	ex Tunbridge Wells, Ipswich, Shawbury, 41, 54, GR.1, Gulf Det, 54, 2. SOC 28-11-05. Cockpit	12-19
☐ XZ400	'FQ'	SEPECAT Jaguar GR.3A	78	ex Ipswich, St Athan, 41, GR.1, 54, Shawbury, 6, 54, Warton	4-19
☐ XZ455		HS Sea Harrier F/A.2	79	ex Queensbury, Ipswich, Yeovilton, FSAIU, 801, 899, 800, 899, 801, 899, 700A. Crashed 14-2-96, Arrived 7-11 [4]	1-16
☐ ZA359	'B-55'	Panavia Tornado GR.1	81	ex Warton, TTTE. Arrived 24-1-14	1-16
☐ ZB601		HS Harrier T.4	82	ex Yeovilton, Dunsfold, St Athan, ETS Yeovilton, 899, 233 OCU. SOC 5-6-00. Arrived 9-9-15. Forward fuselage	8-20
☐ ZD613*	'122'	HS Sea Harrier F/A.2	85	ex Leeds, Shawbury, 800, 899, 801, 899, 801, 800, 899, 801, 899, 801, 899. SOC 8-9-03. Arrived 18-3-21	7-21
☐ ZD899		Panavia Tornado F.2	84	ex Bury, Selby, Boscombe Down, Warton. Arr 12-19	7-21
☐ ZE168		Panavia Tornado F.3	86	ex East Cowes, Leeming RTP, 43, 25, F3 OEU, 23, 5, 11, 111, 229 OCU. Cockpit. Arrived 9-16 [5]	3-18
☐ ZE965		Panavia Tornado F.3	89	ex Church F', Leeming, 111, 111. Cockpit. Arr 17-7-17	3-18
☐ ZH804*	'003'	HS Sea Harrier F/A.2	97	ex Culdrose, Shawbury, Yeovilton, 801, 899, 800, 899, 800. Arrived 29-1-21	7-21
☐ ZH807		HS Sea Harrier F/A.2	98	ex East Cowes, Newport, Basingstoke, St Athan, accident 1-5-02, 899. Cockpit	1-21
☐ ZH811*	'002'	HS Sea Harrier F/A.2	98	ex Culdrose, Shawbury, Yeovilton, 801, 899. Last flight 28-3-06. Arrived by 3-21	7-21
☐ –		V-S Swift CIM	~	ex Newark, Hemswell. Arrived by 6-13	1-16
☐ –		HS Harrier	~	ex Ipswich, Wittering, Warton. Fuselage [6]	2-18
☐ –		HS Harrier GR.1 or 3	~	ex Ruthin. Cockpit, flying control rig	1-16
☐ –*		SEPECAT Jaguar SIM	~	single-seater	7-21
☐ –		BAe/McDD Harrier GR.9	~	ex Welshpool, Hixon, Wittering. Procedure trainer	1-16
☐ A92-255		GAF Jindivik 102BL	~	ex Aberporth, DRA, RAE. Arrived 6-10. [7]	1-18
☐ 163205		BAe/McDD AV-8B Harrier II	88	ex Queensbury, St Athan, USMC, VMA-223. _Spanky._ Forward fuselage [8]	1-16

■ **[1]** XV779 belly-landed at Wildenrath 16-12-74; pilot safely ejected. XV779 was rebuilt with a spare cockpit and is to be found at Wittering Cambs. Original nose was rebuilt and held as a spare. **[2]** VAAC – Vectored-Thrust Aircraft Advanced Control; T.2 airframe transformed under Cranfield Institute guidance 1983-1986 with rear cockpit fitted with a digital fly-by-wire control system and at same time brought up to near-T.4 status. Carried out the first ever deck landing using a unified control system, on HMS _Illustrious_, in 1986. John Farley flew XW175 in VAAC guise during 1999. **[3]** Converted at Cranfield to ASTRA - Advanced Stability Training and Research Aircraft. **[4]** XZ455 flew 58 Falklands combat sorties, scoring two air-to-air 'kills'. Then, in its _second_ war, it crashed on return from a patrol over Bosnia; the pilot ejecting safely. **[5]** ZE168 scored two air-to-air 'kills' against QF-4 Phantom drones during ASRAAM trials out of Elgin AFB in April 2002. **[6]** Unflown airframe built around the time of the GR.1 Development Batch (XV276 to XV281, 1966-1967), Kestrel-like intake side fairings with 'punch-in' doors. Fitted with 'needle' nose during static/wind tunnel trials at Warton. **[7]** A92-255 lost on 5-12-67 on a sortie out of Llanbedr: salvaged it is likely a composite. **[8]** As flown by Capt S C Spang USMC.

Anne and **Nigel Ponsford / Ponsford Collection**: Located in the *general* area and at a *separate* site from Jet Art. See also Breighton, E Yorks. ◆ *Airframes held in deep storage or under restoration in the locality: visits are **not** possible*

❑ G-AEFG	Mignet HM.14 'Flea'	36	BAPC.75, ex Breighton, Leeds, Harrogate, Kirkby Overblow, Accrington. CoA 31-3-38	[1]	1-22
❑ G-APXZ	Payne Knight Twister	r60	ex Breighton, Tumby Woodside, Loughborough, Biggin Hill. De-reg 26-3-73. Frame		1-22
❑ ALX	Hawkridge Dagling	47	BGA.491, ex Leeds, Great Hucklow		1-22
❑ AQY	EoN Primary	48	BGA.588, ex Breighton, Hemel Hempstead. Stored		1-22
❑ BVM	Slingsby Dart 17R	66	BGA.1269, ex Breighton, Rufforth. CoA 25-7-90		1-22
❑ –	Hutter H.17a	36	ex Leeds, Accrington		1-22
❑ –	Dickson Primary	31	BAPC.340, ex Leeds, Harrogate		1-22
❑ –	Addyman STG	34	BAPC.14, ex Leeds, Harrogate, Wigan	[2]	1-22
❑ -	Addyman STG	34	BAPC.15, ex Wigan, Warmingham, Wigan, Harrogate.	[2]	1-22
❑ –	Addyman Ultralight	36	BAPC.16, ex Leeds, Harrogate, Wigan	[2]	1-22
❑ –	Killick Gyroplane	c63	BAPC.18, ex Leeds, Harrogate, Irlam		1-22
❑ –	Addyman Zephyr	33	BAPC.39, ex Leeds, Harrogate. Substantial parts	[2]	1-22

■ **[1]** 'Flea' built by John Nolan at Accrington, tested at Barton by 9-36, Authorisation to Fly No.51. **[2]** Addyman was the prolific E T W Addyman of Harrogate, who designed and built a series of gliders or in the case of the unfinished Ultralight, a powered aircraft based on the STG. STG = Standard Training Glider; the Zephyr was a more refined sailplane.

SHERBURN-IN-ELMET AERODROME on the B1222 east of the town, east of Leeds   EGCJ
The clubhouse serves quite possibly the best aerodrome bacon butties *in the world.*

❑ G-OPTZ*	Pitts S-2A Special	73	ex G-SKNT, G-PEAL, N81LF, N48KA. Aerotek-built. CoA 26-8-17	12-21

SKIPWITH on minor roads east of Riccall and the A19
Yorkshire Paintball Centre: Escrick Park Estate. ◆ *By prior arrangement* **only** | www.ypc.co.uk

❑ G-AXRL	Piper Cherokee 160	62	ex Sturton, North Cave, PH-CHE, D-EFRI. De-reg 12-8-94	12-20

SUTTON BANK AERODROME on the A170 west of Thirsk, engage low gear
Yorkshire Gliding Club ◆ *By prior arrangement* **only** | www.ygc.co.uk

❑ G-BFRY	Piper Pawnee 260	74	ex SE-GIB. CoA 10-7-15	1-22

THORPE UNDERWOOD north of the A59 northwest of York
Queen Ethelburga's School: ◆ *By prior arrangement* **only** | www.qe.org

❑ 'G-BUTX'	Bücker Jungmeister FSM	~	displayed in atrium	12-19

■ **[1]** 'The real G-BUTX is airworthy and is based in the south of England.

WOMERSLEY south of the M62, west of the A19
Blue Lagoon Diving and Leisure Centre: As well as the Hunter displayed on the surface, see also Appendix C : *Submerged.*
◆ *By prior arrangement* **only** | www.divebluelagoon.co.uk

❑ WT799	'879' Hawker Hunter T.8C	55	ex Exeter, N Weald, Ipswich, Shawbury, FRADU, FRU, 759, RAE, F.4, 4, 11. SOC 3-4-95. Displayed	10-21

YORK
Strensall Barracks: Strensall Road, northeast of the city centre. A Puma is used as an embarkation trainer.

❑ XW202	Sud Puma HC.1	71	ex Shawbury, Benson, 33, 230, 33, 27, 230, 1563 Flt, 33, 1563 Flt, 33, 1563 Flt, 33, 240 OCU, 230, A&AEE, 230, 240 OCU, 230, 240 OCU. Westland-built. Arrived 14-5-14	11-21

Also:

❑ G-BICP	Robin DR.360 Chevalier	71	ex F-BSPH. CoA 28-7-08	3-20

SOUTH YORKSHIRE
Includes the unitary authorities of Doncaster, Rotherham and Sheffield

BARNSLEY
FlyMe: During 2019 a Boeing 737 simulator and 'Virtual Airport' was established at the Shortwood Business Park. In addition to the -800 'sim', a former Jet2 737 has been acquired. Another element of the business is 'Sky-Pods', customising airliner fuselage sections as 'posh sheds'. ◆ *By prior arrangement* only | www.flyme.co.uk

❏ G-CELG*	Boeing 737-377	88	ex St Athan, Jet2, S7-ABD, VH-CZN. De-reg 18-5-18. Forward fuselage	9-20

BAWTRY on the A638 south of Doncaster
Bawtry Paintball and Laser Fields ◆ *By prior arrangement* only | www.bawtrypaintballfields.co.uk

❏ XL840	Westland Whirlwind HAS.7	57	ex Long Marston, Norwich, Sibson, Blackpool, Fleetwood, Wroughton, 705, Brawdy SF, Culdrose SF, 705, 820. SOC 26-6-76	12-19
❏ XZ211	Westland Lynx AH.7	79	ex Croft, M Wallop. Boomless, first noted 2-15	12-19
❏ ZD255	Westland Lynx HAS.3GMS	83	ex Croft, Fleetlands, 815	12-19
❏ ZD263 '632'	Westland Lynx HAS.3S	83	ex Croft, Fleetlands, 702, 815, 702. Arrived 7-14	12-19

DONCASTER Leisure Park, Lakeside – former Doncaster aerodrome site
South Yorkshire Aircraft Museum (SYAM): From the very first *CockpitFest*, held at the Newark Air Museum since 2000, SYAM has been a major supporter. Prominent in this has been museum leading light Bill Fern. For the August 2021 event all the stops were pulled out with a line-up entitled 'Civvie Street'. This comprised James Stable's Enstrom and his superbly restored Dart and K.8b gliders plus no less than *five* from Bill: Airedale, Cessna 140, Pup, Starduster and 'Missfire'. This secured a *W&R Spirit of CockpitFest* award for Bill, especially the exceptionally restored Airedale. "'Missfire' what's that?" I hear you utter. A cockpit, firewall and cowling from some sort of homebuild, picked up for a song by Bill during the 'Lockdown'. Camouflaged and given a 'shark's mouth', with Bill's initials flanking RAF roundels, the cockpit is fitted with easily detachable stub wings to make an ideal travelling exhibit. To date, the exact nature of this machine has eluded everyone confronted with it - over to you, reader! (See also Appendix D.)

'Civvie Street' at Newark was 'book ended' by a pair of Buccaneer cockpits, the newly arrived S.2B XX888 resplendent in 16 Squadron colours and German language warning panels from its days at Laarbruch. The other was the stripped-down S.2 previously attributed as XN979, but research has overturned this provenance. It was the author's pleasure to bestow a *W&R Spirit of CockpitFest* award on this project, even though it is only in the formative phase. This cockpit was acquired from Bill Fern in October 2020 by Carolyn Cordran (mum) and the then ten-year-old **Marcus Cordran**. Marcus refers to this venture as a 'rig' with the build/contract number B3-2-69 and that it was most likely within the batch XV870 to XV879 which was cancelled when HMS *Victorious* was decommissioned in March 1968. Two cockpits were built at Brough for use as Redifon simulators; one went to Lossiemouth, *perhaps* this was the other. It was used inside Brough's 'Shed B' - restricted entrance - and was used for cockpit ergonomics trials. It was sold off from Brough in the late 1980s. Any leads on this cockpit's pedigree, or offers of help with kitting it out, via buccaneerxn979@gmail.com

Many airframes that are in store or under restoration are *not* available for public inspection - see beyond the main list. Working with SYAM and co-based is the **Yorkshire Helicopter Preservation Group** - see separate entry. SYAM curator Naylan Moore bases his **Classic Aircraft Collection** here. Naylan has a Hurricane project under way but it is not at the stage of a formal listing. See also Moore's Restorations later.

Departures: After use for spares Dove G-ARHX left to join a new collection in Kent (along with Cessna 120 G-BRJC see the store entry below) Tutor VW529 (BGA.904) was exchanged for Swallow BGA.1008 and departed. Cadet TX.3 XN238 - exchanged for Buccaneer S.2 XX888 - to Barnstaple, Devon, 7-21.
◆ *Off the A638 beyond 'The Dome'* | Dakota Way, Airborne Road, DN4 7FB **but** DN4 7NW for sat-nav junkies | **01302 761616** | **email** via website | Facebook: **AeroventureSYAM** | www.southyorkshireaircraftmuseum.org.uk

❏ 'K-158'	Austin Whippet replica	90	BAPC.207, ex Sunderland, Stoke-on-Trent. Arrived 1-00		1-22
❏ G-ACBH	Blackburn B-2	32	ex Redhill, 'Kent', Ingatestone, W Hanningfield, Wickham Bishops, Downham, Ramsden Heath, Brentwood 2895M. CoA 27-11-41, de-reg 14-7-42. Arrived 21-2-12. Fuselage	[1]	1-22
❏ G-AEJZ	Mignet HM.14 'Flea'	36	BAPC.120, ex Hemswell, Cleethorpes, Brough. CoA 28-5-37, de-reg 12-38. Arrived 2004	[2]	1-22
❏ G-APMY	Piper Apache 160	58	ex Firbeck, Connah's Quay, Halfpenny Green, EI-AJT. CoA 1-11-81, de-reg 25-11-81. Acquired 4-96		1-22

Ercoupe 415 G-AVTT, January 2020.
Ian Humphreys

☐ G-ARYZ		Beagle Airedale	62	ex Spanhoe. CoA 26-2-01. Arrived 12-4-15	[3]	1-22
☐ G-ATXH		HP Jetstream 200	67	ex Cranwell, Finningley, Prestwick, Filton.		
				De-reg 22-4-71. Arrived 2005. Cockpit	[4]	1-22
☐ G-AVAA		Cessna F.150G	67	ex Firbeck, Shobdon, Hurn. Reims-built. CoA 5-7-96,		
				de-reg 16-4-96. Arrived 26-11-97		1-22
☐ G-AVTT		Erco Ercoupe 415D	47	ex Monewden, SE-BFZ, NC3774H. CoA 20-1-86,		
				de-reg 12-4-02. Arrived 21-2-14		1-22
☐ G-BCLW		American AA-1B Trainer	74	ex Finningley. Damaged 12-2-13, CoA 9-6-13. Arrived 27-4-13		1-22
☐ G-DDCD		DH Dove 8	62	ex Cricklade, Little Rissington, Kemble, Staverton, Biggin Hill,		
				G-OEWA, G-DDCD, G-ARUM. CoA 7-10-91, de-reg 24-5-05.		
				Arrived 28-2-20	[5]	1-22
☐ G-DELB		Robinson R22	88	ex Firbeck, Sherburn, Retford, N26461. Cr 27-12-94,		
				De-reg 20-4-95. Acquired 11-97		1-22
☐ G-BNNA		Stolp Starduster Too	73	ex N8SD. Cr 20-6-17, de-reg 11-7-17. Forward fuselage		1-22
☐ G-BTYX		Cessna 140	76	ex Spanhoe, Uckfield. Rochester, N76568. CoA 23-2-98,		
				de-reg 10-4-01. Arrived 12-4-15. Cockpit	[6]	1-22
☐ G-BUUV		Lindstrand LBL.77A HAB	93	ex Lancing. CoA 16-5-97, de-reg 9-6-97. Arrived 2011	[7]	1-22
☐ G-MJKP		Hiway Skytrike	r82	CoA 31-12-86, de-reg 9-12-94. Arrived 2001		1-22
☐ G-MMDK		Mainair Tri-Flyer	83	CoA 30-5-99, de-reg 2-12-10. Arrived 2009		1-22
☐ G-MVNT		Whittaker MW-5-K	90	CoA 5-5-07, de-reg 27-5-11. Arrived 2009		1-22
☐ G-MYJX		Whittaker MW-8	93	de-reg 31-7-01. Arrived 2007	[8]	1-22
☐ G-OPFW		HS HS.748-2A/266	72	ex Haverigg, Emerald, G-BMFT, VR-BFT, G-BMFT,		
				5W-FAO,G-11-10. CoA 16-2-07, de-reg 15-6-09.		
				Parcelforce colours. Arrived 4-9-10. Cockpit		1-22
☐ -*		Cayley glider rep	03	ex Brough. BAE Heritage Group-built. Arrived 10-11-21		1-22
☐ -		Blériot XI replica	09	BAPC.307. Unveiled 2010. 'Delagrange'	[9]	1-22
☐ -		Bensen B-8	c65	BAPC.533. Built in Doncaster. Arrived 2009		1-22
☐ -*	'W-F'	'Missfire'	~	cockpit, travelling exhibit. *Missfire*. See notes above	[6]	1-22
☐ -	'404'	Slingsby Dart 15	66	BGA.1268 / BVL, ex 'Lincs', Shipdham. Travelling exhibit	[10]	1-22
☐ BGA.1008*	BJP	Slingsby Swallow	c61	ex Dunstable	[6]	1-22
☐ BGA.1657		Slingsby Swallow	c69	ex Wroot. Cockpit. Arrived 11-17	[11]	1-22
☐ GGA.522		Schleicher K.8b	~	BGA.3257, ex Stretton, RAFGGA.522, D-0322.		
				Cockpit. Travelling exhibit	[10] [12]	1-22
☐ EI-BBK*		Beagle Airedale	62	ex Spanhoe, Abbeyshrule, G-ARXB, EI-ATE, G-ARXB.		
				CoA 11-11-83. Arrived 6-6-20. Cockpit	[6]	1-22
☐ EI-JWM		Robinson R22	90	ex G-BSLB. Arrived 2004		1-22
☐ HB-NAV	'A'	Beagle Pup 150	71	ex Dover, Stock, Henley, Henlow, Redhill, G-AZCM.		
		G-AZCM		Arrived 2009. Forward fuselage, trailer mounted	[6]	1-22
☐ HB-XMO		Enstrom 280C	80	ex Sudbury, Switzerland. Crashed 23-5-97.		
				Arrived 29-10-15. Travelling exhibit	[10]	1-22

❑ N4565L	Douglas DC-3-201A	39	ex Framlingham, Ipswich, Dublin, LV-GYP, LV-PCV, N129H,		
			N512, N51D, N80C, NC21744. De-reg 7-6-13. Arr 6-8-03		1-22
❑ N9399	DH Tiger Moth	39	ex Old Sarum SF, M Wallop SF, Baginton SF, 1 AACU, 1618 Flt,		
			287. 24 EFTS, 28 EFTS. SOC 28-3-50. Fuselage. Arr 2004	[6]	1-22
❑ FX322	NAA Harvard II	44	ex Worksop, Doncaster, Bruntingthorpe, Stoke, ?,		
			French AF, FX322, n/s. Cockpit	[13]	1-22
❑ LB314	Taylorcraft Plus D	42	ex Denmark, D-ELUS, G-AHHX, Auster I LB314, Llanbedr SF,		
	OY-DSZ		83 GCF, 43 OTU, 656, 652, 654. Arrived 12-2-18		1-22
❑ SN280	Hawker Tempest V	45	ex Napier. SOC 30-12-49. Acquired 2010.		
			Cockpit/firewall and growing!	[14] [15]	1-22
❑ VP519	Avro Anson C.19/2	47	ex W'hampton, 'Manchester', Dukinfield, Hadfield, Stockport,		
	G-AVVR		Peel Green, Cosford, Wigan, Irlam, Halfpenny Green, G-AVVR		
			(de-reg 16-9-72), Shawbury, FCCS, 11 GCF, MCS, 31, Malta CF,		
			TCDU. SOC 19-2-68. Arrived 2011. Cockpit, on loan		1-22
❑ WA662	Gloster Meteor T.7	50	ex Firbeck, Willington, Chalgrove, Llanbedr, Farnborough,		
			FCCS, 3, Wildenrath SF, Gütersloh SF, 3. Acquired 1994		1-22
❑ WB733	DHC Chipmunk T.10	50	ex Firbeck, Sevenoaks, Shawbury SF, G-ATDE (de-reg 19-1-68),		
	G-ATDE		Marham SF, 4 SoTT 'hack', Lyneham SF, Upavon SF, Hull UAS,		
			11 RFS. SOC 12-9-73. Acquired 1995		1-22
❑ WB969	Slingsby Sedbergh TX.1	50	BGA.2036, ex Wroot, RAFGSA.247, WB969, CGIS, 168 GS.		
			Crashed 24-8-80, CoA 8-10-80. Arrived 10-01		1-22
❑ WD935	EE Canberra B.2	51	ex Birdlip, Bridgnorth, Ottershaw, Egham, St Athan 84440M		
			(17-4-75), 360, 97, 151, CSE, EE, BCDU, RAAF A84-1.		
			Arrived 2003. Cockpit		1-22
❑ WE987	DZX Slingsby Prefect TX.1	50	BGA.2517, ex Newport Pagnell, ACCGS, CGS, 633 GS,		
			642 GS, 2 GS. CoA 17-7-89. Arrived 12-01		1-22
❑ WH779	'CK' EE Canberra PR.7	54	ex Winthorpe, Castle Donington, Boscombe D', Farnborough,		
			Marham, RAE, 100, 13, Wildenrath 8129M (10-3-71),		
			Brüggen, 31, 80, 13, 542. Arr 11-1-15. Cockpit. 13 Sqn c/s	[16]	1-22
❑ –	Vickers Valetta	52	ex Cardington, Henlow, ATC unit (?). Arr 2001. Cockpit	[17]	1-22
❑ WJ565	EE Canberra T.17	53	ex Harrington, North Coates, Coventry, North Coates,		
			Binbrook, Bruntingthorpe, Cosford 8871M, St Athan,		
			360, B.2, A&AEE. HP-built. Arrived 22-3-03. Cockpit		1-22
❑ WJ903	Vickers Varsity T.1	52	ex Firbeck, Dumfries, Glasgow Airport, 6 FTS, AE&AEOS,		
			1 ANS, 2 ANS, 3 ANS. SOC 5-2-75. Hurn-built.		
			Acquired 14-3-97. Cockpit, 6 FTS colours by late 2020		1-22
❑ WJ975	EE Canberra T.19	53	ex Hemswell, Cleethorpes, Cambridge, 100, 7, 100, 85,		
			West Raynham TFF, 228 OCU, B.2, 44, 35, 231 OCU.		
			Avro-built. SOC 21-5-80. Arrived 2005. Cockpit	[6]	1-22
❑ WK626	'85' DHC Chipmunk T.10	52	ex Firbeck, Salisbury, Welling, White Waltham 8123M		
			(4-8-72), Bicester SF, Odiham SF, Ox UAS, S Cerney SF, 1 FTS,		
			Bicester SF, Odiham SF, FTCCS, Lon, Cam UASs, Colerne SF,		
			Leeds, Nott UASs, 16 FRS, 18 RFS. Acquired 1997. Fuselage	[6]	1-22
❑ WL131	Gloster Meteor F.8	53	ex Firbeck, Guernsey 7751M, APS Sylt, 601, 111.		
			SOC 16-11-62. Acquired 9-95. Cockpit	[6]	1-22
❑ WT534	EE Canberra PR.7	55	ex Upwood, Doncaster, Boscombe D, Solihull, Halton		
			8549M (10-7-78), St Athan, 17. Short-built. Cockpit	[18]	1-22
❑ WT536	EE Canberra PR.7	55	ex Walcott, Southampton, Bruntingthorpe, Cosford		
			8063M (19-11-69), 80, 31, 13, 17. Short-built. Cockpit		1-22
❑ WT741	'791' Hawker Hunter GA.11	55	ex Hemswell, Macclesfield, Bitteswell, HAS, 738, F.4,		
			118. SOC 13-7-71. Arrived 2005. Cockpit. 738 Sqn c/s	[14]	1-22
❑ 'WV314'	'B' Hawker Hunter F.51	56	ex Firbeck, East Kirkby, Tattershall, Cosford, Dunsfold,		
	E-424		G-9-445 (20-2-76), Danish AF, Esk.724. Acq 1988. 92 Sqn c/s		1-22
❑ XE317	Bristol Sycamore	54	ex Firbeck, Winthorpe, Portsmouth, CFS, 275, G-AMWO		
	HR.14 G-AMWO		(de-reg 30-9-53). SOC 6-5-72. 275 Sqn c/s. Arrived 1997		1-22
❑ XE797	Slingsby Cadet TX.3	53	ex Topcliffe, Dishforth, Catterick, Dishforth, 645 GS, 2 GC,		
			641 GS, 27 GS. SOC 28-9-78. Cockpit. Arrived 30-10-16		1-22
❑ XE935	DH Vampire T.11	55	ex Firbeck, Sibson, Hitchin, Woodford, Chester,		
			St Athan, 8 FTS. Hatfield-built. SOC 8-11-67. Acquired 1986		1-22

☐ XG297	'Y'	Hawker Hunter FGA.9	56	ex Firbeck, Newton-le-Willows, Bacup, Macclesfield, Bitteswell, HSA, 20, 28, 20, F.6, 4. SOC 12-2-76. Acquired 1995. 20 Sqn colours. Cockpit	[6]	1-22
☐ XH584		EE Canberra T.4	55	ex Firbeck, Sunderland, Marham, 231 OCU. SOC 12-7-66. Acquired 1993. Cockpit	[6]	1-22
☐ XL149		Blackburn Beverley C.1	57	ex Winthorpe, Finningley 7988M (7-11-67), 84, 30, 84, 242 OCU. Arrived 2005. Cockpit. 84 Sqn colours		1-22
☐ XL388		Avro Vulcan B.2	62	ex Walpole, Honington 8750M (2-4-82), 50, Wadd Wing, Scampton Wing, 9. Arrived 7-4-03. Cockpit. *Mayflower III*, 9 Squadron colours		1-22
☐ XM350		Hunting Jet Provost T.3A	58	ex Firbeck, Church Fenton 9036M (10-11-89), 7 FTS, 1 FTS, RAFC, A&AEE. Acquired 1995		1-22
☐ XM411		Hunting Jet Provost T.3	60	ex Firbeck, Otterburn, Halton 8434M (10-11-74), St Athan, Shawbury, Kemble, CFS. Acquired 1999. Cockpit		1-22
☐ 'XM651'		Saro Skeeter AOP.12 XM561	59	ex Firbeck, East Kirkby, Tattershall, Moston, M Wallop, Arborfield 7980M (4-8-67), 15 MU, HQ 1 Wing, HQ 2 Wing, 651. Acquired 1993		1-22
☐ XN386	'435'	Westland Whirlwind HAR.9	60	ex Lancaster, Blackpool, Heysham, Wroughton A2713 (10-8-76), Fleetlands, *Endurance* Flt, HAS.7, 846, 814. Arrived 1999. Boomless		1-22
☐ XN511	'12'	Hunting Jet Provost T.3	60	ex Firbeck, Robertsbridge, 'XM426', Lutterworth, Liversedge, Blackpool, Kemble, CFS, 1 FTS, CFS. SOC 28-5-76. Acquired 1997. Cockpit	[6]	1-22
☐ XP190		Saro P.531-2	61	ex Firbeck, Wroughton, Arborfield, M Wallop, BSE Filton, A&AEE. SOC 1-5-72. Acquired 27-8-92		1-22
☐ XP706		EE Lightning F.3	63	ex Hemswell, Strubby, Binbrook 8925M (9-2-87), LTF, 11, 5, LTF, 23, 111, 74. Arrived 19-11-02		1-22
☐ XP902		Westland Scout AH.1	63	ex Firbeck, Otterburn, Edinburgh, Dishforth, Netheravon, Wroughton, Garrison Air Sqn, 3 CBAS. Acquired 1999. Cockpit		1-22
☐ XS216		Hunting Jet Provost T.4	64	ex Goole, Finningley, 6 FTS, CAW. Damaged 7-5-73. Cockpit. Arrived 2003. Marked 'CRAN22/1'		1-22
☐ XS481		Westland Wessex HU.5	63	ex Firbeck, Dishforth, Wroughton, Yeovilton, Culdrose, Yeovilton, 771, 707. SOC 21-7-92. Acquired 6-98		1-22
☐ XS735	'R'	HS Dominie T.1	66	ex Walcott, Penwyllt, St Athan, CTTS, Sealand, Cranwell 9246M (28-10-96), 55, 6 FTS, RAFC, CAW. First noted 8-17		1-22
☐ XV139		Westland Scout AH.1	67	ex Wattisham, 'XV137', Yeovil, Arborfield, Wroughton, 657, Falklands, 656, 662, 653. Arrived 6-09		1-22
☐ XV280	'31121RN'	HS Harrier GR.1	67	ex Yeovilton, Culdrose, Yeovilton A2700[2] (1-11-90), Foulness, Boscombe Down, A&AEE, HSA. Cockpit, Sea Harrier style, trailer-mounted. First noted 6-16		1-22
☐ XV281		HS Harrier GR.1	67	BAPC.484, ex Welshpool, Cannock, Preston, Samlesbury, Dunsfold, Boscombe D', A&AEE, BSE. Forward fuselage.	[19]	1-22
☐ XV677	'269'	Westland Sea King HAS.6	70	ex Gosport A2619 [3] (7-6-99), Fleetlands, 814, 810, 819, 706, 814, 820. Arrived 25-7-06	[20]	1-22
☐ XV752	'B'	HS Harrier GR.3	69	ex Bletchley, Cosford 9078M, 4, 3, 1, 233 OCU, GR.1, 1, 233 OCU. Arrived 5-12-11	[21]	1-22
☐ -		Blackburn Buccaneer S.2 EMU	69	ex Stamford, Croydon, Popham, Brough. Arrived 2005. Cockpit - see notes above		1-22
☐ XW666		HS Nimrod R.1	73	ex Long Marston, Warton, Woodford, Kinloss, 51, A&AEE. Crashed 16-5-95. Arrived 2001. Cockpit		1-22
☐ XX411	'X'	Sud Gazelle AH.1	75	ex Chichester, 3 CBAS. Shot down 21-5-82, San Carlos. Westland-built. Arrived 5-02		1-22
☐ XX495	'C'	HP Jetstream T.1	75	ex Bedford, Shawbury, Cranwell, 45, 3 FTS, 45, 6 FTS, METS. SAL-completed. Arrived 13-2-19		1-22
☐ XX669	'B'	SAL Bulldog T.1	75	ex Halton, Andover, Llantrisant, Bruntingthorpe, Cosford 8997M, 2 FTS, Birm UAS, Man UAS. Damaged 6-9-88. Arrived 2006. Birmingham UAS colours		1-22
☐ XX736		SEPECAT Jaguar GR.1	74	ex Brough, 9110M, Coltishall, Shawbury, Warton, Indian AF JI013, G-27-327, 6, 226 OCU. Arr 2007. Cockpit. 54 Sqn c/s	[6]	1-22

☐ XX888*		Blackburn Buccaneer S.2B	74	ex Barnstaple, Dundonald, Ottershaw, Shawbury, St Athan, 16, 15. SOC 10-10-91. 16 Sqn colours. Cockpit, arrived 7-7-21	1-22
☐ XZ246	'434'	Westland Lynx HAS.3S(ICE)	78	ex Ipswich, 815, *Endurance* Flt, HAS.2, 815, 702. Arrived 8-16. HMS *Endurance* colours	1-22
☐ XZ431		Blackburn Buccaneer S.2B	77	ex Newark, Selby, Newport, Market Drayton, B'thorpe, Marham 9233M, 12, 208, 12, 208. Arrived by 6-16. Nose [22]	1-22
☐ ZD938		Panavia Tornado F.2	85	ex Chester, Market Drayton, Shawbury, St Athan, 229 OCU. Arr 28-6-11. Forward fuselage. 229 OCU c/s [23]	1-22
☐ 0767	'A-4-116'	Aermacchi MB.339AA	81	ex Derby, Mickleover, Filton, Yeovilton, Stanley, Argentine Navy. First noted 11-13 [24]	1-22
☐ AE-406		Bell UH-1H Iroquois	72	ex Valley, M Wallop, Greenford, M Wallop, Fleetlands, Stanley, Arg Army AE-406, 72-21491. Boomless cabin, Griffin colours. Arrived 8-8-18	1-22
☐ N-302		Hawker Hunter T.53	58	ex Firbeck, Chelford, Macclesfield, Leavesden, Elstree, Hatfield, Danish AF Esk.724 ET-273, Netherlands AF N-302. Acquired 1996. Netherlands AF colours. Cockpit [6]	1-22
☐ –		Waco CG-4 Hadrian rep	97	BAPC.443, ex Hatfield, *Saving Private Ryan*. Cockpit [6]	1-22

■ **[1]** At some stage G-ACBH had elements of G-ADFO grafted on - both identities can be discerned on the airframe. (G-ADFO was written off 3-9-40.) **[2]** Built by Leslie Crosland in Hull, flew: Authorisation No.82. **[3]** *Yankee-Zulu* gifted by Carl Tyers/Windmill Aviation. Wings held in store. **[4]** Prototype Jetstream, first flown 18-8-67. **[5]** Served the National Coal Board as G-ARUM from new – 11-61 – to 1-84 when it became G-DDCD. As such, *Uniform-Mike* was a 'regular' as Doncaster. **[6]** Airframes on loan from Bill Fern. **[7]** Balloon on loan from the Mobberley Balloon Collection. **[8]** MW-8 prototype, built by the designer, Mike Whittaker. **[9]** Full-size replica Blériot XI built by Ken Fern to celebrate the 100th anniversary of the first aviation meeting in the UK - at Doncaster racecourse 15/18-10-09. It depicts Léon Delagrange's machine that established a world speed record of 49.9mph at the event. **[10]** Dart, K.8 and Enstrom owned by James Stables. **[11]** Swallow built by Roy Greenslade at nearby Wroot, c/n RG.103. **[12]** GGA - RAF Germany Gliding Association. **[13]** FX322 owned by Phil Jarvis - see Worksop, Notts - restoration by Naylan Moore. **[14]** On loan from Naylan Moore's Classic Aircraft Collection. **[15]** SN280 served exclusively with Napier and was SOC 30-12-49. This may, or may not be, BAPC.536. **[16]** PR.7 WH779 is on loan from Darren Green - **www.wh779.webs.com** **[17]** Valetta came from Cardington and Henlow and is said to have been with an ATC unit before joining SYAM. The 'smart-money' is on this being T.3 WJ476. **[18]** WT534 on loan from Sam Scrimshaw. **[19]** XV281 has the rear of a P.1127 test-rig. **[20]** Sea King ownership transferred to SYAM. **[21]** XV752 on loan from 1053 Sqn ATC, Armthorpe, S Yorks. **[22]** John Hoole's cockpit was 'detached' to Southend, Essex, in 9-21 for a repaint, it will return. **[23]** Tornado owned by Simon Pulford - see Chester, Cheshire. **[24]** MB.339 was fitted with the forward fuselage of 0761 at Yeovilton, circa 1984; its cockpit section was never brought to the UK. Last used by Rolls-Royce as a mock-up for the US Navy JPATS programme, 1995.

Deep Store and **Workshop**: SYAM is happy to offer 'back lot' tours of the storage area - applications in advance **only** - see above for contact details. Auster 5 G-ANFU (missed out from the listing in *W&R27*) moved to Tattershall Thorpe, Lincs, by 11-20; recent arrival, the *original* fuselage of Cessna 120 G-BRJC moved to a collection in Kent (along with Dove G-ARHX – see above); Auster AOP.9 WZ711 moved on to Messingham, Lincs, 13-8-21. Temporarily stored was Robinson R22 G-VOCE, it moved to Storwood, E Yorks, by May 2021.

☐ G-AHHP	Auster J1N Alpha	46	ex Dunkeswell, G-SIME, G-AHHP. De-reg 22-2-99. Arrived by 9-18	[1]	1-22
☐ G-AOKO	Percival Prentice 1	49	ex Coventry, Southend, VS621, CFS, 2 FTS, 22 FTS. CoA 23-10-72, de-reg 9-10-84. Arrived 9-5-00		1-22
☐ G-ARGI	Auster 6A Tugmaster	46	ex Newark-on-Trent, Chirk, Heathfield, AOP.6 VF530, 661. CoA 4-7-76, de-reg 23-8-77. Arrived 1-00. Frame	[2]	1-22
☐ G-BAML	Bell JetRanger	67	ex Walton Wood, N7844S. Crashed 30-5-03, de-reg 7-7-03. Arrived 2004		1-22
☐ G-BBNJ	Cessna F.150L	73	ex Spanhoe, Sherburn. Reims-built. De-reg 10-3-20	[3]	1-22
☐ G-BECE	AD Skyship 500	76	ex Cardington, Old Warden, Cardington, Kirkbymoorside. Gondola, damaged 9-3-79, de-reg 30-5-84. Arrived 1-08		1-22
☐ G-DDEA*	Slingsby T.59D Kestrel	75	ex BGA.2046. De-reg 24-11-15. In trailer. Arrived 7-5-21		1-22
☐ G-FTAX*	Cessna 421C	77	ex Stafford, Cambridge, N8363G, G-BFFM, N8363G. CoA 16-5-01, de-reg 8-7-03. Forward fuselage. F/n 7-21		1-22
☐ G-MJPO	Eurowing Goldwing	82	de-reg 9-4-02. Arrived 2003		1-22
☐ G-TPTR	Bell JetRanger II	79	ex Weston-super-Mare, Lyneham, G-LOCK, N2951N, N2951W, Agusta-built. Cr 1-3-89, de-reg 9-10-94. Arrived 28-4-17		1-22
☐ BGA.1863	Scheibe L-Spatz 55	~	ex Wroot, D-8225, D-6425. Arrived 11-17	[4]	1-22
☐ –	Stewart Ornithopter	c65	BAPC.61, ex Boston, N' Coates, Louth, Tumby Woodside, East Kirkby, Tattershall, Wigan, Irlam, South Reston. Built by Alan Stewart. *Bellbird II*. Arrived 9-5-16		1-22

☐	–	Hawker Typhoon		c42	ex Boscombe Down, Salisbury. Cockpit project	[5] [6]	1-22
☐	–	Hawker Typhoon		c42	ex Staverton. Cockpit	[5] [6]	1-22
☐	WK393	DH Venom FB.1		53	ex Lavendon, Doncaster, CGS, FWS, Silloth, Firbeck, Dumfries, Silloth. Hawarden-built. SOC 28-2-58. Acquired 12-3-17. Cockpit	[5]	1-22
☐	WP255	DH Vampire NF.10		51	ex Haverigg, Firbeck, Ecclesfield, Bingley, C' Fenton, 27 MU, CNCS, 1 ANS, CNCS, 23. SOC 30-11-59. Acq 1991. Cockpit	[5]	1-22
☐	WX788	DH Venom NF.3		54	ex Elvington, Kenilworth, L' Marston, Cardiff, Bledlow Ridge, Connah's Quay, DH. Christchurch-built. SOC 25-11-57. Arrived 2-02		1-22
☐	WZ822	Slingsby Grasshopper TX.1		52	ex Firbeck, Robertsbridge, Halton, London. Acquired 5-97		1-22
☐	XK421	Auster AOP.9		57	ex Woodhall Spa, S Molton, Eggesford, Doncaster, Firbeck, Thurcroft, Firbeck, Hedge End, Fownhope, Long Marston, Innsworth, Bristol, Coldicote, Bristol, 8365M (7-11-63), A&AEE, 1 Wing, M Wallop, LAS. Arrived 2017	[5] [7]	1-22
☐	XP282	Auster AOP.9	G-BGTC	61	ex Worksop, Melton Mowbray, East Dereham, St Athan, 1 Air Despatch Regt, 14 ADR, 2 Flt, 651. SOC 12-2-76. Damaged 2-10-96. Fuselage frame, first noted 12-17	[3] [8]	1-22
☐	XP905*	Westland Scout AH.1		63	ex Ipswich, Arborfield, M Wallop, Wroughton, 656, 655, 652, 654, 652. First noted 7-21		1-22
☐	XT793	Westland Wasp HAS.1	G-BZPP	67	ex Old Sarum, Thruxton, Babcary, Lee-on-Solent, Thruxton, G-BZPP (de-reg 7-9-12), East Dereham, Bruntingthorpe, Fleetlands, HHU, 829, A&AEE, 829, HHU. Arr 16-7-19		1-22
☐	333	DH Vampire T.55		53	ex Barton, Chelford, Hadfield, Dukinfield, New Brighton, Chester, Iraqi AF. Christchurch-built. Arr 2-03. Cockpit	[3] [9]	1-22

■ **[1]** *Hotel-Papa* operated from Doncaster 1969-1973. **[2]** *Golf-India* served as a tug with Doncaster and District Glding Club 1961-1971. **[3]** Airframes on loan from Bill Fern. **[4]** *Likely* identity of the L-Spatz; may well have been flown locally. **[5]** Airframes on loan from Naylan Moore's Classic Aircraft Collection. **[6]** One of these may be BAPC.534 and the other BAPC.535, then again... **[7]** Parts from XP286 - see Molton, Devon - used in restoration. **[8]** Original fuselage frame from XP282 - see Woodhall Spa, Lincs. **[9]** Delivered to Iraq 1953. Airfreighted to Hawarden 1960 for trial installation of ejector seats, not returned.

Yorkshire Helicopter Preservation Group: The Dragonfly continues to be the centre of restoration activity. Not suitable for a 'formal' listing is a Whirlwind hydraulic system training aid constructed from gearbox, rotor head and tail rotor components by Bristow Helicopters trainees at Redhill. This carries the fictitious registration 'G-YHPG' and attracts a lot of attention in the main aircraft hall! As well as the airframes, the group has a wealth of artefacts and documentation.

Wessex HAS.1 XS887 moved to Tattershall Thorpe, Lincs, by December 2021.

◆ *Most airframes on display within SYAM; workshop by appointment only | info@yhpg.co.uk | www.yhpg.co.uk*

☐	WN499	'Y'	Westland Dragonfly HR.5		53	ex Caernarfon, Higher Blagdon, Blackbushe, Culdrose SF, 705. SOC 1-6-44. Arrived 3-6-06. Dismantled	[1]	1-22
☐	XA862	'704'	Westland Whirlwind HAR.1	G-AMJT	53	ex Colerne, Weston-super-Mare, Coventry, Wroughton, Lee-on-Solent A2542 (20-5-66), Seafield Park, Haslar, L-o-S, Fleetlands, 781, 771, 700, 705, G-AMJT (de-reg 13-3-53). Arrived 13-7-05. Cockpit	[2]	1-22
☐	XA870	'911'	Westland Whirlwind HAR.1		54	ex Helston, Predannack, Lee-on-Solent A2543 (18-5-66), 705, 155, 848. Arrived 1-12-02. Sectioned		1-22
☐	XJ398		Westland Whirlwind HAR.10	G-BDBZ	57	ex Elvington, Oxford, Luton G-BDBZ (de-reg 28-3-85), XJ398, Culdrose, RAE, ETPS, DH Engines, A&AEE, HAR.5, HAR.3. Arrived 27-6-03. 202 Sqn colours	[3]	1-22
☐	XP345	'N'	Westland Whirlwind HAR.10		62	ex Elvington, Storwood, Tattershall Thorpe, Lee-on-Solent Cyprus 8792M (2-9-83), 84, 1563 Flt, 202, CFS. Arrived 6-7-02. 84 Sqn UN colours.		1-22
☐	XT150		Bell Sioux AH.1		65	ex Netheravon, M Wallop 7883M, Wimbourne, Andover, Arborfield, Seletar, 42 Cmdo. Arrived 7-8-08. Off-site	[4]	1-22
☐	XT242		Bell Sioux AH.1		66	ex Firbeck, Hooton Park, Warmingham, Long Marston, Wimborne, Middle Wallop, 'Blue Eagles'. Acquired 13-2-03. 'Blue Eagles' colours	[5]	1-22

■ **[1]** WN499 will be restored to represent HC.4 XB251 of 194 Sqn used in Operation FIREDOG, in Malaya. **[2]** Remainder of XA862 - well battered - is/was in the fire training area at Colerne, Wilts. This was the first Yeovil-built S-55, first flown at 12-11-52 by Derrick Colvin. **[3]** XJ398 was the prototype HAR.10. Fitted with a GE T58 it first flew on 28-2-59. **[4]** XT150 is a composite airframe, incorporating elements of the purely instructional 7884M. **[5]** Owned by YHPG's Alan Beattie and is a composite, with parts of XW179 included.

Moore's Restorations: SYAM stalwart, **Naylan Moore**'s workshop is listed here as a 'port of convenience'. As well as airframes, he specialises in classic Minis. ◆ *By prior arrangement only* | Facebook: **mooresrestorations**

☐ G-ASWF	Beagle Airedale	64	ex Newark-on-Trent, Leicester. CoA 27-4-83, de-reg 3-2-89		1-22
☐ N55XJ	Cassutt M11	03	ex Bungay area. Original fuselage		1-22
☐ WD293*	DHC Chipmunk T.10	50	ex St Athan, Aberdare, Newport, Caerleon, Cwmbran, 7645M (4-7-60), Queen's, St And, Glas, St And UASs, Chatham Flt, SoMR, 1 BFTS. Cockpit, arrived 16-1-19		1-22
☐ XP888	Westland Scout AH.1	63	ex Ipswich, Arborfield, M Wallop, Wroughton, 651, 652, 14 Flt. Cabin	[1]	1-22
☐ XV806	HS Harrier GR.3	71	ex Workshop, South Molton, Boscombe Down, Culdrose, A607[3], A2602[2] (18-4-91), Cosford, 4, 3, 4, 20	[2]	1-22
☐ XW927	'02' HS Harrier T.4	72	ex South Molton, Ipswich, Hermeskeil, Brüggen, Gütersloh SF, 4, Gütersloh SF, 3, 233 OCU, 4, Wittering SF, 233 OCU, T.2, 233 OCU. Crashed 7-2-92. Cockpit	[2]	1-22
☐ XZ131	HS Harrier GR.3	76	ex Spark Bridge, Brierley Hill 9174M, St Athan, 1417 Flt, 233 OCU, 4, 1, 4. Cockpit	[2]	1-22
☐ -*	HS Sea Harrier FRS.1 EMU	~	ex Halesworth	[2]	1-22
☐ 162074*	BAe/McDD AV-8B Harrier II	84	ex USMC. Cockpit	[2]	1-22

■ **[1]** Scout for restoration to static display status. **[2]** Harriers being restored for the **4 Squadron Collection** - more details on **www.the4squadroncollection.org** XV806 will be a full fuselage in due course.

DONCASTER town centre

Danum Gallery, Library and Museum: The previous **Museum and Art Gallery** was subsumed into a new edifice which includes the encapsulated former Doncaster High School for Girls, built in 1910, *within* a high-tech loads-of-glass modern building. Opened – virtually – in March 2021, it was fully opened – to organic beings – on 9th July 2021.
◆ *Waterdale and Chequer Road, DN1 2AE* | **01302 734293** | **www.doncaster.gov.uk/museums**

☐ 'G-AEKR'	Mignet HM.14 'Flea'	71	BAPC.121, ex Breighton, Firbeck, Nostell Priory, Crowle, Oakington. Acquired 22-3-97. *This is the 'Flea' that Claybourne's Built*	[1]	7-21
☐ -	Bensen B-7	c61	BAPC.275. Acquired 2001		7-21

■ **[1]** Original G-AEKR, first flew at Doncaster 28-5-36, Authorisation No.87. It became part of the RAF Finningley 'Station Museum' in the 1960s but was burnt out in a hangar fire 5-9-70. Some metal parts incorporated in this 'replacement' built largely at Oakington. Completed project handed over at Finningley 18-9-71, **[2]** Bensen built by S J R Wood of Warmsworth.

DONCASTER SHEFFIELD (ROBIN HOOD) AIRPORT or Finningley, east of A638, north of Bawtry   EGCN

Vulcan to the Sky Trust (VTST): The leading light of the entire VTST programme, from the earliest discussions with the CAA, to engineering endorsement, comprehensive fund-raising, test flight, display flying and establishing the 'base camp' for retirement at Finningley, **Robert Pleming**, died on 2nd February 2021, aged 69. Robert's spirit and negotiating prowess galvanised and steered the project from what many regarded as 'Mission Impossible' to unprecedented achievement.

'Operation Safeguard' was launched in October 2020 to raise funds – reported in the realm of £2.4m – for a hangar-cum-visitor centre plus a so-called 'Green Technology Hub' which is "aimed at the young, the engaged members of Generation Z and specifically in relation to aviation".

The Canberras operated by the Royal Radar Establishment at Pershore were well known for their ever-evolving shapes and rampant swopping of major elements, including cockpits. The record-breaking WK163 is just such an example and on 11th November 2020 VTST succeeded in acquiring its original cockpit from California, and arrangements to bring it to Robin Hood are being completed. In 1971 the nose of WK163 was grafted on to B(I).8 WT327 which served initially at Boscombe Down on laser ranger and marked-target seeker trials. It returned to Pershore and transferred to RAE Bedford. Disposed of from Boscombe Down, WT327 was written out of *W&R16* (p273) when it was ferried to the USA, as G-BXMO, on 7th December 1997. Registered as N30UP in September 2005, it fell into disuse in California, where VTST caught up with it.
◆ *Check website for details of open days and special events* | **enquiries@vulcantothesky.org** | **www.vulcantothesky.org**

☐ WK163	EE Canberra B.2/6 G-CTTS	55	ex Baginton, G-BVWC, DRA Farnborough, RAE Bedford, RRE Pershore, Napier, ASM Bitteswell. Avro-built. CoA 29-6-08, handed over 19-5-16. 617 Sqn colours	[1]	1-22
☐ XH558	Avro Vulcan B.2(MRR) ✈ G-VLCN	60	ex Lyneham, Bruntingthorpe, Waddington, VDF, Marham, Waddington, 50, Wadd Wing, A&AEE, Wadd Wing, 27, 230 OCU, 27, Wadd Wing, 230 OCU. *Spirit of Great Britain*. Last flight 20-10-15, de-reg 19-8-17		1-22

■ **[1]** Registered to VTST. When fitted with a Napier Double Scorpion booster rocket, WK163 clinched the world altitude record on 28-8-57, reaching 70,310ft. While at Pershore, WK163 was substantially re-engineered with B.6 wings, engines and the cockpit of B.6 XH568. In 1971 WK163's original nose was installed on the nose of B(I).8 WT327 – see above for more.

Also:

❑ G-GAVA	BAe Jetstream 3102	87	ex SE-LDI, C-FHOE. De-reg 1-3-18. First noted 4-18	9-21
❑ EC-DDX	Boeing 727-256	79	ex Oakley, Hurn, Iberia. Forward fuselage	9-21
❑ N80364	Cessna 500 Citation	75	ex OY-TKI, N80364, PT-OZX, YV-940CP, N5133K, ZS-MGH,	
			N55AK, N66TR, N3JJ, HB-VEO, D-IVVV. First noted 2016	5-19

Locally: Previously listed under VTST above, Tim Wood's Swift moved off site in May 2019 and is reported to have changed hands by 2022: it is listed here as a 'port of convenience'. Another owner keeps a Chipmunk cockpit in the *general* area.

❑ WK275	V-S Swift F.4	55	ex VTST site, Selby, Upper Hill Hatfield, Filton, C(A).	
			SOC 25-5-59. Arrived 15-5-19: off-site	5-21
❑ WK638	DHC Chipmunk T.10	52	ex Swindon, Long Eaton, Eccleshall, Stamford, Manston,	
	G-BWJZ		9 AEF, RAFC, 9 AEF, York UAS, 1 FTS, 1 AEF, Ox UAS, 1 RFS.	
			Cr 22-8-99, CoA 17-1-02, de-reg 4-4-00. Arr 2015. Cockpit	6-20

HIGH BRADFIELD Lynx AH.7 XZ205 left the paintball site for further duty at <u>Copthorne</u>, W Sussex, 7-4-20.

NETHERTHORPE AERODROME north of the A619, west of Worksop   EGNF

❑ G-ARJT	Piper Apache 160G	62	ex N10F. CoA 18-8-07, de-reg 17-10-17		9-21
❑ G-BBKF*	Cessna FRA.150L	74	ex Sibson. Reims-built. CoA 13-6-91, de-reg 15-2-07.		
			Fuselage in rafters	[1]	9-21
❑ G-BEIA	Cessna FRA.150M	76	ex Sibson. Reims-built. CoA 27-10-03, de-reg 3-3-11.		
			Fuselage in rafters		9-21
❑ G-NIUS	Cessna F.172N	78	ex Morgansfield, EI-BSC, G-NIUS. Reims-built.		
			Damaged 29-1-16, de-reg 12-6-20. Cabin, simulator		2-19

■ **[1]** *Kilo-Fox* was written out of *W&R26* (p31) at Sibson.

SHEFFIELD

Structural Dynamics Laboratory for Verification and Validation: Europa Avenue. Run by Sheffield University, this high-tech facility specialises in acoustic and vibration testing. ◆ *By prior arrangement* **only** | www.lvv.ac.uk

❑ XX184	'CQ' HS Hawk T.1	77	ex Boscombe Down, Portsmouth, B' Down, Portsmouth,	
			B' Down, 100, 208, 234, 4 FTS. SOC 7-8-17. F/n 11-19	12-21
❑ ZE376	Westland Lynx AH.9A	85	ex M Wallop. SOC 3-10-18. First noted 11-19	12-21

WEST YORKSHIRE

Includes the unitary authorities of Barnsley, Bradford, Calderdale, Kirklees, Leeds and Wakefield

---

BIRD'S EDGE on the A629 northwest of Penistone

A pair of Jodels are being worked on at a *private* airstrip in the area.

❑ G-BFXR	Jodel D.112	54	ex F-BFTM. Wassmer-built. CoA 1-9-11	7-21
❑ G-BKIR	Jodel D.117	56	ex F-BIOC. SAN-built. CoA 28-8-92	7-21

BRADFORD Last noted in October 2016, the fuselage of HS.125-800B G-JJSI has been deleted.

DEWSBURY

Two helicopters are stored in a *private* location in the area.

❑ G-BHAR	Bell Sioux AH.1	65	ex XT194. Westland-built. CoA 8-9-11, de-reg 13-2-13	12-19
❑ G-USAI	Bell 47J-2A Ranger	63	ex D-HACK, 5B-CAF, Cyprus CR-1, N83701. Agusta-built	12-19

HUDDERSFIELD AERODROME or Crosland Moor, south of the A670 west of the city

❑ G-AYKK	Jodel D.117	55	ex F-BHGM. SAN-built	N10-18

☐ G-BIIZ*	Great Lakes 2T-1A	29	ex Squires Gate, N603K. Crashed 8-8-98, CoA 4-2-99	1-21
☐ D-AGEK	Boeing 737-700	91	ex Bradford, Kemble, Germania, Air Berlin, SX-BLB, PT-TET, D-AGEK, N799BB, I-TEAI, OO-LTF. Germania and 'International Food and Travel Studio' titles. Forward fuselage. F/n 8-18	10-19

LEEDS
'SHAR' ZD613 left the Cross Green Industrial Estate on 18th March 2021 bound for Selby, N Yorks.

LEEDS-BRADFORD AIRPORT or Yeadon   EGNM

☐ G-PROG	Robinson R44	06	crashed 2-5-06, de-reg 29-9-07, CoA 8-3-08. Rescue tnr	12-18
☐ EI-BPD	Short 360-100	84	ex Southend, Aer Arran, Gill, G-RMCT, Aer Lingus EI-BPD, G-BLPU, G-14-3656. Dam 4-2-01. Rescue trainer, fuselage	12-18

Craven College Aviation Academy: Last noted in 2015 HR.200 'G-OTAA' (G-MFLC) had been disposed of by late 2021.

Locally: A Cessna is still held at a private dwelling in the locality.

☐ G-ATND	Cessna F.150F	66	ex airport. Reims-built. Crashed 9-12-72, de-reg 24-8-73	9-21

LEEDS HELIPORT or Coney Park
Heli Jet Aviation:. Robinson R44 G-OGBF was flying by 2021.
◆ *Has a viewing area, but access to the hangars is* strictly *by prior arrangement* **only | www.helijet.co.uk**

☐ G-CHPA	Robinson R22 Beta	03	ex EI-EHC. CoA 13-9-12	9-19
☐ G-HMPT	Bell JetRanger II	68	ex D-HARO. Agusta-built. CoA 15-10-09	9-19
☐ G-LOLZ	Robinson R22 Beta	87	ex OH-HAF	N5-21
☐ G-MRSN*	Robinson R22 Beta	91	de-reg 2-9-20	10-20
☐ G-RAMI	Bell JetRanger III	79	ex N1080N. CoA 5-9-16, crashed 6-6-15	9-21
☐ G-WIRL	Robinson R22 Beta	87	CoA 5-8-16	9-19
☐ N153H*	Bell 222B	~	first noted 4-20	9-21
☐ N800HL*	Bell 222	~	first noted 4-20	9-21
☐ N911DN*	Bell UH-1H Iroquois	~	first noted 1-11	9-21
☐ DU-103	Bell JetRanger	~	ex Dubai Air Wing. Arrived 23-11-15	9-19

SOWERBY BRIDGE on the A646 west of Halifax
Ryburn Valley High School: It is *thought* that the Cadet-cum-simulator is still extant.
◆ *By prior arrangement* **only | www.rvhs.co.uk**

☐ G-SACU	Piper Cadet 161	88	ex Sherburn, N9162X. Crashed 29-6-96, de-reg 7-6-01. Arrived by 8-16. Simulator	8-16

SCOTLAND

Scotland comprises 32 unitary authorities ranging from Orkney, Shetland to Dumfries and Galloway and Borders

ABERDEEN AIRPORT or Dyce
EGPD

As well as the 'pukka' training aids, there is a purpose-built rig for HUET - Helicopter Underwater Escape Training.

☐ G-BHIC	Cessna F.182Q	80	ex Kemble, Alton, Kidlington. Reims-built. Damaged 9-06, CoA 3-8-08, de-reg 4-5-07. Fuselage, rescue trainer		9-21
☐ -	Sud Dauphin II	~	BAPC.563, ex CHC Scotia. Composite	[1]	11-21
☐ XZ232	Westland Lynx HAS.3GMS	77	ex Ipswich, Fleetlands, 815, 702, HAS.2, 702, 700L. Red scheme	[2]	11-21
	'Falck 4'				
☐ XZ372	'FV' SEPECAT Jaguar GR.3A	76	ex Ipswich, St Athan, 41, 6, GR.1, 6, 226 OCU, 20, 14. Last flown 5-7-05. Rescue trainer		11-21
☐ XZ647	Westland Lynx AH.7	80	ex Falck NUTEC, M Wallop. Red scheme. On site since 2009, rescue trainer on west side since 4-11		9-21
☐ ZA110	'563' HP Jetstream T.2	81	ex Ipswich, Culdrose, 750, F-BTMI. SOC 29-10-10. SAL-built. Fuselage, rescue trainer		11-21

■ **[1]** Dauphin is with Survivex on the western perimeter industrial estate. It is fitted with a 'N2-model tail if that helps. Apparently, it deserves a heritage number. **[2]** Lynx HAS.3 is a fire-trainer on a mock-up oil rig heli-pad with Falck NUTEC on the eastern perimeter.

ABOYNE south of the A93 west of Banchory

Deeside Activity Park ◆ *By prior arrangement only* | www.deesideactivitypark.com

☐ G-OANN	Zenair CH-601 Zodiac	00	ex airstrip, crashed 23-4-06. 'Crash' scene	[1]	9-15

■ **[1]** Zodiac G-OANN was rebuilt and is airworthy - this is the original fuselage.

Also: Stampe SV-4 G-BKRK was flying by August 2020, from Little Gransden, Cambs.

ABOYNE AERODROME south of the A93 west of Banchory

A homebuilt amphibian is stored at a local, *private*, location.

☐ G-BAHP	Volmer Sportsman	73	CoA 18-10-93	10-19

ACHARACLE on the southern tip of Loch Shiel, a long way west of Fort William

W&R27 pondered a possible move for the Sea King at a *private* location in the *general* area: that was not the case.

☐ XV648	Westland Sea King HU.5SAR	69	ex Colsterworth, Fleetlands, 771, Gannet Flt, 819, DERA, 706, HAS.2, 706, Falklands, 825, 706, HAS.1, 706, 737, 826, 700S. First noted 10-16	1-21

ARBROATH AIRFIELD Last noted in November 20212, Cadet TX.3 XE786 has been deleted.

AYR east of the A77 southwest of Kilmarnock

Ayrshire College: Dam Park, off the A79. ◆ *By prior arrangement only* | www.ayrshire.ac.uk

☐ G-AZHK*	Robin HR.100-210B	71	ex Dalcross, G-ILEG, G-AZHK. CoA 22-10-71, de-reg 30-9-21	9-21
☐ XX612	SAL Bulldog T.1	74	ex Prestwick, Dunfermline, Dundee, Wales, S'ton UASs., RNEFTS, QUAS, CFS. CoA 15-1-09, de-reg 5-3-08	4-19
	'03' *and* 'A' G-BZXC			

BALADO AERODROME or Balado Bridge, on the A91 west of Milnathort

☐ XM412	'41' Hunting Jet Provost T.3A	60	ex Ipswich, N Weald, Binbrook, Colsterworth, Halton 9011M (10-8-89), 1 FTS, 3 FTS, 2 FTS. Displayed	11-21
	and '49'			

BANCHORY on the A93 west of Aberdeen

A pair of Airedales are cherished in the *general* area.

☐ G-ARXD	Beagle Airedale	62	ex Netherley. CoA 13-6-86	N4-18
☐ G-ASAI	Beagle Airedale	62	ex Dundee, Islay. CoA 20-5-77	N11-18

BLANTYRE on the A724 south east of Glasgow
A *private* owner has a Gnat in the *general* area.

☐ XM697 'S' Folland Gnat T.1   61 ex Carluke, Market Drayton, Exeter, Hurn, Dunsfold, Hurn
    G-NAAT   Woking, HSA, A&AEE, HSA. SOC 23-9-68, de-reg 10-4-95.
    'Red Arrows' colours. First noted 4-16   9-21

BORGUE on the B727 west of Kirkcudbright
Brighouse Bay Holiday Park: Displayed in the grounds is a Meteor | **www.brighousebayholidaypark.co.uk**

☐ WS792 'K' Gloster Meteor   54 ex Carlisle, Cosford 7965M (19-6-67), 5 MU, 1 ANS,
    NF(T).14   2 ANS, no service as NF.14. AWA-built   1-22

BRIDGE OF WEIR on the A761 northwest of Paisley
Neil Geddes: Has a *private* store/workshop in the locality.

☐ G-AJAJ*   Auster J1N Alpha   46 CoA 12-6-15   7-21
☐ G-CDUW   Aeronca C.3   35 ex F-AZKE, N64765, N14631   7-21
☐ WZ824   Slingsby Grasshopper TX.1   52 ex Dirleton, Strathaven, Ringmer, Dishforth, St Bees.
    SOC 9-3-88   [1] 7-21
☐ XK820   Slingsby Grasshopper TX.1   56 ex Strathallan, Aberdeen, Lancing, Locking. SOC 21-6-88   [2] 7-21
■ **[1]** For WZ824 see under Carlisle, Cumbria. **[2]** XK820 has wings from WZ754 and WZ778.

CARLUKE on the A73 southeast of Motherwell and Wishaw
Reynard Nursery: Within the nursery, the Convair is used by **Runway Studios Makeup Lounge** as a 'surgery'.
◆ *Visitors welcome during open hours, but best to check beforehand* | **www.reynardnursery.co.uk**

☐ G-CONV   Convair CV-440-54   57 ex Coventry, CS-TML, N357SA, N28KE, N4402. De-reg 20-12-06   1-22

CARRUTHERSTOWN on the A75 between Dumfries and Annan
Hetland Garden Centre: A Cessna 310, in the inevitable crash pose, is in the 'Dino Park' segment. This was written out of *W&R25* (p318) as having left Perth by road on 11th December 2014 - address unknown: it *may* have been here ever since. Although technically US registered, it still carries its UK registration. ◆ **www.hetland.co.uk**

☐ N310WT*   Cessna 310R   78 ex Perth, G-BGXK, N6070X. De-reg 17-10-01. First noted 4-21   7-21

CHAPELTON on the A276 northwest of Strathaven
A *private* store of light aircraft in the locality.

☐ G-AOEH   Aeronca 7AC Champion   46 ex Newtownards, OO-TWF, N79854. CoA 19-7-10   6-21
☐ G-AWUS   Cessna F.150J   68 Reims-built. Crashed 22-11-86, de-reg 4-7-94   6-21
☐ G-AYXV   Cessna FRA.150L   68 Reims-built. Crashed 5-9-79, de-reg 24-9-79   6-21
☐ G-AZHT   Victa Airtourer T3   69 ex Glasgow, Abbotsinch. AESL-built. Crashed 29-4-86   6-21
☐ G-BGWV   Aeronca 7AC Champion   46 ex OO-GRI, OO-TWR. Crashed 8-6-86, de-reg 9-1-13   6-21
☐ N170AZ   Cessna 170A   48 ex Strathallan, HB-CAZ   6-21

CULLODEN southeast of Inverness
The Belfair is believed extant in the *general* area.

☐ G-APOD   Tipsy Belfair   58 ex Dundee, OO-TIF. CoA 23-8-88, de-reg 6-9-00   1-12

CUMBERNAULD AERODROME north of the A80, north of Cumbernauld
The Dragon is a major omission. Using original wings, a fuselage commissioned in New Zealand, the long term project was recorded in *W&R18* at the workshop of Aero Antiques and Aero Tech near Southampton, Hampshire, through its test flight in late summer 2016 in *W&R26*. Work continues to return it to flight.

☐ G-ACET   DH Dragon   34 ex Southampton, Bishop's Stortford, 2779M Kingston-upon--
    Thames, AW171, 6 AACU, Ringway SF, G-ACET, Highland AW,
    Midland & Scottish Air Ferries – see notes above   6-20
☐ S7-AAU   BN Islander   77 ex A2-01M, S7-AAD, G-BELB. First noted 8-16   5-19
☐ XV268   DHC Beaver 1   G-BVER 66 ex G-BTDM, XV268, M Wallop. CoA 23-4-95, de-reg 20-12-16   4-19

CUPAR on the A91 west of St Andrews
Scottish Deer Centre: The site' jingle 'For Those with a Wild Side', things got a bit more savage with the arrival of the former Elgin Buccaneer. ◆ Bow of Fife, KY15 4NQ | **email** via website | **https://scottishdeerpark.co.uk**

❑ XW530*	Blackburn Buccaneer S.2B	70	ex Elgin, Lossiemouth, 208, 12, 208, 216, 16, 15, 16. Arrived 11-12-21	1-22

A Victor cockpit is kept at a *private* location in the area.

❑ XA917	HP Victor B.1	56	ex Crowland, Barnham, Marham, Wittering 7827M (13-12-63), A&AEE, HP. Damaged 2-3-61. Cockpit	[1]	7-21

■ **[1]** The first production Victor B.1, XA917 hit the headlines on a sortie out of Radlett 1-6-57 with John Allam at the helm; in a shallow dive at around 40,000ft, it clocked 675mph - Mach 1.02 - becoming the largest aircraft at the time to go supersonic.

CURRIE Spitfire FSM 'L1018' (BAPC.308 moved to <u>Kinloss</u>, 12th December 2021.

DIRLETON on the A198 west of North Berwick
A *private* airstrip in the locality hold two restoration projects.

❑ G-BBBO	SIPA 903	51	ex Eggington, F-BGBQ. CoA 9-9-09	[1]	6-21
❑ G-JIII*	Stolp Starduster Too	75	ex N9043. CoA 15-6-17		6-21

■ **[1]** Written out of *W&R27* (p313) under this heading, as having moved on – not so!

DUMFRIES off the A701 northeast of Dumfries on the former airfield
Dumfries and Galloway Aviation Museum: The restored watch tower that forms the centrepiece of the museum contains a huge array of artefacts, all well presented. The ground floor includes an impressive engine collection. The impressive Airborne Forces Hall is graced with an impressive full-size replica of a Hamilcar assault glider, adding to the Horsa and Hadrian. As the Horsa is a beautifully restored/constructed fuselage section, lacking cockpit, and is not formally listed.
◆ *Heathfield Industrial Estate, DG1 3PH* | **01387 251623** | **email** via website | **www.dumfriesaviationmuseum.com**

❑ G-AWZJ	HS Trident 3B-101	71	ex Prestwick, BA, BEA. CoA 12-9-85, de-reg 7-3-86. Arrived 1999. Forward fuselage	[1]	1-22
❑ G-AYFA	SAL Twin Pioneer 3	58	ex Hooton Park, Morecambe, Mold, Carlisle, Hooton Park, Warmingham, Sandbach, Shobdon, Prestwick, G-31-5, XM285, SRCU, 225, Odiham SF, 230. De-reg 16-5-91. Cockpit. Arrived 9-13	[2]	1-22
❑ G-AZIL	Slingsby T.61A Falke	71	CoA 13-10-14. Arrived 10-2-19		1-22
❑ G-RAYE	Piper Cherokee Six	66	ex Doncaster, Stamford, Tatenhill, G-ATTY, N11C. CoA 27-9-08, de-reg 2-6-08. Arrived by 4-14. Fuselage		3-20
❑ –	HS HS.748-2B	89	ex Perth, Woodford. Cockpit	[3]	7-21
❑ P7540	V-S Spitfire IIa 'DU-W' recreation	40	ex Pickhill, Loch Doon, 312, 266, 609, 66. CBAF-built. Crashed 25-10-41. Salvaged 198. Unveiled 16-7-17	[4]	1-22
❑ –*	Avro Anson I	~	ex Canada, RCAF. Complete frame plus additional cockpit. 'Unveiled' 6-21		7-21
❑ –	HP Halifax rep	~	BAPC.322, ex Linton-on-Ouse. Cockpit. First noted 3-18		1-22
❑ –	GAL Hotspur II	~	BAPC.397, ex Duxford, Aldershot. Cockpit. First noted 6-17		1-22
❑ –*	GAL Hamilcar	~	forward fuselage; entrance to Airborne Forces hall		1-22
❑ WA576	Bristol Sycamore 3 G-ALSS	51	ex East Fortune, Strathallan, Halton 7900M (5-1-66), RAE, A&AEE, G-ALSS de-reg 17-11-50. Arrived 7-6-87		1-22
❑ WJ880	EE Canberra T.4	55	ex Firbeck, N Weald, Halton 8491M (2-4-76), 7, 85, 100, 56, Laarbruch SF, RAE, 16, Laarbruch SF, Gütersloh SF, 104. Arrived 1995. Cockpit, travelling exhibit		1-22
❑ WL375	Gloster Meteor T.7(mod)	52	ex West Freugh, RAE. SOC 16-6-69, acquired 1977	[5]	1-22
❑ WT746	Hawker Hunter F.4	55	ex 'XF506', Saighton, Halton 7770M (28-11-62), St Athan, AFDS. Arrived 1999. 43 Sqn colour scheme, *Clara*		1-22
❑ XL497	'041' Fairey Gannet AEW.3	61	ex Prestwick, Lossiemouth, 849, A&AEE, 849. SOC 7-12-78. Arrived 13-4-05		1-22
❑ XP557	Hunting Jet Provost T.4	62	ex Hemswell, Firbeck, Bruntingthorpe, Halton 8494M (30-6-76), 6 FTS, RAFC. Arrived 25-3-05. 'Dazzle' colours		1-22
❑ XT280	'323' Blackburn Buccaneer S.2B	65	ex Dundonald, Birtley, East Fortune, Lossie', 208, 12, 208, 12, 16, 809, A&AEE, 809. SOC 10-4-94. Arrived 2-03. Cockpit		1-22

Anonymous Anson I cockpit frame (left) and Hamilcar forward fuselage replica. Both July 2021. *David S Johnstone*

❏ XT486		Westland Wessex HU.5	66	ex Altcar, Brize Norton 8919M (3-2-87), Wroughton, 848, 847, 772, 707, 781. Arrived 13-6-07		1-22
❏ XW363	'36'	BAC Jet Provost T.5A	71	ex Haverigg, Swinton, Warton, Samlesbury, Preston, Warton, RAFC, 6 FTS, 1 FTS. SOC 11-1-91. Arrived 2010, off-site		4-18
❏ XX483	'562'	HP Jetstream T.1	74	ex Welshpool, Weston-on-Trent, Shawbury, 750, CFS, 5 FTS. Arrived 2002. 750 Sqn c/s. Cockpit, travelling exhibit		1-22
❏ ZF584		EE Lightning F.53	68	ex Edinburgh, Turnhouse, Warton, Saudi AF 53-682, G-27-52. Last flown 22-1-86, arrived 22-5-06. 111 Sqn c/s		1-22
❏ FT-36		Lockheed T-33A-1-LO	55	ex Sculthorpe, Belgian AF, USAF 55-3047. , Last flew 26-11-79, arrived 8-9-81. *Little Miss Laura*	[6]	1-22
❏ 318	'8-NY'	Dassault Mystère IVA	c57	ex Sculthorpe, French Air Force. Last flown 15-5-79. Arrived 1981. 'Tiger' stripes	[6]	1-22
❏ Fv35075	'40'	SAAB J35A Draken	c61	ex Duxford, Swedish AF F16. Arrived 19-8-05	[7]	1-22
❏ '241079'		Waco CG-4 Hadrian replica	03	BAPC.370, ex Cosford, Shawbury, Lubbock, Texas. Fuselage. Arrived 11-18	[8]	1-22
❏ '54-2005'		NAA F-100D-11-NA Super Sabre	54	ex Sculthorpe, FAF, USAF 54-2163. Last flown 24-5-77, arrived 11-1-79. USAF colours, *Miss Shillelagh*	[6]	1-22
❏ 68-0060		GD F-111E Aardvark	68	ex 20 TFW. Escape pod. Crashed 5-11-75. Arrived 1990		7-21

■ [1] *Zulu-Juliet*'s is open to the public and includes an interior display and 30-seat lecture hall. [2] 'Twin Pin' on loan. [3] HS.748 cockpit is no longer thought to be off the line, but a dedicated customer mock-up. [4] Based at Ayr with 312 (Czechoslovak) Sqn, P7540 was flying ultra-low over Loch Doon, near Craigmalloch, 25-10-41, when a wing tip hit the water and it crashed. [5] Meteor fitted with an FR.9 or PR.10 nose cone. [6] Part of the National Museum of the USAF's Loan Program. [7] Draken was signed over to the museum from the IWM during 2012. [8] From the Assault Glider Trust.

Locally: **No.1153 (Dumfries) Squadron Air Cadets**: Destined to become a simulator, the status of the CoZy is uncertain.

❏ G-CESP	Puffer CoZy Mk.4	07	ex Perth. Unfinished project, de-reg 5-11-10	1-14

DUNDEE AIRPORT or Riverside   EGPN

❏ G-BXET	Piper Tomahawk 112	80	ex N25089. CoA 26-8-11, de-reg 23-6-11. Cockpit, rescue tnr	7-20

EAST FORTUNE AERODROME north of the A1, west of East Linton

National Museum of Flight Scotland: Part of National Museums Scotland - see Edinburgh for the 'headquarters'. As well as the hangars: Hangar 2, military aviation, Hangar 3 - civil aviation, Hangar 4 Concorde and the 'Jet Age' exhibition, several other wartime buildings are open. Hangar 1 is devoted to conservation and is not *generally* available to the public.

◆ *Signed from the A1 near Haddington, EH39 5LF* | **0300 1236789** | **info@nms.ac.uk** | **www.nms.ac.uk/flight**

Hangars 2, 3, 4 and external exhibits:

❏ G-ACYK		Spartan Cruiser III	35	ex Hill of Stake, Largs. Crashed 14-1-38, de-reg 86-38. Arrived 1973. Fuselage	1-22
❏ G-AGBN		GAL Cygnet II	41	ex Strathallan, Biggin Hill, ES915, MCCS, 52 OTU, 51 OTU, 23, G-AGBN. CoA 28-11-80, de-reg 15-11-88. Arrived 11-8-81	1-22
❏ G-AHKY		Miles M.18-2	40	ex Perth, Strathallan, Blackbushe, HM545, U-0224, U-8. CoA 20-9-89, de-reg 19-3-92. Phillips & Powis-built. Arr 1991	1-22
❏ G-ANOV		DH Dove 6	54	ex CAFU, G-5-16. CoA 31-5-75, de-reg 6-7-81. Arr 10-78	1-22
❏ G-APFJ		Boeing 707-436	60	ex Cosford, British Airtours, BOAC. CoA 16-2-82, de-reg 30-5-84. Arrived 4-06. BOAC colours. Forward fuselage	1-22
❏ G-ARCX		Gloster Meteor NF.14	53	ex Ferranti, WM261. CoA 20-2-69, de-reg 25-10-73. AWA-built. Arrived 8-75 [1]	1-22
❏ G-ARPH		HS Trident 1C	64	ex Cosford, BA, BEA. CoA 8-9-82, de-reg 24-5-82. Arrived 2006. BA colours. Cockpit	1-22
❏ G-ASUG		Beech E.18S	56	ex Loganair, N575C, N555CB, N24R. CoA 23-7-75, de-reg 12-5-75. Arrived 1976	1-22
❏ G-ATOY		Piper Comanche 260B	66	ex Elstree, N8893P. Crashed 6-3-79; de-reg 14-5-79. Arrived 1979. *Myth Too*. Fuselage, in 'Fantastic Flight' [2]	1-22
❏ G-AVMO		BAC 111-510ED	68	ex Cosford, Hurn, BA, BEA. *Lothian Region*. CoA 3-2-95, de-reg 12-7-93. Arrived 9-9-06. Outside	1-22
❏ G-AVPC		Druine Turbulent	73	CoA 28-9-99, de-reg 13-9-02. Arrived 4-03	1-22
❏ G-BBVF		SAL Twin Pioneer 2	59	ex Shobdon, XM961 / 7978M, SRCU, Odiham SF, 230, 21. Damaged 11-3-82, de-reg 8-8-83. Arrived 19-8-82	1-22
❏ G-BDIX		DH Comet 4C	62	ex Lasham, Dan-Air, XR399, 216. CoA 11-10-81, de-reg 13-6-83. Hawarden-built. Arrived 30-9-81. Outside	1-22
❏ G-BELF		BN Islander	77	ex Cumbernauld, D-IBRA, G-BELF - CoA 12-3-01, de-reg	
	G-HEBZ			21-3-09. G-HEBZ de-reg 8-11-18. Arrived 7-7-05. Scottish Ambulance colours [3]	1-22
❏ G-BOAA		BAC/Sud Concorde 102	75	ex London, BA, G-N94AA (1-79 to 7-80), G-BOAA. CoA 24-2-01, de-reg 4-5-04. Arrived 19-4-04 [4]	1-22
❏ G-JSSD		HP Jetstream 3100	69	ex Prestwick, N510F, N510E, N12227, G-AXJZ. CoA 9-10-90. De-reg 4-1-96. Arrived 2-96 [5]	1-22
❏ G-SJEN		Icarus C42 FB80	04	ex Strathaven. Last flown 5-10, de-reg 10-8-10. Arr 7-11	3-20
❏ G-UNIV		Montgomerie Two-Place	96	ex Glasgow, G-BWTP. CoA 18-1-05, de-reg 16-1-14 [6]	3-20
❏ W-2		Weir W.2	34	BAPC.85, ex Edinburgh, East Fortune, Glasgow, EF, Hayes, Knockholt, Hanworth, Cathcart. Acquired 1986 [7]	1-22
❏ –		Scotkites Cirrus III hang-glider	77	BAPC.197, ex Lothian Hang Glider Club, Edinburgh. Last flown and arrived 1987	3-20
❏ –		Firebird Sierra h-glider	c83	BAPC.313, ex Huntly. Arrived 2002	3-20
❏ –		Airwave Magic Kiss h-g	89	BAPC.312, ex Biggar. Arrived 2005	3-20
❏ 591		Schleicher Rhönlerche II	59	ex D-0359. Arrived 1987	10-21
❏ VH-SNB		DH Dragon I	42	ex Strathallan, VH-ASK, RAAF A34-13. Arrived 1981 [8]	1-22
❏ VH-UQB		DH Puss Moth	30	ex Strathallan, Bankstown, G-ABDW. Arrived 1981	1-22
❏ N14234		HP Jetstream 1	69	ex Hatfield, East Midlands, N14234, N102SC, N200SC, N1BE, G-BBBV, G-8-12. Arrived 5-94. Fuselage [9]	1-22
❏ TE462		V-S Spitfire XVI	45	ex Ouston 7243M (14-12-54), 101 FRS, Finningley SF. CBAF-built. Arrived 19-2-71. Plinth-mounted	1-22
❏ VM360		Avro Anson C.19	47	ex Strathallan, Thruxton, Kemps, G-APHV (de-reg 21-1-82), TRE, A&AEE. SOC 18-11-57. Arrived 8-77	1-22
❏ VX185		EE Canberra B.5	52	ex Wroughton, South Kensington, EE. Arrived 10-97. *The Record-Breaking Canberra*. Cockpit [10]	1-22
❏ WF259	'171'	Hawker Sea Hawk F.2	54	ex Lossiemouth A2483 (24-6-59), Lossiemouth SF, 736. AWA-built. Arrived 10-7-72	1-22
❏ WW145	'680'	DH Sea Venom FAW.22	55	ex Lossiemouth, 750, 891. Christchurch-built. SOC 13-2-70. Arrived 1972	1-22
❏ XA228		Slingsby Grasshopper TX.1	53	ex store, Glenalmond School. Arrived 6-00	1-22
❏ XM597		Avro Vulcan B.2	63	ex Waddington, 50, 35, 101, 9, 50, 35, Wadd W, 12. Arrived 12-4-84. Outside	1-22
❏ XN776	'C'	EE Lightning F.2A	62	ex Leuchars 8535M (1-4-77), 92, 19. Arrived 8-5-82	1-22

☐ XV277		HS Harrier GR.1	66	ex Ipswich, Yeovilton A2602[2], A2600[2] (28-11-88),	
				Filton, HSA. Arrived 4-00	1-22
☐ XX308		HS Hawk T.1	80	ex Shawbury, 'Red Arrows', 4 FTS. Last flown 18-4-13.	
				SOC 5-12-17. Arrived 30-11-17	[11] 1-22
☐ XZ119	'FG'	SEPECAT Jaguar GR.1A	76	ex Cranwell, Coltishall, 41, Warden Det, 41, Gulf Det,	
				ETPS, 41. Arrived 27-4-09. *Katrina Jane*	1-22
☐ ZE934	'TA'	Panavia Tornado F.3	89	ex St Athan, 56, 111, 11, 43, 11, 111, 5. Arrived 13-9-05	1-22
☐ 9940		Bristol Bolingbroke IVT	42	ex Strathallan, RCAF 5 B&GS. SOC 21-8-46.	
				Fairchild Canada-built. Arrived 8-8-81. RCAF yellow c/s	1-22
☐ 3677	613677	Mikoyan-Gurevich	53	ex Cáslav, Ostravian Air Regt, Czech AF.	
		MiG-15*bis* Fagot		Letov-built S-103	1-22
☐ 191659	'15'	Me 163B-1a Komet	44	ex Cambridge, Cranfield, Brize Norton, RAE, Husum,	
				II/JG400. Arrived 1976	1-22

■ **[1]** *Charlie-Xray* factoids: Built as an NF.11, it was fitted with the NF.14 clear canopy and was the prototype for that variant, first-flying at Bitteswell 15-7-53 and despatched to Boscombe Down for trials 13 days later. With the Ferranti test fleet its colour scheme gave it the nickname *Mentadent*, after a toothpaste of the time! Retired in 1969 with just 346 hours 'on the clock'. **[2]** The unrestored Comanche fuselage, was flown solo around the world by Sheila Scott in 1966. **[3]** Although wearing G-BELF, this registration was cancelled 21-3-07 and on that day it was re-registered as G-HEBZ. **[4]** *Alpha-Alpha* factoids: Withdrawn from BA service 12-8-00, total hours 22,769, landings 8,064. It is on long-term loan from British Airways. **[5]** Handley Page-built as a Series 1, first flown at Radlett 21-7-69; converted to BAe Series 31 prototype and first flown at Prestwick 28-3-80. **[6]** Built in Glasgow, full designation Montgomerie-Parsons Two-Place (mod). Donated by Glasgow University's Department of Aerospace Engineering. Used for a variety of trials, with instrumentation in the second cockpit. **[7]** W-2 coincidently has the 'B Condition' ('B Class' or 'trade-plate') identity W-2, used by G & J Weir Ltd of Cathcart. Previously recorded as on loan from the Science Museum, this was the case until 1986 when it was donated to NMS by Viscount Weir. **[8]** Built by DH Australia at Bankstown, NSW, for the RAAF; *believed* no active service. **[9]** Airframe used as engineering mock-up for the BAE Jetstream Super 31. **[10]** Canberra B.5 VX185 has been quoted in previous editions as 7631M. This 'M' number was indeed allocated to VX185, in 1959. But this was *after* it had lost *this* cockpit, and it was converted to the prototype B(I).8 in 1954; it was broken up at Filton 30-4-64. *With* this cockpit, the crew of Beamont, Hillwood and Wilson made the first-ever out-and-back crossing of the North Atlantic in VX185 on 26-8-52 in an elapsed time of 10 hours 3½ mins, hence the lettering on the nose. **[11]** There is *another* 'XX308' - see Cranwell, Lincs.

Deep store and Hangar 1: Hangar 1 is the conservation workshop and not generally available to the public. The museum also has a storage site at Granton, Edinburgh - also **not** available for inspection. The cockpit of Buccaneer S.1 XK533 moved to Stranraer, Scotland, on 30th October 2021.

☐ G-AMOG		Vickers Viscount 701	53	ex Cosford, Cardiff, BOAC, Cambrian, BEA G-AMNZ.	
				CoA 14-6-77, de-reg 17-5-76. Arrived 17-8-06.	
				BEA colours, *Robert Falcon Scott*	1-22
☐ G-AXEH		SAL Bulldog Srs 1	69	ex Prestwick, Shoreham. CoA 15-1-77,	
				de-reg 19-6-78. Arrived 23-12-84. Beagle-built	[1] 1-22
☐ G-BCFN		Cameron O-65 HAB	74	CoA 15-5-97, de-reg 24-1-19	12-17
☐ G-BDFU		Dragonfly MPA	81	ex Blackpool, Warton, Prestwick. De-reg 15-12-83. Arr 1981	12-17
☐ G-BVWK		Air and Space 18A	65	ex Kinnettles, SE-HID, N6108S. De-reg 18-10-00. Arr 10-04	3-20
☐ G-MBJX		Hiway Super Scorpion	r82	ex Halton. De-reg 13-6-90. Arrived 1998	12-17
☐ G-MBPM		Eurowing Goldwing	80	CoA 21-8-98, de-reg 3-8-00. Arrived 4-99	12-17
☐ G-MMLI		Solar Tri-Flyer / Typhoon	r84	BAPC.244, ex Glasgow. De-reg 7-9-94. Arrived 1998	12-17
☐ BJV		Slingsby T.21A	49	BGA.1014, ex Feshiebridge, SE-SHK. CoA 30-4-81. Arr 28-5-82	12-17
☐ –		Chargus 18/50 h-glider	75	BAPC.160, ex Tranent. Arrived 1975 - from new	12-17
☐ –		Birdman Moonraker h-g	77	BAPC.195, ex Edinburgh. Arrived 1987	12-17
☐ –		Southdown Sigma II h-g	c80	BAPC.196, ex Penicuik. Arrived 1987	12-17
☐ –		Electra Floater h-g	79	BAPC.245, ex Edinburgh. Arrived 1995	12-17
☐ –		Hiway Cloudbase h-g	79	BAPC.246, ex Edinburgh. Arrived 1995	12-17
☐ –		Albatros ASG.21 h-g	77	BAPC.247, ex Edinburgh. Arrived 1995	12-17
☐ -		Eurowing Catto CP-16	c81	BAPC.262, ex Gifford. With wings of G-MJEN. Arrived 1983	12-17
☐ –		Goldmarque Gyr	c82	BAPC.314, ex Huntly. Arrived 2002	12-17
☐ TS291	BCB	Slingsby Cadet TX.2	44	BGA.852, ex Portmoak, TS291. CoA 12-66. Arr 1980	10-21
☐ WV493	'29'	Percival Provost T.1	53	ex Strathallan, G-BDYG (de-reg 4-11-91, CoA 28-11-80),	
				Halton 7696M, 6 FTS. Arrived 11-8-81	1-22
☐ XL762		Saro Skeeter AOP.12	58	ex Wallop, Halton 8017M, 7 Flt, 9 Flt, 652, 22 Flt, 654, 651.	
				SOC 27-5-68. Arrived 1-11-75	1-22
☐ XT288		Blackburn Buccaneer	66	ex Lossiemouth 9134M (10-4-91), A&AEE, 208, 12,	
		S.2B		FAA 800. Arrived 7-94	1-22

☐ XV241		HS Nimrod MR.2	70	ex Kinloss, Kinloss Wing, Kin/St M Wing, 42, MR.1, A&AEE,
				Kin Wing, 203, Kinloss. Arrived 10-2-11. Forward fuselage	1-22
☐ –		Hunting Jet Provost CIM	~	ex Leuchars, Rosyth. Cockpit. Acquired 9-14	9-19
☐ –	'FI+S'	MS Criquet	47	ex Duxford, G-BIRW, OO-FIS, F-BDQS.
				CoA 3-6-83, de-reg 15-11-88. Arrived 9-11-82	1-22
☐ 309	3309	Mikoyan-Gurevich	53	ex Polish AF. WSK-built SBLim-2.
		MiG-15UTI *Midget*		Cockpit	1-22
☐ BF-10		Bristol Beaufighter TF.10	44	ex South Africa, Portuguese AF BF-10, RD220 n/s. Arr 9-12-00	1-22
☐ –		Waco CG-4A Hadrian	44	BAPC.317, ex Aberlady. Arr 1980. Nose. *The Bunhouse*	12-17
☐ 155848	'WT'	McD F-4S-MC Phantom II	68	ex Yeovilton, VMFA-232, USMC, F-4J US Navy.
				Arrived 13-5-99. VMFA-232 colours	[2] 1-22

■ **[1]** Built by Beagle, *Echo-Hotel* was the prototype Bulldog, first flying from Shoreham 19-5-69. See under Sandown, Isle of Wight' for another 'G-AXEH'. **[2]** The F-4 is on loan from the US DoD.

❖

Aviation Preservation Society of Scotland (APSS): The main workshop is at Congalton Gardens Farm, to the north of East Fortune, on the B1367 towards Kingston. (See also under Edinburgh, Scotland, for another workshop.) The main project is a full-scale, flyable, Sopwith 1½ Strutter which is nearing completion. Wassmer-built Jodel D.120 G-BKCW (permit lapsed in February 2020) is also on the stocks and makes good progress. Jodels D.117 G-BDIH and D.120A G-BYBE, having been used for spares for *Charlie-Whisky*, had been stripped down and sold off, respectively, by December 2021. Slingsby T.53B G-DDHE which APSS operated from Portmoak was sold off in 2020. ◆ *By prior arrangement* only | **via Facebook**

EAST LINTON just north of the A1, east of Haddington
The Tin Shed: This 'community focal point' *should* have a Tomahawk. **www.themart.co.uk**

☐ G-BMKG	Piper Tomahawk 112	82	ex Perth, ZS-LGC. CoA 17-1-13, de-reg 5-2-18	3-18

EDDERTON Last noted in October 2010, Rand KR-2 G-BRJY has been deleted.

EDINBURGH
National Museum of Scotland: The National Museum of Flight at East Fortune (above) is a part of the group.
◆ *Chambers Street, Edinburgh, EH1 1JF* | **0300 1236789** | info@nms.ac.uk | **www.nms.ac.uk**

☐ G-ACVA	Kay Gyroplane	35	ex East Fortune, Edinburgh, Glasgow, Strathallan,
			Perth, Glasgow, Perth. De-reg 5-5-59. Acquired 1998	1-22
☐ G-AOEL	DH Tiger Moth	40	ex East Fortune, Strathallan, Dunstable, Mk. II N9510,
			7 FTS, 2 GU,11 RFS, 1 RFS, 7 RFS, 7 EFTS. CoA 18-7-72,
			de-reg 21-1-82. Acquired 1980, first noted 7-16	1-22
☐ G-AXIG	SAL Bulldog 104	71	ex Dirleton, Compton Abbas, Blackbushe, SAL.
			Beagle-built. CoA 12-11-11, de-reg 21-4-11. Acq 7-11	[1] 1-22
☐ G-BGXB	Piper Tomahawk 112	79	ex East Fortune, Alton, Cardiff, N9728N. CoA 16-8-04,
			de-reg 22-2-10. First noted 7-16	3-20
☐ –	Pilcher Hawk	1896	BAPC.49, ex East Fortune, Edinburgh. Accident 30-9-1899.
			On loan from 1909, acquired 24-3-20	[2] 1-22
☐ BED	Slingsby Gull I	38	BGA.902, ex East Fortune, Edinburgh, Newbattle,
			'G-ALPHA'. Acquired 1968. First noted 7-16	[3] 1-22
☐ VF581	'G' Beagle Terrier 2	G-ARSL 46	ex East Fortune, Eggesford, Auster AOP.6 VF581, 664.
			De-reg 4-8-14. First noted 7-16	1-22

■ **[1]** *India-Golf* completed at Prestwick by SAL as the second prototype and first flew 14-2-71. **[2]** Designed and built by Percy Pilcher with help from his sister Ella, the Hawk was first flown in 1896 and is the UK's oldest heavier-than-aircraft. Pilcher crashed this machine while flying at Stanford Hall, Leics, on 30-9-1899 and died of his injuries two days later. (There is a Hawk replica at Stanford Hall - qv.) **[3]** Gull I is *possibly* the former VW912.

Aviation Preservation Society of Scotland: See under East Fortune, Scotland, for more details.

☐ –	Bensen gyroglider	~	BAPC.315, Acquired 2015	10-16
☐ F-AZDH	DH Tiger Moth	44	ex Melun, La Ferté Alais, Brussels, OO-EVM, Belg AF T-19,
			RAF NM199, Belgian TS. Morris-built	10-16

Edinburgh Academy: In Kinnear Road, close to the Botanic Gardens, is *believed* to still have its Grasshopper.

☐ WZ773	Slingsby Grasshopper TX.1	52	SOC 16-6-88	6-12

EDINBURGH AIRPORT or Turnhouse   EGPH

☐ 'L1067' 'XT-D' V-S Spitfire FSM   89 BAPC.227, ex 'L1070', 'XT-A', 603 Sqn colours.
                                                  Blue Peter. Plinth-mounted near entrance   [1] 11-21
■ **[1]** The 603 (City of Edinburgh) Squadron Association look after the Spitfire FSM.

ELGIN

The **Buccaneer Service Station** gave up its namesake on 11th December 2021 was S.2B XW530 moved to Cupar, Scotland.
At the **Highland Gliding Club** Airtourer G-ATJC had gravitated to Perth, Scotland, by November 2021.

ERROL south of the A90, east of Perth

The trio is kept by a *private* collector locally: the Gannet outside, the other two internally.
☐ 'XE897'   DH Vampire T.11   54 ex Leuchars, Errol, Strathallan, Woodford, Chester, 4 FTS,
                                  XD403   1, 7, 8, 5 and 4 FTSs. Christchurch-built. SOC 2-12-68   10-21
☐ XG882   '771' Fairey Gannet T.5   57 ex Lossiemouth 8754M (21-7-82), 845.   [1] 10-21
☐ XN981   Blackburn Buccaneer   65 ex Lossiemouth, 12, 208, 12, 809, 12, 800, 801, 700B.
                 S.2B   SOC 11-4-94   10-21
■ **[1]** Gannet is a composite, including parts from XA463.

EVANTON on the B9176 southwest of Alness

Last noted in May 2017 the fuselages of Jetstream 31 G-EEST and an anonymous Bandeirante have been deleted.

FIFE AERODROME or Glenrothes, on the A92 north of Kircaldy   EGPJ

The Tiger is *believed* to be extant in the general area. Maule G-BHJK was airworthy again by the summer of 2020.
☐ G-AREH   DH Tiger Moth   41 ex Bridge of Weir, Lochwinnoch, Kilkerran, G-APYV, 6746M,
                                              DE241, 22 RFS, 22 EFTS. Morris-built. CoA 19-4-66. Off-site   N1-21

FORFAR east of the A90 north of Dundee

The Cessna and the Kachina are stored at *separate* locations in the area.
☐ G-AVID   Cessna 182K   67 ex N2534Q. CoA 18-4-06, de-reg 25-2-10   5-18
☐ G-DJCR   Varga Kachina   80 ex Perth, EI-CFK, G-BLWG, OO-HTD, N8360J. CoA 3-4-99   N3-18

GLASGOW

Kelvingrove Art Gallery and Museum: There is a huge amount going on within this superb building, but from the *W&R* point
of view, the main attraction is the Spitfire which 'flies' in the main hall.
◆ *Kelvin Park, Argyle Street, G3 8AG* | **0141 276959** | **info@glasgowlife.org.uk** | **www.glasgowmuseums.com**
☐ LA198   V-S Spitfire F.21   44 ex Kelvin Hall-Glasgow, East Fortune, Cardington, St Athan,
        'RAI-G'   Leuchars, Locking, Worcester, 7118M (19-2-54), 3 CAACU,
                                              602, 1. 602 Sqn colours   6-21

Riverside Museum: Sub-titled 'Scotland's Museum of Transport and Travel' and in a whiz-bang new building with many
more exhibits than the previous Museum of Transport, there is, however, little in the way of aeronautical content.
◆ *Pointhouse Place, G3 8RS* | **0141 2872720** | **info@glasgowlife.org.uk** | **www.glasgowmuseums.com**
☐ -   Pilcher Hawk replica   66 BAPC.48, stored   [1] 3-10
☐ -   Pilcher Bat II replica   07 BAPC.316, ex Prestwick. Unveiled 23-11-07   [2] 3-20
■ **[1]** Hawk built by 2175 Squadron ATC, Glasgow, and awaits restoration. **[2]** Bat built by the Pilcher Glider Reproduction Project team;
volunteers from BAE Systems at Prestwick who took 10 years to complete it.

The Experience: Montrose Avenue, Hillington Park. The venue *appears* to have closed.
☐ VP-BRV   Boeing 737-528   ex Kemble, Yamal Airlines, F-GJNB. Forward fuselage.
                                              Arrived 14-10-15, Chequers colour scheme   11-21

Mission Aviation Fellowship (MAF): The charity's base in Challenge House, Canal Street, is home to a Cessna used as a
travelling demonstrator. (See also Irthlingborough, Northants.) ◆ *By prior arrangement* **only** | **www.maf-uk.org**
☐ P2-MFA   Cessna 172   ~ ex Perth, Papua New Guinea, MAF. Accident 2013   [1] 3-21
■ **[1]** Fitted with the wings of 150 G-BTIN.

Locally: Last noted in January 2016, Air Command G-BRGO has been deleted.

GOREBRIDGE on the A7 southwest of Edinburgh
The 'airsoft' site had closed by early 2021: Rallyes G-AZKA and G-BBAK and Robison R22 G-OLIZ are homeless.

GRANGEMOUTH on the M9 east of Falkirk
No.1333 Squadron Air Cadets' memorial to the site of the former RAF Grangemouth, on Bo'Ness Road
❑	'X4859'	'PQ-N'	V-S Spitfire FSM	08 BAPC.319, 2 TEU colours	4-21

HOUSTON on the B790 west of Glasgow Airport
Delta Force Paintball: Turningshaw Road. ◆ *By prior arrangement* **only** | **www.paintballgames.co.uk**
❑	XZ690	'640'	Westland Lynx HMA.8	79 ex Upminster, Ipswich, Fleetlands, 815, HAS.3, 702, HAS.2, 829, 815. SOC 27-10-10. First noted 11-16	11-21

INCHINNAN on the A8, north of Glasgow Airport
Rolls-Royce Heritage Trust Scotland Branch: The branch has a collection of engines and artefacts at the Inchinnan Business Park. This includes material on the Hillington plant that built Merlins 1939 to 1947.
◆ *By prior appointment* only | **www.rolls-royce.com/about/heritage-trust**

INSCH AERODROME west of the B992 at Auchleven
❑	G-BALK		Stampe SV-4C	46 ex Aboyne, 'Cheshire', Liverpool, Littleborough, F-BBAN, French mil No.387. Nord-built. De-reg 4-12-96. Fuselage	9-21
❑	T6830		DH Tiger Moth	43 ex 'A17-376' C-GIZA, N548DH, F-BHIQ, G-ANJI, T6830,	
		G-ANJI		2 RFS, 21 EFTS. Morris-built. Arrived 3-9-18	9-21
❑	479781		Piper L-4H Cub	G-AISS 44 ex D-ECAV, SL-AAA, 44-79781. CoA 25-6-97	9-21

INVERNESS AIRPORT or Dalcross   EGPE
Former **Highland Aviation Museum**: Hunter WT660 departed for West Raynham, Norfolk, on 15th October 2020; Nimrod MR.2 forward fuselage XV254 left for St Athan, Wales, 17th February 2021; Tornado GR.1 ZA362 moved to Coningsby, Lincs, on 14th December 2020. Buccaneer XK532 is expected to move on. A 'JP' has arrived at the former museum compound.

❑	XK532	'632'	Blackburn Buccaneer S.1	61 ex airport, Lossiemouth 8867M, Manadon A2581 (22-2-68), Arbroath, Lossiemouth, 736. Arrived 23-12-02 – see above	12-21
❑	XW375*	'52'	BAC Jet Provost T.5A	71 ex St Athan, Cosford, 9149M (7-6-93), Halton, CFS, 6 FTS, RAFC. Arrived 25-2-21	11-21
❑	XW419	'125'	BAC Jet Provost T.5A	71 ex Bruntingthorpe, Hurn, Basingstoke, Booker, Wickenby, Cosford, Halton 9120M (16-9-91), 7 FTS, 1 FTS, RAFC. Off-site	11-21

Highland Aviation Training: Operates a gyrocopter school from the airport. Most of the 'museum' gyros previously at Rufforth, N Yorks, arrived in February 2021. ◆ *By prior appointment* only | **www.highlandaviation.com**
❑	G-ARTJ*		Bensen B-8M	62 ex Rufforth, Leven, Cupar, East Fortune, Cupar, Currie. De-reg 6-6-75	2-21
❑	G-BXCJ*		Campbell Cricket	97 ex Rufforth. CoA 28-4-09	2-21
❑	G-CDBE*		Bensen B-8M	05 ex Rufforth. CoA 7-9-04	2-21
❑	'PCL-132'*		PFA Rotaglider 001	~ BAPC.440. Ex Rufforth [1]	2-21
❑	-*		'Gyroglider'	~ ex Rufforth. Unknown 'species'	2-21

■ **[1]** Built by Peter Lovegrove, *thought* original design.

Also:
❑	G-AWMT*		Cessna F.150H	68 Reims-built. CoA 5-8-16	8-21
❑	G-BNHG		Piper Tomahawk 112	80 ex N91435. De-reg 27-9-17. Towing training	8-21
❑	G-BTCI		Piper Vagabond	48 ex N4839H, NC4839H. CoA 9-8-05	8-21

KEITH on the A96 between Fochabers and Huntly
A *private* collector has the forward fuselage of a Nimrod at a location in the area.
❑	XV252		HS Nimrod MR.2	71 ex Kinloss, Kinloss Wing, MR.1, Kinloss, 51 (loan), 203, 42, St Mawgan. Forward fuselage	7-21

KILMARNOCK northeast of Ayr

No.**327 Squadron Air Cadets**: The exact nature - and status - of the Hunter - be it synthetic or F.4-based - is unresolved.

❏ -	Hawker Hunter	~ cockpit -see comments above		11-14

KINGSMUIR or Sorbie, on the B9131 southeast of St Andrews

Bensen G-BRFW and Kitfox G-LOST have been deleted. A Super Cub project has arrived.

❏ G-PGEE*	Piper L-18C Super Cub	51	ex Launrencekirk, G-BIYJ, Italian AF MM 51-15303, I-EIST, MM51-15303. CoA 6-6-17. First noted 12-20	12-20

KINLOSS north of the A96, west of Elgin

Morayvia Sci-Tech Experience Project: Morayvia aims to bring together disciplines from aerospace and astronomy to technology and arts-related activities into a single visitor centre, serving the northeast of Scotland, the Highlands and beyond. Not all airframes are on site. There is a workshop along the coast at Spey Bay - _not_ available for inspection.

See under Duxford, Cambs, for Morayvia's timely acceptance of Herald _Whisky-Juliet_. W&R27 (p285) jumped the gun with the Old Sarum end of the innovative 'Sycamore Shuttle' - the full story of 'grass roots' common sense is written up at Sunderland, N&T. With the arrival of XJ380, the line-up of RAF SAR helicopters - Sycamore to Sea King - is completed here. Additionally, there is a Super Puma cockpit sim and an F-35 cockpit, the latter very much a film mock-up and not deserving a formal listing. ◆ _Abbeylands, North Road, IV36 3YA_ | **01309 691916** | admin@morayvia.org.uk | www.morayvia.org.uk

❏ G-APWJ*	HP Herald 201	63	ex Duxford, Norwich, Air UK, BIA, BUIA. Last flight 7-7-85, de-reg 10-7-85. Air UK colours		**due**
❏ G-ASVO	HP Herald 214	64	ex Inverness, Glenrothes, Perth, Shoreham, Hurn, Channel Express, PP-SDG, G-ASVO, G-8-3. Damaged 8-4-97, de-reg 25-9-01. Forward fuselage. Arrived 4-17		1-22
❏ G-MJSV	MBA Tiger Cub 440	r83	ex local scrapyard, Kinloss. De-reg 9-11-89. Arrived 2016		1-22
❏ G-UIST	BAe Jetstream 3102	87	ex Westerton, _Batman - The Dark Knight Rises_, Iver Heath, Inverness, N190PC, N331QH, N840JS, G-31-750. CoA 4-6-10, de-reg 5-5-11. Cockpit. Arrived 16-3-19	[1]	1-22
❏ '14' red	Antonov An-2R _Colt_	74	ex France, Air Foyle, UR-07714, CCCP-07714. WSK PZL-		1-22
	HA-MKE		Mielec-built. Arr 2-6-16. _Mopaúbua_ (cyrillic for Morayvia)		
❏ 'L1018'*	'LO-S' V-S Spitfire FSM	12	BAPC.308, ex Currie. Fuselage. Arr 12-12-21. 602 Sqn c/s		12-21
❏ WJ721	EE Canberra TT.18	53	ex Gairloch, Oban, Dundonald, Bacup, Samlesbury, 7, B.2, 50, 40. SOC 19-11-81. Cockpit. Arrived 3-6-15	[2]	1-22
❏ WM145	Gloster Meteor NF.11	52	ex Durham-TVA, Dinsdale, Gatenby, Great Ayton, Rotherham, Finningley, Finningley, 5, 29, 151, 219. AWA-built. SOC 30-10-63. Cockpit. Arrived 18-12-18	[3]	1-22
❏ WN957	Hawker Hunter F.5	54	ex Stockport, Welshpool, Llanbedr, Stafford, North Weald, Chivenor, Leconfield, St Athan 7407M (21-2-57), RAE. AWA-built. Cockpit. Arrived 5-16. 1 Sqn colours		1-22
❏ WP495	Westland Dragonfly	53	ex 'G-AJOV', Cosford, Biggin Hill, Banstead, Warnham,		
	'915' HR.3		Wimbledon, Blackbushe, Culdrose SF, 705, _Victorious_ Flt, _Centaur_ Flt, _Victorious_ Flt, HR.1, Culdrose SF, Ford SF. SOC 1-6-64. Acquired 27-7-17	[4]	1-22
❏ WZ557	DH Vampire T.11	53	ex Durham-TVA, Dinsdale, Gatenby, Great Ayton, Huntingdon, Acaster Malbis, Woodford, Chester, St Athan, 5 FTS, 16. Hawarden-built. SOC 13-11-67. Arr 18-12-18	[3]	1-22
❏ XD425	'M' DH Vampire T.11	54	ex Seaton Burn, Millom, Dumfries, W Freugh, Stranraer, Woodford, Chester, St Athan, 8, 5, 7 FTs, 202 AFS. Hawarden-built. SOC 30-11-67. Arr 2015. Cockpit	[5]	1-22
❏ XD875	Vickers Valiant B.1	57	ex Inverness, Winthorpe, Bruntingthorpe, Marham, Firbeck, Coventry, Cosford, 7, 138, 207, 49, 207. SOC 9-11-62. Cockpit. Arrived 1-2-18	[3] [6]	1-22
❏ XH563	Avro Vulcan B.2MRR	60	ex Durham-TVA, Dinsdale, Bruntingthorpe, Banchory, Rotherham, Scampton 8744M (31-3-82) 27, 230 OCU, Wadd W, 230 OCU, 12, 83. Cockpit. Arrived 18-12-18	[3]	1-22
❏ XJ380*	Bristol Sycamore HR.14	56	ex Old Sarum, Boscombe Down, Crowland, Montrose, New Byth, Drighlington, Finningley 8628M, Catterick, CFS, MoA, Handling Sqn, 275. SOC 22-3-68. Arr 19-5-21		1-22

☐ XJ723		Westland Whirlwind HAR.10	55	ex Newcastle upon Tyne, Montrose, Wroughton, 202, 228, HAR.4, 155. SOC 29-3-79. Acquired 25-7-17	[7] 1-22
☐ XL875*		Westland Whirlwind HAR.9	58	ex Perth, Wroughton, Lee SAR Flt, Culdrose SAR Flt, 847, HAS.7, 848, 815. SOC 2-5-77. Arrived 21-5-21, off-site	1-22
☐ XM169		EE Lightning F.1A	60	ex Inverness, Great Ayton, Thirsk, Leuchars 8422M (13-6-74), Leuchars TFF, 23, Binbrook TFF, 111, A&AEE. Cockpit. Arrived 1-2-18	[3] 1-22
☐ XN351		Saro Skeeter AOP.12 G-BKSC	59	ex Norwich, Saxmundham, Lossiemouth, Inverness, Shobdon, Cardiff, H' Blagdon, Old Warden, Wroughton, 652, 651. CoA 8-11-84, de-reg 11-10-00. Arr 3-6-19	1-22
☐ XN607		Hunting Jet Provost T.3	61	ex Inverness, Great Ayton, Leuchars. SOC 28-5-76. Grey colours. Cockpit. Arrived 1-2-18	[3] 1-22
☐ XR447*		Northrop Shelduck D.1	61	ex Elgin. Crashed 16-6-61, wreckage. First noted 9-21	[8] 1-22
☐ XR528		Westland Wessex HC.2	64	ex Little Rissington, Lyneham, Gosport, Culdrose, Predannack, St Mawgan, 72, 60, 28, 240 OCU, 78. SOC 5-12-08. Arrived 17-8-17. Yellow, SAR colours	1-22
☐ XS176	'N'	Hunting Jet Provost T.4	63	ex Inverness, Stamford, Luton, Solihull, Bruntingthorpe, Salford, Halton 8514M (24-3-77), CATCS, 3 FTS, 2 FTS. Arrived 11-11-12. Cockpit	1-22
☐ XS510*	'626'	Westland Wessex HU.5	64	ex Crowborough, Gosport, A2676 [2], A2765 (24-3-88), Lee-on-Solent, 772, Lee SAR Flt, 707, 848. Arr 2-19, off-site	1-22
☐ XS713*	'C'	HS Dominie T.1	65	ex Shawbury, Cranwell, 55, 3 FTS, 6 FTS, 1 ANS, CAW, 1 ANS, CAW, 1 ANS. Arrived 18-11-20	1-22
☐ XT466	'528'	Westland Wessex HU.5	65	ex Kemble, Bentwaters, Lichfield, Gosport, A2617 [4], Weeton 8921M (3-2-87), Cosford, Wroughton, 847, 771, 848, 845. Acquired 13-12-17. 771 Sqn c/s, Duke of York	[9] 1-22
☐ XV240		HS Nimrod MR.2	70	ex Kinloss, Kin Wing, St M, 42, Kin, MR.1, Kin, 42, Kin, 203, Kinloss. Acquired 12-11. Forward fuselage	1-22
☐ XV725*	'C'	Westland Wessex HC.2	68	ex Manston, Cosford, Gosport A2707 [2], Shawbury, 72, 18. Arrived 18-12-20	12-20
☐ XV867		Blackburn Buccaneer S.2B	68	ex Inverness, Great Ayton, Leeming, 208, 12, 208, 237 OCU, FAA, 809, 736, 803. Cr 10-9-57. Cockpit. Arr 1-2-18, off-site	[3] 1-22
☐ XZ113	'A'	SEPECAT Jaguar GR.3A	76	ex Musselburgh, Bentwaters, St Athan, FJ&WOEU, SAOEU, 41, GR.1, Granby Det, 41, 2, 41. Arrived 11-5-17. 2 Sqn colours, Samantha Jayne	1-22
☐ XZ592	'H'	Westland Sea King HAR.3	78	ex 202, SKTU, 22, SKTU, 78, 202, SKTU, 78, 1564 Flt, 202. Arrived 16-7-15	1-22
☐ ZH821		EHI Merlin HM.1	97	ex Shawbury, Yeovil. Arrived 26-6-19	1-22
☐ -*		Panavia Tornado GR.4	~	simulator, f/n 7-21. Plus additional Tornado cockpit	[10] 1-22

■ [1] On loan from Paul Gibbs. [2] Canberra on loan from Bruce Hudson. [3] On permanent loan from a N Yorks-based collector. [4] WP495 on long term loan from Surrey and Sussex APS. Names on the nose are of the Lord Lieutenant of Moray, Lt Col Grenville S Johnson, a huge supporter of the project, and his father Lt Col W D Johnston who served at Lossiemouth in the 1950s and was involved with Dragonflies. [5] Wings of XD425 are on XD547 at Cantley, Norfolk. [6] XD875 was the last of 107 - including prototypes - Valiants, issued to the RAF on 27-8-57. [7] On 27-12-65 winchman Sgt John Reeson of 22 Sqn in XJ723 was involved in a rescue of from the collapsed North Sea oil rig Sea Gem and was awarded a GM. [8] Salvaged from a local scrapyard, XR447 crashed on its first UK sortie 16-6-61. [9] XT466 is owned by famed SAR winchman Bob Pountney. [10] GR.4 sim donated by Thales UK.

Kinloss Barracks: The former RAF base displays Morayvia's Nimrod - see above.

☐ XV244		HS Nimrod MR.2	71	ex Kin Wing, 42, Kinloss, 203, 42, Kinloss. Duke of Edinburgh	1-22

KIRKNEWTON Between the A70 and A71 southwest of Edinburgh
Delta Force Paintball ◆ By prior arrangement only | www.paintballgames.co.uk

☐ XZ698	'316'	Westland Lynx HMA.8	80	ex Upminster, Ipswich, Fleetlands, 815, 702, HAS.3, 815, 829, HAS.2, 815, A&AEE. Boom of ZD249. First noted 11-16	5-19

LAURENCEKIRK On the A90 between Brechin and Stonehaven
Neil Butler: Continues to work his magic on a series of projects. Tomahawk G-NCFC was flying again by September 2020. Piper L-18C G-BIYJ was re-registered as G-PGEE in July 2020, prior to moving to <u>Kingsmuir</u>, Scotland.
◆ By prior appointment only

Laurencekirk continues on page 294

Antonov An-2R *Colt* '14' (HA-MKE).

Jaguar GR.3A XZ113 *Samantha Jayne*

Nimrod MR.2 XV244 *Duke of Edinburgh*. All November 2021. *David S Johnstone*

☐ G-AWSS		Druine Condor		69	ex Montrose, Fordoun. Rollason-built. CoA 19-10-94		4-21
☐ G-BHIY		Cessna F.150K		70	ex F-BRXR. Reims-built. CoA 20-5-16		4-21
☐ G-BTDY		Piper Super Cub 150		61	ex N24570. CoA 23-7-94		4-21
☐ VS356		Percival Prentice T.1		50	ex Montrose, Stonehaven, Perth, Strathallan, Biggin Hill,		
			G-AOLU		EI-ASP, G-AOLU, VS356, CFS, 2 FTS. Blackburn-built.		
					CoA 8-5-76. Stored, first noted 8-17		4-21
☐ VS610	'K-L'	Percival Prentice T.1		49	ex Montrose, Old Warden, Bassingbourn, VS610, 1 FTS,		
			G-AOKL		22 FTS, RAFC, 22 FTS. CoA 20-9-96. Stored, f/n 8-17		4-21
☐ 454537		Piper J3C Cub	G-BFDL	45	ex HB-OIF, L-4J 45-4537. CoA 27-6-18		4-21

LEUCHARS AIRFIELD on the A919, northwest of St Andrews   EGQL

Waterloo Barracks: Leuchars still roars, acting as a 'satellite' for Lossiemouth. Within the base **2345 Squadron Air Cadets** has a presence with a Harrier and a Tomahawk that attend local events.

☐ G-CWFB		Piper Tomahawk 112		78	ex G-OAAL, N4471E. CoA 8-2-07, de-reg 8-12-10.		
					Cockpit, first noted 7-16		7-19
☐ XW265	'W'	HS Harrier T.4A		70	ex ??, St Athan, Cosford 9258M (3-10-96), Shawbury,		
					20, 233 OCU, A&AEE. Cockpit		7-16
☐ ZE967	'UT'	Panavia Tornado F.3		89	ex 56, 43, 111, 43, 25, 23, 25, 43, 11, 111. Displayed	[1]	7-21

■ **[1]** Tornado wears 43 Sqn c/s to port, 111 on starboard and 56 on both sides of the tail.

LEVEN Last noted in June 2014, Bölkow Junior G-ATRI has been deleted.

LIMERIGG Last noted in January 2008, Aeronca 11AC G-BRFJ has been deleted.

LONGSIDE AERODROME on the A950 between Peterhead and Mintlaw

| ☐ G-BLDC | | K&S Jungster | | r83 | de-reg 6-3-99 | | 6-21 |
| ☐ G-BYRE | | Rans S10 Sakota | | r91 | de-reg 8-5-99 | | 6-21 |

LOSSIEMOUTH AIRFIELD south of the B4090, west of Lossiemouth   EGQS

RAF Lossiemouth: The resident Typhoon units tend to allocate weapons loading trainers - WLTs - for short periods and then rotate them back into operational service: so *W&R* will avoid them, unless they are seriously long term.

☐ LA255	'JX-U'	V-S Spitfire F.21		45	ex Leuchars, Coningsby, Cottesmore, Wittering 6490M,		
					W Raynham, Cardington, Tangmere, 1. Arrived 11-14	[1]	7-20
☐ ZA463*	'028'	Panavia Tornado GR.4		83	ex Marham, 12, 15, 12, GR.1, 15	[2]	7-20
☐ ZA475		Panavia Tornado GR.1B		83	9311M, ex 12, 27, 20, 17, 9, 16. Displayed since 19-12-01		
					15 Sqn colours to port, 617 Sqn to stb		7-21

■ **[1]** LA255 is owned by the 1 Squadron Association. **[2]** ZA463 fitted with the fin of GR.4 ZA554 - SOC 4-2-19 and scrapped here 7-19. ZA463 carried out last ever RAF Tornado flight, call-sign 'MRM74' on 14-3-19, crewed by S/Ls Ian Dornan and Stephen Boardman: it is destined to be put on display.

MAYBOLE on the A77 south of Ayr

Two airframes are *believed* stored locally, both in shipping containers.

| ☐ G-RWMW | | Zenair CH-601XL Zodiac | | 06 | crashed 14-5-14, de-reg 13-5-16 | | 6-17 |
| ☐ OO-NAT | | MS Rallye Club | | 73 | ex Cumberland, G-BAOK | | 6-17 |

MOFFATT east of the A74(M) north of Lockerbie

Dr Hamish Macleod: The Spitfire is in a *private* garden. A donation to the RAF Benevolent Fund permits photography.

| ☐ 'PT462' | 'SW-A' | V-S Spitfire IX FSM | ~ | BAPC.318. 253 Sqn colours | [1] | 9-21 |

■ **[1]** The *real* PT462 is based at Duxford, Cambs.

MONTROSE on the A92 north of Arbroath

Montrose Air Station Heritage Centre: Montrose was Britain's first operational military air station: the original hangar block, known as 'Burke's Shed' dates from 1913. The restoration workshop is *not* open to the public.
◆ *Broomfield Industrial Estate, Waldron Road, DD10 9BD* | **01674 678222** | **enquiries@rafmontrose.org.uk** | **www.rafmontrose.org.uk**

☐ G-MMLM		MBA Tiger Cub 440	84	ex Dundee. De-reg 22-5-00. Arrived 2011. *Red Baron*	1-22
☐ '471'		Royal A/c Factory BE.2a rep	15	BAPC.321, unveiled 12-8-16. 2 Sqn colours	[1] 1-22
☐ 'B7320'	'P'	Sopwith Camel replica	c72	BAPC.59, ex 'B5577', 'E' Fortune, Cosford, St Athan, 'D3419',	
				St Mawgan, 'F1921', St Athan, Colerne. Arrived 2006	[2] 1-22
☐ DG590		Miles Hawk Major	35	ex Stafford, Cosford, Wyton, Cardington, M Wallop,	
	G-ADMW			Henlow 8379M, Ternhill, G-ADMW, Swanton Morley SF,	
				Wyton SF, G-ADMW. Phillips & Powis-built. CoA 4-6-83,	
				de-reg 16-9-86. Arrived 15-2-17	[3] 1-22
☐ 'EP121'		V-S Spitfire V FSM	12	BAPC.320. GB Replicas-built. Arrived 17-7-13,	
	'LO-D'			unveiled 26-7-13. 602 Sqn colours, *Red Lichtie*	1-22
☐ TX226		Avro Anson C.19	46	ex Coventry, Duxford, Little Staughton, East Dereham,	
				Colerne 7865M (22-1-65), Shawbury, FTCCF, OCTU Jurby,	
				187, Hemswell SF, Coningsby CF, CBE. Arrived 4-18	[4] 1-22
☐ WF825	'X'	Gloster Meteor T.7	51	ex Redhill, Yatesbury, Malmesbury, Monkton Farleigh,	
				Lyneham 8359M, Kemble, CAW, 33, 603. SOC 6-2-69.	
				Arrived 3-12-09	1-22
☐ WT619		Hawker Hunter F.1	54	ex Stafford, Manchester, Henlow, St Athan, Weeton 7525M	
				(22-11-57), 233 OCU, 222, 43. Sectioned. Arrived 28-10-19	1-22
☐ WZ791*		Slingsby Grasshopper TX.1	52	ex Hendon 8944M, Syerston, Halton, High Wycombe,	
				Hove. Arrived by 9-21, under restoration, off-site	9-21
☐ XA109		DH Sea Vampire T.22	53	ex Leuchars, East Fortune, Lossiemouth, Lossie' SF, 831,	
				Culdrose SF, 781. Christchurch-built. SOC 17-3-67. Arr3-8-11	1-22

■ **[1]** Based at Montrose from February 1914, 2 Sqn was the first RFC unit to deploy to France on the outbreak of war. After an epic series of 'hops' southwards, Lt Hubert Dunsterville Harvey-Kelly was the first British airman to touch down 'in anger' in France, landing BE.2a 471 at Amiens on 13-8-14. Construction of the replica took place 2014-2016. **[2]** Camel painted as one flown by Capt John Todd, who instructed at Montrose in 1918. **[3]** Tested by Charles Powis at Woodley on 31-7-35, G-ADMW is the oldest surviving Miles aircraft in Britain (although the Miles-designed Southern Martlet G-AAYX at the Shuttleworth Collection was built in 1930). **[4]** Acquired from Glenn James, owner of airworthy Anson T.21 WD413 (G-VROE).

Petrofac Training Services - Montrose Training Centre: Forties Road. ◆ *By prior application* only | www.petrofac.com
☐ N116WG	Westland WG.30-160	85	ex Weston-super-Mare, Yeovil, PanAm, G-BLLG, G-17-20	9-21

NETHERLEY on the B979 north of Stonehaven

Alba Power: The turbine specialists have a 'guardian' at the Mill of Monquich. www.albapower.co.uk
☐ N-315	Hawker Hunter T.7	58	ex Long Marston, Hucclecote, Batley, Amsterdam, and	
			NLS spares, XM121, n/s	8-21

NORTH ROE on the A970 north of Lerwick, 'Mainland' Shetland Islands

Duncan Feather: After an epic recovery from Sumburgh, Duncan keeps the Potez locally.
☐ F-BMCY	Potez 840	62	ex Sumburgh, N840HP, F-BJSU, F-WJSU. Damaged 29-3-81	6-16

PERTH

BlueSky Experiences ◆ **Strictly** *by prior arrangement* | www.blueskyexperiences.com
☐ XX892	Blackburn Buccaneer S.2B	75	ex Forres, Lossiemouth, 208, 237 OCU, 16. Cockpit	7-21

Perth College - University of the Highlands and Islands: Behan Campus, Crieff Road. Linked with AST at the airport (see below). ◆ *By prior arrangement* | www.perth.uhi.ac.uk
☐ G-BATW	Piper Cherokee 140	72	ex Scone, N742FL. CoA 24-10-14, de-reg 18-11-16	3-20

Also: The **Merlin Extended Reach Drilling Engineers** travelling demonstrator Spitfire FSM 'BR954' is reported to have been returned to Replica Aircraft Fabricators at Newquay, Cornwall. The **Mission Aviation Fellowship** Cessna 172 P2-MFA had moved to Glasgow, Scotland, by 2021.

PERTH AIRPORT or Scone

EGPT

Air Service Training - Perth College: See also Perth College, above. Whirlwind XL875 departed to Kinloss, Scotland, on 21st May 2021. By that time Cessna 310Q G-AYGB had also moved on - fate unknown.
◆ **Strictly** *by prior arrangement* only | www.airservicetraining.co.uk
☐ G-BEWP	Cessna F.150M	77	Reims-built. Crashed 4-10-83, de-reg 5-12-83	1-22
☐ G-BWYE	Cessna 310R II	79	ex F-GBPE, N26369. CoA 10-9-09, de-reg 7-7-11	1-22

❏ G-NFLC	HP Jetstream 1	69	ex Cranfield, G-AXUI, G-8-9. CoA 3-6-05, de-reg 3-8-04		1-22
❏ –	BAe ATP	~	ex Prestwick. Cockpit, simulator	[1]	11-17
❏ ZE413	Agusta 109A	98	ex Ipswich, Lichfield, 8 Flt. Arrived 1-11-16	[2]	1-22
❏ MM81220*	Agusta 109A	~	ex Italy, Guardia di Finanza. Arrived 21-5-21		1-22
❏ MM81335*	Agusta 109A	~	ex Italy, Guardia di Finanza. Arrived 21-5-21		1-22

■ **[1]** The ATP cockpit *could* be from the prototype Jetstream 61 G-JLXI. **[2]** Contributor Jim Simpson found the serial on the 'Hereford Gun Club' Agusta, it's on the entrance door. As he noted: "It's not the ghost of its old serial, it really is white on white!"

Also: Bestmann G-CBKB departed to a location in Herefordshire to complete its restoration by mid-2021.

| ❏ G-ATJC* | Victa Airtourer 100 | 65 | ex Elgin. CoA 21-3-13. First noted 11-21 | 11-21 |
| ❏ EI-APF | Cessna F.150G | 66 | ex Anstruther, Kirknewton, Perth, Sligo. Reims-built. CoA 8-98. Fuselage, rescue trainer | 11-21 |

PETERHEAD on the A90 south of Fraserburgh
Score Energy Ltd: The Lightning 'guards' the GLEN Test Facility, which handles industrial R-R Avons, among other types.
◆ *Private site, entrance **strictly** by prior arrangement* | **www.score-group.com**

| ❏ XR749 | 'DA' EE Lightning F.3 | 65 | ex Tees-side, Chop Gate, Leuchars 8934M, 11, LTF, 11, LTF, Binbrook pool, 29, 226 OCU, 56. Damaged 17-2-87. LTF c/s | 10-21 |

PRESTWICK AIRPORT
EGPK

Chipmunk T.10 G-AORW made its first post-restoration test flight on 1st May 2020. Warrior G-BPFH and Tobago G-TBTN have also been returned to airworthiness. A quintet of former Norwegian Boeing 787s (LN-LNA, 'B, 'D, 'G and 'H) have been in external store since May-September 2019, but are bound to be up and running before too long. Katana G-BXOF was cancelled as sold in the Slovak Republic in November 2021.

❏ G-ARMD	DHC Chipmunk T.10	50	ex Kemble, Redditch area, WD297, 666, 1 BFTS. CoA 5-6-76, de-reg 26-6-15. In ISO container		10-21
❏ G-BCNZ	Fuji FA.200-160	74	CoA 23-2-08, de-reg 11-3-19		4-18
❏ G-BCVC	MS Rallye 100ST	74	ex F-OCZO. CoA 30-7-16		8-19
❏ G-BDEU	DHC Chipmunk T.10	52	ex WP808, Edin, Nott, Edin, Lpl, Nott UASs, Detling SF, Birm UAS, 15 RFS. CoA 27-1-13, de-reg 8-5-14. Cockpit		10-21
❏ G-BFFE	Cessna F.152	77	Reims-built. CoA 29-4-10		4-18
❏ G-CELR	Boeing 737-330	86	ex TF-ELR, D-ABXB. De-reg 8-9-17. Forward fuselage		3-19
❏ G-ORJX	HSA HS.146 RJX85 T1	01	ex Woodford, de-reg 12-12-02	[1]	6-11
❏ G-11-068	BAe ATP	93	fuselage. Rescue trainer		11-21
❏ N1909G	Cessna 310R	77	ex G-TKPZ, G-BRAH, N1909G. first noted 2-11		11-21

■ **[1]** Prototype RJX (first flown 28-4-01), used as an engineering design aid by BAE Regional Aircraft (amends *W&R27*) in support of the 146/RJ fleet. It comprises fuselage, starboard wing, and tail. It arrived on site 8-6-11. It last flew 10-1-02 and clocked 321:59 hours.

Locally: The Wagtail Flying Group keeps its Tipsy in the area.

| ❏ G-AISC | Tipsy B | 48 | ex Cumbernauld, Henstridge, Yeovil. CoA 23-5-79 | N9-18 |

SCALLOWAY on the A970, west of Lerwick, Shetland
Scalloway Museum: As well as displays on the famous 'Shetland Bus', the risky trawler run across the North Sea to re-supply Norwegian partisans during the German occupation 1940-1945, there is an unfinished Luton Minor on show.
◆ *Castle Street, ZE1 0TP* | **01595 880734** | email via website | **www.scallowaymuseum.org**

| ❏ G-AMUW | Luton Minor | 52 | ex Orkney. De-reg 13-4-73. Unfinished, uncovered airframe. Unveiled 5-15 | [1] | 12-20 |

■ **[1]** Project started by Bill Petrie at St Margaret's Hope on Orkney; later to Shetland-based Jim Smith.

SPEY BAY on the B9014 north of Fochabers
Spey Bay Salvage Ltd: A diverse operation combining metal recycling and a fleet of recovery and transport vehicles. The proprietor is an enthusiast and a great supporter of Morayvia (Kinloss, Scotland). This is the 'off-site' facility that stores and prepares exhibits for the museum: like the rest of the Spey Bay site, it is *not* readily open to the public. Additionally, the company has been been engaged in moving Morayvia airframes, for example Nimrod MR.2 forward fuselage XV240.

As *W&R* went to press, the airframes known to have been handled by Spey Bay Salvage include: Canberra B(I).6 WT308 from Predannack, Cornwall (8-21); Wessex HU.5 XT773 from Shawbury, Shropshire (11-20); Phantom FGR.2 XV411 from Manston, Kent (11-20); noseless Merlin HC.3 ZJ128 from Farnborough, Hampshire (8-21). These *may* become more long term in which case they will appear in *W&R29*. ◆ *By prior arrangement* **only**

STRANRAER
Stoneykirk Aviation Museum: Steve Austin and friends have turned their award-winning restorations and many artefacts into a museum. ◆ *Mid Cairngarroch Croft, DG9 9EH. Open 'most Sundays' during the summer – check beforehand – or by prior arrangement* | **steve@2av8.co.uk** | **www.2av8.co.uk**

❑ WE191	EE Canberra T.4	54	ex Dumfries, Warton, Samlesbury, Bracebridge Heath, Kemble, Indian AF B.52 Q497, Samlesbury, Kemble, WE191, 231 OCU, 237 OCU, 231 OCU, 245. SOC 1-2-78. Cockpit [1]	1-22
❑ WV903	'128' Hawker Sea Hawk FGA.6	55	ex Hooton Park, Mold, Yeo'ton, Dunsfold, Lee-on-Solent, Culdrose A2632, Halton 8153M, Sydenham, 801, FGA.4, 802, 897, 811, 804. SOC 20-1-71. AW-built. Cockpit. Arr 6-15	1-22
❑ XA903	Avro Vulcan B.1	57	ex Wellesbourne Mountford, Sidcup, Cardiff, Farnborough. Last flight 22-7-79, SOC 19-7-79. Cockpit [2]	1-22
❑ XE921	'VR' DH Vampire T.11	55	ex St Mawgan, Newbridge, Yarmouth, Welshpool, Stoke, Barton, Firbeck, Retford, Firbeck, Keevil, Exeter, 3/4 CAACU, 1 FTS, CFS. Hatfield-built. SOC 16-12-71. Arrived 3-17. CFS colours. Cockpit	1-22
❑ XK533*	'229' Blackburn Buccaneer S.1	61	ex East Fortune, Arbroath, Lossiemouth, 809, 700Z, A&AEE, 700Z. Crashed 10-10-63. Cockpit. Arrived 30-10-21	1-22
❑ XP558	'20' Hunting Jet Provost T.4	62	ex Sheffield, Ipswich, Norwich, Honington 8627M, St Athan, Culdrose, A2628 (13-5-74), CAW, 3 CAACU, RAFC. Cockpit	1-22
❑ XP925	'752' DH Sea Vixen FAW.2	63	ex Chorley, Haslemere, Farnborough, Tarrant Rushton, FRADU, FRU, 899. Hawarden-built. SOC 19-11-81. Cockpit	1-22

■ **[1]** WE191 was acquired by BAC 24-5-65 and converted to B.52 status for the Indian Air Force. Frustrated by the Indo-Pakistan war of 1965, it was stored at Kemble from 5-7-66 on behalf of BAC, before transferring *back* to the RAF on 15-10-70. It never returned to active service and was declared a non-effective airframe 30-6-72. **[2]** XA903 has a fabulous trials provenance: Blue Steel trials (57-61), Olympus 593 test-bed (64-71), RB.199 test-bed and Mauser cannon static tests (73-79).

STRATHALLAN AERODROME west of the B8062, north of Auchterarder
Skydive Strathallan ◆ *By prior arrangement* only www.skydivestrathallan.co.uk

❑ G-BAGV	Cessna U.206F	72	ex N9667G. Cr 5-5-02, CoA 14-5-04, de-reg 19-9-11. Para-tnr	6-17

STRATHBLANE on the A381 north of Glasgow
Contrary to *W&R27*, the Sea King is *not* with a local outdoor centre. Privately owned, it is kept in the *general* area.
◆ *Inspection* **not** *possible*

❑ XV705*	Westland Sea King HAS.2	71	ex Woodmancote, Colsterworth, Gosport, 824, HAS.1, 814, 824, 737, 706, 771, Gosport A2618 (28-8-01), 771, Gannet Flt, 771. First noted 1-20	1-21

THORNHILL on the A873 northwest of Stirling
Mains Farm Wigwams: Among the choice of exotic places to sleep is a Sea King with a Twin Pioneer due for conversion.
◆ *By prior arrangement* only | **www.mainsfarmwigwams.com**

❑ G-APRS	SAL Twin Pioneer 3	59	ex Coventry, Staverton, G-BCWF, XT610, G-APRS, PI-C430. CoA 15-7-08, de-reg 6-12-17. *Primrose*. 'Raspberry Ripple' c/s. Arrived 13-7-18	11-21
❑ ZA127	'509' Westland Sea King HAS.6	80	ex Colsterworth, Gosport A2846 (19-7-01), 706, HAS.5, 810, A&AEE, 820. Arrived 19-4-16	11-21

TRANENT south of the A1, east of Musselburgh
Written out of *W&R27* (p59) at Rayleigh, Essex, PT-22 G-BPUD was stored in Scotland since perhaps 2009. It was offered for sale during late 2020 and moved to 'Cornwall' in early 2021.

WINCHBURGH on the B9080 east of Edinburgh
A *private* house in the area has a pink HS.125 cockpit, believed used as a simulator and possibly from a Series 400.

❑ -	HSA HS.125	~	cockpit, see note above. First noted 5-16	4-21

WALES

Comprises 22 unitary authorities ranging from Anglesey and Flintshire to Pembrokeshire and Rhondda

AMMANFORD on the A483 north of Swansea
No.2475 Squadron Air Cadets: Penybanc Road.

❑ WH739	EE Canberra B.2	53	ex St Athan, 100, 85, 45, 75 RNZAF, Upwood SF, 50, 101. SOC 27-7-76. Cockpit		12-21

CAERNARFON AERODROME or Llandwrog north of the A499, southwest of Caernarfon   EGCK
Caernarfon Airport Airworld Museum: The museum tells the story of aviation in general and aviation in North Wales in particular. The mountain rescue exhibit is a graphic story of wartime crashes, both Allied and Luftwaffe, and includes a large amount of salvaged wreck items. Among the many interesting exhibits is a 'Turtle' narrow-gauge railway shunting engine, salvaged from what was RAF Hell's Mouth (west of Abersoch on the Lleyn Peninsula).
◆ *Caernarfon Airport, LL54 5TP* | **01286 832154** | **info.airworldmuseum.com** | **www.airworldmuseum.com**

❑ 'G-EGCK'	Mignet HM.14 'Flea'	c36	BAPC.286, ex St Athan, 'local area'. Arrived 12-02	[1]	1-22
❑ G-BSMX	Bensen B-8MR	90	de-reg 17-5-10		1-22
❑ –	Blériot XI replica	11	BAPC.448, unveiled 2011	[3]	1-22
❑ –	Vickers Varsity T.1 EMU	c52	ex Higher Blagdon, Oakington. Arrived 1988	[4]	1-22
❑ 'N5137'	DH Tiger Moth	39	ex Shobdon, Fownhope, N6638, Fairford SF, 27 GCF,		
	G-BNDW		St Mawgan SF, Prestwick SF, 25 EFTS, 22 EFTS, 22 E&RFTS. De-reg 19-7-12. Arrived 26-11-97	[2]	1-22
❑ WM961	'J' Hawker Sea Hawk FB.5	54	ex Higher Blagdon, Culdrose A2517, FRU, 802, FB.3, 811. SOC 17-1-62. Arrived 1988		1-22
❑ WT694	Hawker Hunter F.1	54	ex Newton, Debden 7510M (22-11-57), 229 OCU, DFLS, 54. Arrived 9-95. 245 Sqn colours		1-22
❑ WV781	Bristol Sycamore HR.12	52	ex Finningley, Odiham, Digby 7839M (16-3-61), HDU, CFS, ASWDU, G-ALTD. Arrived 1986. Forward fuselage		1-22
❑ XA282	Slingsby Cadet TX.3	52	ex Syerston, 635 VGS, 617 GS, 1 GC, CGIS, 105 GS. SOC 19-8-86. Arrived 1986		1-22
❑ XH837	Gloster Javelin FAW.7	57	ex Northolt, Ruislip 8032M (21-2-62), 33. Arr 1987. Cockpit		1-22
❑ XJ726	Westland Whirlwind HAR.10	55	ex Sibson, Wroughton, 2 FTS, CFS, ME SAR Flt, 22. SOC 4-2-81. Arrived 1986		1-22
❑ XK623	'56' DH Vampire T.11	56	ex Hurn 'G-VAMP', Moston, Woodford, Hawarden, St Athan, 5 FTS. Hawarden-built. SOC 6-12-68. Arrived 1986		1-22
❑ XW269	'TB' HS Harrier T.4A	71	ex Selby, Queensbury, Boscombe Down, Wittering, SAOEU, 233 OCU, 3, 1, 233 OCU, 4. 4 Sqn c/s, T.2 era. Arr 2-10-12		1-22

■ **[1]** Former University of Wales Air Sqn St Athan 'Flea' is *believed* to be largely new-build, but with Scott A2S engine. From circa 2006 it incorporated the metal elements - including the unique undercarriage - from the Idwal Jones-built example BAPC.201 acquired from nearby Talysarn. The 'registration' is derived from the aerodrome's ICAO Location Indicator. **[2]** Tiger comprises a fuselage and mocked-up port wings. **[3]** Blériot *perhaps* built to a reduced scale. **[4]** Varsity cockpit - within the 'Astra' cinema area *underneath* the mountain rescue display - carries a Marshall of Cambridge mod plate and is *very* substantial.

Store: *Not* available for inspection.

❑ G-MBBB	Skycraft Scout 2	79	de-reg 4-8-17		1-21
❑ G-MJSM	Chotia Weedhopper	~	ex Prestatyn. De-reg 16-6-90. Arrived 1995		6-21
❑ -	Skycraft Scout 2	~	spares for the above		1-21

Others:

❑ G-AWUK	Cessna F.150H	68	ex Shobdon, Stansted, Oaksey Park, Bristol, Biggin Hill. Reims-built. Cr 4-9-71, de-reg 13-4-73. Cockpit, rescue tnr		4-21
❑ XD165	'B' Westland Whirlwind HAR.10	54	ex Doncaster, Storwood, Wattisham, Netheravon, Halton 8673M (2-2-81), SARTS, 202, 228, 22, 225, 155. Rescue tnr		10-21

CARDIFF

Cardiff University School of Engineering: The Parade ◆ *By prior application only* | **www.cardiff.ac.uk/engineering**

❑ XX263	HS Hawk T.1A	79	ex Shawbury, 19, Shawbury, T.1, 2 TWU, 1 TWU, TWU. SOC 11-1-18. First noted 6-19		12-19

CARDIFF AIRPORT or Rhoose   EGFF

Airport: In a compound on the southwest side, the fire crews have a synthetic trainer and a BAC 111. Last recorded in 2018, Airtourer G-AWMI and Warrior G-ESSX have been deleted.

☐ G-AVMT	BAC 111-510ED	68 ex Hurn, European, BA, BEA. CoA 5-12-03, de-reg 17-12-04	9-21

International Centre for Aerospace Training: Part of Cardiff and Vale College, located in a high-tech campus on the main access road to the terminal. ◆ *By prior application only* | www.cavc.ac.uk

☐ D-AGEG	Boeing 737-300	88 ex Kemble, Germania, UR-GAF, D-AGEG, G-EURP.	
		Arrived 14-11-12. Forward fuselage	6-21
☐ XX487	'568' HP Jetstream T.2	74 ex Culdrose, 750, T.1 n/s. SAL-completed. Arrived 18-6-11	9-21
☐ XX687	'F' SAL Bulldog T.1	75 ex Shawbury, EM UAS, Liv UAS. Arrived 18-7-01	9-21

CAREW CHERITON on the A477 east of Pembroke

Carew Control Tower Group: Based at the unique watch tower at the former airfield, visitors are in for a treat at this superbly put-together and very friendly museum. The Anson is a long-term project.
◆ *Edge of the Showground, SA70 8SX* | info@carewcheritoncontroltower.co.uk | www.carewcheritoncontroltower.co.uk

☐ VM325	Avro Anson C.19	47 ex Gloucestershire, Bentham, Staverton, Coventry,	
		Halfpenny Green, WCS, NCS, WCS, TCCF, Upavon CF,	
		173, 4 FP. SOC 19-9-68. Workshop	12-20

CHIRK on the A5 north of Oswestry

Last noted in August 2017, Thruster G-MVBT has been deleted. ◆ **Private** *airstrip; by prior application* **only**

☐ G-AJBJ	DH Dragon Rapide	44 ex Coventry, Husbands Bosworth, Peel Green, Squires Gate,	
		Dominie NF894, 18 MU, HQ TCCF. Brush-built.	
		CoA 14-9-61, de-reg 16-12-91	9-21
☐ 'G-AJCL'	DH Dragon Rapide	45 ex Southend, British Westpoint G-AIUL, Dominie NR749,	
	G-AIUL	Kemble, 2 RS. Brush-built. CoA 29-9-67, de-reg 6-4-73	9-21
☐ G-AKOE	DH Dragon Rapide	42 ex Booker, X7484, PTS. CoA 25-2-82, de-reg 18-6-02.	
		British Airways colours, *Sir Henry Morgan*	9-21
☐ G-ANFC	DH Tiger Moth	42 ex London Colney, Dunstable, DE363, 22 EFTS, 4 FIS.	
		Morris Motors-built. CoA 9-10-03	9-21
☐ G-AZMX	Piper Cherokee 140	68 ex Connah's Quay, Chester, Halfpenny Green, SE-FLL,	
		LN-LMK. CoA 9-1-82, de-reg 9-1-84	9-21
☐ G-BAYL	Nord Norecrin	48 ex Ivychurch, Solihull, Bodmin, F-BEQV. De-reg 14-11-91	9-21
☐ G-BEDB	Nord Norecrin	48 ex Liverpool, Chirk, F-BEOB. CoA 11-6-80, de-reg 14-11-91	9-21

CONNAH'S QUAY on the A548 west of Chester

Coleg Cambria ◆ *By prior application* **only** | www.cambria.ac.uk

☐ N66SW	Cessna 340	~ ex N5035Q. *Flyer* titles	9-21
☐ -	HSA HS.125-1000	~ BAPC.382, ex Hawarden. Unflown forward fuselage	9-21
☐ XW291	BAC Jet Provost T.5	69 ex N Weald, Hurn, SOC 18-3-96, Shawbury, 6 FTS, 3 FTS,	
	G-BWOF	RAFC, CFS, RAFC, CFS. CoA 6-5-16. First noted 7-18	9-21
☐ XW423	'14' BAC Jet Provost T.5A	72 ex Little Snoring, RAF, Shawbury, 3 FTS, RAFC, 1 FTS,	
	G-BWUW	3 FTS. CoA 14-2-02, de-reg 29-6-06	9-21

COWBRIDGE on the A48 west of Cardiff

Task Force Paintball ◆ *By prior application* **only** | www.taskforcepaintball.co.uk

☐ XG592	W'land Whirlwind HAS.7	57 ex Cardiff, Wroughton, 705, 846, 705, 700, HS. SOC 5-5-76	6-21

CWMBRAN on the A4051 north of Newport

Mark Gauntlett: The cockpits are *believed* extant. ◆ *By prior application* **only**

☐ XE985	DH Vampire T.11	55 ex Exeter, Bridgend, Cwmbran, Bridgend, London Colney,	
		Woodford, Chester, St Athan, 5 FTS. Hawarden-built.	
		SOC 17-11-67. Cockpit	7-11
☐ QA-12	Hawker Hunter FGA.78	56 ex Woking, Hurn, Qatar AF, G-9-284, Dutch AF N-222. Cockpit	7-11

FONMON north of the village, on minor road north of the B4265 between St Athan and Cardiff Airport

Fonmon Castle Park and Gardens: Among the growing number of visitor attractions is a 'JP'.
◆ *CF62 3ZN* | info@fonmoncastle.com | www.fonmoncastle.com

❑	XW320*	'71'	BAC Jet Provost T.5A	70	ex St Athan, Cosford, '9015M', 9016M (19-12-89), Halton,		
					1 FTS, Leeming SF, 3 FTS, RAFC. Arrived 13-7-21	[1]	12-21

■ [1] On loan from GJD Services, St Athan.

HAVERFORDWEST on the A4076 north of Milford Haven

Welsh Spitfire Museum: During January 2022 the museum was moving to new premises – check the website for details.
◆ info@welshspitfire.org | www.welshspitfire.org

❑	JG668		V-S Spitfire VIII	44	ex Oxford, Australia, Oakey, RAAF A58-441 (SOC 22-5-46),		
		G-CFGA			JG668 no service	[1]	1-22

■ [1] Registered to TSIB Ltd.

HAVERFORDWEST AERODROME or Withybush, on the A40, north of Haverfordwest   EGFE

❑	G-BLTT	Slingsby T.67B Firefly	85	CoA 5-8-00, de-reg 28-7-04. Rescue trainer	9-21

HAWARDEN AIRFIELD or Broughton, on the B5129 west of Chester   EGNR

North Wales Military Aviation Services: The restoration and operation of jet 'warbirds', especially 'JPs' and Strikemasters, is a speciality. Only those under long-term restoration and storage are listed. MiG-23ML '04' and MiG-27K '71' at the Newark, Notts, are on loan from NWMAS. ◆ *By prior arrangement* only | www.nwmas.com

❑	G-BCOO*		DHC Chipmunk T.10	50	ex WB760, York UAS, 1 FTS, CFS, AAC, Northum UAS, Lpl UAS,	
					AOTS, 1 ITS, RAFC, Nicosia SF, Nott, Birm, Leeds, Notts,	
					Durham, Birm UASs, 9 RFS, 14 RFS. SOC 9-10-74. CoA 25-5-17	10-21
❑	G-OEDB*		Piper Tomahawk 112	78	ex G-BGGJ, N9694N. De-reg 25-5-19. Fuselage	10-21
❑	CCCP-07268	Antonov An-2R	YL-LEV	~	ex Latvia, USSR	10-21
❑	CCCP-17939	Antonov An-2R	YL-LFC	~	ex Latvia, USSR	10-21
❑	CCCP-19731	Antonov An-2R	YL-LEU	~	ex Hooton Park, Chester, Latvia, USSR	10-21
❑	CCCP-19733	Antonov An-2R	YL-LEZ	~	ex Latvia, USSR	10-21
❑	CCCP-20320	Mil Mi-2 *Hoplite*	YL-LHN	~	ex Latvia, Latvian AF 154, USSR	10-21
❑	CCCP-20619	Mil Mi-2 *Hoplite*	YL-LHO	~	ex Latvia, Latvian AF 153, USSR	10-21
❑	CCCP-40748	Antonov An-2R	YL-LFA	~	ex Latvia, USSR	10-21
❑	CCCP-40749	Antonov An-2R	YL-LFD	~	ex Latvia, USSR	10-21
❑	CCCP-40784	Antonov An-2R	YL-LEY	~	ex Latvia, USSR	10-21
❑	CCCP-40785	Antonov An-2R	YL-LFB	~	ex Latvia, USSR	10-21
❑	CCCP-54949	Antonov An-2R	YL-LEX	~	ex Latvia, USSR	10-21
❑	CCCP-56471	Antonov An-2R	YL-LEW	~	ex Latvia, USSR	10-21
❑	'37' yellow	Aviatika MAI 890		~	ex Latvia, USSR	10-21
❑	'38' yellow	Aviatika MAI 890		~	ex Latvia, USSR	10-21
❑	XW409	'123'	BAC Jet Provost T.5A	71	ex St Athan 9047M (29-6-90), 7 FTS, 1 FTS. Off-site	9-14
❑	311*	BAC Strikemaster		70	ex N Weald, N2146J, Singapore ADC 311, G-27-139.	
		Mk.84	G-MXPH		CoA 30-8-18	9-21
❑	323	BAC Strikemaster		69	ex Singapore ADC, S Yemen AF 504, G-27-36, G-AXFX,	
		Mk.81	N21419		G-27-36, S Yemen AF 504	9-14
❑	'18' red	Aero L29 Delfin			YL-PAF, ex Latvia, USSR. (591771)	10-21
❑	'23' red	Mikoyan-Gurevich		81	ex Latvia, USSR.	
		MiG-27M *Flogger*		81	(83712515040)	10-21
❑	'35' red	Sukhoi Su-17M3 *Fitter*		77	ex Latvia, USSR. (25102)	10-21
❑	'54' red	Sukhoi Su-17M *Fitter*		74	ex Latvia, USSR. (69004)	10-21

Also:

❑	G-BYJF*	Thorp T.211	98	ex N2545C. Venture Light A/c-built. CoA 14-6-<u>12</u>	9-21
❑	G-EGEE	Cessna 310Q	69	ex G-AZVY, SE-FKV, N7540Q. CoA 22-3-08, de-reg 15-2-11	9-21
❑	5N-JMA	HSA HS.125-800XP	93	ex N658XP. First noted 6-18	10-21

Aviation Park: The 'Chocks Away Diner' which is well worth a visit: it is 'guarded by MiG-27 '23' see above. Also on the site is **Cokebusters**, nothing to do with fizzy drinks or more powerful stimulants, the company is a specialist in decoking industrial processes and pipe inspection. ◆ *Aviation Park, CH4 0GZ* | **http://cokebusters.com**

❑ 'AB196'*		SA Spitfire Mk.26	G-CCGH 07 CoA 6-6-13. Displayed, first noted 8-20	[1] 10-21

■ **[1]** Australian scale kitplane by <u>S</u>upermarine <u>A</u>ircraft, registered to Cokebusters Ltd.

Tornado Heritage Centre: Offers pre-bookable 'Aircrew' experience days, including 'time' on a Tornado F.3 procedures trainer/simulator. See under Chester, Cheshire, for GR.1 cockpit ZD710. ◆ *Aviation Park, CH4 0GZ* | *email via* Facebook

❑ ZE966	'VT'	Panavia Tornado F.3	89 ex Wroughton, Swinton, St Athan, 111, 56, 11, 25, 11, 43.	
			56 Sqn colours. Acquired 30-9-16, arrived 18-2-17	10-21

No.2247 Squadron Air Cadets: In Manor Lane to the west of the airfield.

❑ BGA.1733*		SZD Pirat	c72 cockpit, first noted 5-21	[1] 10-21
❑ XE852	'H'	DH Vampire T.11	54 ex Woodford, Chester, Shawbury, 1 FTS, 4 FTS.	
			Hatfield-built. SOC 30-10-67	10-21

■ **[1]** Pirat was accepted as a complete airframe – date unknown – and cut down to a cockpit.

Locally: A Chipmunk project is being tackled in the area.

❑ WK620*	'T'	DHC Chipmunk T.10	52 ex Enstone, Twyford, Tattershall Thorpe, M Wallop, BFWF,	
			Hull, Mcr, Queen's and Bristol UASs, 22 RFS. Dam 19-5-93	2-19

KENFIG HILL north of the B4281 east of Pyle
No.2117 Squadron Air Cadets: Off Main Street, and behind Pwll-y-Garth Street.

❑ WT569	Hawker Hunter F.1	55 ex St Athan 7491M (21-11-57), A&AEE, Hawker trials	10-21

KNIGHTON The Gazelle-based 'sculpture' created by Andy Hazell is believed to have been exported.

LLANBEDR AIRFIELD west of Llanbedr and the A496 on the road to Shell Island
Snowdonia Aerospace Centre: ◆ *By prior arrangement* **only**

❑ ZJ503	GAF Jindivik 104AL	c98 ex RAAF A92-908. Trolley-mounted	6-20

LLANDYSUL on the A486 north of Carmarthen
First noted in mid-2020, a *private* owner in the locality kept the cockpit of a former Flag Officer Flying Training Sea Vampire XG775. Travel back to *W&R5* no less and this machine was written out (p40) from Southall Technical College. It went on to an unknown London scrappie - where the wings etc were processed - but the 'pod' lingered and was acquired by a Norfolk-based collector before moving to Wales with **Max Valk**.(This XG775 is not to be confused with former Swiss Air Force Vampire T.55 U-1219, G-DHWW 'XG775' based at Bournemouth, Dorset. That 'XG775' was written out of *W&R22* [p47] as sold in South Africa.) On 21st July 2021 the pod arrived at <u>Fishburn</u>, D&C, for restoration on Max's behalf: it will return.

LLANGEINOR on the A4064 north of Bridgend
IrvinGQ: The rescue equipment manufacturer has a Draken on display. **www.irvingq.com**

❑ 35515	'49' SAAB J35F Draken	c68 ex F10, Swedish AF	10-21

MONA AIRFIELD Last noted in September 2019, Colibri G-PRAG has been deleted.

NANTGARW on the A470 northwest of Cardiff
National Collections Centre: The large object store for the National Museum of Wales.
◆ *By prior appointment* **only** | **www.museumwales.ac.uk**

❑ XM300	Westland Wessex HAS.1	59 ex Cardiff, Cardiff-Wales, RAE Farnborough, RAE Bedford,	
		A&AEE, Westland. SOC 1-8-79. SAR colours	10-19

NEWBOROUGH Anglesey, on the B4421, at the southern tip of the island
Anglesey Transport Museum - Tacla Taid: Amid the cars, armoured vehicles, agricultural machinery and more, is a Hunter.
◆ *Tyddyn Pwrpas, Newborough, LL61 6TN* | **01248 440344** | **email** via website | **www.angleseytransportmuseum.co.uk**

❑ WV396	'91' Hawker Hunter T.8C	55 ex Valley, 9249M, Yeovilton, FRADU, 229 OCU, 20.	
		SOC 16-5-95/ 4 FTS colours. Arrived by 6-17	1-22

NEWBRIDGE-ON-WYE on the A470 north of Builth Wells

Quackers Indoor Play Centre: At Newmead Farm, a 'JP' is in the grounds. | **www.quackersnow.com**

☐ XM358	Hunting Jet Provost T.3A	59	ex Twyford, North Scarle, Colsterworth, Halton 8987M
			(10-1-89), 1 FTS, 3 FTS, 1 FTS, CFS, RAFC, CFS, 7 FTS, 2 FTS 9-21

PEMBREY FOREST RANGES west of the A484 and Llanelli

☐ XR523	'M'	Westland Wessex HC.2	64	ex Torpoint, Fleetlands, Gosport, S'bury, F'lands, 72. Arr 4-16 6-21
☐ XV372		Sikorsky SH-3D Sea King	66	ex St Mawgan, Culdrose, Predannack, St Mawgan,
				Trowbridge, Yeovil, Aston Down, Lee-on-Solent, Pyestock,
				BSE, Westland. SOC 1-11-71, arrived by 4-16 6-21
☐ XX958	'BK'	SEPECAT Jaguar GR.1	75	ex Cosford 9022M, Shawbury, 17, 14. Arrived 2-7-19 6-21
☐ XX966	'JJ'	SEPECAT Jaguar GR.1A	75	ex Cosford, Halton 8904M (23-5-86), Shawbury,
				6, 54, 20, A&AEE, 20, 17 6-21

PEMBROKE DOCK on the A477 northwest of Pembroke

Pembroke Dock Heritage Centre: Administered by the **Pembroke Dock Sunderland Trust**, the centre displays many recovered parts, including two Pegasus radials, from 210 Squadron Sunderland I T9044 which sank in a gale at Pembroke Dock on 21st November 1940. Recovery of other items is on-going. Displays chart the history of this famous flying-boat haven and the general history of the maritime complex.
◆ *Royal Dockyard, SA72 6YH* | **01646 684220** | **enquiries@sunderlandtrust.com** | **www.sunderlandtrust.com**

PYLE on the A48 west of Bridgend, north of junction 37, M4

JBT AeroTech: Village Farm Industrial Estate, a Spitfire FSM is displayed. | **www.jbtaerotech.com**

☐ 'EN398'	'JE-J'	V-S Spitfire IX FSM	~	BAPC.552. Unveiled 6-12-13	[1] 3-19

■ **[1]** Other 'EN398s' can be found at: Coningsby, Lincs; Sleap, Shropshire, Taunton, Somerset.

RADYR south of the M4, west of Cardiff

Delta Force Paintball: Tyla-Morris Farm. ◆ *By prior arrangement* **only** | **www.paintballgames.co.uk**

☐ ZD565	'404'	Westland Lynx HMA.8	80	ex Upminster, Ipswich, Fleetlands, 815, 702, HAS.3, 702.
				First noted 11-17 11-17

REDBERTH on the A477 east of Pembroke Dock

Apple Camping: Never mind the yurts, glamp it up in the JetStar! The site also offers 'Arabian Nights' in the fuselage 'barrel' of a former Etihad A319. Cockpitless, it is beyond the remit of the book, but it is most likely from A6-EID.
◆ *By prior arrangement* **only** | **www.applecamping.co.uk**

☐ N25AG	Lockheed JetStar II	76	ex Kemble, Alton, Kemble, 3C-QRK, P4-CBG, VP-CBH,
			EC-FQX, EC-232, N20GB, N333KN, N717X, N717, N5528L.
			Last flown 26-9-06. Fuselage, arrived mid-2016 1-22

RUTHIN on the A494 southwest of Mold

Phantom Preservation Group: Mark A Jones *should* still have his cockpits in the locality. ◆ *By prior arrangement* **only**

☐ XV419		McD Phantom FGR.2	69	ex Terrington St Clement, Stock, Wattisham, 19, 228 OCU,
				29, 56, 29, 228 OCU, 29, 111, 14, 111, 54, 228 OCU, 54.
				SOC 5-10-92. Cockpit 3-14
☐ ZE788	'HV'	Panavia Tornado F.3	88	ex Selby, Leeming, 111. Cockpit 1-19

ST ATHAN AIRFIELD on the B4265 west of Barry

EGSY

South Wales Aviation Museum (SWAM): Founded by two aviation professionals and helped by an increasing band of supporters, WAM continues to flourish. Gary Spoors is mentioned several times in this book and is the leading light of GJD Services and GJD AeroTech, headquartered at St Athan. GJD provides specialist parting out, maintenance, transport and other engineering tasks – see also below. (A GJD team moved the major exhibits out of the former Air and Space Hall of the Science and Industry Museum, Manchester.) John Sparks runs the resident Horizon Aviation Services and affiliated concerns, with a penchant for the operation and restoration of 'classics' - see separate entry. SWAM occupies the famous Picketston Site - a 'peninsula' that extends northwards from the vast former RAF St Athan site.

Gary Spoors is a great supporter/benefactor of other projects and he has airframes on loan as follows: East Midlands, Leics, VC10 forward fuselage XV108, Jetstream XX494, Sea King ZD477; Filton, Glos: Sea Harrier ZD610; Gloucestershire, Glos: Vulcan cockpit XM569 (along with David Price); Woodford, Gtr Man, VC10 cockpit XV106.

Given that SWAM is part of a large airfield complex, there will be some to-ing and fro-ing of airframes; so please bear this in mind when visiting. Likewise, aircraft given below as 'on show' may well go into restoration or store; or vice versa.

Departures: Jetstream 31 G-BLKP moved to Exeter, Devon, by 5-21; Jetstream 31 G-CONY had moved by 6-20 to a camp site due north of the museum – see below.

◆ *Hangar 872, Picketston Business Park, CF62 4QR* | **01446 789767** | **info@swam.online** | **www.swam.online**

❏ G-APFG	Boeing 707-436	60	ex Pershore, Cove, Bruntingthorpe, Cardington, Stansted, British Airtours, BOAC. Last flight 3-11-80, CoA 24-5-81, de-reg 24-4-81. Flightdeck		1-22
❏ G-APSA*	Douglas DC-6A	58	ex Baginton, 4W-ABQ, HZ-ADA, G-APSA, CF-MCK, CF-CZY. CoA 23-5-09, de-reg 17-5-21. British Eagle c/s. Arr by 9-21		1-22
❏ G-BCTT*	Evans VP-1	77	CoA 25-3-05, de-reg 15-4-14. Arrived 22-4-21		1-22
❏ G-BMMF	Clutton FRED Srs II	90	ex Glamorgan, CoA 18-7-03		1-22
❏ G-BOCB	HSA HS.125-1B/522	66	ex Porthcawl, Doncaster, Cardiff, Hatfield, G-OMCA, G-DJMJ, G-AWUF, 5N-ALY, G-AWUF, HZ-BIN. CoA 16-10-90, de-reg 22-2-95. *Winnie* (port), *Peter* (stb). Cockpit, arr 12-1-19	[1]	1-22
❏ G-BTUS*	Whittaker MW-7	92	CoA 20-6-06. Arrived 10-6-21		1-22
❏ G-BYMT*	Pegasus Quantum 15-912	99	ex Manchester, Strathaven. De-reg 10-8-10. Arr 30-10-21		10-21
❏ G-CLAX	Jurca Sirocco	68	ex Barry, G-AWKB. De-reg 19-7-19. Fuselage, in cafe	[2]	1-22
❏ G-ELLE*	Cameron N90 HAB	98	envelope. CoA 15-6-07, de-reg 4-10-19. Arrived -20		8-20
❏ G-MMNN*	Sherry Buzzard	84	ex Stoke. Unfinished, de-reg 28-7-17. Arrived 13-6-20	[3]	1-22
❏ G-SIXC*	Douglas DC-6A/B	58	ex Baginton, 'DC-6 Diner', Air Atlantique, N93459, N90645, B-1006, XW-PFZ, B-1006. CoA 4-4-05, de-reg 2-8-11. Air Atlantique colours. Arrived 5-8-21		1-22
❏ A7-ABX	Airbus A300B4-622	90	ex Bruntingthorpe, Qatar, Korean HL7537, HL7293, F-WWAU. Last flight 19-11-13. Cockpit		1-22
❏ F-BTGV* '1'	Aerospacelines Super Guppy 201	71	ex Bruntingthorpe, Airbus Skylink, Aeromaritime, N211AS. Last flight 1-7-96. Flightdeck, arrived 4-2-21	[4]	1-22
❏ N858WL	Boeing 737-406	90	ex Bruntingthorpe, KLM PH-BDW. Last flight 16-11-11. Arrived 12-1-19. Cockpit		6-21
❏ WF784*	Gloster Meteor T.7	51	ex Bentham, Staverton, Quedgeley, Kemble 7895M (30-11-65), 5 CAACU, CAW, FTU, 130, 26. Arr 2-9-21		1-22
❏ WK126* '843'	EE Canberra TT.18	54	ex Staverton, Bentham, Staverton, Hucclecote, N2138J, St Athan, FRADU, B.2, 100, 9. SOC 26-10-90		**due**
❏ WK128	EE Canberra B.2	54	ex Pershore, Llanbedr, FRL. Avro-built. Cockpit		9-21
❏ WL405	Gloster Meteor T.7	52	ex 'Liverpool', Hooton Park, Bruntingthorpe, Yatesbury, Chalgrove, Martin-Baker, Farnborough, BCCS, 1 GCF, 231 OCU, Wittering SF, JCU, Hemswell CF. SOC 1-4-69. Cockpit. First noted 10-19		1-22
❏ WP321	Percival Sea Prince T.1 G-BRFC	53	ex Horizon site, Hurn, N7SY, G-BRFC (CoA 28-5-87, de-reg 21-11-99), N Weald, Bourn, WP321, Kemble, 750, 744. SOC 16-9-80	[5]	1-22
❏ WR974* 'K'	Avro Shackleton MR.3/3	57	ex Burtonwood, Charlwood, Cosford 8117M (9-12-70), Kinloss W, 203, 42, 203, SWDU, ASWDU. Arrived 7-20		1-22
❏ XE956	DH Vampire T.11 G-OBLN	55	ex Rochester, Pen-Coed, Bridgend, St Albans, Hatfield, CATCS, 1 FTS, 8 FTS, 3 CAACU, APS, 67. Hatfield-built. SOC 2-2-71. Arrived 9-7-18	[6]	9-21
❏ XK895	DH Sea Devon C.20 G-SDEV	56	ex St Mawgan, G-SDEV (CoA 17-9-01, de-reg 4-1-19), Coventry, Kemble, Swansea, Bruntingthorpe, Cambridge, Culdrose SF, 781 Sqn. Arrived 8-7-18		1-22
❏ XL500	Fairey Gannet AEW.3 G-KAEW	61	ex Horizon site, Exeter, N Weald, Chatham, Culdrose, Fleetlands, Lee-on-Solent, Dowty-Rotol, Culdrose SAH A2701, A&AEE, 849. Last flown 28-2-85	[5]	1-22
❏ XL573	Hawker Hunter T.7 G-BVGH	58	ex Horizon site, Exeter, N Weald, Exeter, Shawbury, 237 OCU, Laarbruch SF, 237 OCU, 4 FTS, 229 OCU, FCS. Arrived St Athan 15-12-11. CoA 6-10-15		9-21

☐ XN584*	'E' and '88'	Hunting Jet Provost T.3A	61	ex Treforest, Bruntingthorpe, Halton 9014M (10-9-90), 1 FTS, CFS, RAFC, CFS, RAFC, TWU, RAFC. Arrived 4-8-21 [7]	1-22
☐ XP672	'03'	Hunting Jet Provost T.4 G-RAFI	62	ex Bruntingthorpe, Retford, Ipswich, N Weald, Hurn, Jurby, Halton 8458M (19-12-75), SoRF, CAW, CATCS, CAW, 2 FTS. CoA 11-3-00, de-reg 22-11-10. Arrived 9-4-18	1-22
☐ 'XR993'		Folland Gnat T.1 XP534 G-BVPP	63	ex Bruntingthorpe, N Weald, Cranfield, G-BVPP, XP534, Halton 8620M, 4 FTS, CFS, 4 FTS, CFS, 4 FTS. Damaged 17-9-04, CoA 14-1-05, de-reg 22-5-09. 'Red Arrows' c/s. Arr6-4-19	1-22
☐ XS507*	'27'	Westland Wessex HU.5	64	ex Higher Purtington, Benson, Gosport, Lee-on-Solent A2674 [2], A2762 (21-3-88), 772, 845, 707, 848, 847, 772, 2 FTS, 772, 707, 846, 845, 707. Arrived 18-5-21	1-22
☐ XV254*		HS Nimrod MR.2	71	ex Inverness, Kinloss, Kinloss Wing, A&AEE, Kin W, St Mawgan W, 42. Arrived 2-21. Forward fuselage	1-22
☐ XV582	'M'	McD Phantom FG.1	69	ex Cosford, Leuchars, 9066M (6-9-90), 43, 228 OCU, 43, 111, 43. Black Mike. All-black colours. Arrived 21-11-18	1-22
☐ XW420	'MU'	BAC Jet Provost T.5A	71	ex Horizon site, Woodvale, Cosford 9194M (7-6-93), 1 FTS, RAFC. Arrived at St Athan 8-9-17	1-22
☐ XX889*	'T'	Blackburn Buccaneer S.2B	75	ex Cosford, Bruntingthorpe, Kemble, Staverton, Bentham, Staverton, Enstone, St Athan, 12, 208, 12, 16. 208 Sqn c/s	due
☐ XZ729	'452'	Westland Lynx HMA.8SRU	80	ex storage site, Fleetlands, 702, HAS.3, 815, HAS.2, Falklands 1982, 815. Arrived 15-4-19	1-22
☐ ZA195	'710'	HS Sea Harrier F/A.2	83	ex Tangmere, Farnborough, Booker, Yeovilton, St Athan, Warton, BAE, 899. Arrived 7-19	1-22
☐ ZA326		Panavia Tornado GR.1	83	ex Bruntingthorpe, Boscombe Down, DERA, RAE Bedford. Arrived 27-10-18. First ground run 7-2-20 [8]	1-22
☐ ZA612*	'074'	Panavia Tornado GR.4	82	ex Winterbourne Gunner, Marham, GR.1. Last flown 21-1-19. Arrived 6-21	1-22
☐ ZE700*		HSA HS.146 CC.2	84	ex Northolt, 32, G-6-201, ZE700, G-5-07, G-5-02. Hatfield-built	due
☐ ZF557	'426'	Westland Lynx HMA.8	87	ex storage site, Fleetlands, 702, 815, HAS.3, 815, 702. First noted 12-19	1-22
☐ ZG822	'WS'	Westland Sea King HC.4	90	ex Bruntingthorpe, Gosport, Yeovilton, 848, 846, 845, 846, 845, 846, 848, 846, 848, 846. Arrived 11-4-18	1-22
☐ –		HS Hawk SIM	~	ex Pershore, Farnborough. First noted 4-19	4-19
☐ –*		Short Tucano cockpit	~	front cockpit procedure tnr, 'shark's mouth'. First noted 5-21	5-21
☐ 55-4439	'WI'	Lockheed T-33A-1-LO	55	ex Sunderland, Sculthorpe, French AF, USAF 55-4439. Last flown 25-1-78. Arrived 1-20 [9]	1-22
☐ 526	25887	Mikoyan-Gurevich MiG-29 Fulcrum	~	ex West Walton Highway, Fairford, Sov AF. Crashed 24-7-93. Cockpit	8-20

■ [1] HS.125 owned and restored by Dean Smith: winner of a W&R Spirit of CockpitFest award 8-21. [2] The fuselage of unfinished project G-CLAX graces the cafe. It has been cut in half vertically and both sides have been mounted on the wall, nose to nose. It is best left to the reader to decide if this is still an airframe or 'installation art'! [3] Buzzard designed and built by Ernie Sherry. [4] Golf-Victor was the first 337SGT conversion, maiden flight 24-8-70. It is composed of Boeing C-97 Stratofreighter wings, cockpit, fin/rudder, and new-build fuselage. [5] Airframes from Mark Stott. [6] Lima-November registered to Jon Vivash. [7] The wings of XN584 are fitted to XP627: see Sunderland, N&T. [8] ZA326 factoids: first flown 31-3-83 and last flown 13-12-05 by which time it was the last flying GR.1. Donated to the Panavia Tornado Preservation Group by Elliott Atkins - keep an eye on www.za326.com [9] Part of the National Museum of the USAF's Loan Program.

Restoration and Store: Chipmunk T.20 cockpit WD293 moved to Doncaster, S Yorks. The cockpit of Hercules C.3 XV221 arrived from White Waltham, Berks, during May 2020. It was exported to Turkey on 3rd March 2021. 'JP' T.5A XW320 arrived from Cosford 16-10-20 before moving on loan to nearby Fonmon, Wales, 13-7-21.

☐ G-AVFM	HS Trident 2E		69	ex Pershore, Cove, Bristol, BA, BEA. CoA 2-6-84, de-reg 20-3-84. Arrived 16-4-19. Flightdeck	9-21
☐ G-AZHJ*	SAL Twin Pioneer 3		59	ex off-site Coventry, Prestwick, Staverton, Prestwick, G-31-16, XP295, Odiham SF, 1310F, Odiham SF, 230. CoA 23-8-90, de-reg 23-7-97. Arrived 11-11-20	9-21
☐ G-BDXG	Boeing 747-236B		78	ex Bruntingthorpe, Hurn, European, Saudia, European, BA. CoA 30-6-06, de-reg 29-3-06. Flightdeck	9-21
☐ G-BDXH	Boeing 747-236B		79	ex Bruntingthorpe, Hurn, Filton, European, BA. Last flight 12-11-04, CoA 13-4-04, de-reg 7-3-06. Flightdeck	9-21

Flightdeck and forward upper fairing of Super Guppy 201 F-BTGV, October 2021. *Tom Davis*

Tornado GR.1 ZA326, August 2020. *Les Woodward*

☐ G-CEAG	Boeing 737-229	75	ex Bruntingthorpe, European, SABENA OO-SDL.	
			CoA 14-6-06, de-reg 23-1-09. Flightdeck	9-21
☐ G-MKCA	Boeing 747-285	80	ex Bruntingthorpe, Kemble, MK Airlines, 9G-MKM. N207BA,	
			Korean HL7454. Last flight 7-8-09, de-reg 30-9-15. Flightdeck	9-21
☐ B-HUE	Boeing 747-467	93	ex Bruntingthorpe, Cathay, VR-HUE. Last flight 5-1-15.	
			Flightdeck, arrived 12-1-19	3-20
☐ B-HUI	Boeing 747-467	93	ex Bruntingthorpe, Cathay, VR-HUI. Last flight 31-10-16.	
			Nick Heard / Simon McGlynn. Flightdeck, arrived 12-1-19	9-21
☐ SX-OAD*	Boeing 747-212B	79	ex Bruntingthorpe, 'G-ASDA', Olympic, 9V-SQH.	
			Olympic Flame. Last flown 12-6-02. Flightdeck. Arr 4-2-21	2-21
☐ N470AC*	Boeing 737-300	90	ex Hurn, HZ-AMC, B-2653, N2332Q, G-OABD, 9V-TRC,	
			OY-MME. Fuselage. Arrived 5-8-20	9-21
☐ N747KD	Boeing 747-236F	80	ex Bruntingthorpe, Kemble, Cathay B-HVY, VR-HVY,	
			BA G-KILO. Last flight 29-4-08. Flightdeck	3-20
☐ 'VH-FDT'	DHA Drover II	51	ex Horizon, Booker, Lasham, Blackbushe, Southend,	
	G-APXX		Squires Gate, G-APXX (de-reg 26-11-73), VH-EAS	[1] 9-21
☐ WJ992*	EE Canberra T.4	53	ex Hurn, DRA Bedford, RAE, 76. Avro-built.	
			Cockpit, arrived 9-2-21	5-21
☐ WZ869	'6' DHC Chipmunk T.10	53	ex Leicester, Bruntingthorpe, South Molton, Handforth	
			8019M, 1 FTS, RAFC, Dishforth SF, Benson SF, Oxf UAS,	
			Dur UAS, 64 GCF, Colerne SF. Crashed 20-5-68. Fuselage,	
			less tail. RAFC colours	9-21
☐ XL472	'044' Fairey Gannet AEW.3	59	ex Horizon site, Charlwood, Boscombe Down, 849 'B',	
			HQ, 'A' Flts. SOC 6-12-78	[1] 9-21
☐ XL929*	Percival Pembroke C.1	56	ex off-site Coventry, Shoreham, Sandown, Shawbury, 60,	
	G-BNPU		Kemble, 207, SCCS, TCCS, FCCS, BCCS. De-reg 11-8-88.	
			Arrived 11-11-20	9-21
☐ XM833	Westland Wessex HAS.3	60	ex Usworth, Lasham, Wroughton, 737, 820, 814, HAS.1,	
			819, 700H. SOC 24-11-81. Arrived 14-5-19	9-21
☐ XP150	'18' Westland Wessex HAS.3	62	ex Moreton-in-Marsh, Lee-on-S' A2764, A2719 (8-8-84),	
			Wroughton, 772, 737, 814, HAS.1, 706. Arrived 22-5-19	9-21
☐ XV104	'U' Vickers VC10 C.1K	67	ex Bruntingthorpe, 101, 10. Arrived 26-1-19. Flightdeck	[2] 3-20
☐ XV109	'Z' Vickers VC10 C.1K	68	ex Bruntingthorpe, 101, 10. Arrived 26-1-19. Cockpit	[2] 3-20
☐ XV499	'I' McD Phantom FGR.2	69	ex RAF enclave, B'thorpe, Hixon, Leeming, 74, 19, 228 OCU,	
			29, 228 OCU, 29, 228 OCU, 23, 19, 92, 41, 228 OCU, 29,	
			228 OCU, 6, 228 OCU. SOC 5-10-92. Cockpit.	3-20
☐ ZD627	'WO' Westland Sea King HC.4	84	ex B'thorpe, Gosport, 848, 846, 707. Cockpit. F/n 10-18	3-20
☐ M25-04	SAL Bulldog 102	72	ex Kemble, R Malaysian AF FM1224. Fuselage. F/n 7-19	9-21

■ **[1]** Airframes from Mark Stott. **[2]** The centre fuselage of XV106 is also on show: its cockpit is as Woodford, Gtr Man.

Horizon Aviation Services: (See introductory notes to SWAM above.) Operates jet warbirds and other types, on behalf of a series of owners: these are not given a formal listing. Only long-term restoration projects or stored airframes are presented. **Mark Stott** operates Pembroke C.1 WV740 (G-BNPH) from the Horizon ramp and has a collection of airframes several of which are with SAWM: Drover 'VH-FDT', Sea Prince T.1 WP321, Gannet AEW.3s XL472 and XL500.

　　Departures: Hunter PR.11 WT723 moved to Birmingham, W Mids, by 9-21; T.8M XL602 exported to Canada during 2019; **Hawk** T.1s XX175, XX226, XX290 departed for Selby, N Yorks, 14-10-20; T.1 XX237 and T.1W XX312 departed 6-21 bound for instructional use in Qatar; T.53 ZK534 shipped to the USA during 9-21.

◆ *By prior arrangement* only | www.horizonaircraft.co.uk

☐ G-AKVF*	Chrislea Super Ace	48	ex Dublin, Coventry, Dunsfold, AP-ADT, G-AKVF. CoA 31-5-13,	
			de-reg 15-5-18. Arrived 3-7-20	7-20
☐ G-FLSH*	Yakovlev Yak-52	87	ex N Weald, RA-44550. IAR Bacau-built. CoA 29-10-10,	
			de-reg 26-3-10. Arrived 20-11-18	11-18
☐ G-FLYY*	BAC Strikemaster Mk.80	69	ex Saudi AF 1112, G=27-31. CoA 30-9-20. Arrived 25-9-20	[1] 6-21
☐ G-FRCE	Folland Gnat T.1	63	ex N Weald, Halton 8604M, XS104, 4 FTS, CFS, 4 FTS.	
			CoA 28-8-08. 'Red Arrows' colours	[2] 11-16
☐ G-JIBO	BAe Jetstream 3102	86	ex OY-SVJ, G-BTYG, N415MX, G-31-711. CoA 29-4-16	[3] 9-21
☐ WF118	'569' Percival Sea Prince T.1	51	ex Charlwood, Staverton, G-DACA (de-reg 15-12-09), Kemble,	
			750, A&AEE, 727, A&AEE, RAE. SOC 1-8-80. Off-site	[4] 8-21

☐ XL954*	Percival Pembroke		57	ex Weston, Coventry, N4234C, Tatenhill, W Waltham, 9042M,	
	C.1	G-BXES		Northolt, 60, RAFG CS, 2 TAF CS. CoA 4-10-17, de-reg 4-3-21.	
				Arrived 14-12-21	10-21
☐ XW289	'MU' BAC Jet Provost		71	ex N Weald, Cranfield, G-BVXT, Shawbury, 1 FTS, 3 FTS,	
	T.5A	G-JPVA		RAFC, 1 FTS, RAFC, CFS. CoA 6-1-17, de-reg 4-11-16. Arr 11-16	9-21
☐ XW436*	'68' BAC Jet Provost T.5A		72	ex Cosford, Halton 9148M (18-5-92), 1 FTS, CFS, 3 FTS,	
				Leeming SF, 3 FTS, RAFC. Arrived 16-10-20	10-20
☐ XX342	HS Hawk T.1	G-HAWC	81	ex Boscombe Down, ETPS. First noted 7-19	[5] 6-21
☐ ZD990	HS Harrier T.8		87	ex Culdrose, St Athan, 899, T.8, 20, 3, T.4.	
	'DDT90'	G-RNTB		Arrived 15-8-17	[6] 6-21
☐ ZH803	HS Sea Harrier F/A.2		96	ex Culdrose, Shawbury, Yeovilton, 801, 800.	
	'DD03'	G-RNFA		Arrived 8-8-17	[6] 11-21

■ [1] Registered to High G Jets of Blackpool, Lancs. [2] G-FRCE registered to Red Gnat Ltd. [3] Registered to K B leasing. [4] Owned by Mark Stott. [5] Registered to L39 Aviation Ltd. [6] Registered to Fly Harrier Ltd.

MoD Saint Athan: (W&R will continue to call it St Athan!) Operating as an enclave within the Welsh Government-owned site is **4 School of Technical Training** - formed here on 1st September 1938.

☐ VN-A190	Boeing 737-4H6	94	ex Kemble, Jet Star Pacific, Malaysian 9M-MQJ.	
			Arrived 6-13. Training airframe	6-20
☐ 'JP098'	Eurofighter Typhoon EMU	~	dumped out on the East Camp. First noted 7-11	6-19

Airliner parting out: Both **GJD Services** and **GJD AeroTech** – see narrative for the South Wales Aviation Museum, above and **eCube Solutions** have extensive facilities and operations at St Athan. With the pandemic airliner storage increased considerably, but the main activity has remained the decommissioning and recycling of jetliners. This work is relatively rapid and beyond the scope of W&R but a much-travelled Boeing 767 has proved more tenacious than most. eCube took on custodianship of the last-ever BA 747 and plans for its long-term future are being formulated.
◆ **Strictly by prior arrangement only** | www.gjdservices.co.uk | https://ecube.aero

☐ G-BYGC*	Boeing 747-436	99	ex Cardiff, BA. BOAC colours. De-reg 5-1-21. Arr 11-12-20	[1] 1-22
☐ ZS-DJI*	Boeing 767-200	86	ex J2-KBE, ZS-DJI, N480JC, G-SJET, G-FJEC, N769BC, TJ-AAC,	
			N769BC, TJ-AAC, N769BC, 5R-MFE, N151LF, PT-TAH,	
			CC-CJV, N4528Y. Arrived 7-10-15	8-20

■ [1] With eCube Solutions; last-ever BA 747 flight – total time 91,023 hours.

Happy Jakes Touring Caravan Park: At Flemingston, just north of the SWAM site, took delivery of a Jetstream 31 fuselage from the museum, ready for the 2020 season. ◆ By prior arrangement only | www.happyjakes.wales

☐ G-CONY*	BAe Jetstream 3101	87	ex SWAM, N22746, N331QE, G-31-745. De-reg 27-2-17.	
			Fuselage. First noted 6-20	1-22

SEALAND on the A494 north of Queensferry
Defence Electronics and Components Agency: The former RAF Sealand has a GR.4 as a 'guardian'.

☐ ZA607	'EB-X' Panavia Tornado GR.4	82	ex Marham, GR.1, 9. Arrived 18-2-19, unveiled 22-2-19	1-22

SWANSEA
National Waterfront Museum: Part of the National Museum of Wales.
◆ Oystermouth Road, SA1 3RD | 0300 1112333 | waterfront@museumwales.ac.uk | www.museumwales.ac.uk/swansea

☐ –	Watkins CHW	1909	BAPC.47, ex Nantgarw, Cardiff, St Athan, Cardiff.	
			Robin Goch	[1] 1-22

■ [1] Single-seat monoplane designed and built by C H Watkins at Maendy, Cardiff, 1907-1909. Fitted with a 40hp 3-cylinder also designed by Watkins. Claimed to have made its first hop in 1909, a cross-country in 1910 and flown extensively until 1916.

SWANSEA AIRPORT or Fairwood Common   EGFH

☐ 'G-STNR'	Aero L29 Delfin	RA-01611	~	ex St Athan, Germany, Sov AF. 'Tiger' colours	
				Arrived 7-15, displayed	[1] 9-21

■ [1] The real G-STNR is a Yak-52 - see Henstridge, Somerset

TALGARTH AERODROME east of the A479 south of the town
Black Mountains Gliding Club: ◆ By prior arrangement only | www.southwales.ac.uk

☐ G-BLDG*	Piper Pawnee 235	68	ex Rufforth, SE-FLB, LN-VYM. CoA 4-9-15. Arrived 30-10-19	10-19

TREFOREST on the A473 southeast of Pontypridd
University of South Wales: The Jetstream is *believed* to be still ensconced in the purpose-built Aerospace Centre at the Faculty of Advanced Technology. Jet Provost T.3A XN584 departed to St Athan, Wales, on 4th August 2021.
◆ *By prior arrangement* **only** | **www.southwales.ac.uk**

❑ G-JXTC	BAe Jetstream 31	86	ex Eindhoven, PH-KJG, G-JXTC, G-LOGT, G-BSFH,
			PH-KJG, G-31-690. De-reg 7-10-11 4-12

VALLEY AIRFIELD south of the A5, southeast of Holyhead
RAF Valley: With the wind-down of the Hawk T.1 fleet, the resident Aircraft Maintenance Repair and Overhaul (AMRO) organisation will handle the reduce to produce (RTP) programme, although it is doubted airframes will endure here long. Hawk XX157 arrived from Shawbury for prep for the 'Red Arrows' but the 45-year-old was deemed not up to the work required: it awaits a decision on its future. A 'synthetic' Hawk training aid is on the dump.

❑ XX156	HS Hawk T.1	75	ex CFS, 19, DTEO/DRA, A&AEE, RAE, HS, A&AEE.
			SOC 10-7-17. Displayed from 29-8-18 [1] 9-21
❑ XX157*	HS Hawk T.1A	76	ex Shawbury, 736, FRADU, 208, 92, 7 FTS, 63, TWU,
			A&AEE. Arrived 10-21 – see notes above 10-21

■ **[1]** Second prototype Hawk, first flown at Dunsfold 19-5-75.

WELSHPOOL on the A483 west of Shrewsbury
Military Aircraft Cockpit Collection: Run by Sue and Roy Jerman. ◆ **Private** *collection, by prior arrangement* **only**

❑ WH775	EE Canberra PR.7	54	ex Bruntingthorpe, Cosford 8868M/8128M (11-3-71),
			100, 13, 31, 17, 31, 13, 82, makers. Cockpit 12-19
❑ WK102	EE Canberra T.17	54	ex Bruntingthorpe, Cosford 8780M, 360, B.2, 45,
			RNZAF, 207. SOC 18-2-83. Avro-built. Cockpit 12-19
❑ XJ758	Westland Whirlwind HAR.10	56	ex Oswestry, Shrewsbury, Shawbury 8464M (10-2-76), CFS, 230, CFS, HAR.2, 217, 1360F, 22. Cockpit [1] 12-19
❑ XM652	Avro Vulcan B.2	64	ex Burntwood, Sheffield, Waddington, 50, Wadd Wing,
			Cott Wing. SOC 20-2-84. Cockpit 12-19
❑ XM692	Folland Gnat T.1	60	ex S Molton, East Tilbury, Boscombe D', Robertsbridge, Salisbury, Southampton, Fareham, Foulness, A&AEE. SOC 28-3-69. Forward cockpit 3-13
❑ XS923	'BE' EE Lightning F.6	66	ex Bruntingthorpe, Cranfield, Binbrook, 11, LTF,
			5-11 pool. SOC 24-6-88. Cockpit 12-19
❑ XT277	Blackburn Buccaneer S.2B	65	ex Bruntingthorpe, Cosford 8853M (21-5-85), Shawbury, 237 OCU, 12, 800, 809, 801. Cockpit 12-19
❑ XZ356	'FU' SEPECAT Jaguar GR.3A	76	ex Ipswich, St Athan, 41, SAOEU, 54, GR.1, Shawbury, 6, Gulf Det, 41, 14, 17, 41 12-19

■ **[1]** Whirlwind cockpit is on loan from Dave Higgins - see also Norwich, Norfolk.

Also: Based locally is a Robinson R22 used as a travelling fund-raiser for the Wales Air Ambulance.

❑ G-GDAY*	Robinson R22 Beta	87	ex Squires Gate. Crashed 24-4-99, de-reg 28-9-19.
			Red scheme, trailer-mounted 11-21

WREXHAM
Glyndŵr University: In Mold Road ◆ *By prior arrangement* **only** | **www.glyndwr.ac.uk**

❑ XP585	'24' Hunting Jet Provost T.4	62	ex Halton 8407M (7-10-74), St Athan, RAFC, 6 FTS, RAFC 9-21

YSTRAD MYNACH on the A469 south of Pontllanfraith
Coleg y Cymoedd: The Jetstream is *believed* to still serve. ◆ *By prior arrangement* **only** | **www.cymoedd.ac.uk**

❑ –	HP Jetstream 41 EMU	67	ex Rhoose, Luton, G-ATXJ, HP. CoA 8-2-71, de-reg 11-4-72.
	G-ATXJ		.Fuselage. 'Ystrad Mynach Airways' titles 3-10

■ **[1]** Jetstream factoids: Based on G-ATXJ, the third prototype; first flying 28-12-67. Became the Srs 200/300 prototype: maiden flight 16-12-69. Last flight 5-3-70, total time 636 hours. Was an exhibit with the former Wales Aircraft Museum.

CHANNEL ISLANDS
*The Islands are self-governing British Crown Dependencies - part of the British Isles,
but not part of the United Kingdom*

ALDERNEY AIRPORT
EGJA

☐ G-ASHV	Piper Aztec 250B	63	ex Guernsey, N5281Y. CoA 22-7-85, de-reg 20-6-88.	
			Rescue trainer	11-19
☐ G-BDTN	BN Trislander	76	ex Guernsey, Aurigny, S7-AAN, VQ-SAN, G-BDTN.	
			CoA 10-6-98, de-reg 5-1-11. Rescue trainer	11-19

GUERNSEY

Mark Hollingsworth: Is restoring the front 21ft of a Herald.

| ☐ G-BAZJ | HP Herald 209 | 74 | ex airport, Air UK, 4X-AHR, G-8-1. CoA 24-11-84, | |
| | | | de-reg 4-1-85. Forward fuselage | 1-20 |

Oatlands Visitor Centre: At St Sampsons, within Oatey and Joey's Playbarn is the dramatically posed Trislander. Grub's good at the café too! | www.oatlands.gg

| ☐ G-JOEY | BN Trislander | 75 | ex airport, Aurigny, G-BDGG, C-GSAA, G-BDGG. FBN-built. | |
| | | | Last service 28-6-14. De-reg 19-10-16. Arrived 10-4-18 | 9-21 |

Others: Some references are long-in-the-tooth but *believed* current. Each is held at a different *private* venue.

☐ G-ATEP	EAA Biplane	67	CoA 18-6-73, de-reg 14-7-86	5-03
☐ G-ATHN	Nord Noralpha	48	ex F-BFUZ, Fr mil No.84. CoA 27-6-75, de-reg 16-12-91	1-20
☐ G-FTSE	BN Trislander	77	ex airport, Aurigny, G-BEPI. Fairey BN-built. Crashed 17-1-11,	
			de-reg 14-8-14. Forward fuselage, trailer-mounted	1-20
☐ 5N-AHN	Bell JetRanger	68	ex Bristow, G-AWFV. Forward fuselage - sim	5-11

GUERNSEY AIRPORT
EGJB

Missed for at least two decades, Cessna 303 N11FV departed by road in July 2020 bound for the ferry to the UK. It was destined for the owner's British home – no more details.

☐ GBDTO	BN Trislander	76	ex Aurigny, G-RBSI, G-OTSB, G-BDTO, 8P-ASC, G-BDTO,	
			C-GYOX, G-BDTO. De-reg 10-2-17. Rescue trainer	1-20
☐ N97121	Embraer Bandeirante	~	ex City-Link, PT-SDK. Rescue trainer	1-20
☐ XM409	Hunting Jet Provost T.3	60	ex Firbeck, Moreton-in-Marsh, Halton 8082M	
			(13-5-70), Shawbury, 2 FTS. Cockpit	1-20

JERSEY AIRPORT
EGJJ

Jersey Airlines Duchess of Brittany Heritage Group: The Heron was registered to the airline on 20th September 2021 amid a 'push' to get it airworthy again. The 'JP' *should* still serve the fire crews.

☐ G-AORG*	DH Sea Heron C.1	56	ex Coventry, XR441, *Heron* Flt, 781, G-AORG, G-5-16.	
			Jersey Airlines c/s, *Duchess of Brittany*. CoA 24-7-19	9-21
☐ XP573	Hunting Jet Provost T.4	62	ex Halton 8336M (21-3-73), '8236M', Kemble, Shawbury,	
			R-R, 1 FTS, CFS. Rescue trainer	9-18

NORTHERN IRELAND

ANTRIM on the M22 northwest of Belfast
At a *private* location in the *general* area David and Matthew McCullough have mounted the cockpit of a tri-gear Europa on a gimbal – Link Trainer fashion. It is bedecked in NASA colours, has small delta wings, a long, pointed, nose from the firewall and 'rockets' mounted at the rear – Gordon's alive!

☐ G-TAGR*	Shaw Europa XS	04	crashed 19-4-14, de-reg 27-11-15. Cockpit	12-21

ARMAGH on the A3 / A28 northwest of Newry
Tidying up: Rans S.7 G-BWKJ (last noted 10-13), Gemini Flashes G-MJYF and G-MVRB (both 8-13) and Cessna 152 EI-CGT (10-13) have been deleted. That leaves the following at a *private* location in the *general* area.

☐ G-APXR	Piper Tri-Pacer 160	60	CoA 31-3-11	N2-19
☐ G-ARDO	Jodel D.112	60	ex F-PBTE, F-BBTE, F-WBTE. CoA 30-5-07	N8-18

AUGHNACLOY at the A5/A28 junction, north of Monaghan
AWOL Outdoor Adventure: ◆ *By prior arrangement* only | www.awolpaintball.ie

☐ EI-BDK	MS Rallye Club 100ST	ex Abbeyshrule, F-BXMZ. De-reg 25-11-08	8-14

BALLYMAGORRY on the N14 northwest of Strabane
A long out-of-use microlight lingers in the area.

☐ G-MTCZ	Solar Wings Tri-Pacer 250	r87	de-reg 3-8-94	1-20

BALLYMONEY on the A26 southeast of Coleraine
A yard in the area should still hold a Sierra. Last noted in November 2016, X'Air G-CCGR has been deleted.

☐ G-BBSC	Beech Sierra 200	73	ex Aldergrove. Damaged 4-12-97, de-reg 27-7-01. Fuselage	7-19

BANN FOOT Last noted in September 2015, Rallye G-BDWA and FRED G-PFAL have been deleted.

BELFAST

Crumlin Road Gaol: Boasting it was the scene of umpteen executions, less gory attractions include a Wessex.
◆ *Tour-based - see website* | *Crumlin Road, BT14 6ST* | info@crumlinroadgaol.com | www.crumlinroadgaol.com

☐ XR529	'E' Westland Wessex HC.2	64	ex Aldergrove 9268M, 72, SARTU, 2 FTS, 18, 78, 72. Arrived 15-1-19	1-19

BELFAST AIRPORT or Aldergrove   EGAA

☐ G-AVFE	HS Trident 2E	67	ex BA, BEA. CoA 6-5-85, de-reg 20-3-85. Rescue trainer, forward fuselage by 11-19	11-19
☐ PH-PTD	Piper Navajo 350	78	ex Quick Airways, N27583. Fuselage, rescue trainer	11-19
☐ XT456	'XZ' Westland Wessex HU.5	65	ex 8941M (11-11-87), Wroughton, Yeovilton, Wroughton, 845, 847, 846, 845, 707. Rescue trainer	4-14

Joint Helicopter Command Flying Station Aldergrove. The cockpits are used by RAF Careers and do 'the rounds'. In July 2021 the Defender and Islander fleet was paid off, departing to Lee-on-Solent... sorry, Solent, Hampshire, for disposal. That included Defender R.2 ZG995, stored since October 2017, which reverted to G-SURV in the process.

☐ XE643	Hawker Hunter FGA.9	56	ex Abingdon 8586M, 208, F.6, 56, 63, 66, 92. Crashed 9-12-61. Cockpit	9-19
☐ XR700	Hunting Jet Provost T.4	63	ex Abingdon 8589M, Shawbury, CATCS, 3 FTS, 1 FTS. SOC 1-10-71. Cockpit	9-19
☐ XX443	'Y' Sud Gazelle AH.1	76	ex Gosport, M Wallop, 658, 662, 663, 3 Regt, 669, 659. Westland-built. Crashed 28-9-97. Displayed, first noted 3-17	3-17

Also: Close to the airport, a *private* collector *should* have a Vampire cockpit.

☐ XD525	DH Vampire T.11	54	ex Belfast, Holywood, Belfast, Aldergrove 7882M (8-4-65), 1 FTS, 4 FTS, 5 FTS, 7 FTS. Christchurch-built. Cockpit	2-14

BELLARENA AERODROME north of Limavady

☐ G-ARAP		Champion 7EC Traveler	60	ex Londonderry, Eglinton. Cr 22-9-81, de-reg 30-5-84	7-21
☐ BGA.327*	AAF	Slingsby Kirby Kite	37	BGA.327, ex Eaton Bray, Ilkley Moor, Tibenham,	
				RAFGSA.182, VD218, BGA.310	[1] 10-21

■ [1] BGA.310 rebuilt using elements of BGA.327, which is at Shuttleworth, Beds - qv. The *original* fuselage, tail feathers and an aileron, after a crash in 1970, are here, hence the change of BGA identity.

BROUGHSHANE, on the A42, northeast of Ballymena

☐ G-MZGB	Cyclone AX2000	97	ex Blackhill. CoA 19-5-08, de-reg 6-11-15	12-21

BUSHMILLS Last noted in May 2016, FRED G-BDSA has been deleted.

CAUSEWAY AERODROME near Aghadowey, south of Coleraine

☐ G-BASO	Lake LA-4-180	67	ex Londonderry, N2025L. CoA 19-6-06	12-21
☐ G-BOLL*	Lake LA-4-180	64	ex EI-ANR, N1133L. CoA 29-8-18	12-21
☐ G-BVRY	Cyclone AX3/582	95	crashed 9-7-98. CoA 2-3-99, de-reg 21-11-02	2-20
☐ N216HK	CGS Hawk Arrow	r92	G-MWYP, de-reg 9-2-93	12-21
☐ N217HK	CGS Hawk Arrow	r92	G-MWYR, de-reg 9-2-93	2-20

DUNGANNON Last noted in July 2015, Scout AH.1 XW281 (G-BYNZ) had moved to <u>Moy</u>, N Ireland, by July 2021. Cessna 337 G-AVJG, last noted in July 2013, has been deleted.

ENNISKILLEN

South West College: Technology and Skills Centre, Dublin Road. ◆*By prior arrangement* **only | www.swc.ac.uk**

☐ EI-BBI	MS Rallye Commodore	75	de-reg 5-4-17	1-20

ENNISKILLEN AERODROME or St Angelo

				EGAB
☐ G-SWAT	Robinson R44 Raven	03	ex N75097. CoA 14-11-15	2-20
☐ EI-AVC	Cessna F.337F	~	ex Dungannon, Castlerock, Abbeyshrule, N4757.	
			Reims-built. De-reg 26-6-03. Rescue trainer	2-20

FINTONA on the B46 / B122 south of Omagh

☐ G-BMYF	Bensen B-8M	86	de-reg 6-4-09	10-18

FIVEMILETOWN on the A4 east of Enniskillen

Blessingbourne Carriage and Costume Museum: Within the Blessingbourne Estate.
◆ *Prior appointment* **only** | *Tyrone, BT75 0QS* | **info@blessingbourne.com | www.blessingbourne.com**

☐ XT208	Bell Sioux AH.1	66	ex Sek Kong, 656. Ditched 16-3-72, cabin	[1]	3-19
☐ XW795	Westland Scout AH.1	72	ex M Wallop, Almondbank, Wroughton, 659, 655, 669		3-19

■ [1] A door opened in flight while low over Tolo Harbour, Hong Kong. Distracted while closing the door, the chopper struck the water.

GILFORD on the A51 north of Newry

Two airframes are stored at a *private* house in the *general* area.

☐ G-BKAF	Clutton FRED Srs II	83	CoA 30-5-97	6-21
☐ EI-AUT	Forney F.1A Aircoupe	60	ex Bann Foot, Cork, G-ARXS, D-EBSA, N3037G. De-reg 27-5-11	6-21

HOLYWOOD on the A2 east of Belfast

Ulster Transport Museum: Part of National Museums NI, the transport element is co-located with the **Ulster Folk Museum**, on either side of the A2 Belfast to Bangor road. Time really should be taken to visit *both*. The Transport Museum is on the banks of Belfast Lough and a series of halls take the visitor through railways, buses, trams, cars, horse-drawn vehicles, shipping models, a special *Titanic* exhibition and then to the small, but pleasing aviation section.
◆ *Cultra Manor, Holywood, BT18 0EU* | **028 90428428 | uftm.info@nmni.com | www.nmni.com/uftm**

☐ G-AKLW	Short Sealand 1	51	ex USA, Jeddah, Saudi AF, SU-AHY, G-AKLW. Acquired 8-86		1-22
☐ G-ATXX	McCandless M4	68	ex Killough. De-reg 9-9-70. Acquired 1987		1-22
☐ G-BKMW	Short Sherpa	82	ex Belfast City, CoA 14-9-90, de-reg 14-11-96. Cockpit		1-22
☐ G-BREL	Cameron O-77 HAB	78	de-reg 12-10-98. Basket. First noted 11-18		1-22
☐ XG905	Short SC.1	57	ex Sydenham, Thurleigh, BLEU, RAE. Acquired 20-5-74	[1]	1-22
☐ –	Ferguson Mono replica	73	IAHC.6, ex Dublin. Acquired 4-5-76		1-22

■ [1] XG905 made the type's first full transition from vertical to horizontal flight at Thurleigh 6-4-60. It crashed fatally following an autostabilsation failure at Sydenham 2-10-63. It was rebuilt and flying again in 1966.

Deep store sites: not available for inspection.

☐ G-AJOC	Miles Messenger 2A	47	ex East Fortune, Strathallan, Dunottar, U-9.		
			CoA 18-5-72, de-reg 5-1-82	[1]	12-18
☐ G-AKEL	Miles Gemini 1A	47	ex Kilbrittain Castle. CoA 29-4-72, de-reg 30-5-84.		
			Cockpit and wings	[2]	12-18
☐ G-ALCS	Miles Gemini 3	47	ex 'Limerick', Kilbrittain Castle. CoA 30-11-72,		
			de-reg 30-5-84. Cockpit and wing stubs.	[3]	12-18
☐ G-AOUR	DH Tiger Moth	43	ex Belfast, NL898, 15 EFTS. Morris -built.		
			Crashed 6-6-65, de-reg 8-7-65		12-18
☐ G-ARTZ (1)	McCandless M2	66	ex Killough	[4]	12-18
☐ ALA	Short Nimbus I	47	BGA.470, ex Bishop's Stortford, Duxford. CoA 8-75		12-18
☐ –	Ferguson Mono replica	75	IAHC.9, ex Belfast Airport, Holywood. Off-site		12-18
☐ VH-UUP	Short Scion I	34	ex East Fortune, Strathallan, G-ACUX, VH-UUP, G-ACUX		11-19

■ [1] Built at the Miles plant at Newtownards, N Ireland. [2] As well as G-AKEL, the rear fuselage and tail 'feathers' of G-AKGE - see under Dromod, Ireland - are held. [3] Thanks to Ian Thompson the other Gemini cockpit can be confirmed as Wolverhampton Aviation-completed G-ALCS. [4] Registration G-ARTZ has been used twice, both times on Rex McCandless' products. The second candidate was last recorded at St Merryn, Cornwall.

KILKEEL on the A2 east of Newry and Warrenpoint

Cub G-BFHI was flying by September 2020. The tail section of the Twinstar had stopped serving as a 'water feature' at a house near Armagh by June 2020 and was up for sale four months later.

| ☐ G-BYTA | Kolb Twinstar Mk.3 | 00 | crashed 16-11-07, CoA 14-2-08, de-reg 21-3-11. See above | 12-21 |

LETTERKENNY on the N56, west of Londonderry

A collection of microlights is *believed* extant in the area at a *private* address.

☐ G-MBWL	Huntair Pathfinder 1	r84	de-reg 6-1-93		1-16
☐ G-MJBT	Eipper Quicksilver	~	de-reg 24-1-95		3-17
☐ G-MVXW	Rans Coyote	90	ex Frosses. CoA 14-9-06, de-reg 6-2-07	[1]	12-16
☐ G-MZFI	Lorimer Iolaire	97	de-reg 25-3-09		3-17

■ [1] The Coyote was de-registered as sold in Ireland.

Others: A local scrapyard has/had a Rallye.

| ☐ EI-AWU | MS Rallye Club | 67 | ex Rosnakill, G-AVIM. De-reg 27-6-08 | 2-19 |

LISBELLAW on the A4 east of Enniskillen

Last recorded in August 2014, Crickets G-BSPJ and G-BTEI have been deleted. The Whittaker is *thought* to be extant.

| ☐ G-BUOA | Whittaker MW-6 Fatboy A | 93 | CoA 4-10-06 | N7-18 |

LONDONDERRY / DERRY

Greater Shantallow Community Arts at Studio2: On the Skegoe Industrial Estate, keeps an AA-5 as a travelling exhibit.
◆ *By prior arrangement* only | www.gscaderry.com

| ☐ EI-BNR | American AA-5A | r83 | ex Abbeyshrule, N9992Q, CS-AHM. Crashed 21-2-88 | 6-19 |

Oakfire Adventures: ◆ *By prior arrangement* only | www.oakfireadventures.com

| ☐ G-BFWK | Piper Warrior 161 | 78 | ex Belfast, N9589N. CoA 8-12-99, de-reg 26-5-98 | 8-13 |

LONDONDERRY AIRPORT or Eglinton, on the A2 east of Londonderry   EGAE

| ☐ G-BWWX | Yakovlev Yak-50 | 85 | ex LY-AOI, Sov AF. CoA 11-6-09, de-reg 4-2-15 | 12-19 |
| ☐ EI-DIF | Piper Navajo 350 | 77 | ex G-OAMT, G-BXKS, N350RC, EC-EBN, N27230 | 12-19 |

LONG KESH west of Lisburn, close to J7 of the M1

Ulster Aviation Society Heritage Collection (UAS). Major refurbishment of the hangars was ongoing during late 2021. This work serves to underline the importance of this often under-rated museum: here is a collection of *national* status – be that Northern Ireland, the Island of Ireland or the British Isles. The Irish Air Corps continues to honour the collection with retired examples of its fleet. The team conduct a vigorous outreach policy and is engaged in an extensive restoration programme.

For three decades chairman of UAS and always at the heart of this incredible organisation, **Ernie Cromie** died on 16th July 2021, aged 79. Forever modest, Ernie was a historian of great repute, a man of vision and quiet inspiration. His 'mark' can be found in every aspect of the collection and all that it stands for.

Nearly three years of planning and, at times, hoping, came to fruition on 29th September 2021 when a convoy of low-loaders courtesy of the Boscombe Down-based Joint Aircraft Recovery and Transport Squadron arrived at Long Kesh bringing Tornado GR.4 ZG771 to join the collection – another feather in the UAS cap. Covid-19 meant a prolonged stay at Boscombe and, indeed, *W&R27* quoted a 'due to arrive' date of 24th March 2020. Digging into ZG771's history, UAS volunteers pleasantly discovered that the specially-marked aircraft was the last Tornado to visit Northern Ireland, on 13th February 2019, with a classic low-level 'beat up' at Aldergrove.

One-off abbreviation for this section: LL = Langford Lodge, the collection's previous home.

◆ *Maze Long Kesh, Halftown Road, BT27 5RF. Only available on pre-arranged basis –* **bookvisit@ulteraviationSociety.org | hello@ulteraviationsociety.org | www.ulsteraviationsociety.org**

❑ G-AVCS	Beagle Terrier 1	52	ex Lisburn, Auster AOP.6 WJ363, Odiham SF, AAC, 1900 Flt. Crashed 18-10-81, de-reg 3-4-89. Arrived 8-7-17			1-22
❑ G-BDBS	Short 330	75	ex LL, Belfast City, Short, G-14-3001. CoA 2-9-92, de-reg 1-7-93. Acquired 7-4-93			1-22
❑ G-BEHX	Evans VP-2	81	ex Coalisland. CoA 22-1-90, de-reg 16-12-02. *Ulster Flyer.* Arrived 5-6-16			1-22
❑ G-BNZR	Clutton FRED II	91	ex Belfast. CoA 25-5-99, de-reg 11-8-10. Acquired 31-5-10			1-22
❑ G-BTUC	Embraer Tucano	83	ex LL, Belfast City, Short, G-14-007, PP-ZTC. CoA 20-8-91, de-reg 20-12-96. Acquired 16-1-01			1-22
❑ G-CDUX	Piper Cherokee Six	73	ex Newtownards, EC-DUX. De-reg 29-1-15, crashed 6-6-14. Fuselage. Arrived 21-11-17			1-22
❑ G-CJEN	Ferguson Mono rep	16	built at Long Kesh. Flown 5-16, de-reg 1-6-16. Handed over 28-9-16	[1]		1-22
❑ G-MBJV	Rotec Rally 2B	r82	ex Armagh. De-reg 13-6-90. Arrived 12-10-13	[2]		1-22
❑ G-MJWS	Eurowing Goldwing	r83	ex LL, Newtownards. De-reg 23-6-97. Acquired 29-7-00	[3]		1-22
❑ G-MZHM	Team Hi-Max 1700	97	CoA 26-10-06. Acquired 13-9-07	[4]		1-22
❑ G-RENT	Robinson R22	88	ex LL, Newtownards, N2635M. Damaged 30-9-92, de-reg 11-12-03. Acquired 28-2-03	[5]		1-22
❑ G-TANK	Cameron N-90 HAB	95	CoA 28-5-14, de-reg 25-5-16. *DFDS Hoyer*	[6]		1-22
❑ G-14-1	Short SB.4 Sherpa	53	ex Flixton, Rochester, Duxford, Staverton, Bristol, G-36-1, Cranfield, G-14-1. Fuselage, replica wings. Arrived 16-7-08, acquired 10-12			1-22
❑ EVN	Monnett Monerai	r85	ex Bellarena, BGA.2988. CoA 6-11-88. Arrived 15-3-17	[7]		1-22
❑ -	Mignet HM.14 'Flea'	35	ex Moneymore. Fuselage, arrived 1-18	[8]		1-22
❑ –	Chargus Cyclone	79	BAPC.263, ex LL, Ballyclare. Last flight 4-4-88, acq 11-94			1-22
❑ –	Eipper Quicksilver	80	arrived 18-2-12. Ross's (mineral water) logos	[9]		1-22
❑ –	Rogallo hang glider	77	BAPC.266, ex LL Last flown 1978, acquired 2-00			1-22
❑ 'NI-UAS'	Aerosport Scamp	~	arrived 31-8-13	[10]		1-22
❑ –	Hapi Cygnet SF-2A	~	unassembled, in kit form. Arrived 31-8-13	[11]		1-22
❑ –	Short Tucano EMU	c86	ex Sydenham, Sydenham. Acquired 1-12			1-22
❑ EI-BUO	Aero Composites Sea Hawker	87	ex LL, Newtownards. Ditched Strangford Lough 9-91. Acquired 1998. Stored	[12]		1-22
❑ EI-CNG	Air and Space 18A	66	ex Sligo, Knock, G-BALB, N6170S. Last flown 11-2007. Arrived 17-11-12			1-22
❑ N80BA	Pitts S-1A	~	ex Killinchy, Newtownards. Cr 7-11-99. Arr by 9-13. Stored			1-22
❑ 'P7823' 'FT-M'	V-S Spitfire FSM	13	BAPC.369, ex 'P7895', Seaton Burn, Linton-on-Ouse. GB Replicas-built. Arrived 21-12-13. 504 Sqn colours, *Belfast Telegraph – Down*			1-22
❑ HB612 G-AJSN	Fairchild Argus II	43	ex Dromore, Cork, HB612, ATA, 43-14885. Dam 10-6-67, de-reg 12-3-73. Arrived 3-3-12			1-22
❑ JV482 'S-C'	Grumman Wildcat V	44	ex LL, Newtownards, Castlereagh, Lough Beg, 882. Crashed 24-12-44. Acquired 30-4-84			1-22

❑ VP957	DH Devon C.2/2	48	ex Lisburn, Bishop's Court 8822M, Belfast, Northolt, 207, 21, C.1, WCS, SCS, NCS, SCS, WCS, SCS, Andover SF, 38 GCF, AAFCE, 2 TAF CS, BAFO CS. Last flown 4-7-84. Cockpit. Arrived 2-14
			1-22
❑ WF122	'575' Percival Sea Prince T.1	51	ex Doncaster, Bruntingthorpe, Helston, Culdrose A2673 (5-2-79), 750, Sydenham SF, Arbroath SF, Lossiemouth SF, 700Z Flt, Lossiemouth SF, FOFT, 750, Eglinton SF, 744. Arrived 13-10-17. Sydenham SF colours
			1-22
❑ WF911	'CO' EE Canberra B.2	52	ex Alveley, Gloucester, Hooton Park, Charnock Richard, Bacup, Preston, Samlesbury, G-27-161, 231 OCU. SOC 21-5-69. Arrived 19-10-13. Cockpit
			1-22
❑ WN108	'033' Hawker Sea Hawk FB.3	54	ex LL, Sydenham, Hurn, FRU, 806, 895, 897, 800. SOC 26-9-63, acquired 17-10-89
			1-22
❑ WZ549	'F' DH Vampire T.11	53	ex LL, Sydenham, Coningsby, Tattershall, Coningsby 8118M (last flight 19-12-70), CATCS, 1 FTS, 8 FTS, FTU, C(A). Christchurch-built. Acquired 10-91
			1-22
❑ XA460	'768' Fairey Gannet AS.4	56	ex Doncaster, Connah's Quay, Brawdy, Gannet Supp Unit, 849, AS.4, 831, ECM.6, 849, AS.4. SOC 10-2-71, Last flight 22-1-71. Acquired 29-10-11
			1-22
❑ XH131	EE Canberra PR.9	59	ex Kemble, Marham, 39, 1 PRU, 39, 13, 39, MoA. Short-built. Last flight 31-7-06, acquired 13-12-10
❑ XM414	'101' Hunting Jet Provost T.3A	60	ex LL, Dundonald, Binbrook, Colsterworth, Halton 8996M (10-4-89), 7 FTS, RAFC, 1 FTS, RAFC, 2 FTS. Acquired 23-12-04	1-22
❑ XR517	'N' Westland Wessex HC.2	64	ex LL, Shoreham, Ipswich, Fleetlands, 60, 72, 18. Acquired 3-12-05
			1-22
❑ XT864	'007' McD Phantom FG.1	68	ex Leuchars 8998M, 111, 892, 767, 700P. Arrived 15-6-15. Unveiled 28-4-18, in 892 Sqn colours
			1-22
❑ XV136	'X' Westland Scout AH.1	68	ex Netheravon, Almondbank, Wroughton. Arrived 2-3-14	1-22
❑ XV361	Blackburn Buccaneer S.2B	68	ex LL, Lossiemouth, 208, 15, 208, 12, 15, 809, 800. Last flight 18-4-94
			1-22
❑ XW222	Sud Puma HC.1	72	ex Benson, 230, 33, 230, 33, 230, 27, 1563 Flt, 18, 230. Last flown 12-11. Westland-built. Arrived 29-7-14
❑ 'XX530'	'F' SAL Bulldog T.1	74	ex Glasgow, Kinloss, Cranwell, St Athan 9197M,
	XX637		North UAS, 2 FTS. Arrived 1-12-19
			1-22
❑ ZF167	Short Tucano T.1	89	ex Sydenham, Shawbury, 1 FTS, 7 FTS. Arrived by 9-14	1-22
❑ ZG771	Panavia Tornado GR.4	91	ex Boscombe Down, Marham, 9, 31, 12, 15, Warton, 15, 617, 14, 617, 12, 9, 13, 15, GR.1, 9, 13, 9, 2, 9, 13, 9, 31, 9, 14, 31, 17, 31, 17, 31. Last flown 28-2-19, arrived 29-9-21
			1-22
❑ 202	Sud Alouette III	72	ex Baldonnel, IAC. Ditched 20-10-95. Acquired 27-5-09 [13]	1-22
❑ 203*	Cessna FR.172H Rocket	72	ex Baldonnel, IAC. Reims-built. Last flew 4-10-19. Arrived 6-11-21
			1-22
❑ 218*	Fouga CM.170-1 Magister	~	ex Baldonnel, Shannon, Baldonnel, IAC, Austrian AF 4D-YU. Last flew 30-4-98. Arrived 6-11-21
			1-22
❑ -	Fieseler Fi 103 (V-1) FSM	c09	BAPC.403, acquired 1-10 [14]	1-22

■ **[1]** Ferguson replica built for BBC Belfast for a documentary screened in 9-16. Based on Harry Ferguson's second design of 1911. Construction led by boat-builder Alastair Duffin at Long Kesh 2-16. Piloted by William McMinn, it was flown at Bellarena in 5-16. Civil registration very brief, allocated 9-5-16, de-registered 1-6-16! **[2]** Rotec donated by Stuart Wilson. **[3]** Eurowing Goldwing donated by Jeff Salter. **[4]** Hi-Max built and donated by Maurice McKeown. **[5]** Robinson is on loan from Harold Hassard. **[6]** Cameron donated by Robin Mercer. **[7]** Monerai donated by Loudon Blair. **[8]** 'Flea' was built by the late Robert Wilbert Harris in the town in 1937. It was powered by a converted Austin 7, but is now fitted with an original Scott A2S. It is believed to have flown, at least once. It was used as a 'floatplane' in the 1936 coronation pageant at Moneymore. Reports that the wings and a propeller survive are being tracked down. **[9]** Quicksilver was built by Ernie Patterson. In August 1980 he flew it from the sands of Dundrum Bay, Newcastle, NI, to commemorate Harry Ferguson's flight of three miles on 8-8-1910. **[10]** Scamp partly built by Don Chisholm and finished by UAS volunteers. [11] Cygnet kit acquired by Don Chisholm; not assembled. **[12]** Jon Horswell notes that this machine was initially registered in 3-93) as a Glass S005E, the Sea Hawker having originated as the QuikKit Glass Goose = hence the nearly spelt-out S005E. **[13]** Alouette taken on charge by the IAC 22-3-72, ditched on 20-10-95 and struck off charge 31-10-95, with 7,100 hours on the clock. **[14]** V-1 was built by member James Herron.

Also: Last noted as far back as February 2014, Rallye EI-BGB has been deleted.

MOY on the A29 southeast of Dungannon
Moy Antiques: In The Square; has taken delivery of a Scout. ◆ **https://moyantiques.com**
- ❏ XW281* 'T' Westland Scout AH.1   69 ex Dungannon, Gortin, Plymouth Thruxton, G-BYNZ
                          G-BYNZ   (crashed 24-9-00, de-reg 5-2-01). Arrived 27-7-21   [1]   7-21
- ■ **[1]** Scout is/was fitted with the boom of XP883 - the rest of the latter is at Wymeswold, Leics.

NEWTOWNARDS AERODROME south of the town, between the A20 and A21   EGAD
- ❏ G-ARSX   Piper Tri-Pacer 160   56 ex Rathfriland, N2907Z. CoA 19-5-02, de-reg 12-2-02. Frame   1-20
- ❏ G-BANF   Luton Minor   77 ex Moneymore. CoA 5-6-92   1-20

PORTADOWN on the A3 southwest of Belfast
Gerald Hamill and Sons: The prototype Short 330 *may* linger at the yard. ◆ *By prior arrangement* **only**
- ❏ G-BSBH   Short 330   74 ex Sydenham, G-14-3000. De-reg 8-12-88   [1]   5-15
- ■ **[1]** *Bravo-Hotel* was the prototype, first flown 22-8-74.

RANDALSTOWN at the end of the M22 west of Antrim
Escarmouche Action Park: A *thinking* paintball site - escarmouche is French for skirmish!
◆ *By prior arrangement* **only** | www.escarmouche.com
- ❏ G-KNAP   Piper Warrior II   81 ex Aldergrove, G-BIUX, N9507N. Cr 13-7-99, de-reg 12-1-10.   5-15

SAINTFIELD on the A7 southwest of Belfast
The Wessex is *believed* still current in the general area.
- ❏ XS865   Westland Wessex HAS.1   65 ex Ballykinler, Lee-on-Solent, A2694, Wroughton, 771, 820.
                                         SOC 10-10-80. Camouflaged. First noted 6-13   1-18

STRABANE on the A5 south of Londonderry
Within the area, in *separate* locations, are two airframes. Last noted in July 2014, McCandless M4 G-BVLE has been deleted.
- ❏ G-BDRL   Stits Playboy   62 ex Londonderry, N730GF. CoA 17-6-98, de-reg 11-5-01   1-20
- ❏ G-BSZI   Cessna 152   84 ex N95139. De-reg 20-6-13   1-20

UPPER BALLINDERRY on the A26 north of Moria
A collector at a *private* location in the area *should* still have two airframes.
- ❏ EI-BAG   Cessna 172A   60 ex Langford Lodge, Upper Ballinderry, Portadown, Enniskillen,
                                         Abbeyshrule, G-ARAV, N9771T. CoA 26-6-79   2-14
- ❏ WD386   'O' DHC Chipmunk T.10   51 ex Dumfries, Firbeck, Cranfield, Tenby, St Athan, 1 FTS,
                                         Oxf UAS, 22 RFS, 2 BFTS. SOC 29-7-70   [1]   2-14
- ■ **[1]** WD386 has the rear fuselage of WD377 - see under Balcombe W Sussex.

IRELAND

ABBEYSHRULE AERODROME northwest of Mullingar, south of the N4 EIAB

Time for a tidy up: Rallye EI-AYT (last noted 11-13) and Cessna 172s EI-BIC and EI-CAA (both 9-15) have been deleted. Although very dated, the Tiger Moth is *believed* extant locally. Stored locally for many years, Taylorcraft Plus C2 EI-ALH is thought to have moved to East Anglia for restoration.

☐ EI-AOP	DH Tiger Moth	40	ex Dublin, G-AIBN, T7967, 18 EFTS, 1667 CU, 1 GCF,	
			16 PFTS. Morris Motors-built. Crashed 5-5-74, off-site	7-14
☐ F-GAIF	Wassmer Piranha	~	de-reg 6-07	9-20
☐ ZK-EVC	Piper Tomahawk	~	first noted 9-18	1-20

ARDAGH on the R521 south of Foynes

A *private* airstrip and glider store includes a long retired Rallye.

☐ EI-BNG*	MS Rallye Commodore	~	ex Abbeyshrule, D-EDZO, F-BRGY. De-reg 5-8-87	6-21

ASHBOURNE between the N2 and the N3 northwest of Dublin, Meath

Leo Murray's *private* and eclectic collection, the **Meath Aero Museum**. Dove 6 VP-YKF was due to move to <u>Shannon</u>, Ireland, by the time *W&R* was published: this has been anticipated. ◆ *By prior arrangement* **only**

☐ 'EI-ABH'	Mignet HM.14 'Flea'	99	fuselage and rudder	12-21
☐ EI-AWR	Malmo MFI-9 Junior	~	ex Bray, LN-HAG, SE-EBW	12-21
☐ VM657	Slingsby Tutor	IGA.6 47	ex Galway, Gort, Castlebridge, Cork, IGA,6, IAC.6, VM657,	
			126 GS, 146 GS. SOC 23-5-57. Arrived 20-3-01	12-21

■ [1] In 1962 the Tutor had a 'bit part' in the film *The Running Man* (Laurence Harvey, Alan Bates, Lee Remick, et al) in yellow colours.

The Ark Puddenhill: The activity centre *may* still have its airframes. ◆ *By prior arrangement* **only** | www.puddenhill.com

☐ EI-BHM	Cessna F.337E	77	ex Dublin, Farranfore, OO-PDC, OO-PDG. CoA 9-7-82	11-14
☐ E-402	Hawker Hunter F.51	56	ex Farnborough, Hurn, Kemble, Hurn, Macclesfield,	
			Dunsfold, G-9-433 (8-8-76), Danish AF Esk.724	7-17

ASKEATON Last noted in June 2017, the hulks of Cessna 337s N1CD and N3119K have been deleted.

BALDONNEL AIRFIELD or Casement, west of Dublin EIME

Irish Air Corps Museum and Heritage Centre: CM.170 216 moved to <u>Shannon</u>, Ireland, on 10th December 2021. CM.170 218 was delivered by road to <u>Long Kesh</u>, N Ireland, 6th November 2021.
◆ *By prior arrangement* **only** | *Baldonnel, Dublin 22, Ireland*

☐ C-7	Avro Cadet ✈	34	ex New Zealand ZK-AVR, Southampton, Abbeyshrule,	
			Terenure, EI-AGO, EI-AFO, IAC C-7	10-20
☐ '98'	Cessna 172B	61	ex Southend, G-ARLU, N8002X. Damaged 30-10-77,	
			de-reg 6-8-80. Instructional	10-18
☐ 141	Avro XIX Srs 2	46	ex Dublin, Baldonnel	10-20
☐ 164	DHC Chipmunk T.20	52	-	11-17
☐ 172	DHC Chipmunk T.20	52	ex Castle Archdale, Baldonnel. Fuselage	3-17
☐ 183	Percival Provost T.51	55	ex Dublin, Baldonnel	[1] 11-17
☐ 191	DH Vampire T.55	61	ex Gormanston, Dublin, Baldonnel. Hawarden-built	10-18
☐ 195	Sud Alouette III	63	ex F-WJDH. '30 Years' markings. Training aid	10-18
☐ 199	DHC Chipmunk T.20	51	ex Gormanston, G-APTF, T.10 WG320, TTCCF, Wyton SF,	
	G-APTF		18 RFS. Fuselage	3-17
☐ 206	Cessna FR.172H Rocket	72	Reims-built	10-19
☐ 215	Fouga CM.170-1 Magister	~	ex Dublin, Baldonnel, Katanga AF not delivered,	
			Austrian AF 4D-YJ. First noted 1-19	1-19
☐ 219	Fouga CM.170-1 Magister	~	-	10-18
☐ 231	SIAI-M SF-260WE Warrior	77	-	11-17
☐ WZ762	Slingsby Grasshopper TX.1	~	EI-135, ex Gowran Grange, Cosford, Rugby	[2] 3-17
☐ - c/no 1012	Sud Alouette III	~	non-flying training rig.	[3] 3-17

| ☐ | - | '3-KE' | Fouga CM.170-2 Magister | ~ | ex French Air Force No.79. 221 allocated. Fuselage | 11-17 |
| ☐ | - | | Wright Flyer replica | 03 | built on site | 9-18 |

■ **[1]** Provost 183's wings are fitted to fellow 184 at Dromod, Ireland – which see. The ones it is fitted with now have no attribution. **[2]** Grasshopper WZ762 is fitted with the wings of WZ756. **[3]** Alouette has the constructor's number 1153 painted on it.

Irish Air Corps Headquarters: By August 2020 Cessna FR.172H 210 had joined the museum at <u>Shannon</u>, Ireland. FR.172H 203, which took part in the farewell flypast on 4th October 2019 moved to <u>Long Kesh</u>, N Ireland, on 6th November 2021.

☐	205*	Cessna FR.172H Rocket	72	Reims-built. Last flew 4-10-19	10-19
☐	208*	Cessna FR.172H Rocket	72	Reims-built. Last flew 4-10-19	10-19
☐	EI-BXO	Fouga CM.170-2 Magister	c62	ex Dungannon, Saggart, Swords, Shannon, N18FM, Finnish AF FM-28. Valmet-built. Arrived by 4-14	6-17
☐	EI-RJZ*	HSA HS.146-RJ85	98	ex CityJet, N512XJ, G-6-326. Woodford-built. Flew in 17-4-20. Instructional	4-20
☐	G-ASNG	DH Dove 6	57	ex Waterford, Cork, (EI-BJW), Coventry, HB-LFF, G-ASNG, HB-LFF, G-ASNG, PH-IOM. Fuselage with Garda	9-15

Irish Historical Flight Foundation: See under Ballyboy, Ireland.

BALLINAMORE on the R199/R202 northeast of Carrick-on-Shannon

At a *private* workshop in the *general* area, a Bell Ranger is being restored.

| ☐ | G-BFPP* | Bell 47J-2 Ranger | 63 | ex Lee-on-Solent, F-BJAN, TR-LKD, F-OCBU. Crashed 11-7-97, CoA 11-11-99. First noted 8-21 | 8-21 |

■ **[1]** Tail boom of AB 47J-3B-1 EC-AXZ also present.

BALLYBOY east of the N52 southwest of Tullamore

Irish Historic Flight Foundation: The organisation officially moved in on 14th August 2020 – it was previously listed in *W&R* under Baldonnel. Construction of a hangar began at that time, with plans for a 'surfaced' runway. The fleet currently stands at: Chipmunk T.20s 168 (EI-HFA), 169 (EI-HFB) and '170' (EI-HFC), Boeing N2S-5 EI-AFD and the 'custodianship of Dragon EI-ABI – see under Dublin, Ireland. At the time of going to press public access was not possible but it was hoped to stage the occasional event and to attend other aviation gatherings. Keep an eye on: **www.irishhistoricflight.com**

Last noted in April 2011 Quasar G-MWJS has been deleted.

☐	EI-CUB	Piper J3C-65 Cub	46	ex G-BPPV, N88392. Off-site	2-17
☐	EI-ETC	Aeronca 15-AC Sedan	49	N915TC. ex G-CETC, HB-ETC	8-20
☐	G-MTKE*	Thruster TSM Mk.1	87	CoA 27-8-03, de-reg 20-3-09	8-20
☐	G-MVMM*	Aerial Arts Chaser	88	CoA30-7-04, de-reg 29-1-19	8-20

BANDON off the N71 southwest of Cork

ICP NewTech: The company builds remotely operated vehicles (ROVs) and has an ATR 42 in use for training 'drivers'.

◆ **Strictly** *by prior arrangement* **only** | www.icpnewtech.com

| ☐ | EC-LMX | ATR 42-320 | 88 | ex Shannon, EI-SLI, 5Y-BVD, EI-SLI, CS-TLR, PT-MTO, XA-TPZ, XA-MAR, F-WWEL. Fuselage. Arrived 23-5-15 | 6-21 |

CARLOW on the N9 southwest of Dublin

Carlow Institute of Technology: Kilkenny Road ◆ *By prior arrangement* **only** | www.itcarlow.ie

☐	EI-AMI	Piper Colt 108	61	ex Wexford, G-ARSU, EI-AMI, G-ARSU	9-19
☐	EI-AUE	MS Rallye Club	69	ex Kilkenny, G-AXHU	11-18
☐	EI-BGJ	Cessna F.152 II	r79	ex Kilrush. Reims-built	11-18
☐	EI-CUP	Cessna 335	80	ex Sligo, N2706X	11-18
☐	–	Monnett Sonerai II-LW	~	fuselage frame, c/n SAAC.23. Arrived during 2013	11-18
☐	G-HUGS	Robinson R22	90	ex Enniskillen. CoA 23-3-11, de-reg 21-2-11	11-18
☐	220	Fouga CM.170-1 Magister	~	ex Baldonnel, IAC	11-18

CELBRIDGE south of the M4, west of Dublin

A pair of dismantled Duchesses are held in store at a *private* location in the locality.

| ☐ | G-WACI* | Beech Duchess | 79 | ex Weston, N6703Y. CoA 22-11-12, de-reg 5-9-17 | 10-21 |
| ☐ | G-WACJ* | Beech Duchess | 80 | ex Weston, N6700Y. Damaged 10-7-11. CoA 22-7-11, de-reg 15-2-18 | 10-21 |

CLOGHAN on the N52 northeast of Mullingar
A Whirlwind *may* still be stored at a *private* location in the area.
☐ XP354   W'land Whirlwind HAR.10   62 ex Cricklade, Colsterworth, Halton 8721M (4-11-81), 22, 202   11-14

CLONBULLOGUE AERODROME on the R401 south of Kinnegad   EICL
By late 2021 Rallye EI-BKN and Cessna U206G EI-HOG had been cleared. The former moved to Craddenstown, Ireland.
☐ EI-BNK   Cessna U206F   71 ex G-HILL, PH-ADN, D-EEXY, N9506G. De-reg 31-10-12   10-21

CORK
Munster Airsoft ◆ *By prior arrangement* only | www.munsterairsoft.com
☐ EI-BBO   MS Rallye 180G   75 ex Limerick, F-BVNM. Fuselage, identity confirmed   7-18
☐ EI-BPJ   Cessna 182A   58 ex Limerick, Abbeyshrule, G-BAGA, N4849D. *The Hooker*   1-20

Locally: A VP-2 is stored at a *private* location in the *general* area.
☐ EI-BVT*   Evans VP-2   c76 ex G-BEIE (de-reg 2-8-91). Birdy   3-21

CORK AIRPORT   EICK
Irish Aviation Historians: Keep a Spitfire cockpit FSM at the airport.
☐ -   'FY-Y' V-S Spitfire FSM   ~ cockpit   6-19

COURTMACSHERRY Last noted in July 2017, Antonov An-2 G-BTCU has been deleted.

CRADDENSTOWN north of the R156, between Mullingar and Trim
☐ EI-BKN*   MS Rallye 100ST   ~ ex Clonbullogue, Weston, F-GBCK. De-reg 5-11-10. Fuselage   9-21
☐ EI-BVK*   Piper Tomahawk 112   ~ ex Newcastle (Wicklow), OO-FLG, OO-HLG, N9705N   9-21
☐ EI-DXN*   Zenair CH-601   ~ ex Newcastle (Wicklow). De-reg 201-20   9-21

CROOKSTOWN on the N9, south of Newbridge
Crookstown Craft Village: Should have a Cessna 401 on display | www.crookstowncraftvillage.com
☐ N9146N   Cessna 401B RAM   70 ex Weston   11-18

DROGHEDA on R132 north of Dublin
A gyrocopter is *thought* still to be stored in the locality.
☐ G-BRVR   Barnett J4B-2   89 ex Frosses. De-reg 21-4-09   5-19

DROMOD on the N4, north of Longford
South East Aviation Enthusiasts Group (SEAEG): Thanks to the **Cavan and Leitrim Railway** SEAEG has a great base within this extensive and friendly railway and transport centre. Due to Covid-19 restrictions and lockdowns the site closed in 2020 and it is hoped that it will open up again by the time *W&R* is published. Aeronautical and railway volunteers have not been idle, taking the time to refine the site and exhibits. See also Dublin, Ireland, for more of Phil Bedford's collection.
◆ *On the L1600 out of Dromod, alongside the mainline railway station* | *SEAEG: Philip Bedford,* **pbedford@tcd.ie** | *Cavan and Leitrim: Station Road, Dromod,* | **00 353 9638599** | **dromodrailway@gmail.com** | **www.cavanandleitrim.com**

☐ EI-BDM	Piper Aztec 250D	69	ex New Ross, Waterford, Kildimo, G-AXIV, N6826Y	[1]	1-22
☐ EI-CVW*	Bensen B-8V	98	arrived 14-8-21	[2]	1-22
☐ EI-ETE	MS Rallye Club	71	ex Newcastle (Wicklow), G-BXZT, OO-EDG, D-EBDG, F-BSVL. Arrived 23-6-17.		1-22
☐ EI-100	SZD Mucha	58	ex OY-XAN. CoA 1-7-97		1-22
☐ EI-139	Slingsby Cadet TX.3 EI-GMH	53	ex New Ross, Gowran Grange, BGA.3485, Falgunzeon, Motor Cadet III G-BOKG, TX.3 XE789, 553 GS, 662 GS, 663 GS, 661 GS, 31 GS. CoA 2-8-97	[1] [3]	1-22
☐ –	Mignet HM.14 'Flea'	35	IAHC.1, ex New Ross, Waterford, Dublin, Coonagh. *St Patrick*. Off-site	[4]	1-22
☐ G-AKGE	Miles Gemini 3C	47	ex New Ross, Waterford, Kilbrain, EI-ALM, G-AKGE. CoA 7-6-74, de-reg 30-5-84. Cockpit	[1] [5]	1-22

☐ G-ANIS	Taylorcraft Auster 5	44	ex Longford, AOP.V TJ375, 1952 Flt. CoA 19-9-76, de-reg 8-10-81		1-22
☐ G-AOIE	Douglas DC-7C	56	ex 'EI-AWA', New Ross, Waterford, Shannon, PH-SAX, G-AOIE Caledonian. *County of Perth*. Forward fuselage	[1]	1-22
☐ G-OGGS	Thunder Colt Ax-8 HAB	89	CoA 10-2-95, de-reg 12-12-01		1-22
☐ CBK	DFS Grunau Baby III	c48	BGA.1410, ex New Ross, Naas, Breighton, Stoke-on-Trent, Firbeck, RAFGSA.378, D-4676. CoA 2-4-83	[1]	1-22
☐ CBZ	Slingsby Tutor	c44	BGA.1424, ex New Ross, Naas, Gowran Grange, Jurby, RAFGSA.214, RA877. CoA 4-4-78. Stored in a bus	[1] [6]	1-22
☐ VP-BDF	Boeing 707-321	61	ex New Ross, Waterford, Dublin, N435MA, G-14-372, G-AYAG, N759PA. *Spirit of 73*. Cockpit	[1]	1-22
☐ NC285RS	NAA Navion	46	ex New Ross, Naas, Abbeyshrule, N91488. Crashed 11-6-79. *My Way*. Cockpit, rear fuselage, tail	[1]	1-22
☐ 173	DHC Chipmunk T.20	52	ex New Ross, Waterford, Gormanston, IAC	[7]	1-22
☐ 184	Percival Provost T.51	55	ex New Ross, Waterford, Baldonnel, IAC	[7] [8]	1-22
☐ 187	DH Vampire T.55	56	ex New Ross, Waterford, Baldonnel, IAC. Hawarden-built. Cockpit	[7] [9]	1-22
☐ 192	DH Vampire T.55	61	ex New Ross, Waterford, Baldonnel, IAC. Hawarden-built. Dismantled	[7] [9]	1-22
☐ RA881	Slingsby Cadet TX.1	c44	ex New Ross, Breighton, Halfpenny Green, RAFGSA 163. Cockpit, stored	[1] [6]	1-22

■ **[1]** Airframes on loan from the leading light of the group, Philip Bedford. **[2]** Built, and owned by, Fergus Kavanagh. **[3]** EI-139 has been brought back to Cadet TX.3 status. It is hoped to fly it again and it has the registration EI-GMH reserved for it. **[4]** 'Flea' is on loan from the Aviation Society of Ireland Preservation Group. A 1935 Douglas flat twin has been acquired for it. **[5]** See also Holywood, Northern Ireland, for more on G-AKGE. **[6]** Phil Bedford is restoring T.8 Tutor CBZ to its original 1944 condition as a long-span Cadet TX.2. CBZ was converted into an enclosed cockpit motor glider and will use the cockpit of RA881 in the rebuild. Phil owns CBZ along with Damian Smyth. **[7]** Airframes on loan from the Department of Defence. **[8]** Provost 184 has the wings of 183 (see Baldonnel) Ireland. **[9]** Vampire 187's 'pod' came on site 30-1-2011. Its wings are fitted to 192.

DUBLIN

National Museum of Ireland: Within the impressive Collins Barracks. ◆ *Benburb Street* | www.museum.ie

☐ 34	Miles Magister	39	ex Baldonnel, Dublin, Baldonnel, RAF N5392 n/s. Phillips & Powis-built	[1]	9-21
☐ 198	DH Vampire T.11	55	ex Baldonnel, XE977, 8 FTS. Hawarden-built	[2]	9-21

■ **[1]** Magister 34 was delivered from new 22-2-39 and became an instructional airframe 11-3-52. **[2]** Vampire 198 was never operated by the IAC, having been acquired ex-RAF as a training aid 30-8-63.

Philip Bedford: Keeps his Auster and Proctor at a *private* site in the locality. See also Dromod, Ireland.

☐ EI-ACY	Auster J1 Autocrat	46	ex Dromore, G-AIBK. Crashed 6-4-67	[1]	1-22
☐ G-AHWO	Percival Proctor V	46	ex Whitehall, Dublin, (EI-ALY). Cr 5-5-59, de-reg 17-11-60		1-22

■ **[1]** Philip is now the sole owner of *Charlie-Yankee*.

Merchants Arch Bar and Restaurant: Wellington Quay. A Sonerai 'soars' over the diners. www.merchantsarch.ie

☐ -	Monnet Sonerai II	78	c/n SAAC.6. Unflown, installed 3-16	3-20

Others: Last noted in November 2014 at the Civil Defence School in Phoenix Park, Skipper EI-BHT has been deleted. The Portlaoise Plane Restoration Project Aldritt Monoplane moved to Portlaoise, Ireland, early in 2021. A Viscount cockpit is preserved at a *private* location. in the general area.

☐ EI-AOH	Vickers Viscount 808	67	ex Dublin Airport, Aer Lingus, PH-VII. Scrapped 12-72. *St Fiacre*. Cockpit	10-18

DUBLIN AIRPORT or Collinstown

Dragon EI-ABI is stored at the airport. Technically it is part of the Irish Historic Flight Foundation - see Ballyboy, Ireland.

☐ EI-ABI	DH Dragon	36	ex EI-AFK, G-AECZ, AV982, EE, 7 AACU, 110 Wing, G-AECZ. *Iolar*. Stored by 9-19	[1]	8-20
☐ EI-CJD	Boeing 737-204	83	ex Ryanair, G-BKHE, G-BKGU. Rescue / tow-training		1-20

■ **[1]** EI-ABI represents the first Aer Lingus aircraft, 1936. Factoid: The original EI-ABI was previously G-ACPY and returned to the UK in 1938. It was shot down by a Ju 88 off the Scilly Isles on 3rd June 1941.

Technological University Dublin - Aviation Technology Centre: Within the Dublin Airport Business Park.
◆ *By prior arrangement* only | www.tudublin.ie

☐ EI-AWH	Cessna 210J Centurion	69	ex Rathcoole, G-AZCC, 5N-AIE, N616FN, N1734C.	
			De-reg 13-4-99. Arrived 14-1-19	1-19
☐ EI-CGU	Robinson R22	81	ex Dublin, G-BSNH, N9065D. De-reg 16-4-97. DIT titles	1-19
☐ N829AA	Learjet 25B	72	ex N25TK, N741F, N741E, N262JE	1-19
☐ N7205R	Beech A36 Bonanza	~	ex Dublin, Ballingarry. Accident 9-8-02. Cockpit, simulator	9-12

Simtech Flight Crew Training: At the Airport Logistics Park operates ATR72, A320 and 737-800 sims. Last noted in August 2011 the cockpit of HS.146 G-NJIB is no longer used. ◆ *By prior arrangement* only |www.simtech.ie

Also: Super Ace G-AKVF moved to St Athan, Wales on 3rd July 2020. Venom FB.50s 'VV612' (G-VENI) and 'WR421' (G-BHTT) made the trek to Shannon, Ireland.

DUBLIN WESTON AIRPORT near Leixlip   EIWT

Last recorded in April 2019, JetRanger II G-JBDB had moved off-site by mid-2020. Duchesses G-WACI and 'J had moved to Celbridge, Ireland, by late 2021. Pembroke XL954 (G-BXES) departed in December, arriving at St Athan, Wales, on the 14th. Efforts to find a new home for Buccaneer S.2B XV863 were exhausted by the end of December 2021 and it was broken up in mid-January 2022.

☐ EI-AUH	Cessna F.172H	~	ex Kilkenny. Reims-built. Cr 10-5-72, de-reg 28-8-86.	
			Fuselage	10-21
☐ EI-BSF	HS HS.748-1/105	62	ex Baldonnel, Dublin, Ryanair, EC-DTP, G-BEKD, LV-HHF,	
			LV-PUM. *Spirit of Tipperary*. CoA 21-5-87, de-reg 26-7-94.	
			Fuselage, rescue trainer. Arrived 10-14	10-21
☐ EI-BUA*	Cessna 172M	~	ex N5458H. First noted 10-21	10-21
☐ EI-CCK	Cessna 152 II	~	ex N24251. De-reg 5-11-12. Fuselage	10-21
☐ EI-CDV	Cessna 150G	~	ex N2777S. First noted 4-19	10-21
☐ EI-CFN*	Cessna 150G	~	ex N5446K. De-reg 13-11-07. Rescue tnr, first noted 10-21	10-21
☐ EI-CGG	Forney Aircoupe 415C	~	ex N2522H. CoA 10-00. de-reg 6-11-12. Rescue trainer	10-21
☐ EI-GSE*	Cessna F.172M	~	ex D-EDXO. De-re 27-1-14. First noted 10-21	10-14
☐ G-BHIA	Cessna F.152 II	80	de-reg 23-7-92. Reims-built. Fuselage	10-21
☐ G-BPBI	Cessna 152	79	de-reg 11-2-91. Fuselage	10-21
☐ G-SEAI	Cessna U.206G	77	ex N756FQ. CoA 12-6-08, de-reg 20-5-21. Floatplane	10-21
☐ N4575C	Grumman Goose	45	ex Superior Oil, USAF OA-13B 45-49088, USN JRF-5 87726	10-21

DUN LAOGHAIRE Last noted in November 2014, Super Cruiser EI-ADV has been deleted.

DUNSHAUGHLIN on the N3 northwest of Dublin

A cache of French types is held at a *private* storage site in the locality.

☐ EI-ATS	MS Rallye Club	~	de-reg 14-6-11	1-20
☐ EI-BBJ	MS Rallye Club	~	ex Clonbullogue, Weston, F-BUVX. De-reg 5-11-10	1-20
☐ EI-BMJ	MS Rallye Club	~	ex Coonagh, F-BXTG. De-reg 6-10-09	1-20
☐ EI-BNU	MS Rallye Club	~	ex Weston, F-BPQV	1-20
☐ EI-BUG	SOCATA ST-10 Diplomate	71	ex Weston, G-STIO, OH-SAB. CoA 8-98	1-20
☐ G-HOLY	SOCATA ST-10 Diplomate	70	ex F-BSCZ. CoA 26-9-05, re-reg 22-10-15	1-20

Others: Also in the locality are three other aircraft, at *separate* locations.

☐ EI-AKM	Piper J-3C-65 Cub	~	ex N88194. CoA 30-6-60	12-21
☐ EI-AUS	Auster J5F Aiglet Trainer	52	ex Powerscourt, G-AMRL. CoA 2-12-75, de-reg 18-11-12	2-16
☐ EI-FFT	Forney F.1A Aircoupe	61	ex G-AROO, N25B	1-20

EDGEWORTHSTOWN on the N4 between Longford and Mullingar

Midland Karting and Paintballing ◆ *By prior arrangement* only | www.actionsports.ie

☐ EI-ATK	Piper Cherokee 140	67	ex G-AVUP. De-reg 22-2-11	2-19
☐ EI-BKE	MS Rallye	~	ex F-BKUN, F-WKUN. De-reg 16-9-86	2-19
☐ EI-CFV	MS Rallye Club	71	ex Abbeyshrule, G-OLFS, G-AYYZ	2-19
☐ EI-CHN	MS Rallye	67	ex Abbeyshrule, G-AVIO. Fuselage	2-19

ENNISCRONE or Inishcrone, on the R297 north of Ballina
Quirky Nights Glamping Village: Development of this ambitious site, which includes railway carriages, buses and specialised 'pods', continues. ◆ *By prior arrangement* **only**

❏ EI-CZD	Boeing 767-216ER	86 ex Shannon, Transaero, N762TA, CC-CJU, N4529T	
		Arrived 5-16	9-19

FOYNES on the N69 west of Limerick
Foynes Flying-Boat and Maritime Museum: This exceptional venue is within the former transatlantic flying-boat terminal and control tower. The fantastic Boeing 314 'Clipper' 'walk-in' exhibit must be sampled to be believed. Two grants approved in April 2021 look set to further transform this venue. A total of €2.25m from the Rural Regeneration and Development Fund and the Department of Tourism, Culture and Arts will go towards a €4.2m plan to create a viewing gallery, 112-seat cinema, archive zone and conference facilities.
◆ *Foynes, Limerick, Ireland* | **00 353 69 65416** | **email** via website | **www.flyingboatmuseum.com**

❏ -	Boeing 314 'Clipper' FSM	06 BAPC.594, PanAm colours	3-20

FROSSES on the R262 between Killybegs and Donegal
A Tiger Cub is stored at a *private* site in the locality.

❏ G-MMJS	MBA Tiger Cub	c87 ex Drogheda, Newry. De-reg 7-9-94	1-22

GLENTIES Last noted in October 2018 KB.2 EI-CVY has been deleted.

Thruster T600 G-MZNY, July 2021.
Ian Thompson

KILKENNY on the N76 / N10, north of Waterford
National Reptile Zoo: The entrance hall is graced by a microlight, in a suitably reptilian colour scheme.
◆ *Hebron Business Park* | **info@nationalreptilezoo.ie** | **www.nationalreptilezoo.ie**

❏ G-MZNY*	Thruster T600 450N	98 de-reg 17-3-21. First noted 7-21	7-21

Also: Aeronca Sedan EI-BJJ had moved on by August 2020 - no 'forwarding address'.

KILTIERNAN Last noted at Skirmish Paintball in November 2014 the hulk of Cessna 182 EI-BDP has been deleted.

KNOCK IRELAND WEST AIRPORT on the N17, southwest of Charlestown   EIKN

❏ YU-AON	Boeing 737-3Q4	87 ex Air Serbia, JAT, N181LF, S7-RGL, PT-TEF.	
		Last flight 28-3-14. Rescue trainer	5-21

LIMERICK on the N24 southwest of Shannon

A Silvaire is kept in the *general* area. The cockpit of a former Shannon 727 may still be at the United Metals yard.

☐ G-AFZK	Luscombe 8A Silvaire	39	ex N25118. CoA 15-6-09	N9-20
☐ EC-CFA	Boeing 727-256	73	ex Shannon, N907RF, Iberia. *Jeres Xeres Sherry.*	
			Cockpit. Arrived mid-2018	6-19

LIMETREE AERODROME north of Portlaoise

Last noted in August 2014 the following have been deleted: Cessna 140 G-BSUH, Puma Sprint G-MMTJ, Pegasus G-MMTK.

| ☐ G-MNGB | Mainair Gemini Flash | 84 | CoA 19-4-98, de-reg 4-5-01 | 11-18 |

LOUGHREA Last noted in September 2016 EC120 EI-PJW and Bell 222 N222WX have been deleted.

MAYNOOTH AERODROME or Dolly's Grove, north of the M4 and the town, south of the R156

The three airframes are dramatically mounted alongside the hangars.

☐ ES-YLK	Aero L29 Delfin	~	ex Cork	9-19
☐ LY-AFO	Antonov An-2 *Colt*	~	ex Cork	9-18
☐ XZ995	'3G' HS Harrier GR.3	86	ex Lowestoft, Shoreham, Ipswich, St Mawgan 92220M,	
	G-CBGK		Chivenor, 1417 Flt, 4, 3, 233 OCU, 3. De-reg 14-3-05	9-19

Also: An Auster is *believed* stored in the area.

| ☐ EI-AMY | Auster J1N Alpha | 50 | ex Powerscourt, Kells, G-AJUW. De-reg 18-10-12. Fuselage | 12-15 |

MILTOWNPASS AERODROME on the N6 west of Dublin

| | | | | EIMP |
| ☐ EI-DUV* | Beech Baron B55 | 73 | ex N3045W. Fuselage | 8-20 |

NEWBRIDGE north of the M7, southwest of Dublin

A Venom cockpit is kept in the *general* area.

| ☐ 'WR360' | 'K' DH Venom FB.50 | 56 | ex Portarlington, Hurn, Swiss AF J-1626. CoA 22-4-03, | |
| | G-DHSS | | de-reg 5-3-13. Swiss-built. Cockpit. | 1-20 |

NEWCASTLE AERODROME on the R671 north of Wicklow

| | | | | EINC |
| ☐ G-BTSN | Cessna 150G | 67 | ex N3806J. CoA 16-12-14, de-reg 4-6-18. Fuselage, rescue tnr | 5-19 |

PORTLAOISE at the N7 / N8 junction southwest of Dublin

Portlaoise Plane Restoration Project: Early in 2021 the Aldritt Monoplane project moved to a location in the *general* area. The plan is to display the monoplane at a suitable venue; negotiations are on-going.

◆ *Visits **not** possible - keep an eye on the website* | **www.portlaoiseplane.com**

| ☐ -* | Aldritt Monoplane | 1909 | IAHC.2, ex Donabate, Wannock, Portlaoise. | |
| | | | Acquired 27-11-18; unveiled 21-8-21 | [1] 8-21 |

■ [1] Designed and built by motor engineers Frank and Louis Aldritt at Portlaoise, it carried out a limited number of flights from 11-09.

RATHCOOLE AERODROME south of the N72 and Dromagh

| | | | | EIRT |

Although dated, both airframes are *thought* to be current.

| ☐ EI-AFN | BA Swallow 2 | 38 | ex G-AFGV. Off-site | 5-16 |
| ☐ G-AXVV | Piper J3C-65 Cub | 44 | ex F-BBQB, L-4H 43-29572. CoA 16-6-73, de-reg 12-4-99 | 7-17 |

ROSCOMMON Last noted in October 2018 Demon G-MBCM has been deleted.

ROSCREA at the N7 northeast of Limerick

A Jodel is held at a *private* location in the *general* area.

| ☐ G-BMLB* | Jodel D.140A Paris-Nice | 65 | ex F-BNCI. CoA 20-10-09, de-reg 16-5-11. Wassmer-built | [1] 8-20 |

■ [1] De-registered as sold in Ireland.

ROUNDWOOD on the R765 west of Newtown Mount Kennedy
Special Ops East - North Wicklow: ◆ *By prior arrangement* only | **www.specialops.ie**

❑ -	MS Rallye		~ camouflaged fuselage	11-17

SHANNON AIRPORT on the N19 between Limerick and Ennis   EINN
Atlantic Airadventures: Shannon Aviation Museum and **Shannon Flight Simulation Centre**, on the airport industrial area. The Irish Aviation Foundation CLG - the organisation behind the museum - initiated a new hangar in August 2020. Seneca G-GFCD was used as the basis of a fixed based simulator and was effectively scrapped.
◆ *Aviation Education Centre, Link Road* | **00 353 061363687** | **info@shannonaviationmuseum.com** | **https://shannonaviationmuseum.com**

❑ EI-CIA	MS Rallye	68	ex Toomyvara, G-MONA, G-AWJK. De-reg 3-2-11			1-22
❑ EI-CIN*	Cessna 150K	70	ex Shannon Training Centre, Weston, G-OCIN, EI-CIN,			
			G-BSXG, N6228G. Stored			1-22
❑ EI-COZ	Piper Cherokee 140C	70	ex Abbeyshrule G-AYMZ, N11C. De-reg 16-5-13			1-22
❑ EI-SLM	ATR 42-310	94	ex Aer Lingus, Air Contractors, N643AS, F-WWLC.			
			Accident 17-7-11. Forward fuselage			1-22
❑ G-AVMZ	BAC 111-510ED	69	ex Alton, Hurn, European, BA, BEA. CoA 17-2-02, de-reg			
			10-6-03. Forward fuselage			1-22
❑ G-BAHI	Cessna F.150H	68	ex Little Staughton, PH-EHA. Reims-built. CoA 14-12-07.			
			Fuselage			1-22
❑ G-BTVV	Cessna F.337G	73	ex Weston, PH-RPD, N1876M. Reims-built. CoA 12-1-03			1-22
❑ G-CDPF	HSA HS.146-300	89	ex Lasham, Southend, Air Wisconsin N614AW, G-5-132.			
			Hatfield-built. Cockpit - simulator. De-reg 23-6-07			1-22
❑ -	Monnett Monerai	~	fuselage	[1]	1-22
❑ -	Bede BD-5B Micro	~	ex Glasgow. Long-span wings			1-22
❑ -*	Dragon 150	~	arrived 10-21	[2]	1-22
❑ C-GAPW	Boeing 737-275	74	ex Canadian, N127AW, C-GAPW. Simulator	[3]	1-22
❑ D-3229	Scheibe Bergfalk 55/II	~	suspended in main building			1-22
❑ 5N-ABJ	Boeing 707-3F9C	71	ex Limerick, Shannon, Nigeria Airways. Cockpit.			
			Arrived 2-9-15	[4]	1-22
❑ VP-YKF*	DH Dove 6	50	ex Ashbourne, '176', Omagh, New Ross, Waterford, Cork,			
			Dublin, 3D-AAI, VQ-ZJC, G-AMDD. Accident, Cork, 8-82			**due**
❑ 210*	Cessna FR.172H Rocket 72		ex IAC, Baldonnel. Reims-built. Last 'op' 4-10-19. F/n 8-20			1-22
❑ 216*	Fouga CM.170-1 Magister	~	ex Baldonnel, Cork, Baldonnel, Austrian AF 4D-YK.			
			Arrived 10-12-21			1-22
❑ -	V-S Spitfire FSM	c98	ex Lytham St Annes. Cockpit, built by Richard Jones			1-22
❑ VS562	Avro Anson T.21	48	ex Market Drayton, Coventry, Crowland, Llanbedr,			
			Portsmouth, Llanbedr 8012M (9-4-65), A&AEE.			
			Forward fuselage			1-22
❑ 'VV612'*	DH Venom FB.50	55	ex Dublin area, Portarlington, Hurn, 'WE402', Swiss AF			
	G-VENI		J-1523. CoA 25-7-01, de-reg 5-3-13. Swiss-built.			
			Silver colours. First noted 12-21			1-22
❑ 'WR421'*	DH Venom FB.50	56	ex Dublin area, Portarlington, Hurn, G-BMOC, Swiss AF			
	G-DHTT		J-1611. Swiss-built. CoA 17-7-99, de-reg 5-3-13.			
			Red colours. First noted 12-21			1-22
❑ 'WR410'	DH Venom FB.50	54	ex Portarlington, Hurn, G-BMOD, Swiss AF J-1539.			
	G-DHUU		Swiss-built. CoA 24-5-02, de-reg 5-3-13. 6 Sqn c/s			1-22
❑ XM144	EE Lightning F.1	60	ex Spark Bridge, Pershore, Booker, Eaglescott,			
			Burntwood, Leuchars 8417M (28-5-74), Leuchars TFF,			
			23, Leuchars TFF, 226 OCU, 74. Cockpit. 74 Sqn c/s.			1-22
❑ XX826	'JH' SEPECAT Jaguar GR.1	75	ex Market Drayton, Welshpool, Ipswich, Cosford			
			9021M (10-1-90), Shawbury, 2, 20, 14. Cockpit			1-22
❑ XX897	Blackburn Buccaneer S.2B	76	ex Hurn, DRA Bedford, RAE, RRE. Tornado nose	[5]	1-22
❑ XZ654	Westland Lynx AH.7	80	ex Ipswich, M Wallop. First noted 6-15			1-22

■ **[1]** Monerai on loan from Larry Kelly. **[2]** Dragon donated by Olly Conway. **[3]** *Papa-Whisky* factoids: 71,151 hours, 74,613 landings and is now a fixed-base trainer for a 737-800 series. **[4]** The 707 cockpit is a returnee to Shannon, it flew in there in 1989 and was scrapped in 1998. It was latterly at the University of Limerick. **[5]** XX897 converted by Marshall of Cambridge in 1980 with Tornado F.2 style nose as part of the Foxhunter radar development programme.

Shannon Training Centre: Cessna 150K EI-CIN moved to the museum - above. ◆ *By prior arrangement* **only.**
❑ G-ORHE	Cessna Citation 1	74	ex Enniskillen, N619EA, G-OBEL, G-BOGA, N932HA, N93WD, N5220J. CoA 24-7-08, de-reg 19-8-11. Arr 22-10-18	10-18

SLIGO on the N16 west of Enniskillen
Gerry O'Hara: The airframes are *thought* to be still stored at a *private* location in the area.
❑ EI-BOV	Rand KR-2	r84	*Kitty Hawk*	3-16
❑ –	Sligo Concept	~	IAHC.7, single seat low wing monoplane, unflown	3-16
❑ –	O'Hara Gyroplane	~	IAHC.8, on Bensen lines, unflown	3-16

SLIGO AIRPORT or Strandhill, west of the town   EISG
Last noted in May 2014, Rallye G-BDEC has been deleted.
❑ G-ECAT	Fokker Friendship 500	86	ex G-JEAI, VH-EWY, PH-EXL. Damaged 2-11-02. CoA 16-12-02, de-reg 12-8-03. Rescue trainer	4-17
❑ XX631	'W' SAL Bulldog T.1	74	ex Northum UAS, 9 AEF, Northum UAS, CFS.	
	G-BZXS		CoA 7-5-10	N3-21

TRIM on the R154 northwest of Dublin, Meath
A Tri-Pacer is in the area, becoming a tail-dragger.
❑ EI-UFO	Piper Tri-Pacer 150	57	ex G-BRZR, N7045D	1-20

TUAMGRANEY on the R463/ R352 north of Killaloe, on the western shores of Lough Derg
Wastelands Salvage: An amazing recycling/upcycling/industrial-and-architectural salvage site, always worth a browse, still holds the exotic T-37 'Tweet'. **https//wastelandssalvage.com**
❑ 0931	Cessna T-37C	70	ex Brazilian Air Force. Fuselage, first noted 2-18	8-20

Opposite: The prototype Beagle Pup G-AVDF (see Turweston, Bucks) and Shuttleworth's Sopwith Pup '9917' (G-EBKY) performing at Old Warden, Beds, June 2021. *Paul Middleton*

APPENDIX
AND
INDEX SECTION

Appendix A : RAF OVERSEAS

British military aircraft in the *W&R* categories to be found on *Crown* territory or property.

CYPRUS
RAF Akrotiri:

☐ XD184		W'land Whirlwind HAR.10	54	ex 8787M (2-9-83), 84 'A' Flt, 1563F, 228, 155. Displayed	12-21
☐ XR504		Westland Wessex HC.2	63	ex 9327M, 84, 22, SARTS, 18, 1 FTU. Displayed	12-21
☐ XS929	'L'	EE Lightning F.6	67	ex 8970M (20-5-88), Binbrook, 11, LTF, 11, 56, 11. Displayed	12-21
☐ XV470	'BD'	McD Phantom FGR.2	69	ex 9156M, 56, 228 OCU, 11, 43, 228 OCU, 56, 228 OCU, 18, 228 OCU, 29, 228 OCU, 92, 228 OCU, 92, 56, 228 OCU, 31, 17, 14. Stored	10-21

GIBRALTAR
RAF North Front: *W&R27* (p354) recorded the removal of Jaguar GR.1 XX956 by mid-February 2020 and stated it was not known if it returned to the UK: it was in store at Boscombe Down, Wilts, by October 2021.

Appendix B : EXPORTS

All known exports are of course listed in the text, but not highlighted as such. This table highlights 'heritage' and former military exports: excluding general aviation types. Column 4 gives the location under which it was to be found within *W&R* and Column 5 the destination.

G-BKSX		Stampe SV-4C	Eggesford, Devon	Belgium 25-2-19, becoming OO-RTC	
N475EL	'EV-RAMP'	Boeing 737-500	Bournemouth, Dorset	China 6-20	
N733UK		Boeing 737-300	Bournemouth, Dorset	China 6-20	
MJ755	G-CLGS	Spitfire IX ✈	Biggin Hill, Gtr Lon	Greece 25-5-21	
MJ772	G-AVAV	Spitfire Tr.IX ✈	Biggin Hill, Gtr Lon	Netherlands 25-8-21	
PL344	G-IXCC	Spitfire IX	Northampto0n, Northants	Australia as VH-IUK 9-20	
WR985		Shackleton MR.3/3	St Mawgan, Cornwall	Russia, 28-10-21	[1]
XL602	G-BWFT	Hunter T.8M	St Athan, Wales	Canada 2019	
XV221		Hercules C.3 cockpit	St Athan, Wales	Turkey 3-3-21	
XX237		Hawk T.1	St Athan, Wales	Qatar, 6-21	
XX292		Hawk T.1W	Ipswich, Suffolk	USA mid-2020	
XX312		Hawk T.1W	St Athan, Wales	Qatar, 6-21	
XX445		Gazelle AH.1	Stapleford, Essex	Mozambique AF FA-085 2-21	
XZ130		Harrier GR.3	Selby, N Yorks	USA 4-20	
XZ996		Harrier GR.3	Ipswich, Suffolk	Germany by 10-20	
ZB673		Gazelle AH.1	Stapleford, Essex	Mozambique AF FA-083 2-21	
ZF510		Tucano T.1	Boscombe Down, Wilts	USA N889KT 6-20	
ZF511		Tucano T.1	Boscombe Down, Wilts	USA N511ZF 6-20	
ZJ649		Dassault Alpha Jet	Boscombe Down, Wilts	Canada C-GMBU 12-19	
ZJ650		Dassault Alpha Jet	Boscombe Down, Wilts	Canada C-GYMT 2-20	
ZJ651		Dassault Alpha Jet	Boscombe Down, Wilts	Canada C-GLZW 12-19	
ZJ652		Dassault Alpha Jet	Boscombe Down, Wilts	Canada C-GKFN 2-20	
ZJ653		Dassault Alpha Jet	Boscombe Down, Wilts	Canada 2-20	
ZJ654		Dassault Alpha Jet	Boscombe Down, Wilts	Canada C-GHZH 2-20	
ZJ655		Dassault Alpha Jet	Boscombe Down, Wilts	Canada C-GXNB 2-20	
ZJ656		Dassault Alpha Jet	Boscombe Down, Wilts	Canada C-GZEH 2-20	
ZK534		Hawk T.53	St Athan, Wales	USA 9-20	

■ [1] Along with the forward fuselage of Lancaster replica '976' (BAPC.553).

Appendix C : SUBMERGED

Unless readers are wet suit-equipped, airframes at dive sites are inaccessible. For completeness, this section gives brief details of 'aquatic' aircraft: 'Last noted' dates are given in brackets. Thanks to Anthony Mills for much of this material.

BLETCHLEY south of the A5, near Milton Keynes. **Blue Lagoon Diving Centre**: Cessna 150E G-ASVF was sunk here in 1984 (6-15). **www.mksac.co.uk**

CAPERNWRAY on the A6 north of Carnforth. **Capernwray Diving Centre**: Cessna F.150L G-BFWL (4-10); HS.748-2A G-BVOV (sunk 29-3-10); Dragonfly HR.3 WP503 (4-10); Wessex HU.5 XS491 (4-10). **www.dive-site.co.uk**

CLIFFE at the end of the B2000, north of Rochester. **Buckland Lake Reserve - Polaris Scuba**: Aztec 250E N54211 (submerged circa 5-12, it was last noted dumped on the lakeside 8-13) and the fuselage of Falcon 20 9M-BCR (8-13).

CROMHALL east of Thornbury. **Cromhall Quarry Diving Centre**: The cockpit of HS.125 VR-BMB had been removed by 2021. Wessex HU.5 XS488 (with the rear end of XR497) from Layer Marney, Essex, had arrived by late 2020, Also reported was Commander N5834N. **www.cromhallquarry.co.uk**

CROUGHTON on the B4031 southwest of Brackley. *W&R24* (p174) covered the 'emergence' of Piper Apache G-BFSK which had been submerged in a lake by a diving club in 1994. No news since...

ECCLESTON on the B5250 south of Leyland. **Delph Scuba Diving Centre:** The forward fuselage of a Short 330 G-SSWR and Jet Provost T.4 XP688, both noted 6-16. **www.thedelph.com**

GODSTONE junction of A22/A25 east of Redhill. **Divers Cove**: Cherokee 140 G-ZANG (8-16) and Cherokee 180C G-ATXM cockpit (ex Southend), the later first noted 8-16. **www.diverscove.co.uk**

HARLECH Known as *The Maid of Harlech*, **Lockheed P-38F Lightning 41-7677** became the first legally designated crash site during 2019. This 14th FG machine force-landed just off the coast on 27th September 1942, the pilot was rescued.

LOUGH FOYLE Northern Ireland. Sometimes visible off shore is the hulk of **Corsair II JT693** 'R' of 1837 Flight, which crashed on 9th October 1944. A good viewpoint is from a car park at Engine Corner, Shore Road, north of Ballykelly.

NORTH CAVE west of Hull. **Eight Acre Lake**: Unidentified Puma HC.1 circa 2014. **www.scubadream.co.uk**

PORTSMOUTH Defence Diving School: Since 1997 Wessex HU.5 XT760 has been in a lake off Horsea Island. It is/was fitted with the rear fuselage of XT604 - see East Midlands Airport, Leics.

STONEY STANTON on the B581 east of Hinckley. **Stoney Cove - The National Diving Centre**: Wessex HU.5 XT768 (4-17), the forward fuselage of Viscount 814 G-AWXI (4-17) and Partenavia P.68 G-LOUP (4-17). There is only one Wessex here, the other: HU.5 XT770 is reported to have come here from Shawell, Leics, in 2008. **www.stoneycove.com**

TAMWORTH Dosthill Diving Centre: The fuselage of Jetstream 31 G-WMCC (7-17) was delivered from Sandwell, W Mids, on 12-4-15 for submerging in the lake. **www.divedozzi.com**

TIDENHAM, on the A48 northeast of Chepstow. **National Diving and Activity Centre**: HS.146-100 G-JEAU (sunk 17-12-07); an Aztec; Sea Devon C.20 XK896 fuselage (G-RNAS - 2-08); Wessex HAS.3 XS122 (12-13) and Wessex HC.2 XT607 (1-12). **www.ndac.co.uk**

UPPER VOBSTER on minor road west of Frome. **Vobster Quay**: Sea King HC.4 ZA299 (submerged 23-1-18) and HS.748-2A G-AVXJ (5-17) is split into three sections. **www.vobsterquay.co.uk**

WHITTLESEY on the A605 east of Peterborough. **Dive In**: Short 360 G-ROOM (7-17) and Jet Provost T.3 XM467 (7-17). **www.divein.co.uk**

WOMERSLEY south of the M62, west of the A19. **Blue Lagoon Diving and Leisure Centre**: As well as Hunter T.8C WT799 on show on the surface (see main section) in the depths is MS Rallye G-BLIY (sunk 2012) and Hunter F.6A XJ639, (sunk 7-06). **via Facebook**

WRAYSBURY south of Colnbrook. **Wraysbury Dive Centre**: The forward fuselage of Boeing 737 G-CELA arrived from Cotswold (Kemble) 5-19 and submerged 26-8-20. **www.wraysbury.ws**

Appendix D : 'COCKPITFEST'

Staged at the Newark Air Museum, *CockpitFest* is a unique occasion in the aviation 'year'. Awards are as follows: 'Grand Champion' (GC) as judged by the attending public; 'Cockpiteers' Cockpit' (CC) voted for by the attending 'cockpiters'; and *Wrecks & Relics* 'Spirit of *CockpitFest*' (*W&R*) awarded by the author of this 'ere book! Occasionally, a 'Spirit' prize is also given by the museum. Presentations are also made for flying clothing etc, but these are not applicable here.

Information is given as follows: Column 1 gives type and identity plus award (if applicable); Column 2 location at that time. Readers seeking more information should look at: **www.newarkairmuseum.org**

CockpitFest XXI Newark, 20th-21st June 2020
Postponed due to the Boris-19 Pandemonium - see below

CockpitFest XXI reprise Newark, 28th-30th <u>August</u> 2021

Airedale EI-BBK	*W&R*	Doncaster, S Yorks*
Buccaneer S.2 EMU	*W&R*	Doncaster, S Yorks
Buccaneer S.2B XX899		resident
Canberra PR.9		resident
Cessna 140 G-BTYX		Doncaster, S Yorks*
Dove 6 G-ANAP		March, Cambs
Dragon Rapide FSM 'G-AJCL'		Liverpool, Merseyside
Enstrom 280 HB-XMO		Doncaster, S Yorks
Harrier GR.3 XV810		Walcott, Lincs
Harvard II FX322		Doncaster, S Yorks
HS.125-1B/522 G-BOCB		
	W&R	St Athan, Wales
Jet Provost T.5 G-BYED		Metheringham, Lincs
Lightning F.2A XN728	GC CC	Binbrook, Lincs
Lightning F.6 XR757		resident
'Missfire'		Doncaster, S Yorks*
P-51D Mustang SIM		Amesbury, Wilts
Phantom FGR.2 XV490		resident

Provost T.1 'XF545'	Leicester, Leics**
	Newark 'Spirit'
Pup HB-NAV	Doncaster, S Yorks*
Schleicher K.8b '522'	Doncaster, S Yorks
Sea Vixen FAW.2 XN651	Lavendon, Bucks
Slingsby Dart '404'	Doncaster, S Yorks
Starduster G-BNNA	Doncaster, S Yorks*
Tempest V SN280	Doncaster, S Yorks

Notes: * Airedale, Cessna, 'Missfire', Pup and Starduster were part of the South Yorkshire Aircraft Museum's 'Civvie Street' line-up. Owner Bill Fern was presented with a *W&R Spirit* award for these, particularly the Airedale. ** Also with the Provost was the instrument facia and controls of a Brasov IS-28M2A motor glider, beyond the remit of *W&R*, but as it is designed for 'small people' and disabled access, well worthy of a mention.

Any ideas? Bill Fern's 'Missfire' cockpit, August 2021. (See page 273) *Ken Ellis*

South Yorkshire Aircraft Museum's 'Civvie Street' line-up at *CockpitFest XXI*, August 2021. Front to back: Schleicher K.8b '552', Slingsby Dart 15 '404', Enstrom 280 HB-XMO, Airedale EI-BBK, Cessna 140 G-BTYX, Pup 150 HB-NAV, Starduster Too G-BNNA, 'Missfire' 'W-F'. In the foreground is Tempest V SN280 and in the background Buccaneer S.2B XX899, Harvard II FX322, T-33A 51-9036, MiG-27K '71' and MiG-23M '458'. *Ken Ellis*

Magazines

Air North, North East Branch of Air-Britain, monthly | ajmurray1967@blueyonder.co.uk | www.airnorth.org
Aviation News and Review, LAAS International, monthly | laasint@btinternet.com | www.laasdata.com
FlyPast, monthly magazine from Key Publishing | **01780 480404** | subs@keypublishing.com | www.key.aero/flypast
Humberside Air Review, Humberside Aviation Society, monthly 'e-zine', also publish an excellent annual *Residents Review*
  | pwildf117@yahoo.com
Irish Air Letter, published by Paul Cunniffe, Karl E Hayes and Eamon C Power, monthly (also available as an 'e-zine')
  | ial.magazine@upcmail.ie
Military Aviation Review, Military Aircraft Photographs, monthly and 'e-zine' plus sister journal *@MAR* |
  redbrae99@gmail.com
Scottish Air News, Central Scotland Aviation Group, monthly (also available as an 'e-zine') and also publishes the annual
  Scottish Register | scansubs@googlemail.com | www.scottishairnews.co.uk
Ulster Air Mail, published by the Ulster Aviation Society, monthly | **membership@ulsteraviationsociety.org** |
  www.ulsteraviationsociety.org

Books

The following have been on and off the shelves with great speed and are regarded as trusted friends:
British Civil Aircraft Register 1919-1999, Michael Austin, Air-Britain, 1999
Category Five, RAF Aircraft Losses 1954 to 2009, Colin Cummings, Nimbus Publishing, 2010, plus *Final Landings* (2001) and
  Last Take-off (2000) in this exceptional series
Fleet Air Arm Fixed-Wing Aircraft since 1946, Ray Sturtivant with Mick Burrow and Lee Howard, Air-Britain, 2004 –
  a masterpiece!
Fleet Air Arm Helicopters since 1943, Lee Howard, Mick Burrow and Eric Myall, Air-Britain, 2010 - likewise!
Great Aviation Collections of Britain, Ken Ellis, Crécy Publishing, Manchester, 2013
Local Aviation Collections of Britain, Ken Ellis, Crécy Publishing, Manchester, 2017
Royal Air Force Aircraft XA100 to XZ999, Jim Halley, Air-Britain, 2001 – and others in the series
Royal Air Force Flying Training & Support Units since 1912, Ray Sturtivant, John Hamlin, James J Halley, Air-Britain, 2007
Royal Air Force Squadrons, Wg Cdr C G Jefford, Airlife, 1988
Royal Navy Instructional Airframes, Ray Sturtivant and Rod Burden, British Av Research Group/Air-Britain, 1997
Squadrons and Units of the Fleet Air Arm, Theo Ballance, Lee Howard and Ray Sturtivant, Air-Britain, 2016

Websites

Many web sites are mentioned within the main narrative, but the following have been of great use and proven worth.
www.caa.co.uk - the excellent GINFO database run by the Civil Aviation Authority
www.demobbed.org.uk - great database on former British military aircraft from the stalwarts of the Wolverhampton
Aviation Group. Not content with this, the group also runs the UK Serials Resource centre - **www.ukserials.com**
www.flyinginireland.com - comprehensive site devoted to Irish aviation

Without the use of abbreviations for the 'potted' histories of the aircraft listed in *W&R*, the book would be twice the size. To save repetition, abbreviations that are clearly combinations of others are not listed in full, eg MEAFCS, breaks into MEAF and CS, ie Middle East Air Force Communications Squadron.

AA	Air Attaché
A&AEE	Aeroplane and Armament Experimental Establishment. From the late 1980s became the Aircraft and Armament Evaluation Establishment.
AAC	Army Air Corps
AACU	Anti-Aircraft Co-operation Unit
AAFCE	Allied Air Forces Central Europe
AAIU	Air Accident Investigation Unit
ABDR	Aircraft Battle Damage Repair
ABG	Air Base Group (USAF)
ACC	Allied Control Commission
acq	Acquired by organisation listed, not necessarily at the venue given
ACSEA	Allied Command, South East Asia- *see Note 1*
ACU	Andover Conversion Unit
ADS	Air Director School
AE&AEOS	Air Engineers and Air Electronic Operators School
AEF	Air Experience Flight
AES	Air Engineers School
AES	Air Engineering School
AETW	Air Engineering Training Wing
AFDS	Air Fighting Development Squadron,
AFDU	Air Fighting Development Unit
AFEE	Airborne Forces Experimental Establishment
AFN	Air Forces North
AFNE	Air Forces Near East
AFS	Advanced Flying School
AFTS	Advanced Flying Training School
AFU	Advanced Flying Unit
AFWF	Advanced Fixed Wing Flight
AIU	Accident Investigation Unit
ALAT	Aviation Legere de l'Armee de Terre
ALE	Aviation Legacy Enthusiast
AMARC	Aerospace Maintenance& Regeneration Center, Arizona, USA
AMIF	Aircraft Maintenance Instruction Flight
AMS	Air Movements School - see DMS / DMTS
ANG	Air National Guard
ANS	Air Navigation School
AONS	Air Observer and Navigator School
AOTS	Aircrew Officers Training School
APS	Aircraft Preservation Society
APS	Armament Practice Station
AR&TF	Aircraft Recovery and Transportation Flight, St Athan – tri-service 'mover' of fixed-wing airframes. (See MASU)
arr	Arrived at venue, by road or air
ARW	Air Refueling Wing (USAF)
ARWF	Advanced Rotary Wing Flight,
AS	Aggressor Squadron
AS&RU	Aircraft Salvage and Repair Unit
ASF	Aircraft Servicing Flight
ASS	Air Signals School
AST	Air Service Training
ASWDU	Air-Sea Warfare Development Unit
ATA	Air Transport Auxiliary
ATAIU	Allied Technical Air Intelligence Unit
ATC	Air Training Corps (Air Cadets)
ATDU	Air Torpedo Development Unit
ATF	Airframe Technology Flight
Att	Air Attache

AuxAF	Auxiliary Air Force
aw/cn	AWaiting CollectioN - *see Note 2*
AWFCS	All Weather Fighter Combat School
AWOCU	All Weather Operational Conversion Unit
AWRE	Atomic Weapons Research Establishment,
BA	British Airways
BAAT	British Airways Airtours
BAC	Bristol Aero Collection
BAC	British Aircraft Corporation
BAe	British Aerospace
BAE	BAE Systems - the 'B' 'A' and'E' apparently standing for nothing!
BAF	British Air Ferries
BAFO	British Air Forces of Occupation
BAH	British Airways Helicopters
BAM	Booker Aircraft Museum
BANS	Basic Air Navigation School
BAOR	British Army of the Rhine
BAPC	British Aviation Preservation Council
BATUS	British Army Training Unit, Suffield (Can)
BBMF	Battle of Britain Memorial Flight
BBML	British Balloon Museum and Library
BC	Bomber Command.
BCBS	Bomber Command Bombing School
BDRF	Battle Damage Repair Flight
BDTF	Bomber Defence Training Flight
BDU	Bomber Development Unit
BEA	British European Airways
BEAS	British Executive Air Services
BFTS	Basic Flying Training School
BFWF	Basic Fixed Wing Flight
B&GS	Bombing & Gunnery School (RCAF)
BG	Bomb(ardment) Group (US)
BLEU	Blind Landing Experimental Unit
BMA	British Midland Airways now bmi
BOAC	British Overseas Airways Corporation
BPPU	Bristol Plane Preservation Unit
BRNC	Britannia Royal Naval College
BSE	Bristol Siddeley Engines
B&TTF	Bombing & Target Towing Flight
BTF	Beaver Training Flight
BTU	Bombing Trials Unit
BUA	British United Airlines
BW	Bomb(ardment) Wing (US)
C(A)	Controller (Aircraft) see also CS(A) - *see Note 3*
CAA	Civil Aviation Authority
CAACU	Civilian Anti-Aircraft Co-operation Unit
CACF	Coastal Artillery Co-operation Flight
CACU	Coastal Artillery Co-operation Unit
CAF	Canadian Armed Forces
CAFU	Civil Aviation Flying Unit
Cam Flt	Camouflage Flight
CATCS	Central Air Traffic Control School
CAW	College of Air Warfare
CBAF	Castle Bromwich Aircraft Factory
CBE	Central Bombing Establishment
CC	Coastal Command
CCAS	Civilian Craft Apprentices School,
CCF	Combined Cadet Force
CF	Communications Flight as suffix with other unit, or for an airfield

332 – W&R28 – **Appendix F** Abbreviations   www.crecy.co.uk

CFCCU	Civilian Fighter Control and Co-op Unit	ETS	Engineering Training School
CFE	Central Fighter Establishment - see CFE-EAF.	ETU	Experimental Trials Unit
CFE-EAF	Central Fighter Establishment - Enemy Aircraft Flight	EWAD	Electronic Warfare and Avionics Detachment
		EWE&TU	Electronic Warfare Experimental & Training Unit
CFS	Central Flying School	F / Flt	Flight, suffix to number
C&TTS	Communications and Target Towing Sqn	FAA	Fleet Air Arm
CGS	Central Gliding School	FAA	Fuerza Aerea Argentina
CGS	Central Gunnery School	FAAHAF	Fleet Air Arm Historic Aircraft Flight
CIFAS	Centre d'Instruction des Forces Aeriennes Strategiques	FAAM	Fleet Air Arm Museum
		FAF	French Air Force.
CIT	Cranfield Institute of Technology	FAH	Fuerza Aerea Hondurena
CNCS	Central Navigation and Control School	FC	Fighter Command.
CoA	Certificate (or Permit) of Airworthiness.	FC&RS	Fighter Control and Reporting School
Cott	Cottesmore, in relation to V-Bomber wings	FCS	Fighter Control School
CPF	Coastal Patrol Flight	FCTU	Fighter Command Trials Unit
cr	crashed, or other form of accident	FEAF	Far East Air Forces - see Note 1
CR	Crash Rescue, training airframe.	FECS	Far East Communications Flight
CRD	Controller, Research and Development	FF	Ferry Flight
C&RS	Control and Reporting School	FF&SS	Fire Fighting and Safety School
CS	Communications Squadron, as a suffix with other units, or for an airfield.	FGF	Flying Grading Flight
		FLS	Fighter Leader School
CS(A)	Controller, Supplies (Air), see also CA - Note 3	f/n	first noted
CSDE	Central Servicing Development Establishment	FOAC	Flag Officer, Aircraft Carriers
CSE	Central Signals Establishment	FOCAS	Friends of Cardington Airship Station
CSF	Canberra Servicing Flight	FOFT	Flag Officer, Flying Training
CTE	Central Training Establishment	FONA	Flag Officer, Naval Aviation
CTTS	Civilian Technical Training School	FONAC	Flag Officer, Naval Air Command
C&TTS	Communications & Target Towing Squadron	FP	Ferry Pool
CU	Communications Unit, as suffix	FPP	Ferry Pilots Pool
CU	Conversion Unit, as suffix	FRADU	Fleet Requirements and Direction Unit
DARA	Defence Aviation Repair Agency, Fleetlands, St Athan, Sealand	FRL	Flight Refuelling Ltd
		FRS	Flying Refresher School
dbr	damaged beyond repair, to distinguish an aircraft that was written off but did not crash	FRU	Fleet Requirements Unit
		FS	Fighter Squadron (US)
deH	de Havilland	FSM	Full Scale Model
de-reg	de-registered (from a civilian identity)	FSS	Ferry Support Squadron
DEMS	Defence Explosives Ordnance Disposal, Munitions and Search School	FSS	Flying Selection Squadron
		FTC	Flying Training Command
DERA	Defence Evaluation and Research Agency — replaced DRA and DTEO.	FTS	Flying Training School
		FTU	Ferry Training Unit
Det	Detachment, flight or other unit detached from main base	FU	Ferry Unit
		FW	Fighter Wing (USAF)
DFLS	Day Fighter Leader School	FWS	Fighter Weapons School
dism	dismantled	GIA	Ground Instructional Airframe
DLO	Defence Logistics Organisation	GS	Glider School
DMA	Doesn't Mean Anything	GSU	Group Support Unit
DMS /DMTS	Defence Movements School, later Defence Movements Training Squadron	GTS	Glider Training School
		GU	Glider Unit
DPA	Defence Procurement Agency replaced MoD(PE)	GWDS	Guided Weapons Development Squadron
DRA	Defence Research Agency – see DERA	HAB	Hot air balloon
DSA	Disposal Ss Agency	HAM	Historic Aircraft Museum, Southend
DSDA	Defence Storage and Distribution Agency	HC	Home Command
DTEO	Defence Test and Evaluation Organisation – see DERA	HCEU	Home Command Examining Unit
		HCF	Hornet Conversion Flight
DU	Development Unit, as suffix	HDU	Helicopter Development Unit
EAAS	East Anglian Aviation Society	HGSU	Heavy Glider Servicing Unit
EASAMS	European avionics consortium	HHU	Helicopter Holding Unit
ECTT	Escadre de Chasse Tous Temps	HMTS	Harrier Maintenance Training School
EE	English Electric	HQ	Headquarters
EFTS	Elementary Flying Training School	HS	Handling Squadron
EOD	Explosive Ordnance Disposal	HSA	Hawker Siddeley Aviation
EP&TU	Exhibition, Production and Transport Unit	HTF	Helicopter Training Flight
E&RFTS	Elementary & Reserve Flying Trng School	IAAC / IAC	Irish Army Air Corps / Irish Air Corps
ERS	Empire Radio School	IAF	Indian Air Force
Esc	Escadre, French squadron	IAM	Institute of Aviation Medicine
ETPS	Empire Test Pilots School	IAP	(Russian) Fighter Aviation Regiment

IA-PVO	(Russian) Air Defence Fighter Force		(P)AFU	(Pilot) Advanced Flying Unit
IFTU	Intensive Flying Trials Unit		PAX	Passenger, as used in Chipmunk PAX trainer
IGN	Institut Geographique National		PCSS	Protectorate Comms and Support Squadron
IHM	International Helicopter Museum		PEE	Proof & Experimental Establishment
ITF or 'S	Instrument Training Flight / Squadron		PFA	Popular Flying Association
IWM	Imperial War Museum		PFS	Primary Flying School
JASS	Joint Anti-Submarine School		PFTS	Primary Flying Training School
JADTEU	Joint Air Delivery Test and Evaluation Unit -		PP	Pilots' Pool
	replaced JATEU		PPS	Personal Plane Services
JATE	Joint Air Transport Establishment - see JATEU		PRDU	Photo Reconnaissance Development Unit
JATEU	Joint Air Transport Evaluation Unit – see JADTEU		PRU	Photographic Reconnaissance Unit
JCU	Javelin Conversion Unit		PTC	Personnel and Training Command
JEHU	Joint Experimental Helicopter Unit		PTF	Phantom Training Flight
JMU	Joint Maritime Unit		PTS	Primary Training School
JOCU	Jaguar Operational Conversion Unit		PVO	(Russian) Air Defence Force
JTU	Joint Trials Unit		QF	Queen's Flight
JWE	Joint Warfare Establishment		RAAF	Royal Australian Air Force
LAS	Light Aircraft School		RAE	Royal Aircraft / Aerospace Establishment
LC	Logistics Command		RAeS	Royal Aeronautical Society
LCS & 'U	Lightning Conversion Squadron / Unit		RAF	Royal Air Force
l/n	last noted		RAFA	Royal Air Force Association
LRWE	Long Range Weapons Research Est		RAFC	Royal Air Force College
LTF	Lightning Training Flight		RAFEF	Royal Air Force Exhibition Flight
LTW	Lyneham Tactical Wing (Hercules)		RAFFC	Royal Air Force Flying College
MAM	Midland Air Museum		RAFG	Royal Air Force Germany
MASL	Military Aircraft Spares Ltd		RAFGSA	Royal Air Force Gliding & Soaring Assoc
MASU	Mobile Aircraft Support Unit – DARA Fleetlands,		RAFHSF	Royal Air Force High Speed Flight
	tri-service 'mover' of helicopters See AR&TF		RAFM	Royal Air Force Museum
MBA	Museum of Berkshire Aviation		RAN	Royal Australian Navy
MC	Maintenance Command		RC	Reserve Command
MCS	Metropolitan Communications Squadron		RCAF	Royal Canadian Air Force
MEAF	Middle East Air Force- *see Note 1*		RCN	Royal Canadian Navy
MECS	Middle East Communications Squadron		RCS	Rotary Conversion Squadron
METS	Multi-Engine Training School		Regt	Regiment
MGSP	Mobile Glider Servicing Party		RFS	Reserve Flying School
MinTech	Ministry of Technology, see also MoA, MoS		RHK	Royal Hong Kong
	- *see Note 3*		RMAF	Royal Malaysian Air Force
MoA	Ministry of Aviation, see also MinTech, MoS		RNAY	Royal Naval Aircraft Yard
	- *see Note 3*		RNEC	Royal Naval Engineering College
MoD(PE)	Ministry of Defence (Procurement Executive) –		RNEFTS	Royal Navy Elementary Flying Training School
	see DPA		RNGSA	Royal Navy Gliding and Soaring Association
MoS	Ministry of Supply, see MinTech, MoA - *see Note 3*		RNHF	Royal Navy Historic Flight
MoTaT	Museum of Transport & Technology, NZ		RNoAF	Royal Norwegian Air Force
MOTU	Maritime Operational Training Unit		RNZAF	Royal New Zealand Air Force
MPA	Man-powered aircraft		ROC	Royal Observer Corps
MU	Maintenance Unit - *See Note 4*		RPRE	Rocket Propulsion Research Establishment
NAAS	Navigator and Airman Aircrew School		RRAF	Royal Rhodesian Air Force
NACDS	Naval Air Command Driving School		RRE	Royal Radar Establishment
NASA	National Aeronautical and Space Admin		RRF	Radar Reconnaissance Flight
NASU	Naval Aircraft Servicing Unit		RRHT	Rolls-Royce Heritage Trust
NBC	Nuclear, Bacteriological and Chemical		RS	Radio School
NCS	Northern Communications Squadron		RSRE	Radar and Signals Research Establishment
nea	Non effective airframe - *See Note 2*		RSS & 'U	Repair & Servicing Section / Unit
NECS	North Eastern Communications Squadron		RTR	Royal Tank Regiment
NFLS	Night Fighter Leaders School		RWE	Radio Warfare Establishment
NGTE	National Gas Turbine Establishment		SAAF	South African Air Force
NIBF	Northern Ireland Beaver Flight		SAC	School of Army Co-operation
n/s	No service - UK military only		SAF	School of Aerial Fighting
NSF	Northern Sector Flight		SAH	School of Aircraft Handling
ntu	Not taken up, registration applied for, but not		SAOEU	Strike Attack Operational Evaluation Unit
	worn, or paperwork not concluded		SAR	Search and Rescue
(O)AFU	(Observers) Advanced Flying Unit		SAREW	Search and Rescue Engineering Wing
OCTU	Officer Cadet Training Unit		SARTS	Search and Rescue Training Squadron
OCU	Operational Conversion Unit		SARTU	Search and Rescue Training Unit
OEU	Operational Evaluation Unit		SC	Signals Command
OFU	Overseas Ferry Unit		Scamp	Scampton, to distinguish a V-Bomber wing
OTU	Operational Training Unit		SCBS	Strike Command Bombing School

SCS	Southern Communications Squadron	Thum Flt	Temperature and HUMidity Flight
SEAE	School of Electrical and Aeronautical Engineering	TLA	Three-letter abbreviation
SF	Station Flight, usually with an airfield name	TMS	Tornado Maintenance School
SFDO	School of Flight Deck Operations	TMTS	Trade Management Training School
SFTS	Service Flying Training School	TOC	Taken on charge - *See Note 2*
ShF	Ship's Flight	TOEU	Tornado Operational Evaluation Unit
SHQ	Station HQ	TRE	Telecommunications Research Establishment
SKTU	Sea King Training Unit	TS	Training Squadron
SLAW	School of Land/Air Warfare	TTC	Technical Training Command
SMR	School of Maritime Reconnaissance	TTF	Tanker Training Flight
SOC	Struck off charge - *See Note 2*	TTTE	Tri-National Tornado Training Establishment
SoRF	School of Refresher Flying	TTTE	Thomas The Tank Engine
SoTT	School of Technical Training - *See Note 5*	TTU	Torpedo Training Unit
SRCU	Short Range Conversion Unit	TWDU	Tactical Weapons Development Unit
SRW	Strategic Reconnaissance Wing	TWU	Tactical Weapons Unit
SS	Signals Squadron	UAS	University Air Squadron - *See Note 6*
SS	Support Squadron	UNFICYP	United Nations Forces In Cyprus
SU	Support Unit	USAAC	United States Army Air Corps
SVAS	Shuttleworth Veteran Aeroplane Society	USAAF	United States Army Air Force
TAC	The Aeroplane Collection	USAF	United States Air Force
TAF	Tactical Air Force	USMC	United States Marine Corps
TAW	Tactical Airlift Wing	USN	United States Navy
TC	Transport Command	VAFA	Vintage Aircraft Flying Association
TCS	Troop Carrier Squadron (USAAF)	VAT	Vintage Aircraft Team
TCW	Troop Carrier Wing (USAAF)	VGS	Volunteer Gliding School – and, from 2005:
TEE	Trials and Experimental Establishment		Volunteer Gliding *Squadron*
TES	Tri-Partitie Evaluation Squadron	VVS KA	(Russian) Soviet Army Air Force
TEU	Tactical Exercise Unit	VVS VMF	(Russian) Soviet Naval Air Force
TF	Training Flight	Wadd	Waddington, denoting a V-Bomber wing
TFF	Target Facilities Flight	WCS	Western Communications Squadron
TFS	Traget Facilities Squadron	wfu	Withdrawn from use
TFS	Tactical Fighter Squadron	Witt	Wittering, denoting a V-bomber wing.
TFTAS	Tactical Fighter Training Aggressor Squadron	WLT	Weapons Loading Trainer
TFU	Telecommunications Flying Unit	WSF	Western Sector Flight
TFW	Tactical Fighter Wing		
TGDA	Training Group Defence Agency		

Notes on UK military airframes

1 **RAF 'Holding Units'**: For administrative purposes, the history cards of some RAF aircraft become fairly vague when transferred to either Middle East or Far East theatres of operations. Accordingly, the following abbreviations denote the 'operator' for the segment of an aircraft's life in that theatre, even though it may have been used by several front-line units: ACSEA, FEAF, MEAF.

2 **History Card 'milestones'**: There are several RAF aircraft history card 'milestones' referred to in the main text. Essentially an aircraft starts off as AWaiting Collection (Aw/cn) - a signal from the manufacturer that the aircraft is ready for issue to service; it is then taken on charge (toc) and becomes a part of the RAF; after service life, it may eventually to be declared a non-effective airframe (nea) and down-graded to instructional or fire-training use; the final act is for it to be struck off charge (SOC), either being written-off in an accident, scrapped, sold to another user etc etc.

3 **Government 'owning' bodies**: Technical 'owner' of UK military machines is the C(A) or CS(A) and at times these are noted within the aircraft history cards instead of a unit, although it may well be a pointer to the aircraft being operated at that time of its life by a test or trials unit. In similar manner, MinTech, MoA or MoS can appear, frequently meaning operation by the RAE, or DRA.

4 **Maintenance Unit** (MU): Frequently mentioned in the text are: 2 - Sealand, 5 - Kemble, 6 - Brize Norton, 7 - Quedgeley, 8 - Little Rissington, 9 - Cosford, 10 - Hullavington, 12 - Kirkbride, 13 - Henlow, 14 - Carlisle, 15 - Wroughton, 16 - Stafford, 18 - Dumfries, 19 - St Athan, 20- Aston Down, 22 - Silloth, 23 - Aldergrove, 24 - Tern Hill, 25 - Hartlebury, 27 - Shawbury, 29 - High Ercall, 32 - St Athan, 33 - Lyneham, 34 - Montford Bridge, 36 - Sealand, 37 - Burtonwood, 38 - Llandow, 39 - Colerne, 44 - Edzell, 45 - Kinloss, 46 - Lossiemouth, 47 - Sealand, 48 - Hawarden, 51 - Lichfield, 52 - Cardiff, 54 - Cambridge, 57 - Wig Bay, 60 - Leconfield, 71 - Bicester. Note that several locations had more than one MU, eg Sealand, St Athan.

5 **School of Technical Training** (SoTT): The following are mentioned in the main text: 1 - Halton, 2 - Cosford, 3 - Manston, 4 - St Athan, 5 - Locking, 6 - Hednesford, 7 - Innsworth, 8 - Weeton, 9 - Newton, 10 - Kirkham, 11 - Credenhill, 12 - Melksham, 14 - Henlow, 21 - Burtonwood.

6 **University Air Squadron** (UAS): Prefixed with a university name: Abn - Aberdeen, Dundee and St Andrews, Bir - Birmingham, Bri - Bristol, Cam - Cambridge, Dur - Durham, Edn - Edinburgh, Elo - East Lowlands, Ems - East Midlands, G&S - Glasgow & Strathclyde, Lee - Leeds, Liv - Liverpool, Lon - London, Man - Manchester and Salford, Nor - Northumbrian, Not - Nottingham, Oxf - Oxford, QUB - Queen's University Belfast, Sotn - Southampton, Wal - Ws, Yor - Yorkshire.

Index I : BY TYPE

For the purposes of this index, no distinction is made for replicas, full-scale models etc.

Awaiting the developers: VC10 K.3 ZA150 and Boeing 747-436 G-CIVW, Dunsfold, June 2021. *Ian Haskell*

Index II : LOCATIONS

This index also includes a decode of alternative names to help you find Robin Hood!

All generalisations are wrong
- including this one
Attributed to Mark Twain,
but perhaps only generally

Top: English Electric P.1A WG763 awaiting re-assembly.
Bottom: Avro 707A WG763 settling in to the BDAC hangar. Both Old Sarum, Wilts, February 2022, *Hugh Trevor*

Britain's Aircraft Industry

Triumphs and Tragedies since 1909

Britain established the world's first aircraft factory in 1909 after the Short brothers met with the American Wright brothers and struck a deal. The industry expanded rapidly to rise to the challenge of World War One with such thoroughbreds as the Camel and the SE.5. The post-conflict slump proved to be difficult but classics such as the Moths, the Hart family and the Gladiator maintained Britain's leadership. Another war loomed and iconic types such as the Hurricane, Lancaster, Mosquito, Spitfire and the Meteor jet appeared.

With the return of peace over 20 major manufacturers faced inevitable contraction. The misguided Bristol Brabazon airliner was a dead end but the superb de Havilland Comet and Vickers Viscount led the field. Canberras, Hunters, Lightnings and the V-bombers met the Cold War confrontation.

For the first time *Britain's Aircraft Industry* provides a readable, highly illustrated, examination of the entire industry; its heritage and the changes it faces in the 21st century, both technical and political. The life and times of the 40 'big names' from Airbus to Westland: aircraft, designers, factories, failures and successes, mergers and closures are all explained, supported by statistical tables and copious illustrations. Here is a celebration of a world class industry that remains at the cutting edge of excellence.

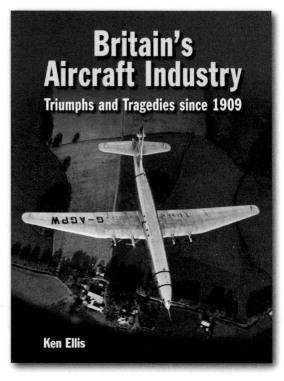

368 Pages | hardback
280mm x 216mm
Over 450 b/w and colour photographs
ISBN 9 781910 809426
£27.95

Local Aviation Collections of Britain

The UK's Regional Aeronautical Treasures

Britain has a wealth of museums of all sizes, all with incredible exhibits, yet the 'big' collections tend to get the limelight. All over the UK are amazing aircraft collections, containing aircraft of world, national or regional importance, many of which the curators of the national institutions would love to have.

With region-by-region coverage, the backgrounds of the formative museums of Great Britain are highlighted along with the pedigrees of their most significant exhibits. Included are such icons as the de Havilland Aircraft Museum, the Brooklands Museum and The Helicopter Museum.

Across Britain are many local collections that helped to pioneer this country's incredible aviation heritage and the role of enthusiasts is highlighted with a profile of the first of them all - the Northern Aircraft Preservation Society and its lineage. Among the 'regionals' covered are the Dumfries and Galloway, Solway, North East, Newark, Norfolk and Suffolk, Yorkshire and Berkshire museums.

Over 150 museums and their most important exhibits are profiled with over 250 photographs, both archive and in full colour. Like the other titles in the series, *Britain's Local Aviation Treasures* is a unique reference for anyone interested in Britain's aviation heritage and it provides inspiration for a tour of discovery of the 'unknown' gems of the UK.

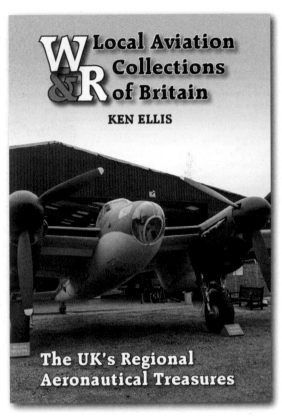

W & R

Local Aviation Collections of Britain

KEN ELLIS

The UK's Regional Aeronautical Treasures

352 pages | hardback
234mm x 156mm
180 B/w and 96 colour photographs
ISBN 9 781910 809112
£18.95

Testing to the Limits

British Test Pilots Since 1910

Tentative flights hops by Edwardian-era pioneers led to the development of a world-class industry. Spearheading this were the test pilots who ventured into the unknown in British-built aircraft for their maiden flights. As well as those that became household names, *Testing to the Limits* also brings to the fore many 'unknowns' who risked everything to take a prototype into the skies.

The culmination of a 20-year project, in two volumes *Testing to the Limits* charts the careers and endeavours of over 400 company test pilots. Inter-related biographies brim with types first flown, incidents and anecdotes, including first-hand quotes. It is the most comprehensive study on the subject ever produced.

From Short biplanes of 1909, the book traverses the abundance of prototypes in the 1920s and 1930s, the advances of WW2 from Spitfire to Vampire, the post-war challenges of the 'sound barrier' and the pressures of the 'Cold War' to the supersonic Concorde, the Harrier 'jump-jet' and today's fly-by-wire Typhoon.

Designer-pilots, flight test observers, the Empire Test Pilots' School, the relentless pace of production tests, engine test-beds and the origins of the ejector seat, the service test institutions and a glimpse of the future – all aspects of these extraordinary flyers are examined.

Chris Yeo, BAE Systems Typhoon test pilot and John Farley former Hawker Siddeley & British Aerospace Harrier test pilot, provide forewords to volume 1 and 2 respectively. *Testing to the Limits* is not just a tribute to a band of elite aviators it is also a vibrant commentary on the failures and successes of the British aircraft industry.

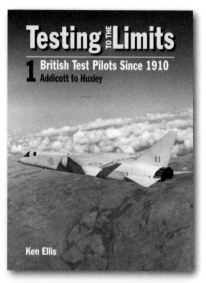

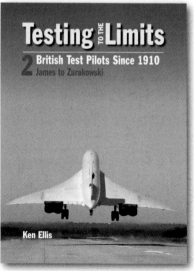

Volume 1: 256pp | hbk | 290mm x 216mm
Over 300 photos/illustrations
ISBN 9 780859 791847 | **£24.95**

Volume 2: 336pp | hbk | 290mm x 216mm
Over 400 photos/illustrations
ISBN 9 780859 791854 | **£24.95**

Lost Aviation Collections of Britain

A tribute to the UK's bygone aviation museums and collections

Britain's diverse aviation heritage owes much to the pioneer museums and collections that preserved irreplaceable aircraft from the 1930s onwards and to celebrate the 50th anniversary of the first publication of *Wrecks & Relics*, this special edition of 'W&R' commemorates the most important of these collections.

Warbird pioneers such as Richard Nash, Spencer Flack and Charles Church feature together with important institutions, such as Cranfield and Loughborough, that helped kick-start the aircraft preservation 'booms' of the 1960s and 1970s. Additionally, many much-loved museums that are no more are described, including Colerne, Skyfame, Southend, Strathallan and Torbay. Over 40 such organisations, large and small, are covered.

Lost Aviation Collections of Britain also examines 'Ones that Got Away' – important types that slipped through the preservation 'net' and into extinction, such as the ATEL Carvair, Miles Marathon and the Westland Whirlwind fighter.

Lavishly illustrated with over 200 period images, 96 in full colour, *Lost Aviation Collections of Britain* provides a wonderful record of the UK's aircraft preservation movement, a unique reference book from the author who knows its history better than anybody else.

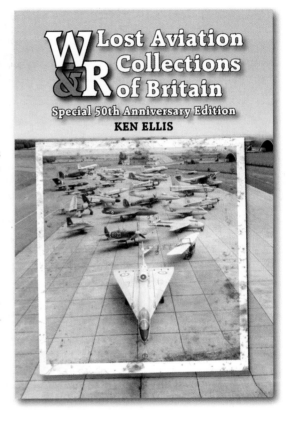

224 pages | hardback
234mm x 156mm
Over 100 b/w and 96 colour photos
ISBN 9 780859 791595
£16.95

Tel: **+44 (0)161 499 0024**

 Crécy

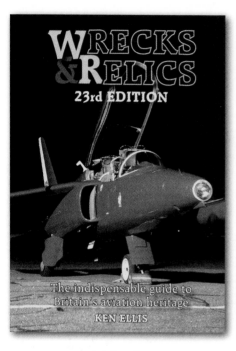 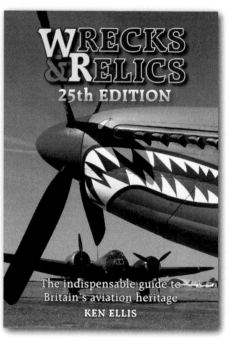